Language Arts

CONTENT AND TEACHING STRATEGIES

Kenneth Hoskisson
Virginia Polytechnic Institute and State University

Gail E. Tompkins
The University of Oklahoma

MERRILL PUBLISHING COMPANY
A BELL & HOWELL INFORMATION COMPANY
COLUMBUS   TORONTO   LONDON   MELBOURNE

To my wife Virginia, and my children,
Heather, Mark, and Tamora.

K.H.

To Mac.
G.E.T

Cover Art: Leslie Beaber

Published by Merrill Publishing Company
A Bell & Howell Information Company
Columbus, Ohio 43216

This book was set in Garamond.

Administrative Editor: Jeff Johnston
Production Coordinator: Pamela Hedrick-Bennett
Cover Designer: Cathy Watterson

Library of Congress Catalog Card Number: 86-62489
International Standard Book Number: 0-675-20434-8
Printed in the United States of America
6   7   8   9—91   90   89

Credits

Chapter 1   p. 8: "Hair-hare" by Jaclyn Cooley, Hubbard Elementary School, Noble, OK. Reprinted by permission. p. 20: From *Language and maturation* (p. 70) by P. Menyuk, 1977, Cambridge, MA: MIT Press. Copyright 1977 by MIT Press. p. 32: "Is is red?" By Chris Weaver, Ranchwood Elementary School, Yukon, OK. Reprinted by permission.

Chapter 2   p. 37: From *Language assessment in the early years,* (p. 23) by C. Genishi and A. H. Dyson, 1984, Norwood, NJ: Ablex. Copyright 1984 by Ablex. Reprinted by permission. p. 46: "Edith, No!" by Mr. John McCracken's third-grade class, Nevin Coppock School, Tipp City, OH. Reprinted by permission. p. 58: From "Selecting software for your LD students" by P. L. Smith and G. E. Tompkins, 1984, *Academic Therapy, 20,* pp. 221–224. Copyright 1984 by *Academic Therapy.* Reprinted by permission.

Chapter 3   pp. 74–77, 79: From "Strategies for more effective listening" by G. E. Tompkins, M. Friend, and P. L. Smith. In C. R. Personke and D. D. Johnson (Eds.) *Language arts and the beginning teacher* (Chapter 3). Englewood Cliffs, NJ: Prentice-Hall, in press. Adapted by permission. pp. 82–83, 85: From Listening skills schoolwide: Activities and programs (pp. 39–40) by T. G. Devine, 1982, Urbana, IL: ERIC Clearinghouse on Reading and Communication Skills and NCTE. Copyright 1982 by ERIC/ NCTE. Adapted by permission. p. 84: From "Some examples of doublespeak" by W. D. Lutz, n.d., unpublished ms. distributed by NCTE. Reprinted by permission. pp. 85–86: From *Listening instruction* by A. D. Wolvin and C. G. Coakley, 1979, Urbana, IL: ERIC Clearinghouse on Reading and Communication Association. Copyright 1979 by ERIC/NCTE. Adapted by permission.

Chapter 4   p. 113: "I am the Frog" by Whitney Mohaffay, Norman Christian Academy, Norman, OK. Reprinted by permission. p. 123: "Mr. Kirtley came down. . ." by Tomara Trett, Sulphur Elementary School, Sulphur, OK. Reprinted by permission. p. 124: "Ghost town gazette" by Betsy Rice's classes, Sumner School, Sumner, OK. Reprinted by permission.

Chapter 5   p. 135: From "The Uses of Language" by F. Smith, 1977, *Language Arts, 54,* p. 640. Copyright 1979 by NCTE. Reprinted by permission. p. 137: "One morning Danny woke. . ." by Tamara Hoskisson, Blacksburg, VA. Reprinted by permission. p. 143: "Dear Diary" by Stephanie Camp, Ranchwood Elementary School, Yukon, OK. Reprinted by permission. p. 144: From "Exciting children about literature through creative storytelling techniques" by L. M. Morrow, 1979. *Language Arts, 56,* pp. 237, pp. 237–240. Copyright 1979 by NCTE. Reprinted by

Houghton Mifflin. pp. 353–355: Adapted from *Wishes, Lies, and Dreams* by K. Koch, 1970, New York: Chelsea House Publishers. p. 354: From "Class Collaboration Wish Poems" by Ms. Kim Schmidt's class of 5- and 6-year-olds, La Petite Academy, Oklahoma City, OK. Reprinted by permission. p. 354: From "I Wish" by Johnny Pickard, Monroe Elementary School, Norman, OK. Reprinted by permission. p. 354: From "Wish Poems Written in Music Class" by Christy Allbritton and Mark Bauman, Lincoln Elementary School, Norman, OK. Reprinted by permission. p. 355: From "Red Seasons" by Thomas Johns, *The McGuffey Writer*, Winter, 1985, p. 1, The McGuffey Laboratory School, Oxford, OH. Dr. Eileen Tway, editor. Reprinted by permission. p. 355: From "If I Were Poems" by Robbie Neal and Heather Hughes, *The McGuffey Writer*, March 1980, p. 4. The McGuffey Laboratory School, Oxford, OH. Dr. Eileen Tway, editor. Reprinted by permission. p. 356: From "I Used to/But now" poems by Tony Brown, Cristina Foster, Jeanie Barber, and Kristie Phillips, John Adams Elementary School, Lawton, OK. Reprinted by permission. p. 356: From "Class Collaboration Poem" by Mrs. Glenda LoBaugh's fifth-grade class, Ranchwood Elementary School, Yukon, OK. Reprinted by permission. p. 357: From "Class Collaboration Noise Poem" by Mrs. Carol Ochs' second-grade class, Hubbard Elementary School, Noble, OK. Reprinted by permission. p. 358: From "Loneliness" by Maureen Cooley, *The McGuffey Writer*, January 1982, p. 8, The McGuffey Laboratory School, Oxford, OH. Reprinted by permission. p. 358: From "Elephant Noises" by Christopher Anderson, *The McGuffey Writer*, March 1980, p. 12, The McGuffey Laboratory School, Oxford, OH. Dr. Eileen Tway, editor. Reprinted by permission. p. 359: From "Students' Haiku Poems" by Shawn Ware, Shannon Roy, and Larissa Eversgerd, *The McGuffey Writer*, Fall, 1983, p. 5 and May 1981, p. 11, The McGuffey Laboratory School, Oxford, OH. Dr. Eileen Tway, editor. Reprinted by permission. p. 360: From "Students' Tanka Poems" by Amy Bowen, Randal Wright, Quenton Maddux, *The Regal Collection*, 1984, Watonga Oklahoma Public Schools, Peggy Givens, editor. Reprinted by permission. p. 361: From "Students' Cinquain Poems" by Lisa Elliot, Alison Scott, and Stephanie Shirley, *The McGuffey Writer*, March 1980, p. 8, and *The Regal Collection* 1984. Reprinted by permission. p. 362: From "Students' Diamante Poems" by Ms. Nancy Hutter's third-grade class, Tioga Elementary School, Bensenville, IL; Scott Ketchum, Ranchwood Elementary School, Yukon, OK; and Chad Feurborn, Ranchwood Elementary School, Yukon, OK. Reprinted by permission. p. 363: From "Students' Hink-pink Poems" by Marshall Owen, Tara Dillman, and Mark Anderson, *The Regal Collection*, 1984, Watonga Oklahoma Public Schools, Peggy A. Givens, editor; and Burgundy Gregg, Irving Middle School, Norman, OK. p. 363: From "What Do You Call a Finicky Chicken?" by Robin Cox, Irving Elementary School, Norman, OK. Reprinted by permission. p. 364: From "Students' Limericks and Clerihews" by Kim Berry and Joe Peach, *The McGuffey Writer*, Fall 1983, p. 4 and Spring 1984, p. 12, The McGuffey Laboratory School, Oxford, OH, Dr. Eileen Tway, editor; Johnny Whisler and Heather Adkins, *The Regal Collection*, 1984, Watonga Oklahoma Public Schools, Peggy A. Givens, editor. Reprinted by permission. p. 366: From "Students' Model Poems" by Nicole Dobbins and Jennifer Rickey, *Revelations*, 1985, Watonga Oklahoma Public Schools, Peggy A. Givens, editor; David Fisher and Mattson Woodruff, *The McGuffey Writer*, May 1981, p. 6, The McGuffey Laboratory School, Oxford, OH. Dr. Eileen Tway, editor. Reprinted by permission. p. 367: From "Students' Concrete Poems" by Randy Roman Nose, *The Regal Collection*, 1984. Watonga Oklahoma Public Schools, Peggy A. Givens, editor; Brian McGuire and Chris Hogan, *The McGuffey Writer*, January 1981, pp. 11 and 6, The McGuffey Laboratory School, Oxford, OH, Dr. Eileen Tway, editor. Reprinted by permission.

Chapter 13 pp. 406–407, 408: *Spelling for Word Mastery— Grade 3* (pp. 90–93; 1) by G. E. Cook, M. Esposito, T. Gabriel-son, E. G. Turner, 1984, Columbus, OH: Merrill. Copyright 1984 by Merrill. Reprinted by permission. p. 408: From a Writing Vocabulary for Elementary Children, (p. xiii) by R. L. Hillerich, 1978, Springfield, IL: Charles C. Thomas, Publisher. Reprinted by permission. pp. 416–417: From *Spelling: An Application of Research Findings*, (pp. 27–28) by R. A. Allred, 1977, Washington, D. C.: National Education Association. Reprinted by permission. pp. 418–419: From "Reading, Writing, and Phonology" by C. Chomsky, 1970, *Harvard Educational Review, 40*, pp. 287–309. Copyright 1970 by *Harvard Educational Review*. Reprinted by permission. pp. 422–423: From "Spelling Strategies of Primary School Children and their Relationship to Piaget's Concept of Decentration" by J. Zutell, 1978, *Research in the Teaching of English, 13*, pp. 69–79. Copyright 1978 by NCTE. Reprinted by permission.

Chapter 14 p. 442: Used with permission from *Handwriting: Basic Skills and Application*. Copyright © 1984, Zaner-Bloser, Inc., Columbus, OH. pp. 443, 444: From *D'Nealian Handwriting (Grades K–8)* by D. N. Thurber, 1981, Glenview, IL: Scott, Foresman. Copyright 1981 by Scott Foresman. Reprinted by permission. p. 447–450: From "Let's Go on a Bear Hunt" by G. E. Tompkins, 1980, *Language Arts, 57*, pp. 782–786. Copyright by NCTE. Reprinted by permission. p. 452: From "Students' Copy Books" by Jennifer Lee, Sulphur Elementary School, Sulphur, OK: and Aaron Ochs, Pioneer Elementary School, Noble, OK. Reprinted by permission.

Chapter 15 p. 471: From "Learning Disabilities . . . A Puzzlement" by M. Summers, 1977, *Today's Education, 66*, pp. 40–42. Reprinted by permission of the National Education Association. p. 473: From "My Name Is Ryan . . ." by Ryan Gorman, Southgate Elementary School, Moore, OK. Reprinted by permission. p. 475: From "Out! Out! Out!" by Lisa Smith, JD McCarthy Center, Norman, OK. Reprinted by permission. p. 475: From "Survival Words for Disabled Readers" by C. H. Polloway and E. A. Polloway, 1981, *Academic Therapy, 16*, pp. 443–448. Reprinted by permission. p. 481: From "Doing What Comes Naturally: Recent Research in Second Language Acquisition" by C. Urzua, 1980. In G. S. Pinnell (Ed.), *Discovering Language with Children*, (pp. 33–38). Urbana, IL: NCTE. Reprinted by permission. p. 482: From "Beginning English Reading for ESL Students" by P. Gonzales, 1981, *The Reading Teacher, 35*, pp. 156–157. Reprinted by permission of IRA. p. 483: From "How to Begin Language Instruction for Non-English Speaking Students" by P. Gonzales, 1981, *Language Arts, 58*, pp. 175–180. Reprinted by permission of NCTE. p. 486: From "I Have Butterflies . . ." by Robert Ochs, Noble, OK. Reprinted by permission. pp. 490–491: From "Launching Nonstandard Speakers into Standard English" by G. E. Tompkins and L. M. McGee, 1983, *Language Arts, 60*, pp. 463–469. Reprinted by permission of NCTE. p. 492: From "Spelling and Grammar Logs" by R. Van DeWeghe, 1982. In C. Carter (Ed.), *Non-native and Nonstandard Dialect Students: Classroom Practices in Teaching English*, 1982–1983, (pp. 101–105). Urbana, IL: NCTE. Reprinted by permission. p. 494: From "Giftedness" by L. Silverman, 1982. In E. L. Meyer (Ed.), *Exceptional Children in Today's Schools: An Alternative Resource Book*, (pp. 485–528). Denver: Love. Reprinted by permission. p. 498: From "Tropical Forest Survival Activities" by Brian Johnson and Brady Toothaker, Irving Middle School, Norman, OK. Reprinted by permission.

Foreword

Those of us who began our teaching careers with Dick and Jane and remember the continual command to "see Spot run" have a deep appreciation for the impact of recent research on emerging instructional strategies. The first 60 years of this century were characterized by the controversies of phonics versus the sight word method and whether to diagram sentences or fill in the blank. The wealth of research over the past two decades has finally provided educators with new insight into how children acquire language and how they use language skills in learning to read and write. The proliferation of studies has consistently pointed out the phenomenal development that takes place during the preschool years. Between birth and the first day of kindergarten, children somehow internalize the rules of language without benefit of formal classroom instruction. They come to school completely able to understand spoken language and able to generate original sentences that make sense and communicate a message. School curriculum writers are beginning to realize that children's natural ability with language should be the foundation for instruction, not the "prepared" commercial materials that promote random activities with scant theoretical bases.

This book embodies both theory and practice. The numerous strategies offered within these pages were developed through years of research and successful application in hundreds of classrooms. Teachers employing the strategies have found that these natural, whole language methods elicit an enthusiastic response from students, resulting in a more effective understanding and use of language than the typical "fill-in-the-blank" approach can ever achieve.

Reading aloud daily to children from carefully selected children's literature is an ideal starting point for teachers who are serious about using the ideas in this book. The heart of this integrated language approach is to immerse children in the many forms of language in their world. Children must hear or read many samples of stories, poems, speeches, and reports before they will be able to imitate or manipulate the language in each model. Lists of suggested tradebooks are offered throughout this text to assist teachers in this selection.

Frequent experimentation with the various functions of language is an essential component of this language arts program. After each model is introduced, children are engaged in carefully structured activities that employ the ideas being studied. For example, after reading many story beginnings and discovering the characteristics of the beginning of a story, children are invited to apply those story rules in writing a beginning for an original story.

Individualization of instruction may be achieved by modifying the pace and/or expectations for students. For instance, some children will be ready to write original story beginnings immediately; others will require the comfort and security of additional practice with retelling the beginnings of familiar stories. Both activities develop the use of language and enable young writers to discover their own talents and abilities. Few teachers can share these experiences with children without feeling rewarded.

I am a firm believer in the whole language program described in this text. These activities stimulate the thinking of teachers and students, and produce a new depth in children's language skills at all grade levels. These ideas stem from a strong theoretical base, which deserves attention. Teachers should frequently review Chapters 1 and 2 as they first employ the strategies presented in later chapters. Understanding the concepts will enable teachers to experiment with each strategy more effectively to best meet the needs of their students.

I have been sharing the strategies in this book with students and teachers for over 10 years. The teachers' enthusiasm, the students' eagerness to write or to give oral presentations, and the quality of the final products continue to affirm the value of this approach to language arts instruction. Each time teachers read through these pages, they will be challenged to look at children's acquisition of language and the direction of their classroom instructional program in a new way.

Sharon Ackerman
Loudoun County Public Schools
Leesburg, Virginia

Preface

Language Arts: Content and Teaching Strategies is a language arts methods text designed for preservice and inservice teachers who work (or will work) with students in kindergarten through eighth grade. An integrated or "whole language" approach is taken in the book, based on cognitive, developmental, and psycholinguistic theories about how children learn, and how they learn language, in particular. An instructional strategy based on these theories is developed in the first chapter and then applied throughout the text.

Our goal is to present the content of the language arts curriculum and strategies for teaching this content in order for teachers to help students develop communicative competence, the complementary abilities to transmit meaning through talking and writing, and to comprehend meaning through listening and reading. We will discuss language processes, as well as present genuine communication activities to help students develop communicative competence. These activities include conducting oral interviews of community residents; participating in informal debates on relevant topics; writing stories and sharing these stories with classmates and other genuine audiences; keeping learning logs in science classes; and writing simulated newspapers in conjunction with social studies units. We believe that students must actively engage in whatever it is they are to learn.

This text takes a structured approach because we believe students should *learn* how to use language rather than simply *practice* using language. In the past, teachers have admonished students to listen critically, and then assigned them oral reports to give and stories to write. Often the results were disastrous, not because students did not apply themselves, but because they did not know how to comprehend and evaluate the message they listened to, how to prepare and present oral reports, or how to write well-organized and interesting stories.

While the content of the text is divided into traditional chapters on listening, writing, and so on, we have blurred the distinctions between the language modes because students integrate them as they learn language and learn through language. Reading and literature have been integrated throughout the text rather than being placed in separate chapters. Six of the chapters have been devoted to reading and writing, with special emphasis on reading and writing stories. Many student samples have been included and across-the-curriculum applications have been suggested throughout the book.

The final chapter describes how to adapt the content and teaching strategies presented in the text for three types of students with special learning needs—mildly handicapped, language different, and gifted students.

This text has been prepared with the preservice and inservice teachers who will read it in mind, and special features have been included to increase the book's readability. "Points to Ponder" questions are posed before each major section in each chapter to focus readers' attention on key concepts, and newly introduced terms are highlighted and defined in the text. Lists of characteristics, tradebooks, and steps in teaching strategies are presented in figures to highlight them for readers.

Extension activities are included at the end of each chapter. Readers may apply the information that was presented in the chapter through these activities. Many of the extensions invite readers to observe and interact with students in elementary classrooms while others ask them to prepare instructional materials, to consult outside readings, or to examine how they use language themselves. Also, a list of additional readings under the title "If You Want to Learn More" is included at the end of each chapter.

Acknowledgments

Many people helped and encouraged us during the development of this text, and to them we offer our heartfelt thanks. First, we want to thank our graduate and undergraduate students who taught us as we taught them. Their insightful questions challenged and broadened our thinking, and their willingness to experiment with the teaching strategies we were developing furthered our own learning. In particular, we want to acknowledge Sharon Ackerman and Carol Wimmer, who were Ken's students at Virginia Tech, and Chris Edge-Christensen, Sandy Harris, and Carol Ochs who were Gail's students at the University of Oklahoma. We owe a special debt of gratitude to Gail's doctoral student, Donna Camp, who spent many hours researching topics, tracking down books and journal articles, and laboriously verifying references.

We want to express our appreciation to the children whose writing samples and photographs appear in the book and to the teachers and administrators who welcomed us into their schools to take photographs and collect writing samples: Linda Bessett, Sulphur Elementary School, Sulphur, OK; Sherre Carson, George Lynn Cross Academy, Norman, OK; Chris Edge-Christensen, Whittier Elementary School, Lawton, OK; Susan Fields, Noble Junior High School, Noble, OK; Peggy Givens, Watonga Middle School, Watonga, OK; Sandra Harris, Anadarko Middle School, Anadarko, OK; Paula Harrington, Southgate Elementary School, Moore, OK; Beth Hough, Pioneer Intermediate School, Noble, OK; Annette Jacks, Blanchard Elementary School, Blanchard, OK; Janet Kretschmer, McGuffey Foundation School, Oxford, OH; Glenda LoBaugh, Ranchwood Elementary School, Yukon, OK; John McCracken, Nevin Coppock School, Tipp City, OH; Carol Ochs, Patty Cejda, Mike King, David White, and Pam McCarty, Hubbard Elementary School, Noble, OK; Sandra Pabst, Monroe Elementary School, Norman, OK; Audra Paris and Katherine Daily, Crosstimbers Elementary School, Noble, OK; Cindy Perez, John Adams Elementary School, Lawton, OK; Jelta Reneau and M'Lynn Emanuel, Lincoln Elementary School, Norman, OK; Betsy Rice, Sumner School, Sumner, OK; Kim Schmidt, La Petite Academy, Oklahoma City, OK; Letty Watt, Jefferson Elementary School, Norman, OK; Jeanne Webb, Norman Christian Academy, Norman, OK; MaryBeth Webeler and Nancy Hutter, Tioga Elementary School, Bensenville, IL; Jean Winters, Diane Lewis, and Kenneth Muncy, Irving Middle School, Norman, OK. And, thanks, too, to the parents who welcomed us into their homes to take photographs of their children and shared their children's writing samples with us: Regina Blair, Sherry Bynum, John and Lois McCracken, Kendra Magness, Faye Richard, and Susan Steele.

We also thank our colleagues and administrators. In particular, Gail is indebted to Dr. Thomas H. Gallaher, Chair of Instructional Leadership and Academic Curriculum; Fred H. Wood, Dean of the College of Education; and Jack F. Parker, Regents' Professor and former Interim Dean of the College of Education for their appreciation of her work and encouragement on this project.

Our secretaries deserve special recognition for their tireless efforts, typing and editing the many drafts of this book: Bonnie Guthrie and David Starkey at Virginia Tech and Patti Kroenke, Shirley Hodges, Reneé Heath, and Liz Smith at the University of Oklahoma. We also thank the Instructional Services Center at the University of Oklahoma and its director, Dr. Jay Smith, for providing Timothy J. Bernard, a staff photographer, who took many of the photographs that appear in the text.

We also want to recognize our colleagues. Marilyn Friend, Northern Illinois University; Sara Lundsteen, North Texas State University; Lea M. McGee, Louisiana State University; Lee McKenzie, Weber State College; Patricia L. Smith, University of Texas; and Eileen Tway, Miami University, encouraged, listened, and shared their ideas with us. For this collegial support, we are especially grateful. We also want to thank our colleagues who served as reviewers, carefully reading and critically reacting to the several drafts of this book: Lana Smith, Memphis State University; Tim Shanahan, University of Illinois at Chicago; Rebecca P. Harlin, State University College of Arts and Sciences; Pamela Farris, Northern Illinois University; Nancy C. Millett, Wichita State University; and Lavern Warner, Sam Houston University.

Finally, we want to express sincere appreciation to our editors at Merrill Publishing Company. We want to thank our editor, Jeff Johnston, for seeing the project to completion. We also want to thank Pam Bennett, our production editor, who moved the book so efficiently through the maze of production details, and Cindy Peck, our copyeditor, who capably wielded her red pen to smooth out many of the rough spots in the text.

Contents

CHAPTER ONE

How Children Learn

*O*VERVIEW. *In this chapter we will introduce the basic concepts underlying the cognitive and psycholinguistic learning theories that provide the foundation for this textbook. Cognitive development will be discussed in terms of Piaget's concepts of schemata and equilibration. The three modes of learning—experience, observation, and language— will be presented to emphasize that elementary students are concrete thinkers and learn best through active involvement. A model of instruction based on the cognitive processes of assimilation and accommodation will also be presented. Next, we will briefly review the stages of language acquisition and discuss children's oral language development during the elementary grades. We will conclude by describing how parents can best enhance their children's language development and how they can use assisted reading to help their children learn to read.*

Understanding how children learn and how they learn language in particular influences the way language arts is taught. The approach taken in this textbook is a cognitive psycholinguistic view of learning. This view couples the cognitive theories of learning proposed by Jean Piaget, Jerome Bruner, and others with the psycholinguistic theories of language acquisition developed by Roger Brown, Carol Chomsky, David McNeill, and others. Psycholinguistics is a discipline that combines cognitive psychology with linguistics (the study of language) to focus on the cognitive or mental aspects of language learning.

Jean Piaget (1886–1980) was a Swiss psychologist who developed a new theory of learning, or cognitive development, which radically changed conceptions of child development and learning. Piaget's theoretical framework differs substantially from conventional behavioral theories that have influenced education for decades. Central to Piaget's theory are the concepts of cognitive structure, schemata, and equilibration. He describes learning as the modification of students' cognitive structures as they interact with and adapt to their environment. This re-definition of learning requires a re-examination of the teacher's role, too. Instead of dispensing knowledge, the teacher must engage students with experiences and environments that require them to modify their cognitive structures and construct their own knowledge. The teaching strategies set out in this book are designed to help teachers establish learning environments that help their students develop and use oral and written language effectively.

Psycholinguists view language as an example of children's cognitive development, of their ability to learn. Young children learn to talk by being immersed in a language-rich environment and without formal instruction. In the period of only three or four years, children acquire a sizeable vocabulary and internalize the grammar of our language. Studying preschoolers' oral language development provides a model of language learning that can be used in discussing how children learn to read and write.

POINTS TO PONDER
How Do Children Learn?
How Do Children Process Stimuli in Their Environments?
How Do Children Organize Their Knowledge?
What Motivates Children to Learn?

THE COGNITIVE STRUCTURE

The *cognitive structure* is the organization of knowledge in the brain, and knowledge is organized into category systems called *schemata.* Within the schemata are three components: (a) categories of knowledge, (b) the features, or rules for determining what constitutes a category and what will be included in each category, and (c) a network of interrelationships among the categories (Smith, 1975). These schemata may be compared to a conceptual filing system in which children and adults organize and store the information derived from their past experiences.

Children learn by developing their schemata through the dual processes of assimilation and accommodation.

As children learn, they invent new categories, and while each person has many similar categories, schemata are personalized according to individual experiences and interests. For example, some people may have only one general category, *bugs,* into which they lump their knowledge of ants, butterflies, spiders, and bees, while other people distinguish between *insects* and *spiders* and develop a category for each. Those people who distinguish also develop a set of rules based on the distinctive characteristics of these animals for classifying them into one category or the other.

Diagrams called *semantic maps* (Pearson & Johnson, 1978) can be drawn to illustrate these categories or segments of them. Two semantic maps are presented in Figure 1–1. The first map is for a *bug* category in which insects and spiders are grouped together. This semantic map is undeveloped and is characteristic of the thinking of young children as well as of adults who have little knowledge of insects or arachnids. In contrast, the second semantic map for the category *spider* is more sophisticated. It indicates that the person can not only distinguish between bugs in general and spiders in particular but can also list the distinctive characteristics of the more narrow category of spiders. For example, the characteristics of spiders are identified and examples of a few kinds of spiders are listed together with the distinguishing features of each.

Semantic maps can be drawn to illustrate any concept. The complexity of information included in each semantic map depends on the person's past experiences and knowledge of the particular concept. For example, the information included in the *spider* semantic map in Figure 1–1 may differ dramatically from a *spider* map any other individual would draw. Perhaps another person would include the names of spiders indigenous to their community. A gardener making this semantic map would know that spiders are useful because they kill and eat harmful insects and might include that information. Another person, whose knowledge about spiders is limited to having read E. B. White's *Charlotte's web* (1952) might include completely different information.

In addition to *bug* or *spider* categories, a network of interrelationships connect these categories to other categories. Networks, too, are individualized, depending on each person's unique knowledge and experiences. In the *spider* semantic web in Figure 1–1, for instance, spiders are listed as a subcategory of arachnids and animals, and ticks, scorpions, and daddy-longlegs are listed as other examples of the *arachnid* category. The class relationship between scorpions and spiders is shown in the map. Other networks, such as a line to a *poisonous animals* category, could have been included in the semantic map, but overlapping lines, ovals, and rectangles make the map extremely difficult to decipher. In reality, networks that link categories, characteristics, and examples with other categories, characteristics, and examples are very complex.

Assimilation and Accommodation

As children adapt to their environment, they add new information about their experiences, requiring them to enlarge existing categories or to construct new ones. According to Piaget (1969), two processes, assimilation and accommodation,

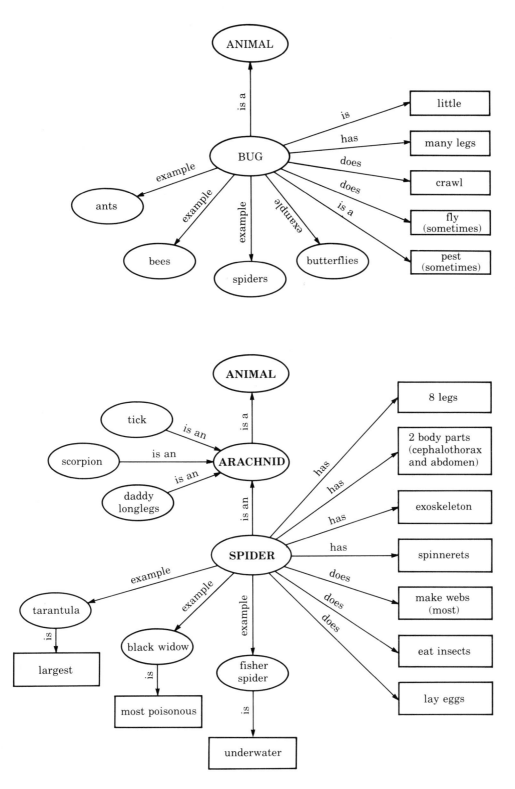

Figure 1–1 Semantic Maps of *Bug* and *Spider*

make this change possible. *Assimilation* is the cognitive process by which information from the environment is integrated into existing schemata. In contrast, *accommodation* is the cognitive process by which existing schemata are modified or new schemata are restructured to adapt to the environment. Through assimilation, children add new information to their picture of the world; through accommodation, they change their picture of the world on the basis of new information.

Development of Schemata

The sucking reflex provides a good example of the processes of assimilation and accommodation. Sucking begins as a reflex activity when babies are born. An infant will suck on anything that is put into its mouth. This suggests that the *schema* (singular for schemata) for sucking is undifferentiated. A few weeks after birth, however, the baby soon distinguishes the nipple that gives milk from other objects that do not. The baby may be content to suck on other objects between feedings, but at feeding time it seeks only the milk-dispensing nipple.

The baby has developed two schemata: (a) a schema for the nipple that produces milk and (b) a schema for objects that do not produce milk. The baby has assimilated and differentiated the milk-producing stimulus from the non milk-producing stimulus and has accommodated both stimuli by changing the original sucking schema to match the environment. The new schemata are related to each other because they both are differentiated forms of the sucking schema.

The processes of assimilation and accommodation also operate as students develop language arts-related schemata for concepts such as homonyms, verbs, and haiku poetry. For example, second and third graders are typically introduced to the concept of homonyms*, or sets of words that are pronounced alike but are spelled differently and have different meanings, such as *to-two-too, bear-bare,* and *one-won.* These and other examples of homonyms are listed in Figure 1–2. Most primary grade students are aware that some words sound alike, and there may have been occasions when they used the incorrect spelling in their writing. Other sets of homonyms will be unfamiliar to them. The teacher may present homonyms by listing examples on the chalkboard for students to compare. Students begin to assimilate information about the concept by relating these words to the information in their existing schemata.

Next, the teacher provides the label *homonyms,* defines the concept, and provides additional examples. Books illustrating homonyms may also be shared with students. Figure 1–3 lists homonym books appropriate for second and third graders. Students may also look for examples of correct or incorrect homonym

---

Homonyms, or the general category of words that sound alike, is a label typically used in the primary and intermediate grades. More specifically, there are several kinds of homonyms. *Homophones* are words, such as *to-two-too,* that are pronounced alike but spelled differently. *Homographic homophones* are words that are pronounced and spelled alike, such as *bat* (baseball *bat* and nocturnal animal *bat*). In contrast, *homographs* are words that are spelled alike but pronounced differently, such as *read* (present tense and past tense).

ail-ale	hear-here	rap-wrap
ate-eight	heard-herd	read-red
bail-bale	hi-high	right-write
ball-bawl	hoarse-horse	ring-wring
bare-bear	hole-whole	root-route
be-bee	hour-our	sail-sale
beat-beet	knight-night	scene-seen
berry-bury	knot-not	sea-see
blew-blue	know-no	sew-so
board-bored	knows-nose	soar-sore
braid-brayed	lead-led	son-sun
brake-break	made-maid	stake-steak
ceiling-sealing	marry-Mary-merry	stares-stairs
cell-sell	meat-meet	steal-steel
cent-scent-sent	might-mite	tacks-tax
chili-chilly	moose-mousse	tail-tale
Claus-clause-claws	none-nun	tea-tee
dear-deer	oar-or-ore	to-too-two
die-dye	one-won	toe-tow
faint-feint	pain-pane	their-there-they're
fairy-ferry	pair-pare	told-tolled
find-fined	peak-peek	vain-vane-vein
flea-flee	peal-peel-peil	wail-whale
flour-flower	pedal-peddle-petal	waist-waste
for-fore-four	pole-poll	wait-weight
gorilla-guerrilla	praise-prays-preys	wear-where
grate-great	presence-presents	which-witch
hair-hare	prince-prints	wood-would
hay-hey	rain-rein-reign	
heal-heel	raise-rays	

Figure 1–2   A List of Homonyms

use in their own writing. Accommodation occurs as students change their schemata to incorporate new information about homonyms and examples of homonyms.

Students refine their understanding of homonyms as they experiment with them in their writing. Students can experiment with homonyms by compiling a homonym book in which a set of homonyms is illustrated with drawings or sentences on each page. Each student in the class could contribute one page for the book, or they could compile individual booklets. Figure 1–4 presents a page from

Figure 1–3 Books About Homonyms

Basil, C. (1980). *How ships play cards: A beginning book of homonyms.* New York: Morrow. (M)

Gwynne, F. (1976). *A chocolate moose for dinner.* New York: Windmill. (P–M–U)

Gwynne, F. (1970). *The king who rained.* New York: Windmill. (P–M–U)

Hanlon, E. (1976). *How a horse grew hoarse on the site where he sighted a bare bear.* New York: Delacorte. (M)

Hanson, J. (1972). *Homonyms.* Minneapolis, MN: Lerner. (P–M)

Howe, D. & Howe, J. (1979). *Bunnicula: A rabbit-tale of mystery.* New York: Atheneum. (M)

Terban, M. (1982). *Eight ate: A feast of homonym riddles.* Boston: Houghton Mifflin. (M)

P = primary grades (K–2)
M = middle grades (3–5)
U = upper grades (6–8)

Figure 1–4 A Page from a Second Grader's Homonym Book

Jaclyn, age 7

a homonym book written and illustrated by a second grader. Students might also write their own homonym riddle books following the model provided in Marvin Terban's *Eight ate: A feast of homonym riddles* (1982).

The schemata that children develop and refine during the elementary grades include both general knowledge concepts as well as specialized language concepts and concepts related to other content areas. Children develop schemata for language skills such as how to use punctuation marks (see Chapter 6) and for language processes and strategies, such as taking notes (see Chapter 3) and using the writing process (see Chapter 6).

Equilibration

The mechanism for cognitive growth or learning is the process of *equilibration* (Piaget, 1975). When children experience something they do not understand or cannot assimilate, it causes *disequilibrium,* or cognitive conflict. Disequilibrium typically produces confusion and agitation, feelings that impel children to seek *equilibrium,* or a comfortable balance with the environment. In other words, when confronted with new or discrepant information, children (as well as adults) are intrinsically motivated to try to make sense out of it. If the children's schemata can accommodate the new information, then the disequilibrium caused by the new experience will motivate the children to learn. Equilibrium is thus regained at a higher developmental level. The steps of this process are summarized in Figure 1–5.

If however, the new information is too difficult, and children cannot relate it to what they already know, they will not learn. The important implication for teachers is that the new information being presented must be puzzling, challenging, or to use Piaget's words, *"moderately novel."* Information that is too easy is quickly assimilated, and information that is too difficult cannot be accommodated and will not be learned. Bybee and Sund (1982) suggest that teachers strive for an "optimum mismatch" between what children already know and the new information being presented.

---

1. Equilibrium is disrupted by the introduction of new or discrepant information.
2. Disequilibrium occurs, and the dual processes of assimilation and accommodation function.
3. Equilibrium is attained at a higher development level.

Figure 1–5   Steps in the Equilibration Process

Motivation

The motivation to learn is intrinsic, based on the need to seek equilibrium. The cognitive structure is self-regulating; that is, children motivate themselves. Outside forces—including teachers—do not motivate; they can only stimulate. The focus of development and growth, however, is on children's own abilities to construct for themselves rather than upon the environment shaping them. The environment merely provides the stimuli; it is not the cause or agent of development and growth. Children's development is the result of creating and enlarging schemata by means of assimilation and accommodation.

Anticipatory and Predictive Behavior

If we refer to the example of a baby using the sucking schema to act on an environment in which some stimuli are milk producing and others are not, we can see the beginnings of children's abilities to anticipate events and organize their behaviors accordingly. The baby at feeding time comes in contact with the milk-dispensing nipple. It has accommodated its sucking schema to act on the nipple to produce the desired effect—getting some milk.

Gradually, however, greater and greater differentiation of stimuli will occur. The reflexive schemata of sucking, grasping, and looking will be used to assimilate and accommodate new stimuli. New schemata will continue to develop and greater elaboration of existing schemata will occur.

Children's anticipatory behaviors become more refined as they develop additional schemata. The reflexive activity of anticipating milk from the nipple becomes generalized to other schemata. Children's knowledge then enables them to anticipate discrepant or unfamiliar stimuli in situations for which they have previously developed schemata.

Anticipatory behavior occurs as children put their schemata to use in interpreting their environment. They anticipate what will happen if they act in certain ways and predict the results of their actions. When children enter any situation, they organize their behavior according to what they can anticipate, using those schemata that would be appropriate to assimilate whatever is in the environment that interests them. If their schemata can assimilate all stimuli in the situation, they relax because they are in a comfortable state of equilibrium. However, if there are stimuli in the environment for which they cannot predict the results, they will proceed more cautiously, trying to discover the meanings of the stimuli they cannot anticipate. Children seek equilibrium, but they are always undergoing disequilibrium because they cannot assimilate discrepant stimuli without some accommodation.

Learning

Piaget has provided the framework for learning through his ideas of schemata, assimilation, and accommodation. The schemata provide the structures for adapting to and organizing information. Learning takes place when existing schemata must be enlarged because of assimilated information and when the schemata must be restructured to account for new data and experiences being acted on and accommodated.

As students engage in learning activities, they are faced with learning and discovering some new element in an otherwise known or familiar system of information. Students recognize or seek out the information embedded in a situation that makes sense and is moderately novel. By being forced to contend with the novel part of the information, students' schemata are disrupted or put in a state of disequilibrium. The accommodation of the novel information causes a reorganization of the schemata, resulting in students having more complex schemata and being able to operate on more complex information than was previously possible.

Frank Smith (1975) has suggested a metaphor that is useful in describing schemata. He likens the cognitive structure to a "theory of the world in the head." This theory summarizes everything that has been learned, determines how new data will be perceived and interpreted, and provides information for making hypotheses about the future.

Students learn by relating the known to the unknown as they try to make sense out of what they encounter in their environment. Instruction should be focused on helping students relate what they know to what they do not know. The amount of new information in a lesson should be within students' capacity to assimilate and accommodate without experiencing long periods of disequilibrium.

Teachers can create optimal conditions for learning in the lessons they prepare for their students. When students do not have the schemata for predicting and interpreting the new information, they must relate what they know to what they do not know. Therefore, the new information must be included in a situation that makes sense to students, and the information must be moderately novel. It must not be too difficult for them to accommodate to it.

Students process information or learn by three modes: (a) experience, (b) observation, and (c) language (Smith, 1975). For example, imagine that a boy has just received a new two-wheel bicycle for his fifth birthday. How will he learn to ride it? Will his parents read a book about bicycles to him? Will his father demonstrate how to ride the new bicycle while the boy observes? Will the boy get on his new bicycle and learn to ride it by trial and error? Of course, he will get on his new bicycle and learn to ride it by riding, through direct experience. Later, his father might demonstrate a tricky maneuver his son is having trouble mastering, or the boy may become so interested in bicycle riding that he will be motivated to read a book to learn more about it. Yet, the learning process begins with experience for both in-school and out-of-school learning.

Experience is the most basic, concrete way of learning. According to Piaget (1969), elementary students are concrete thinkers and learn best through active involvement. The second and third learning modes, observation and language, are progressively more abstract and further removed from experience. Activities involving observation and language can be made more meaningful when used in conjunction with direct experience and real-life materials. A list of school experiences using each mode is presented in Figure 1–6.

Experience	*Observation*	*Language*
interviewing	creating filmstrips	brainstorming
manipulating objects	drawing and painting	choral speaking/reading
participating in dramatic	pictures	debating
play	making diagrams,	dictating stories
participating in field trips	clusters, and story maps	discussing
participating in informal	"reading" and using non-	listening to audiotapes
drama activities	verbal language	listening to stories read
using puppets	"reading" wordless	aloud
using the five senses	picture books	participating in
writing simulated journals	viewing films, filmstrips,	conversations
and newspapers	and videotapes	participating in readers
	viewing charts, maps, and	theater
	models	reading
	viewing plays and puppet	taking notes
	shows	talking
	viewing and writing	writing
	concrete poetry	
	watching demonstrations	
	writing class	
	collaboration stories	

Figure 1–6   Activities Using the Three Learning Modes

POINTS TO PONDER

How Can a Model of Instruction Be Constructed from the Concepts of Assimilation and Accommodation?

What Effect Will a Model of Instruction Have on the Language Arts Program?

AN INSTRUCTIONAL MODEL

The processes of assimilation and accommodation can be used to develop a model of instruction that can be adapted to various teaching strategies used in a language arts program. As noted earlier, assimilation begins after children perceive something in the environment. If they do not have schemata that fit the information being assimilated, cognitive conflict occurs; they must either restructure an existing schema to fit the information or develop a new schema that fits the information. They then adjust the interrelationships among existing schemata to accommodate the new schema.

A model of instruction can be developed that incorporates the main aspects of cognitive theory discussed in this chapter. The model establishes a sequence of instruction for the interaction of students, teacher, and materials in an environment that promotes the assimilation and accommodation of the information presented. The steps in the sequence of instruction are (a) *initiating*, (b) *structuring*, (c) *conceptualizing*, (d) *summarizing*, (e) *generalizing*, and (f) *applying*. The steps are described in the following sections and summarized in Figure 1–7.

Steps in the Instructional Sequence

Initiating. In this step, teachers introduce the information they want students to use in learning a concept or in understanding some type of information. The initiating step includes the initial questions, statements, and activities that teachers use to stimulate interest in the lesson materials and to obtain the participation of students. The process of assimilation begins when students are stimulated to participate in the lesson, and it will continue until cognitive conflict occurs.

Structuring. In this step, teachers structure the information so that students can begin to overcome the cognitive conflict they experienced in the initiating

1. *Initiating*

   Introduce new information and stimulate students' interest.

2. *Structuring*

   Structure information to facilitate accommodation.

3. *Conceptualizing*

   Establish relationships between information presented in steps 1 and 2.

4. *Summarizing*

   Review major points.

5. *Generalizing*

   Present new information as a comprehension check.

6. *Applying*

   Use newly learned concept or information in an activity.

Figure 1–7   Steps in the Instructional Model

step. To overcome their cognitive conflict, students begin to enlarge or restructure an existing schema to fit the information, or they begin to develop new schema to organize the information. The information must be moderately novel and be related in some way to what students already know. By relating new information to what students already know, teachers have more assurance that students will be able to assimilate and accommodate it. Teachers must explore with students what information they already have in their schemata. Teachers can only infer students' existing schemata from what they say and do.

Conceptualizing. In this step, teachers focus students' attention on the relationships among the pieces of information they present. In the previous step, teachers located and established the information; in the conceptualizing step, teachers try to organize and make explicit the relationships that exist among the facts and further the process of accommodation begun during structuring. When the accommodation process is completed, the existing schemata have been enlarged or a new schema has been developed that fits the new information. In either case the cognitive conflict that was begun in the initiating step has been eliminated.

Summarizing. Teachers review the major points of the lesson in this step. The material used in the structuring step and the relationships established during the conceptualizing step are organized and summarized for use in reviewing the concept. This step allows students to make any needed adjustments in the concept or information and in the interrelationships established within their cognitive structures with this information. For those students who did not complete the accommodation process in the conceptualizing step, summarizing presents another opportunity to accommodate the information.

Generalizing. Here teachers present information similar to that introduced in the initiating step. The same concept or information is contained in this new material. This step is a check on students' understanding of the concept presented in the lesson. Students demonstrate their understanding by generalizing from the first material to this new material.

Applying. In this step, students incorporate the concept or information in an activity that allows them to demonstrate their knowledge by using the concept in a novel or unique way.

Using the Instructional Model

Students do not, of course, learn in such neat little steps. Rather, learning is a process of ebb and flow in which assimilating and accommodating processes move back and forth as pieces of information are grasped. Students may grasp a new concept in any of the steps of the instructional model; some students may not learn it at all. Teachers will need to plan additional lessons for those students who do not learn. Whether or not they learn depends on the closeness of the fit between their schemata and the information being presented. Information that does not relate to an existing schema in some way is almost impossible to learn. Information must be just moderately novel to fit students' existing cognitive structures.

Some lessons may not lend themselves readily to this six-step sequence of instruction. For certain concepts, one or more of the steps may not be appropriate, and some adjustments may be necessary. Assimilation and accommodation, however, will be operating as students process the informaton being presented.

One element of story structure, motifs, will be used to develop a lesson sequence using this instructional model. Briefly, a *motif* is the structural main idea of a story. One of the basic motifs in children's literature is "a character's journey from home to a confrontation with a monster." *Little Red Riding Hood* (Hyman, 1983) is a good example of this motif. As you read through the following steps in teaching motifs, you may notice that the initiating and structuring steps overlap somewhat. The material presented in the initiating step is already structured so that the students can begin the processes of assimilation and accommodation. Also, the summarizing step is not crucial to this lesson because students seem to have little difficulty grasping motifs.

Initiating.   Display a chart containing the motif, "A character's journey from home to a confrontation with a monster." Read the motif and discuss it with your students. Define a motif as the structural main idea of a story. Students will begin the assimilation process and have some cognitive conflict with the term *motif* and its definition. Kindergarten or first-grade teachers may need to simplify the terminology in the definition of the motif. It might be phrased as "someone leaves home and meets a monster." Even though the terminology may need to be simplified for young children, they can understand the motif and can tell stories using it.

Structuring.   Have students read two or three stories that contain the "monster" motif, or read these stories aloud to them. For example, folktales such as *The three billy goats Gruff, The three little pigs,* and *Little Red Riding Hood* can be used. Explain the motif in each story. Use the names of the story characters and explain the journey and the confrontation. Reading the stories and explaining the motif help students accommodate the information about motifs and develop a schema for them.

Conceptualizing.   Read two or three other stories and ask students to describe the motif. Have students explain the motif in terms of a journey, a monster, or a confrontation. If they can explain the motif, they have assimilated and accommodated the information presented in the initiating step. Students may not be able to repeat the motif exactly as it was presented, but they will know what it is.

Summarizing.   Review the definition of a motif. Have a student read the motif from the chart. Ask various students to explain the motif in each of the stories read and discussed in the structuring and conceptualizing steps. Students should be able to assimilate any variations on the motif and relate them to their newly developed schema.

Generalizing. Read additional stories to the students and have them explain the motif, including the characters, the journey, the nature of the monster, and elements of the confrontation.

Applying. Have students tell, dictate, or write stories using the motif. Let them model their stories after those read to them in the generalizing step. If students structure their stories on the basis of the monster motif, it will verify that they have developed the schema for motifs.

POINTS TO PONDER

What Is the Relationship Between Cognitive Development and Language?

What Are the Three Language Systems?

How Do Children Develop Language?

What Language Competencies Do Children Acquire During the Elementary School Years?

LANGUAGE DEVELOPMENT

Even in the first moments of life, infants begin to categorize their experiences to try to organize and control their world. They learn to recognize and name objects in their environments; they learn to understand and communicate with other fellow beings; they learn to cooperate as they assume roles as members of families, communities, countries, and the world.

Language becomes children's primary means of classifying and exerting control over their experiences. With words, they can begin to label their categories of experience, create more elaborate categories as they learn new information, and relate all of these different categories that make up their cognitive structures. It is with words that children organize their experiences and make, confirm, or reject predictions that lead to their continued cognitive development. Language enables children to learn about their world, to understand it, to control it. It is indeed a powerful tool.

The Three Language Systems

As children learn to talk, they implicitly develop knowledge about three language systems: (a) the phonological system, (b) the syntactic system, and (c) the semantic system. Children develop the *phonological,* or sound system, as they learn to pronounce each of the approximately 40 English speech sounds. These individual sounds are called phonemes, and they are represented in print with diagonal lines to differentiate them from letters (or graphemes). Thus, the first letter in *mother* is written *m* while the first phoneme is written /m/. The second language system is the *syntactic,* or grammar, system. The word *grammar* (also referred to as *syntax*) is used here to mean the rules governing how words are combined in sentences

Language is both a means of classifying experiences into categories and communicating experiences to other people.

rather than the grammar textbooks used in school or the correct etiquette of language. Children use the syntactic system as they combine words to form sentences, and they learn to comprehend and produce statements, questions, and other types of sentences during the preschool years.

Another aspect of syntax is *morphology,* the study of word forms. Children quickly learn to combine words and word parts such as adding -*s* to *dog* to create a plural and -*ed* to *play* to indicate past tense. These words and word parts are *morphemes,* the smallest units of meaning in language. *Dog* and *play* are *free morphemes* because they convey meaning while standing alone. The endings -*s* and -*ed* are *bound morphemes* because they must be attached to free morphemes to convey meaning. Prefixes and suffixes are also bound morphemes. In addition to combining bound morphemes with free morphemes, two or more free morphemes can be combined to form compound words. *Birthday* is an example of a compound word created by combining two free morphemes.

The third language system is the *semantic,* or meaning, system. Vocabulary and the arrangement of words in sentences are the key components of this system.

As children learn to talk, they acquire a vocabulary which is continually increasing through the preschool years. It has been estimated that children have a vocabulary of 5,000 words by the time they enter school. As children are acquiring these vocabulary words, they are also learning how to string them together to form English sentences. For instance, children say "The dog has a bone" not "A has dog bone the." In English, word order and the relationships among words are crucial in comprehending the message.

As children learn to talk, and later to read and write, these are the three language systems they learn to control. During this chapter and throughout this book, we will refer to these systems using the terminology introduced in this section. Because the terminology can be confusing, the words are also defined in Figure 1–8.

Stages of Development

Young children acquire oral language in a fairly regular and systematic way. All children pass through the same stages, but they do so at widely different ages. The ages mentioned in this section are estimates, for reference only.

Phonological System

phonology	The study of the sounds in a language.
phoneme	The smallest unit of sound.
grapheme	The written representation of a sound using one or more letters.

Syntactic System

syntax or grammar	The rules governing how words are combined to form sentences.
morphology	The study of morphemes or word forms.
morpheme	The smallest unit of meaning in a language.
free morpheme	A morpheme that can stand alone as a word.
bound morpheme	A morpheme that cannot stand alone as a word and must be attached to a free morpheme.

Semantic System

semantics	The study of the meaning of a language.

Figure 1–8 Terminology for the Three Language Systems

The first real evidence that children are developing language occurs when they speak their first words. Prior to that time, they have experimented with sounds, a stage known as "babbling." Typically, during the first year of life, babies vocalize a wide variety of speech-like sounds. The sounds they produce are repeated strings of consonant plus vowel syllables. Amazingly, babies' vocalizations include English sounds as well as sounds used in German, Russian, Japanese, and other languages. The sounds not common to English gradually drop out, probably the result of both listening to sounds in the environment and parents' reinforcement of familiar sounds such as the eagerly awaited *ma-ma* and *da-da*.

One-Word Utterances.   Beginning at approximately 12 months of age, young children begin to use one-word utterances, or *holophrastic speech,* to express complex ideas. This is the first stage in which children use words to communicate. These first words are most often nouns, adjectives, or invented words (McNeill, 1970). Examples of one-word utterances include "Milk" and "Ball." While anxious parents often try to read meaning into babies' babbling, it is difficult to understand children's meaning without observing their accompanying actions or gestures. For example, "Ball" may mean "Look, I see a ball," "I want that ball," or "Oops, I dropped my ball, and I can't reach it."

Greenfield and Smith (1976) suggest that as children begin using one-word utterances to communicate meaning, they make their system of nonlinguistic communication more powerful with the addition of language. A relationship is believed to exist between the cognitive structure and language that enables children to systematically combine their words with nonverbal clues.

Two-Word Utterances.   In this stage, children use two-word utterances such as "bye-bye car," "light off," and "allgone cookie." This speech is called *telegraphic* because nonessential words are omitted as they are in telegrams. Children use nouns, verbs, and adjectives—all high information words. Low information words—prepositions, articles, and conjunctions—are omitted.

The emergence of children's two-word utterances at approximately 18 months of age signals the beginning of word order patterns in children's speech. Their words can be classified into two functional categories: open class (O) and pivot class (P) words. Most words fall into the *open* class, which includes nouns, verbs, adjectives, and adverbs. The *pivot* words are similar to pronouns, prepositions, conjunctions, and auxiliary verbs in adult speech.

Researchers have identified several basic syntactic patterns in children's telegraphic speech (Braine, 1963; McNeill, 1970). They have found that young children combine words in the following ways:

Combinations	Sample Utterances
P + O	"allgone milk"
O + P	"shirt off"
O + O	"baby sleep"
O	"Daddy"

These syntactic patterns, known as *pivot grammar,* indicate that young children's speech is rule governed, and that they create their own ways to represent meaning rather than simply imitating adult language. However, a serious shortcoming of pivot grammar is that the meanings of children's utterances are far more complex than the pivot and open class combinations suggest.

An alternate way to analyze young children's early language is to consider the semantic or functional relationships between the words that the child says. For example, the phrase "Mommy hat" may indicate a possessive relationship between the words, as in "Here is Mommy's hat," or may show an agent-object relationship, as in "Mommy has a hat," depending on the child's intention. Researchers have identified a number of relationships in children's two-word utterances. A partial list of these relationships include:

Relationships	Sample Utterances
agent-action	"daddy eat"
agent-object	"hit ball"
possessive	"baby shoe"
demonstrative	"that book"
attributive	"big truck"
location-object	"book table"
location-action	"put floor" (Menyuk, 1977, p. 70)

The researchers who describe two-word utterances in terms of semantic relationships are interested in discovering the underlying meanings that are represented in children's speech.

Utterances Longer Than Two Words.   The development of syntax proceeds from the base of the semantic functions of holophrastic speech that are part linguistic, part nonlinguistic. Word order, the basis of syntax in English, becomes important when children begin using utterances of three and four words. At this point grammatical relations such as subject, verb, and object begin to appear in overt syntactic structures. Syntactic structures are differentiated from adult speech and integrated into children's grammars. The phonological, syntactic, and semantic systems are constructed as development continues to come closer and closer to the adult form of the language used in their speech communities.

Children's use of negatives is an example of how their perceptions change and they gradually develop the adult form of a syntactic structure. At first young children simply negate positive statements by adding the word *no,* and they may say "no milk" or "he no go." With additional experiences with language, their perceptions change, and they learn to combine *not* with auxiliary verbs such as *have* and *do* to produce sentences such as "I don't have any milk" and "He didn't go." These changes illustrate that children perceive new forms and develop new ways to express them.

The processes of assimilation and accommodation are active in the hypothesis testing that children do as they work out the syntax of their language. As they perceive some new element of grammatical structure, such as the negative, they assimilate what they can and then accommodate their current linguistic structure.

Their accommodation amounts to working out a structure that fits the reality they perceive. At first the structure is a hypothesis. If the hypothesis fits the reality perceived, it is retained, and the linguistic information is assimilated. As children's perceptions change, the structure that once served them adequately no longer can handle the linguistic information being assimilated. Their perceptions must be changed, that is, accommodated to match the new reality. As in the case of the negative structure, the processes of assimilation and accommodation continue until the structure matches the adult form used in the children's speech community.

Children's use of past tense follows a similar pattern. At first they use the unmarked form of irregular verbs such as *ate* or *ran* that they hear in the speech of those around them. After they perceive that past tense is marked with the *-ed* inflection, they begin to use it with practically all past tense verbs (e.g., *eated* and *runned*). It is not until much later that children return to using the correct form of the irregular verbs again. The tendency to overgeneralize the *-ed* inflection that marks the past tense of regular verbs continues even when children enter school.

As children continue to develop their language competence, their semantic and grammatical relations become more complex. Their sentences grow in length and complexity; they develop the auxiliary system and transformations; they develop the ability to change the word order of their sentences to express the meanings desired. The initial physical and emotional context of speech with objects, people, events, and locations continues to play an important role in their language development. By the time children enter school, they are comprehending and producing utterances that are like the adult forms in their syntactic characteristics.

Children use speech for social purposes, that is, to communicate with others. Researchers have just recently begun to study children's language in social context, a field called pragmatics. Preschoolers learn language routines, courtesy words such as *please* and *thank you,* and other language conventions. They also learn about the appropriateness of language in varied situations—that some things are appropriate to talk about with people outside the family while others are not. Later during the elementary school years, children learn the social conventions of school language as well as playground language.

Development in the Elementary Grades

While the most critical period in oral language acquisition is during the preschool years, children's phonological, syntactic, and semantic development continues through the elementary grades and beyond. They continue to acquire additional sentence patterns, their vocabularies expand tremendously, and they master the remaining sounds of English.

Phonological Development.   Children have mastered a large part of the phonological system by the time they come to school. However, a few sounds, especially in medial and final positions, are not acquired until after age 5. These sounds include /v/, /th/, /ch/, /sh/, and /zh/. Even at age 7 or 8, students still make some sound substitutions, especially in consonant clusters. For example, they may substitute /w/ for /r/ or /l/ as in *cwack* for *crack* (DeStefano, 1978). The implication for teaching language arts is clear: Students will read words aloud the same way they say them. Also, they will spell words phonetically the same way they say them.

Syntactic Development.   During the elementary grades, students acquire a variety of sentence patterns. They begin to construct complex sentences and use embedding techniques to combine ideas. While primary grade students use the connector *and* to string together a series of ideas, middle and upper grade students learn to use dependent clauses and other connectors. For example, a young child might say, "I have a gerbil *and* he is brown *and* his name is Pumpkin *and* he likes to run on his wheel." An older student can embed these ideas: "My brown gerbil named Pumpkin likes to run on his wheel." Older students learn to use connectors such as *because, if, unless, meanwhile, in spite of,* and *nevertheless* (Loban, 1976). The constructions students learn to use in their talk also appear in their writing. Ingram (1975) found that fifth- and seventh-grade students used more complex, embedded structures in writing than in talk. This makes sense because when students write, they must organize their thoughts and, for efficiency, embed as much information as possible.

Students also learn more about word order in English sentences. Consider these two sentences:

Ann told Tom to leave.

Ann promised Tom to leave.

Who is going to leave? According to the Minimal Distance Principle (MDP), the noun closest to the complement verb (i.e., *to leave*) is the subject of that verb. In the first sentence, *Tom* is the person who will leave. Substitute these other verbs for *told: asked, wanted, tried, urged, commanded, implored.* In each case *Tom* is the person to leave. However, *promise* is an exception to the MDP, and in the second sentence, it is *Ann,* not *Tom* who will leave. Chomsky (1969) found that primary grade students overgeneralize the MDP principle and equate *promise* sentences with *tell* sentences. During the middle grades, however, students learn to distinguish the exceptions to the rule.

As students learn to read, they are introduced to the more complex syntactic forms and other conventions found in written language. One form unique to writing is the passive voice. The active voice is almost always used in talk (e.g., "Bobby broke the vase") rather than the passive voice (e.g., "The vase was broken by Bobby").

Children's syntactic development during this period suggests several implications for language arts instruction. Through reading and writing activities, students investigate the syntactic forms and other conventions unique to written language. Children's literature provides a rich source of written language material. As they read, students will encounter the language forms they are learning. Also, sentence combining activities allow students the opportunity to experiment with the many ways ideas can be combined, related, and embedded in sentences.

Semantic Development.   Of the three language systems, Lindfors (1980) says that semantic growth is the most vigorous in the elementary grades. Children's semantic system develops at a slower rate and over a longer period of time than their phonological and syntactic systems. During the elementary grades, children's vocabulary increases at a very rapid rate. It has been estimated to increase at the rate of 1,000 to 2,000 words per year!

Vocabulary growth is only one aspect of semantic development. A second aspect is the meanings of words. Very few words have only one meaning; the meaning of words is usually based on context, or the words surrounding them. The common word *run,* for instance, has more than 30 meanings listed in *The American Heritage Dictionary* (1983). The meaning of the word is tied to the context in which it is used:

> Will the mayor *run* for re-election?
>
> The bus *runs* between Dallas and Houston.
>
> The advertisement will *run* for three days.
>
> The plane made a bombing *run.*
>
> Will you *run* to the store and get a loaf of bread for me?
>
> The dogs are out in the *run.*
>
> Oh, no! I got a *run* in my new pair of pantyhose!

Researchers have found that children do not have the full, adult meaning of many words. For example, very young children call all men *daddy,* but with more experience, they refine their meaning of *daddy* to refer to only one very special man. Clark (1971) suggests that children learn the meanings of words through a process of refinement. They add "features" or layers of meaning. In the elementary grades, students use this refinement process to distinguish between pairs of words such as *ask* and *tell* to expand their range of meanings for many common words.

In the elementary school, vocabulary instruction focuses both on acquiring new words as well as learning the multiple meanings of commonly used words. Children need to learn both denotative (explicit) as well as connotative (implied) meanings, euphemisms (substituting a more pleasant expression for an offensive one, e.g., *passed away* for *died*), and the figurative versus literal meanings of idioms (e.g., "in hot water"). They also learn about the relationships among words by studying the *nyms*—antonyms (words that are opposite in meaning, e.g., *love-hate*), synonyms (words that are similar in meaning, e.g., *street-road*), and homonyms (words that sound alike but have different meanings, e.g., *bat-bat, to-two-too*). Vocabulary activities should be much more than mechanical, look-it-up-in-the-dictionary assignments; they should be tied to work with concrete materials, informal drama, and literature.

POINTS TO PONDER
What Contributions Do Parents Make to Their Children's Language Development?

How Can Parents Introduce Their Children to Books and to Reading?

Why Should Parents Read Aloud to Their Preschoolers?
What are the Steps in the Assisted Reading Strategy?
What are Predictable Books?

PARENTS AND LANGUAGE DEVELOPMENT

Parents play a crucial role in their child's language development, and this role begins as soon as the child is born. In addition to being the main source of language for their child, parents expand and extend the child's speech and provide experiences that enhance the child's cognitive development. They also introduce their preschooler to books and reading.

From the onset of the holophrastic stage of language development, parents take a more active role in providing the linguistic raw material children use in learning to talk. When children begin using two-word utterances, parents begin to expand their sentences (Brown & Bellugi-Klima, 1971). For example, when a child says "Baby highchair," the mother often expands the sentence to "Yes, baby is in the highchair." The process of expanding young children's speech supplies them with function words: prepositions, pronouns, and articles. Parents also introduce some auxiliary verbs in the expansions they make. The expansions preserve the word order of the children's sentences but add the functions they have dropped from their sentences.

Another contribution that parents make to their children's language development is in extending the children's utterances. In contrast to expansions which are limited to the information contained in the utterance, extensions add information for the child to process. For example, to the child's utterance, "Dog bark," a parent may respond, "Yes, the dog is barking at the kitty," and provide information about why the dog is barking (Cazden, 1972). This extension helps the child interpret what is happening in the environment and adds grammatical information. Expansions supply function words while extensions supply both environmental and grammatical information.

Jerome Bruner (1978) used the term *scaffold* as a metaphor to explain the value of parents' expansions and extensions of their children's language. These expansions and extensions are scaffolds, or temporary launching platforms that support and encourage children's language development to more complex levels. In addition, Bruner noted that parents use these interactions to keep their children from sliding back once they have moved onto higher platforms and more complex language constructions. This concept of scaffolding has also been applied to teachers' interactions with students.

During the process of their children's language development, parents teach vocabulary both indirectly and directly. They teach indirectly by talking to their children in all types of situations. They teach directly when they say words to their children and have them repeat the words. For example, while a child is eating, the mother may hold up a spoon, pronounce the word *spoon,* and then ask the child to say *spoon.* In this way, parents can teach many words that have direct references in the child's environment.

Parents and Reading

Parents can become further involved with their children's cognitive and language development by reading to them. Reading aloud to children gives them access to information about the world and introduces reading and writing to them. This reading should begin very early. Both fathers and mothers should begin reading aloud to their children soon after birth. When parents read to their babies, a special kind of closeness develops that continues throughout the years as they are read to. In the beginning, it is the cuddling and sound of their parents' voices to which babies respond. Later, they respond to the illustrations as well as the sounds and meanings of the words.

Reading aloud to young children contributes directly to their early literacy development. This belief is widely accepted by educators and is increasingly being accepted by the general public (c.f., Holdaway, 1979). Researchers have documented the development of preschoolers who were read to frequently and found that these children understand the functions, structures, and processes of reading and writing better and at an earlier age than children without these experiences. These preschoolers thus expand their cognitive structure by developing a schema for reading (Bissex, 1980; Clay, 1979; Taylor, 1983; Teale, 1984).

*Preschool children gain a valuable introduction to
reading and writing when their parents read to them.*

Involving Children in Reading.   There are different ways to share a book with a child, and it is important to consider what happens while reading to children. Parents can simply read through the book while the child sits passively or they can actively involve the child in the reading experience. Active involvement is the recommended approach. Parents can involve their children in the reading process in these ways:

■   focusing the child's attention on particular elements

■   providing and requesting labels and other words

■   listing features of objects and experiences

■   relating the text to the child's experiences

■   asking interpretive questions

■   demonstrating book handling skills and concepts about print

■   encouraging the child to respond to the story

Through these interactions, parents assume the role of a teacher and in that role children are introduced to the routines and language patterns that teachers will use in the elementary grades (Heath, 1983). Thus, in addition to providing preschoolers with an introduction to reading and writing, parents can prepare young children for schooling. A list of books with guidelines for reading with young children and reading lists is presented in Figure 1–9.

Butler, D. (1982). *Babies need books.* New York: Atheneum.

Butler, D. & M. Clay. (1982). *Reading begins at home: Preparing children for reading before they go to school.* Auckland, New Zealand: Heinemann.

Coody, B. (1973). *Using literature with young children.* Boston: Little, Brown.

Hearne, B. (1981). *Choosing books for children: A commonsense guide.* New York: Delacorte.

Kimmel, M.M. & E. Segel. (1983). *For reading out loud: A guide to sharing books with children.* New York: Delacorte.

Lamme, L.L. (1980). *Raising readers: A guide to sharing literature with young children.* New York: Walker.

Larrick, N. (1982). *A parent's guide to children's reading* (5th ed.). New York: Doubleday.

McMullan, K.H. (1984). *How to choose good books for kids.* Reading, MA: Addison-Wesley.

Trelease, J. (1985). *The read-aloud handbook* (revised ed.). New York: Viking.

Figure 1–9   Reading with Young Children—
Books for Parents and Educators

In addition to reading to their children, parents can use a more structured approach known as assisted reading to introduce their preschoolers to reading (Hoskisson, 1974, 1975a, 1975b, 1977; Hoskisson & Krohm, 1974; Hoskisson, Sherman, & Smith, 1974). *Assisted reading* is the process by which parents read to their young children and allow them to handle books. Children learn that books have front and back parts and top and bottom dimensions. They discover that parents begin at the front of the book and turn pages toward the back of the books. They learn this by holding books while listening to stories, by playing with books, and by trying out the behaviors they have experienced while being read to.

Pictures also play an important role in books read to young children because they provide contextual situations that bridge the gap between children's actual experiences and the abstract language presented by authors. Pictures provide the context, the visual images that help children relate what they know to what is being presented in the story. Eventually children will be able to supply their own context to the stories they read, but in the beginning, pictures help bridge the gap from the abstract to the real.

As children learn that pictures relate the meaning of the story to their own experiences, they begin to attend to the words they hear and consider the meaning they have constructed via the pictures. They want stories read over again and again. Before long they can "read" a book by using the pictures as prompts in retelling the story. Most parents have succumbed to the temptation to skip pages of a story they have read for the twentieth time only to have children correct them. Parents may call this memorization. However, the children are storing the meaning of the story rather than memorizing exact words. Any part that is skipped disrupts this meaning and results in the correcting feedback they give to their errant parents.

Stage 1. The first stage in assisted reading is reading to children and having them repeat the phrases and sentences. At first most children's attention will *not* be on the lines of print as they repeat the words being read. They may be looking around the room, at the pictures in the book, or at other parts of the book. To direct their attention to the lines of print, the reader points to the words on each line as they are read. This allows children to see that lines of print are read from left to right, not in a random fashion. During this stage, many different books are reread. Rereading is important because the visual images of the words must be seen and read many times to ensure their recognition in other stories. Later, one repetition of a word may be sufficient for subsequent recognition of the word in context.

Stage 2. As children begin to notice that some words occur repeatedly, from story to story, they enter the second stage of assisted reading. In this stage, the reader reads and the children repeat the words. However, now the reader does not read the words that the children seem to recognize. The reader leaves out those words, and the children fill them in. The fluency, or flow, of the reading should not be interrupted. If the fluency is not maintained during this stage, children will not grasp the meaning of the passage because the syntactic, semantic, and punctuation cues that come from a smooth flow of language will not be evident to them.

Stage 3.   The transition to stage 3 occurs when children begin to ask the reader to let them read the words themselves. Stage 3 may be initiated in this manner by the children or it may be introduced by the person assisting the children. When children know enough words to do the initial reading themselves, they read and the person assisting supplies any unknown words. It is important to assist children so that the fluency of the reading is not disrupted. In stage 3, children do the major portion of the reading, but they tire more easily because they are struggling to use all the information they have acquired about the written language. Children at this stage need constant encouragement; they must not feel a sense of frustration or failure. Moving to independent reading is a gradual process. The stages of assisted reading are summarized in Figure 1–10.

Predictable Books

While a variety of books can be used with assisted reading, one type of children's literature is especially effective. These books are known as *predictable books.*

Stage 1

Select a story to read, encouraging the child to help select stories. Choose stories that are short enough to be read in one sitting.

Sit beside the child, holding the storybook in a comfortable position for him to see. Move your fingers slowly under the line of text as you read. Do not become concerned if at first the child's attention wanders and he does not focus on the lines of text.

Read many, many stories and reread them at least once to help the child become familiar with the words.

Stage 2

Take note of the words the child remembers. When you read the story again, omit these words, having the child fill them in. If the child does not remember a word, say the word and continue reading.

Stage 3

When a child wants to do the reading himself, let him read at a natural pace and supply any words that are new or unfamiliar.

Continue to read many, many stories with the child.

Figure 1–10   The Assisted Reading Process

They contain repetitive phrases or sentences, repetitive sentences in a cumulative structure, or sequential events that make them easier for young children to read. Youngsters enjoy the repetition device, and it is a natural part of storytelling. Predictable books are a valuable tool for beginning readers because the repetitive patterns enable children to predict the next sentence or episode in the story (Bridge, 1979; Rhodes, 1981; Tompkins & Webeler, 1983).

A list of predictable books appropriate for beginning readers is presented in Figure 1–11. These books are arranged into three categories. Books in the first category, repetitive sentences, include phrases or sentences that are repeated throughout the story. An example is Wanda Gag's *Millions of cats* (1956) in which the refrain "Cats here, Cats there, Cats and kittens everywhere, Hundreds of cats, Thousands of cats, Millions and billions and trillions of cats" is repeated again and again. The second category, repetitive sentences in a cumulative structure, includes books in which phrases or sentences are repeated and expanded in each episode. In *The gingerbread boy* (Galdone, 1975), for instance, the gingerbread boy repeats and expands his boast as he meets each character. Books included in the third category, sequential patterns, use cultural sequences such as letters of the alphabet, numbers, and days of the week to structure the story. For example, *The very hungry caterpillar* by Eric Carle (1969) combines the number and day of week sequences. Children may also use rhyme to anticipate events as they are reading. Many of the well-known Dr. Seuss stories use rhyme extensively.

Not only are predictable books useful as reading material for young children, but they also provide patterns for their writing. Children often create their own books following the repetitive sentence patterns, cumulative story episode structures, and other sequential patterns they have learned. A first grader dictated the question-answer pattern book presented in Figure 1–12.

Summary

In the cognitive view of learning, knowledge is organized into schemata or category systems. The three components of schemata are (a) categories, (b) features, and (c) networks of interrelationships. Semantic maps can be used to diagram categories or segments of them. Children use the dual processes of assimilation and accommodation to enlarge their existing schemata and to add new schemata. They interpret what occurs in the environment on the basis of their past experiences and the organization of their schemata.

Children learn by three different modes—experience, observation, and language. Elementary students learn best with concrete learning modes. The first mode, experience, is concrete and involves students' active involvement. The second and third learning modes, observation and language, are progressively abstract and should be used in conjunction with experience for the most effective learning.

An effective, six-step instructional model that uses the dual processes of assimilation and accommodation to develop language arts-related schemata was presented. The steps in the model include (a) initiating, (b) structuring, (c) conceptualizing, (d) summarizing, (e) generalizing, and (f) applying. While the model may not fit every language arts lesson that teachers develop, it provides

REPETITIVE SENTENCES

Balian, L. (1972). *Where in the world is Henry?* Nashville, TN: Abingdon.

Brown, M. W. (1947). *Goodnight Moon.* New York: Harper and Row.

Brown, R. (1981). *A dark, dark tale.* New York: Dial.

Cauley, L. B. (1982). *The cock, the mouse, and the little red hen.* New York: Putnam.

Charlip, R. (1969). *What good luck! What bad luck!* New York: Scholastic.

Gag, W. (1956). *Millions of cats.* New York: Coward-McCann.

Galdone, P. (1973). *The little red hen.* New York: Seabury.

————. (1973). *The three billy goats Gruff.* Boston: Houghton Mifflin.

Ginsburg, M. (1972). *The chick and the duckling.* New York: Macmillan.

Hill, E. (1980). *Where's Spot?* New York: Putnam.

Hutchins, P. (1972). *Good-night, owl!* New York: Macmillan.

Martin, B. (1983). *Brown bear, brown bear, what do you see?* New York: Holt.

Peek, M. (1981). *Roll over!* Boston: Houghton Mifflin.

Tafuri, N. (1984). *Have you seen my duckling?* New York: Greenwillow.

Viorst, J. (1972). *Alexander and the terrible, horrible, no good, very bad day.* New York: Atheneum.

REPETITIVE SENTENCES IN A CUMULATIVE STRUCTURE

Carle E. (1971). *Do you want to be my friend?* New York: Crowell.

Ets, M. H. (1972). *Elephant in a well.* New York: Viking.

Flack, M. (1932). *Ask Mr. Bear.* New York: Macmillan.

Figure 1–11   Predictable Books for Beginning Readers

teachers with a means of conceptualizing the instructional process.

Language provides a glimpse into children's cognitive development. Some of the highlights of children's language development during the preschool years and elementary grades were reviewed in the second part of the chapter. Researchers have documented that children move through a series of stages as they acquire language. As they move through one- and two-word utterances to longer and more complex utterances, children develop their phonological, syntactic, and semantic language systems. Children's language is well developed by the time they enter school, and during the elementary grades, the major emphasis is on expanding the semantic system. The way children learn oral language also provides valuable information about how they learn to read and write.

Parents play an important part in their children's language development. They provide the raw materials from which their children construct language as well as "scaffolds" to

REPETITIVE SENTENCES IN A CUMULATIVE STRUCTURE *(Continued)*

Galdone, P. (1975). *The gingerbread boy.* New York: Seabury.

Hutchins, P. (1968). *Rosie's walk.* New York: Macmillan.

Kellogg, S. (1974). *There was an old woman.* New York: Parents.

Peppe, R. (1970). *The house that Jack built.* New York: Delacorte.

Tolstoi, A. (1968). *The great big enormous turnip.* New York: Watts.

Westcott, N. B. (1980). *I know an old lady who swallowed a fly.* Boston: Little, Brown.

Zemach, H. & Zemach, M. (1966). *Mommy, buy me a china doll.* Chicago: Follett.

———. (1969). *The judge.* New York: Farrar.

SEQUENTIAL PATTERNS

Alain. (1964). *One, two, three, going to sea.* New York: Scholastic.

Baskin, L. (1972). *Hosie's alphabet.* New York: Viking.

Carle, E. (1969). *The very hungry caterpillar.* Cleveland: Collins-World.

———. (1977). *The grouchy ladybug.* New York: Crowell.

Domanska, J. (1985). *Busy Monday morning.* New York: Greenwillow.

Keats, E. J. (1973). *Over in the meadow.* New York: Scholastic.

Mack, S. (1974). *10 bears in my bed.* New York: Pantheon.

Martin, B. (1970). *Monday, Monday, I like Monday.* New York: Holt.

Schulevitz, U. (1967). *One Monday morning.* New York: Scribner.

Sendak, M. (1975). *Seven little monsters.* New York: Harper and Row.

Figure 1–11   *Continued*

support that development. Reading to children and using the assisted reading strategy are probably the easiest and most beneficial things that parents can do to help develop their children's language ability.

Extensions

1. Observe a language arts lesson being taught in an elementary classroom. Try to determine when students are assimilating new information into already existing schemata and when accommodation is taking place and new schemata are being created. What conclusions can you draw about students who are confused or do not understand the information being presented?

Figure 1–12   A Dictated Question and
Answer Book Using a Repetitive Pattern

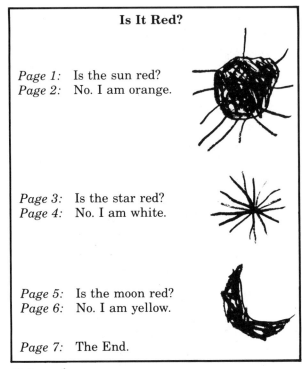

Is It Red?

Page 1:   Is the sun red?
Page 2:   No. I am orange.

Page 3:   Is the star red?
Page 4:   No. I am white.

Page 5:   Is the moon red?
Page 6:   No. I am yellow.

Page 7:   The End.

Chris, age 6

2. Choose a topic that you know very little about (e.g., kangaroos or Norse myths) and draw a semantic map similar to the semantic maps presented in Figure 1–1. Then study the topic and draw a second semantic map that reflects your increased knowledge. Compare the two maps and consider how your schema for that topic has changed. How have you developed the concept? What new features have you added? What new relationships with other schemata have you developed?

3. Teach a lesson on homonyms to a small group of second or third graders using the instructional strategy presented in this chapter. Share some of the homonym books listed in Figure 1–3 with students and have them write a homonym book.

4. Observe and tape-record several young children's talk. Analyze the development of their phonological, syntactic and semantic language systems. Repeat with school age children. If possible compare primary grade students' language with middle and upper grade students' language.

5. Use the assisted reading strategy with a young child just learning to read or with an older child who is having difficulty learning to read. Read with the child over a two- or three-week period, moving from stage 1 to stage 2 or 3, if possible. Keep a journal documenting the child's progress and the books that are read and reread.

References

The American heritage dictionary (2nd ed.). (1985). Boston: Houghton Mifflin.

Bissex, G. L. (1980). *Gyns at wrk: A child learns to write and read.* Cambridge, MA: Harvard University Press.

Braine, M. (1963). The ontogeny of English phrase structure: The first phase. *Language, 39,* 1–13.

Bridge, C. (1979). Predictable materials for beginning readers. *Language Arts, 56,* 503–507.

Brown, R., & Bellugi-Klima, U. (1971). Three processes in the child's acquisition of syntax. In A. Bar-Adon & W. F. Leopold (Eds.), *Child language: A book of readings* (pp. 307–318). Englewood Cliffs, NJ: Prentice-Hall.

Bruner, J. S. (1978). The role of dialogue in language acquisition. In A. Sinclair, R. J. Jarvella, & W. M. Levelt (Eds.), *The child's conception of language* (pp. 241–256). New York: Springer-Verlag.

Bybee, R. W., & Sund, R. B. (1982). *Piaget for educators* (2nd ed.). Columbus, OH: Merrill.

Carle, E. (1969). *The very hungry caterpillar.* Cleveland: Collins-World.

Cazden, C. (1972). *Child language and education.* New York: Holt.

Chomsky, C. (1969). *The acquisition of syntax in children from 5 to 10.* Cambridge, MA: MIT Press.

Clark, E. V. (1971). On the acquisition of the meaning of *before* and *after. Journal of Verbal Learning and Verbal Behavior, 10,* 266–275.

Clay, M. M. (1979). *Reading: The patterning of complex behavior* (2nd ed.). Auckland, New Zealand: Heinemann.

DeStefano, J. S. (1978). *Language, the learner and the school.* New York: Wiley.

Gag, W. (1956). *Millions of cats.* New York: Coward-McCann.

Galdone, P. (1975). *The gingerbread boy.* New York: Seabury.

Greenfield, P. M., & Smith, J. H. (1976). *The structure of communication in early language development.* New York: Academic Press.

Heath, S. B. (1983). *Ways with words: Language, life, and work in communities and classrooms.* Cambridge, England: Cambridge University Press.

Holdaway, D. (1979). *The foundations of literacy.* New York: Scholastic.

Hoskisson, K. (1974). Should parents teach their children to read? *Elementary English, 51,* 295–299.

_____. (1975a). The many facets of assisted reading. *Elementary English, 52,* 312–315.

_____. (1975b). Successive approximation and beginning reading. *Elementary School Journal, 75,* 442–451.

_____. (1977). Reading readiness: Three viewpoints. *Elementary School Journal, 78,* 44–52.

Hoskisson, K., & Krohm, B. (1974). Reading by immersion: Assisted reading. *Elementary English, 51,* 832–836.

Hoskisson, K., Sherman, T., & Smith, L. (1974). Assisted reading and parent involvement. *The Reading Teacher, 27,* 710–714.

Hyman, T. S. (1982). *Little Red Riding Hood.* New York: Holiday House.

Ingram, D. (1975). If and when transformations are acquired by children. In D. P. Dato (Ed.), *Developmental psycholinguistics: Theory and applications* (pp. 99–127). Washington, DC: Georgetown University Press.

Lindfors, J. W. (1980). *Children's language and learning.* Englewood Cliffs, NJ: Prentice-Hall.

Loban, W. (1976). *Language development: Kindergarten through grade twelve* (Research Report No. 18). Urbana, IL: National Council of Teachers of English.

McNeill, D. (1970). *The acquisition of language: The study of developmental psycholinguistics.* New York: Harper and Row.

Menyuk, P. (1977). *Language and maturation.* Cambridge, MA: MIT Press.

_____. (1980). What young children know about language. In G. S. Pinnell (Ed.), *Discovering language with children* (pp. 5–8). Urbana IL: National Council of Teachers of English.

Miller, W. R., & Ervin, S. M. (1971). The development of grammar in child language. In A. Bar-

Adon & W. F. Leopold (Eds.), *Child language: A book of readings* (pp. 331–339). Englewood Cliffs, NJ: Prentice-Hall.

Pearson, P. D., & Johnson, D. D. (1978). *Teaching reading comprehension.* New York: Holt.

Piaget, J. (1969). *The psychology of intelligence.* Patterson, NJ: Littlefield, Adams.

_____. (1975). *The development of thought: Equilibration of cognitive structures.* New York: Viking.

Rhodes, L. K. (1981). I can read! Predictable books as resources for reading and writing instruction. *The Reading Teacher, 34,* 511–518.

Smith, F. (1975). *Comprehension and learning.* New York: Holt.

Taylor, D. (1983). *Family literacy: Young children learning to read and write.* Exeter, NH: Heinemann.

Teale W. H. (1984). Reading to young children: Its significance for literacy development. In H. Goelman, A. Oberg, & F. Smith (Eds.), *Awakening to literacy* (pp. 110–121). Exeter, NH: Heinemann.

Terban, M. (1982). *Eight ate: A feast of homonym riddles.* Boston: Houghton Mifflin.

Tompkins, G., & Webeler, M. (1983). What will happen next? Using predictable books with young children. *The Reading Teacher, 36,* 498–502.

White, E. B. (1952). *Charlotte's web.* New York: Harper and Row.

IF YOU WANT TO LEARN MORE

Bissex, G. L. (1980). *Gyns at wrk: A child learns to write and read.* Cambridge, MA: Harvard University Press.

Bybee, R. W., & Sund, R. B. (1982). *Piaget for educators* (2nd ed.). Columbus, OH: Merrill.

deVilliers, P. A., & deVilliers, J. G. (1984). *Early language.* Cambridge, MA: Harvard University Press.

Garnica. O. K. (1975). How children learn to talk. *Theory into Practice, 14,* 229–305.

Lindfors, J. W. (1980). *Children's language and learning.* Englewood Cliffs, NJ: Prentice-Hall.

Taylor, D. (1983). *Family literacy: Young children learning to read and write.* Exeter, NH: Heinemann.

Tompkins, G., & Webeler, M. (1983). What will happen next? Using predictable books with young children. *The Reading Teacher, 36,* 498–502.

Williams, F., Hopper, R., & Natalicio, D. S. (1977). *The sounds of children.* Englewood Cliffs, NJ: Prentice-Hall.

CHAPTER TWO

Teaching Language Arts in the Elementary School

OVERVIEW. In Chapter 2 we will introduce the concept of communicative competence and identify the four traditional language modes and the seven functions of language. Next, we will discuss the goal of language arts education and the principles underlying language arts instruction. Also included are the three components of the language arts curriculum, the role of textbooks and computers in teaching language arts, and how to evaluate students' progress in language arts. We will conclude the chapter with a list of resources for language arts teachers.

> It seems to me that the most important general goal for education in the language arts is to enable each child to communicate, as effectively as he or she can, what he or she intends and to understand, as well as he or she can, what others have communicated, intentionally or not. (Brown, 1979, p. 483)

Roger Brown's statement succinctly states the goal for language arts instruction at all grade levels. The teacher's goal, then, is to help students learn to communicate effectively with others through oral and written language. This language ability is known as *communicative competence* (Hymes, 1974), and it involves two components. The first component is the ability to transmit meaning through talking and writing, and the second is the ability to comprehend meaning through listening and reading. Communicative competence also refers to students' fluency in the different *registers,* or variances, of language as well as knowing when it is socially appropriate to use language in each register (Smith, 1982). For example, we use language informally as we talk with family members and close friends while we use more formal language with people we know less well or when giving a speech. Similarly, in writing we use different registers. We write letters to close friends in a less formal register than we would use in writing a letter to the editor of the local newspaper.

Genishi and Dyson (1984) distinguish between communicative and linguistic competence. They define communicative competence as students' ability to use language in various social situations and linguistic competence as students' unconscious knowledge of the phonological, syntactic, and semantic systems. This distinction becomes important when we consider that students may use language for purposes other than communication. For example, they often use language to talk or think aloud to themselves and to write notes or lists of homework assignments that only they will ever read. Similarly, students may communicate with others through nonlanguage means, such as pantomime and gestures, as well as through language. Figure 2–1 illustrates the overlap of communicative and linguistic competence as well as the unique dimensions of each.

The content and teaching strategies discussed in this book capitalize on students' cognitive and language abilities to help students develop communicative competence. We emphasize that teachers should provide opportunities for students to use language in situations that are meaningful, functional, and genuine.

Figure 2–1 Linguistic and Communicative Competence

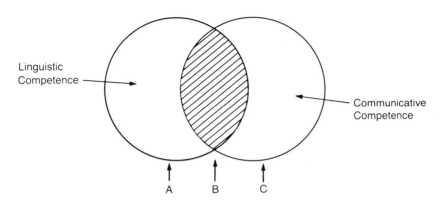

A = language not used for communication with others

B = language used for communication with others

C = nonlanguage used for communication with others

Genishi & Dyson, 1984, p. 23.

These three characteristics are important determinants in learning. Walter Loban (1979) echoes our beliefs:

> The path to power over language is to use, to use it in genuinely meaningful situations, whether we are reading, listening, writing, or speaking. (p. 485)

We will discuss a variety of language activities designed to help students develop communicative competence. These include the following suggestions:

1. conducting oral interviews of community residents with special interests or talents

2. participating in a speechmaster's club

3. writing a simulated journal as the character while reading a story, autobiography, or biography

4. writing stories using the writing process and then sharing their stories with classmates and other genuine audiences

5. analyzing word choice or other aspects of language in the stories they read as well as in their own writing

6. compiling class newspapers or simulated newspapers set in the historical period being studied

These activities exhibit the three characteristics of all worthwhile experiences with language. They use language in meaningful rather than contrived situations. They are functional, or real-life, activities. They are genuine rather than artificial activities such as those we often find in workbooks and on ditto sheets.

POINTS TO PONDER
What Are the Language Modes?
What Relationships Exist Among the Language Modes?
What Are the Implications for Instruction in Listening, Talking, Reading, and Writing?
What Are the Seven Language Functions?

THE FOUR LANGUAGE MODES

Traditionally, language arts educators have defined *language arts* as the study of the four modes of language: listening, talking, reading, and writing. Thinking is sometimes referred to as the fifth language mode, but, more accurately, it permeates all the language modes.

Key Concepts

Listening.   Listening is children's first contact with language, beginning as soon as the child is born. Listening instruction is often neglected in elementary classrooms because teachers feel that students have already learned to listen and that instructional time should be devoted to reading and writing. An alternative view of listening and listening instruction will be presented in Chapter 3. We will present the following key concepts:

- Listening is a process of which hearing is only one part.
- There are many purposes for listening.
- Students listen differently according to their purpose.
- Students need to learn strategies for these different listening purposes.

Talking.   As with listening, teachers often neglect instruction in talk during the elementary grades because they feel students have already learned to talk and that they should focus on reading and writing instruction. However, students need to refine their oral language skills and learn to use talk for more formal purposes and in different settings. In Chapter 4 we will discuss these key concepts about talk:

- Talk is an essential part of the language arts curriculum.
- Talk is necessary for success in all academic areas.
- Talk ranges from informal conversations and discussions to more formal oral presentations including oral reports, panel discussions, and speeches.

Reading.   Until recently, teachers have focused their instructional time almost exclusively on reading. Because separate courses and numerous textbooks are devoted to teaching reading, we will not devote a separate chapter to reading in this book. Instead, we will focus on ways to integrate reading with the other language arts. Key concepts about reading that will be included throughout this book include the following:

- Reading allows children to experience and appreciate literature.
- Reading involves both reading aloud to students and students reading silently.
- The most effective reading strategies are meaning-oriented.
- Informational books are resources for content area-related language activities (e.g., oral and written research reports).
- Proofreading is a unique type of reading that writers use as they edit their compositions.

Writing. The new emphasis on writing focuses on the process approach, and elementary students can learn to use this approach to draft, revise, and share their writing. Chapters 6 through 11 focus on writing with special emphasis on story writing. Grammar, spelling, and handwriting (presented in Chapters 12 through 14) are viewed as tools that writers need to communicate effectively with their readers. We will present the following key concepts about writing:

- Writing is a process in which students cycle recursively through prewriting, drafting, revising, editing, and sharing stages.
- Elementary students can experiment with many different written language forms.
- Students can learn to write stories, poems, and other forms using literature as a model.
- Students can examine the stylistic devices and words that authors use in the stories they read as well as in their own writing.
- Grammar, spelling, and handwriting are tools for writers.

Comparisons Among the Language Modes

The four language modes can be compared and contrasted in a variety of ways. First, oral versus written; listening and talking are oral while reading and writing are written. Second, primary versus secondary; the oral language modes are learned informally at home before children come to school while the written language modes are typically considered to be the school's responsibility and are taught more formally. Listening and talking are called primary language modes; reading and writing are called secondary language modes. The third way to compare the modes is receptive versus productive. Two language modes, listening and reading, are receptive while talking and writing are productive. In the receptive language modes, students receive or comprehend a message orally through listening or in writing as they read. In the productive language modes, students produce a message, orally through talking or in writing as they write. These three sets of relationships are shown graphically in Figure 2–2.

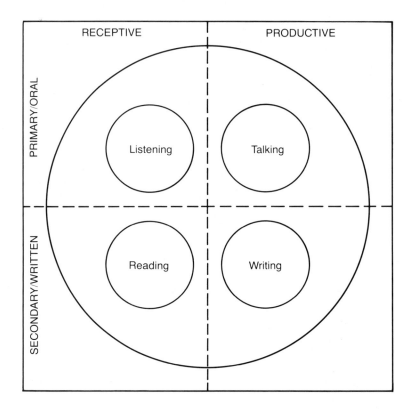

Figure 2–2 Relationships Among the Four Language Modes

Even though we devote chapters in this book to specific language modes, the grouping of the four language modes is both arbitrary and artificial. This arrangement wrongly suggests that there are separate stages of development for each language mode and that children use different mental processes for listening, talking, reading, and writing (Smith, 1979). It has generally been assumed that the four language modes develop in sequence from listening to talking to reading to writing. While listening is the first form of language to develop and talking develops soon after, parents and preschool teachers have recently documented children's early interest in both reading and writing (Baghan, 1984; Bissex, 1980; Lass, 1982). Also, Carol Chomsky (1971) and other researchers have observed young children experimenting with writing earlier than with reading. On the basis of reports from parents, teachers, and researchers, we can no longer assume that there is a definite sequence in learning to use the four language modes.

This grouping also suggests a division among the language modes, as though they could be used separately. In reality, they are used simultaneously and reciprocally. In almost any language arts activity, more than one language mode is involved. For instance, in learning about stories, students use all four language modes. They begin by listening as stories are read aloud first by parents and teachers and later by reading stories themselves. Next, they retell familiar stories as well as original stories. They make puppets to dramatize and role-play favorite stories. From telling stories, they move to writing stories and sharing their stories with classmates or other genuine audiences. The cluster diagram in Figure 2–3 lists these and other activities related to learning about stories that involve all four of the language modes.

Also, this grouping does not account for other subjects, such as grammar, literature, and drama, that are considered part of the language arts. These subjects do indeed play an important role in language learning. Grammar is the foundation of language because conventional structures such as word order are necessary in order to comprehend and produce English sentences. Literature is the content of reading and writing, and students listen to, tell, dramatize, and write it. Drama is another means of communicating as well as a way of learning, and in Chapter 5 we will repeat John Stewig's suggestion that drama should be the fifth language mode. The traditional four modes are simply inadequate to describe all that is language; the language arts are more than the sum of the four parts. Frank Smith (1979) concludes an article in which he examines our traditional system of the four language modes by saying that these categories "are useful perhaps in the way we want to

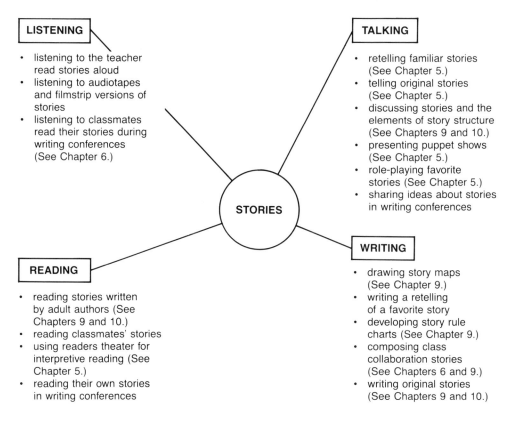

Figure 2–3   How the Language Modes Are Used in Learning
About Stories

organize our schools, but they are not a reflection of a categorization in the learner's mind. . . To a child, language and the world must be indivisible" (p. 125).

Walter Loban's Study.   Over a 13-year period, researcher Walter Loban (1976) documented the language growth and development of a group of 338 students from kindergarten through 12th grade (ages 5–18). Two of the purposes of his longitudinal study were (a) to examine differences between students who used language effectively and those who did not and (b) to identify predictable stages of language development for these students. While it is not possible to report fully the results of his study in this chapter, three conclusions are especially noteworthy to our discussion about the relationship among the language modes. First, Loban reported positive correlations among the four language modes. Second, he found that students with less effective oral language (listening and talking) abilities tended to have less effective written language (reading and writing) abilities. And, third, he found a strong relationship between students' oral language ability and their overall academic ability. Loban's seminal study demonstrates clear relationships among the language modes and emphasizes the need to teach oral language in the elementary school language arts curriculum.

The Functions of Language

A new and different way to categorize language is according to function. In contrast to the four traditional language modes, the language functions focus on how language is used in communicating with others. We use language for a variety of purposes—to communicate, to find out about things, to give information, to persuade, and to interact with others—and often talk and writing can be used for the same purpose as listening and reading. M.A.K. Halliday (1973, 1975) has identified seven language function categories that apply to oral and written language and even to nonlanguage forms of communication such as gestures and pantomime. These seven language functions and some language arts activities that exemplify each are listed and described in Figure 2–4. Frank Smith (1977) has made a number of observations about these language functions:

1. Language is learned in genuine communication experiences, rather than through practice activities that lack functional purposes.
2. Skill in one language function does not generalize to skill in other functions.
3. Language is rarely used for just one function at a time; typically two or more language functions are involved in talk or in a writing activity.
4. These language functions involve an audience, listeners for talk and readers for writing.
5. Language is one communication alternative, and there are other alternatives including gestures, drawings, pantomime, and rituals.

When children are using language functionally, they are using language for genuine communication and they are interacting with others (Pinnell, 1975). These two characteristics of functional language are apparent whether students

Figure 2–4   The Seven Functions of Language

Function	Description	Sample Language Arts Activities
1. Instrumental Language	Language to satisfy needs	Conversations Business letters Letters to the editor Advertisements
2. Regulatory Language	Language to control behavior of others	Directions Gestures Dramatic play
3. Interactional Language	Language to establish and maintain social relationships	Conversations Friendly letters Gestures Discussions
4. Personal Language	Language to express personal opinions	Personal journals Panel discussions Show and tell Response to literature activities
5. Imaginative Language	Language to express imagination and creativity	Storytelling Pantomime Readers theater Dramatic play Stories, scripts, poems
6. Heuristic Language	Language to seek information and to find out about things	Learning logs Interviews Role playing Discussions
7. Informative Language*	Language to convey information	Oral and written reports Panel discussions Show and tell Discussions

*The label for the seventh function is used by Pinnell (1985).

use oral or written language. In addition, drama and other forms of nonlanguage communication can be used functionally, for genuine communication purposes and to interact with others.

The teacher's role is two-fold: (a) to foster a wide range of language use in the elementary classroom, and (b) to find ways to extend children's language in real-life situations (Pinnell, 1985). Because children's ability to use one language function does not generalize to ability in other functions, it is essential that students have opportunities to use each of the seven language functions. In her study of the functions of talk in a primary grade classroom, Pinnell (1975) found that the first graders she studied used interactional language or language for social purposes most commonly and they rarely used heuristic language or language to seek information as they talked and worked in small groups. Pinnell concluded that students need to experiment with all seven language functions and learn what they can do with language. Some of the language functions may not occur spontaneously in students' talk and writing, and teachers need to plan genuine communication experiences that incorporate these language functions. Many of the language activities suggested in this book, such as interviewing, designing advertisements, and writing letters to pen pals, involve students in genuine oral and written language communication activities that involve interaction with others.

The concept of language functions is relatively new, and research is currently underway that will undoubtedly affect the way language arts is taught in the future. For instance, Gere and Abbott (1985) categorized students' talk in writing conferences, and Florio and Clark (1982) examined the language functions in elementary students' compositions. One drawback of much of this recent research is that several different frameworks are being used to categorize children's language samples, and it is difficult to compare the findings.

POINTS TO PONDER

What Are the Three Components of the Language Arts Curriculum?

What Are the Characteristics of a "Whole Language" Classroom?

What Role Do Language Arts Textbooks and Computers Play in Language Arts Instruction?

How Can Language Arts Be Integrated with Content Areas Such as Social Studies, Science, Art, and Music?

How Can Students' Language Development Be Evaluated?

LANGUAGE ARTS INSTRUCTION

Carl Lefevre (1970) advises that language learning in school should "parallel [children's] early childhood method of learning to speak [their] native tongue—playfully, through delighted experiences of discovery—through repeated exposure to language forms and patterns, by creating imitation and manipulation, and by personal trial and error, with kindly (and not too much) correction from adults" (p. 75). Language arts instruction should be based on how children learn and how they learn language in particular. Teachers need to provide opportunities for discovery as Lefevre suggests. First, students need repeated exposure to the many and varied forms of oral and written language. Second, they need opportunities to imitate and manipulate these oral and written language forms. In the following chapters of this book, we will identify a variety of oral and written language forms and suggest strategies and activities that encourage students to imitate and manipulate these forms.

A unit on mystery stories, for example, provides the types of discovery experiences Lefevre suggests. Students begin by reading mystery stories or listening to them read aloud. Many mystery stories have been written for elementary students, and they especially enjoy reading these suspense stories. The *Nate the great* series of stories by Marjorie Weinman Sharmat (c.f., *Nate the great goes undercover,* 1974) is popular with beginning readers, and middle grade students enjoy the *Encyclopedia Brown* series by Donald J. Sobol (c.f., *Encyclopedia Brown, boy detective,* 1963). Mystery stories have unique characteristics, which students can learn to identify after reading and discussing several mysteries. Some characteristics of mystery stories are presented in Figure 2–5. With this information, students are prepared to write their own stories. Students can publish their stories by binding them into hardcover books and adding them to the school library. Figure 2–6 presents a class collaboration mystery story composed by a class of third graders. This class story was composed by the teacher and students working together, and it is an effective way to begin writing.

These mystery reading and writing activities provide many opportunities for students to imitate and manipulate language in a situation that is meaningful, functional, and genuine. Moreover, both the mystery stories students read and ones they write can later be used in studying specific language skills. For example, they can examine how authors use alliteration, sentence structure, and punctuation. Students can also examine their own stories for similar conventions. Within the context of stories children have read and others they have written, they can examine how language is used to communicate effectively.

1. Mysteries have crimes or problems to solve. Some types of crimes and problems are something lost or stolen, someone killed, or someone kidnapped.
2. Mysteries have clues. Some examples include torn papers, footprints, fingerprints, dead bodies, and tire tracks.
3. Mysteries have detectives to solve the crimes or problems. (They *always* solve the crime, too!)
4. Detectives have unusual names, such as Encyclopedia Brown and Nate the Great.
5. Detectives have something special about them such as having a dog for an assistant and loving to eat pancakes.
6. Detectives have special equipment, including magnifying glasses, secret codes, knives and guns, costumes, and masks.

Figure 2–5 Characteristics of Mystery Stories

Figure 2–6 A Class Collaboration Mystery Story

"Edith, No!"

The mud oozed around Ed Trail's boots as he beached his canoe. It was 10:00 Saturday evening as Ed made his way home through the woods from his fishing trip. He only walked a few steps when . . . SNAP . . . an old trap caught his foot and pulled him down.

As he turned over to free himself, the last thing he saw was a rock.

From the other side of the woods, Sam Baker, well-known detective, was searching for Ed at the request of his worried wife, Sally. He found the place where Ed docked his boat and followed the path from there.

A short distance up the path led Sam to where Ed Trail lay dead with a rock crushing his head.

While Sam was running to tell what had happened, he discovered a torn scarf stuck on a bush. As he observed the scarf, he discovered the initials E.T.

Sam stuck the scarf in his pocket because he knew it was a clue and went to tell Sally Trail what had happened.

Out of breath, Sam arrived at the Trails' and told Sally the horrible details. When Sam showed her the scarf, Sally got a far away look in her eyes and went upstairs. Finding this strange, Sam Baker waited outside the Trail home to see what he might find.

Meanwhile, Sally went upstairs to the room of Aunt Belle who lived with the Trails. Aunt Belle had taken care of Sally as a little girl and knew everything about Sally. Now she was crippled and in a wheelchair.

"Well, hello dear," said Aunt Belle. "What are you doing here?" "Where are you taking me?" said Aunt Belle worriedly as Sally wheeled her to the stairs. As Sally gave the final shove Aunt Belle screamed . . . .

"EDITH, NO!"

At that moment Sam Baker knew that the initials stood for *Sally Edith Trail*. The S had been ripped off in her rush to leave the place of the crime.

Sam rushed in just in time to catch Aunt Belle before Sally Edith Trail sent another victim to her death.

Quickly Sam grabbed Sally and took her to the police station.

At the station house the chief found out that Sally killed her husband to keep him from giving all his money to Aunt Belle to take care of her. Sally tried to kill Aunt Belle because she was the only one who could connect Sally with the initials E.T.

Another case wrapped up by Sam Baker.

Third graders

Components of the Language Arts Curriculum

M.A.K. Halliday (1980) has identified three components of the language arts curriculum: (a) learning language, (b) learning through language, and (c) learning about language. The first component, learning language, might seem to be the primary responsibility of the language arts curriculum. Certainly, students do need to develop communicative competence in listening, talking, reading, and writing; instruction in each of the four language modes is essential. But, language learning does not occur in isolation, and the second and third components are equally important.

Learning through language is defined as "how we use language to build up a picture of the world in which we live" (Halliday, 1980, p. 13). It involves using language to learn in content areas across the curriculum—social studies, science, mathematics, art, music, and so on. Throughout this book, we will point out content area-related applications of the language arts such as learning logs, oral and written informational reports, role-playing, and simulated journals.

The third component, learning about language, may be the most controversial. This component involves "coming to understand the nature and function of language itself" (Halliday, 1980, p. 16). Students develop intuitive knowledge about language and its forms and purposes through school experiences, and they develop the ability to control or talk about this knowledge. Students' ability to reflect upon their knowledge of any subject is known as *metacognition* (Brown, 1980) and to reflect on language as *metalanguage* or *metalinguistic awareness* (Yaden & Templeton, 1986). Some educators have suggested that elementary students are not prepared cognitively to study language at an abstract level, and that some types of language analysis should be postponed. However, research has shown that young children develop concepts about "letter" and "word" (Yaden, 1984), and other children in the elementary grades can examine the forms of oral and written language, functions of language, language registers, and language processes such as the listening process and the writing process.

Sometimes teachers assume that students have developed intuitive knowledge about various aspects of language and do not make these understandings explicit. However, research studies have shown that students do not always develop knowledge about language concepts intuitively. For example, most teachers in the middle and upper elementary grades assume that their students can sense by the teacher's mannerisms when information being presented is important. However, researchers have found that students are unable to identify commonly used techniques to emphasize important information such as writing it on the chalkboard, repeating it, and saying it in a louder voice (Tompkins, Friend, & Smith, 1984). Learning about language is an essential component of the language arts curriculum because children do have misconceptions that must be clarified.

Also, in the mystery stories example, students were learning about language as they examined the characteristics of mystery stories. In Chapters 9 and 10 we will suggest ways to help students learn about the elements of story structure and stylistic devices. By learning about the language of stories, students learn to write better organized and more interesting stories.

Instructional Models

Instructional models for language arts reflect a wide range of instructional philosophies. At one end of the continuum, we find teachers who have assumed the traditional role of instructional leaders. They teach for children to learn. A daily schedule is often posted on the chalkboard. According to that schedule, reading, language arts, literature, spelling, and handwriting are taught separately and at different times during the school day. Textbooks, workbooks, and ditto sheets are frequently used instructional materials. John Hemphill (1981) classifies these classrooms as segmented, content-centered classrooms.

Educators have questioned the value and transfer of teaching skills through textbooks, workbooks, and other drill activities that are a part of the segmented, content-centered approach. Russell Stauffer (1980) explains:

> Because conventional instructional activities are all too often referred to as "skills" and are assembled in "skillbooks" they deserve a critical look. What we find is this: Skillbook activities are brief; they do not stem from an immediate learner need and are seldom process oriented; they do not provide for transfer of learning to other types of situations; and usually they are administered in a setting devoid of communication context. (p. 47)

Also, Donald Graves (1976), a leading researcher in writing, argues against teachers providing a welfare program for their students. By doing for students—whether it is preparing dittos or selecting topics for story writing—teachers make students dependent on them. Rather, our aim must be to make children independent learners and to provide them with both the language arts content and strategies they need to communicate effectively through oral and written language.

At the other end of the continuum, are integrated, child-centered classrooms in which curricular areas are interrelated with each other and children's oral and written language provides the foundation for the curriculum. Figure 2–7 lists the features that characterize this type of classroom environment. This "whole language" classroom (Goodman, 1986; Newman, 1985) is the type of environment that we will advocate in this book. It functions equally well in self-contained or in open space schools with a single teacher, in classrooms with aides and parent volunteers, in old school buildings, as well as in new, modern buildings.

In addition to characteristics presented in Figure 2–7, we will also consider how language skills are taught, how the language arts are integrated across the curriculum, and how textbooks and computers are used in whole language classrooms.

Teaching Language Skills.   Language and language skills are not synonymous terms (Genishi, 1979). *Language* is a means of communication and specific *language skills* such as note-taking or using punctuation marks correctly are skills that enhance students' communicative competence. Other traditional language skills such as parts of speech are used for a different purpose in whole language classrooms than in traditional classrooms. For example, in a traditional, segmented classroom, parts of speech are taught with the objective of learning to define them and identify them in a sentence. In contrast, in whole language classrooms, the purpose is different: Students learn the labels and uses of parts of speech to better understand how authors write and how they communicate effectively in their writing. Similarly, students who write need to know these labels to discuss their own writing and their classmates' writing. Nouns, verbs, adjectives, and other parts of speech become functional labels for writers rather than simply words to circle in textbooks or on ditto sheets.

In whole language classrooms, students use language in situations that are meaningful, functional, and genuine, the three characteristics of language experiences mentioned earlier in this chapter. Students continue to learn skills such as parts of speech and punctuation marks, but they learn them as they are needed for genuine language activities rather than because they are presented in the next chapter of a language arts textbook. Figure 2–8 presents a cluster diagram that shows options for teaching punctuation marks. Notice that the suggested activities involve students in language they write as well as language written in books they read. Both large and small group activities are suggested and textbooks are listed as *one* resource. Many other resources are suggested, such as informational books, students' journals and letters, and cartoons. Teachers can choose among these and other activities to provide necessary experiences, and they can also provide one-on-one tutoring or individualized practice activities for students who need additional work.

Integrating the Language Modes.   Just as children learn to talk in the context of the real world, not in special "learning to talk" classes, children learn other language modes by using language in meaningful situations. Busching and Lundsteen (1983) warn that "dividing classroom instruction into separate classes, textbooks, and lessons for individual language skills is a violation of how we use language" (p. 3). The example of learning about stories discussed earlier and summarized in Figure 2–3 shows how the language modes can be integrated.

Integrating Across the Curriculum.   Although this is a book about language arts, it is impossible to confine it to the language modes alone. Halliday (1980) reminds us that students use language to learn in all areas of the curriculum. Throughout this book, then, we will draw connections to other content areas such as social studies, science, art, and music. For example, in learning about the American Revolution, students read stories set in the historical period as well as informational books. They dramatize events of the period and learn about key figures of the period, perhaps by keeping a simulated journal in the role of that person. Handwriting practice can even be integrated by having students copy slogans from the historical period. These and other language arts activities that might be used in conjunction with a social studies unit on the American Revolution are presented in Figure 2–9.

Language arts-related activities can be used in music class, too. Students may listen to music and discuss it, read and write song lyrics, research the lives of composers, and use the information gathered for oral or written reports. They may interview local musicians and summarize the interview for the school newspaper, and write poems to music. Two "If I were" poems in which students write what it would be like to be musical instruments are included in Chapter 11.

The Students

work independently and in small groups
work at different types of activities at the same time
talk with their classmates
work at their own pace
meet together in conferences about their work
share their projects with genuine audiences
move freely in the classroom
participate in making decisions

The Teacher

serves as facilitator or guide
understands that children learn written language competencies in the
    same ways they learned oral language competencies
provides information on language arts-related concepts as students
    need the information to continue working on projects
listens to and responds to students
shows respect for students and learning
encourages students to explore areas of special interest
uses a flexible schedule
meets with students informally
keeps anecdotal records about students as well as samples of their work

The Classroom

has an abundance of tradebooks and other reading materials
includes puppets, puppet stages, and other props for drama activities
has an abundance of writing paper, notebooks, pencils, marking pens,
    and other writing materials
includes an art area with a variety of art materials
has a variety of manipulative materials, collections, and content-area re-
    lated materials
includes audio-visual equipment and software for students to use
includes microcomputers for word processing and other uses
displays charts with information about language concepts, such as story
    elements, in the room
displays students' work throughout the room

Figure 2–7　Characteristics of Integrated or Whole
Language Classrooms

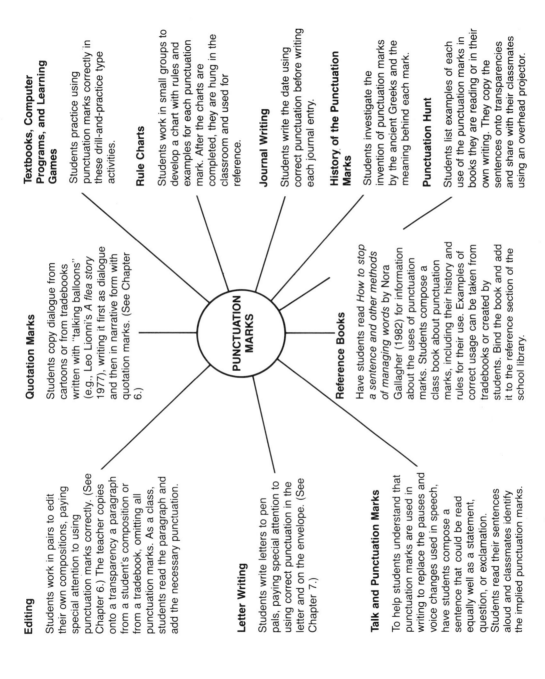

Textbooks, Computer Programs, and Learning Games

Students practice using punctuation marks correctly in these drill-and-practice type activities.

Rule Charts

Students work in small groups to develop a chart with rules and examples for each punctuation mark. After the charts are completed, they are hung in the classroom and used for reference.

Journal Writing

Students write the date using correct punctuation before writing each journal entry.

History of the Punctuation Marks

Students investigate the invention of punctuation marks by the ancient Greeks and the meaning behind each mark.

Punctuation Hunt

Students list examples of each use of the punctuation marks in books they are reading or in their own writing. They copy the sentences onto transparencies and share with their classmates using an overhead projector.

Quotation Marks

Students copy dialogue from cartoons or from tradebooks written with "talking balloons" (e.g., Leo Lionni's *A flea story* 1977), writing it first as dialogue and then in narrative form with quotation marks. (See Chapter 6.)

Reference Books

Have students read *How to stop a sentence and other methods of managing words* by Nora Gallagher (1982) for information about the uses of punctuation marks. Students compose a class book about punctuation marks, including their history and rules for their use. Examples of correct usage can be taken from tradebooks or created by students. Bind the book and add it to the reference section of the school library.

Editing

Students work in pairs to edit their own compositions, paying special attention to using punctuation marks correctly. (See Chapter 6.) The teacher copies onto a transparency a paragraph from a student's composition or from a tradebook, omitting all punctuation marks. As a class, students read the paragraph and add the necessary punctuation.

Letter Writing

Students write letters to pen pals, paying special attention to using correct punctuation in the letter and on the envelope. (See Chapter 7.)

Talk and Punctuation Marks

To help students understand that punctuation marks are used in writing to replace the pauses and voice changes used in speech, have students compose a sentence that could be read equally well as a statement, question, or exclamation. Students read their sentences aloud and classmates identify the implied punctuation marks.

Figure 2–8 Ways to Teach Students About Punctuation Marks

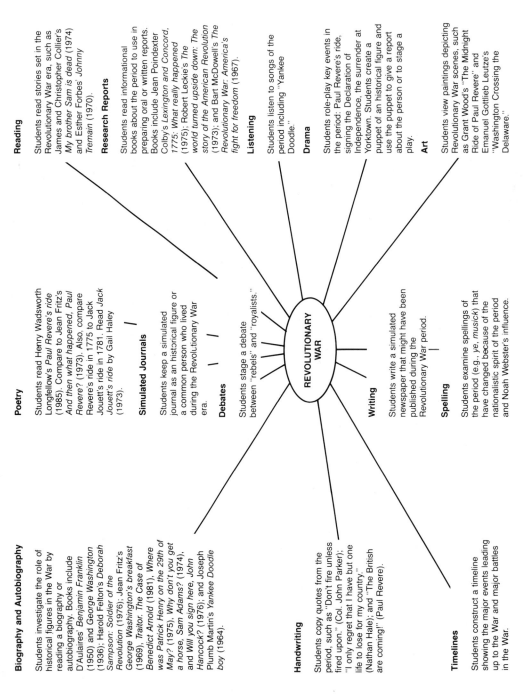

Reading

Students read stories set in the Revolutionary War era, such as James and Christopher Collier's *My brother Sam is dead* (1974) and Esther Forbes' *Johnny Tremain* (1970).

Research Reports

Students read informational books about the period to use in preparing oral or written reports. Books include Jean Poindexter Colby's *Lexington and Concord, 1775: What really happened* (1975); Robert Leckie's *The world turned upside down: The story of the American Revolution* (1973); and Bart McDowell's *The Revolutionary War: America's fight for freedom* (1967).

Listening

Students listen to songs of the period including "Yankee Doodle."

Drama

Students role-play key events in the period: Paul Revere's ride, signing the Declaration of Independence, the surrender at Yorktown. Students create a puppet of an historical figure and use the puppet to give a report about the person or to stage a play.

Art

Students view paintings depicting Revolutionary War scenes, such as Grant Wood's "The Midnight Ride of Paul Revere" and Emanuel Gottlieb Leutze's "Washington Crossing the Delaware."

Poetry

Students read Henry Wadsworth Longfellow's *Paul Revere's ride* (1985). Compare to Jean Fritz's *And then what happened, Paul Revere?* (1973). Also, compare Revere's ride in 1775 to Jack Jouett's ride in 1781. Read *Jack Jouett's ride* by Gail Haley (1973).

Simulated Journals

Students keep a simulated journal as an historical figure or a common person who lived during the Revolutionary War era.

Debates

Students stage a debate between "rebels" and "royalists."

Writing

Students write a simulated newspaper that might have been published during the Revolutionary War period.

Spelling

Students examine spellings of the period (e.g., *ye*, *musick*) that have changed because of the nationalistic spirit of the period and Noah Webster's influence.

Biography and Autobiography

Students investigate the role of historical figures in the War by reading a biography or autobiography. Books include D'Aulaires' *Benjamin Franklin* (1950) and *George Washington* (1936); Harold Felton's *Deborah Sampson: Soldier of the Revolution* (1976); Jean Fritz's *George Washington's breakfast* (1969). *Traitor: The Case of Benedict Arnold* (1981), *Where was Patrick Henry on the 29th of May?* (1975), *Why don't you get a horse, Sam Adams?* (1974), and *Will you sign here, John Hancock?* (1976); and Joseph Plumb Martin's *Yankee Doodle boy* (1964).

Handwriting

Students copy quotes from the period, such as "Don't fire unless fired upon." (Col. John Parker); "I only regret that I have but one life to lose for my country." (Nathan Hale); and "The British are coming!" (Paul Revere).

Timelines

Students construct a timeline showing the major events leading up to the War and major battles in the War.

REVOLUTIONARY WAR

Figure 2–9 Integrating the Language Arts in Teaching About the American Revolution

Textbooks are not the language arts curriculum; rather, they are a tool for teaching language skills.

Textbooks

Textbooks are one tool for teaching language skills. They are the most accessible resource that teachers have and they have some benefits, providing a sequence of skills for each grade level and throughout the elementary grades, security for beginning teachers, and practice activities. However, there are also drawbacks, and textbooks cannot be the only instructional material used in teaching language arts (Graves, 1977). The format of textbooks, themselves, is a major drawback for language learning. The format does not allow meaningful, functional, and genuine situations for using language (Loban, 1979). Collections of tradebooks, tape recordings, puppets, concrete materials, notebooks, paper, and pencils are other necessary materials. A list of strengths and weaknesses of textbooks is presented in Figure 2–10.

Teachers cannot assume that textbooks are equivalent to the total language arts program. To start on the first page of the language arts textbook on the first day of school and to continue page-by-page through the textbook fails to consider the language needs of students. Instead, we recommend that textbooks serve as only one resource for the language arts program. For example, as illustrated in Figure 2–8, textbooks are one resource in teaching about punctuation marks. Many other types of activities and resources are suggested in that figure.

Strengths

Textbooks include information about language skills.
A clear sequence of language skills is provided.
Models and examples are included.
Student exercises are included.
Textbooks are especially useful for beginning teachers.

Weaknesses

The textbook format is inappropriate for many language activities.
There is limited emphasis on talking and listening.
There is a strong emphasis on grammar and usage skills.
There is emphasis on rote memorization of skills rather than on effective communication.
There is emphasis on correctness rather than on experimentation with language.
Few opportunities are provided to individualize instruction.

Figure 2–10   Strengths and Weaknesses of Language Arts Textbooks

Evaluating Language Arts Textbooks.   Several elements must be carefully considered in evaluating language arts textbooks or choosing a textbook series for a school or school district. The conceptual framework of the textbook and the instructional philosophy of its authors is of primary importance. Is the textbook more content-centered or is it child-centered? Textbooks should be consistent with teachers' views of language arts education and how they organize and conduct their classrooms. It is also important to consider whether or not the latest research on how children learn language has been incorporated.

The theoretical orientation is reflected in the content of the textbook, and the content is the second critical consideration. Textbooks that are based on the segmented, content-centered model typically emphasize language skills more than textbooks based on the child-centered or whole language model. It is essential to examine textbooks carefully to determine whether their activities include the three components of the language arts curriculum identified by M.A.K. Halliday (1980). The types of listening, talking, reading, and writing activities that are included are also very important. Consider, too, what other types of activities, such as grammar activities, are included and compute the percentage of space devoted to each language mode. Other considerations include whether the textbook invites students to use language in genuine ways or whether the majority of activities involve copying sentences from the textbook or filling-in-the-blank with single letters and words.

Other considerations include the physical features of the textbook, its organization, its adaptability for special students, and its style. A list of these guidelines is presented in Figure 2–11. Some of the questions included in the figure can be an-

Physical Features

_____ Is the textbook attractive, durable, and interesting to students?

_____ Do the size, use of margins, print style, and graphics increase the usability of the textbook?

_____ Do the illustrations enhance interest in the textbook?

_____ What supplemental materials (e.g., teacher's editions, resource books, skill handbooks, computer programs, posters, tests) are included with the textbook?

Conceptual Framework

_____ What is the theoretical orientation of the textbook?

_____ Does the textbook reflect the latest research in how language is learned?

_____ Are the instructional goals of the textbook presented clearly?

_____ How well do these goals mesh with your own views of language arts education?

Content

_____ Does the textbook include lessons on learning language, learning through language, and learning about language, the three components of the language arts curriculum identified by M.A.K. Halliday?

_____ What types of listening, talking, reading, and writing activities are included in the textbook?

_____ How much emphasis is placed on each of the four language modes?

_____ How much emphasis is placed on grammar?

_____ Is quality children's literature included in the textbook?

_____ Is drama included in the textbook?

_____ Are the language and language skill activities appropriate for the grade level at which they are presented?

_____ Are activities provided that require students to use language in genuine ways or do most activities require students to only copy sentences from the textbook or fill in the blanks with letters and words?

_____ Are across the curriculum activities suggested?

_____ Does the textbook invite student involvement?

_____ Does the textbook encourage students to think critically and creatively?

Organization

_____ How is the textbook organized?

_____ Must each lesson or unit be taught in sequence?

_____ Does the scope and sequence chart provide a reasonable organization of language skills?

Adaptability

_____ Is information provided on how to adapt the textbook to meet students' individual needs?

_____ Can the textbook be adapted for gifted students?

_____ Can the textbook be adapted for learning disabled students?

_____ Can the textbook be adapted for speakers of nonstandard English?

Style

_____ Will students like the writing style of the textbook?

_____ Does the textbook avoid stereotypes and stereotypical language?

Figure 2–11   Guidelines for Evaluating Language Arts Textbooks

swered simply with "yes" or "no." Other questions, however, require a more careful and in-depth review.

Computers

Computers are becoming more and more a part of elementary classrooms. At first, they were used primarily in mathematics, but they have great potential for all areas of the curriculum, including language arts. Several different instructional uses are possible with computers. Robert Taylor (1980) suggests that computers have three educational applications: They can serve as tool, tutor, and tutee.

Perhaps the most valuable application of the computer in the language arts classroom is as a tool. Students can use microcomputers with word processing programs to write stories, poems, and other types of compositions. The computer simplifies revising and editing and eliminates the tedium of recopying compositions. Several word processing programs, such as *The Bank Street writer* (1982), *The writing workshop* (1986), and *QUILL* (1983), have been developed especially for elementary students and are easy to learn to use. See Chapter 6 for more information about using the computer as a writing tool.

A second application is as tutor. This use is also known as computer assisted instruction (CAI). Instructional software programs are available for drill and practice, educational games, simulations, and tutorials. Programs that provide pro-

Students are eager to use microcomputers with word processing programs to write stories, poems, and other compositions.

grammed instruction in language skills such as letter sounds, parts of speech, and affixes are becoming increasingly available today. Many of these programs resemble language arts textbook exercises with the exception that they are presented on a monitor screen rather than in a book. It is important to remember, though, that while students enjoy using computers, some of these activities are little more than electronic workbooks and are subject to the same criticisms as language arts textbooks. However, high quality software programs can be useful in providing individualized practice on a particular skill.

The number of software programs has increased tremendously in the past few years; some are very effective while others are of inferior quality. Chomsky (1984) suggests that the primary criterion in identifying high quality software programs is whether they stimulate students to think about language in new and creative ways. Because of both quality and cost considerations, it is important to preview software carefully before purchasing it. A list of guidelines for selecting and evaluating language arts software is provided in Figure 2–12. Students should also assist in previewing software programs and offering their opinions and recommendations.

A third application is as tutee. Students can learn computer languages such as LOGO and how to program computers. In Chapter 15 we will suggest that gifted students, in particular, should learn computer languages as a way of extending their repertoire of communication modes.

In summarizing the promises and pitfalls of microcomputers in the language arts classroom, Jane Ann Zaharias (1983) concludes that there are two factors restricting the usefulness of this technology. The quantity of high quality instructional software available is still limited, and very few computers are available in most elementary schools. Because so few computers are available, students are rarely able to use them regularly. In the next few years, however, educators predict that the availability of high quality software will improve and computers will be added to most elementary classrooms.

Evaluating Students' Language Development

Evaluating students' progress in the language arts is a difficult task. While it may seem fairly easy to develop a criterion-referenced test, administer it, and grade it, tests often measure language skills rather than language. It is extremely difficult to measure students' communicative competence with a test. Tests do not measure listening and talking very well, and a test on punctuation marks, for example, does not indicate students' ability to use punctuation marks correctly in their own writing. Instead, tests typically evaluate students' ability to add punctuation marks to a set of sentences created by someone else or to proofread and spot punctuation errors in someone else's writing. An alternative and far better approach is to examine how students use punctuation marks in their own writing.

In this book, we suggest several alternative approaches to documenting children's language development and evaluating students' progress. Instead of using tests, we suggest that teachers become "kid watchers." Yetta Goodman (1978) coined the term, which she defined as direct and informal observation of students. To be an effective kid watcher, teachers must understand how children develop

Figure 2–12 Guidelines for Selecting Language Arts Software

Computer Compatibility

Is the software program compatible with the computer students will be using?
Does the computer have sufficient memory to run the software program?
Which peripherals are needed (e.g., color monitor, printer, voice synthesizer)?

Theoretical Rationale

Is the software consistent with the philosophy of your language arts program?
Can it be integrated into your program to instruct rather than merely to entertain?

Computer Capabilities

Does the software program take advantage of the unique capabilities of the computer?
Does it provide for extensive student interaction?
Does it provide for immediate feedback?
Does it provide for dynamic text display in which text can be built paragraph by paragraph,
      sentences and words can be highlighted, and text can be moved about?

Frame Display

Is the text in the software program presented in both upper and lower case letters?
Is between-line spacing adequate for easy reading?
Do letters resemble regular type rather than stylized lettering?
Are highlighting and other attention-getting devices overused?

Rate of Presentation

Is the rate at which text is advanced controlled by the student rather than by the program?

Readability

Is the text (especially the directions) written at students' reading level?

Graphics

Do the illustrations and animation used in the software program support the instruction or
      serve only to gain the students' attention?

Game Format

Does the software program require students to learn or practice a skill to play the game suc-
      cessfully or can students simply make random choices?
Does it allow students to play against themselves and compete against their previous perfor-
      mances rather than with another student?

Instructions to Students

Does the software program provide information on each frame of text on how students can
      quit the program, get help, and see the menu?

Documentation

Does the documentation (or printed materials) accompanying the software program con-
      tain information on objectives, description of the program, the target population, pre-
      requisite language and computing skills, suggested introductory and follow-up activi-
      ties, and the results of field testing and validation studies?

Adapted from Smith & Tompkins, 1984.

language and understand the role of errors in language learning. In the first chapter, we discussed language development and described it as a natural, hypothesis-testing process. Children often make *miscues* or "errors" (Goodman & Burke, 1972) as they learn to talk. For instance, they may say "keeped" or "goodest" as they are learning rules for forming past tense or superlatives. Instead of being errors, these words are clues to children's language development. Children's sentence structure, spelling, and other errors provide equally valuable clues to their written language development. Teachers use kid watching spontaneously as they interact with children and are attentive to students' behavior and their comments. However, other observation times should be planned when the teacher focuses on particular children and makes anecdotal notes about the child's use of language.

In addition to kid watching, several other methods of documenting students' oral and written language development are available. Teachers can use checklists as they observe students. For example, as students participate in writing conferences in which they read their compositions to small groups of classmates and ask for suggestions about how to improve their writing, teachers can check that students participate fully in these groups, that they share their writing with classmates, that they gracefully accept suggestions about how to improve their own writing, and that they make substantive changes in their writing based on some of their classmates' suggestions. Students can even help to develop these checklists so that they understand the types of behavior expected of them. Checklists based on the elements of legibility presented in Chapter 14 can also be designed to use in evaluating students' handwriting.

Teachers can interview or talk with students about language to try to understand their perceptions and to clarify misunderstandings. Teachers can ask factual questions about language and language skills, but more valuable questions focus how the students use language. Questions such as "Do you listen the same way to something that compares one thing to another (such as alligators and crocodiles) as you do to something that has a lot of descriptive words (such as what a swamp looks like)? Why or why not?" or "What do you do when you're writing and don't know how to spell a word? What else can you do?" These questions probe students' awareness of language processes and strategies for comprehending and producing language.

Teachers should also keep samples of students' language. Audiotapes of children's reading, oral reports, and storytelling can be kept as well as children's writing and handwriting samples. Over the period of a school year, patterns of growth can be found in these language samples.

A final approach to evaluating students' progress in language arts is to examine how well students have applied their knowledge about listening, talking, reading, and writing to other areas of the curriculum. For example, too often students score 100% on weekly spelling tests but continue to spell the words incorrectly in science learning logs and research reports on social studies topics.

To evaluate students' language development systematically using alternative techniques, teachers should use at least three different evaluation approaches. The process by which an evaluation is approached through at least three different points of view is called *triangulation*. In addition to tests, we have suggested kid watching, keeping anecdotal records, using checklists, interviewing students, tape-recording students' talk, keeping writing samples, and across the curriculum applications. These alternative approaches are summarized in Figure 2–13. Through a variety of approaches, teachers are much more accurate as they chart and evaluate students' language growth.

POINTS TO PONDER

How Can You Keep Up-to-Date on New Research Findings and Innovative Strategies for Teaching Language Arts?

Which Organizations Are Dedicated to Improving the Quality of Language Arts Instruction?

RESOURCES FOR TEACHERS

As you begin teaching, you will want to learn as much as possible about how to teach language arts. Most schools provide inservice or staff development programs, some of which will be devoted to language arts instruction. There are also two organizations dedicated to improving the quality of instruction in reading and the other language arts. These two organizations are the National Council of Teachers of English (NCTE) and the International Reading Association (IRA). As an undergraduate student majoring in elementary education or as an elementary language arts teacher, you will find that these organizations can help you keep in touch with new ideas in the field of language arts education. Both organizations publish journals that include articles of interest to preservice and classroom teachers. These journals include articles suggesting innovative teaching practices, reports of significant research studies, reviews of recently published books of children's literature, techniques for using computers in the classroom, and reviews of recently published professional books and classroom materials. *Language Arts* is published by NCTE and *The Reading Teacher* by IRA. These journals are for elementary teachers. These two organizations also publish other journals for high school language arts and reading teachers, college faculty, and researchers. A list including these and other journals and magazines of interest to language arts teachers is presented in Figure 2–14. The editors of most of these journals and magazines invite readers to share their classroom-tested ideas by submitting manuscripts for possible publication. Information for authors is included in each publication that invites unsolicited manuscripts.

NCTE and IRA also organize yearly national conferences held in major cities around the United States on a rotating basis. At these conferences, teachers can listen to presentations given by well-known authorities in language arts and by children's authors and illustrators as well as by other classroom teachers who have developed innovative programs in their classrooms. Teachers can also meet together in special interest groups to share ideas and concerns. Commercial publishers also display textbooks and other instructional materials at these conferences.

Classroom Observations

Teachers can observe students as they listen, talk, read, and write in the classroom and note their competencies as well as their miscues. Students' behavior during testing situations often does not reflect their ability to communicate using the language modes.

Anecdotal Records

Teachers can make anecdotal records noting students' performance in listening, talking, reading, and writing activities as well as questions students ask and concepts and skills they indicate confusion about. These records document students' growth as well as pinpointing problem areas that need direct instruction from the teacher.

Checklists

Teachers can develop process and product checklists. Process checklists are used to observe students as they listen, talk, read, and write, and product checklists are used to evaluate their written products—stories, poems, and reports as well as their spelling and handwriting.

Interviews

Teachers can interview students to gauge their understanding of language processes and to have students evaluate their own progress. It is important to note, however, that often students are harsher in evaluating themselves than teachers are.

Language Samples

Teachers can collect students' oral and written language samples to use in evaluating students' progress. Oral language samples can be tape-recorded and written language samples can be kept in writing folders. Samples from the first month of the school year can be compared with more recent samples to identify areas of growth as well as areas needing instruction. When language samples are to be graded, students should choose the ones to be evaluated from the samples that have been collected.

Across the Curriculum Applications

Perhaps the truest evaluation of progress in language arts is whether students apply what they have learned about listening, talking, reading, and writing to other content areas. Observations should be made throughout the school day and language samples should be collected from other content areas, including social studies, science, math, art, and music.

Figure 2–13   Alternative Approaches to Evaluate Students' Language Development

CBC Features
Childrens' Book Council, Inc.
67 Irving Place
New York, NY 10003

Childhood Education
Association for Childhood
  Education International
11141 Georgia Avenue, Suite
  200
Wheaton, MD 20902

*Computers, Reading, and
  Language Arts*
1308 East 38th Street
Oakland, CA 94602

Early Years
P. O. Box 1266
Darien, CT 06820

The Elementary School Journal
University of Chicago Press
P. O. Box 37005
Chicago, IL 60637

The Good Apple Newspaper
P. O. Box 299
Carthage, IL 62321

The Horn Book
Park Square Building
31 Saint James Avenue
Boston, MA 02116

Instructor
757 Third Avenue
New York, NY 10017

Language Arts
National Council of Teachers of
  English
1111 Kenyon Road
Urbana, IL 61801

Learning
530 University Avenue
Palo Alto, CA 94301

The Middle School Journal
National Middle School
  Association
P. O. Box 14882
Columbus, OH 43214

The Reading Teacher
International Reading
  Association
800 Barksdale Road
P. O. Box 8139
Newark, DE 19711

*The WEB: Wonderfully Exciting
  Books*
The Ohio State University
200 Ramseyer Hall
Columbus, OH 43210

Figure 2–14   Journals and Magazines for Language Arts Teachers

In addition, these two organizations have state and local affiliate groups that teachers can join. These groups also publish journals and organize conferences. In these ways teachers can meet other teachers with similar interests and concerns.

Elementary teachers can also learn more about teaching writing by participation in workshops sponsored by affiliate groups of the National Writing Project (NWP). The NWP began as the Bay Area Writing Project at the University of California at Berkeley in 1974. It was conceived by James Gray and a group of English teachers who wanted to improve the quality of writing instruction in elementary and secondary schools. In less than 15 years, the NWP has spread to more than 150 affiliate groups located in almost every state and in Canada, Europe, and Asia. For example, the Gateway Writing Project serves the St. Louis area, the Capital Writing

Project serves the Washington, D.C. area, and the Oklahoma Writing Project serves the state of Oklahoma. Inservice workshops are scheduled in school districts located near each affiliate group. One of the principles on which the NWP is based is that the best teacher of other teachers is a teacher, and teachers who have been trained by the affiliate groups give the presentations at the inservice workshops.

Each NWP affiliate group recruits experienced elementary teachers who have a special interest and/or expertise in teaching writing to participate in special summer training institutes. These teachers then serve as teacher/consultants and make presentations at the inservice workshops. Many NWP affiliate groups also sponsor other workshops and study tours, young author conferences and workshops for student writers, and teacher-as-researcher projects which have direct classroom applications. For additional information about the National Writing Project or for the location of the NWP affiliate group nearest you, contact the National Writing Project, School of Education, University of California, Berkeley, CA 94720.

Summary

The goal of language arts education is to help students develop communicative competence or the ability to communicate effectively with others using the four traditional language modes: listening, talking, reading, and writing. This traditional grouping is inadequate in several ways: (a) it is arbitrary and artificial, (b) it inaccurately suggests a fixed sequence of acquisition, and (c) it implies a division rather than an integration of the language arts. A more realistic approach to classifying language is the seven language functions identified by M.A.K. Halliday.

The language arts curriculum includes three components: (a) language learning, (b) learning through language, and (c) learning about language. Language learning has been the commonly accepted component of traditional language arts instruction, but the other two components are equally important. Students learn through language in all areas of the curriculum, and it is essential to integrate the language arts with other content areas.

A continuum of language arts instructional models ranging from segmented, content-centered classrooms to integrated, child-centered classrooms was discussed, and the characteristics of integrated or whole language classrooms were presented. In whole language classrooms, textbooks are only one of many possible resources for teaching language arts.

The question of how to evaluate students' learning is an important one for language arts teachers. Because it is extremely difficult to evaluate students' language development using traditional testing measures, alternative approaches to evaluation have been suggested. "Kid watching" or informal classroom observations, anecdotal notes, checklists, interviews, audiotapes, writing samples, and across the curriculum applications are possible alternatives.

We also discussed resources available to language arts teachers. Two organizations dedicated to improving the quality of reading and language arts instruction are the National Council of Teachers of English (NCTE) and the International Reading Association (IRA). Both organizations publish journals of interest to elementary teachers and organize yearly conferences. Also, the National Writing Project has sites in most cities and states where teachers can learn new strategies for teaching composition.

Extensions

1. Observe in an elementary classroom classified as segmented and content-centered and in another classroom described as integrated or whole language. Compare the language arts activities in the two classrooms, focusing on the activities the students engage in, the instructional materials used, the teacher's role, and the classroom environment.

2. Choose a language skill (e.g., plurals, synonyms) and design a cluster diagram similar to the one presented in Figure 2–8, which illustrates at least six ways to teach the skill in addition to using language arts textbooks. Include activities using each of the four language modes.

3. Examine several language arts textbooks for the grade level at which you teach or expect to teach using the guidelines presented in Figure 2–11. Evaluate the value of the textbooks and consider how they should be used in teaching language arts.

4. Preview language arts software programs using the guidelines presented in Figure 2–12. Three highly rated programs that you might want to preview are *Story tree* (1984), *M-ss-ng l-nks: Young people's literature* (1983), and *Jabbertalky* (1983). Also examine word processing programs such as *The writing workshop* (1986), and *QUILL* (1983).

5. Review at least six of the language arts journals and magazines listed in Figure 2–14. Summarize your review of each publication on an index card and include the following information:

   ■ title, mailing address, and sponsoring organization of the publication

   ■ number of issues published each year

   ■ cost of yearly subscription

   ■ types of articles in each issue

   ■ evaluation of the journal and its value for elementary teachers

References

Baghban, M. (1984). *Our daughter learns to read and write: A case study from birth to three.* Newark, DE: International Reading Association.

The Bank Street writer [Computer program]. (1982). San Rafael, CA: Broderbund Software.

Bissex, G. L. (1980). *Gnys at wrk: A child learns to write and read.* Cambridge, MA: Harvard University Press.

Brown, A. L. (1980). Metacognitive development and reading. In R. Spiro, B. Bruce, & W. F. Brewer (Eds.), *Theoretical issues in reading comprehension.* New York: Erlbaum.

Brown, R. (1979). Some priorities in language arts education. *Language Arts, 56,* 483–484.

Busching, B. A. & Lundsteen, S. W. (1983). Curriculum models for integrating the language arts (Chapter 1). In B. A. Busching and J. I. Schwartz (Eds.), *Integrating the language arts in the elementary school,* (pp. 3–27). Urbana, IL: National Council of Teachers of English.

Chomsky, C. (1971). Write now, read later. *Childhood Education, 47,* 296–299.

———. (1984). Finding the best language arts software. *Classroom Computer Learning, 4,* 61–63.

Colby, J. P. (1975). *Lexington and Concord, 1775: What really happened.* New York: Hasting House.

Collier, J. & Collier, C. (1974). *My brother Sam is dead*. New York: Four Winds.

D'Aulaire, I. & D'Aulaire, E. P. (1936). *George Washington*. New York: Doubleday.

_____.(1950). *Benjamin Franklin*. New York: Doubleday.

Felton, H. (1976). *Deborah Sampson: Soldier of the revolution*. New York: Dodd.

Florio, S. & Clark, C. M. (1982). The functions of writing in an elementary classroom. *Research in the Teaching of English, 19*, 115–130.

Forbes, E., (1970). *Johnny Tremain*. Boston: Houghton Mifflin.

Fritz, J. (1969). *George Washington's breakfast*. New York: Coward.

_____. (1973). *And then what happened, Paul Revere?* New York: Coward.

_____. (1974). *Why don't you get a horse, Sam Adams?* New York: Coward.

_____. (1976). *Will you sign here, John Hancock?* New York: Coward.

_____. (1981). *Traitor. The case of Benedict Arnold*. New York: Putnam.

Fritz, J. (1981). *Where was Patrick Henry on the 29th of May?* New York: Coward.

Gallagher, N. (1982). *How to stop a sentence and other methods of managing words*. Reading, MA: Addison-Wesley.

Genishi, C. (1979). Letting children communicate: The synthesis of language skills and language. *Language Arts, 56*, 628–633.

Genishi, C. & Dyson, A. H. (1984). *Language assessment in the early years*. Norwood, NJ: Ablex.

Gere, A. R. & Abbott, R. D. (1985). Talking about writing: The language of writing groups. *Research in the Teaching of English, 19*, 362–381.

Goodman, K. (1986). *What's whole in whole language?* Portsmouth, NH: Heinemann.

Goodman, Y. M. (1978). Kid watching: An alternative to testing. *National Elementary Principals Journal, 57*, 41–45.

Goodman, Y. M. & Burke, C. L. (1972). *The reading miscue inventory manual*. New York: Richard C. Owen.

Graves, D. H. (1976). Let's get rid of the welfare mess in the teaching of writing. *Language Arts, 53*, 645–651.

_____. (1977). Research update: Language arts textbooks: A writing process evaluation. *Language Arts, 54*, 817–823.

Haley, G. (1973). *Jack Jouett's ride*. New York: Viking.

Halliday, M. A. K. (1973). *Explorations in the functions of language*. London: Edward Arnold.

_____. (1975). *Learning how to mean: Explorations in the development of language*. London: Edward Arnold.

_____. (1980). Three aspects of children's language development: Learning language, learning through language, learning about language. In Y. M. Goodman, M. M. Haussler, & D. S. Strickland (Eds.), *Oral and written language development research: Impact on the schools* (pp. 7–19). Proceedings from the 1979 and 1980 IMPACT Conferences sponsored by the International Reading Association and the National Council of Teachers of English.

Hemphill, J. (1981). Language arts instruction: A continuum of possible models. *Language Arts, 58*, 643–651.

Hymes, D. (1974). *Foundations in sociolinguistics: An ethnographic approach*. Philadelphia: University of Pennsylvania Press.

Jabbertalky: The programmable word game [Computer program]. (1983). Sunnyvale, CA: Automated Simulations.

Lass, B. (1982). Portrait of my son as an early reader. *The Reading Teacher, 36*, 20–28.

Leckie, R. (1973). *The world turned upside down: The story of the American revolution*. New York: Putnam.

Lefevre, C. A. (1970). *Linguistics, English, and the language arts*. Boston: Allyn and Bacon.

Lionni, L. (1977). *A flea story*. New York: Pantheon.

Loban, W. (1976). *Language development: Kindergarten through grade twelve* (NCTE Research Report No. 18). Urbana, IL: National Council of Teachers of English.

_____. (1979). Relationships between language and literacy. *Language Arts, 56*, 485–486.

Longfellow, H. W. (1985). *Paul Revere's ride.* New York: Greenwillow.

Martin, J. P. (1964). *Yankee doodle boy.* New York: Scott.

McDowell, B. (1967). *The Revolutionary War: America's fight for freedom.* Washington, DC: National Geographic Society.

M-ss-ng l-nks: Young people's literature [Computer program]. (1983). Pleasantville, NY: Sunburst Communications.

Newman, J. M. (Ed.). (1985). *Whole language: Theory in use.* Portsmouth, NH: Heinemann.

Pinnell, G. S. (1975). Language in primary classrooms. *Theory into Practice, 14,* 318–327.

_____. (1985). Ways to look at the functions of children's language. In A. Jaggar & M. T. Smith (Eds.), *Observing the language learner,* (pp. 57-72). Newark, DE: International Reading Association and National Council of Teachers of English.

QUILL [Computer program]. (1983). Lexington, MA: DC Heath.

Sharmat, M. W. (1974). *Nate the great goes undercover.* New York: Coward.

Smith, F. (1977). The uses of language. *Language Arts, 54,* 638–644.

_____. (1979). The language arts and the learner's mind. *Language Arts, 56,* 118–125.

_____. (1982). *Writing and the writer.* New York: Holt.

Smith, P. L. & Tompkins, G. E. (1984). Selecting software for your LD students. *Academic Therapy, 20,* 221–224.

Sobol, D. J. (1963). *Encyclopedia Brown, boy detective.* New York: Dutton.

Stauffer, R. G. (1980). Process-oriented instructional activities: Pre-kindergarten through grade 5 (Chapter 5). In B. J. Mandel (Ed.), *Three language-arts curriculum models: Pre-kindergarten through college* (pp. 47-60). Urbana, IL: National Council of Teachers of English.

Story tree [Computer program]. (1984). New York: Scholastic.

Taylor, R. (1980). *Computers in the schools: Tool, tutor, and tutee.* New York: Teachers College Press.

Tompkins, G. E., Friend, M., & Smith, P. L. (1984). Children's metacognitive knowledge of listening. American Educational Research Association 1984 Convention, New Orleans, LA.

The writing workshop [Computer program]. (1986). St. Louis: Milliken.

Yaden, Jr. D. B. (1984). Research in metalinguistic awareness: Findings, problems, and classroom applications. *Visible Language, 18,* 5–47.

Yaden, Jr. D. B. and Templeton, S. (Eds.). (1986). *Metalinguistic awareness and beginning literacy: Conceptualizing what it means to read and write.* Portsmouth, NH: Heinemann.

Zaharias, J. A. (1983). Microcomputers in the language arts classroom: Promises and pitfalls. *Language Arts, 60,* 990–996.

IF YOU WANT TO LEARN MORE

Busching, B. A. & Schwartz, J. I. (Eds.). (1983). *Integrating the language arts in the elementary school.* Urbana, IL: National Council of Teachers of English.

Dickson, W. & Raymond, M. (1984). *Language arts computer books: A how-to guide for teachers.* Reston, VA: Reston.

Genishi, C. & Dyson, A. H. (1984). *Language assessment in the early years.* Norwood, NJ: Ablex.

Goodman, K. (1986). *What's whole in whole language?* Portsmouth, NH: Heinemann.

Jaggar, A. & Smith-Burke, M. T. (Eds.). (1985). *Observing the language learner.* Newark, DE: International Reading Association and National Council of Teachers of English.

Lindfors, J. W. (1984). How children learn or how teachers teach? A profound confusion. *Language Arts, 61,* 600–606.

Loban, W. (1976). *Language development: Kindergarten through grade twelve.* (NCTE Research Report No. 18). Urbana, IL: National Council of Teachers of English.

Mandel, B. J. (Ed.). (1980). *Three language-arts curriculum models: Pre-kindergarten through college.* Urbana, IL: National Council of Teachers of English.

Newman, J. M. (Ed.). (1985). *Whole language: Theory in use.* Portsmouth, NH: Heinemann.

Smith, F. (1983). *Essays into literacy.* Portsmouth, NH: Heinemann.

Stanford, G. (Ed.). (1979). *How to handle the paper load* (Classroom Practices in Teaching English 1979-1980). Urbana, IL: National Council of Teachers of English.

Staniford, S. N., Jaycox, K., & Auten, A. (1983). *Computers in the English classroom: A primer for teachers.* Urbana, IL: ERIC Clearinghouse on Reading and Communication Skills and the National Council of Teachers of English.

CHAPTER THREE

Listening to Learn

*O*VERVIEW.   *In this chapter we will consider listening, the first language mode that children acquire and the most frequently used mode by both children and adults. Because listening plays a significant role in education, it is crucial that teachers understand the listening process. Too often teachers equate instruction with practice activities, but we will suggest instructional strategies to help students develop listening skills for comprehensive, critical, and appreciative listening.*

Listening is the first language mode that children acquire, and it provides the basis for the other language arts (Lundsteen, 1979). Infants use listening to begin the process of learning to comprehend and produce language. From the beginning of their lives, they listen to sounds in their immediate environment, attend to speech sounds, and construct their knowledge of oral language. Listening is also important in learning to read. Children are introduced to reading by having stories read to them. As children are being read to, they begin to see the connection between what they hear and what they see on the printed page. Reading and listening comprehension skills—main ideas, details, sequence, and so on—are similar in many ways.

Listening also indirectly influences writing. Writing begins as talk written down, and the stories that students read become models for their writing. Listening ability also is essential as students share their writing in conferences and receive feedback on how to improve their writing. Inner listening, that is, dialoguing with yourself, also occurs as students write and revise their writing, and is also a form of listening.

Listening is "the most used and perhaps the most important of the language (and learning) arts" (Devine, 1982, p. 1). Researchers have found that more of children's and adults' time is spent listening than reading, writing, or talking. The chart in Figure 3–1 illustrates the amount of time we communicate in each language mode. Both children and adults spend approximately 50% of their communication time listening. Language researcher Walter Loban compares the four language modes this way: We listen a book a day, we speak a book a week, we read a book a month, and we write a book a year (cited in Erickson, 1985).

Despite the importance of listening in our lives, listening has been called the "neglected" or "orphan" language art for 35 years or more (Anderson, 1949). Little

---

POINTS TO PONDER

What Is Listening?

How Is Listening Different from Hearing?

What Are the Steps in the Listening Process?

What Are Five Purposes for Listening?

Figure 3–1 Percentage of Communication Time in Each Language Mode

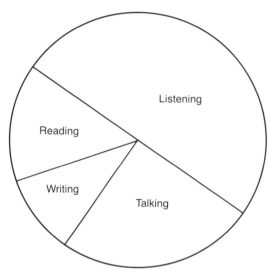

Data from Rankin, 1926; Wilt, 1950; Werner, 1975.

Listening centers provide a valuable opportunity for students to practice listening skills, but they cannot substitute for listening instruction.

time has been devoted to listening instruction in most classrooms, listening is not stressed in language arts textbooks, and teachers often complain that they do not know how to teach listening (Devine, 1978; Landry, 1969; Wolvin & Coakley, 1985).

THE LISTENING PROCESS

Listening is elusive because it occurs internally. Sara Lundsteen (1979) describes listening as the "most mysterious" language process. In fact, teachers often do not know whether listening has occurred until they ask students to apply what they have listened to by answering questions, completing assignments, or taking tests. Even then, there is no guarantee that the students' responses indicate that they have listened.

What Is Listening?

Listening is a highly complex, interactive process that has been defined as "the process by which spoken language is converted to meaning in the mind" (Lundsteen, 1979, p. 1). As this definition suggests, listening is more than just hearing, even though children and adults often use the two terms, *hearing* and *listening*, synonymously. Rather, hearing is an integral component, but only one component, of the listening process.

Wolvin and Coakley (1985) describe three steps in the listening process: (a) receiving, (b) attending, and (c) assigning meaning. In the first step, the listener receives the aural stimuli or the aural and visual stimuli presented by the speaker. Next, the listener focuses on selected stimuli while ignoring other distracting stimuli. Because so many stimuli surround students in the classroom, they must attend to the speaker's message, focusing on the most important information in that message. In the third step, the listener assigns meaning to, or understands, the speaker's message. Listeners assign meaning using assimilation and accommodation to fit the message into their existing cognitive structures or to create new structures if necessary. Responding or reacting to the message is not considered part of the listening process: The response occurs afterward, and it sets another communication process into action in which the listener becomes the message sender.

The second step of Wolvin and Coakley's listening process model may be called the "paying attention" component. Elementary teachers spend a great deal of instructional time reminding students to pay attention to the listening task. Unfortunately, however, children often do not understand the admonition. When asked to explain what "paying attention" means, some children equate it with physical behaviors such as not kicking their feet or cleaning off their desks. Learning to attend to the speaker's message is especially important because researchers have learned that students can listen to 250 words per minute, 2 to 3 times the normal rate of talking (Foulke, 1968). This differential allows listeners the time to tune in and out as well as to become distracted during listening.

Furthermore, the need of students to attend to the speaker's message will vary with the purpose for listening. Some types of listening require more attentiveness than others. For example, effective listeners will listen differently to directions on how to reach a friend's home than to a poem or story being read aloud.

Purposes for Listening

Why do you listen? Often students answer that question by explaining that they listen to learn or to avoid punishment (Tompkins, Friend, & Smith, 1984). While these are two purposes of in-school listening, children seem to be unaware of many other purposes for listening. Wolvin and Coakley (1979, 1985) list five major purposes for listening:

1. *Discriminative listening* is listening to distinguish sounds and develop a sensitivity to nonverbal communication.
2. *Comprehensive listening* is listening to understand a message.
3. *Therapeutic listening* is listening to allow a speaker to talk through a problem.
4. *Critical listening* is listening to comprehend and evaluate a message.
5. *Appreciative listening* is listening to a speaker or reader for enjoyment.

While all five purposes are important, we will focus in this chapter on only three listening purposes: (a) comprehensive listening, or the type of listening required in many instructional activities; (b) critical listening, or learning to detect propaganda devices and persuasive language; and (c) appreciative listening, or listening to conversation and to literature read aloud for pleasure.

POINTS TO PONDER
Can Comprehensive Listening Be Taught?
What Is the Difference Between Practice Activities and Listening Instruction?
What Comprehensive Listening Strategies Can Elementary Students Learn?
What Is the Directed Listening Activity (DLA)?

COMPREHENSIVE LISTENING

Activities involving listening can be observed in almost every language arts classroom. Students listen to the teacher giving directions and instruction, to tape-recorded stories at listening centers, to classmates during discussions, and to the teacher reading stories and poetry aloud. Since listening plays a significant role in these and other classroom activities, listening is not neglected. However, while these activities provide opportunities for students to practice listening skills, they do *not* teach students how to be more effective listeners.

Language arts educators have repeatedly cited the need for systematic instruction in listening (Devine, 1978; Lundsteen, 1979; Pearson & Fielding, 1982; Wolvin & Coakley, 1985). Most of what has traditionally been called listening instruction has been only practice. For example, when students listen to a story at a listening center and then answer questions about it, teachers assume that the students know *how* to listen so they will be able to answer the questions. Students practice listening at a listening center, but they do not learn how to be more effective listeners. Too often instruction has been equated with practice. Perhaps one reason listening has not been taught is simply that teachers do not know how to teach listening. In a recent study, only 17% of the teachers surveyed recalled receiving any instruction in how to teach listening in their language arts methods class (Tompkins, Smith, & Friend, 1984). Instead, the teachers surveyed reported using practice activities instead of listening instruction.

A Strategies Approach

In contrast to practice activities, listening instruction should teach students specific strategies they can use for comprehensive listening and other types of listening tasks. These strategies help students attend to the important information in the message and understand it more easily. Teachers have assumed that students acquire these strategies intuitively. Certainly some students do. However, many students do not recognize that different listening purposes require different strategies. Many students have only one approach to listening, no matter what the purpose is. They say that they listen as hard as they can and try to remember everything. Such a strategy seems destined to fail for at least two reasons. First, remembering everything places an impossible demand on a student's short-term memory, and second, many items in a message are not important enough to be remembered. Still other students equate listening with intelligence, assuming that they "just aren't smart enough" if they are poor listeners.

Six listening strategies that elementary students can learn and use for comprehensive listening activities are (a) creating imagery, (b) categorizing, (c) asking questions, (d) organizing, (e) note-taking, and (f) attention-directing.* These strategies are primarily aimed at comprehensive listening, but they can also be used with discriminative listening, critical listening, and other listening purposes as well. Information about each of the six listening strategies is presented in the following paragraphs.

Creating Imagery: Forming a Picture in Your Mind.   Students can draw a mental picture to help them remember while listening. The imagery strategy is especially useful when a speaker's message has many visual images, details, or descriptive words. Excerpts from stories and pictures can be used in teaching this strategy.

Categorizing: Putting Information into Groups.   Students can categorize to group or cluster information when the speaker's message contains many pieces of information, comparisons, or contrasts. For example, students could use this strategy as they listen to a comparison of reptiles and amphibians. Students can divide

---

*Adapted from Tompkins, Friend, & Smith, in press.

a sheet of paper into two columns, labeling one column *reptiles* and the other *amphibians.* Then they make notes in the columns as they listen to the speaker or immediately after listening. When students are listening to presentations that contain information on more than two or three categories, such as a presentation on the five basic food groups, they can make a cluster diagram and take notes about each food group. An example of a cluster diagram is presented in Figure 3–2. More information about clustering is presented in Chapter 6.

Asking Questions.   Students can also use questions to increase their understanding of a speaker's message. Two types of questions can be asked: (a) students can ask the speaker about any unclear information, and (b) they can ask themselves questions to monitor their listening and understanding. While most students are familiar with asking the speaker questions, the idea of self-questions is usually new to students. Develop a list of self-questions similar to those that follow to help students understand the self-questioning procedure and how to monitor their understanding:

> Why am I listening to this message?
>
> Do I know what _____ means?
>
> Does this information make sense to me?

Organizing: Discovering the Plan.   Speakers use one of several types of organization to structure their message. Five commonly used organizational patterns are (a) description, (b) sequence, (c) comparison, (d) cause and effect, and (e) prob-

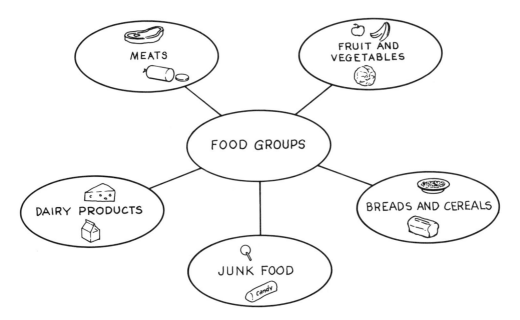

Figure 3–2   A Cluster Diagram on the Food Groups

lem and solution. Students can learn to recognize these patterns and use them to understand and remember a speaker's message more easily. Graphic organizers can be developed for each of these five organizational patterns. Three possible graphic organizers for the cause and effect pattern are presented in Figure 3–3. To help students visualize the organization of the message, they can devise graphic organizers to display the messages representing each pattern. Excerpts from social studies and science textbooks as well as from informational books can be used in teaching this strategy.

In addition, speakers often use special words to signal the organizational patterns they are following. These signal words include *first, second, third, next, in contrast,* and *in summary.* Students can learn to attend to these signals to identify the organizational pattern the speaker is using as well as to better understand the message.

Note-taking: Writing down Important Information.   Note-taking is a strategy that helps students become more active listeners. Devine (1981) describes note-

1. Single Cause Leading to Single Effect

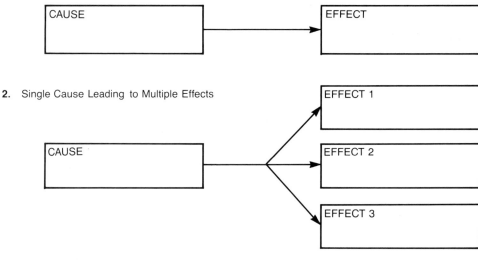

2. Single Cause Leading to Multiple Effects

3. Multiple Causes Contributing to a Single Effect

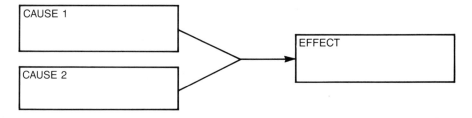

Figure 3–3   Possible Graphic Organizers for Cause and Effect

taking as "responding-with-pen-in-hand" (p. 156). Students' interest in note-taking begins with the realization that they cannot store unlimited amounts of information in their minds; some sort of external storage system is needed.

Teachers introduce note-taking by taking notes with the class on the chalkboard. During an oral presentation, the teacher stops periodically, asks students to identify the important information that was presented, and lists their responses on the chalkboard. Teachers often begin by writing notes in a list format, but the notes also can be written in outline or cluster formats. Similarly, the teacher can use key words, phrases, or sentences in recording notes. After an introduction to various note-taking strategies, students develop personal note-taking systems in which they write notes in their own words and use a consistent format.

Outlining is a useful note-taking strategy, but it has gained a bad reputation from misuse in secondary and college English classes (Devine, 1981). It may be preferable to use print materials to introduce outlining because oral presentations are often less structured than print materials. However, teachers who want to teach outlining through oral presentations should begin with a very simple organization of perhaps three main ideas with two subordinate ideas for each main idea. Teachers can also give students a partial outline to complete as they give an oral presentation.

The information in the notes that students take depends on their purpose for listening. Thus, it is essential that students understand the purpose for listening before they begin to take notes. For some listening tasks, main ideas or details should be noted; for other tasks, sequence, cause and effect, or comparisons are noted.

Most language arts textbooks limit instruction in note-taking to taking notes from textbooks and reference materials (Tompkins, Smith, & Friend, 1984). However, taking notes from a speaker is an equally important strategy. In note taking from a speaker, students cannot control the speed at which information is presented. They usually cannot relisten to a speaker to complete notes, and the structure of oral presentations is often not as formal as in print materials. Students need to become aware of these differences so that they can adapt their note-taking system to the presentation mode.

Attention-directing: Getting Clues from the Speaker. Speakers use both visual and verbal cues to convey their messages. Visual cues include gesturing, writing or underlining important information on the chalkboard, and changing facial expressions. Verbal cues include pausing, raising or lowering the voice, slowing speech down to stress key points, and repeating important information. Students can use these cues to increase their understanding of a message.

Instructional Strategy

Students need to learn to use each of these six comprehensive listening strategies and apply them in a variety of listening tasks. The following instructional strategy, developed from the instructional model presented in the first chapter, can be used to teach these listening strategies.

Step 1: Initiating.   Explain the listening strategy, how it is used, and the types of listening activities for which it is most effective. Develop a chart listing the characteristics or steps involved in the strategy. For example, the information about organizational patterns presented in Figure 3–3 can be listed in a chart for students to refer to.

Step 2: Structuring.   Demonstrate the strategy as you give an oral presentation or as students listen to a tape-recorded presentation or a film presentation. Stop the presentation periodically to talk aloud about what you are doing as you are listening, to ask yourself questions, to take notes, or to comment on cues. After completing the activity, discuss your use of the strategy with students.

Step 3: Conceptualizing.   Have students model the strategy during other presentations. Stop the presentation periodically to ask students to describe how they are listening. After several large-group presentations, students can work in small groups, and later individually to practice the strategy.

Step 4: Summarizing.   After each listening activity, have students explain the strategy and how they use it.

Step 5: Generalizing.   Present a variety of listening activities, and have students experiment to determine if the strategy is effective or if a different strategy should be tried. Introduce additional strategies to meet these other listening purposes. After all six strategies have been presented and practiced, continue to the next step.

Step 6: Applying.   After students develop a repertoire of these six comprehensive listening strategies, they need to learn to select an appropriate strategy for specific listening purposes. Their choice depends both on their purpose for listening as well as the speaker's purpose. Students may want to generate a list of questions similar to the questions presented in Figure 3–4 to select a strategy and monitor the effectiveness of their choice. Repeat the first five steps of this instructional strategy to teach students how to select an appropriate listening strategy for various listening activities.

Directed Listening Activity

In addition to teaching students strategies that they can use while listening, teachers can also structure their oral presentations to facilitate students' comprehension. One strategy for teachers is the Directed Listening Activity (Cunningham, Cunningham, & Arthur, 1981). This strategy is an adaption of the Directed Reading Activity, the instructional approach used in many reading textbooks. This strategy has three steps: (a) prelistening, (b) listening, and (c) follow-up. In the prelistening step, the teacher sets the stage for listening by presenting background information, introducing terms related to the presentation, and setting the purpose for listening. During the second step, the teacher gives the presentation, and as they lis-

Figure 3–4 How to Choose an Appropriate Listening Strategy

Before Listening

What is the speaker's purpose?
What is my purpose for listening?
What am I going to do with what I listen to?
Will I need to take notes?
Which strategies could I use?
Which one will I select?

During Listening

Is my strategy still working?
Am I putting information into groups?
Is the speaker giving me clues about the organization of the message?
Is the speaker giving me nonverbal cues such as gestures and varied facial expressions?
Is the speaker's voice giving me other cues?

After Listening

Do I have questions for the speaker?
Was any part of the message unclear?
Are my notes complete?
Did I make a good choice of strategies? Why or why not?

Tompkins, Friend, & Smith, in press.

ten, students are directed to try to relate it to the purposes set in the first step. After the presentation, the teacher asks comprehension questions to check that students have understood and provides further explanation when necessary. Students are also encouraged to offer comments about the presentation, and discussions often develop. In the follow-up step, the teacher provides opportunities for students to engage in activities that apply the concepts presented during the first two steps. These activities may include reading and writing activities, small group discussions, as well as project work. This approach lends itself to social studies and science concepts as well as language arts concepts presented in the middle and upper elementary grades.

POINTS TO PONDER
How Can Elementary Students Become Critical Listeners?
What Types of Propaganda Devices and Persuasive Language Can Students Identify?

CRITICAL LISTENING

Children, even primary grade students, need to develop critical listening skills because they are exposed to advertising and propaganda devices as they watch television. Because many commercials are directed to children, it is essential that they listen critically to the commercials and learn to judge their claims. For example, do the jogging shoes actually help you to run faster? Will the breakfast cereal make you a better football player? Will a particular toy make you a more popular child?

As the commercials are telecast repeatedly, children learn to sing the jingles associated with the commercials and beg their parents to buy the advertised products. Children can learn to be critical listeners and detect propaganda devices and persuasive language to judge the claims of the sponsors. Even first graders can develop their critical listening skills.

Propaganda Devices

Advertisers use propaganda devices such as testimonials, the bandwagon effect, and rewards to sell their products. Nine devices that elementary students can learn to identify are listed in Figure 3–5. Students can listen to commercials to locate examples of each propaganda device and discuss the effect the device has on them. They can also investigate to see how the same devices are varied in commercials directed to youngsters, teenagers, and adults. For instance, while a snack food commercial with a sticker or toy in the package will appeal to youngster, a videotape recorder advertisement with a factory rebate will appeal to an adult. The propaganda device for both ads is the same: a reward! These devices can be used to sell ideas as well as products. Public service announcements about not smoking or wearing seat belts as well as political advertisements, endorsements, and speeches use these same devices.

Persuasive Language

People seeking to influence us often use words that evoke a variety of responses. They claim something is *improved, more natural,* or *50% better.* These commercial words are called *loaded words* because they are suggestive. For example, when a product is advertised as 50% better, consumers need to ask, "50% better than what?" That question is rarely answered in commercials or advertisements.

Another type of persuasive language is known as doublespeak. *Doublespeak* is characterized as deceptive, evasive, euphemistic, confusing, and self-contradictory language. For example, janitors may be called *maintenance engineers* and repeats of television shows are termed *encore-telecasts.* William Lutz (1984) cites a number of kinds of doublespeak. Elementary students can easily understand two kinds of doublespeak, euphemisms and inflated language. Other kinds of doublespeak, such as jargon specific to particular groups, overwhelming an audience with words, and language that pretends to communicate but does not, may be more appropriate for older students. *Euphemisms* are words or phrases, such as *passed away,* that are used to avoid a harsh or distasteful reality. They are often used out of concern for someone's feelings rather than to deceive. *Inflated language* includes words designed to make the ordinary seem extraordinary. For example, *car mechanics* become *automotive internists* and *used cars* become *pre-owned* or *experienced cars.* Some loaded words and examples of doublespeak are listed in Figure 3–6. Children need to learn that people sometimes use words that only pretend to communicate; at other times, they use words to intentionally misrepresent. For instance, a wallet advertised as *genuine imitation leather* is a vinyl wallet. Children need to be able to interpret this persuasive language and to avoid using it themselves.

Instructional Strategy

The steps in teaching students to be critical listeners are similar to the steps in teaching the comprehensive listening strategies presented earlier. In this instructional strategy, students view commercials and examine the propaganda devices and persuasive language used in them.

Step 1: Initiating. Begin by talking about commercials and asking students about familiar commercials. Videotape a set of commercials and view them with your students. Discuss the purpose of each commercial. Use the questions about commercials presented in Figure 3–7 to probe students' thinking about propaganda and persuasive language.

Step 2: Structuring. Introduce the propaganda devices and view the commercials again to look for examples of each device. Introduce loaded words and doublespeak and view the commercials for a third time to look for examples of persuasive language.

Step 3: Conceptualizing. Have students work in small groups to critique a commercial, listing the propaganda devices and persuasive language used. Students might also want to test the claims made in the commercial.

Step 4: Summarizing. Review the concepts about propaganda devices and persuasive language introduced in the first three steps.

Step 5: Generalizing. Present a new set of videotaped commercials for students to critique. Ask students to identify propaganda devices and persuasive language used in the commercials.

Step 6: Applying. Have students apply what they have learned about propaganda devices and persuasive language by creating their own products and writing and producing their own commercials. As the commercials are presented, have classmates act as critical listeners to detect propaganda devices, loaded words, and doublespeak.

Figure 3–5   Nine Propaganda Devices

1. *Glittering Generality*

   Generalities such as "motherhood," "justice," and "The American Way" are used to enhance the quality of a product or the character of a political figure. Propagandists select a generality so attractive that listeners do not challenge the speaker's real point. If a candidate for public office happens to be a mother, for example, the speaker may say, "Our civilization could not survive without mothers." The generalization is true, of course, and listeners may—if they are not careful—accept the candidate without asking these questions: Is she a mother? Is she a good mother? Does being a mother have anything to do with being a good candidate?

2. *Testimonial*

   To convince people to purchase a product, an advertiser associates it with a popular personality such as an athlete or film star. For example, "Bozo Cereal must be good because Joe Footballstar eats it every morning." Similarly, film stars endorse candidates for political office and telethons to raise money for medical research and other causes. Consider these questions: Is the person familiar with the product being advertised? Does the person offering the testimonial have the expertise necessary to judge the quality of the product, event, or candidate?

3. *Transfer*

   In this device, which is similar to the testimonial technique, the persuader tries to transfer the authority and prestige of some person or object to another person or object that will then be accepted. Good examples are found regularly in advertising: A film star is shown using Super Soap, and viewers are supposed to believe that they too may have healthy, youthful skin if they use the same soap. Likewise, politicians like to be seen with famous athletes or entertainers in hopes that the luster of the stars will rub off on them. This technique is also known as guilt or glory by association. Questions to determine the effect of this device are the same as for the testimonial technique.

4. *Name-calling*

   Here the advertiser tries to pin a bad label on something they want listeners to dislike so that it will automatically be rejected or condemned. In a discussion of health insurance, for example, an opponent may call the sponsor of a bill a socialist. Whether or not the sponsor is a socialist does not matter to the name-caller; the purpose is to have any unpleasant associations of the term rub off on the victim. Listeners should ask themselves whether or not the label has any effect on the product.

Figure 3–5 *Continued*

5. *Plain Folks*

   Assuming that most listeners favor common, ordinary people (rather than elitist, stuffed shirts), many politicians like to assume the appearance of common folk. One candidate, who really went to Harvard and wore $400 suits, campaigned in clothes from J.C. Penney's and spoke backcountry dialect. "Look at me, folks," the candidate wanted to say, "I'm just a regular country boy like you; I wouldn't sell you a bill of goods!" To determine the effect of this device, listeners should ask these questions: Is the person really the type of person he or she is portraying? Does the person really share the ideas of the people with whom he or she professes to identify?

6. *Card Stacking*

   In presenting complex issues, the unscrupulous persuader often chooses only those items that favor one side of an issue. Any unfavorable facts are suppressed. To consider the argument objectively, listeners must seek additional information about other viewpoints.

7. *Bandwagon*

   This technique appeals to many people's need to be a part of a group. Advertisers claim that everyone is using this product and you should, too. For example, "more physicians recommend this pill than any other." (Notice that the advertisement doesn't specify what "any other" is.) Questions to consider include the following: Does everyone really use this product? What is it better than? Why should I jump on the bandwagon?

8. *Snob Appeal*

   In contrast to the plain folks device, persuaders use snob appeal to try to appeal to the people who want to become part of an elite or exclusive group. Advertisements for expensive clothes, cosmetics, and gourmet foods often use this technique. Listeners should consider these questions in evaluating the commercials and advertisements using this device: Is the product of high quality or does it have an expensive nametag? Is the product of higher quality than other non-snobbish brands?

9. *Rewards*

   Increasingly, advertisers offer rewards for buying their products. For many years, snack food and cereal products offered toys and other gimmicks in their product packages. More often, adults are being lured by this device, too. Free gifts, rebates from manufacturers, low-cost financing, and other rewards are being offered for the purchase of expensive items such as appliances and automobiles. Listeners should consider the value of these rewards and whether they increase the cost of the product.

Techniques 1–6 adapted from Devine, 1982, pp. 39–40.

Figure 3–6 Examples of Persuasive Language

Loaded Words

best buy	longer lasting
better than	lowest
carefree	maximum
discount	more natural
easier	more powerful
extra strong	new/newer
fortified	plus
fresh	stronger
guaranteed	ultra
improved	virtually

Doublespeak — *Translations*

Doublespeak	*Translations*
bathroom tissue	toilet paper
civil disorder	riot
correctional facility	jail, prison
dentures	false teeth
disadvantaged	poor
encore telecast	re-run
funeral director	undertaker
genuine imitation leather	vinyl
inner city	slum, ghetto
inoperative statement or misspeak	lie
mobile home	house trailer
memorial park	cemetery
nervous wetness	sweat
occasional irregularity	constipation
passed away	died
people expressways	sidewalks
personal preservation flotation device	life preserver
pre-owned or experienced	used
pupil station	student's desk
senior citizen	old person
terminal living	dying
urban transportation specialist	cab driver, bus driver

Lutz, n.d.

Figure 3–7   Questions to Detect Propaganda

1. What is the speaker's purpose?
2. What are the speaker's credentials?
3. Is there evidence of bias?
4. Does the speaker use persuasive language?
5. Does the speaker make sweeping generalizations or unsupported inferences?
6. Do opinions predominate the talk?
7. Does the speaker use any propaganda devices?
8. Do I accept the message?

Devine, 1982, pp. 41–42.

Using Advertisements.   Students can use the same procedures and activities with advertisements they have collected from magazines and product packages. Have children collect examples of advertisements and display them on a bulletin board. The same types of propaganda devices, loaded words, and doublespeak are used in written advertisements. Students examine advertisements and then decide how the writer is trying to persuade them to purchase the product. They can also compare the amount of text to the amount of pictures. Fox and Allen (1983) reported that children who examined advertisements found that, in contrast to advertisements for toys, cosmetics, and appliances, ads for cigarettes had comparatively little text and pictures were used prominently. The students quickly speculated on the reasons for this approach.

POINTS TO PONDER
Why Read Aloud to Students?
What Is the Directed Listening Thinking Activity?
What Types of Response to Literature Activities Can Students Participate In?
What Is the Reflective Discussion Strategy?

APPRECIATIVE LISTENING

Students listen appreciatively when they listen for enjoyment. Appreciative listening includes listening to music played on a radio, to a comedian tell jokes, to friends as they talk, and to a storyteller or to stories read aloud. In this section, we will focus on reading stories aloud to students. Wolvin and Coakley (1979) have identified some basic skills related to appreciative listening that students develop as they listen to stories read aloud. These skills include the ability to visualize, identify the speech rhythm, identify the speaker's style, interpret character from dialogue, recognize tone and mode, understand the effect of the speaker or reader's vocal qualities and physical action, and understand the effect of the audience on the listeners' own responses.

Reading Aloud to Students

Sharing books orally is a valuable way to help students enjoy literature. Reading stories to children is an important component in most kindergarten and first-grade classrooms. Unfortunately, too often teachers think that they need to read to children only until they learn to read for themselves; however, reading aloud and sharing the excitement of books, language, and reading should remain an important part of the language arts program at all grade levels. The common complaint is that there is not enough time in the school day to read to children, but reading aloud can take as little as 10 or 15 minutes a day. Many educators (Kimmel & Segel, 1983; Sims, 1977; Trelease, 1982) point out the necessity of finding time to read aloud because of its many benefits for students. Some of these benefits include the following:

1. stimulating children's interest in books and reading
2. broadening children's reading interests and developing their taste for quality literature
3. introducing children to the sounds of written language and expanding their vocabulary and sentence patterns
4. sharing books "too good to miss" with children
5. allowing children to listen to books that would be too difficult for them to read on their own or books that are "hard to get into"
6. expanding children's background of experiences
7. introducing children to concepts about written language, different genres of literature, poetry, and elements of story structure
8. providing a pleasurable, shared experience
9. modeling to children that adults read and enjoy reading in order to increase the likelihood that children will become lifelong readers

By reading aloud to students daily, you can introduce them to all types of literature and the enjoyment of reading. The guidelines for choosing books to read aloud are simple: Choose books that you like and you think will appeal to your students. Jim Trelease, author of *The read-aloud handbook* (1982), suggests four additional criteria of good read-aloud books: They should (a) be fast-paced to hook children's interest as quickly as possible; (b) contain well-developed characters; (c) include easy-to-read dialogue; and (d) keep long descriptive passages to a minimum. A number of annotated guidebooks have been prepared to help teachers se-

Teachers should share stories by reading aloud to students every day, even to middle- and upper-grade students.

lect books for reading aloud as well as for independent reading. A list of these guides is presented in Figure 3–8.

Repeated Readings.　Children, especially preschoolers and kindergartners, often beg to have a familiar book reread. While it is important to share a wide variety of books with children, researchers have found that children benefit in specific ways from repeated readings. Through these repetitions, students gain control over the parts of a story and are better able to synthesize the story parts into a whole. The quality of children's responses to a repeated story also changes (Beaver, 1982).

In a recent study, Martinez and Roser (1985) examined young children's responses to stories and found that as stories become increasingly familiar, students' responses indicate a greater depth of understanding. They found that children talked almost twice as much about familiar books that had been reread many times as about unfamiliar books that had been read only once or twice. The form and focus of children's talk changed, too. While children tended to ask questions about unfamiliar stories, they made comments about familiar stories. In unfamiliar stories, children's talk focused on characters; the focus changed to details and word meanings when children talked about familiar stories. These researchers also found that children's comments after repeated readings were more probing and more specific, suggesting that they had greater insights into the story. Researchers

Books

Bauer, C.F. (1983). *This way to books.* New York: Wilson.

Carroll, F.L. & Mecham, M. (Eds.). (1984). *Exciting, funny, scary, short, different, and sad books kids like about animals, science, sports, families, songs, and other things.* Chicago: American Library Association.

Christensen, J. (Ed.). (1983). *Your reading: A booklist for junior high and middle school students.* Urbana, IL: National Council of Teachers of English.

Freeman, J. (1984). *Books kids will sit still for.* Hagerstown, MD: Alleyside Press.

Kimmel, M.M. & Segel, E. (1983). *For reading out loud! A guide for sharing books with children.* New York: Delacorte.

McMullan, K.H. (1984). *How to choose good books for kids.* Reading, MA: Addison-Wesley.

Monson, D.L. (Ed.). (1985). *Adventuring with books: A booklist for pre-K–grade 6* (new ed.). Urbana, IL: National Council of Teachers of English.

Roser, N. & Frith, M. (Eds.). (1983). *Children's choices: Teaching with books children like.* Newark, DE: International Reading Association.

Stensland. A.L. (1979). *Literature by and about the American Indian: An annotated bibliography* (2nd ed.). Urbana, IL: National Council of Teachers of English.

Trelease. J. (1982). *The read-aloud handbook.* New York: Penguin.

Tway, E. (Ed.). (1981). *Reading ladders for human relations* (6th ed.). Urbana, IL: National Council of Teachers of English.

Journals and Newsletters

CBC Features, The Children's Book Council, 67 Irving Place, New York, NY 10003.

The Horn Book, Park Square Building, 31 St. James Avenue, Boston, MA 02116.

Language Arts, National Council of Teachers of English, 1111 Kenyon Road, Urbana, IL 61801.

The Reading Teacher, International Reading Association, P.O. Box 8139, Newark, DE 19711.

Figure 3–8   Resources about Choosing Books for Students

investigating the value of repeated readings have focused mainly on preschool and primary grade students. However, rereading favorite stories may have similar benefits for older students as well.

Other Oral Presentation Modes.   Students can also benefit from other forms of oral presentations, such as tape recordings of stories and filmstrip and film versions of stories. Audio-visual story presentations are available from Weston Woods (Weston, CT 06883), Random House/Miller Brody (400 Hahn Road, Westminster, MD 21157), Pied Piper (P.O. Box 320, Verdugo City, CA 91046), and other distributors. For more information about audio-visual materials, check *Films and film-strips for language arts: An annotated bibliography* (May, 1981).

Directed Listening Thinking Activity

The Directed Reading Thinking Activity (DRTA) is a procedure developed by Russell Stauffer (1975) in which students make predictions about a story and then read to confirm or reject them. The DRTA can be easily adapted for reading aloud to students in a Directed Listening Thinking Activity (DLTA). Instead of reading the stories themselves, students listen while the teacher reads the story. Students continue to make predictions about a story and listen to confirm or reject them in DLTA. The following steps illustrate this strategy.

Step 1: Predicting.   After showing students the cover of the book and reading the title, the teacher begins by asking students to make a prediction about the story using questions such as:

- What do you think a story with a title like this might be about?
- What do you think might happen in this story?
- Does this picture give you any ideas about what might happen in this story?

If necessary, the teacher may read the first paragraph or two of the story to provide more information for students to use in making their predictions. After a brief discussion in which all students commit themselves to one or another of the alternatives presented, the teacher asks these questions:

- Which of these ideas do you think would be the likely one?
- Why do you think that idea is a good one?

Step 2: Reasoning and Predicting from Succeeding Pages.   After students set their purposes for listening, the teacher reads part of the story, and then students begin to confirm or reject their predictions by answering questions such as the following:

- What do you think now?
- What do you think will happen next?
- What would happen if . . . ?
- Why do you think that idea is a good one?

The teacher continues reading the story aloud, stopping at key points in the story to repeat this step.

Step 3: Proving.   Students give reasons to support their predictions by answering questions such as the following:

- What in the story makes you think that?
- Where in the story do you get information to support that idea?

The teacher can ask these "proving" questions during the story or after it has been read.

The DLTA strategy illustrates the processes of adaption and organization that were discussed in the first chapter. Students make predictions based on their knowledge of stories. As they listen, they confirm or reject their hypotheses. When their predictions are confirmed, the information is assimilated into their existing schemata, but when their predictions are rejected, disequilibrium occurs and students modify their schemata through accommodation.

Responding to Literature

Listening to literature for enjoyment is reason enough to read aloud to children. However, several kinds of activities can be used to extend children's interest in a story even further. These activities can be spontaneous expressions of interest and delight in a book as well as teacher-planned activities. Janet Hickman (1980) cites the example of a kindergartner named Ben who spontaneously responded to a favorite story when his teacher shared *Pezzetino* (Lionni, 1975):

> Ben says, "I like *Pezzetino* because of all the colors 'n stuff, and the way it repeats. He keeps saying it. And there's marbelizing—see here? And this very last

Two students present their "movie" retelling of a favorite story for an audience of their classmates.

page . . . " Then Ben turns to the end of the book and holds up a picture for the group to see. "He cut paper. How many think he's a good cutter?" Ben conducts a vote, counting the raised hands that show a majority of the group believes Leo Lionni to be "a good cutter." (p. 525)

Ben's knowledge of the text and illustrations in the story as well as his enjoyment are obvious. Through his comments and the class vote, Ben is involving his class-mates in the story, and it seems likely that *Pezzetino* will be passed from student to student in the class. Spontaneous responses to literature similar to Ben's occur at all grade levels in supportive classrooms where students are invited to share their ideas and feelings.

Teacher-planned response activities include having students make puppets to use in retelling a favorite story, writing letters to authors, creating a mobile for a favorite story, and reading other books by the same author or on a similar theme, to name only a few possibilities. A more complete list of response to literature activi-ties is presented in Figure 3–9. These activities can be used equally well with books students have listened to read aloud as with books they have read them-selves. Traditional activities such as having students answer factual recall level questions or completing a fill-in-the-blanks book report form should not automati-cally be a follow-up to reading aloud. Instead, students should engage in activities that grow out of their enjoyment of a particular book.

Discussions are another type of response to literature. They can be valuable when the talk causes students to think analytically about the stories to which they have listened. The purpose of discussions should always be on higher level think-ing skills, not factual recall questions.

Reflective Discussions*

Reflective discussions of stories take place after students have listened to a story read aloud. Teachers then guide the discussion with questions that cause students to think about what the story has meant to them. As students respond, they reflect on the questions as well as on the responses given by classmates. Students' re-sponses probe the meaning of the topic under discussion. Students also justify their responses, causing them to think more critically and probe more deeply into the meaning of the story.

Categories of Questions.   The kinds of questions asked in a reflective discus-sion can be grouped into three categories. These categories are factual questions, inferential questions, and experiential questions.

1. *Factual questions* refer to the exact information the author has supplied in the story. They are used to clarify any confusion about what the author has said about the topic under discussion.

---

*Reflective discussions are based on the method of reading and discussion developed by the Great Books Foundation for its Adult and Junior Great Books programs and is adapted from *A manual for co-leaders,* The Great Books Foundation (1965). Currently published under title, *Handbook on interpre-tive reading and instruction* (1984).

Art Activities

Create a series of illustrations for a favorite book or story episode and compile the illustrations to form a wordless picture book.

Practice the illustration techniques (e.g., collage, styrofoam prints, watercolors, line drawing) used in the favorite book. Also, examine other books that use the same illustration technique.

Create a collage to represent the theme of a favorite book.

Design a book jacket for a favorite book, laminate it, and place it on the book.

Construct a shoebox or other miniature scene of an episode from a favorite story.

Create a filmstrip to illustrate a favorite story.

Create a game based on a favorite story or series of stories. Possible game formats include card games, board games, word finds, crossword puzzles, and computer games.

Draw a map or make a relief map of a book's setting. Some stories, such as Kathryn Lasky's *Beyond the Divide* (1983), include a map, usually on the book's end papers.

Create a mobile illustrating a favorite book.

Make a movie of a favorite book by drawing a series of pictures on a long strip of paper. Attach ends to rollers and place in a cardboard box.

Writing Activities

Assume the role of a book character and keep a simulated journal from that character's viewpoint.

Write a book review of a favorite book for the class newspaper.

Write a letter to a pen pal about a favorite book.

Create a poster to advertise a favorite book.

Write another episode for the characters in a favorite story.

Create a newspaper with news stories and advertisements based on characters and episodes from a favorite book.

Write a letter to the author of a favorite book. Check the guidelines for writing to children's authors presented in Chapter 6.

Write a simulated letter from one book character to another.

Select five "quotable quotes" from a favorite book and list them on a poster or in copy books.

Reading Activities

Research a favorite author and compile the information in a brief report to insert in the author's book.

Figure 3–9   Types of Response Activities

Read other stories by the same author.

Read other stories with a similar theme.

Tape-record a favorite book or excerpts from a longer story to place in a listening center.

Read a favorite story to children in the primary grades.

Compare different versions of the same story.

Talk and Drama Activities

Give a readers theater presentation of a favorite story. See Chapter 5 for more information about readers theater.

Write a script and produce a play or puppet show about a favorite book.

Dress as a favorite book character and answer questions from classmates about the character and the story.

Retell a favorite story or episode from a longer story using puppets or other props. See Chapter 5 for information about retelling stories.

Give a chalk talk by sketching pictures on the chalkboard or on a large sheet of paper as the story is retold.

Discuss a favorite book informally with several classmates.

Tape-record a review of a favorite book using background music and sound effects.

Videotape a commercial for a favorite book.

Interview classmates about a favorite book.

Other Activities

Plan a special day to honor a favorite author with posters, publicity information from the author's publishers, letters to and from the author, a display of the author's books, and products from other activities listed above.

If possible, arrange to place a conference telephone call to the author or have the author visit the school on that day.

Conduct a class or school vote to determine students' 10 most popular books. Also, many states sponsor annual book awards for outstanding children's books such as Ohio's Buckeye Book Award and Oklahoma's Sequoia Book Award. Encourage students to read the books nominated for their state's award and to vote for their favorite books.

Cook a food described in a favorite book, such as gingerbread cookies after reading Galdone's *The gingerbread boy* (1975) or spaghetti after reading de Paola's *Strega nona* (1975).

Figure 3–9 *Continued*

2. *Inferential questions* refer to the ideas or assumptions that can be derived from the information supplied by the author. Inferential questions, however, are not answered with the information direct from the story; the answers must be inferred. Students should be able to justify their answers to these questions. Response justification gives teachers insight into their students' thinking. It also helps students probe their deepest insights about the meaning of the story being discussed.

3. *Experiential questions* refer to common experiences students have had, and are designed to elicit students' opinions rather than the author's inferred meaning. By relating the content of the story to the students' experiences, experiential questions help students to accommodate new information and extend their knowledge.

Interactive Categories.   Reflective discussions also include an interactive dimension. The *main question* is the question a teacher uses to initiate the discussion and to introduce the topic to students. All other questions are used to probe the main question. *Probing questions* are used to examine the topic in as much depth as possible.

Students will explore a topic in depth only to the degree that the questions they are asked require them to think deeply. The main question and the probing questions should be inferential questions, requiring students to probe for meaning. Factual questions are used only to clarify facts if students do not remember something or get the facts twisted. Teachers ask experiential questions after they probe the meaning of the story and relate the topic to students' own experiences.

Preparing the Questions.   The questions teachers develop should stimulate students to reflect on the topic being discussed. Instead of asking questions that have only one "correct" answer, prepare questions that encourage students to consider alternatives and resolve issues raised by the main question. These are called thought-provoking, or "true," questions, in contrast to "false" questions, ones with only one correct answer (Hoskisson, 1973). The difference between the two types of questions is purpose. If the purpose is to have students answer questions for which the teachers have the correct answer, then the teachers are simply fishing for facts or opinions that agree with their own; they are asking "false" questions. "True" questions are those for which a teacher has preliminary answers but is willing to accept students' points of view.

The steps involved in writing main and probing questions are as follows:

1. Read the selection twice.

2. The first time you read the selection, read it for information and for understanding.

3. The second time, write as many questions about the selection as you can.

4. Examine the questions you have written for ones with the most interesting ideas.

5. Select two or three questions that have the most potential for being rewritten as main questions.

6. Check that the remaining questions relate to one or both of the potential main questions.

7. Rewrite the main question so that it is an inferential question, making sure that it is concise and easy to understand.

8. Rewrite your potential probing questions, relating them directly to the main question and ensuring that they probe the topic in depth.

9. Develop as many additional probing questions as you can. A good discussion requires at least 10 probing questions. This number of probing questions related to the main question indicates a strong main question and the potential for an interesting discussion.

Content and Structure Questions.   Ideas for main questions may be drawn from many sources in a story. The reflective discussion strategy lends itself very effectively to discussing the themes of stories. Possible themes include good versus evil, love, friendship, loyalty, honesty, doing good to others, being honest with yourself, and respecting the rights of others. For example, in the fable of "The Ant and the Grasshopper," the main question might be developed using the theme of responsibility: "Is the ant responsible for the life of the grasshopper, or is the grasshopper responsible for its own life?"

The main question is an inferential question beginning with a form of the verb *be*. Using the auxiliary verbs *do* or *be* forces teachers to develop their ideas more fully and to write stronger questions. Questions beginning with a form of *do* or *be* generally result in *yes* or *no* responses and require justification. To follow up a *yes* or *no* response, simply ask *why* or *why not*. Eventually students will answer *yes* or *no* and follow with the justification, "because . . . ."

Avoid using *what* or *how* at the beginning of main and probing questions. Both *what* and *how* tend to favor responses that require facts or lists of reasons. Similarly, avoid the phrase "do you think" in developing questions because it changes a would-be inferential question into an experiential question asking students for their opinions. Also, "why" questions should be used sparingly. It is very easy to put an implied assumption into a *why* question and lead students away from the topic under discussion. A list of guidelines for preparing questions is presented in Figure 3–10.

The following examples should help to clarify the use of assumptions in questions. In the fable "The Ant and the Grasshopper," a possible *what* question could be: "What did the grasshopper want the ant to do?" The response might be, "to share its food." Instead of asking the *what* question, put the probable response into a question such as: "Did the grasshopper want the ant to share its food?" and then ask for justification using *why* or *why not*. An implied assumption in this fable might be: "The grasshopper believes the ant should share its food." Instead of asking the question as a *why* question: ("Why does the grasshopper believe the ant should share its food?"), pose the question so that the assumption can be accepted or rejected rather than risk the chance of the whole question being rejected if the students do not believe the assumption. State the assumption as part of a *yes* or *no* question: "Did the grasshopper believe the ant should share its food?" Follow the response with a justification request using *why* or *why not*. Do not assume that stu-

1. Write one main question and at least 10 probing questions.
2. Tie the main question to the topic being discussed.
3. Relate all probing questions to the main question.
4. Write concise and easy-to-understand questions.
5. Write "true" questions that encourage students to think deeply and consider alternatives.
6. Use inferential questions that begin with some form of the auxiliary verbs *do* or *be*.
7. Avoid using "what" or "how" questions, which lead to factual responses.
8. Avoid using the phrase "do you think," which leads to opinion responses.

Figure 3–10 Guidelines for Preparing Questions

Book: *Alexander and the wind-up mouse* by Leo Lionni (1969)

Main Question

According to the story, is it more important to love someone or to be loved by someone?

Probing Questions

Why does Alexander want to be like Willy?
Is Alexander loved by anyone?
Does Alexander love anyone?
Is Willy loved by anyone?
Does Willy love anyone?
Why was Willy put in the box of old toys if Annie loved him?
Why does Alexander feel sorry for Willy?
Does Alexander have the lizard change Willy into a live mouse so that he will have someone to love him?
Is Alexander or Willy loved the most?
Is it more important for Willy to love or to be loved?
Is it more important for Alexander to love or to be loved?

Book: *The nightingale* by Hans Christian Andersen (1972)

Main Question

Does Hans Christian Andersen believe it is better to be a real nightingale or a jeweled toy bird?

Figure 3–11 Reflective Discussion Questions

dents will accept any assumptions made by the teacher, and be aware of the feelings and opinions of students. While their backgrounds and experiences may differ from those of the teacher, their opinions must be respected.

Inferential questions should be designed to free the students from the tyranny of correct responses. Leaving questions open to *yes* or *no* responses allows students to respond freely. There is no reward for right answers or punishment for wrong answers. There is, however, challenge to students' thinking because they must justify their responses and clarify or defend them. If students are to think deeply, the discussions they participate in must be open and accepting of their best thinking.

Reflective discussion questions have been developed for *Alexander and the wind-up mouse* (Lionni, 1969) and *The nightingale* (Andersen, 1972) using the steps for preparing questions presented earlier. These sets of questions are shown in Figure 3–11.

Guiding a Discussion. Initiate the reflective discussion by calling a student by name and asking the main question. This alerts the student and helps focus atten-

---

Probing Questions

Was the real nightingale or the toy bird more beautiful? Why?

Did the Chinese agree with the Japanese Emperor's statement that the toy bird was a poor copy of the real nightingale? Why?

Was the real nightingale or the toy bird more content in the Emperor's court? Why?

Did the Emperor ever try to get the real nightingale back after it flew away? Why?

Were the Chinese content with the toy bird's music or did they long for the real nightingale? Why?

Did the toy bird care about what people thought of it or was it content with itself? Why?

If the toy bird had not been given to the Emperor, would the real nightingale have been happy? Why?

Did the toy bird have as good a life as it was possible for it to have? Why?

Did the real nightingale have as good a life as it was possible for it to have? Why?

Could the toy bird have served as a trusted advisor as the real nightingale did? Why?

Would the Emperor have survived without the real nightingale's song? Why?

Would the Emperor have come to appreciate the real nightingale if it hadn't saved his life? Why?

Was the real nightingale as valuable as the toy bird was even though it had no jewels? Why?

Figure 3–11 *Continued*

tion on the question. Ask four or five students the main question before asking probing questions. Try to get at least one opposing opinion from students; however, if they do not express an opposing opinion after they have heard the main question four or five times, begin asking the probing questions. After asking two or three probing questions, ask the main question again to one or two other students.

In conducting a reflective discussion, ask the main question of every student at sometime during the discussion. Ask the main question of only some of the students at first to sample their thinking and to generate ideas to begin the discussion. Try to determine in advance which students will hold opposing or contradictory views and ask those students the main question first. It is also important to re-ask the main question of those students who appear to be changing their minds during the discussion. If students decide to modify their initial responses to the main question, make certain they have the opportunity to do so. A change of opinion indicates a deeper level of thinking if it is justified.

As the probing questions are asked, it may be necessary to ask questions that require students to clarify their responses, relate their responses to other responses, and develop their responses in more depth. Making up new questions while conducting a discussion is difficult; nevertheless, students' responses must be turned into questions, or questions directly related to the responses must be constructed. If enough thinking has gone into the preparation of the questions, you will have anticipated many of the ideas the students will propose as responses to your questions.

When asking probing questions, re-ask the same probing question of more than one student. However, if there are many probing questions, it may not be necessary to ask the same probing question more than once. If a probing question must be re-asked, try asking it of a student who takes a different view of the topic being discussed. The more contradictory the opinions expressed, the deeper the thinking will go.

Students should participate freely in a reflective discussion. They may ask each other questions. They may challenge the responses others make. They may request that a question be repeated, but they may not ask the teacher to answer a question, except relating to procedures. While discussing a topic, students do not need to raise their hands or wait to be called on. They may talk freely whenever they wish as long as someone else is not responding. If students begin to wander away from the topic, ask a probing question or ask the main question again. Asking the main question is the best way to keep the discussion focused on the topic.

Conclude the discussion with the experiential questions. In this way, students summarize what they have learned and tie their understanding to their own experiences.

Summary

In this chapter we described listening as the most basic and the most used of the language modes. Despite its importance, listening instruction has been neglected in elementary classrooms. Too often practice activities have been substituted for instruction.

Listening was defined as a process involving three steps: (a) receiving, (b) attending, and (c) assigning meaning. Listening and hearing are not synonymous terms; rather hearing is part of the listening process. A student's need to attend to the speaker's message varies with the listening purpose. Five purposes for listening were presented: (a) discriminative listening, (b) comprehensive listening, (c) therapeutic listening, (d) critical listening, and (e) appreciative listening.

Comprehensive listening was described as the type of listening required in many instructional activities. Six strategies for comprehensive listening were discussed and an instructional strategy for teaching students to use these strategies was presented. These strategies help students attend to the important information in a message and understand it more easily.

Learning to be critical listeners involves learning to detect propaganda devices and persuasive language. Nine types of propaganda devices, loaded words, and examples of doublespeak were presented to help students learn to detect these devices in commercials and advertisements.

Appreciative listening was described as listening for enjoyment. Reading aloud is one important way to share literature with students and to provide an opportunity for appreciative listening. Several response activities were presented, including art, drama, and discussions. Conducting reflective discussions was presented as a way to respond to literature that involved listening, talking, and higher level thinking skills.

Extensions

1. Keep a record of how much time you spend listening, talking, reading, and writing for a day or two. Compare your time allotments with the chart presented in Figure 3–1. Also, record how much time students spend using each of the four language modes while you are observing in an elementary classroom.

2. Visit a classroom and observe how listening is taught or practiced. Consider how practice activities might be changed into instructional activities.

3. Interview primary, middle, and upper grade students about listening and the strategies they use while listening, using questions such as these:

- What is listening?
- What is the difference between hearing and listening, or are they the same?
- Why do people listen? Why else?
- What do you do while you are listening?
- What do you do to help you remember what you are listening to?
- Do you always listen in the same way, or are there different ways to listen?
- How do you know what is important in the message you are listening to?
- What is the hardest thing about listening?

■ Are you a good listener? Why? Why not?

Compare students' responses across grade levels. Are older students more aware of the listening process than younger students are? Can older students identify a greater variety of listening strategies than younger students can?

4. Plan and teach a lesson on one of the six comprehensive listening strategies presented in this chapter. Or, plan and teach a content-area lesson using the Directed Listening Activity.

5. Read one or more stories aloud to a group of students and involve them in several of the response activities listed in Figure 3–9.

Also, use the Directed Listening Thinking Activity in which students make and confirm predictions for one of the stories read aloud.

6. Become a pen pal with several students and correspond about books their teacher is reading aloud to them. Read "Sixth graders write about reading literature" by Lewis B. Smith (1982) for a description of a pen pal program Dr. Smith was involved with.

7. After reading a story aloud to a small group of students, direct a reflective discussion with those students. Be sure to choose a book that will stimulate discussion.

References

Andersen, H. C. (1972). *The nightingale.* New York: Van Nostrand Reinhold.

Anderson, H. (1949). Teaching the art of listening. *School Review 57,* pp. 63–67.

Beaver, J. M. (1982). *Say it!* over and over. *Language Arts, 59,* 143–148.

Cunningham, J. W., Cunningham, P. M., & Arthur, S. V. (1981). *Middle and secondary school reading.* New York: Longman.

dePaola, T. (1975). *Strega nona.* Englewood Cliffs, NJ: Prentice-Hall.

Devine, T. G. (1978). Listening: What do we know after fifty years of theorizing? *Journal of Reading, 21,* 296–304.

_____. (1981). *Teaching study skills: A guide for teachers.* Boston: Allyn and Bacon.

_____. *Listening skills schoolwide: Activities and programs.* (1982). Urbana, IL: ERIC Clearinghouse on Reading and Communication Skills and the National Council of Teachers of English.

Erickson, A. (1985). Listening leads to reading. *Reading Today 2,* 13.

Foulke, E. (1968). Listening comprehension as a function of word rate. *Journal of Communication, 18,* 198–206.

Fox, S. E. & Allen, V. G. (1983). *The language arts: An integrated approach.* New York: Holt.

Galdone, P. (1975). *The gingerbread boy.* New York: Seabury.

Hickman, J. (1980). Children's response to literature: What happens in the classroom. *Language Arts, 57,* 524–529.

Hoskisson, K. (1973). 'False' questions and 'right' answers. *The Reading Teacher, 27,* 159–162.

Kimmel, M. M. & Segel, E. (1983). *For reading aloud! A guide for sharing books with children.* New York: Delacorte.

Landry, D. (1969). The neglect of listening. *Elementary English, 46,* 599–605.

Lasky, K. (1983). *Beyond the divide.* New York: Macmillan.

Lionni, L. (1969). *Alexander and the wind-up mouse.* New York: Pantheon.

Lionni, L. (1975). *Pezzetino*. New York: Pantheon.

Lundsteen, S. W. (1979). *Listening: Its impact on reading and the other language arts* (rev. ed.). Urbana, IL: National Council of Teachers of English.

Lutz, W. (1984). Notes toward a description of doublespeak. *Quarterly Review of Doublespeak, 10,* 1–2.

———. (n.d.). *Some examples of doublespeak.* Unpublished manuscript, National Council of Teachers of English.

Martinez, M. & Roser, N. (1985). Read it again: The value of repeated readings during storytime. *The Reading Teacher, 38,* 782–786.

May, J. P. (1981). *Films and filmstrips for language arts: An annotated bibliography.* Urbana, IL: National Council of Teachers of English.

Pearson, P. D. & Fielding, L. (1982). Research update: Listening comprehension. *Language Arts, 59,* 617–629.

Rankin, P. R. (1928). The importance of listening ability. *English Journal, 17,* 623–640.

Sims, R. (1977). Reading literature aloud. In B. E. Cullinan & C. W. Carmichael (Eds.) *Literature and young children,* (pp. 108–119). Urbana, IL: National Council of Teachers of English.

Smith, L. B. (1982). Sixth graders write about reading literature. *Language Arts, 59,* 357–363.

Stauffer, R. G. (1975). *Directing the reading thinking process.* New York: Harper and Row.

Tompkins, G. E., Friend, M., & Smith, P. L. (1984). Children's metacognitive knowledge about listening. Presentation at the American Educational Research Association Convention, New Orleans, LA.

———. (in press). Strategies for more effective listening. In C. R. Personke & D. D. Johnson (Eds.); *Language arts and the beginning teacher,* (Chapter 3). Englewood Cliffs, NJ: Prentice-Hall.

Tompkins, G. E., Smith, P. L., & Friend, M. (1984). Three dimensions of listening and listening instruction in the elementary school. Paper presented at the Southwestern Educational Research Association Annual Meeting, Dallas, TX.

Trelease, J. (1982). *The read-aloud handbook.* New York: Penguin.

Werner, E. K. (1975). A study of communication time. Unpublished master's thesis, University of Maryland, College Park.

Wilt, M. E. (1950). A study of teacher awareness of listening as a factor in elementary education. *Journal of Educational Research, 43,* 626–636.

Wolvin, A. D. & Coakley, C. G. (1979). *Listening instruction* (TRIP Booklet). Urbana, IL: ERIC Clearinghouse on Reading and Communication Skills and the Speech Communication Association.

IF YOU WANT TO LEARN MORE

Devine, T. G. (1978). Listening: What do we know after fifty years of research and theorizing? *Journal of Reading, 21,* 296–304.

———. (1981). *Teaching study skills: A guide for teachers.* Boston: Allyn and Bacon.

———. (1982). *Listening skills schoolwide: Activities and programs.* Urbana, IL: ERIC Clearinghouse on Reading and Communication Skills and the National Council of Teachers of English.

Friedman, P. G. (1978). *Listening processes: Attention, understanding, evaluation.* Washington, DC: National Education Association.

Lundsteen S. W. (1979). *Listening: Its impact at all levels on reading and the other language arts* (rev. ed.). Urbana, IL: National Council of Teachers of English.

Pearson, P. D. & Fielding, L. (1982). Research update: Listening comprehension. *Language Arts, 59,* 617–629.

Wolvin, A. D. & Coakley, C. G. (1979). *Listening instruction* (TRIP Booklet). Urbana, IL: ERIC Clearinghouse on Reading and Communication Skills and the National Council of Teachers of English.

———. (1985). *Listening* (2nd ed.). Dubuque, IA: William C. Brown.

CHAPTER FOUR

Sustaining Talk in the Classroom

*O*VERVIEW.   *We consider talk to be a major part of the elementary school experience. Children talk to each other, discuss problems, ask questions, give examples, share opinions, and so on. Talk is used for a wide range of purposes. The teacher's role is to provide opportunities for students to use informal types of talk such as conversations and discussions and to introduce students to more formal types including reports, interviews, speeches, and debates.*

Talk is the primary expressive language mode. Stewig (1983) lists three reasons for the primacy of talk. First, talk is used more frequently than writing by both children and adults. Next, children learn to talk before they learn to read and write. Third, talk is the communication mode that all peoples around the world develop. Stewig reports that while there are 2,796 languages spoken today, only a fraction of them—approximately 153—have developed written forms.

When they come to school, most children are fluent oral language users. They have had four or five years of extensive practice talking and listening. Because students have acquired basic oral language competencies, teachers often assume that they do not need to emphasize talk in the elementary school curriculum. However, research shows that students benefit from participating in both informal and formal talk throughout the schoolday (Heath, 1983). Students converse in peer

Students participate in both informal and formal talk situations during the elementary grades.

groups as they work on projects, tell and discuss stories with classmates, partici-pate in role-play activities that involve talk, give reports related to social studies and science units, and participate in formal panel discussions. Many of these talk activities are integrated with other language modes and content area subjects as well. For instance, to give an oral report related to a science unit, students research the topic by reading informational books as well as by interviewing persons in the community with special expertise on the topic. Students write notes and compile the information on notecards in preparation for giving the report. They may also construct charts, models, and other visuals to use in giving their reports.

Shirley Brice Heath (1983) questioned whether talk in elementary classrooms is "talk about nothing" and concluded that children's talk is an essential part of the language arts curriculum and is necessary for academic success in all content areas. Too often, quiet classrooms are considered the most conducive to learning even though research shows that talk is a necessary ingredient for learning. Marvin Klein (1979) argues that "talk opportunities must be consciously structured into [the language arts] curriculum and done so in the most likely manner to encourage children to use talk in a wide variety of contexts and for a variety of purposes" (p. 656).

Halliday (1973) stresses that elementary students need to learn to control all seven of the language functions presented in Chapter 2 to become competent lan-guage users. In her research, however, Pinnell (1975) found that some of the lan-guage functions did not occur as frequently as might be expected in many class-rooms. In this chapter, five types of talk activities which represent the language functions are discussed. The five types are (a) conversations, (b) discussions, (c) oral reports, (d) interviews, and (e) speechmasters club. These activities have several benefits. First, they expand children's oral language skills. Next, they de-velop students' abilities to use talk for a variety of language functions, and third, they work to dispel the fear most adults have about speaking before a group.

POINTS TO PONDER

In What Types of Conversation Activities Can Elementary Students Participate?

Why Should Teachers Talk Informally with Their Students?

How Can Formal Conversation Activities Be Tied to Science or Social Studies Lessons?

How Can Show-and-Tell Activities Be Made Worthwhile?

CONVERSATION

Conversation is a social activity, involving the exchange of ideas, information, opinions, and feelings about people, places, things, and events. It is the most basic form of talk and should be more than an incidental activity. In school, conversa-tion can be either informal or formal. Informal conversations take place in the classroom, on the playground, during playtime, during snacktime, during lunch—

anywhere, anytime. Formal conversations occur when the teacher plans for students to converse about specified topics. While informal conversations take care of themselves, formal conversations, including simulated conversations, must be planned.

Reading Diane Stanley's cozy little book, *The conversation club* (1983), is a good way to introduce conversation activities. The book emphasizes the need for listeners to listen to each other and to take turns talking. Students may want to organize their own conversation club, too, after listening to the story.

Informal Conversations

Teachers can hold informal conversations with students at odd moments during the day. Some special times may need to be planned for teachers to talk with quiet children or children who need extra attention. Teachers may find it helpful to have a list of topics to which they can refer when they want to plan a special time for conversations. The items in Figure 4–1 offer suggestions for such a list. By holding conversations with their students, teachers can make them feel important, find out about their interests, likes and dislikes, and become their friend. Teachers

---

What do you do in your free time?

What books do you like best?

What television shows do you watch?

Do you have a hobby?

What sports do you play? (or would like to play)

What games are your favorites?

Do you have a pet? Tell me about it.

Do you like movies? What ones do you like the most? Tell me about those.

What kind of work do you think you will do when you finish school?

If you could live anywhere in the world, where would it be?

What magazines do you like to read?

What do you like to do on the weekends?

Do you like to travel? Where have you been?

Have you been to any museums?

What do you like to do with your brothers and sisters?

What things don't you like?

What makes you happy? (or unhappy)

Figure 4–1   Topics for Informal Conversations

must decide on the appropriateness of a particular topic for each student and the best time to use it. When holding informal conversations with students, teachers must show a genuine interest in their students.

Peer Group Conversations

Teachers often group students in pairs and small groups to work on reading and math assignments as well as for projects in other content areas. As they work collaboratively, students naturally converse with their classmates whether they were instructed to talk or not. Wilkinson (1984) has studied children's language in small-group situations and has made several insightful observations about their language use. First, she found that students use language representing several different language functions in their conversations. They ask and answer questions using informative language, make requests to satisfy their own needs using instrumental language, and use regulatory language to control classmates' behavior. Students also use interactional and personal language as they talk informally.

Wilkinson has identified three characteristics of effective speakers in peer group conversations. While her characteristics focus on students' use of one language function, instrumental language, her findings may be generalizable to the wider context of peer group conversations. Wilkinson found that effective speakers' comments were (a) directly and clearly stated to particular students, (b) related to the task at hand, and (c) interpreted as being sincere by classmates.

Wilkinson recommends that teachers "listen in" on students' conversations to learn about students' language competencies and their understanding of the assignment as well as their ability to work with classmates in peer groups. Teachers can identify students who are not effective speakers and plan additional group activities for them to develop their conversational skills.

Pairing students to work on science experiments is an effective way to develop conversational abilities that involve problem solving situations. Students can use a discovery approach to solve a problem that has been set up for them. For example, an easy concept to begin with is magnets and the attraction a magnet has for materials made of iron. The instructional strategy is outlined in the following paragraphs.

Instructional Strategy

Step 1: Initiating.   Divide the class into pairs or small groups of students. Give each pair a shoe box containing one magnet, some materials that are attracted by a magnet, and other materials that are not attracted by the magnet. Instruct students to see what they can find out about the magnet and the materials they have been given in their science kit.

Step 2: Structuring.   Let students manipulate the materials for a few minutes and then give the following instructions:

1. Talk with your partner about the materials in the science kit. Decide what you can do with them.

2. Keep a record of your investigations.

3. Write down what you discover.

Step 3: Conceptualizing.   After students have had sufficient time to record what they found, give the following instructions:

1. Read over what you have written about what you discovered.

2. Think about it.

3. Write a paragraph that explains what you discovered, what you think about your discovery, and if possible, why you think so.

Step 4: Summarizing.   After students have had time to write their paragraphs, call the class together and have each pair of students share what they discovered and what they think about their discoveries.

Step 5: Generalizing.   After the students have discussed what they learned, have them discuss how they can use this approach to solve other problems.

By having students work in pairs and small groups, they will all have more experience in conversing about the problems they are trying to solve. Teachers can begin problem solving by pairs and small groups in science and extend it to other content areas.

Show-and-Tell

A daily sharing time is a familiar ritual in many kindergarten and primary grade classrooms. Children bring favorite objects to school and talk about them. This is a nice bridge between home and school, and the value of show-and-tell is that children have something familiar to talk about.

Teachers must play an active role to make show-and-tell a worthwhile activity. Too often sharing time becomes repetitive, and children lose interest. To make the activity more worthwhile, teachers can discuss the roles and responsibilities of both speakers and listeners with students. A second-grade class developed the list of responsibilities for speakers and listeners presented in Figure 4–2.

Some children will need prompting even if they are advised to plan in advance two or three things to say about the object they have brought to school. It is very tempting for teachers to speed things up by asking questions and, without realizing it, to answer their own questions, especially for a very quiet child. For example, show-and-tell could go like this:

Teacher:	Jerry, what did you bring today?
Jerry:	(Holds up a stuffed bear.)
Teacher:	Is that a teddy bear?
Jerry:	Yeah.
Teacher:	Is it new?

Rules for Show-and-Tell

What a speaker does

Brings something interesting to talk about.
Brings the same thing *only* one time.
Thinks of three things to say about the thing.
Speaks loudly so everyone can hear.
Passes what he/she brought around so everyone can see it.

What listeners do

Be interested.
Pay attention.
Listen.
Ask the "5 Ws plus one": *who, what, where, when, why,* and *how.*
Say something nice.

Figure 4–2   Responsibilities of Speakers and Listeners

Jerry:	(Shakes head yes.)
Teacher:	Can you tell us about your bear?
Jerry:	(Silence.)
Teacher:	Jerry, why don't you walk around and show your bear to everyone.

While Jerry needed prompting, the teacher in this example clearly dominated the conversation, and Jerry only said one word, "yeah." Two strategies may help. First, talk with children like Jerry and help them plan something to say. Second, invite listeners to ask the speakers the "5 Ws plus one" (Calderonello & Edwards, 1986, p. 29). These questions, also referred to as reporters' or journalists' questions, include *what, who, when, where, why,* and *how.* It is crucial that the conversation be among the students!

Show-and-tell can evolve into an informal type of oral reports for middle grade students. When used effectively, older students gain valuable practice talking in an informal and nonthreatening situation. Beginning as a sharing activity, students' talk about a collection of shark's teeth, a program from an Ice Capades Show, a recently found snake's skin, or snapshots of last summer's vacation at Yellowstone National Park can lead to informal dramatics, reading, and writing activities. One student may act out the dances recalled from the Ice Capades Show; another student may point out the location of Yellowstone National Park on a map or check an almanac for more information about the park. A third student may write about the prized collection of shark's teeth and how they were collected. Experience plus oral rehearsal help students gear up for other language activities.

POINTS TO PONDER
How Can Children's Literature Be Used to Stimulate Discussions?
How Can You Integrate Discussions with Content Area Lessons?
What Kinds of Discussions Can Your Students Lead?

DISCUSSIONS

Discussions are an effective means of helping students learn to express themselves in small groups or in whole class settings. They are usually more purposeful than conversations. Teachers can use literature and content area-related discussions, informal debates, and panel discussions to enhance students' thinking.

Discussions Stimulated by Literature

Discussions often follow reading stories aloud to students or students reading stories silently. The reflective discussions described in Chapter 3 point out how discussion can be a valuable response to literature. In addition, a number of books have been created that stimulate discussions and talk activities for children. For instance, John Burningham's *Would you rather. . .* (1979) invites primary grade students to consider silly and absurd possibilities and talk about them while older students are challenged to create stories for Van Allsburg's *The mysteries of Harris Burdick* (1984). A list of these and other books that encourage talk is presented in Figure 4–3.

Wordless Picture Books.   Other books that are especially useful for developing students' oral language competency are wordless picture books. In these books, the story is told entirely through pictures, as the name suggests. Few words other than the title are included in the book. Well-known illustrators including Mitsumasa Anno, Tomie de Paola, Fernando Krahn, John Goodall, and others have created a number of these marvelous stories. For instance, Tomie de Paola's *Pancakes for breakfast* (1978) is a charming story of a little old woman who tries to cook pancakes for breakfast but runs into a series of problems as she tries to assemble the ingredients. In the end, her neighbors invite her to their home for pancakes. The book encourages young children to tell the story and to talk about it as well as introducing them to some of the elements of stories. The rustic New England setting and the repetition of events are essential to the story's success. Young children may begin by pointing out familiar objects in the pictures and follow along as the teacher tells the story. Soon, however, they are telling the story themselves, using "book language" such as dialogue and stylistic devices. Cooking pancakes is a natural follow-up activity. A list of wordless picture books is presented in Figure 4–4.

Teachers typically use these books with young children because even nonreaders can enjoy and understand many of them. Students can tell the story for a

Figure 4–3   Books that Encourage Talk

Ahlberg, J. & Ahlberg, A. (1978). *Each peach pear plum: An "I spy" story.* New York: Scholastic. (P)

Anno, M. (1970). *Topsy turvies: Pictures to stretch the imagination.* New York: Walker. (P–M)

Burningham, J. (1979). *Would you rather. . .* New York: Crowell. (P)

Gardner, B. (1984). *The look again . . . and again, and again, and again book.* New York: Lothrop. (P)

Hoban, T. (1971). *Look again!* New York: Macmillan. (P)

Hoguet, S.R. (1983). *I unpacked my grandmother's trunk: A picture book game.* New York: Dutton. (P–M)

Kroll, S. (1976). *The tyrannosaurus game.* New York: Holiday House. (P–M)

Strauss, J. (1984). *Imagine that!!! Exploring make-believe.* Chicago: Human Sciences Press. (P–M–U)

Van Allsburg, C. (1981). *Jumanji.* Boston: Houghton Mifflin. (P–M)

_____. (1984). *The mysteries of Harris Burdick.* Boston: Houghton Mifflin. (M–U)

Zolotow, C. (1967). *Summer is . . .* New York: Crowell. (P–M)

P = primary grades (K–2)
M = middle grades (3–5)
U = upper grades (6–8)

small group of classmates, role-play the story, and dictate or write their own versions. However, many wordless picture books have sophisticated storylines, often presented on several levels of understanding, which are more appropriate for older students. For example, John Goodall's *Above and below stairs* (1983) compares the lifestyle of English lords and peasants during the Middle Ages. This book is a very useful resource for a unit on medieval life for upper grade students, but hardly appropriate for primary grade students even though there are no words in the book.

While students typically discuss and retell wordless picture books, students often use the books for writing activities as well (Abrahamson, 1981; D'Angelo, 1979; Degler, 1979). Students can write dialogue for the characters using cartoon-like balloons or write their own versions of the story. These books are also especially valuable in teaching point of view. Because there is no text to "bias" the reader, students can tell, dictate, or write the story from different viewpoints more easily. Figure 4–5 presents an 8-year-old's version of Mercer Mayer's *Frog goes to dinner* (1974) in which a frog travels to a fancy restaurant hiding in the pocket of a boy's jacket. The results are hilarious! Notice that this child wrote the story from the frog's point of view.

Alexander, M. (1968). *Out! out! out!* New York: Dial. (P)

_____. (1970). *Bobo's dream.* New York: Dial. (P)

Anno, M. (1983). *Anno's USA.* New York: Philomel. (M–U)

Aruego, J. (1971). *Look what I can do.* New York: Scribner. (P)

Bang, M. (1980). *The grey lady and the strawberry snatcher.* New York: Four Winds. (P–M–U)

Briggs, R. (1980). *The snowman.* New York: Random House. (P)

Carle, E. (1971). *Do you want to be my friend?* New York: Crowell. (P)

Carroll, R. (1965). *What whiskers did.* New York: Walck. (P)

deGroat, D. (1977). *Alligator's toothache.* New York: Crown. (P–M)

de Paola, T. (1979). *Flicks.* New York: Harcourt Brace Jovanovich. (P)

_____. (1981). *The hunter and the animals: A wordless picture book.* New York: Holiday House. (P–M)

_____. (1983). *Sing, Pierrot, sing.* New York: Harcourt Brace Jovanovich. (M–U)

Goodall, John S. (1975). *Creepy castle.* New York: Macmillan. (M)

_____. (1979). *The story of an English village.* New York: Atheneum. (M–U)

_____. (1980). *Paddy's new hat.* New York: Atheneum. (M)

_____. (1983). *Above and below stairs.* New York: Atheneum. (U)

Henstra, F. (1983). *Mighty mizzling mouse.* New York: Lippincott. (P–M)

Hoban, T. (1971). *Look again.* New York: Macmillan. (P)

Krahn, F. (1970). *A flying saucer full of spaghetti.* New York: Dutton. (P–M)

_____. (1977). *The mystery of the giant footprints.* New York: Dutton. (P–M)

_____. (1978). *The great ape.* New York: Penguin. (P–M–U)

Mayer, M. (1967). *A boy, a dog, and a frog.* New York: Dial. (P–M)

_____. (1974). *Frog goes to dinner.* New York: Dial. (P–M–U)

Spier, P. (1982). *Rain.* New York: Doubleday. (P–M)

Turkle, B. (1976). *Deep in the forest.* New York: Dutton. (P–M)

Winters, P. (1976). *The bear and the fly.* New York: Crown. (P–M–U)

_____. (1980). *Sir Andrew.* New York: Crown. (P–M)

Young. E. (1984). *The other bone.* New York: Harper and Row. (P–M)

Figure 4–4   Wordless Picture Books

Even though these books are wordless, they are also a valuable tool in teaching reading (McGee & Tompkins, 1983). Students can dictate a story to accompany a wordless picture book; the teacher records the story, page by page, and clips the text to each page of the book. Then students read and reread the story. This approach works well, even with older students who are experiencing reading difficulties.

Figure 4–5 A Retelling of *Frog goes to dinner* (Mayer, 1974)

I Am the Frog

Once there was this boy. His family was going to dinner. They had a dog named Jerry and a turtle and his name was Jeff. And they had a frog which was me! Then the boy takes me to dinner. I jumped out of the boy's pocket. I flew out to the man that was playing the saxophone. And boy WAS he mad! And boy, did I get in trouble! The other musicians fell into the drum. Then I jumped into some salad. And the girl who was served the salad screamed! She screamed so loud that I almost popped my ears! And I jumped right in a man's cup. When the man was about to get a drink, I kissed him. Then the man who served the dinner got mad. And we had to leave.

Whitney, age 7

Content Area Discussions

The reflective discussions presented in Chapter 3 can easily be adapted for discussions related to social studies, current events, and science. Issues such as slavery, acid rain, social security, and nuclear weapons can be used instead of children's literature. The main difference is in the source of information. Instead of using a single story as the basis for the discussion, the teacher uses textbooks, informational books, newspapers, and television news reports as sources of information. Teachers can follow the same procedures used for reflective discussions in writing sets of questions and in guiding the discussions.

Informal Debates

Informal debates are very useful when the whole class is excited about an issue and most or all of the students have taken supporting or opposing positions. The class decides what the issue is, clarifies it, and identifies positions that support the issue or oppose it. Class members who wish to speak in favor of the issue move to a side of the room designated for supporters. Class members who wish to speak against the issue move to a side designated for those in opposition. The class members who have not yet formulated a position sit in the middle of the room. When anyone wishes to participate, he or she goes to the side of the room for the position he or she supports. Students may change their minds as a result of the arguments put forth and move to the opposite side of the room. If they are no longer certain what side they are on, they may take a seat in the middle. The teacher initiates the debate by asking someone from the supporting side of the issue to state that side. After this opening statement, the opposing side makes a statement. From then on, each side takes a turn making statements. It is permissible to ask the person who has just made a statement a question before a side makes a return statement. The sixth graders we observed who were using this informal debate procedure in their social studies class enjoyed the experience and increased their abilities to express themselves effectively.

More Formal Debates

A more formal type of debate is appropriate for students in the upper elementary grades. Debates take the form of arguments between opposing sides of a proposition. A *proposition* is a debate subject that can be discussed from opposing points of view. An example of a proposition would be the following statement:

> Resolved, that students should have a role in setting up standards of behavior in classes and in disciplining those students who disrupt classes.

Once the proposition is determined, teams of two to four students each are designated to support the proposition (the affirmative team) or to oppose it (the negative team).

Depending on the number of members on each team, this order is followed:

1. The first and third statements support the proposition.
2. The second and fourth statements attack the proposition.
3. The first and third rebuttal statements are made by the affirmative team.
4. The second and fourth rebuttal statements are made by the negative team.

Each member makes both a statement about the proposition and a rebuttal statement to the opposite team. Normally there are as many rebuttal statements as there are statements about the proposition. Teachers may vary these procedures to fit their class and their purposes. Donoghue (1985) also suggests that students choose judges to determine the winning team.

If judges evaluate the debates, let students decide on the criteria for making the judgments. Have them brainstorm questions that form the basis for their criteria. Questions similar to the following might be used to initiate the brainstorming sessions:

- Did the speakers communicate their ideas to listeners?
- Was a mastery of information evident in the presentations and rebuttals?
- Was there evidence that the speakers knew the topic well?
- Was the team courteous?
- Did the team work well together?
- Did the second speaker on each team pick up and extend the statement of the first team member?

Students may want to interview the high school debating team for ideas on judging and presenting their topics. They might also enjoy attending a high school debate.

Panel Discussions

Panel discussions are also used to develop students' ability to present ideas in a group and for an audience. Panel members are experts on the topic to be discussed. Students can become experts on the topic by studying for the panel discussion. The panel members enter into a free-flowing discussion directed by a moderator who begins the discussion by making a statement about the topic to be discussed and then calls on various members of the panel to elicit preliminary opinions about the topic. The moderator ensures that all panel members get the opportunity to discuss their ideas concerning the topic. The moderator also ensures the quality of the discussion by asking panel members to respond to questions that will bring out points that might otherwise be skimmed over. A panel usually consists of four to eight members, but the actual number will depend on the topic, how knowledgeable the panel members are, and the ability of the panel members to express themselves. A panel discussion is also a good vehicle for students to present opposing or supporting views on any topic of interest to the class.

POINTS TO PONDER
What Are the Steps in Preparing and Presenting Oral Research Reports?
How Can You Integrate Oral Reports with Social Studies and Science Units?

ORAL REPORTS

Learning how to prepare and present an oral report is an important language skill for middle and upper grade students. However, too often students are simply assigned to give an oral report without any classroom preparation. They often fail miserably, copying the report verbatim from an encyclopedia and then reading it aloud. The result is that students learn to fear speaking in front of a group instead of building confidence in their oral language abilities.

In this section, the steps in teaching students how to prepare and present two types of formal, oral reports are presented. The first type includes research reports on social studies or science topics such as Indians, the solar system, or Canada. The second type includes book reviews, television shows, and movies. These oral reports have genuine language functions—to inform or to inform and persuade.

Research Reports

Students can prepare and give oral reports about topics they are studying in social studies, science, and other content areas. Giving oral reports helps students to learn about topics in specific content areas as well as to develop their oral language abilities. Students need much more than just an assignment to prepare a report for presentation on a particular date; they need to *learn* how to prepare and present research reports. The four steps involved in preparing reports are (a) choosing a topic, (b) gathering information, (c) organizing information, and (d) making the presentation.

Choosing a Topic.   The class begins by choosing a topic for the reports. For example, if a second-grade class was studying the human body, then each student might select a different part of the body for a report.

Once students have chosen their topics, they need to *inventory,* or think over, what they know about the topic and decide what they need to learn about it. Students can learn to focus on the key points for their reports in several ways. One strategy is a data chart (McKenzie, 1979). In this strategy, the teacher provides a chart listing three or more key points to guide students as they gather information for their reports. An example of a data chart for a report on a part of the human body is shown in Figure 4–6. Another strategy is brainstorming ideas for possible key points by asking questions about the topic prefaced with the "5 Ws plus one": *who, what, when, where, why,* and *how.* The number and complexity of the key

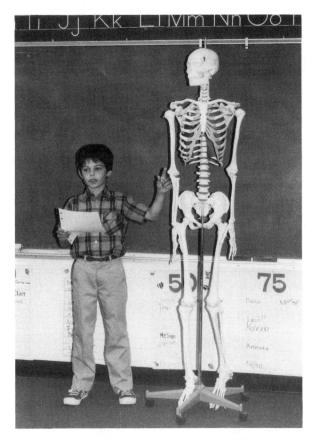

A student presents an oral report on the lungs for his classmates using a skeleton as a prop.

HUMAN BODY REPORT DATA CHART				
Body part _____		Reporter _____		
Source of information	What does it look like?	Where is it located?	What job does it do?	Other important information

Figure 4–6   A Data Chart

points depend on students' age or level of experience. If students do not use data charts, they can write each key point on a notecard and use the cards in gathering information.

Gathering Information.   Students gather information using a variety of reference materials including, but not limited to, informational books, magazines, newspapers, encyclopedias, almanacs, and atlases. While encyclopedias are a valuable resource, they are only one possible source, and other reference materials must be made available to students. In addition to print sources, students can view filmstrips, films, and videotapes and can interview people in the community who have special expertise on the topic.

For students who have had limited experience locating information in a library, a class trip to the school and public library to collect reference materials is useful. Numbering each reference checked out of the library (place a notecard with a number or other code printed on it in the card pocket) is a convenient way to keep track of materials and to simplify recording bibliographic information. It is extremely important that students learn to give appropriate credit for information they have used in preparing their reports.

Elementary students are not too young to understand what plagiarism is and why it is wrong. Even primary grade students understand that they should not "borrow" items belonging to classmates and pretend they are theirs. Similarly, students should not "borrow" or "steal" someone's words, especially without asking permission or giving credit in the composition. Writing key words and phrases on data charts and closing the book before taking notes are two strategies that students can use to take notes without copying entire sentences and paragraphs from reference books.

As students read and gather information, they fill in the blocks on their data charts or record important information on the notecards they prepared in the previous step. Students should be instructed to jot down main ideas and interesting details without copying directly from the reference. It is often helpful to demonstrate how to take notes by *paraphrasing* information, or writing only words or short phrases instead of direct quotations. Students should keep track of the sources they consult by recording the numbers of the references on their data charts or on the notecards. In this way, they are giving credit to their references, can go back to check any inconsistencies, and can use the information to prepare a bibliography.

Organizing the Information.   The preliminary organization—deciding on the key points—completed in the first step provided the direction for gathering the information. Now students review the information they have gathered and decide how to best present it so that the report will be both interesting and well organized. Students who used notecards can review their cards, sort them in order for the presentation, and eliminate any unnecessary cards. Students who used data charts can transfer the information they want to use for their reports onto notecards. Remind students that only key words should be written on the cards.

Students may also develop visuals such as charts, diagrams, maps, pictures, models, and timelines to use in presenting their reports. For example, the second graders giving reports on the parts of the body made drawings and clay models of the body parts, and they also used a large skeleton hanging in the classroom to show the location of the organ in the body. Visuals are useful as they provide a "crutch" for the speaker and add an element of interest for the listeners.

Making the Presentation.   The final step is to rehearse and then give the presentation. Students can rehearse the presentation several times by reviewing key points and reading over the notecards they have prepared. Students might want to choose a particularly interesting fact to use at the beginning of their presentations.

Before the presentations begin, discuss the important things that speakers should remember. For instance, speakers should talk loudly enough for all to hear, keep to the key points, refer to their notecards for important facts, and use the visuals they have prepared.

Through these four steps, elementary students can learn to prepare and present well-organized and interesting reports. The steps are summarized in Figure 4–7.

Written Reports

The same steps used in preparing oral research reports are used for preparing written research reports. Only the final step is different. Instead of rehearsing and presenting

---

Choose a topic

Choose a specific topic.
Decide on the key points to be covered in the report.

Gather information

Consult a variety of reference materials, including nonprint sources.
Use a data chart or notecards to record the information.

Organize the information

Sort notecards in the order of presentation.
Construct visuals.

Make the presentation

Rehearse the presentation several times.
Give the presentation, keeping in mind to focus on the key points and
    use visuals.

Figure 4–7   Steps in Preparing a Research Report

an oral report, the report is written and revised. Preparing or creating a report is a composition activity, and compositions can be presented in either the oral or the written mode. For more information on written research reports, see Chapter 8.

Reviews

Students can give oral reports to review books they have read or television shows and films they have viewed. However, it is important to remember that giving oral reports is only one way to respond to literature. Other ideas for sharing and responding to literature include informal dramatics, storytelling, art, and writing activities, all of which are described in other chapters.

The steps in preparing and presenting reviews are similar to those for informational reports:

1. Read or view the selection.

2. Select information for the report, including (a) a brief summary of the selection including bibliographic information; (b) comparisons with other selections (e.g., with similar themes, written by the same author, starring the same actor); (c) strengths and weaknesses; and (d) opinions and conclusions.

3. Record and organize the information on notecards.

4. Give the presentation after a brief rehearsal.

POINTS TO PONDER

How Can Questioning Skills Be Taught Through Interviewing?
What Are the Three Steps in the Interview Process?
How Can Interviewing Be Integrated with Other Content Areas?

INTERVIEWING

Almost all children have watched interviews on television news programs and are familiar with the interviewing techniques that reporters use. Interviewing is an exciting, real-life communication activity. Through interviewing, students refine their questioning skills and practice all four language modes—listening, talking, reading, and writing.

Interviewing is an important language tool that can be integrated effectively with almost any area of the curriculum. Primary grade students, for instance, can interview community helpers as part of a social studies unit on the community, and older students can interview long-time area residents about local history. Students can also interview people who live far away, such as a favorite author, a legislator, or an Olympic athlete, using a long-distance telephone conference call.

One way to introduce interviewing is by watching interviews conducted on a television news program and discussing the purpose of the interview, what the reporter does before and after an interview, and the types of questions that are asked. While interviewers use a variety of questions—some to elicit facts and others to probe for feelings and opinions—all questions are open-ended. Rarely, if ever, do they ask questions that require only a *yes* or *no* answer.

The Interview Process

Interviewing involves far more than the actual interview. There are three steps in the interview process: (a) planning the interview, (b) conducting the interview, and (c) sharing the results. The first step, planning, involves arranging for the interview and developing a list of questions to be asked during the interview. The second step is the interview itself. Students conduct the interview by asking questions they have prepared in advance and taking notes or tape recording the answers. The third step, sharing the results, involves preparing a report based on the information learned in the interview. The report can take many different forms, ranging from oral reports to class newspapers to published booklets. The activities involved in each of the three steps are outlined in Figure 4–8.

Interviewing Activities

Students need to practice developing and asking questions before they interview people outside the classroom. One way to get this practice is for students to interview their classmates. The proverbial "How I Spent My Summer Vacation" report that teachers have their students give during the first few days of school can be

Planning the Interview

Make arrangements for the interview.

Brainstorm a list of questions to ask the person being interviewed.

Write the questions on notecards, using one card for each question. Be sure that the questions are open-ended, not *yes* or *no* questions.

Organize the questions so that related questions will be asked together.

Read over the questions, making sure they will elicit the information you are seeking.

Conducting the Interview

After a friendly greeting, explain the reason for the interview and begin asking the questions.

Allow the person being interviewed to answer each question fully before asking another question.

Ask follow-up questions on the points that are not clear.

If the answer to one question brings up another question that has not been written down, do not hesitate to ask it.

Be polite and respectful of the answers and opinions of the person being interviewed.

Take notes on the notecards or take notes and tape-record the interview.

Limit the time involved in the interview.

Thank the person for participating in the interview.

Sharing the Results

Read over the notes or listen to the tape recording of the interview.

Organize the information collected during the interview.

Share the results of the interview through an oral or written report, a newspaper article, or another presentation form.

Figure 4–8   Steps in the Interview Process

turned into an interviewing opportunity. Have the class, as a group, brainstorm a list of possible questions. Then pair students to interview each other about their summer activities. They can then report their interviews to the class. Other possible topics for class interviews include favorite films, hobbies, or games.

Class Interviews.   Next, invite someone such as a police officer, the manager of the local McDonald's restaurant, or even a television news reporter to visit the classroom and be interviewed. Have students follow the three-step interview process presented earlier. Instruct them to prepare in advance for the interview by developing a list of questions, deciding who will greet the visitor, and how the questions will be asked. After the interview, work together to prepare a class collaboration or group report about the interview that can be published in the class or community newspaper.

A class interview is a useful practice activity for all students, but it is an especially valuable introduction to interviewing for kindergartners and first graders.

For example, after studying interviewing skills, a class of first graders invited the local high school principal to visit their class and be interviewed. The principal, who had been blinded several years earlier, brought his guide dog with him. The children asked questions about how visually impaired people manage everyday tasks as well as how he does his job as a high school principal. They also asked questions about his guide dog. After the interview, students drew pictures and wrote summaries of the interview. One first grader's report is shown in Figure 4–9.

To follow up on an interview, children could also discuss what they learned through the interview or dictate a report which the teacher prints on the chalkboard. Later, the report could be written on chart paper or photocopies of it could be made for each child and drawings added.

Outside Interviews.   Students can conduct interviews with family members and other members of the community on a variety of topics. One of the most interesting topics is community histories popularized by the Foxfire project (Wigginton, 1972, 1985). Kay Cooper's *Who put the cannon in the courthouse square? A guide to uncovering the past* (1985) and David Weitzman's *My backyard history book* (1975) are excellent books to use with students in planning a community history project. Students work individually or in small groups to interview long-time community residents about the community's history, growth and changes, modes of dress, transportation, communication, types of work, and ways to have fun. After gathering information through interviews, they write reports that are published in a class or community newspaper or in a book. Figure 4–10 is an example of a local history newspaper written and produced by upper grade students in a rural Oklahoma community.

POINTS TO PONDER

How Can Upper Grade Students Give Formal Talks?

SPEECHMASTERS CLUB*

The Speechmasters Club approach is an excellent way to stimulate interest in preparing and giving formal talks. The approach helps students become more aware

---

*The Speechmasters Club uses procedures that are similar to the Toastmasters International Clubs. Teachers who are interested in their organization may write to Toastmasters International, P.O. Box 10400, Santa Ana, CA 10400.

Figure 4–9   A First Grader's Interview Summary

Mr. Kirtley came down. We asked him questions. He answered them. He is blind. His dog's name is Milo.

Tomara, age 7

of their audience and understand the importance of being well prepared and using audience feedback. It also provides the opportunity to improve the quality of the feedback that the audience provides the speakers.

In many upper grade classes, the Speechmasters Club meets weekly for approximately 45 minutes. Four speakers are assigned to speak during each session. This schedule gives students adequate time to prepare their speeches in advance. The speakers are selected on a rotating basis so that the same speakers do not come

Figure 4–10 A Local History Newspaper

GHOST TOWN GAZETTE

Written by Sumner School
Upper-Grade Students
1982

Ghost town in Noble County

by HERB MATHESON

What is a ghost town? According to John Morris's book, Ghost Towns of Oklahoma, there is no definite answer to this question.

Many people make the assumption that a ghost town must be where nobody lives. Lots of writers, however, don't consider this point at all. A large number of ghost towns that have been written about still have several hundred inhabitants.

The place called a ghost town could have been a camp, or village, or in a few instances, an old, run down town with a few remains of old buildings or stores.

In John Morris's book he tells what a ghost town is. It is (1) a place that has been destroyed or covered by water, (2) a place where buildings are not used anymore, or (3) a place where the population has gone down at least eighty percent from the highest average.

Sumner is considered a ghost town by Morris. Also, Sumner has been featured as a ghost town in an exhibit at the Oklahoma Territorial Museum.

There are few people living in Sumner now, and the post office and businesses are gone. But Sumner still has an active church and school.

We wonder if we are the only ghost town in Oklahoma that still has a school.

Do these people look like ghosts? Sumner School, 1982.

Sumner History

By JANELLE HYATT, REJINA JAMES, VALERIE QUICK

Mr. and Mrs. Lloyd Lambert said that there are fifteen Sumners in the United States.

One source says that Sumner, Oklahoma was named after a Kansas senator. But another source says that Sumner was named after a man in Perry. Still another source says that it was named by people in Washington, D.C.

Sumner originally was a mile and a half south from the Sumner School. It was a post office site.

According to the Lamberts, the first post office was started by a man named Youree. Youree had let some people camp on his land by Mule Creek.

When he told them to get off, they told him to get off because they needed the land and he was old and didn't need it. When he disagreed, they shot him. He died in his post office.

His body was taken to Perry in a spring wagon. There were no charges pressed against the people who shot him, because there was a lot of shooting in those days.

There were a lot of postmasters, but Neva Rupp was the last. J.E. Dawson and Edith Dawson ran the post of-

fice for a long time. It was always in a store. The post office closed in July, 1957.

Mr. Chet Speer said that when the Frisco Railroad moved in in 1903-4, Sumner was moved by the railroad tracks. A town called Robertall had been planned, but Sumner decided to move there instead.

Some things that were in Sumner at its height are two blacksmiths, one thirteen-room hotel, one stockyard, 1 post office, 1 school, 2 churches (a Christian and a Baptist), 2 lumber yards, 2 banks, 2 grocery stores, 1 cotton gin, 2 elevators, 1 feed lot, 1 garage, and people had smokehouses.

The Frisco Railroad was very important to Sumner. There were four passenger trains daily and many freight trains.

Henry Rieman remembers being able to ride to Perry and back for 25¢.

It was a lot easier to go by train than it was by the roads, because the roads were often in bad shape.

One recent state map said that Sumner had a population of 19, but we made a count, and we think that there are 37 people now. That's good, for Sumner.

Kids' views of ghost towns

Ideas about ghost towns and local attitudes of living or attending school in an official ghost town vary greatly among Sumner residents. When asked, "What is a ghost town?", kindergarten students attending Sumner School gave the following replies:

"Where ghosts come out of broken houses, and broken schools, and broken stores. Sumner is a ghost town cause there are old houses. I'm no ghost; I live in a new house." Scott King.

"Where people live. There really aren't any ghosts in Sumner." Joy Rieman.

"Part of Sumner is a ghost town. No ghosts live here, it is just an old town." Holly Longan.

"Sumner is a ghost town and ghosts live here. I'm a ghost 'cause I live in Sumner." Cheryl Taylor.

"Someone might live in a ghost town. No ghosts live in a ghost town, because Grandma said there is no such thing as ghosts." Jamie Rieman.

"A ghost town looks real spooky and sounds real spooky 'cause ghosts live there. Sumner is a ghost town and sometimes I am a ghost and I scare people." Amy Rieman.

"Looks real old and spiders and snakes that bite you are in there, and it's real, real scary. I'm not a ghost and if the ghosts try to come to my house they will die." Jennifer Leigh.

"A ghost town is real old. Ghosts live there, but they are nice ghosts. Sumner isn't a ghost town 'cause no ghosts live here." Frankie Mitchell.

Sumner School — 1920. Because the new Sumner School was not quite finished, pupils went to school at the Christian Church and a downtown business for a few months. Notice the school trucks, called Speedwagons, in the background. These had woven metal panels in place of windows, with canvas curtains to roll down in case of bad weather. We call these school busses today.

Fifth, sixth, seventh, and eighth graders

together more than once or twice during the year. A schedule is posted several months or a semester in advance so that all students know when they will be speaking and have time to prepare their speeches.

In addition to the four speakers, four evaluators are selected for each session. These evaluators will be the speakers for the following week. Having the evaluators follow the speakers helps them to profit by the feedback they give the speakers. A schedule should also be posted for the evaluators.

The teacher is the leader or speechmaster for the first meeting. Subsequent speechmasters are selected by the evaluators each week according to the standards determined by the class. Criteria for evaluating the effectiveness of the speakers are discussed by the class and standards are selected. As students gain more experience speaking, the standards may be added to or changed. One class selected the following standards:

1. Choose an interesting topic.
2. Be well prepared.
3. Speak clearly.
4. Stand straight.
5. Speak for at least 2 minutes but not over 5 minutes.

Standards for Evaluators

The class also selects standards for evaluators. These standards guide the evaluators in pinpointing what makes one speaker's speech and delivery better than another's. The standards used by the evaluators are similar to those used by the speakers to prepare themselves for their presentations.

In addition to the standards themselves, point values are assigned to each standard. The highest points are assigned to the time limits because it is essential that students do not exceed the 5-minute time limit. When the time limit is not adhered to, the Speechmasters Club is prolonged, and students tend to lose interest. Moreover, by adhering to a time limit, students must gather and organize a certain amount of information about their topics. The time limits encourage students to think through their material and either add to it, reorganize, or condense it to stay within the time restrictions.

One class developed the following standards and point values:

1. Did the speaker choose an interesting topic? (10 points)
2. Was the speaker well prepared? (20 points)
3. Did the speaker speak clearly? Could the speech be understood? (10 points)
4. Did the speaker keep within the time limits? (50 points)

Evaluators are also instructed to give positive feedback when presenting their evaluations to the class.

The class also evaluates the evaluators. Evaluating the evaluators is a check to ensure that they are striving to help the speakers improve their presentations. The class sets standards for evaluators and the best evaluator is selected each week. One class used the following standards:

1. Speak clearly.
2. Make favorable comments.
3. Suggest ways of making the speech better.

Conducting the Meeting

The speechmaster, the speakers, the evaluators, and the class as a whole all participate in a Speechmasters Club meeting. The speechmaster finds out a little about the speakers and the topics they selected in order to introduce each speaker and give a lead-in about the topic. The speaker thanks the speechmaster and gives the speech. The speechmaster thanks the speaker and makes a concluding comment. The class can decide in advance whether to have all the speakers speak before getting the feedback from the evaluators or to have the evaluators give the feedback after each speech. After all the speakers have spoken and the evaluators have given their feedback, the class evaluates the evaluators. The speaker who received the most points is selected and announced the following day. This adds a little suspense to the selection.

A timekeeper is needed to time the talks. The timekeeper's job is to keep track of the time and flash warning cards that warn the speaker when a certain amount of time has passed. Try using color-coded cards using the colors on a traffic light:

Timing Cards
Green — 3 minutes have passed
Yellow — 4 minutes have passed
Red — 5 minutes have passed

Selecting the Topics

The topics that students select for their speeches may be handled in various ways. Students may be given free choice of any topic they wish to investigate, a certain theme may be selected for all class members, or the speeches may be correlated with content area subjects. It is preferable to let students choose their own topics. By having free choice of topics, students can talk about their hobbies or any subject they happen to be interested in at the time.

Through free choice of topics, teachers can also gain additional insights into the lives of their students. As students share their hobbies and outside experiences, teachers may discover that students who do poorly in school have hobbies that require patience, skill, and understanding. Teachers can use this information in planning instructional activities that build on these students' interests. Free choice of topics will also ensure that many of the weakest students can give speeches successfully.

Summary

Talk is an important part of the language arts curriculum, and the activities presented in this chapter are essential for improving students' abilities to express themselves effectively. Teachers, unfortunately, tend to assume that students have already developed their oral language abilities and overlook the importance of helping them develop the abilities to express themselves through talk in many situations. Because reading and math instruction takes precedence over most other aspects of the school curriculum, talk is often not interwoven into content areas. Conversation is probably the first of the components to be disregarded. Because we talk all the time, teachers may fail to recognize the value of conversation. The informal and formal uses of conversation discussed in this chapter will help teachers get to know their students better and provide them with the means of solving problems.

Discussions move students from conversations to more formal types of talk and help them to develop their abilities to look at both sides of an argument, to respond to questions, and to clarify their thinking. Discussions take many forms, from informal debates in which the whole class participates to debates and panel discussions in which an audience is involved.

Oral reports and interviews are formal types of talk. They offer valuable ways to integrate oral language with the other language arts as well as with other content areas. The Speechmasters Club was introduced as an organized and formal way of giving students practice in presenting speeches. This approach provides an audience and feedback that students can use to improve their oral language abilities.

Extensions

1. In an elementary classroom observe what types of oral language activities students participate in and what language functions they use.

2. Plan and direct a science-related lesson similar to the magnet lesson described in this chapter. Divide students into pairs or small groups for the lesson and observe the interactions that occur among students. Which students communicated effectively with their classmates? Why were they successful?

3. Observe a show-and-tell activity in a primary grade classroom. What are the characteristics of students who are effective speakers? What questions could the teacher use to generate conversation from less verbal or shy students?

4. Collect and "read" ten or more wordless picture books. Summarize each book on an index card and list possible talk activities related to each book.

5. Share several wordless picture books with a small group of students. "Read" the books and discuss them with the students.

6. Plan and conduct an informal debate or panel discussion with a group of upper grade students. Topics can be drawn from current events, school and community issues, or social studies units.

7. Assist a small group of middle or upper grade students as they prepare and give oral reports on topics related to a science or social studies unit. Follow the four-step procedure described in the chapter.

References

Abrahamson, R.F. (1981). An update on wordless picture books with an annotated bibliography. *The Reading Teacher, 32,* 417–421.

Burningham, J. (1979). *Would you rather. . .* New York: Crowell.

Calderonello, A.H., & Edwards, B.L., Jr. (1986). *Roughdrafts: The process of writing.* Boston: Houghton Mifflin.

Cooper, K. (1985). *Who put the cannon in the courthouse square? A guide to uncovering the past.* New York: Walker.

D'Angelo, K. (1979). Wordless picture books: Also for the writer. *Language Arts, 56,* 813–814, 835.

Degler, L.S. (1979). Putting words into wordless books. *The Reading Teacher, 30,* 399–402.

de Paola, T. (1978). *Pancakes for breakfast.* New York: Harcourt Brace Jovanovich.

Donoghue, M.R. (1985). *The child and the English language arts* (4th ed.). Dubuque, IA: William C. Brown.

Goodall, J.S. (1983). *Above and below stairs.* New York: Atheneum.

Halliday, M.A.K. (1973). *Explorations in the functions of language.* London: Arnold.

Heath, S.B. (1983). Research currents: A lot of talk about nothing. *Language Arts, 60,* 999–1007.

Klein, M.L. (1979). Designing a talk environment for the classroom. *Language Arts, 56,* 647–656.

Mayer, M. (1974). *Frog goes to dinner.* New York: Dial.

McGee, L.M., & Tompkins, G.E. (1983). Wordless picture books are for older readers, too. *Journal of Reading, 27,* 120–123.

McKenzie, G.R. (1979). Data charts: A crutch for helping pupils organize reports. *Language Arts, 56,* 784–788.

Pinnell, G.S. (1975). Language in primary classrooms. *Theory into Practice, 14,* 318–327.

Stanley, D. (1983). *The conversation club.* New York: Macmillan.

Stewig, J.W. (1983). *Exploring language arts in the elementary classroom.* New York: Holt, Rinehart and Winston.

Van Allsburg, C. (1984). *The mysteries of Harris Burdick.* Boston: Houghton Mifflin.

Weitzman, D. (1975). *My backyard history book.* Boston: Little Brown.

Wigginton, E. (1972). *The foxfire book.* Rabun Gap, GA: The Foxfire Fund, 1972. (See also subsequent editions of *Foxfire.*)

_____. (1985). *Sometimes a shining moment: The foxfire experience.* New York: Doubleday.

Wilkinson, L.C. (1984). Research currents: Peer group talk in elementary school. *Language Arts, 61,* 164–169.

IF YOU WANT TO LEARN MORE

Bingham, A., & Dusenbery, B. (1979). Just talking isn't enough. *Language Arts, 56,* 275–277.

Enright, L. (1982). Only talking. In M. Barr, P. D'Arcy, & M.K. Healy (Eds.), *Language/learning episodes in British and American classrooms, grades 4–13* (pp. 15–35). Montclair, NJ: Boynton/Cook.

Haley-James, S.M. & Hobson, C. D. (1980). Interviewing: A means of encouraging the drive to communicate. *Language Arts, 57,* 497–502.

Heath, S.B. (1983). Research currents: A lot of talk about nothing. *Language Arts, 60,* 999–1007.

Klein, M.L. (1977). *Talk in the language arts classroom.* Urbana, IL: ERIC Clearinghouse on Reading and Communication Skills and the National Council of Teachers of English.

McKenzie, G.R. (1979). Data charts: A crutch for helping pupils organize reports. *Language Arts, 56,* 784–788.

Olson, M. & Hatcher, B.A. (1982). Cultural journalism: A bridge to the past. *Language Arts, 59,* 46–50.

Roth, R. (1986). Practical use of language in school. *Language Arts, 63,* 134–142.

Wigginton, E. (1985). *Sometimes a shining moment: The foxfire experience.* New York: Doubleday.

Yonan, B. (1982). Encyclopedia reports don't have to be dull. *The Reading Teacher, 36,* 212–214.

CHAPTER FIVE

Learning Through Drama

OVERVIEW. Drama has great potential both as a means of communicating and as a way of learning. In this chapter, drama activities that include dramatic play, informal drama, interpretive drama, and script writing are discussed. Puppets and other props that can be used to enhance drama activities are also presented.

Imagine the following experiment: A teacher reads a familiar folktale to the class, and then divides the students into three groups. The first group draws pictures about the story, the second group discusses the story, and the third group dramatizes the story. Will one of the three response activities be more valuable than the other two? Lee Galda (1982) conducted this study with primary grade students and, according to students' scores on a comprehension test and their retellings of the story, one activity was significantly more beneficial than the other two. Which activity? Drama!

Not only is drama a powerful form of communication, but it is also a valuable way of knowing. According to Dorothy Heathcote, a highly acclaimed British drama teacher, drama "cracks the code" so the message can be understood (Wagner, 1976). We can suggest three reasons why drama has this power:

1. Drama involves both logical left-brain and creative right-brain thinking.
2. Drama requires active experience, the basic, first way of learning.
3. Drama integrates the four language modes.

In the back-to-basics movement, drama is often neglected, considered a nonessential part of the language arts curriculum. However, many educators argue that drama *is* a "basic" because of its power as a learning tool and as a means of communication. Indeed, drama might be called the fifth language art.

There is a wide variety of dramatic activities, ranging from young children's dramatic play to scripted plays. These activities can be grouped into four categories which can be distinguished from one another in three significant ways: (a) spontaneity, (b) process versus product orientation, and (c) level of formality. The four categories include the following:

1. *Dramatic play.* The natural, make-believe play activities of young children are called dramatic play. This kind of drama is spontaneous, unrehearsed, process-oriented, and very informal.
2. *Informal drama.* This includes activities "in which students invent and enact dramatic situations" (NCTE, 1983, p. 370). Informal drama is the natural outgrowth of dramatic play. Like dramatic play, it is spontaneous, unrehearsed, process-oriented, and informal. Informal drama activities include movement, pantomime, characterization, improvisation, dramatizing stories, and role-playing. An example of informal drama is Lee Galda's experiment described at the beginning of this chapter.
3. *Interpretive drama.* These are activities in which students interpret literature, using voice, facial features, and gestures. Interpretive drama involves some re-

hearsal and is somewhat formal. It is a transition between informal drama and theatrical productions; some examples include storytelling and readers theater. As students participate in these activities, they refine their concept of "story," learn the elements of story structure (e.g., characterization, plot, and setting,) and are introduced to the conventions used in scripts.

4. *Theatrical productions.* These productions are the polished performances of a play on a stage and before an audience. They require extensive rehearsal, are product-oriented, and are quite formal. Because the purpose of theatrical productions is the polished presentation of a play, they are audience-centered rather than child-centered. They also require that students memorize lines rather than encourage them to be spontaneous and improvisational. They are not recommended for use by students in elementary grades and will therefore not be discussed in this chapter.

Again and again, educators caution that drama activities should be informal during the elementary school years (Stewig, 1983; Wagner, 1976; Way, 1966). The one exception is when students write their own play and puppet show scripts and want to perform them.

POINTS TO PONDER

What Is Dramatic Play?

How Can Dramatic Play Be Used to Introduce Young Children to the Functions of Reading and Writing?

How Can Dramatic Play Be Integrated with Social Studies, Science, and Other Content Areas?

DRAMATIC PLAY

Playing in the housekeeping corner and putting on dress-up clothes—a bridal veil or a police officer's coat and hat—are familiar activities in preschool and kindergarten classrooms. Young children use these activities to re-enact familiar, everyday activities and to pretend to be someone or something else. These activities are called *dramatic play,* and they represent children's first attempt at drama (McCaslin, 1984).

A housekeeping corner is only one possible dramatic play center. *Prop kits,* which contain collections of materials for dramatic play, can be set out for children to experiment with. For example, a detective prop kit with a Sherlock Holmes hat, raincoat, flashlight, magnifying glass, notepad, and pencil becomes a popular center after children read Marjorie Weinman Sharmat's *Nate the great* series of easy-to-read mystery stories. Even middle grade students are drawn to prop kit materials after reading *Encyclopedia Brown* detective stories by Donald J. Sobol and writing their own mystery stories. A variety of prop kit ideas are provided in Figure 5–1. Many of the prop kits involve reading and writing materials such as the notepad and pencil in the detective kit, menus in the restaurant kit, and a typewriter

1. *Post Office Kit*

mailboxes (use shoeboxes)	wrapping paper	package seals
envelopes	tape	address labels
stamps (use Christmas seals)	packages	cash register
pens	scale	money
string		

2. *Hairdresser Kit*

hair rollers	posters of hair styles	ribbons, barrets, clips
brush and comb	wig and wig stand	appointment book
mirror	hairdryer (with cord cut off)	open/closed sign
empty shampoo bottle		
towel	curling iron (with cord cut off)	

3. *Office Kit*

typewriter	hole punch	telephone
calculator	file folders	message pad
paper	in/out boxes	rubber stamps
notepads	pens and pencils	stamp pad
scotch tape	envelopes	
stapler	stamps	

4. *Medical Kit (doctor, nurse, paramedic)*

white shirt/jacket	thermometer	prescription bottles and labels
medical bag	tweezers	
stethoscope	bandages	walkie-talkie (for paramedics)
hypodermic syringe (play)	prescription pad	

5. *Grocery Store Kit*

grocery cart	cash register
food packages	money
plastic fruit and artificial foods	grocery bags
	marking pen
price stickers	

Figure 5–1 Materials for Prop Kits

6. *Restaurant Kit*

   tablecloth   napkins   apron for waitress
   dishes   menus   vest for waiter
   glasses   tray   hat and apron for chef
   silverware   order pad and pencil

7. *Travel Agency Kit*

   travel posters   wallet with money and
   travel brochures   credit cards
   maps   cash register
   airplane, train tickets suitcases

8. *Veterinarian Kit*

   white shirt/jacket   empty medicine bottles
   stuffed animals   prescription labels
   cages (cardboard boxes) bandages
   medical bag   popsicle stick splints
   stethoscope   hypodermic syringe (play)

9. *Library Kit*

   children's books and   book return box
        magazines (with   sign for book fines
        card pockets and cash register
        date due slips)   money
   date stamp and stamp pad
   library cards

10. *Bank Kit*

   teller window (use a puppet   roll papers for coins
        stage)   deposit slips
   passbooks   money bags
   checks
   money

Figure 5–1   *Continued*

Young children working in a grocery store dramatic play center learn some of the functions of reading and writing.

in the office kit. Thus, through dramatic play with these materials, young children are introduced to some of the functions of reading and writing.

The props for these kits can be collected, stored in boxes, and then used in social studies, science, math, or literature activities. They can also be used in conjunction with field trips and class visitors. For example, for a unit on community helpers, teachers could arrange a field trip to the post office and invite a mail carrier to the classroom to be interviewed. Then a mail carrier prop kit can be set up. With the information they have learned from the field trip, the in-class interview, and through books, children have many experiences to draw on when they experiment with the props.

Dramatic play has all the values of other types of informal drama (Schickedanz, 1978). Children have the opportunity to use talk in a meaningful context as well as to learn new vocabulary words. As with other talk activities, dramatic play helps children develop socialization skills. They are integrating all of the language modes—listening, talking, reading, and writing—through their play activities, and they are also learning content area material.

INFORMAL DRAMA

Informal drama is a versatile form of drama that includes both language and non-language activities for students. The language activities we identify as informal drama—characterization, improvisation, and role-playing—are those that traditionally receive the most instruction in elementary classes. Too often, nonlanguage activities in drama, such as movement and pantomime, are ignored even though researchers have noted their importance.

Frank Smith (1977) has identified nonlanguage alternatives for each of the language functions presented in Chapter 2. These nonlanguage alternatives are presented in Figure 5–2. Stewig (1979) has estimated that as much as 65% of a message is communicated through nonlanguage means; only 35% uses language. These nonlanguage means include facial expressions, gestures, tone of voice, and societal rituals such as shaking hands, looking at the speaker, and putting hands

Figure 5–2 Language Functions and Their Nonlanguage Alternatives

Language Function	*Nonlanguage Alternatives*
1. Instrumental	Pantomime, facial expressions, screaming, pointing, grabbing
2. Regulatory	Pushing and pulling people around; modeling behavior for others to copy
3. Interactional	Waving, smiling, linking arms, holding hands, shaking fists
4. Personal	Art, music, dress, cosmetics, ornamentation
5. Heuristic	Exploration, investigation, experimentation
6. Imaginative	Play, art, pantomime
7. Informational	Pointing, rituals, diagrams, maps, mathematics

Smith, 1977, p. 640.

over hearts when pledging allegiance to the flag. People in certain occupations also use "professional gestures" (Stewig, 1979). For example, police officers, orchestra conductors, television directors, and airport ground crews will use gestures to communicate. Stewig's informative book, *Sending messages: The many ways people use to communicate ideas* (1978) illustrates these professional gestures as well as many other types of nonlanguage communication. This book and others related to nonlanguage communication are listed in Figure 5–3.

Using and interpreting nonlanguage communication is a necessary part of children's communicative competence. Sometimes talking without words is the loudest way to talk! It is important to explore with students the range of ways they can communicate without language by exploring the nonlanguage activities of movement and pantomime. Students can then better understand how language and nonlanguage can be integrated for more effective communication.

Movement

Movement is an easy and nonthreatening way to introduce elementary students to informal drama. According to Blatt and Cunningham (1981), movement is a valuable way "to help children communicate . . . in a setting in which language is used without barriers drawn between reading, writing, speaking, and listening" (p. 4). A first step is to ask children to explore the ways in which they can move their bodies (creep, glide, shake, twist, and dart, for example). The second step is to combine these movements with the sounds of rhythm instruments. Students close their eyes and listen to the sound of a rhythm instrument and then invent movements for the sounds. They visualize a movement that the sound brings to mind, and then they move as the sound is repeated. Teachers will want to repeat this procedure with a variety of instruments. The culminating activity is to play all the rhythm instruments consecutively, having students make the appropriate movement as each individual instrument is played. The number of instruments used de-

Figure 5–3   Books About Nonlanguage Communication

Castle, S. (1977). *Face talk, hand talk, body talk.* New York: Doubleday. (M–U)

Charlip, R., Ancona, M. B., & Ancona, G. (1964). *Handtalk: An ABC of finger spelling and sign language.* New York: Parents. (M–U)

Ets, M. H. (1968). *Talking without words.* New York: Viking. (P)

Stewig, J. W. (1978). *Sending messages: The many ways people use to communicate ideas.* Boston: Houghton Mifflin. (P–M–U)

P = primary (grades K–2)
M = middle (grades 3–5)
U = upper (grades 6–8)

pends on students' grade level. Young children may be able to put only three or four movements together.

Another movement activity encourages students to pretend they are animals, performing the movements that they think different animals would make to the sounds of the rhythm instruments. Visualizing movements and then performing them allows students to use their creativity to invent the movements they put with the sounds.

Movement stories (McIntyre, 1974; Way, 1966) offer yet another interesting way to combine movement activities with stories. Students can compose their own movement stories in which they include as many movement words as possible. They leave short lines in their movement stories to indicate pauses for students to perform the actions. An example of a student's movement story is presented in Figure 5–4.

Before students begin to write movement stories, brainstorm a list of all the movement words. Some possible words include *step, run, jump, crawl, leap, whirl, spin, fall, plop, stretch, slide, slip, catch, hop, roll,* and *gallop.* To increase the number of words on the list, students can check synonyms in a thesaurus.

Figure 5–4   A Movement Story

One morning Danny woke up and wanted to go exploring. He jumped out of bed _____ and pulled on his pants _____. He brushed his teeth with rapid strokes _____ and ran out the door. When he looked up at the sky _____, birds were flying all around. "I bet I can fly too," Danny thought _____. He threw out his arms _____ and flapped them up and down _____. He started to run across his backyard _____. He began to leap _____ and jump _____ so he could get into the air. "Whew!" Danny fell to the ground _____. He was exhausted. After Danny rested, he jumped up _____ and galloped into the woods behind the house _____.

There was a big tree directly in his path. "I'll be a monkey," he thought. He stretched up to catch a branch _____. Soon he was swinging _____ fast _____ then slowly _____. Then Danny fell down _____ and landed in a heap _____. "I'll be a turtle now," he thought. He crawled over to a stream _____. It was a wide stream. Not wanting to swim, Danny slowly got to his feet _____. He saw some rocks going across so he stepped up to the bank _____ and delicately placed one foot on the first stone. Then Danny became brave and hopped over to the next _____. But then he slipped _____ and, splash, fell smack into the middle of the stream _____. It was cold and Danny shivered _____. He stumbled _____ up on the bank and sank down _____. "That's enough exploring for one day," he thought. He gathered himself up _____ and trudged _____ back to his home.

Tamora, age 14

In the primary grades, the movement stories could be class collaboration stories. Have students as a class develop a story in general terms. Have one student begin the story and other students continue telling it. Write down each part. Have students put a movement into each part of the story they tell. When the story is completed, read it with the students and ask them for suggestions to revise it. Then reread it using assisted reading. Have the students perform the story. After performing the story, they can decide if the story or any of their movements need to be changed.

Pantomime

Pantomime, or "the art of conveying ideas without words" (McCaslin, 1984, p. 64), is similar to movement. Movement begins with general actions and, as it leads into movement stories, begins to shade into pantomime. Pantomime, however, makes a greater attempt to communicate feelings, ideas, and meaning. More imagination and concentration are required for pantomime since there is a need to communicate the feelings and ideas of the experience through movement.

Instruction in pantomime can be started with ordinary activities. For example, students might pantomime someone reading a paper, fishing in a lake, charming a cobra snake, eating a lemon, brushing teeth, fixing a peanut butter sandwich, flying a kite, or washing a car. They might also pretend to be a door, a bird, a toaster, or an elephant. Pantomime activities can be extended further when teachers invent unusual situations. For example, one teacher had students pretend they were pieces of bacon frying in a pan. This activity opened up the doors of creativity, and students began to let their imaginations go. It was difficult, however, for the students to perform the pantomimes without making any sounds since their enthusiasm was so high. In all pantomimes, encourage students to use as many of the senses as possible and to clearly communicate their intended feelings and ideas.

Pantomime can be a fruitful source for creativity if students invent their own pantomimes. Explain what a pantomime is, and encourage students to think of things they want to pantomime. Tell them to visualize what they are pretending to be, and to make certain they know what they are and what they will do. When they are ready to perform, classmates become the audience.

In addition to suggesting activities for pantomiming or having students invent their own, teachers can also have students act out stories. Well-known nursery rhymes such as "Humpty Dumpty" and "Jack and Jill," folktales, hero stories, and other stories lend themselves to pantomime. A list of suggested stories for use in pantomime activities is presented in Figure 5–5. Students in a reading group may also pantomime the stories they are reading in basal readers. Integrating drama activities with the reading program will help students to interpret story lines and the feelings of story characters.

Characterization

Pantomime leads to characterization. In pantomime, students focus on creating feelings and ideas to communicate to their audience. When students begin to con-

Figure 5–5   Stories to Pantomime

Aardema, V. (1975). *Why mosquitoes buzz in people's ears: A West African folk tale*. New York: Dial. (P–M)

de Paola, T. (1983). *The legend of the bluebonnet*. New York: Putnam. (P–M)

Farmer, P. (1971). *Daedalus and Icarus*. New York: Harcourt Brace Jovanovich. (U)

Galdone, P. (1972). *The three bears*. Boston: Houghton Mifflin. (P)

_____. (1973). *The three billy goats Gruff*. Boston: Houghton Mifflin. (P)

Hailey, G. (1970). *A story, a story*. New York: Atheneum. (P–M)

Hastings, S. (1981). *Sir Gawain and the green knight*. New York: Lothrop, Lee and Shepard. (M–U)

Hodges, M. (1984). *Saint George and the dragon*. Boston: Little, Brown. (M–U)

Hogrogian, N. (1971). *One fine day*. New York: Macmillan. (P)

Keats. E. J. (1965). *John Henry: An American legend*. New York: Pantheon. (P–M)

Ross, T. (1977). *The pied piper of Hamelin*. New York: Lothrop, Lee and Shepard. (M–U)

Sendak, M. (1963). *Where the wild things are*. New York: Harper and Row. (P)

Stevens, J. (1984). *The tortoise and the hare*. New York: Holiday House. (P–M)

Tolstoy, A. (1968). *The great big enormous turnip*. New York: Watts. (P)

P = primary grades (K–2)
M = middle grades (3–5)
U = upper grades (6–8)

sider characterization, they focus their imagination and concentration on the characters themselves—what they look like, how they think, and how they act.

Students may choose to portray individual characters or characters who need the interrelationships of others in order to be developed. The first characters they attempt should be familiar so that the students will have little trouble developing their role. For example, they might assume the role of a person watching a baseball game with different types of fans, eating in a restaurant, buying something at a sale, being sent to the principal's office, or playing store. Students might also portray characters from children's literature: the troll in *The three billy goats Gruff* (Galdone, 1973), Big Anthony in *Strega nona* (de Paola, 1975), Wilbur in *Charlotte's web* (White, 1952), or Bilbo Baggins in *The hobbit* (Tolkien, 1966).

So that more students can be involved in the dramatic activities, divide the class into small groups, and make each group responsible for acting out a particular situation. Situations from a social studies unit (e.g., the night before a Civil War battle or a day in the life of an Egyptian pharoah) can be used as well as everyday activities. Social studies situations give students the opportunity to apply the information they have learned and to try to understand how people in other situations might feel. When each group has chosen a situation to portray and has identified the characters they need, have them close their eyes and visualize the characters they are going to portray. Tell them first to think about how the character looks to get good physical image. Then have them imagine how that character would walk, talk, feel, act, think, and treat others. Afterward, students open their eyes and discuss the characters they have visualized.

Brainstorm possible questions to use to help students probe and develop each character in each situation that they try out. Questions about the characters being developed would have to do with their physical description, their actions, possible dialogue, and what they might be thinking. Questions prefaced with *who, what, where, why,* and *how* will probe as many facets of each character's personality as possible. Questions such as the following would be appropriate: (a) What does the character do? (b) How would he or she act in this situation? and (c) What kind of a person is the character? Have students evaluate the development of each character and their responses to the characters. Discuss which questions were the most helpful and why they were helpful.

Improvisation

Improvisation builds on the work students have done with pantomime and characterization by adding dialogue. *Improvisation* is the act of inventing, composing, or reciting a drama without preparation, reading, or memorizing a script. Students can re-enact the situations they worked through with pantomime and characterization and add dialogue to them. Since they have already done much work in the pantomime stage, and are familiar with the roles they have played, dialogue comes easily.

Students should review the situations for which they want to improvise dialogue by discussing the feelings, moods, and personalities of the characters. Since they have previously acted out the situations, they can fill out and enhance any parts of the plot and action that need work. After students discuss the type of speech they expect from each character and any speech habits the character might have, have them take a practice run through. Students should then review what they did, what they said, and what they think about it. Further discussion should help them work on the spots that they felt did not convey the feelings, ideas, and meanings they were trying to communicate. A replay is helpful after they complete any restructuring. Do not, however, hound an improvisation to death. Teachers will want to push on to develop new ideas and create more drama.

Teaching Language Skills.   Improvisation is an effective technique for teaching many language skills. For example, students can learn about adverbs by demonstrating all the different ways they can walk—slowly, quietly, rapidly, and so on. (Ehrlich, 1974). Students can also compare the literal and figurative meanings of idioms through improvisation. First, have pairs or small groups of students act out the literal meanings of these idioms: "get off my back," "catch a cold," "in a pickle," and "horsing around" (Foerster, 1974, cited in Ehrlich, 1974). Drama provides an active, concrete way to experience many language skills. Improvisation can also be used to teach compound words, homonyms, and other language skills.

Dramatizing Stories.   Acting out stories is one type of improvisation. Students choose very familiar stories—folktales, fables, legends—and act them out using both dialogue and body movements. The same stories suggested for pantomime activities (see Figure 5–5) can also be used for dramatizing stories. Cumulative tales including *The three little pigs* (Galdone, 1970) and *The gingerbread boy* (Galdone, 1975) are good for younger children to dramatize because they are repetitious in sequence, plot, and dialogue. Middle and upper grade students can act out favorite scenes from longer stories such as *The wind in the willows* (Grahame, 1961) and *Mrs. Frisby and the rats of NIHM* (O'Brien, 1971). Students can also read biographies and dramatize events from these people's lives. Ingri and Edgar Parin d'Aulaire's *Columbus* (1955) and Jean Fritz's *And then what happened, Paul Revere?* (1973) are two biographies that can be dramatized by elementary students.

Keep in mind that a good story for dramatizing has a simple beginning that moves directly into action. A long introduction in a story necessitates a narrator who would have too much to read before the other students got involved in the dramatization. The action should vary as the story progresses. Variation in action is especially important for upper grade students. The conversation in the story should be appealing to the students and easy for them to duplicate in their own words because they will not be memorizing the dialogue. They will dramatize the events in the story and make up the conversation as they go along. They must, however, be familiar with the characters if they are to faithfully re-create the story line and dialogue.

Students must get excited about a story if the dramatization is to be successful. Their mood should be sustaining and infectious. Planning the dramatization will take patience and guidance. As students prepare the story, they will need to decide which parts to enact and which to read. They will need guidance when dramatizing the story and when giving themselves feedback. The teacher's role is to facilitate the development of the story for dramatization and to guide them in their execution of the story. Remember, dramatization is work, but it should also be fun.

Role-playing

Role-playing means what it says: one person takes the role of another person. We are not talking about roles in a story, but rather the roles people play in society. Role-playing is an educational experience designed to help students gain insights about how to handle real-life problems and understand historical and current events.

Dorothy Heathcote has developed an innovative approach to use role-playing so that students can experience and better understand historical events (Wagner, 1976). Through a process she calls "funneling," Heathcote chooses a dramatic focus from a general topic (e.g., ancient Rome, the Civil War, the Pilgrims). She begins by thinking of all the aspects of the general topic and then decides on a dramatic focus, a particular critical moment. For example, using the topic of the Pilgrims, one possible focus is the night of December 20, 1620, eleven weeks after the Pilgrims set sail from England on the *Mayflower* and the night before the ship reached Plymouth.

The improvisation begins as students assume roles, and the teacher becomes a character, too. As they begin to role-play the event, questions are used to draw students' attention to certain features and to prove their understanding. Questions about the Pilgrims might include:

> Where are you?
>
> After 11 weeks sailing the Atlantic Ocean, I wonder what will happen?
>
> How are you feeling?
>
> I wonder why you left England?
>
> What kind of life do you dream of in the new land?
>
> Can you survive in this cold winter weather?

These questions also provide information such as reminding students of the time of year and the length of the voyage.

Sometimes Heathcote stops students in the middle of role-playing and asks them to write what they are thinking and feeling. As a part of the Pilgrim improvisation, students might be asked to write an entry in their simulated diaries for December 20, 1620. (For more information on diaries and journals, see Chapter 7.) An example of a simulated diary entry written by a fourth-grade "Pilgrim" is shown in Figure 5–6. After the writing activity, students continue the role-playing activity.

Heathcote uses drama to begin study on a topic rather than as a culminating activity in which students apply all they have learned. Heathcote suggests that role-playing experiences stimulate children's curiosity and make them want to read books and learn more about an historical or current event. Whether role-playing is used as an introduction or as a conclusion, it is a valuable activity because students become immersed in the event. By reliving it, they are learning far more than mere facts.

POINTS TO PONDER
How Does Interpretive Drama Differ from Informal Drama?
What Are the Types of Interpretive Drama?
What Are the Steps in Telling Stories?
What Is Readers Theater?

Figure 5–6   A Pilgrim's Diary Entry for December 20, 1620

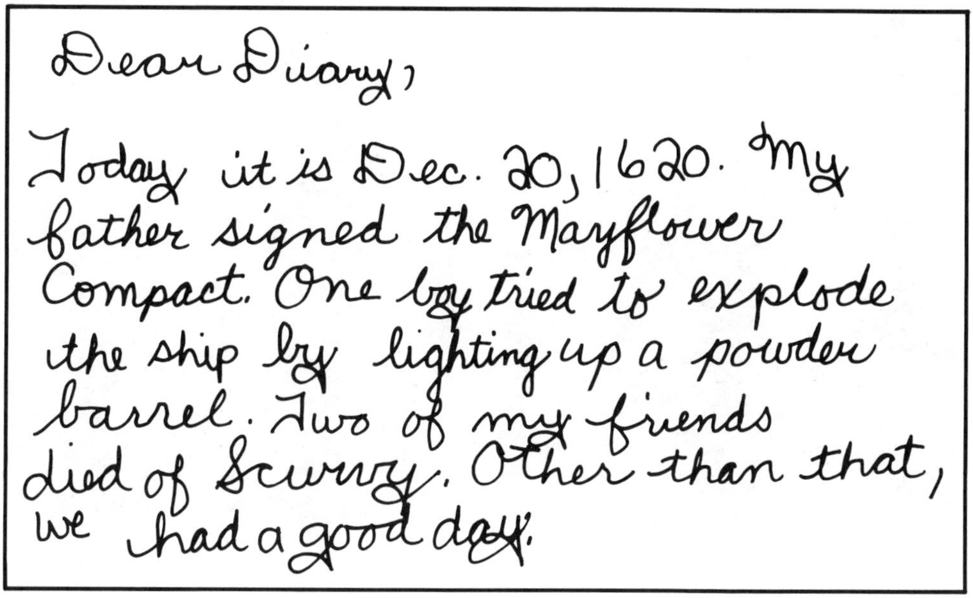

Dear Diary,

Today it is Dec. 20, 1620. My father signed the Mayflower Compact. One boy tried to explode the ship by lighting up a powder barrel. Two of my friends died of Scurvy. Other than that, we had a good day.

Stephanie, age 10

INTERPRETIVE DRAMA

Movement, pantomime, dramatizing stories, and the other types of drama already discussed are classified as informal drama. They are relaxed, spontaneous, and natural extensions of children's dramatic play. In contrast, interpretive drama is more structured. Teachers and students do not create the material; they create an interpretation of ideas and words already written (Busching, 1981). The two types of interpretive drama presented in this section, storytelling and readers theater, both involve students in interpreting literature.

Storytelling

Storytelling is an ancient art that is a valuable instructional tool. Not only should teachers share literature with their students using storytelling techniques, but students can and should tell stories, too. Storytelling is entertaining and stimulates children's imaginations. It expands their language abilities and helps them internalize the characteristics of stories (Morrow, 1985). Storytelling involves four steps: (a) choosing a story, (b) preparing to tell the story, (c) adding props, and (d) telling the story.

Choosing a Story.   Traditional stories such as folktales are often chosen for storytelling activities; however, any type of literature can be used. The most im-

Students use stick puppets in retelling the story of "The Gingerbread Man."

portant consideration in choosing a story is to select a story you like and want to tell. Morrow (1979) has listed other considerations:

1. The story has a simple, well-rounded plot.
2. The story has a clear beginning, middle, and end.
3. The story has an underlying theme.
4. The story has a small number of well-defined characters.
5. The story contains dialogue.
6. The story uses repetition.
7. The story uses colorful language or "catch phrases."

A list of suggested stories that contain many of these characteristics is presented in Figure 5–7.

Preparing to Tell the Story.   It is not necessary for teachers or students to memorize a story to tell it effectively. Kingore (1982) lists the following six steps as preparation for storytelling:

1. Choose a story you really like.
2. Memorizing is not necessary. Just read the story a few times to get a "feel" for the sequence and major events in the story.
3. Plan interesting phrases or repeated phrases to enliven the language of your story.

Brown, M. (1947). *Stone soup.* New York: Scribner. (P–M)

Brown, M. W. (1972). *The runaway bunny.* New York: Harper and Row. (P)

Carle, E. (1970). *The very hungry caterpillar.* Cleveland: Collins-World. (P)

Flack, M. (1932). *Ask Mr. Bear.* New York: Macmillan. (P)

Gag, W. (1956). *Millions of cats.* New York: Coward McCann. (P)

Galdone, P. (1973). *The three billy goats Gruff.* Boston: Houghton Mifflin. (P)

_____. (1975). *The gingerbread boy.* New York: Seabury. (P)

Grimm, The Brothers. (1971). *The Bremen town musicians.* New York: Greenwillow. (P–M)

Johnson, O. (1955). *Harold and the purple crayon.* New York: Harper and Row. (See also other books in this series.) (P)

Kellogg, S. (1973). *The island of the skog.* New York: Dial. (P)

Low, J. (1980). *Mice twice.* New York: Atheneum. (P–M)

Slobodkina, E. (1947). *Caps for sale.* New York: Scott. (P)

Steig, W. (1982). *Doctor DeSoto.* New York: Farrar. (P)

Still, J. (1977). *Jack and the wonder beans.* New York: Putnam. (M)

Thurber, J. (1974). *Many moons.* New York: Harcourt. (P–M)

Turkle, B. (1976). *Deep in the forest.* New York: Dutton. (P–M)

Wildsmith, B. (1972). *The owl and the woodpecker.* New York: Watts. (P–M)

Zemach, H. & Zemach, M. (1973). *Duffy and the devil.* New York: Farrar. (P–M)

Zemach, M. (1976). *It could always be worse.* New York: Farrar. (P–M–U)

Figure 5–7 Stories to Tell

4. Plan simple props or gestures to increase your audience's interest.

5. Prepare a brief introduction that relates the story to your audience's experiences.

6. Practice telling your story in front of a mirror. (p. 29)

This process can be abbreviated when very young children tell stories. They may choose a story they already know well and make props to guide the telling. (Try a set of puppets representing the main characters or a series of drawings.) They are then ready to tell their stories.

Adding Props.   Several techniques can make the story come alive as it is being told. Morrow (1979) describes four types of props that add variety and interest to stories:

1. *Flannel board.* Place drawings or pictures cut from books and backed with flannel on the flannel board as the story is told.

2. *Puppets.* Use puppets representing the main characters to tell a story with dialogue. (For ideas on how to construct puppets, check the section in this chapter on puppets.)

3. *Chalk talks.* Draw pictures on the chalkboard to illustrate the story as it is being told. This technique is especially effective in telling Crockett Johnson's series of *Harold* stories.

4. *Other props.* Use stuffed animals to represent animal characters or other small objects to represent important things in the story being told. Try, for instance, using a pile of caps in telling Slobodkina's *Caps for sale,* (1947) or a small gold ball for Thurber's *Many moons* (1974).

Telling the Story.   Students can tell the stories they have prepared to small groups of their classmates or to younger children. Try dividing the audience into small groups so that more students can tell stories at one time.

Readers Theater

Readers theater is "a formalized dramatic presentation of a script by a group of readers" (Busching, 1981, p. 330). Students each assume the role of a character, and they read the character's lines in the script. The reader's responsibility is to interpret a story without using much action. Students may stand or sit but must carry the whole communication of the plot, characterization, mood, and theme by using their voices, gestures, and facial expressions.

Readers theater avoids many of the restrictions inherent in theatrical productions. Students do not memorize their parts; elaborate props, costumes, and backdrops are not needed; and long, tedious hours are not spent rehearsing.

There are three steps in developing readers theater presentations. They are (a) selecting a script, (b) rehearsing the play, and (c) staging the play.

Selecting a Script.   Quality play scripts exhibit the same characteristics as do other types of fine literature. Manna (1984) lists five essential characteristics: (a) an interesting story, (b) a well-paced plot, (c) recognizable and believable characters, (d) plausible language, and (e) a distinct style. The arrangement of the text on the page is also an important consideration when selecting a script. There should be a clear distinction between the stage directions and dialogue through adequate spacing and by varying the print types and colors. This distinction is especially important for primary grade students and for older students who are not familiar with the script format.

Readers theater is a relatively new idea, and the number of quality scripts available is limited, although more are being published each year. A list of scripts that can be used for readers theater is presented in Figure 5–8. Play scripts found in basal reading textbooks are another source of material for readers theater presentations. Also, stories and folktales that heavily emphasize dialogue, such as *The three billy goats Gruff* (Galdone, 1973) and *The little red hen* (Galdone, 1973), can be used as scripts. Students portraying each character can pick out their lines and a narrator can read the remaining text (Post, 1979).

Figure 5–8 Scripts for Readers Theater

Aiken, J. (1973). *The mooncusser's daughter.* New York: Viking.

Bradley, A. & Bond, M. (1977). *Paddington on stage.* Boston: Houghton Mifflin.

Falls, G. A. (1983). *The pushcart war.* New Orleans, LA: Anchorage Press. (Book that the script is based on was written by Jean Merrill.)

Gackenback. D. (1980). *Hattie, Tom, and the chicken witch.* New York: Harper and Row.

George, R. E. (1976). *Roald Dahl's Charlie and the chocolate factory.* New York: Knopf.

George, R. E. (1982). *Roald Dahl's James and the giant peach.* New York: Knopf.

Jennings, C. A. & Harris, A. (Eds.). (1981). *Plays children love: A treasury of contemporary and classical plays for children.* New York: Doubleday.

Korty, C. (1975). *Plays from African folktales.* New York: Scribner.

Laurie, R. (1980). *Children's plays from Beatrix Potter.* New York: Warne.

Rockwell, T. (1980). *How to eat fried worms.* New York: Delacorte.

Sendak, M. (1975). *Really Rosie: Starring the nutshell kids.* New York: Harper and Row.

Zindel, P. (1974). *Let me hear you whisper.* New York: Harper and Row.

Manna, 1984, pp. 714–716.

Rehearsing the Play.   Begin by assigning readers for each character and a narrator (if needed in the script). Read through the play once or twice and then stop to discuss the story. Busching (1981) recommends using what has been called the "5 Ws plus one" questions—*who, what, where, when, why,* and *how*—to probe students' understanding. Through this discussion, students gain a clearer understanding of the story and make decisions about how to interpret their characters.

After students decide how to use their voice, gestures, and facial expressions to interpret their characters, the script should be read one or two more times. Obviously less rehearsal is needed for an informal, in-class presentation than for a more formal production. Nevertheless, interpretations should always be developed as fully as possible.

Staging the Play.   Readers theater can be presented on a stage or in a corner of the classroom. Students stand or sit in a row and read their lines in the script. They must stay in position through the presentation or enter and leave as their lines are read. If readers are sitting, they may stand to read their lines, or if they are standing, they may take a step forward before reading. The emphasis is not on production quality; rather, it is on the interpretive quality of the readers' voices and expressions. Costumes and props are unnecessary; however, a few can be added to increase interest and enjoyment as long as they do not interfere with the interpretive quality of the reading.

Readers theater provides an excellent introduction to scripts and preparation for script-writing. Through reading scripts, students become familiar with script conventions (e.g., lists of characters, stage directions), and they become more sensitive to language styles.

POINTS TO PONDER

How Do Students Learn to Write Play Scripts and Film/Video Scripts?
What Are the Characteristics of Scripts?
How Can Script Conventions Be Used to Teach Quotation Marks?

SCRIPTWRITING

Scripts are a unique written language form, one that elementary students need opportunities to explore. Scriptwriting often grows out of informal and interpretive dramatics activities. Soon students recognize the need to write notes to help them as they prepare for plays, puppet shows, readers theater, and other dramatic productions. This need provides the impetus for introducing students to the unique dramatic conventions and for encouraging students to write scripts. Two types of scripts — play scripts and film/video scripts — will be discussed in this section.

Play Scripts

Once students want to write scripts, they will recognize the need to add the structures unique to dramatic writing to their repertoire of written language conventions. Students begin by examining scripts. (A list of scripts was presented in Figure 5–8.) It is especially effective to have students compare narrative and script versions of the same story. For example, Richard George has adapted two of Roald Dahl's fantastic stories, *Charlie and the chocolate factory* (1976) and *James and the giant peach* (1982) into scripts. Then students discuss their observations and compile a list of the unique characteristics of scripts. An upper grade class compiled the list of unique dramatic conventions presented in Figure 5–9.

The next step is to have students apply what they have learned about scripts by writing a class collaboration or group script. With the whole class, develop a script by adapting a familiar story. As the script is being written, refer to the chart of dramatic conventions and ask students to check that these conventions are being used. Collaborative writing provides teachers with unique teaching opportunities and needed practice for students before asking them to write individually. After the script is completed, have students read it using readers theater procedures, or produce it as a puppet show or play.

Important Characteristics of Scripts

1. Scripts are divided into acts and scenes.
2. Scripts have these parts: (a) a list of characters (or cast); (b) the setting (at the beginning of each act or scene); (c) stage directions (written in parentheses); and (d) dialogue.
3. The dialogue carries the action.
4. Description and other information are set apart in the setting or in stage directions.
5. Stage directions give actors important information about how to act and how to feel.
6. The dialogue is written in a special way:
   CHARACTER'S NAME: Dialogue
7. Sometimes a narrator is used to quickly fill in parts of the story.

Figure 5–9 Dramatic Conventions Used in Scripts

Once students are aware of the dramatic conventions and have participated in writing a class collaboration script, they can write scripts individually or in small groups. Often, students will adapt familiar stories for their first scripts. Later they will create original scripts. "The Lonely Troll," a script written by a team of five upper grade students is presented in Figure 5–10 as an example of the type of scripts older students can compose. While most of the scripts that students write are narrative, students can also create scripts about famous people or historical events.

Teaching Quotation Marks. Script writing conventions are also useful in teaching primary and middle grade students about punctuation marks. Students can take dialogue written in "talking balloons" as in comics and rewrite it in script form as an intermediary step in learning to use quotation marks in writing dialogue. A few stories use text written in talking balloons such as *A flea story* (Lionni, 1977) and *The bionic bunny show* (Brown & Brown, 1984). Children copy a talking balloon from the text and rewrite it first in script form and then in narrative form. An example of this approach is presented in Figure 5–11 (page 152). This approach helps students isolate the dialogue and learn which words to put in quotation marks by using meaningful text from a story they have read and enjoyed.

Film/Video Scripts

Students use a similar approach in writing scripts that will be filmed or videotaped. However, in writing these scripts, students must consider the visual component of the film as well as the written script. They often compose their scripts on story

Figure 5–10 A Script Written by a Group of Upper Grade Students

---

The Lonely Troll

NARRATOR: Once upon a time, in a far, far away land, there was a troll named Pip-
                 pin who lived all alone in his little corner of the woods. The troll hated
                 all the creatures of the woods and was very lonely because he didn't
                 have anyone to talk to since he scared everyone away. One day, a
                 dwarf named Sam wandered into Pippin's yard and . . .

PIPPIN: Grrr. What are you doing here?

SAM: Ahhhhh! A troll! Please don't eat me!

PIPPIN: Why shouldn't I?

SAM: (Begging) Look, I'm all skin and bones. I won't make a good meal.

PIPPIN: You look fat enough for me. (Turns to audience) Do you think I should
                 eat him? (Sam jumps off stage and hides in the audience.)

PIPPIN: Where did he go? (Pippin jumps off stage and looks for Sam. When he
                 finds Sam, he takes him back on stage, laughing; then he ties Sam up.)
                 Ha, ha, ha. Boy, that sure did tire me out. (Yawn) I'll take a nap. Then
                 I'll eat him later. (Pippin falls asleep. Lights dim. Sam escapes and runs
                 behind a tree. Lights return, and Pippin wakens.)

PIPPIN: (To audience) Where's my breakfast? (Sam peeps out from behind a
                 tree and cautions the audience to be quiet.) Huh? Did someone say he
                 was behind that tree? (Points to tree. Pippin walks around. Sam kicks
                 him in the rear. Pippin falls and is knocked out.)

SAM: I must get out of here, and warn the queen about this short, small,
                 mean, ugly troll. (Sam leaves. Curtains close.)

NARRATOR: So Sam went to tell Queen Muffy about the troll. Meanwhile, in the
                 forest, Pippin awakens, and decides to set a trap for Sam. (Open cur-
                 tains to forest scene, showing Pippin making a box trap.)

PIPPIN: Ha, ha, ha! That stupid dwarf will come back here looking for me.
                 When he sees this ring, he'll take it. Then, I'll trap him! Ha, ha, ha ha.
                 (Pippin hides.)

NARRATOR: The dwarf finally reaches Queen Muffy's castle and hurries to tell her
                 his story.

SAM: (Open curtains to Queen Muffy sitting on a throne, eating. Sam rushes
                 in, out of breath.) I have some very important news for you.
                 There's . . .

QUEEN: I don't have time for you.

SAM: But, I . . .

QUEEN: Come, come. Don't bother me with small things.

SAM: There's an ugly old . . .

QUEEN: You're wasting my time.

SAM: I just wanted to warn you, there's a big, ugly, mean . . .

Figure 5–10 *Continued*

QUEEN:	Hurry up.
SAM:	. . . man-eating . . .
QUEEN:	This had better be important.
SAM:	(Angry, he yells) THERE'S A TROLL IN THE FOREST!!!
QUEEN:	Who cares if there's a . . . a . . . (Screams) A TROLL!!!
SAM:	That's what I've been saying. A troll—in the forest.
QUEEN:	Then I must send out my faithful knight . . . Sir Skippy . . . to kill him. I shall offer a reward. (Queen exits.)
SAM:	A reward, huh? Hmmmm. I think I'll go out and get that troll myself— and collect that reward! (Close curtains.)
NARRATOR:	So Sam sets out to capture the troll, not knowing that Pippin set a trap out for him. (Open curtains to trap scene.)
SAM:	(Carries a huge net) Ohhh Mr. Troll. (He spots the ring and reaches for it.) Wow! A ring! (Pippin sneezes.) What was that? Aha! (Sam sees Pippin, and swings the net. Pippin dives for Sam and gets trapped in his own trap.)
SAM:	He's trapped! I did it! Oh boy, now I can get that reward. I get a hundred dollars . . . or maybe a thousand dollars . . . possibly a million.
SKIPPY:	(Comes in smiling) I am here to rid the forest of this mean, awful, ugly troll. I also want the reward. (Said in an evil way)
SAM:	The reward is mine. I caught him. It's all mine.
SKIPPY:	I want that reward, and I shall get it. (Takes sword) I will carve your throat if you don't hand him over. I'll kill him and take him to the queen, so she will see what a great warrior I am.
SAM:	You're going to kill him? I won't let you!
SKIPPY:	Do you think I'm stupid? I won't take a live troll to Queen Muffy.
SAM:	If you are going to kill him, I will release him. (Throws off box) Hey, Pippin, he's going to kill you. Run away, run for your life, and I shall protect you.
PIPPIN:	(Confused) You are trying to save me, after I tried to kill you?
SAM:	I don't want to see you hurt.
PIPPIN:	Then I will stay here and help you defeat Skippy.
SAM AND PIPPIN:	Friends, forever! (Skippy steps forward and swings at Pippin. Pippin ducks. Pippin and Sam give Skippy the Three Stooges treatment. Skippy is defeated.)
PIPPIN:	Leave my forest, now, Sir Skippy, before we kill you. (Skippy leaves.)
SAM:	Thank you, my friend. We will stay together always, and you will never be lonely again. (Close curtains.)
NARRATOR:	Pippin and Sam became best friends, and the queen never bothered them. They lived happily ever after.

Eighth graders: Raymond, Lisa, Jeff, Kathy, Larry.

Step 1: Dialogue in Talking Balloons

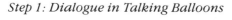

(From Leo Lionni's *A flea story,* 1977, n.p.)

Step 2: Dialogue in Script Form

> THE BLUE FLEA: Where are you? Help! I can't see a thing!

Step 2: Dialogue in Narrative Form

> The blue flea cried, "Where are you? Help! I can't see a thing!"

Figure 5–11   How to Use Script Conventions to Teach
Quotation Marks

boards which focus their attention on how the story they are creating will be filmed (Cox, 1983, 1985). *Story boards,* or sheets of paper divided into three sections, are used by students to sketch in scenes. A series of three or four large squares are placed in a row down the center of the sheet of paper, with space for dialogue and narration on the left side and shooting directions on the right side. Carole Cox compares story boards to road maps because they provide directions for the filming of the script. The scene renderings and the shooting directions help students tie the dialogue to the visual images that will appear on the film or videotape. A sample story board form is presented in Figure 5–12, and an excerpt from a fourth-grade class collaboration script is presented in Figure 5–13.

The script can be produced in several different ways. It can be produced as a live-action play, as a puppet show, or through animation. After writing the script on the story boards or transferring a script they have written previously to story boards, students collect or construct the properties they will need to produce the script. As with other types of drama, the properties do not need to be extensive. A simple backdrop can be constructed and costumes collected. Students should also print the title and credits on large posters that will be filmed at the beginning of the film. After several rehearsals, the script is filmed using either a movie camera or a video camera.

As video cameras and VCR playback systems become common equipment in elementary schools, we anticipate that they will be chosen more often than movie cameras for filming student scripts. Video cameras and tapes are easier and less expensive to use than movie cameras and film. Videotapes do not need to be devel-

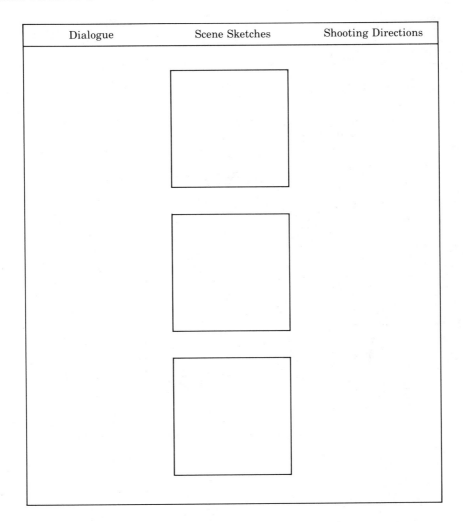

Figure 5–12   A Story Board for Film and Video Scripts

oped as film does and can be re-used. Also, the audio component can be recorded at the same time as the video component on videotapes. Many teachers prefer videotapes to movie films because they can tape rehearsals, which allows students to review their own performance and make any needed changes before the final taping.

POINTS TO PONDER

What Types of Puppets Can Elementary Students Construct?

How Do Students Use Puppets in Drama Activities?

Figure 5–13   Excerpt from a Class Collaboration Story Board Script

Third graders

PUPPETS AND OTHER PROPS

Puppets have long been favorites of children. The delightful combinations of colorful language, novel body constructions, fantasy, and imaginative characters fascinate children. Watching all kinds of puppets perform brings them pleasure. The variety of characters that can be developed by using puppets is endless. The only limitations are the students' imagination, their ability to construct things, and the materials at hand. Puppets can be used not only in all types of drama activities, but also as a novel way to introduce a language skill such as quotation marks. Teachers can use puppets to improvise a dialogue, and then record it using quotation marks. Puppets can be very useful, especially with shy students.

Simple puppets provide children with the opportunity to develop both creative and dramatic ability. The simpler the puppet, the more is left to the imagination of the audience and the puppeteer. Constructing elaborate puppets is beyond the resources of both teachers and students. The type of puppets that students construct, however, depends on how they will be used.

Students can construct puppets using all sorts of scrap materials. Directions for making eight types of hand and finger puppets are presented in this section. These eight types of puppets are illustrated in Figure 5–14.

Stick Puppets.   Stick puppets are very versatile and perhaps the easiest to make. Sticks, tongue depressors, dowels, and straws can be used. The rest of the puppet that is attached to the stick can be constructed from papier-mache, Styrofoam balls, pictures that students have drawn, or pictures cut from magazines and mounted on cardboard. Students draw or draw and paint the features on the materials they have selected to use for the head and the body. Some puppets may need only the head; others may need the whole body. Making stick puppets provides the opportunity to combine art and drama.

Paper Bag Puppets.   This is another simple puppet for students to make. The paper bags should be the right size to fit students' hands. Lunch-size paper bags are a convenient size although smaller bags are better for kindergartners. The characters portrayed and the emphasis placed on the size of the character should be the determining factor, however. The mouth of the puppet can be placed at the fold of the paper bag. Paint on faces and clothes, add yarn for hair, and attach arms and legs. Students should choose ways to decorate their bag puppets to match the characters they develop.

Cylinder Puppets.   Cylinder puppets are made from cardboard tubes that are used as the base for bathroom tissue, paper towels, and aluminum foil. The diameter of the cylinder and its length will determine the size of the puppets that students will make. The cylinders can be painted and various appendages and clothing can be attached. Again, the character's role should determine how the puppet is costumed. Students insert their fingers in the bottom of the cylinder to manipulate the puppet.

Sock Puppets.   Sock puppets are quite versatile. The sock can be used the way it is with button eyes, yarn hair, pipe cleaner antennae, and other features added. The sock can also be cut at the toes to create a mouth, and whatever else is needed to give the impression of the character can be added.

Cup Puppets.   Even primary grade students can make puppets using Styrofoam cups. They glue facial features, hair, wings, and other decorations on the cup. Pipe cleaners, toothpicks, and Q-tips tipped with glitter can easily be attached to Styrofoam cups. Then sticks or heavy-duty straws are attached to the inside of the cup as the handle.

Paper Plate Puppets.   Paper plates can be used for face puppets as well as for masks. Students add junk materials to decorate the puppets. Then sticks or rulers are taped to the back of the paper plate as the handle.

Figure 5–14 Types of Puppets

Finger Puppets.   Students can make several different types of finger puppets. For one type, students can draw, color, and cut out small figures, and then add tabs to either side of the figure and tape the tabs together to fit around the student's finger. Larger puppets can be taped to fit around the student's hand. For a second type of finger puppet, students can cut the finger section from a glove and add decoration. The pointed part separating the compartments in an egg carton can also be used for a finger puppet.

Cloth Puppets.   Students can make cloth puppets if parents are available to assist with the sewing. Two pieces of cloth are sewn together on all sides except the bottom, and then students personalize the puppets using scraps of fabric, lace, yarn, and other materials.

Stages

Puppetry is so versatile it can be performed almost any place. Students can make their own stages from empty appliance packing crates or an empty television cabinet. They can also use classroom tables and desks by draping blankets or cloths in front of them. Some tables can be turned on their sides and be used. There may be other classroom objects your students can use as makeshift stages.

Other Props

A collection of dress-up clothes, hats, and common objects can be used in the drama activities discussed in this chapter. Both young and old children will enjoy using costumes and props. Enlist parents' aid in collecting props. Very simple objects can serve many different functions. For instance, an old towel can become a king's royal cape, a seat on an airplane, a baby wrapped in a blanket, or even the wind. Consider the possible uses for a pair of chopsticks: knitting needles, horns on a goat, a sword, oars in a rowboat, or a baton (Ehrlich, 1974). Encourage students to be imaginative and devise ways to use whatever props are available to add interest to their drama activities.

Summary

Drama is an essential part of the language arts curriculum and is a way of learning as well as a communication mode. Drama activities are essential for improving students' dramatic abilities, for helping them to develop their creative potential, and for allowing them to explore various means of expression.

The drama activities discussed in this chapter fall into two major classifications, informal drama and interpretive drama. Informal drama is relaxed and spontaneous, growing out of young children's dramatic play. Movement, pantomime, characterization, and improvisation are examples of informal drama. Students can also use informal drama to re-enact historical events. The second type, interpretive drama, is more structured and involves students' interpretations of stories. Two types of interpretive drama are storytelling and readers theater.

As students' interest in dramatic activities increases, they will begin to write dialogue and scripts. Scripts are a unique written language form, and through reading and writing scripts, students learn the dramatic conventions used in this form. The first scripts that students compose are often adaptions of familiar stories written as class or group collaborations. Students can write scripts that are performed as plays or puppet shows as well as scripts that are produced as films or videotapes.

Students can construct a variety of types of puppets and use them in most types of drama activities. Puppets as well as other props can be used to increase students' interest in drama activities.

Extensions

1. Stock a dramatic play center in a kindergarten or first-grade classroom with one of the prop kits listed in Figure 5–2. Observe children over several days as they interact in the center and keep a log of the activities they participate in and how they use language in their play.

2. Plan and direct a role-playing activity with a group of students in conjunction with a social studies unit. Follow the guidelines presented in the chapter and integrate a writing activity with the role-playing (e.g., by having students keep a journal or writing a letter).

3. Prepare and tell a story to a group of students following the four-step procedure presented in the chapter. As you work through the procedure, imagine yourself in the role of an elementary student to gain an appreciation for the work students must do to prepare to tell a story.

4. Assist a small group of middle or upper grade students as they prepare to tell stories to a class of primary grade students. Help students use the four-step procedure presented in the chapter.

5. Assist a small group of students as they use readers theater to present an interpretive reading. Use the three-step procedure presented in the chapter. Choose a script from students' basal reading textbooks or from the list of scripts presented in Figure 5–8.

6. Introduce script writing to a group of middle or upper grade students by having them compile a list of the unique dramatic conventions used in script writing and then write a class collaboration script by adapting a familiar folktale.

7. Assist a small group of students as they make finger, stick, paper bag, or other types of puppets. Then have students use the puppets to retell a familiar story or to dramatize another activity.

References

Blatt, G. T. & Cunningham, J. (1981). *It's your move: Expressive movement activities for the language arts class.* New York: Teachers College Press.

Brown, M. & Brown, L. K. (1984). *The bionic bunny show.* Boston: Little, Brown.

Busching, B. A. (1981). Readers theatre: An education for language and life. *Language Arts, 58* 330–338.

Cox, C. (1980). Making films without a camera. *Language Arts, 57,* 274–279.

———. (1983). Young filmmakers speak the language of film. *Language Arts, 60,* 296–304, 372.

———. (1985). Filmmaking as a composing process. *Language Arts, 62,* 60–69.

Dahl, R. (1961). *James and the giant peach.* New York: Knopf.

———. (1964). *Charlie and the chocolate factory.* New York: Knopf.

d'Aulaire, I. & d'Aulaire, E. P. (1955). *Columbus.* New York: Doubleday.

de Paola, T. (1975). *Strega nona.* Englewood Cliffs, NJ: Prentice-Hall.

Ehrlich, H. W. (1974). *Creative dramatics handbook.* Philadelphia: Office of Early Childhood Programs, The School District of Philadelphia. (Distributed by NCTE.)

Farnsworth, K. (1981). Storytelling in the classroom—Not an impossible dream. *Language Arts, 58,* 162–167.

Fritz, J. (1973). *And then what happened, Paul Revere?* New York: Coward.

Galda, L. (1982). Playing about a story: Its impact on comprehension. *The Reading Teacher, 36,* 52–55.

Galdone, P. (1970). *The three little pigs.* New York: Seabury.

———. (1973). *The little red hen.* New York: Seabury.

———. (1973). *The three billy goats Gruff.* Boston: Houghton Mifflin.

———. (1975). *The gingerbread boy.* New York: Seabury.

George, R. E. (1976). *Roald Dahl's Charlie and the chocolate factory.* New York: Knopf.

———. (1982). *Roald Dahl's James and the giant peach.* New York: Knopf.

Grahame, K. (1961). *The wind in the willows.* New York: Scribner.

Johnson, C. (1955). *Harold and the purple crayon.* New York: Harper and Row.

Joint Committee on the Role of Drama in the Classroom. (1983). *Informal classroom drama.* Urbana, IL: NCTE.

Kingore, B. W. (1982). Storytelling: A bridge from the university to the elementary school to the home. *Language Arts, 59,* 28–32.

Lionni, L. (1977). *A flea story.* New York: Pantheon.

Manna, A. L. (1984). Making language come alive through reading plays. *The Reading Teacher, 37,* 712–717.

McCaslin, N. (1984). *Creative dramatics in the classroom* (4th ed.) New York: Longman.

McIntyre, B. (1974). *Creative drama in the elementary school.* Itasca, IL: Peacock.

Morrow, L. M. (1979). Exciting children about literature through creative storytelling techniques. *Language Arts, 56,* 236–243.

———. (1985). Reading and retelling stories: Strategies for emergent readers. *The Reading Teacher, 38,* 870–875.

O'Brien R. C. (1971). *Mrs. Frisby and the rats of NIHM.* New York: Atheneum.

Post, R. M. (1979). Children's readers theatre. *Language Arts, 56,* 262–267.

Schickedanz, J. (1978). 'You be the doctor and I'll be sick': Preschoolers learn the language arts through play. *Language Arts, 55,* 713–718.

Sharmat, M. W. (1977). *Nate the great and the phony clue.* New York: Coward.

Slobodkina, E. (1947). *Caps for sale.* New York: Scott.

Smith, F. (1983). The uses of language. *Language Arts, 54,* 638–644.

Sobol, D. J. (1980). *Encyclopedia Brown carries on.* New York: Scholastic.

Stewig, J. W. (1978). *Sending messages: The many ways people use to communicate ideas.* Boston: Houghton Mifflin.

———. (1979). Nonverbal communication: 'I *see* what you say.' *Language Arts* 56, 150–155.

———. (1983). *Informal drama in the elementary language arts program.* NY: Teachers College Press.

Thurber, J. (1974). *Many moons.* New York: Harcourt.

Tolkien, J. R. R. (1966). *The hobbit.* NY: Houghton Mifflin.

Wagner, B. J. (1976). *Dorothy Heathcote: Drama as a learning medium.* Washington, DC: National Education Association.

Way, B. (1966). *Development through drama.* New York: Humanities Press.

White, E. B. (1952). *Charlotte's web.* New York: Harper and Row.

IF YOU WANT TO LEARN MORE

Blatt, G. T. & Cunningham, J. (1981). *It's your move: Expressive movement activities for the language arts class.* New York: Teacher's College Press.

Champlin, C. (1980). *Puppetry and creative dramatics.* Austn, TX: Nancy Renfro Studios.

Cox, C. (1985). Filmmaking as a composing process. *Language Arts, 62,* 60–69.

Davies, G. (1983). *Practical primary drama.* Exeter, NH: Heinemann.

Johnson, L. & O'Neill, C. (1984). *Dorothy Heathcote: Collected writings on education and drama.* London: Hutchinson.

Judy, S. and Judy, S. (1982). *Putting on a play: A guide to writing and producing neighborhood drama.* New York: Scribner.

Renfro, N. & Armstrong, B. (1979). *Make amazing puppets.* Santa Barbara, CA: The Learning Works.

Ross, R. R. (1980). *Storyteller* (2nd ed.). Columbus, OH: Merrill.

Stewig, J. W. (1983). *Informal drama in the elementary language arts program.* New York: Teachers College Press.

Straw, C. & Straw, M. (1984). *Mime: Basics for beginners.* Boston: Plays.

Wagner, B. J. (1976). *Dorothy Heathcote: Drama as a learning medium.* Washington, DC: National Education Association.

_____. (1983). The expanding circle of informal classroom drama. In B. A. Busching & J. I. Schwartz, (Eds.). *Integrating the language arts in the elementary school,* pp. 155–163. Urbana, IL: NCTE.

Wiemann, M. O. & Wiemann, J. M. (1975). *Nonverbal communication in the elementary classroom.* Urbana, IL: ERIC Clearinghouse on Reading and Communication Skills and NCTE.

CHAPTER SIX

The Writing Process

OVERVIEW.   *In Chapter 6 we will describe the writing process, an approach that focuses on the process writers use rather than on their finished products. Microcomputers will be discussed as valuable tools for writers who use the process approach. An important component of the writing process for children is their concept of "author," which they develop by publishing their writing for genuine audiences and by learning about authors. Finally, we will discuss five basic ingredients of a process-oriented writing program.*

Most of the writing activities provided for children in the elementary grades have fallen under the rubric of "creative writing." Using this approach, teachers select a creative topic such as, "If I were a leprechaun," write it on the chalkboard, and direct their students to write a story about being a leprechaun. Next they provide students with 30 minutes to write a single-draft story. Then teachers collect the papers to grade. However, they are often disappointed with the results. There are usually three or four papers in which students have written clever and creative stories. These papers are fun to read, and the teachers feel gratified. Next there are two or three students who turn in papers with only several words or a single sentence written. This is not surprising because these students never complete assignments. The teachers' biggest disappointment, however, is in the remaining 20 papers; they are mediocre. These students' compositions include a few descriptive sentences, but overall they lack interesting ideas and cannot be classified as stories.

Unsuccessful experiences with writing often lead teachers to believe that their students cannot write stories. They then decide to return to the workbooks to teach their students the mechanics of written language—capitalization, punctuation, grammar, and spelling—before they attempt writing again, thinking that teaching the mechanical skills will prepare students for writing. Teachers in the past have not learned how to teach writing, only to assign writing and teach spelling, grammar and other mechanical skills.

The problem is not with the students, but with the traditional approach to writing. These students are not learning how to write; they are simply trying to perform their best on a difficult task that has not been explained to them. In this chapter, we will present an alternative approach to teaching writing, the writing process. It is the same process that adult writers use. By using the writing process, students learn how to write, not how to hate writing!

POINTS TO PONDER

What Is the Writing Process?

How Does the Process Approach Differ from the Traditional Approach to Writing?

How Can Students Learn to Revise and Edit Their Writing?

How Can Students Share Their Writing with Genuine Audiences?

THE PROCESS APPROACH*

The traditional approach to writing instruction, often called "creative writing," has been used in elementary schools for the past 20 years and is characterized by the following elements:

> the assignment of a writing topic, often using a story starter or other gimmick
>
> a single-draft composition written in a 30-minute period
>
> emphasis on creative content rather than on writing forms and structural elements
>
> either no emphasis on mechanical skills or the requirement that the composition be error free
>
> either no evaluation of the composition or a teacher's written evaluation of the content and mechanics after the composition is completed

This traditional approach has emphasized the finished product, not what students did while they were writing. Students practiced writing; they did not learn how to write. In recent years, however, the emphasis in writing instruction has shifted from the product of writing to the process involved in creating that product. The teacher's role has shifted from merely evaluating this end product to working with students throughout the writing process.

The *writing process* is a series of stages or activities that writers move through as they compose. These stages have been delineated by such authorities in the field of composition as James Britton (1978), Janet Emig (1971), Donald Graves (1983), and Donald Murray (1984). The names given to the stages vary, but they generally fall into five categories: (a) prewriting, (b) drafting, (c) revising, (d) editing, and (e) sharing. The key features of each stage are presented in Figure 6–1. Labeling and numbering the stages may be misleading, however, since in practice the writing process is not a linear series of neatly packaged categories. Rather, the process is cyclical, involving cycles that recur throughout the stages.

Stage 1: Prewriting

Prewriting is the getting-ready-to-write stage, which has, in the past, been the most neglected step in the writing process. However, prewriting is as crucial to writers as a warm-up is to athletes. Murray (1982) believes that up to 70% of writing time should be spent in prewriting. Prewriting provides the background for writing. At this stage, students learn about the structure of stories, poems, letters, and other written language forms. It is at this stage that students choose topics and generate ideas for writing. For the best work, students should choose their own

---

*Adapted from Tompkins & McKenzie, 1985, pp. 1–6.

Stage 1: Prewriting

Students write on topics based on their own experiences.
Students engage in rehearsal activities before writing.
Students identify the audience to whom they will write.
Students identify the purpose of the writing activity.
Students choose an appropriate form for their compositions based on
    audience and purpose.

Stage 2: Drafting

Students move through successive drafts.
Students emphasize content rather than mechanics.

Stage 3: Revising

Students share their writing in conferences.
Students participate constructively in discussions about classmates'
    writing.
Students make changes in their compositions to reflect the reactions
    and comments of both teacher and classmates.
Between the first and final drafts, students make substantive rather than
    only minor changes.

Stage 4: Editing

Students proofread their own compositions.
Students help proofread classmates' compositions.
Students increasingly identify their own mechanical errors.

Stage 5: Sharing

Students publish their writing in an appropriate form.
Students share their finished writing with an appropriate audience.

Figure 6–1   Key Features of the Writing Process

topics. They also make decisions about their purpose for writing and the audience
to whom the composition will be directed. Good writing grows out of this thor-
ough preparation.

Choosing Topics.   Choosing topics for writing can be a stumbling block for students who have become dependent on teachers to supply their topics for writing.
In the traditional writing approach, teachers supplied topics for writing, suggested
gimmickey story starters and relieved students of the burden of topic selection.
Often these "creative" topics stymied students who were forced to write on topics
they knew little about or were not interested in. Donald Graves (1976) calls this
traditional approach of supplying topics for students "writing welfare." As an al-

Students who use the process approach to writing move back and forth through five stages: prewriting, drafting, revising, editing, and publishing.

ternative, he argues that students need to take responsibility for choosing their own topics for writing.

At first these dependent students will argue that they do not know what to write about. However, teachers can help them brainstorm a list of three or four topics and then choose the one topic they are most interested in and know the most about. Students who feel they cannot generate any writing topics are often surprised that they have so many options available. Then through prewriting activities, students talk, draw pictures, read, and even write to develop their topics.

Asking students to choose their own topics for writing does not mean that teachers should never give writing assignments. Teachers can specify the writing form—journals, stories, poems, reports, and so on—but students should choose their own content. In writing journals, for instance, students should decide if they want to complain about the quality of the food in the cafeteria, write a review of a movie they saw last weekend, or write the next chapter in their adventure story. Similarly, after reading myths and examining their characteristics, teachers may assign students to write myths, but students choose their own characters, setting, and plot to write their own unique stories that embody the characteristics of myths.

Writing Folders. Students need writing folders, manila folders with their names on them, to hold their notes, rough drafts, and completed writings. Graves (1983) suggests stapling a sheet of paper inside the folder so students can list possible topics for future compositions based on their personal experiences, interests, and reading. They update the list with new ideas throughout the school year.

Considering Audience and Purpose.   As they prepare to write, students need to know for whom and why they are writing. Is it primarily for themselves, to express and clarify their own ideas and feelings? Or are they writing for others, to entertain, to inform, or to persuade to a particular course of action? Students need real purposes for writing, and their writing must be shared with genuine audiences. Teachers are only one possible audience. Classmates, younger children, parents, the community, children's authors, and pen pals are also possible audiences. Other audiences are more distant and less well known. For example, students can write letters to NASA or to businesses to request information, or they can submit stories and other pieces of writing for possible publication in literary magazines. These audiences and considerations of purpose will influence the decisions students make throughout the writing process.

Considering the Form of Writing.   One of the most important considerations is the form the writing will take: a story? a letter? a poem? or a diary entry? It is possible that the same writing assignment could be handled in any one of these ways. For example, for a social studies unit on the Roman Empire, students could write a story set in ancient Rome, write a simulated letter from Julius Caesar to Cleopatra, write a poem about a Roman god or goddess, or assume the role of a Roman—a slave, a soldier, a ruler, or a god—and keep a simulated diary for that person.

While these considerations change as students write and revise, writers must begin with at least a tentative concept of audience, purpose, and form as they move into the drafting stage.

The teacher's role in this stage is two-fold: (a) to allow students to participate in decisions about purpose, audience, topic, and form; and (b) to provide a variety of idea-gathering activities. These activities, which Donald Graves (1983) calls "rehearsal," help students prepare for writing. They may take many forms, including brainstorming, drawing, talking, note-taking, clustering, role-playing, and class collaboration compositions. These rehearsal activities are elaborated in the following paragraphs.

Brainstorming.   One good way to generate and collect ideas for writing is *brainstorming,* a way of rapidly listing all the things that come to mind about a particular subject. Students can brainstorm individually, in small groups, or as a class to help them discover what they already know about a topic. Brainstorming encourages the free flow of ideas; all ideas are accepted without criticism or judgment. For example, brainstorming can be used to generate lists of benefits and dangers of nuclear energy, characteristics of folktales, or descriptions of the hardships of traveling west on the Oregon Trail. Brainstorming takes only a few minutes, but after the list is complete, students will have many ideas and words they can use in their writing.

Drawing. For young children drawing is an excellent way to gather and organize their ideas for writing. Primary grade teachers often notice that students draw before they begin to write and, thinking that they are eating their dessert before their meat and vegetables, insist that they write first. But many young children cannot. Drawing is a necessary form of organizing compositions for these young writers (Dyson, 1983).

Talking. Too often the value of talk is ignored in the classroom. Students can talk with their classmates to share ideas about possible writing topics, try out ways to express an idea, and ask questions. Students read and react to each other's writing. They also participate in class discussions about writing forms, elements of story structure, and other writing-related issues. Students continue to talk throughout the writing process as they discuss their compositions in conferences and peer-edit each other's writing.

Note-taking. When students are preparing to write reports, they take notes to remember important pieces of information to include in their reports. Students can also note key words to help them prepare to write in other forms, too. For example, before writing a story, students may want to list four or five characteristics of their main character or to write down the refrain a character will repeat in a repetition story.

Clustering. Another technique that students can use to help them start writing is *clustering* (Rico, 1983). The process is similar to brainstorming except that all the words generated are circled and linked to the nucleus word. The result is a web-like diagram rather than a list. Clustering is designed to capture as many associations as possible in a short amount of time. This strategy, like other prewriting strategies, helps students discover what they already know about a topic. In clustering, the ideas are triggered by associating one idea with another. A middle grade student's cluster about her bedroom is shown in Figure 6–2. The nucleus words for the cluster are *my bedroom.* The student used the ideas she developed in the cluster to write a composition about her bedroom. The composition is also presented in Figure 6–2 to illustrate how a cluster can be used to organize a composition and how the cluster words and phrases are expanded into sentences in the composition.

Reading. Reading and writing are closely linked activities. Children read to get ideas for their writing and to investigate the structure of various written forms. Reading is another form of experience, and writers need a variety of experiences to draw on as they write. Often students will retell a favorite story in writing, write new adventures for favorite story characters, or experiment with a stylistic device used in a book they have read.

Reading informational books also provides the raw material necessary for writing. For example, if students are going to write a story set in Russia, they need background information about the country, its people, and its customs; if they are

Figure 6–2 A Cluster Diagram on "My Bedroom" and the
Composition Written from the Cluster

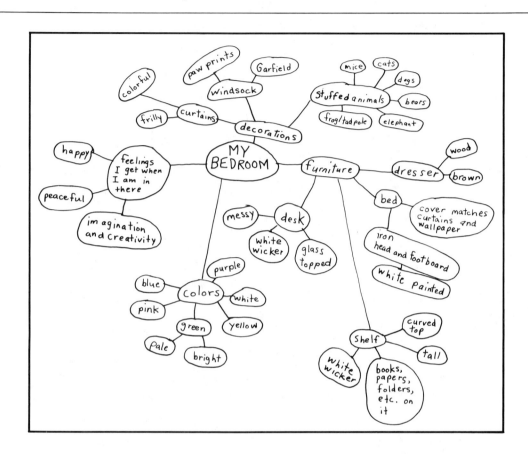

My Bedroom

My bedroom has a variety of different decorations. Among them are my stuffed animals. I have bears, dogs, cats, mice, an elephant, a frog/tadpole, and many others. I also have some colorful and frilly curtains that match my wallpaper and bedcover. Another decoration in my room is a Garfield windsock with pawprints on it. Its colors go very nicely with my bedroom.

Of course, my room also has furniture in it. There is a brown wooden dresser, a bed with a white iron headboard and footboard and a bedcover that matches my wallpaper and curtains, and a tall white wicker shelf with a curved top. The shelf is loaded with books, papers, folders, and other things. I also have a desk which is white wicker, glass-topped, and messy.

My bedroom has lots of colors in it. There are pale and bright greens. There are yellows, pinks, blues, purples, and whites.

When I am in my room, I get happy, peaceful, imaginative, and creative feelings. My room is a fun place for me to be.

Elizabeth, age 11

going to write a report on Albert Einstein, they need to read biographies to gather information about his life.

Role-playing. Through informal drama, children experiment and re-enact events that they might later use in their writing. In Chapter 5, for example, we discussed how role-playing and writing could be integrated with study about the Pilgrims sailing to America on the *Mayflower.* Activities such as role-playing provide the concrete experiences necessary for learning and for writing.

Class Collaboration Compositions. Another prewriting activity is writing a *class collaboration* or group composition. When students write a composition together with the teacher, they have the opportunity to rehearse before writing a similar composition independently. The teacher reviews concepts and clarifies misconceptions as the group composition is written, and students offer ideas for writing as well as suggestions about how to tackle common writing problems. In addition, the teacher models or demonstrates the writing process stages and provides an opportunity for the students to practice the process approach to writing in a supportive environment.

First, the teacher introduces the idea of writing a group composition and reviews the assignment. Students compose the class collaboration composition, moving through drafting, revising, editing, and publishing stages of the writing process. The teacher records students' dictation, noting any misunderstandings students may have about the writing assignment or the writing process. When necessary, the teacher can review concepts and offer suggestions. Students first dictate a rough draft which the teacher records on the chalkboard or on chart paper. Then the teacher and students read the composition and identify ways to revise it. Some parts of the composition will need reworking and other parts may be deleted or moved. More specific words will be substituted for less specific ones and redundant words and sentences will be deleted. Also, students may want to add new parts to the composition. After making the necessary content-related changes, students proofread the composition, checking for capitalization, punctuation, and spelling errors. These errors are corrected, and the teacher or a student copies the completed composition on chart paper or on a sheet of paper. Copies of the composition can be duplicated and given to each student.

Writing class collaboration compositions is an essential part of many writing experiences, especially when students are learning to use the process approach or a new writing form. Group compositions serve as a "dry-run" for independent writing, and students' questions and misconceptions are clarified.

Stage 2: Drafting

In the process approach to writing, students write and refine their compositions through a series of drafts. During the *drafting* stage, students focus on getting their ideas down on paper. Because writers do not begin to write with their compositions already composed in their minds, they usually begin with tentative ideas which they developed through prewriting activities. The rough draft stage is the time to pour out ideas, with little concern about spelling, punctuation, and other mechanical errors. As students move through successive drafts, they delete sections of text, add others, and rearrange them. Students should skip every other line as they write to leave adequate space for making revisions. They can use arrows to move sections of text, cross-outs to delete sections, and scissors and tape to cut apart and rearrange text just as adult authors do. As word processors become more accessible in elementary classrooms, this drafting process, with all its shifting of text, will be made much easier.

As students draft their compositions, they may need to modify their earlier decisions about purpose, audience, and especially the form their writing will take. For example, a composition that began as a story may be transformed into a letter or poem. A new format may allow the student to communicate more effectively. This process of modifying earlier decisions also continues into the revising stage.

During the drafting stage, teachers provide support, encouragement, and feedback for ideas and problems. It is important in this stage not to emphasize correct spelling and neatness. In fact, when teachers point out mechanical errors during the drafting stage, they send a false message to students that mechanical correctness is more important than content (Sommers, 1982). Later, during editing, students can clean up mechanical errors and put their composition into a neat, final form.

Stage 3: Revising

During the *revising* stage, writers refine their ideas. Often student writers break the writing process cycle as soon as they complete a first draft of their compositions, believing that once their ideas are jotted down their writing task is complete. Experienced writers, however, know they must turn to readers for reactions and revise on the basis of these comments. Revision is not just polishing writing; it is meeting the needs of readers through changing, adding, deleting, and rearranging material.

Using Conferences. A good way to obtain readers' reactions is by using *conferences* in which students read their compositions to small groups of classmates, who then respond to them. At first the teacher sits in on these writing conferences to model appropriate behavior. Students need to learn how to react to others' writing in these conferences so that their comments are not destructive. Their first responses must be positive, such as telling what they like best about the piece. Asking the writer questions is often helpful in clarifying ideas and generating new directions. Students may ask the writer questions about parts of the draft that were unclear and about interesting parts that they would like to see developed more fully. Some questions that students may ask the writer are presented in Figure 6–3. Writers may ask questions too. In this way they can check how well they are communicating and get help with particularly troublesome passages. Often these conferences conclude with the writer explaining what he or she plans to do next with the composition.

Figure 6–3   Questions to Ask Writers During Conferences

What is your favorite part?

What problems are you having?

Which part are you having trouble with?

How do you feel about this piece of writing?

Does your writing end abruptly? Does it need a closing?

Do you show feelings or events with specific examples or do you only tell about them?

Does your lead sentence "grab" your audience?

Do your paragraphs seem to be in the right order?

Is each paragraph on one topic?

Can you leave out parts that repeat or that fail to give details about your subject?

Can you combine some sentences?

Can you use precise verbs such as *sprinted* instead of *ran quickly* in places?

What do you plan to do next with this piece of writing?

Adapted from Russell (1983, p. 335).

Writers use the reactions they receive in these conferences to improve their work, to make it clearer and more interesting. Some students repeat the conference-revision cycle several times before they are satisfied with their work, while others move on more quickly to the next stage. However, it is always the students themselves who should decide which suggestions to accept and incorporate into their writing and when to move to the next stage.

The teacher is a reader and reactor just as students are, responding, as Sommers suggests, "as any reader would, registering questions, reflecting befuddlement, and noting places where we are puzzled about the meaning" (1982, p. 155). It is at this conference-revision stage, rather than at the end of the process, that teachers should offer suggestions for improvement. At this point students still have the opportunity to benefit from the suggestions and incorporate changes.

Other Types of Conferences.   There are other types of writing conferences as well as the small-group revising conference. Anytime a student meets with the teacher or a classmate about a piece of writing, the interaction is called a *conference* (Graves, 1983). Often these conferences last only a minute or two, but they help a writer solve a problem or make a decision in order to continue writing. Sometimes, too, the teacher will hold a conference with the entire class. These

Two students share their compositions, ask questions, and offer suggestions on ways to revise the pieces.

conferences occur throughout the writing process. During the prewriting stage, for instance, a student might have a conference with a teacher about which of several possible topics to develop in a composition. The teacher might ask the student to talk a little or to brainstorm five key words about each topic under consideration. Quickly, one topic will emerge as the most promising. Usually the teacher and other students in a conference serve as a sounding board, helping the writer make his or her own decisions. The range of possible types of writing conferences is listed in Figure 6–4.

Stage 4: Editing

Editing is putting the piece of writing into its final form. Until this stage, the focus has been on the content of students' writing. In this stage, the focus changes from content to form, and students polish their writing by rearranging words and correcting spelling, punctuation, and other mechanical errors. The goal here is to make the writing "optimally readable" (Smith, 1982).

The Mechanics of Writing. *Mechanics* are the conventions used to make writing "optimally readable." They include capitalization, punctuation, spelling, usage, and formatting considerations specific to the presentation of poetic forms, scripts, and letters. The use of commonly accepted conventions is a courtesy to those who will read the composition.

As soon as young children begin to write, they learn to capitalize the first letter of their names and the word *I*. They also learn to capitalize the first word in a sentence and other important words. During the elementary grades, students learn the additional functions of capital letters. These functions are listed in Figure 6–5. Interestingly, the most common problem associated with capitalization is students' tendency to capitalize too many words!

Punctuation marks serve as signals to help readers interpret the flow of written words, and as soon as students begin to write, they use these signals. Writers need to know the functions of these signals and to use them correctly. Students are typically introduced to nine punctuation marks during the elementary grades: the period, quotation marks, exclamation point, question mark, apostrophe, comma, colon, parentheses, and hyphen. The functions that students learn for each punctuation mark are listed in Figure 6–6.

The most effective way to teach these mechanical skills is during the editing stage of the writing process rather than through workbook exercises. When editing a composition that will be shared with a genuine audience, students are more interested in using capitalization and punctuation skills correctly so that they can communicate effectively. In a study of 2 third-grade classes, Calkins (1980) found that the students in the class who learned punctuation marks as a part of editing their writing could define or explain many more marks than the students in the other class who were taught punctuation skills in a traditional manner with instruction and practice exercises on each punctuation mark. In other words, the results of this research as well as other studies (Elley, 1976; Bissex, 1980; Graves,

Proper nouns including names of people, days of
    week, months of year, and geographic names

Pronoun *I*

First word in a sentence

Titles such as *Mr., Mrs., Miss, Ms., Dr.*

Abbreviations

Initials

Important words in titles of compositions

First word of a greeting and closing of a letter

Commerical trade names

First word in a direct quotation

Figure 6–5   Functions of Capital Letters

1. *On-the-Spot Conferences*

   The teacher visits briefly with a student at his or her desk to monitor some aspect of the writing assignment or to see how the student is progressing. The teacher begins by asking the student to read what he or she has written and then asks a question or two about the writing. Usually the teacher has several questions in mind before having the conference with the student. These conferences are brief; the teacher spends less than a minute at a student's desk before moving away.

2. *Drafting Conferences*

   Students bring their rough drafts and meet with the teacher at a table set up in the classroom specifically for that purpose. Students bring to the conference examples of specific writing problems that they would like to talk to the teacher about. These short, individual conferences often last less than 5 minutes so it is possible for a teacher to meet with 8 to 10 students in 30 minutes. Often students sign up for these conferences in advance.

3. *Revising Conferences*

   A small group of students and the teacher meet together in writing group conferences. Students read what they have written and ask for specific suggestions from classmates and the teacher about how to revise their compositions. These conferences offer student writers an audience to provide feedback on how well they have communicated. These small-group conferences last approximately 30 minutes or as long as necessary for each student to share his or her writing. Many elementary teachers schedule these conferences periodically in place of reading groups. After all, the purpose of reading and writing groups is virtually the same: to read and react to a piece of writing.

4. *Editing Conferences*

   Students meet with the teacher for an editing conference. In these individual or small-group conferences, the teacher reviews students' proofread compositions and helps them to correct spelling, punctuation, capitalization, and other mechanical errors. The teacher takes notes during these conferences about the problems students are having with mechanical skills in order to plan individual, special instruction conferences.

5. *Instructional Conferences*

   Ten- to fifteen-minute conferences are scheduled with individual students to provide special instruction. Teachers prepare for these conferences by reviewing students' writing folders and by planning instruction on one or two skills (e.g., capitalizing proper nouns, using commas in a series) that are particularly troublesome for individual students.

6. *Conferences with Classmates*

   Students meet with one or two classmates to ask for advice, to share a piece of writing, or to proofread a composition in much the same way that they hold a conference with the teacher. In these student conferences, students are expected to maintain a helpful and supportive relationship with their classmates.

7. *Class Conferences*

   Conferences with the entire class are held periodically to write and revise class collaboration compositions, to practice new conferencing strategies, and to discuss concerns relating to all students. Sometimes, these conferences are planned, and at other times they occur spontaneously as the need arises.

Figure 6–4 Types of Writing Conferences

Period

at the end of a sentence
after abbreviations
after numbers in a list
after an initial

Question Mark

at the end of a question

Exclamation Mark

after words or sentences showing excitement or
strong feeling

Quotation Marks

before and after direct quotations
around the title of a poem, short story,
song, or
television program

Apostrophe

in contractions
to show possession

Comma

to separate words in a series
between day and year
between city and state
after the greeting in a friendly letter
after the closing of a letter
after an initial yes or no
after a noun of direct address
to separate a quote from the speaker
before the conjunction in a compound
sentence
after a dependent clause at the beginning
of a sentence

Colon

before a list
in writing time
after the greeting of a business letter
after an actor's name in a script

Parentheses

to enclose unimportant information
to enclose stage directions in a script

Hyphen

between parts of a compound number
to divide a word at the end of a line
between parts of some compound words

Figure 6–6   Functions of Punctuation Marks

1983) suggest that a functional approach to teaching the mechanics of writing is
more effective than direct instruction.

Proofreading.   Students begin editing each composition by proofreading and
marking possible errors. Next, they seek help from another student, and finally
they have a conference with the teacher. Proofreading requires special reading
skills. King (1985) points out that proofreading is not the same as regular reading
because "reading is taking meaning from the printed page—not words" (p. 109).
In contrast, proofreading requires word-by-word reading and attention to form—
letters, spelling, capital letters, and punctuation marks—rather than to meaning.
It is important, therefore, to take time to explain what proofreading is and to dem-

onstrate how it differs from regular reading. Teachers can take a piece of student writing and copy it on the chalkboard or display it on an overhead projector. Then they read it through slowly, softly pronouncing each word, circling possible misspellings, and marking other mechanical errors. Some errors can be corrected with special proofreader's marks. Students enjoy using these marks, the same ones that adult authors use. A list of proofreader's marks that elementary students can learn to use in editing their writing is presented in Figure 6–7.

Editing checklists can also be used to help students focus on particular categories of error in their compositions. Teachers can develop these checklists with items appropriate for their grade level. A first-grade checklist, for example, might include items about capital letters at the beginning of sentences and periods at the end of sentences. In contrast, a middle grade checklist might include items about paragraph indentation and spelling homonyms correctly. During the school year, teachers often need to revise their checklists to focus attention on skills that have recently been taught. An example of an editing checklist for third graders is illustrated in Figure 6–8. In this checklist, the author signs that he or she has completed the checklist, and a classmate who serves as "editor" also completes the checklist and signs his or her name.

Proofreader's marks and editing checklists are two tools for helping students learn to locate and correct the mechanical errors in their compositions. A page

Function	*Mark*	*Example*
Delete	ℓ	The boy was at ~~in~~ home.
Insert	∧	The weather today ∧ cold and windy. (is)
Indent paragraph	⌗	⌗Spiders are not insects. They are arachnids.
Capitalize	≡	I was born in dallas, Texas.
Add period	⊙	The princess lived in a castle high in the mountains⊙
Add comma	⋏	I have two cats⋏a dog and a parakeet.
Add apostrophe	⩒	My brothers name is Bill.

Figure 6–7   Proofreader's Marks

Editing Checklist

Author   *Editor*

☐ ☐ 1. I have circled the words that might be misspelled.

☐ ☐ 2. I have checked the spelling of each homonym. (*to-two-too   there-their-they're   its-it's   where-wear*)

☐ ☐ 3. I have checked that all sentences begin with capital letters.

☐ ☐ 4. I have checked that all sentences end with punctuation marks.

☐ ☐ 5. I have checked that all proper nouns begin with a capital letter.

☐ ☐ 6. I have checked that paragraphs are indented.

Signatures:

*Author:*_____   *Editor:*_____

Figure 6–8   A Third Grade Editing Checklist

from a 10-year-old's edited composition is shown in Figure 6–9 to illustrate how students can learn to use proofreader's marks to make corrections.

It is unrealistic to expect students to locate and correct every mechanical error in their compositions. Many teachers find it more practical to focus on particular categories of error in each composition. They can quickly review a particular problem area such as quotation marks with a student and help that student make

Figure 6–9 A Page from a 10-year-old's Edited Manuscript

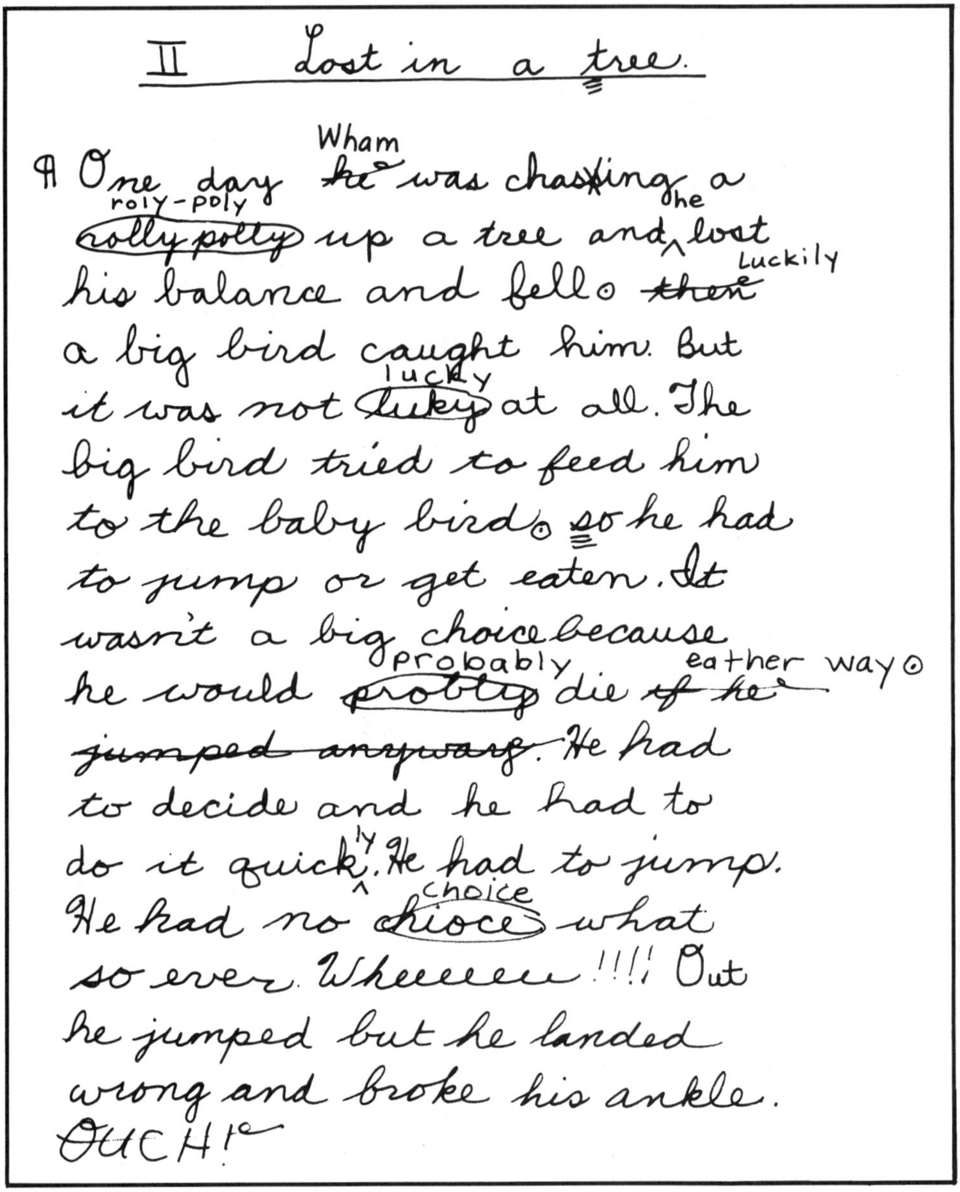
II Lost in a tree.

¶ One day ~~he~~ Wham was cha~~s~~ing a
~~rolly polly~~ roly-poly up a tree and he lost
his balance and fell. ~~then~~ Luckily
a big bird caught him. But
it was not ~~luky~~ lucky at all. The
big bird tried to feed him
to the baby birds. so he had
to jump or get eaten. It
wasn't a big choice because
he would ~~probly~~ probably die ~~if he~~ eather way.
~~jumped anyway~~. He had
to decide and he had to
do it quickly. He had to jump.
He had no ~~chioce~~ choice what
so ever. Wheeeeee!!!! Out
he jumped but he landed
wrong and broke his ankle.
OUCH!

Kristin, age 10

the necessary corrections. Using this procedure, teachers individualize instruction, and throughout the school year, review the mechanical skills that each student needs. When mechanical correctness is crucial in a composition, teachers use simple check marks in the margin to note any remaining errors or problems, so that students can complete the correcting.

Stage 5: Sharing

In this final stage, *sharing,* students bring the composition to life by publishing their writing or sharing it orally with an appropriate audience. Students read their writing to classmates, or share it with larger audiences through hardcover books that are placed in the class or school library, class anthologies, letters, newspapers, plays, or puppet shows. In each of these cases, students are communicating with a genuine audience. Again and again researchers report that although teachers are the most common audience for student writing, they are one of the worst audiences because they often read with a red pen in their hands (Lundsteen, 1976).

As students share their writing with genuine audiences, they develop a greater appreciation of audience and its role in the writing process (Hubbard, 1985). Publishing their writing in small hardbound books is one way that children develop a concept of "author." By copying their stories and other compositions in book form, students identify with adult authors who have their compositions published in books.

Bookmaking.   One of the most popular ways to share students' writing in the elementary grades is by making and binding books. Simple booklets can be made by folding a sheet of paper into quarters, like a greeting card. Students write the title on the front and have three sides remaining for their compositions. They can also construct books by stapling sheets of writing paper together and adding a construction paper cover. Sheets of wallpaper cut from old sample books also make good, sturdy covers. These stapled books can be cut into various shapes, too. Students can make more sophisticated hardcover books by covering cardboard covers with contact paper, wallpaper samples, or cloth. Pages are either sewn or stapled together, and the first and last pages are glued to the cardboard covers to hold the book together. The directions for making one type of hardcover book are outlined in Figure 6–10.

Magazines for Student Writing.   Students can also submit their stories, poems, and other pieces of writing to magazines that publish children's writing. Some magazines also accept artwork accompanying the compositions. A list of these magazines is presented in Figure 6–11 (pages 182–183). Students should check a recent issue of the magazine or write to the editor of the magazine for a complete set of guidelines before submitting compositions.

Responding to Student Writing.   The teacher's role should not be restricted to that of evaluator. Instead, teachers should read students' writing for information, for enjoyment, and for all of the other purposes that other readers do. Indeed, much of students' writing should never by evaluated, but should simply be shared with the teacher as a "trusted adult" (Martin, D'Arcy, Newton, & Parker, 1976). When evaluation is necessary, teachers might ask students to choose several pieces from their writing folders that they wish to submit for grading.

To measure students' growth in writing, it is not always necessary to evaluate their finished products (Tway, 1980). Teachers can make judgments about students' progress in other ways. One of the best ways is by observing students as

Figure 6–10   Directions for Making Hardcover Books

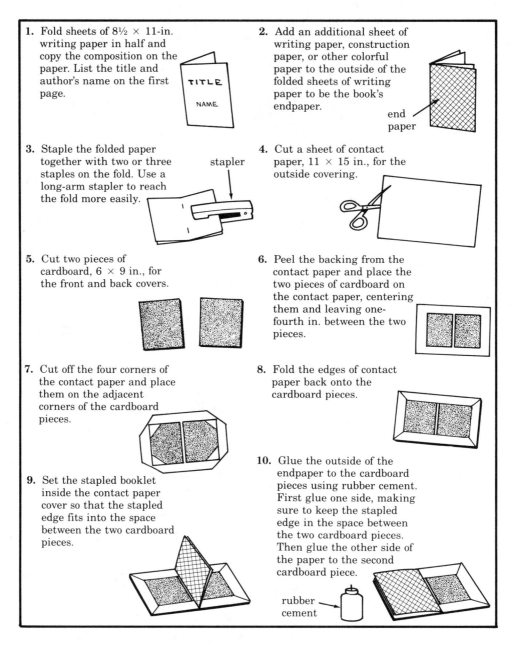

1. Fold sheets of 8½ × 11-in. writing paper in half and copy the composition on the paper. List the title and author's name on the first page.

2. Add an additional sheet of writing paper, construction paper, or other colorful paper to the outside of the folded sheets of writing paper to be the book's endpaper.

3. Staple the folded paper together with two or three staples on the fold. Use a long-arm stapler to reach the fold more easily.

4. Cut a sheet of contact paper, 11 × 15 in., for the outside covering.

5. Cut two pieces of cardboard, 6 × 9 in., for the front and back covers.

6. Peel the backing from the contact paper and place the two pieces of cardboard on the contact paper, centering them and leaving one-fourth in. between the two pieces.

7. Cut off the four corners of the contact paper and place them on the adjacent corners of the cardboard pieces.

8. Fold the edges of contact paper back onto the cardboard pieces.

9. Set the stapled booklet inside the contact paper cover so that the stapled edge fits into the space between the two cardboard pieces.

10. Glue the outside of the endpaper to the cardboard pieces using rubber cement. First glue one side, making sure to keep the stapled edge in the space between the two cardboard pieces. Then glue the other side of the paper to the second cardboard piece.

they write, noting whether or not they engage in prewriting activities, whether or not they focus on content rather than mechanics in their rough drafts, and whether or not they participate in revision conferences. The key features of each stage of the writing process presented in Figure 6–1 can be changed into questions to use as a checklist in evaluating students' progress in using the process approach

(McKenzie & Tompkins, 1984). Copies of the writing process checklist presented in Figure 6–12 (pages 184–185) can be attached to students' writing folders and then used to measure students' growth in using the process approach.

When teachers evaluate students' progress in using the process approach, they chart students' development and use this information in determining students' grades and the quality of their written products. Learning to use the writing process is of far greater importance to students' future writing achievement than the quality of a particular composition.

To illustrate how the writing process can be used when students write stories, poems, and other types of writing, we have outlined how the five stages of the process are involved in four different types of writing assignments. The analysis is presented in Figure 6–13 (pages 186–187).

Teachers must realize that the writing process is merely a tool and, like all tools, must be adapted to individual situations and writers. Not all writing needs to go through all the stages. For example, sometimes a piece such as a journal entry is abandoned after the drafting stage, or students may pay less attention to editing when they plan to share their compositions orally.

However, teachers will want to impress upon students the usefulness of the writing process approach. Students need to be taken through the entire process again and again until it becomes second nature to them. For this tool becomes most effective when students own it, when they become so familiar with the writing process that they can manipulate it to meet the differing demands of particular writing assignments and modify it to accommodate their unique style and habit of writing.

POINTS TO PONDER
Why Is the Word Processor a Valuable Writing Tool?
How Do Students Use Word Processing in the Elementary Classroom?
How Does Word Processing Facilitate the Writing Process?

COMPUTERS AND WRITING*

Word processing is one of the most important classroom applications for microcomputers. Computers have been found to be a valuable tool for student writers (Daiute, 1985; Engberg, 1983; Newman, 1984). Teachers and researchers have found that students write more and that their writing and their attitude toward writing is improved when they compose on computers. Several reasons for these improvements seem obvious. First of all, it is fun to use computers. They allow students to experiment with language, thus reducing their fear of making errors. In addition, computers allow students to revise and refine their writing without the chore of having to recopy the final draft.

---

*Adapted from Smith & Tompkins, unpublished ms., 1983.

Magazine	Ages	Types of Writing Accepted
American Girl 830 Third Avenue New York, NY 10022	12–14	Short stories, poems, and letters to the editor
Boys' Life 1325 Walnut Hill Lane Irving, TX 75062	all	Real-life stories
Children's Digest P.O. Box 567 Indianapolis, IN 46206	8–10	Poetry, short stories, riddles, and jokes
The Children's Album P.O. Box 262 Manchester, CA 95459	all	Short stories, poems, and nonfiction
Child Life P.O. Box 567 Indianapolis, IN 46206	7–9	Short stories, poetry, riddles, jokes, and letters to the editor
Cricket 1058 8th Street LaSalle, IL 61301	6–12	Letters and Cricket League monthly; short story and poetry contests
Ebony Jr! 820 S. Michigan Ave. Chicago, IL 60605	all	Essays, short stories, poems, jokes, riddles, and cartoons
Highlights for Children 803 Church Street Honesdale, PA 18431	5–10	Poetry, short stories, jokes, riddles, and letters to the editor
Jack and Jill P.O. Box 567 Indianapolis, IN 46206	5–10	Short stories, poems, riddles, and letters to the editor

Figure 6–11   Magazines that Publish Children's Writing

What Is Word Processing?

Word processing is a method of producing written compositions using a computer to facilitate revising and formatting the text. Using a computer for word processing is much like using an electric typewriter: writers plan their compositions, sit at a keyboard and type in words, and then revise and edit their work. Instead of seeing their words appear on a piece of paper, writers using computers see their words appear on a video screen. Computers have several capabilities that make

Magazine	Ages	Types of Writing Accepted
Kids Magazine P.O. Box 3041 Grand Central Station New York, NY 10017	all	Short stories, reports, poems, cartoons, puzzles, and most other forms of writing
The McGuffey Writer 400A McGuffey Hall Miami University Oxford, OH 45056	all	Poetry, short stories, essays, and cartoons
Merlyn's Pen P.O. Box 716 East Greenwich, RI 02818	12–14	Essays, poems, and short stories
Scholastic Voice 50 West 44th Street New York, NY 10036	13–14	Short stories and poems; also writing contests
Stone Soup Children's Art Foundation P.O. Box 83 Santa Cruz, CA 95063	all	Poetry, short stories, and book reports (books to be reviewed are provided by the magazine)
Wombat 365 Ashton Drive Athens, GA 30606	all	Short stories, poems, essays, puzzles, cartoons, and book reports
Young World P.O. Box 567 Indianapolis, IN 46206	10–14	Poetry, short stories, jokes, and letters to the editor

Figure 6–11 *Continued*

the tasks of formatting, revising, and editing mechanically easier. Five of these capabilities are described in the following paragraphs.

1. *Typeover.* Word processing programs allow writers to back up and type over mistakes when typing their compositions. This process is like using a self-correcting electric typewriter. Undesired letters are simply replaced by the new letters typed during the correcting.

Figure 6–12 A Writing Process Checklist

Student: _____	Dates									
Prewriting										
Can the student identify the specific audience to whom he/she will write?										
Does this awareness affect the choices the student makes as he/she writes?										
Can the student identify the purpose of the writing activity?										
Does the student write on a topic that grows out of his/her own experience?										
Does the student engage in rehearsal activities before writing?										
Drafting										
Does the student write rough drafts?										
Does the student place a greater emphasis on content than on mechanics in the rough drafts?										
Revising										
Does the student share his/her writing in conferences?										

Does the student participate in discussions about classmates' writing?							
In revising, does the student make changes to reflect the reactions and comments of both teacher and classmates?							
Between first and final drafts, does the student make substantive or only minor changes?							

Editing

Does the student proofread his/her own papers?							
Does the student help proofread classmates' papers?							
Does the student increasingly identify his/her mechanical errors?							

Publishing

Does the student publish his/her writing in an appropriate form?							
Does the student share this finished writing with an appropriate audience?							

McKenzie & Tompkins, 1984, p. 211.

	Write a story (using repetition)	Write a report (in social studies)	Write a limerick (poem)	Write a business letter (to request free materials)
Stage 1 Prewriting	1. Read stories using the repetition device. 2. Analyze the use of repetition in the stories. 3. Develop a "story rule" about repetition. 4. Write a story using repetition together as a class.	1. Choose a topic and collect reference materials. 2. Take notes on a data chart or on notecards. 3. Review and sequence the notes.	1. Explain the structured form of a limerick. 2. Read examples of limericks composed by Edward Lear and others. 3. Write a limerick together as a class.	1. Review the form of a business letter. 2. Brainstorm a list of the pieces of information to include in the letter.
Stage 2 Drafting	5. Write a rough draft of a story using the repetition device.	4. Write a rough draft of the report.	4. Write a limerick individually or in small groups.	3. Write a rough draft of the letter.
Stage 3 Revising	6. Share the rough draft in a conference with classmates.	5. Read the draft to a small group of classmates in a conference.	5. Share the rough draft in a conference. Ask classmates to	4. Have a conference with classmates to check how well the letter communicates

	Story	Report	Poem	Letter
	7. Make revisions based on classmates' suggestions.	6. Make revisions based on classmates' suggestions.	comment on both the content and rhyme schemes. 6. Make revisions based on classmates' comments.	and that all necessary information has been included. 5. Make revisions according to classmates' suggestions.
Stage 4 Editing	8. Proofread with a classmate and the teacher to correct mechanical errors.	7. Proofread with a classmate and the teacher to correct mechanical errors. 8. Add a bibliography.	7. Proofread with a classmate and the teacher to correct mechanical errors and check the line arrangement.	6. Proofread with a classmate and the teacher to correct mechanical errors and letter forms.
Stage 5 Sharing	9. Recopy the story and share with classmates. 10. Alternative: Make stick puppets to use in sharing the story in a puppet show.	9. Construct a hardbound book. 10. Recopy the report in the book. 11. Add the book to the school library.	8. Recopy the limerick. 9. Compile poems to form a class book. 10. Add the book to the class library.	7. Recopy the letter and address the envelope. 8. Mail the letter.

Figure 6–13 An Analysis of Four Writing Activities

2. *Insert and delete.* Word processing programs allow writers to insert or delete letters, words, sentences, and paragraphs within the body of the text. These changes require only a few keystrokes. The remainder of the text automatically adjusts to the changes by shifting lines up, down, or over.

3. *Block move.* The block function allows writers to define a block of text and move it from one location in the text to another. The more sophisticated the program, the larger the amount of text that can be moved in this manner. Usually the program allows writers to move this block of text back to its original location if they regret their move. Some word processing programs even allow writers to leave the text in its current location and move a copy of the block of text or portions of text to another location.

4. *Search and replace.* Sometimes authors wish to locate every occurrence of a certain word within the text and to replace it with a more appropriate word. For example, writers who find that a word has been consistently misspelled throughout the composition can use the search and replace function to correct the misspelling. Most word processing programs have an option that allows writers to specify a particular word to be searched for throughout the composition and to identify a word or phrase to replace it.

5. *Dictionary programs.* Many dictionary programs are available for use with some word processing programs. After students have completed a piece of writing, a dictionary program can be used to search through the composition for misspelled words. Thesaurus programs are also available that allow students to highlight specific words in their compositions and request the computer to supply synonyms.

Using Word Processing with Elementary Students

The first step in using computers for word processing in the elementary classroom is to introduce students to the computer using the tutorial lessons that accompany most word processing programs. Have students work through the tutorial lesson in groups of two or three. Then have them summarize what they have learned by making word processing reference charts that include (a) general directions on operating the word processing program (e.g., how to access a file, save a file, and print out a hard copy) and (b) a list of commands (e.g., insert, delete, move, search, and replace) and key strokes that allow students to execute these commands. Students can use these charts for quick reference as they work at the computers.

It is a good idea for the teacher to complete the first writing assignment with the students as a large-group collaboration so that all students can review the word processing procedures. A large screen is especially useful for class collaborations and group teaching sessions but a regular monitor can be used. The next several writing assignments should be short, generally no longer than a paragraph or two. In this way, students can concentrate on working through the word processing procedure rather than having to focus on the demands of the writing assignments as well as the demands of learning to use the computer.

Electronic Mail.   Students can use the word processor to write notes and letters to classmates and pen pals. They write these letters on the computer, revise and edit them, and then transmit them using a modem hooked up to the computer. The *QUILL* (1983) word processing program, for instance, includes a Mailbag for exchanging messages.

Word Processing with Young Children.   Computers with word processing programs can be used very effectively to record young children's language experience stories (Barber, 1982; Smith, 1985). Teachers take children's dictation as they do in traditional language experience activities but using a computer rather than paper and pencil. After entering the child's dictation, the child and the teacher read the text using assisted reading and make any needed additions, deletions, or substitutions. Next the text is printed out and the child can add a drawing. If the child has already drawn a picture, the print-out can be cut and taped onto the drawing. The computer simplifies the process of taking children's dictation because teachers can record dictation more quickly than they can write, the dictation can be revised easily, and a clean copy of the revised story can be printed out.

While teachers can use computers to record language experience stories for children, even young children can learn to use computers for word processing themselves. Daiute (1985) reports that children as young as 6-years-old can learn the positions of the keys on the keyboard and learn to type. They can also use a graphic tablet (a device that attaches to the computer) to draw and handwrite letters and words directly onto the monitor screen.

In first and second grade, students can write their own compositions on the word processor. For a very interesting report of first graders writing on a computer, check Phenix and Hannan's article, "Word processing in the grade one classroom" (1984). They found that their first graders wrote and revised a variety of compositions on computers and "learned that writing does not have to come out right the first time, that it can be manipulated by the author, that a writer has to take risks, that revising is a normal way writing is done" (p. 812). These are the same process approach generalizations that teachers work toward at all grade levels.

Computers and the Writing Process

In the process approach to writing, students write by developing and refining their compositions. The word processor is a valuable tool in each of the five stages of the writing process. In prewriting, students use a computer to take notes, to freewrite, to brainstorm, and for other rehearsal activities. As students pour out and shape their ideas in the drafting stage, the computer is a more efficient tool than pen and paper. Students who have good typing skills can input text more quickly than they can write by hand, and they make changes in the text more easily. Even students who have not learned to type very well prefer to write using the word processor (Kane, 1983).

In the revising stage, students print out copies of their rough drafts to use in conferences. After reading and discussing their compositions during a conference, they return to the computer to make substantive revisions that reflect the reactions and suggestions received in the conference. Word processing allows students to make revisions easily, without the work of cutting and pasting changes in their rough drafts.

Computers are especially useful during editing when students work to correct mechanical errors in their compositions. Students have "clean" texts to proofread, whether they read them on the monitor screen or on printed copies. After proofreading and editing, students return again to the computer to make their corrections quickly and easily.

After students have completed all corrections, they decide about formatting their compositions (e.g., margins, types of print, spacing) and print out the final copy to share with an audience. Using word processing relieves students from the tedium of recopying their final copies by hand. The professional-looking final copies often boost students' feelings of accomplishment, especially students with poor handwriting skills.

Typically, two or three students work together in a buddy system, taking turns using each computer. While this system is often necessitated by the small number of computers available for student use, there is an added benefit. Students working together are more inclined to collaborate with each other. They provide support, assistance, and feedback to each other as they compose.

Many teachers have expressed the hope that computers will encourage students to use a process approach and write and revise a series of drafts. However, Kane (1983) found that students in her study composed the same way on the computer that they composed with pen and paper. In other words, students who normally write single-draft papers or who limit revisions to making minor changes are likely to continue to do so. This finding reinforces the idea that the computer is only a tool and that good teaching is required for students to learn to write well.

POINTS TO PONDER

Why Should Students View Themselves as Authors?

How Can Students Learn About Authors and Illustrators of Children's Books?

How Can You Arrange a Young Authors' Conference in Your School?

CONCEPT OF AUTHOR

Most of the time children assume the role of "student" in school. However, children take more interest in a subject and learn more about it when they can assume a more active role in learning. Our aim in teaching language arts is to provide opportunities for students to assume real-life roles. And, for writing, that real-life role is "author." Authors write for real purposes and for genuine audiences. Students, in contrast, often write so the teacher will have something to grade. Explaining to students that the writing process they are learning is the same one that authors use is one step in the right direction. In this section, we will discuss other ways to help children move from the "student" role to the "author" role.

Becoming an Author

One way to help students develop the concept of author is by using an "author's chair" (Graves & Hansen, 1983). In a first-grade classroom they visited, one chair was designated as the author's chair. Whenever someone—either the teacher or a child—read a book, he or she sat in that special chair. At the beginning of first grade, most of the books read from that chair were picture books written by authors of children's books such as Dr. Seuss. However, as children began to write and construct their own books, they would sit in that special chair to share the books they had written. Through sitting in the special author's chair and sharing their books, children realized that they had become authors! Graves and Hansen describe children's transition from "student" to "author" in three steps:

1. *Replication: Authors write books.* As children listen to books written by adult authors shared from the author's chair, they develop the concept that authors are the people who write books.

2. *Transition: I am an author.* Children come to see themselves as authors as they write their own books and share them with classmates from the author's chair.

3. *Option-Awareness: If I wrote this published book now, I wouldn't write it this way.* Through additional experience reading and writing stories, children learn that they have options when they write. This awareness grows as they experiment with various writing forms.

In a classroom where reading, writing, and sharing writing are valued activities, students become authors. Often they recopy a story or other piece of writing into a stapled booklet or hardcover book. These published books can be added to the classroom or the school library. Sometimes students want to form a classroom publishing company and add the name of the publishing company and the year the book was made on the title page. In addition, students can add "About the Author" information and even a photograph at the end of their books just as information about the author is often included on the jackets of books written by adult authors.

Learning About Authors

Another way to help students develop the concept of "author" is by learning about favorite authors and the artists who illustrate these books. Students can learn about authors and illustrators in several different ways.

First, students can read about authors and illustrators. A number of biographies and autobiographies of well-known authors and illustrators including Beatrix Potter (Aldis, 1969), Jean Fritz (1982), and Margot Zemach (1978) are available for elementary students. Students can also read profiles of favorite authors in books such as Lee Bennett Hopkins' *Books are by people* (1969) and *More books are by people* (1974). Increasingly, filmstrips, videotapes, and other audio-visual materials about authors and illustrators are becoming available. A list of books and audio-visual materials about authors and illustrators is presented in Figure 6–14. In addition, students can read journal articles to learn about favorite writers. Many ar-

Books

Aldis, D. (1969). *Nothing is impossible: The story of Beatrix Potter.* New York: Atheneum. (M)

Blegvad. E. (1979). *Self-portrait: Erik Blegvad.* Reading, MA: Addison-Wesley. (P–M–U)

Boston, L. M. (1979). *Perverse and foolish: A memoir of childhood and youth.* New York: Atheneum. (U)

Dahl, R. (1984). *Boy: Tales of childhood.* New York: Farrar. (M–U)

Duncan, L. (1982). *Chapters: My growth as a writer.* Boston: Little, Brown. (U)

Fritz, J. (1982). *Homesick: My own story.* New York: Putman. (M–U)

Godall, J. S. (1981). *Before the war, 1908–1939. An autobiography in pictures.* New York: Atheneum. (wordless picture book) (M–U)

Henry, M. (1980). *The illustrated Marguerite Henry.* Chicago: Rand McNally. (M–U)

Lewis, C. S. (1985). *Letters to children.* New York: Macmillan. (M–U)

Hyman, T. S. (1981). *Self-portrait: Trina Schart Hyman.* Reading, MA: Addison-Wesley. (P–M–U)

Naylor, P. R. (1978). *How I came to be a writer.* New York: Atheneum. (U)

Singer, I. B. (1969). *A day of pleasure: Stories of a boy growing up in Warsaw.* New York: Farrar. (U)

Yates, E. (1981). *My diary—My world.* New York: Westminister. (M–U)

Zemach, M. (1978). *Self-portrait: Margot Zemach.* Reading, MA: Addison-Wesley. (P–M–U)

Collections of Profile Articles

Commire, A. (1971–1985). *Something about the author* (38 volumes). Chicago: Gale Research. (M–U)

Hoffman, M., & Samuels, E. (Eds.). (1972). *Authors and illustrators of children's books.* New York: Bowker. (M–U)

Hopkins, L. B. (1969). *Books are by people: Interviews with 104 authors and illustrators of books for young children.* New York: Citation. (M–U)

———. (1974). *More books by more people: Interviews with 65 authors of books for children.* New York: Citation. (M–U)

Jones, C., & Way, O. R. (1976). *British children's authors: Interviews at home.* Chicago: American Library Association. (M–U)

Weiss, M. J. (Ed.). (1979). *From writers to students: The pleasures and pains of writing.* Newark, DE: International Reading Association. (U)

Wintle, J. & Fischer, E. (1975). *The pied pipers: Interviews with the influential creators of children's literature.* London: Paddington Press. (M–U)

Audio-visual Materials

"Bill Peet in his studio," Houghton Mifflin (videotape).

"The case of a Model-A Ford and the man in the snorkel under the hood: Donald J. Sobol," Random House (sound filmstrip).

Figure 6–14   Books and Audiovisual Materials About Children's Authors and Illustrators

Audio-visual Materials *(Continued)*

"Charlotte Zolotow: The grower," Random House (sound filmstrip).

"David Macaulay in his studio," Houghton Mifflin (videotape).

"Edward Ardizzone," Weston Woods (film).

"Ezra Jack Keats," Weston Woods (film).

"First choice: Authors and books," set of nine sound filmstrips from Pied Piper featuring Judy Blume, Clyde Bulla, Beverly Cleary, John D. Fitzgerald, Sid Fleischman, Virginia Hamilton, Marguerite Henry, E. L. Konigsburg, and Theodore Taylor.

"First choice: Poets and poetry," set of five sound filmstrips from Pied Piper featuring Nikki Giovanni, Karla Kuskin, Myra Cohn Livingston, David McCord, and Eve Merriam.

"Gail E. Haley: Wood and linoleum illustration," Weston Woods (sound filmstrip).

"James Daugherty," Weston Woods (film).

"Laurent de Brunhoff: Daydreamer," Random House (sound filmstrip).

"Maurice Sendak," Weston Woods (film).

"Meet Stan and Jan Berenstain," Random House (sound filmstrip).

"Meet the Newbery author," collection of 22 individual sound filmstrips from Random House featuring Lloyd Alexander, William H. Armstrong, Natalie Babbitt, Carol Ryrie Brink, Betsy Byars, Beverly Cleary, James Lincoln and Christopher Collier, Susan Cooper, Eleanor Estes, Jean Craighead George, Bette Green, Virginia Hamilton, Marguerite Henry, Jamake Highwater, Madeleine L'Engle, Arnold Lobel, Scott O'Dell, Katherine Paterson, Isaac Bashevis Singer, Laura Ingalls Wilder, Elizabeth Yates, and Laurence Yep.

"Mr. Shepard and Mr. Milne," Weston Woods (film).

"Poetry explained by Karla Kuskin," Weston Woods (sound filmstrip).

"Robert McCloskey," Weston Woods (film).

"Steven Kellogg: How a picture book is made," Weston Woods (sound filmstrip).

"Tomi Ungerer: Storyteller," Weston Woods (film).

"A visit with Scott O'Dell," Houghton Mifflin (videotape).

"Who's Dr. Seuss? Meet Ted Geisel," Random House (sound filmstrip).

Addresses for Audio-visual Manufacturers

Houghton Mifflin Co.
2 Park Street
Boston, MA 02108

Random House
School Division
400 Hahn Road
Westminster, MD 21157

Weston Woods
Weston, CT 06883

Pied Piper
P.O. Box 320
Verdugo City, CA 91046

Figure 6–14 *Continued*

ticles profiling authors and illustrators have been published in *Language Arts, Horn Book,* and other journals. Teachers can clip and file these articles about children's authors and illustrators. A last source of information about authors and illustrators is the publicity brochures prepared by book publishers. These brochures can be requested from publishers and are usually free of charge.

A second way to learn about authors and illustrators is by writing letters to them. Students can write letters to favorite authors and illustrators to share their ideas and feelings about the books they are reading. They can ask questions about how a particular character was developed or why the illustrator used a particular art medium. Students can also write about the books they have written and illustrated. Most authors and illustrators will reply to children's letters. However, they receive thousands of letters from children every year and do not have the time to become pen pals with students. Beverly Cleary's award-winning book, *Dear Mr. Henshaw* (1983), provides a worthwhile lesson about what students (and teachers) can and cannot expect from the authors and illustrators. Guidelines for writing letters to authors and illustrators are presented in Figure 6–15.

A third way that children can learn about authors is by meeting them in person. Often authors and illustrators make public appearances at libraries, bookstores, and schools. Many students also meet authors at young authors' conferences, often held in schools as the culminating event for a year's work in writing or

Students talk with Caldecott-winning author and illustrator Gail Haley during a visit to their school.

in libraries to spotlight an author and his or her books. Typically students are selected to attend the special conference on the basis of their interest or expertise in writing. Students share their writing and listen to the guest author talk about his or her work. Usually special interest sessions are organized for students to hone their

Figure 6–15 Guidelines for Writing Letters to
Authors and Illustrators

1. Follow the correct letter format with return address, greeting, body, closing, and signature.
2. Use the process approach to write, revise and edit the letter. Be sure to proofread the letter and correct errors.
3. Recopy the letter as a courtesy to the reader so that it will be neat and easy to read.
4. Include the return address both on the envelope and on the letter.
5. Include a stamped, addressed envelope for a reply. (Authors and illustrators receive thousands of letters and it is unfair to expect them to pay postage to reply to all these letters.)
6. Be polite in the letter; ask, don't demand. As a courtesy, use the words "please" and "thank you."
7. Write genuine letters to share thoughts and feelings about the author's writing or the illustrator's artwork. Students should only write to authors or illustrators whose work they are familiar with.
8. Avoid these pitfalls:
   Do not write a long list of questions for the author or illustrator to answer. (Authors and illustrators are busy people; they do not have time to write lengthy responses.)
   Do not ask personal questions such as how much money he or she earns.
   Do not ask for advice on how to be a better writer or artist.
   Do not send stories or artwork for the author or illustrator to critique.
   Do not ask for free books. (Authors and illustrators do not give books away. They pay for the books like everyone else.)
9. Send letters to the author or illustrator in care of the publisher. Publishers' names are listed on the title page of books, and addresses are usually located on the copyright page after the title page. If the complete mailing address is not listed, check the public library. Publishers' mailing addresses are listed in two reference books, *Books in print,* and *Literary market place,* which are available in most public libraries.

Adapted from Cleary, 1983, 1985.

writing skills or experiment with new writing techniques. These conferences give students recognition for their work and emphasize the importance of writing. They also stimulate community interest in writing. Special sessions for parents and teachers are often included to teach parents how to encourge their children's writing and to introduce teachers to new strategies for teaching writing.

POINTS TO PONDER

What Are the Basic Ingredients Necessary for a Process-Oriented Writing Program?

How Can Teachers Organize Their Classrooms to Help Students Learn to Write?

BASIC INGREDIENTS OF A WRITING PROGRAM

We will discuss five basic ingredients of process-oriented writing programs: (a) time, (b) experience, (c) literature, (d) structure, and (e) audience. These writing programs are described as "authentic" (Edelsky & Smith, 1984) because students are involved in real-life writing activities for genuine audiences. In contrast, "inauthentic" writing occurs when the writing process and the five basic ingredients are ignored.

Time

An essential ingredient in a program for helping students learn to write is time (Tway, 1984). Writing about exciting places, realistic characters, and powerful ideas cannot be chopped up into half-hour periods, nor can expression be called forth by giving a few directions and the dictum, "now get busy." If students are to write, to find out about themselves, their thoughts, their feelings—to become aware of themselves and their abilities—they must be given all the time they need. Our recommendation is to throw away the fill-in-the-blank workbooks and dittos that clutter students' in-school world and give them time to write, time to experience life and literature, and time to think.

Another way to find time to write is by integrating writing with content area study. Students can write in conjunction with social studies, science, art, music, and other areas of the curriculum. In the area of art, for instance, students can use writing in many different ways. Ten ways that students can integrate art and writing are presented in Figure 6–16. Writing is a powerful way of learning, and by linking writing with art and other content areas, students can better learn the subject matter and gain valuable writing experience.

Experience

If students are to write, they must have something to write about. However self-evident this appears on the surface, it is rarely acknowledged in practice. Not many teachers actually set about to provide for their students continuous experiences that will provide background for writing. Often teachers attempt to stimulate their students in some way before having them write, but they do not provide in-depth rehearsal activities.

1. Students write captions for the artwork they create.

2. Students write directions explaining how to complete an art project. For example, they can list the steps in making linoleum or Styrofoam prints to illustrate a class book. This activity might be accompanied by finding examples of block print illustrations in books such as Marcia Brown's *Once a mouse* (1961).

3. Students read to learn about artists such as Vincent Van Gogh. An excellent biography of Van Gogh for middle and upper grade students is Dorbin's *I am a stranger on Earth: The story of Vincent Van Gogh* (1975). Later students can write biographical sketches of Van Gogh, relating the turbulence of his paintings to what they have learned about his life and feelings.

4. Students write letters to Tomie de Paola, Eric Carle, or other artists who illustrate children's books.

5. As students view paintings, sculptures, and other artwork, they brainstorm a list or cluster of impressions and write a poem about the piece of artwork. Students can view these paintings and sculptures during a field trip to an art museum or examine copies of these artworks in the classroom.

6. Alice and Martin Provensen have created a fascinating pop-up book, *Leonardo da Vinci* (1984). After reading and manipulating the Provensens' book and learning some basic paper engineering skills, students create their own pop-up or movable books. For an annotated bibliography describing other movable books, check "Books with movables: More than just novelties" (McGee & Charlesworth, 1984).

7. Students plan a class art exhibit and write invitations and make posters announcing it.

8. Students interview a local artist and then write a report about the interview for a class or community newspaper.

9. Students create filmstrips to illustrate stories, poems, reports, and other compositions. Commercially prepared kits are available with blank filmstrips, which students draw on using pencils and marking pens. Then students tape-record their compositions and add "beeps" to indicate when to advance the film.

10. Students create greeting cards using a variety of art media.

Figure 6–16   Ten Ways to Integrate Art and Writing

Providing students with experiences that they can use as a basis for writing may be frustrating if the teacher and the curriculum are not geared to help students learn to write. One change would be to incorporate content area activities, such as social studies- and science-related field trips, into the writing program. A second way is to use audio-visual materials, such as films and filmstrips, to bring the world into the classroom. In addition, students must have access to stories and informational books related to the writing assignment. Students cannot write compositions or invent stories that have believable characters, accurate settings, and interesting plots without a wealth of experience.

Literature

Literature is one type of experience, and a valuable source of information for writers. Classrooms where students are writing should have an abundance of books (Graves, 1983). All types of books should be included—stories, informational books, books of poetry and word play, folktales, fables, biographies, autobiographies, and hero stories. Donald Graves explains that literature is fundamental to both reading and writing. Children bring literature to life through reading, interpretive dramatics, choral reading, and writing. Also, children create literature through writing. Moreover, through their experience with literature, children develop concepts about authors, stories, and writing.

Structure

A basic premise being set forth in this book is that students need to know the structure of different writing forms and that these structures can best be learned using literature as a source of information. Students learn to write by writing and reading, and they learn the form of writing by asking questions about that form and by finding answers to those questions in children's literature. By seeking answers to questions in literature and in their classmates' writing rather than in the textbooks, students can learn whatever forms or structures will help them most effectively express their thoughts and feelings to their audiences.

Audience

Students need a purpose for writing just as adult authors do. In addition to the obvious reason for writing in school, learning how to write, students need to experience the pleasure others can get from their writing. Teachers who encourage students to write and place their compositions in classroom and school libraries soon find that students love to read classmates' compositions. Having an appropriate audience is important. Students are the best audience for other students and they can be helped to accept each others' work and give encouraging feedback to each other. Teachers can be the worst audience if they feel they must correct all the mistakes students make.

Summary

In this chapter we discussed the writing process. The process approach involves five interrelated stages that both students and adult authors work through as they write. Students choose their own topics for writing, engage in rehearsal activities, develop their compositions in a series of drafts, and revise and edit their writing with assistance from their classmates. In contrast to the traditional approach to writing, the emphasis is on the process, not the finished product. Microcomputers are a valuable tool for writers who use the process approach. Revising, editing, and formatting are simplified using the word processor.

Learning to use the writing process is one way to help students develop a concept of "author." One approach, the author's chair, can be used to introduce the concept to primary grade students. Other ways to help students develop the concept of authorship include learning about authors and illustrators,

writing letters to favorite authors, and meeting authors. Young authors' conferences are one of the most successful ways to recognize the achievements of student authors and to provide opportunities for them to interact with favorite authors.

The five basic ingredients—time, experience, literature, structure, and audience—are intrinsically tied to the writing process. Students need time to write, more time in fact than they needed in the traditional approach to writing, because the writing process stages take more time than writing single-draft compositions. Through concrete experiences, reading literature, and learning about the structure of stories, poems, and other writing forms, students gain valuable information that is necessary for writing. Also, students write for appropriate audiences rather than simply to receive a grade in the process approach.

Extensions

1. Observe students using the writing process in an elementary classroom. In what types of rehearsal activities are students involved? In what types of conferences do students and the teacher participate? How do students share their writing with a genuine audience?

2. Interview several students who use a process approach to writing and several other students who use a traditional approach. Ask questions similar to the following and compare students' answers:

   ■ How do you choose a topic for writing?

   ■ How do you get started writing?

   ■ Do you ask your classmates or the teacher to read your writing?

   ■ What do you do when you are having a problem while you are writing?

   ■ What is easiest about writing for you?

   ■ What is hardest about writing for you?

   ■ What is the most important thing to remember when you are writing?

   ■ What happens to your writing after you finish it?

   ■ What kinds of writing (e.g., stories, poems, reports) do you like best?

3. Sit in on a writing conference in which students share their writing and ask their classmates for feedback in revising their compositions. Make a list of the questions and comments students make. What conclusions can you draw about students' in-

teractions with each other? You might want to compare your findings with those reported in "Talking about writing: The language of writing groups" (Gere & Abbott, 1985).

4. Examine language arts textbooks to see how writing is approached. Is the process approach to writing used? Do some steps in the writing process lend themselves to the textbook format better than others? What types of prewriting activities are included in the textbooks? Which writing forms (e.g., letters, stories, advertisements) do these textbooks include?

5. Help a small group of students to learn more about their favorite authors. Students can consult reference books in the library and other resources. Also check Figure 6–14 for possible sources of information. Students may want to write to the authors' publishers for brochures or to write to the authors themselves. When writing to authors, be sure to follow the guidelines presented in Figure 6–15.

6. Reflect on your own writing process. Do you write single-draft papers or do you write a series of drafts and refine them? Do you ask friends to read and react to your writing as well as to help you proofread your writing? Write a two- to three-page paper comparing your writing process to the process described in this chapter. How might you modify your own writing process in view of the information presented in this chapter?

References

Aldis, D. (1969). *Nothing is impossible: The story of Beatrix Potter.* New York: Atheneum.

Barber, B. (1982). Creating BYTES of language. *Language Arts, 59,* 472–475.

Bissex, G. (1980). Gyns at wrk: A child learns to write and read. Cambridge, MA: Harvard University Press.

Britton, J. (1978). The composing process and the functions of writing. In C. R. Cooper & L. Odell. (Eds.). *Research on composing: Points of departure.* Urbana, IL: National Council of Teachers of English.

Brown, M. (1961). *Once a mouse.* New York: Scribner.

Calkins, L. M. (1980). When children want to punctuate: Basic skills belong in context. *Language Arts, 57,* 567–573.

Cleary, B. (1983). *Dear Mr. Henshaw.* New York: Morrow.

———. (1985). Dear author, answer this letter now . . . *Instructor, 95,* 22–23, 25.

Daiute, C. (1985). *Writing and computers.* Reading, MA: Addison-Wesley.

Dobrin, A. (1975). *I am a stranger on Earth: The story of Vincent Van Gogh.* New York: Warne.

Dyson, A. H. (1983). Early writing as drawing: The developmental gap between speaking and writing. American Educational Research Association Annual Meeting, Montreal, Canada.

Edelsky, C., & Smith, K. (1984). Is that writing—Or are those marks just a figment of your curriculum? *Language Arts, 61,* 24–32.

Elley, W. B., Barham, I. H., Lamb, H., & Wyllie, M. (1976). The role of grammar in a secondary school English curriculum. *Research in the Teaching of English, 10,* 5–21.

Emig, J. (1971). *The composing processes of twelfth graders* (NCTE Research Report No. 13). Urbana, IL: National Council of Teachers of English.

Engberg, R. E. (1983). Word processors in the English classroom. *Computers, Reading and Language Arts, 1,* 17–20.

Fritz, J. (1982). *Homesick: My own story.* New York: Putnam.

Gere, A. R., & Abbott, R. D. (1985). Talking about writing: The language of writing groups. *Research in the Teaching of English, 19,* 362–381.

Graves, D. H. (1976). Let's get rid of the welfare mess in the teaching of writing. *Language Arts, 53,* 645–651.

———. (1983). *Writing: Teachers and children at work.* Exeter, NH: Heinemann.

Graves, D., & Hansen, J. (1983). The author's chair. *Language Arts, 60,* 176–183.

Hopkins, L. B. (1969). *Books are by people: Interviews with 104 authors and illustrators of books for young children.* New York: Citation.

———. (1974). *More books by more people: Interviews with 65 authors of books for children.* New York: Citation.

Hubbard, R. (1985). Second graders answer the question 'Why publish?' *The Reading Teacher, 38,* 658–662.

Kane, J. H. (1983). Commputers for composing. In *Chameleon in the classroom: Developing roles for computers* (Technical Report No. 22). New York: Bank Street College of Education.

King, M. (1985). Proofreading is not reading. *Teaching English in the Two-Year College, 12,* 108–112.

Lundsteen, S. W. (Ed.). (1976). *Help for the teacher of written composition: New directions in research.* Urbana, IL: National Conference on Research in English and the ERIC Clearinghouse on Reading and Communication Skills.

Martin, N., D'Arcy, P., Newton, B., & Parker, R. (1976). *Writing and learning across the curriculum 11–16.* London: Ward Lock Educational Publishers.

McGee, L., & Charlesworth, R. (1984). Books with movables: More than just novelties. *The Reading Teacher, 37,* 853–859.

McKenzie, L., & Tompkins, G. E. (1984). Evaluating students' writing: A process approach. *Journal of Teaching Writing, 3,* 201–212.

Murray, D. (1982). *Learning by teaching.* Montclair, NJ: Boynton/Cook.

———. (1984). *Write to learn.* New York: Holt.

Newman, J. M. (1984). Language learning and computers. *Language Arts, 61,* 494–497.

Phenix, J. & Hannan, E. (1984). Word processing in the grade one classroom. *Language Arts, 61,* 804–812.

Provensen, A. & Provensen, M. (1984). *Leonardo da Vinci.* New York: Viking.

QUILL [Computer program]. (1983). Lexington, MA: DC Heath.

Rico, G. L. (1983). *Writing the natural way.* Los Angeles: Tarcher.

Russell, C. (1983). Putting research into practice: Conferencing with young writers. *Language Arts, 60,* 333–340.

Smith, F. (1982). *Writing and the writer.* New York: Holt.

Smith, N. J. (1985). The word processing approach to language experience. *The Reading Teacher, 38,* 556–559.

Smith, P. L., & Tompkins, G. E. (1983). *Computers and writing.* Unpublished manuscript.

Sommers, N. (1982). Responding to student writing. *College Composition and Communication, 33,* 148–156.

Tompkins, G. E., & McKenzie, L. (1985). The writing process. In G. E. Tompkins & C. Goss (Eds.), *Write angles: Strategies for teaching composition* (pp. 1–6). Oklahoma City: The Oklahoma Writing Project and the Oklahoma State Department of Education.

Tway, E. (1980). Teacher responses to children's writing. *Language Arts, 57,* 763–772.

———. (1984). *Time for writing in the elementary school* (TRIP Booklet). Urbana, IL: ERIC Clearinghouse on Reading and Communication Skills and the National Council of Teachers of English.

Zemach, M. (1978). *Self-portrait: Margot Zemach.* Reading, MA: Addison-Wesley.

IF YOU WANT TO LEARN MORE

Bissex, G. (1980). Gyns at wrk: A child learns to read and write. Cambridge, MA: Harvard University Press.

Bruce, B., & Michaels, S., & Watson-Gegeo, K. (1985). How computers can change the writing process. *Language Arts, 62,* 143–149.

Calkins, L. M. (1983). *Lessons from a child: On the teaching and learning of writing.* Exeter, NH: Heinemann.

Cleary, B. (1985). Dear author, answer this letter now . . . *Instructor, 95,* 22–23, 25.

Daiute, C. (1985). *Writing and computers.* Reading, MA: Addison-Wesley.

Gordon, N. (Ed.). (1984). *Classroom experiences: The writing process in action.* Exeter, NH: Heinemann.

Graves, D. H. (1983). *Writing: Teachers and children at work.* Exeter, NH: Heinemann.

_____. (1984). *A researcher learns to write: Selected articles and monographs.* Exeter, NH: Heinemann.

Hansen, J., Newkirk, T., & Graves, D. (1985). *Breaking ground: Teachers relate reading and writing in the elementary school.* Portsmouth, NH: Heinemann.

Hoskisson, K. (1979). Writing is fundamental. *Language Arts, 56,* 892–896.

Murray, D. (1984). *Write to learn.* New York: Holt.

Newkirk, T., & Atwell, N. (Eds.). (1982). *Understanding writing: Ways of observing, learning and teaching K–8.* Chelmsford, MA: The Northeast Regional Exchange.

Rico, G. L. (1983). *Writing the natural way.* Los Angeles: Tarcher.

Smith, F. (1982). *Writing and the writer.* New York: Holt.

Tway, E. (1980). How to find and encourage the nuggets in children's writing. *Language Arts, 57,* 299–304.

Weaver, C. (1982). Welcoming errors as signs of growth. *Language Arts, 59,* 438–444.

CHAPTER SEVEN

Expressive Writing

OVERVIEW. In this chapter, we will discuss expressive writing, the type of writing that is most like children's talk. Young children's writing and older students' journal entries, freewriting, and friendly letters are usually classified as expressive. Students' expressive writing is for and about themselves and is often very personal. The emphasis is on students' experiences, their ideas, and their feelings.

Children's writing assumes many different forms, depending on their purpose and audience. These forms range from journals to newspapers, directions to poems, stories to research reports. Figure 7–1 lists a variety of writing forms appropriate for elementary students. Too often students' writing is limited to writing stories, poems, and several other forms. Instead, they need to experiment with a wide variety of writing forms and to explore the functions and formats of these forms. The forms can be used in creative ways as well as traditional ones. Recipes are a good example. Most adults think of recipes simply as a list of instructions and ingredients for preparing a food, and they may question the appropriateness of elementary students learning to write recipes. Older students who are learning to cook read recipes in cookbooks and copy or write food recipes, but kindergartners and primary grade students can dictate humorous recipes that parents and teachers enjoy reading. Students can also write more creative and more interesting recipes. For instance, they can write a recipe for a war in conjunction with a social studies unit, which would probe students' understanding of the causes and events leading to wars. Students can also write recipes for success in a particular grade, which they leave for the next year's class, or a recipe for a best friend, a football player, or a hero. Through these recipe-writing activities, students learn to write directions clearly and in sequence. For example, a fourth grader's recipe for friendship is presented in Figure 7–2.

There are many ways to categorize these writing forms. The traditional classifications are narration, description, exposition, and persuasion. However, this classification seems artificial when we consider that students use these forms for different purposes—to enjoy, to describe, to explain, to inform, to inquire, to direct, and to persuade (Klein, 1985). Often, students combine two or more categories in a single piece of writing. In writing class newspapers, for instance, students usually involve all four categories. Audiences vary, too. Sometimes the audience is oneself, and at other times it may be a trusted adult, classmates, or the community.

James Britton and his colleagues (1975) examined a large corpus of student writing, and on the basis of their investigations, they have devised another classification system. Their system is based on the function of the piece of writing, and it includes three categories: expressive, transactional, and poetic writing. *Expressive writing* is the writing that is closest to talk, and much of children's early writing as well as older students' journals, freewriting, and friendly letters fits into this category. From the expressive category, students' writing moves into the transactional or the poetic categories. *Transactional writing* is informative while *poetic writ-*

advertisements	fables	postcards
advice columns	folktales	posters
applications	fortune cookies	questionnaires
autobiographies	greeting cards	questions
ballots	horoscopes	quizzes
bibliographies	interviews	recipes
biographies	invitations	research reports
book reports	jokes	reviews
books	journals	riddles
brochures	lab reports	science fiction
bumper stickers	labels	stories
captions	learning logs	scripts
cartoons	letters	sentences
catalogues	letters to the	signs
character sketches	editor	slogans
charts	lists	study guides
comics	lyrics	tall tales
computer programs	maps	telegrams
coupons	memoirs	telephone
crossword puzzles	memory writing	directories
definitions	menus	thank-you's
descriptions	mysteries	thesauruses
dialogue/conversations	myths	thumbnail sketches
diagrams	newspapers	valentines
diaries	notes	weather reports
dictionaries	obituaries	word-finds
directions	outlines	wordless picture
editorials	paragraphs	books
essays	poetry	words

Figure 7–1   A List of Possible Writing Forms

ing is creative. Examples of transactional writing include research reports, newspaper articles, and directions. (These forms of writing are discussed in Chapter 8.) Stories, poems, and scripts are examples of poetic writing. (These forms of writing are discussed in Chapters 9, 10, and 11.)

The boundaries of the three categories are fuzzy at best. Friendly letters, for example, have characteristics of all three categories even though we have classified them as expressive writing. They are usually written for a small and trusted audience. The writing style is informal, often rambling. At the same time, friendly letters are written using a particular form, and the letters provide information and tell stories.

Britton's three categories may more realistically be considered as two continuums, one from informal, private writing to formal, public writing, and a second continuum from informational to creative writing. The two continuums are presented in Figure 7–3 with sample writing forms marked along the continuums.

Figure 7–2   A Fourth Grader's Recipe

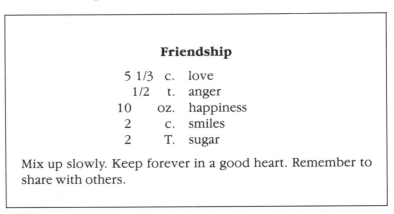

Friendship

5 1/3	c.	love
1/2	t.	anger
10	oz.	happiness
2	c.	smiles
2	T.	sugar

Mix up slowly. Keep forever in a good heart. Remember to share with others.

Misti, age 11

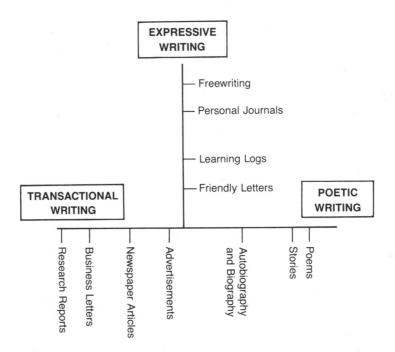

Figure 7–3   The Continuum of Britton's Categories of Writing with Sample Writing Forms

---

POINTS TO PONDER
What Types of Diaries and Journals Can Elementary Students Write?
Why Should Students Keep Diaries and Journals?
***How Can Students Use Learning Logs and Simulated Journals in Conjunction
with Science, Social Studies, and Other Content Areas?***

JOURNAL WRITING

Diaries and journals are two very similar forms of expressive writing. A diary is a private day-to-day record of the events in a person's life and is intended for personal use. In contrast, a journal is slightly more public and may be shared with trusted classmates and adults. In both forms, students record the day-to-day events of their lives as well as their feelings and ideas in notebooks or booklets of paper stapled together. The events that students write about may include common events such as getting a haircut or having dinner at a local pizza parlor, or they may be about "monumental" events such as a pet's death, parents' divorce, or a move to a new town. Susan and Stephen Tchudi (1984) explain that by writing in diaries and journals, children can both "save" and "savor" experiences.

Whether the records that children write are called diaries or journals is not important. For convenience, we will use the term *journal* in this chapter to refer to both types of expressive writing.

Many famous writers, scientists, and presidents have kept journals. Also, characters in children's literature, such as Harriet in *Harriet the spy* (Fitzhugh, 1964) and Catherine Hall in *A gathering of days* (Blos, 1979), keep journals in which they record the events in their lives, their ideas, and dreams. A list of stories in which characters keep journals is presented in Figure 7–4. In these stories, the characters demonstrate the process of journal writing as well as illustrating both the pleasures and difficulties of keeping a journal (Tway, 1981).

Students gain valuable writing experience by recording daily the events in their lives, by exploring the personal meanings of these events, and by analyzing their values, beliefs, and opinions. The raw material for journal writing is extensive. The Tchudis (1984) suggest possible writing activities that explore students' experiences, investigate the world around them, and play with language:

recording past experiences

recording dreams

analyzing opinions to better understand one's values and beliefs

using the senses—seeing, hearing, feeling, smelling, tasting—to write more vividly

recording impressions about people, places, and other new experiences

analyzing experiences by asking *how* and *why*

responding to newspaper/magazine articles, TV shows, or movies

Figure 7–4   Diaries and Journals in Children's Literature

Blos, J. (1979). *A gathering of days: A New England girl's journal, 1830–1832.*
New York: Scribner. (U)

Bourne, M. A. (1975). *Nabby Adams's diary.* New York: Coward. (U)

Cleary, B. (1983). *Dear Mr. Henshaw.* New York: Morrow. (M)

Crusoe, R. (1972). *My journals and sketchbooks.* New York: Harcourt Brace Jovanovich. (U)

Fisher, L. E. (1972). *The death of evening star: Diary of a young New England
whaler.* New York: Doubleday. (M–U)

Fitzhugh, L. (1964). *Harriet the spy.* New York: Harper and Row. (M)

Frank, A. (1952). *Anne Frank: The diary of a young girl.* New York: Doubleday.
(U)

George, J. C. (1959). *My side of the mountain.* New York: Dutton. (M–U)

Glaser, D. (1976). *The diary of Trilby Frost.* New York: Holiday House. (U)

Mazer, N. F. (1971). *I, Trissy.* New York: Delacorte. (U)

Orgel, D. B. (1978). *The devil in Vienna.* New York: Dial. (U)

Reig, J. (1978). *Diary of the boy king Tut-Ankh-Amen.* New York: Scribner. (M)

Sachs, M. (1975). *Dorrie's book.* New York: Doubleday. (M)

Wilder, L. (1962). *On the way home.* New York: Harper and Row. (M)

Williams, V. B. (1981). *Three days on a river in a red canoe.* New York: Greenwillow. (P–M)

P = primary grades (K–2)
M = middle grades (3–5)
U = upper grades (6–8)

collecting examples of dialogues and dialects

conducting a dialogue with oneself, friends, and historical personalities

collecting words, puns, riddles, and other word plays

copying quotes

making lists of possible writing topics

In addition, students gain valuable practice in writing through journal writing. They can experiment with new writing styles and formats without worrying about the conventions of writing (i.e., spelling, punctuation, and capitalization) that must be considered in more public writing. If they decide to make an entry "public," students can later revise and edit their writing.

Journals may be used in a variety of ways in elementary classrooms. Students can write in journals independently with little or no sharing with the teacher, or they can make daily entries which the teacher monitors regularly. Tway (1984), describes four different arrangements for using journals with elementary students:

1. Students keep personal journals as a place to write primarily for themselves or as a notebook for jotting ideas. Sharing is on a voluntary basis, and the teacher does not read the journals unless invited.

2. Students keep personal journals, as above, but the teacher monitors, at least to see that regular entries are being made. The teacher may simply monitor for entries and not read unless passages are specially marked, or the teacher may read on a regular basis (all except passages marked "private") and offer encouragement and suggestions. This kind of arrangement requires an atmosphere of mutual trust in the classroom.

3. Students keep writing journals, where they are expected to develop their writing ideas on an on-going basis. This arrangement brings journal keeping into the curriculum as a language arts requirement, and teachers check regularly and write evaluative comments. The checking usually occurs once a week and many teachers write their comments each time in note form in the margins of the journal pages. Specific strengths are pointed out and praised or encouraged, and constructive suggestions or helpful suggestions are given for trouble spots.

4. Students keep journals on a continuing basis; the writing is part of the requirement of the language arts program. However, because of other projects or because the students are older and prolific, the teacher does not read everything that is entered. Each week, or each regular checking time, the teacher asks the students to mark what they feel is their best writing of the lot (written since last check), and *that* is what the teacher reads and evaluates. This adds writing practice time for students by not limiting them in any way as to *quantity* and saves time for busy teachers who cannot find time for reading lengthy journals. Teachers simply spend time reading what students choose as their best *quality.* (pp. 15–16)

In all of these arrangements, specific periods of time are set aside daily or at least several times a week for journal writing. These arrangements can be used for different types of journal writing. Students can keep personal journals in which they record daily events, can write stories and poems in writing journals, and can converse with the teacher in dialogue journals. Students can reflect on what they are learning in learning logs, and they can take the role of historical figures in simulated journals. Young children can also write and draw in journals. These six types of journals are discussed in the following sections.

Personal Journals

Students can keep *personal journals* in which they recount events in their lives and write about topics of their own choosing. An excerpt from a sixth grader's personal journal in which she lists things she is afraid of is presented in Figure 7–5. It is often helpful to keep a list of possible journal writing topics on a chart in the class-

> *Things I fear*
>
> I'm afraid of the dog across the street.
>
> I'm afraid of having a bike wreck.
>
> I'm afraid of getting locked out of my house.
>
> I'm afraid of loosing my friends.
>
> I'm afraid of snakes.
>
> I'm afraid of insects.
>
> I'm afraid of bad weather.
>
> I'm afraid of being mugged.
>
> I'm afraid of my locker getting broken into.

Figure 7–5   A Personal Journal Entry

room or on sheets of paper clipped inside each student's journal notebook. A list of possible journal writing topics developed by a class of fourth and fifth graders is presented in Figure 7–6. These students add to their list of journal writing topics throughout the year, and the list may include more than one hundred topics by the end of the school year. In personal journals, students choose their own topics and they can write about almost anything, but the list of topics provides a crutch to students who believe they have nothing to write about.

   To monitor students' personal journal entries, the teacher simply checks to see that the entries were made or reads selected entries. Students' journal entries are not graded for quality or mechanical correctness because they are informal, private writings. When considered as part of the writing process, most journal en-

Figure 7–6   Fifty-one Journal Writing Topics

my favorite place in town	if I had three wishes
boyfriends/girlfriends	my teacher
things that make me happy or	TV shows I watch
sad	my favorite holiday
music	if I were stranded on an island
an imaginary planet	what I want to be when I grow up
cars	private thoughts
magazines I like to read	how to be a super hero
what if snow were hot	dinosaurs
dreams I have	my mom/my dad
cartoons	my friends
places I've been	my next vacation
favorite movies	love
rock stars	if I were an animal or
if I were a movie/rock star	something else
poems	books I've read
pets	favorite things to do
football	my hobbies
astronauts	if I were a skydiver
the president	when I get a car
jokes	if I had a lot of money
motorcycles	dolls
things that happen in my school	if I were rich
current events	wrestling and other sports
things I do on weekends	favorite colors
a soap opera with daily episodes	questions answered with "never"

or ANYTHING else I want to write about

Fourth and fifth graders

tries are prewriting or rehearsal activities. Students can select entries from their journals and develop them into polished compositions if they wish, but the journal entries themselves are rarely revised and edited. Evaluation should be based on whether students have written the assigned entries.

Privacy is an important issue as students grow older. Most young children are very willing to share what they have written, but by third or fourth grade, students grow less willing to read what they have written aloud to the class. Usually, they are willing to share their journal entries with a trusted teacher. Teachers must be scrupulous about protecting students' privacy and not insist that students share

A student reflects on daily events as he writes in his personal journal.

their writing when they are unwilling to do so. It is also important to talk with students about respecting each other's privacy and not reading each other's journals.

Writing Journals

In *writing journals,* or author's notebooks, students write drafts of stories, poems, and other pieces of writing. Some students write longer stories, which they write in chapters or episodes, day after day after day. Students also keep lists of ideas for future compositions, interesting settings, or character descriptions to be used later. They also include information about writing that authors need to know in order to write well. For example, as students examine the elements of story structure (see Chapters 9 and 10), they take notes about the characteristics of the elements to which they can refer as they write stories. Students also make charts listing poetic formulas (see Chapter 11) to refer to when writing poetry.

Dialogue Journals

Another approach to journal writing is *dialogue journals.* In this approach, students and teachers converse with each other through writing (Gambrell, 1985; Kreeft, 1984; Staton, 1980). Each day the student writes to the teacher about a concern or something of interest, and the teacher responds and asks questions. Teachers' responses do not need to be lengthy; a sentence or two is often enough. Even so, it is very time-consuming for teachers to respond to 25 journal entries every day. Often, teachers read and respond to students' journal entries on a rotating basis. An entry from a dialogue journal is presented in Figure 7–7. Joy Kreeft suggests that the greatest value of dialogue journals is that they bridge the gap between talk and writing. A second value must be the strong bonds that develop between students and the teacher through writing back and forth to each other.

Figure 7–7 An Excerpt from a Dialogue Journal

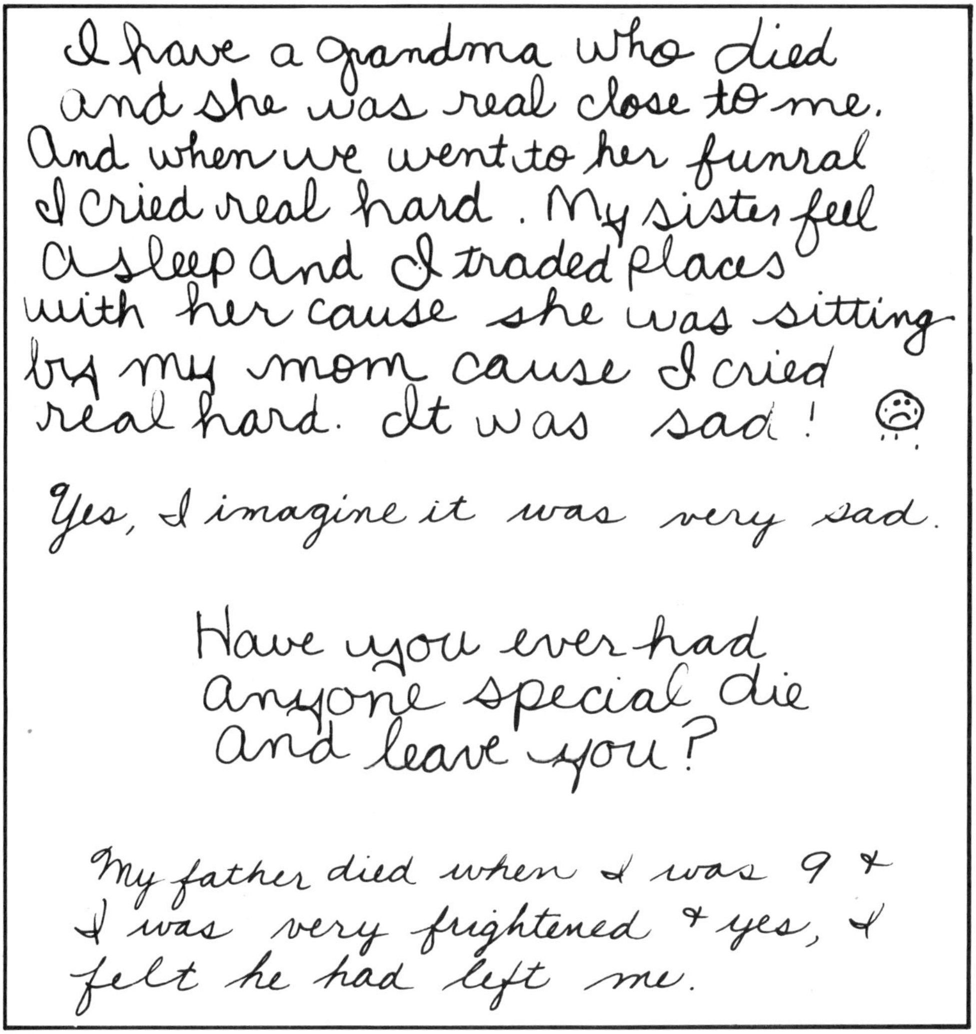

> I have a grandma who died and she was real close to me. And when we went to her funral I cried real hard. My sister feel asleep and I traded places with her cause she was sitting by my mom cause I cried real hard. It was sad! ☹
>
> Yes, I imagine it was very sad.
>
> Have you ever had anyone special die and leave you?
>
> My father died when I was 9 & I was very frightened & yes, I felt he had left me.

Kim, age 12

Learning Logs

Students can also use journals to record or react to what they are learning in language arts, science, math, or other content areas (Fulwiler, 1985). These journals are known as *learning logs.* Writing can be a valuable learning tool, and in these journals, students use writing to reflect on their learning, to discover gaps in their knowledge, and to explore relationships between what they are learning and their past experiences.

In language arts, learning logs can be used as a response to literature activity. As students read stories or listen to them read aloud, they react to the story or relate it to events in their own lives. They can list unfamiliar vocabulary words and jot down quotable quotes in their reading logs. Students can also take notes about characters, plot, or other elements of the story.

In science, students can make daily records of the growth of seeds they have planted or animals they are observing, such as meal worms, gerbils, or caterpillars. For instance, a second-grade class observed and studied caterpillars as they changed from caterpillars to chrysalis to butterflies over a period of 4 to 6 weeks. Students each kept a log with daily entries. They were to describe the changes they observed using shape, color, size, and other property words. Two pages from a second grader's log documenting the caterpillars' growth and change are presented in Figure 7–8. As students write in these science logs, they are assuming the role of scientists, learning to make careful observations and to record them accurately in their logs.

Students can also use learning logs to write about what they are learning in math (Salem, 1982). They record explanations and examples of concepts presented in class and react to the mathematical concepts they are learning and any problems they may be having. Some upper grade teachers allow students the last 5 minutes of math class to summarize the day's lesson and react to it in their learning logs. Through these activities, students practice taking notes, writing descriptions and directions, and other writing skills. They also learn how to reflect on and evaluate their own learning.

Simulated Journals

Students assume the role of another person as they write in *simulated journals* from that person's viewpoint. In connection with social studies units or as students read biographies, they can assume the role of an historical figure and as they read stories, they can assume the role of a character in the story. In this way, students gain insight into the lives of other people and into historical events. Ira Progoff (1975) uses a similar approach, which he calls *dialoguing,* in which students converse with an historical figure or other character in a journal by writing both sides of the conversation. He suggests focusing on a milestone in the person's life and starting the journal at an important point. A dialogue with Paul Revere, for instance, might take place in April, 1775, the month of his famous ride.

Figure 7–8 Two Entries from a Student's
Science Log

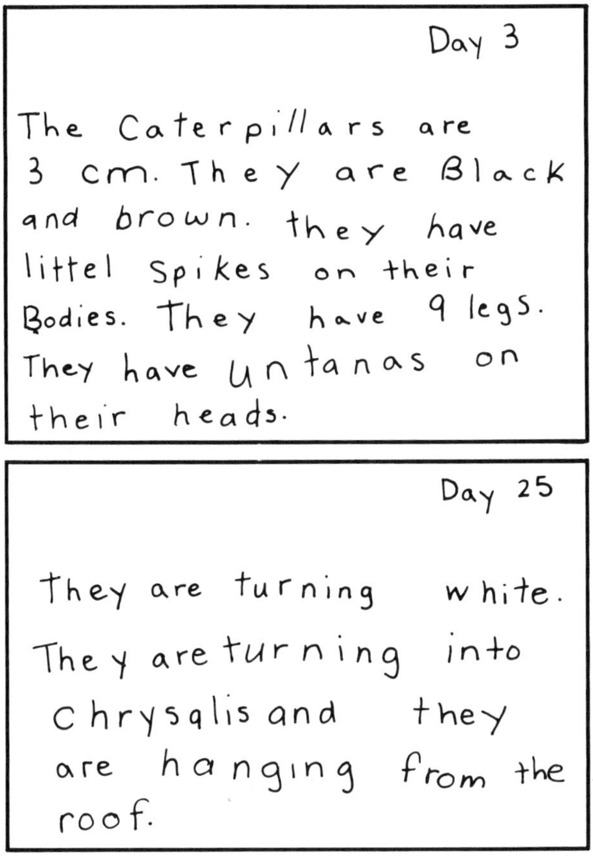

Day 3

The Caterpillars are
3 cm. They are Black
and brown. they have
littel Spikes on their
Bodies. They have 9 legs.
They have untanas on
their heads.

Day 25

They are turning white.
They are turning into
Chrysalis and they
are hanging from the
roof.

Angela, age 8

Young Children's Journals

Teachers have used journals effectively with preschoolers, kindergartners, and other young children who are emergent readers or who have not yet learned to read (Elliott et al., 1981; Hipple, 1985). Young children's journal entries include drawings as well as some type of text. Some children write scribbles, random letters and numbers, simple captions, or extended texts using invented spelling. (Children create spellings for words using their knowledge of the phonological system. The spellings often seem bizarre by adult standards, but are reasonable in terms of children's knowledge of phoneme-grapheme correspondences and spelling patterns.) Other children want parents and teachers to take their dictation and write the text. After the text is written, children read it and then reread it to classmates using the assisted reading strategy.

POINTS TO PONDER
What Is Freewriting?
How Can Students Use Freewriting to Generate Ideas for Writing?
Why Is Freewriting a Good Way to Combat the "Blank Page Syndrome"?

FREEWRITING

Freewriting is just what the name suggests, a technique in which students simply begin to write and let their thoughts flow from their minds to their pens without focusing on mechanics or revisions. Freewriting allows students to ramble on paper, generating words and ideas and developing fluency. This strategy, popularized by Peter Elbow (1973), is a way to help students focus on content rather than mechanics. Even by second or third grade, students have learned that many teach-

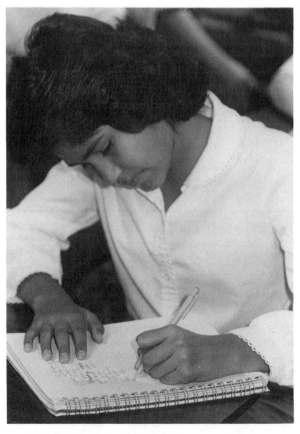

As she freewrites, the student lets her ideas flow,
developing writing fluency.

ers emphasize correct spelling and careful handwriting more than the content of a composition. Elbow explains that focusing on mechanics makes writing "dead" because it does not allow students' natural voices to come through. In freewriting, students focus on content and later, if they choose, can revise and polish their composition using the writing process.

Freewriting is essentially a prewriting or rehearsal activity. Typically, students are directed to keep their pens or pencils moving on the sheet of paper for 5 or 10 minutes. They may write about anything that comes to mind. But, no matter what, they may not stop—not to look back, not to cross something out, not to check the spelling of a word. If students cannot think of anything to write, they write just that over and over:

> I can't think of anything to write . . . I can't think of anything to write
> . . . I can't think of anything to write . . . .

Sooner or later, ideas and the words to express them will come. These "freewrites" often ramble, have jumbled ideas or even unrelated ideas. Elbow uses the term "unfocused" to describe these freewrites.

A sixth grader's unfocused freewrite is presented in Figure 7–9. In this sample, the student has allowed his mind to wander, focusing briefly on several different things—exotic automobiles, school, and a book he is reading—before returning to exotic automobiles, his original idea. In many ways, this student's freewrite is much like a personal journal entry. The content of freewriting and personal journal writing is similar; in both, students write about their thoughts and experiences. The major difference is that in freewriting the student must keep writing throughout a specified period of time.

Figure 7–9   An Unfocused Freewrite

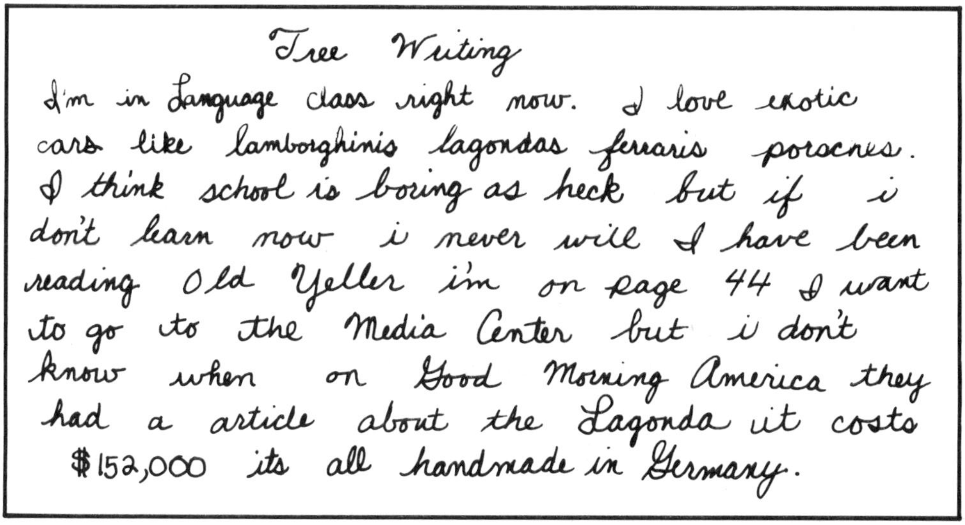

> Free Writing
> I'm in Language class right now. I love exotic cars like lamborghinis lagondas ferraris porsches. I think school is boring as heck but if i don't learn now i never will I have been reading Old Yeller i'm on page 44 I want to go to the Media Center but i don't know when on Good Morning America they had a article about the Lagonda it costs $152,000 its all handmade in Germany.

Sam, age 11

The freewriting activity can end after the first freewrite, or students can write a second, more focused freewrite that develops and expands one of the ideas mentioned in the first, unfocused freewrite. If students are going to continue with a second freewrite, they reread what they have written and choose one idea to develop in the second freewrite. It is often helpful for students to circle a word, phrase, or sentence in the first freewrite that will become the topic for the second. In the freewrite sample presented in Figure 7–9, the student would probably focus on exotic cars in his second, focused freewrite. Freewriting can end after these second freewrites, or students can focus again and write a third freewrite. These second or third freewrites can be developed into polished compositions using the writing process.

Through this unstructured writing, students collect ideas and words that eventually may be used in a polished composition. Even if they are never developed, however, the freewriting experience is valuable because students are developing writing fluency. Students, too, have their own reasons for liking to freewrite. One class of sixth graders listed these reasons why they like to freewrite:

"The best thing about freewriting is that you can write things that are hard to say out loud and you can say what you feel." (Kathi, age 12)

"The best thing about freewriting is being able to show your feelings." (Bethany, age 11)

"The best thing about it is to let my mind go free and make it just dream on and I like that and I like telling about myself." (Beth, age 11)

"I think freewriting relaxes the mind." (Tami, age 12)

"I like it 'cause we can write down things and not have to write it correctly. But I wish we had more time to write." (Doug, age 12)

Clearly, these students enjoy freewriting and recognize its value as a writing strategy.

Student writers as well as adult writers often suffer from the "blank page syndrome" or an inability to start writing. Too often when writers begin writing, they look at a clean, blank sheet of writing paper and freeze. They discard sentence after sentence as they try to create a "perfect" first sentence. Freewriting is a good prescription for the blank page syndrome. Writers simply begin to write without concern for quality and with the confidence that after three or four sentences, a usable, if not perfect, sentence will emerge.

POINTS TO PONDER
How Can Elementary Students Become More Careful Observers?
How Can Students Use Sensory Words to Make Their Writing More Vivid?

SENSORY WRITING

Professional writers are careful observers. To make their writing more vivid, they record descriptions and details and use comparisons. In contrast, children's writing is often bland because it lacks this specificity (Hillocks, 1975). By focusing on the five senses—sight, hearing, smell, touch, and taste—students can learn to write more descriptively and more vividly. The activities suggested in this section are informal, focusing on students' observations and sensory explorations.

Observations

Students can collect descriptive words to use in their writing through observational activities. They can observe pictures, objects, or events, and then brainstorm lists of descriptive words about their observations. In the classroom, students can observe pictures such as art prints, objects such as seashells, and events such as role-playing episodes. They can also practice their observational skills outside of school. For example, students in one fifth-grade class were asked to observe their bedrooms carefully and brainstorm a list of words to bring to class for a writing activity. This activity provides a good opportunity to introduce students to thesauruses, books that provide lists of word options.

Observational activities are an important component of the elementary science curriculum. As students observe a science experiment, they are often asked to describe how the substances changed. For example, in a primary class, students watched as sugar was heated and they listed words and phrases on the chalkboard to describe the changes they observed in the sequence in which they occurred. Their list included the following descriptive words and phrases:

shiny	dark, dark brown
clear	little bubbles
watery	bigger bubbles
yellow like butter	bubbles popping
brown like honey	smoke coming out of the bubbles
dark brown	almost black

These students used language descriptively and precisely. As you read their list, you can almost visualize the scene. Students can also list descriptive words in small groups and individually as they observe other experiments.

Students also use their observational skills as they examine attributes. They make charts with categories such as size, color, shape, and texture, and then list words under each category. Under size, for instance, students might include words such as *length, short, tall, large,* and *tiny,* and they list examples of each. A sample attribute chart is presented in Figure 7–10. In addition to using these property words to understand scientific concepts, students acquire a wealth of precise vocabulary words that they can use in their writing.

Sensory Explorations

Observation involves only one sense, sight. For more complete descriptions, the other four senses—touch, smell, hearing, and taste—should be involved as well (Tompkins & Friend, 1986). Teachers can plan activities similar to the ones described for sight to enhance students' awareness of these other four senses. Stu-

Size	Color

Shape	Texture

Figure 7–10   Attributes Chart

dents can collect objects with different textures (e.g., sandpaper, velvet, pine-cones) and then brainstorm words to use in describing the textures. Lists of these sensory words can be hung in the classroom for students to refer to as they write, or students can write the words in their writing journals to refer to as they write. Similarly, spices and other scents can be collected and sounds can be tape-recorded. Foods can also be sampled.

After students have worked with each of the five senses individually, they can combine the senses in other activities. Food is especially well suited for these explorations because students can use all five senses to explore food. To be sure that students give attention to each sense, prepare a five senses chart or cluster diagram as illustrated in Figure 7–11. This chart or diagram can be drawn on the chalkboard or students can make individual copies. Next, distribute a food sample, such as popcorn, apples, lemons, or chocolate, to each student. Ask them to brainstorm words in the *Look* column of the chart or the *Look* ray of the cluster. Popcorn, for example, is often described as "puffy" or "white clouds." Continue filling in the chart or cluster, listing several words or phrases for each sense. Make sure to save the *Taste* column or ray for last. (It is difficult to look at or feel a food that has already been eaten!) After students complete the chart or cluster, they can use the words and impressions they have recorded for a story, an "If I Were . . ." poem, a concrete poem, or some other writing assignment.

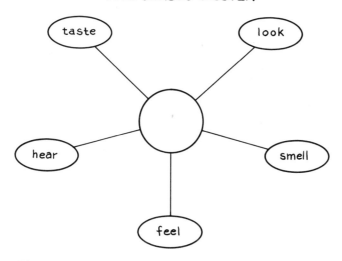

FIVE SENSES CHART				
Look	Smell	Feel	Hear	Taste

FIVE SENSES CLUSTER

Figure 7–11   Two Ways to Organize Sensory Words

Sensory explorations can also be tied to social studies topics. For instance, students can list words and phrases representing each of the five senses before beginning to write simulated journal entries as pioneers on the Oregon Trail, Arctic explorers with Commander Peary, Egyptian slaves building the Great Pyramid, or soldiers fighting in the Battle of Gettysburg. Listing sensory words before writing often helps students sharpen the focus of their writing and make it more authentic.

POINTS TO PONDER
What Types of Letters Can Elementary Students Write?
How Can Letter Writing Be Integrated with Social Studies and Science Lessons?

Students brainstorm a list of sensory words while popping popcorn.

LETTER WRITING

Letters are a way of talking to people who live too far away to visit in person. Letter writing represents a transition from expressive to transactional writing. While letters may be personal, they involve a genuine audience of one or more persons. Not only do students have the opportunity to sharpen their writing skills through writing letters, but they also develop a greater awareness of audience. Because letters are written to communicate with a specific and important audience, students take more care to think through what they want to say, are more inclined to use spelling, capitalization, and punctuation conventions correctly, and to write legibly. Letters written by elementary students are typically classified as friendly or business letters.

Friendly and business letters follow particular forms which are presented in Figure 7–12. Before students write letters, they need to learn about these forms.

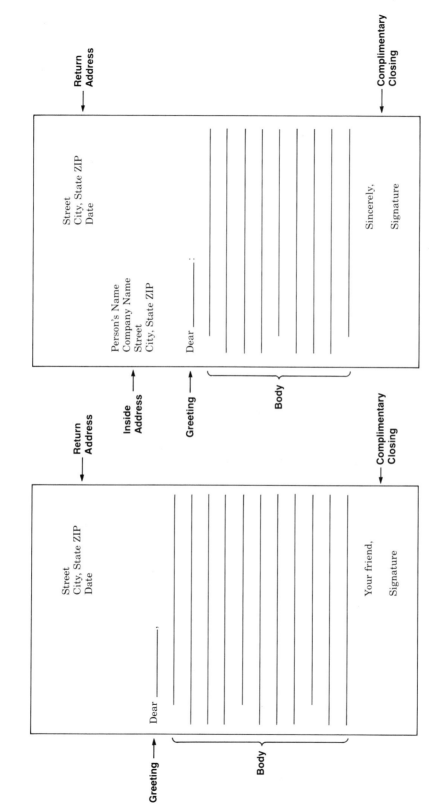

Figure 7-12 Forms for Friendly and Business Letters

223

Prepare a set of charts showing each of the forms as well as how to correctly address an envelope and present this information to students. It may also be helpful to write a class collaboration letter before writing individual letters.

Friendly Letters

Children can write friendly letters to classmates, friends who live out of town, relatives, and pen pals. Students may want to keep a list of addresses of people to write friendly letters to on a special page in their journals or in address booklets. In these casual letters, they share news about events in their lives and ask questions to learn more about the person they are writing to and to encourage that person to write back. Receiving mail is the real reward for letter writing!

After introducing the friendly letter form, students need to choose a "real" someone to write to. Writing authentic letters that are delivered is much more valuable than writing practice letters to be graded by the teacher. Students may draw names and write letters to classmates, to pen pals (exchange with students in another class in the same school or in a school in another town), or to friends and relatives. Next discuss the types of information that children might want to include in their letters. Brainstorming is an effective technique to help students consider possible ideas of what to say and what questions to ask. After writing, revising, editing, and writing final copies of their letters and addressing envelopes, students deliver their letters, by hand or by mail.

Examples of two friendly letters are presented in Figure 7–13. The first letter was sent from a second grader in one school to a pen pal in a nearby school. Notice how the writer tried to involve his reader by asking questions and constructing *yes/no* answer boxes. The second letter was written by an upper grade student to a pen pal in another country. Notice that this student also asked several questions for the pen pal to answer.

Teachers can arrange for their students to write and exchange pen pal letters with students in another class by contacting a teacher in a nearby school, through local education associations, or by answering advertisements in education magazines. Individual students can also arrange for pen pals by contacting one of the following organizations:

International Friendship League, 22 Batterymarch, Boston, MA 02109

League of Friendship, P.O. Box 509, Mt. Vernon, OH 43050

Student Letter Exchange, 910 Fourth Street SE, Austin, MN 55912

World Pen Pals, 1690 Como Avenue, St. Paul, MN 55108

Students should write to one of the organizations describing their interests and including their name, address, age, and sex. Also, they should inquire if a fee is required and enclose a self-addressed, stamped envelope for a reply.

Young children can compose class collaboration letters. The children brainstorm ideas and then the teacher records their ideas on a large chart. After the letter is finished, children add their signatures. In this way, kindergartners and other young children are introduced to the format of and the types of information in-

Figure 7-13 Pen Pal Letters

Jan. 16

Dear Chris,

I'm sorry I have not whriten.
Do you like to draw? [YES/NO] I got Legos
for Christmas. Do you like Trans Formers?
[YES/NO] I'm good at drawing. See. 
Did you git my pen pal letter?

Your Friend,
Landon

Landon, age 7

P.O. Box 177
Anadarko, OK 73005
February 11

Dear Penpal,

Hello, my name is Todd Wells.
I'm a 12 year old 7th grade boy. I've
got blond hair, blue eyes, and I
weigh about 100 lbs. I live in
Anadarko, The Heart of the Indian
Culture, in Oklahoma. The main reason
I wrote this is because I just
wanted somebody I could talk to.
I don't have very many
interests. I like most sports
like wrestling, baseball, track,
Tennis, Football. I also like to
work with my hands, be creative.
I would like to know a
little more about your Country.
Like is Canada a very good
place to go on a vacation?
I would like to have your
Address because either this summer
or next summer I'm going to take
a trip to Canada, and I might be
able to come to your house and
visit you.

Your Friend,
Todd Wells

Todd, age 12

cluded in a letter. Class collaboration letters can also be used as pen pal letters. Lillian Hoban's story *Arthur's pen pal* (1982) is a delightful way to explain what it means to be a pen pal to primary grade students.

Students may also write friendly letters to favorite TV and movie personalities as well as to favorite authors. Letters to television personalities should be sent to the network on which the personality's show appears, and letters to movie stars to the studio that produced the movie. Similarly, letters to authors should be sent in care of the author's publisher. Addresses of the television networks, movie studios, and publishers are available in reference books in public libraries. (For more information about writing letters to authors and illustrators of children's books, see Chapter 6.)

Business Letters

Business letters are more properly classified as transactional writing, but for convenience they have been included with friendly letters in this chapter. Students write business letters to seek information, to complain and compliment, and to transact business. These more formal letters are used to communicate with businesses, local newspapers, and governmental agencies. Students write to businesses to order products, to ask questions, and to complain about or compliment specific products. Students write letters to the editor of local newspapers and magazines to comment on recent articles and to express their opinions on a particular issue. It is important that students back up their comments and opinions with facts if they hope to have their letters published. Students can also write to local, state, and national government leaders to express their concerns, make suggestions, or to seek information.

Addresses of local elected officials are listed in the telephone directory. Addresses of state officials are available in the reference section of the public library, and the addresses of the president and United States senators and representatives are listed here:

Name of President, The White House, Washington, DC 20500

Name of Senator, Senate Office Building, Washington, DC 20510

Name of Representative, House of Representatives Office Building, Washington, DC 20515

Students may also write other types of business letters to request information and free materials. Figure 7–14 lists catalogues describing free and inexpensive materials that children can write for. One very popular book on the list is *Free stuff for kids* (Lansky, 1986), which lists more than 250 free or inexpensive materials that elementary students can write for. This book is updated yearly. In addition, children can write to NASA, the National Wildlife Federation, publishers, state tourism bureaus, and other businesses to request materials. Usually students are advised to enclose long, stamped, self-addressed envelopes with their requests. Sometimes, students are asked to send their requests on postcards—another letter writing form.

Catalogs

Albert, B. (1983). *Clubs for kids.* New York: Ballantine Books.

Feinman, J. (1983). *Freebies for kids.* New York: Wanderer Books.

Jorpeland, E. (1980). *The freebies book: Hundreds of things you can get free (or almost free).* New York: Holt.

Lansky, B. (1986). *Free stuff for kids.* New York: Simon & Schuster.

Moore, N. R. (1983). *Free and inexpensive learning materials.* Nashville, TN: Incentive Publications.

Osborn, S. (1982). *Free things for teachers.* New York: Perigree Books.

U.S. Government Publications

"Consumer's guide to federal publications," available from the Superintendent of Documents, Government Printing Office, Washington, DC 20402.

"Consumer information," available from the Consumer Information Center, Pueblo, CO 81009.

Figure 7–14 Sources of Free and Inexpensive Materials

Simulated Letters

Students can also write *simulated letters*—letters in which students assume the identity of a famous person or in which students communicate with inanimate objects. They can write letters as though they were Davy Crockett or one of the other men defending the Alamo, or they can write letters to their desks or a favorite toy. Even though these letters are never mailed, they provide an opportunity for students to focus on a specific audience as they write. Students can write both the original letters and the response letters or they can exchange letters with a classmate and respond to each other's letters. Students may also write letters from one book character to another as illustrated in Figure 7–15. In this letter written by a fifth grader, Charlotte, the spider in *Charlotte's web,* writes to Wilbur.

Greeting Cards

In addition to letters, students can create greeting cards to send to friends and relatives. Too often, creating greeting cards becomes a Friday afternoon activity before Mother's Day or Valentine's Day, and students are directed to glue a dittoed picture that they have colored to the front of the card and to copy a verse from the chalkboard on the inside of the card. Instead, students should create their own greeting cards to express their individuality and sentiments.

Creating greeting cards can be coordinated with a unit on word play, poetry, or even a unit on economics. One class of middle grade students studied the

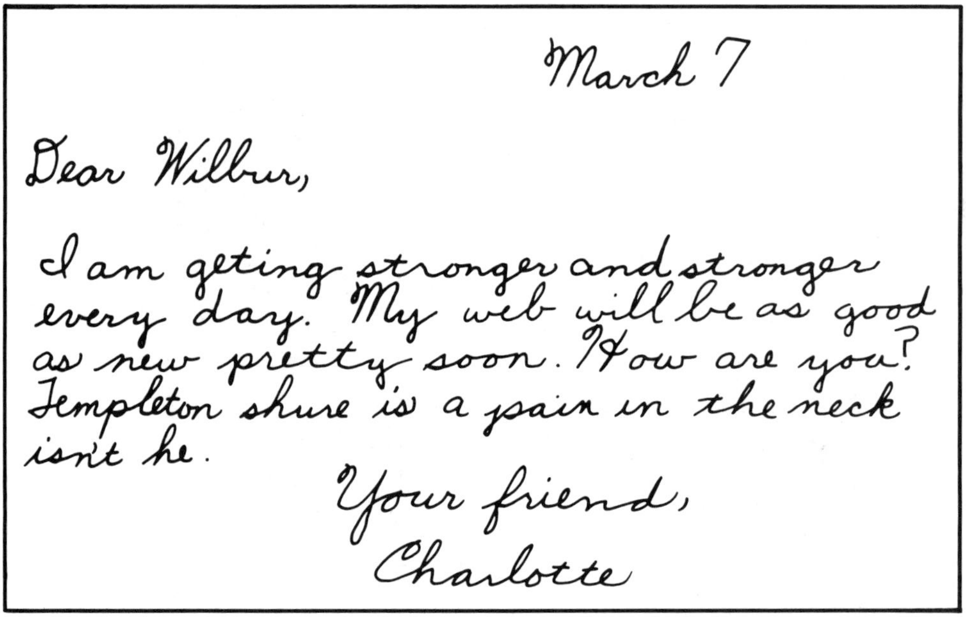

March 7

Dear Wilbur,

I am geting stronger and stronger every day. My web will be as good as new pretty soon. How are you? Templeton shure is a pain in the neck isn't he.

Your friend,
Charlotte

Figure 7–15   A Letter from Charlotte to Wilbur

American enterprise system by creating and operating a greeting card company. They sold shares of stock in the company to classmates for 25 cents to gain the money necessary to operate the company, elected a president and board of directors, assigned jobs to each class member, and then created and sold greeting cards at a profit. They sold the cards they created to other students in the school during lunch period and to people in the community. The company used the profit to pay a dividend—a pizza party—to its stockholders. While the class could have chosen other businesses to engage in while learning these economic concepts, their greeting card company provided an opportunity to expand their knowledge of a special form of written language. They examined greeting cards created by card companies and the techniques that writers use in designing these cards before they designed their own greeting cards. One of the greeting cards that the students created is presented in Figure 7–16. This card uses a play on the word *myth* for its effectiveness. Other cards that the students created used multiple-choice questions and rhyming verses, two of the devices commonly used in the commercially designed greeting cards.

Figure 7–16 Middle Grade Students' Greeting Card

Front

Inside

Third, fourth, and fifth grade classes

Summary

Expressive writing is writing that students do for and about themselves. It grows out of children's talk and is the most personal type of writing. In this chapter, we discussed four types of expressive writing: (a) journals and diaries, (b) freewriting, (c) sensory writing, and (d) letter writing.

Students use journal writing to learn more about themselves, to practice writing, and to record the events in their lives. Literature also plays a role in journal writing. Students can read stories in which characters keep diaries and journals, and they can record their reactions to the stories they are reading in learning logs.

Freewriting is a writing strategy developed by Peter Elbow. In this strategy, students write for a period of time without stopping. Students' first freewrites are unfocused; they can choose an idea from these first writings and write additional, more focused freewrites. One value of freewriting is that stu-dents develop writing fluency and learn a strategy they can use to combat the blank page syndrome.

Through sensory writing activities, students can become more careful observers and use descriptions, details, and compari-sons to make their writing more vivid. Sug-gestions were given for helping students de-velop their powers of observation and their other four senses. Some observation activi-ties can be tied to science lessons and other sensory explorations can be expanded into writing poetry and across the curriculum ac-tivities.

Students can share their thoughts and feel-ings with friends and pen pals in friendly let-ters and write to request information or to complain about a product in business letters. They can also write simulated letters, post-cards, and greeting cards. Letter writing re-presents a transition from expressive to transactional writing.

Extensions

1. Choose 18 or 20 of the writing forms pre-sented in Figure 7–1 and plan how they could be incorporated at the grade level you teach or plan to teach. Consider ways to integrate them with other language arts activities or with social studies and other content area subjects.

2. Have students keep one or more of the six types of journals described in the section on "Journal Writing" for a period of 4 to 6 weeks.

3. Keep a personal journal in which you re-cord personal experiences and feelings or a learning log in which you reflect on the material presented in this book as well as your teaching or aiding experiences for the remainder of the school term.

4. Have a small group of students participate in several unfocused and focused free-writing experiences. Explain to students that the goal of freewriting is to generate ideas and the words to express those ideas, and that correct spelling and careful handwriting are not important during freewriting. Later, students can polish one of their focused freewrites and share it with their classmates.

5. Plan and teach a sensory exploration ac-tivity to a small group of students using food such as popcorn, apples, or choco-late to generate words and phrases for each sense. Then have students use the words and phrases they have generated to write a story, poem, or other composition.

6. Arrange for a group of students to write friendly letters to pen pals in another school. Review the friendly letter form and how to address an envelope. Use the writing process in which students draft, revise, and edit their letters before mailing them.

References

Blos, J. (1979). *A gathering of days: A New England girl's journal, 1830–1832.* New York: Scribner.

Britton, J., Burgess, T., Martin, N., McLeod, A., & Rosen, H. (1975). *The development of writing abilities (11–18).* London: Macmillan Education Ltd. for the Schools Council.

Elbow, P. (1973). *Writing without teachers.* London: Oxford University Press.

Elliott, S., Nowosad, J., & Samuels, P. (1981). 'Me at home,' 'me at school': Using journals with preschoolers. *Language Arts, 58,* 688–691.

Fitzhugh, L. (1964). *Harriet the spy.* New York: Harper and Row.

Fulwiler, T. (1985). Writing and learning, grade 3. *Language Arts, 62,* 55–59.

Gambrell, L. B. (1985). Dialogue journals: Reading-writing interaction. *The Reading Teacher, 38,* 512–515.

Hillocks, G., Jr. (1975). *Observing and writing.* Urbana, IL: ERIC Clearinghouse on Reading and Communication Skills and National Council of Teachers of English.

Hipple, M. L. (1985). Journal writing in kindergarten. *Language Arts, 62,* 255–261.

Hoban, L. (1982). *Arthur's pen pal.* New York: Harper and Row.

Klein, M. L. (1985). *The development of writing in children: Pre-K through grade 8.* Englewood Cliffs, NJ: Prentice-Hall.

Kreeft, J. (1984). Dialogue writing — Bridge from talk to essay writing. *Language Arts, 61,* 141–150.

Lansky, B. (1986). *Free stuff for kids.* New York: Simon and Schuster.

Progoff, I. (1975). *At a journal workshop: The basic text and guide for using the intensive journal process.* New York: Dialogue House.

Salem, J. (1982). Using writing in teaching mathematics. In M. Barr, P. D'Arcy, & M. K. Healy (Eds.), *What's going on? Language/learning episodes in British and American classrooms, grades 4–13,* (pp. 123–134). Montclair, NJ: Boynton/Cook.

Staton, J. (1980). Writing and counseling: Using a dialogue journal. *Language Arts, 57,* 514–518.

Tchudi, S., & Tchudi, S. (1984). *The young writer's handbook: A practical guide for the beginner who is serious about writing.* New York: Scribner.

Tompkins, G., & Friend, M. (1986). On your mark, get set, write! *Teaching Exceptional Children, 18,* 82–89.

Tway, E. (1981). Come, write with me. *Language Arts, 58,* 805–810.

———. (1984). *Time for writing in the elementary school.* Urbana, IL: ERIC Clearinghouse on Reading and Communication Skills and the National Council of Teachers of English.

IF YOU WANT TO LEARN MORE

Barr, M., D'Arcy, P., & Healy, M. K. (Eds.). (1982). *What's going on? Language/learning episodes in British and American classrooms, grades 4–13.* Montclair, NJ: Boynton/Cook.

Beach, R. (1977). *Writing about ourselves and others.* Urbana, IL: ERIC Clearinghouse on Reading and Communication Skills and National Council of Teacher of English.

Burrows, A. T., Jackson, D. C., & Saunders, D. O. (1984). *They all want to write: Written English in the elementary school* (4th ed.). Hamden, CT: Library Professional Publications.

Gere, A. R. (Ed.). (1985). *Roots in the sawdust: Learning to write across the disciplines.* Urbana, IL: National Council of Teachers of English.

Jackson, J. (1974). *Turn not pale, beloved snail: A book about writing among other things.* Boston: Little, Brown.

Newkirk, T., & Atwell, N. (Eds.). (1982). *Understanding writing: Ways of observing, learning and teaching K–8.* Chelmsford, MA: The Northeast Regional Exchange.

P. S. write soon! All about letters. (1982). Urbana, IL: United States Postal Service and the National Council of Teachers of English.

Tchudi, S., & Tchudi, S. (1983). *Teaching writing in the content areas: Elementary school.* Washington, D.C.: National Education Association. (See also *Teaching writing in the content areas: Middle school/junior high.*)

Tway, E. (1985). *Writing is reading: 26 ways to connect.* Urbana, IL: ERIC Clearinghouse on Reading and Communication Skills and National Council of Teachers of English.

CHAPTER EIGHT

Reading and Writing Transactional Texts

O*VERVIEW.   In this chapter, we will consider transactional writing, another of the three categories proposed by James Britton (1970). Transactional writing is both practical and public. We will present a variety of transactional texts which students read and write, including research reports, newspapers, autobiographies, and biographies. We will examine both the general form and function of these transactional texts as well as organizational patterns used within them. Newspaper articles, for instance, are typically organized to answer the 5 Ws plus one—who, what, when, where, why, and how.*

As children gain experience and expertise with reading and writing, their writing moves from informal writing for themselves to more formal and more public writing. Using James Britton's categories presented in the last chapter, we say that children's writing moves from expressive writing to transactional and poetic writing. In this chapter, we will focus on *transactional writing,* writing that has as its purpose to get things done. Britton (1970) describes transactional writing as writing used "to interact with people and things and to make the wheels of the world, for good or ill, go round" (p. 8).

Transactional writing is not a discrete category. Elements of poetic writing are found in transactional writing just as elements of transactional writing are found in poetic writing. Many newspaper articles, for instance, seem to tell a story as well as report facts. In this chapter, we will discuss three major types of transactional texts: (a) research reports, (b) newspapers, and (c) biographies and autobiographies.

POINTS TO PONDER

What Are the Five Organizational Patterns Used in Content Area Textbooks, Informational Tradebooks, and Research Reports?

How Do Elementary Students Write Class Collaboration Research Reports?

How Do Students Write Individual and Small Group Reports?

How Are Written Research Reports Similar to Oral Reports?

RESEARCH REPORTS

One of the most common types of school writing is the research or informational report. The preparation of written reports is very similar to oral reports, which were discussed in Chapter 4. In preparing both oral and written reports, students choose a topic, gather information, and organize the information. The main difference is in the method of presentation: Instead of presenting the reports orally, students write these research reports using the process approach to writing.

Too often students are not exposed to research reports until they are faced with writing a report in high school. Then they are overwhelmed with learning how to take notes on notecards, to organize and write the paper, and to compile a bibliography. There is no reason to postpone report writing until students are in high school. Students in the elementary grades can write class collaboration and individual reports. Through early and successful experiences with report writing, students not only learn how to write research reports but they also learn about content areas through research and writing.

Organizational Patterns

Most forms of transactional and poetic writing are organized or structured in particular ways. Many students are familiar with story structures, such as beginning-middle-end and plot, through telling and reading stories as well as watching them on television. They write poems such as haiku and cinquain which follow syllable-counting formulas, and they read and write biographies and autobiographies which usually follow a chronological sequence.

Transactional texts, which include social studies and other content area textbooks, informational tradebooks, and encyclopedias, follow particular organizational patterns. Reading educators have examined content area reading materials that elementary and high school students read to devise ways to help students comprehend those materials more easily. Through their examination, they have identified a number of patterns or structures used in these textbooks and in tradebooks. These organizational patterns are called *expository text structures*. Five of the most commonly used organizational patterns are (a) description, (b) sequence, (c) comparison, (d) cause and effect, and (e) problem and solution (Niles, 1974; Meyer & Freedle, 1984). In Figure 8–1, these patterns are described and sample passages and a list of cue words that signal authors' use of each pattern are presented.

These organizational patterns correspond to the traditional organization of main ideas and details within paragraphs. The main idea is embodied in the organizational pattern and the details are the elaboration. For example, in the sample passage for the comparison pattern presented in Figure 8–1, the main idea is that the modern Olympics is very different than the ancient Olympic games. The details are the specific comparisons and contrasts. The main idea and details for the comparison passage are illustrated in Figure 8–2. Similar *graphic organizers,* or diagrams with key words from the passage, can be developed for the other four organizational patterns.

Information in content area textbooks, informational tradebooks, and encyclopedias is easier to understand and remember when authors use a clear organizational structure. Unfortunately, not all reading material is clearly structured, but students who are familiar with the five organizational patterns will understand even poorly organized reading material better than students who are not aware of the patterns. Researchers have found that many elementary students are unaware of these five organizational patterns and do not use them to comprehend information they are reading (Taylor & Samuels, 1983).

Figure 8–1 The Five Organizational Patterns

Pattern	Description	Cue Words	Sample Passage
Description	The author describes a topic by listing characteristics, features, and examples.	*for example* *characteristics are*	The Olympic symbol consists of five interlocking rings. The rings represent the five continents—Africa, Asia, Europe, North America, and South America—from which athletes come to compete in the games. The rings are colored black, blue, green, red, and yellow. At least one of these colors is found in the flag of every country sending athletes to compete in the Olympic games.
Sequence	The author lists items or events in numerical or chronological order.	*first, second, third* *next* *then* *finally*	The Olympic games began as athletic festivals to honor the Greek gods. The most important festival was held in the valley of Olympia to honor Zeus, the king of the gods. It was this festival that became the Olympic games in 776 B.C. These games were ended in A.D. 394 by the Roman Emperor who ruled Greece. No Olympic games were held for more than 1,500 years. Then the modern Olympics began in 1896. Almost 300 male athletes competed in the first modern Olympics. In the games held in 1900, female athletes were allowed to compete. The games have continued every four years since 1896 except during World War II, and they will most likely continue for many years to come.
Comparison	The author explains how two or more things are alike and/or how they are different.	*different* *in contrast* *alike* *same as* *on the other hand*	The modern Olympics are very unlike the ancient Olympic games. Individual events are different. While there were no swimming races in the ancient games, for example, there were chariot races. There were no female contestants and all athletes competed in the nude. Of course, the ancient and modern Olympics are also alike in many ways. Some

236

events, such as the javelin and discus throws, are the same. Some people say that cheating, professionalism, and nationalism in the modern games are a disgrace to the ancient Greek Olympic tradition. But according to the ancient Greek writers, there were many cases of cheating, nationalism, and professionalism in their Olympics, too.

There are several reasons why so many people attend the Olympic games or watch them on television. One reason is tradition. The name *Olympics* and the torch and flame remind people of the ancient games. People can escape the ordinariness of daily life by attending or watching the Olympics. They like to identify with someone else's individual sacrifice and accomplishment. National pride is another reason, and an athlete's or a team's hard earned victory becomes a nation's victory. There are national medal counts and people keep track of how many medals their country's athletes have won.

One problem with the modern Olympics is that it has become very big and expensive to operate. The city or country that hosts the games often loses a lot of money. A stadium, pools, and playing fields must be built for the athletic events and housing is needed for the athletes who come from around the world. And all of these facilities are used for only 2 weeks! In 1984, Los Angeles solved these problems by charging a fee for companies who wanted to be official sponsors of the games. Companies like McDonald's paid a lot of money to be part of the Olympics. Many buildings that were already built in the Los Angeles area were also used. The Coliseum where the 1932 games were held was used again and many colleges and universities in the area became playing and living sites.

Cause and Effect	The author lists one or more causes and the resulting effect or effects.	*reasons why* *if . . . then* *as a result* *therefore* *because*
Problem and Solution	The author states a problem and lists one or more solutions for the problem. A variation of this pattern is the question-and-answer format in which the author poses a question and then answers it.	*problem is* *dilemma is* *puzzle is solved* *question . . .* *answer*

Adapted from McGee & Richgels, 1985, pp. 741–742.

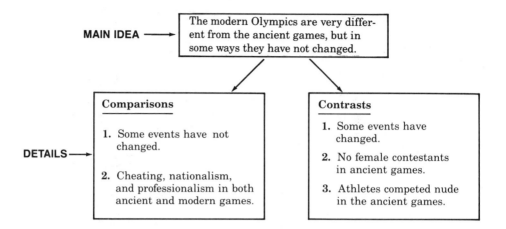

Figure 8–2   Graphic Organizer for Comparison

Students can be taught to recognize these patterns and to use the patterns to improve reading comprehension and organize their writing (McGee & Richgels, 1985; Flood, Lapp, & Farnan, 1986; Taylor & Samuels, 1983). The instructional strategy for teaching students about the five organizational patterns is based on the same instructional model presented in Chapter 1. Students are introduced to a pattern, they read sample passages using the pattern, and then apply what they have learned in writing their own passages using the pattern. The steps in the instructional strategy are detailed in Figure 8–3. The process is repeated for each of the organizational patterns. As a final step in the strategy, students learn how to choose the appropriate organizational pattern to communicate their message most effectively. They can experiment by trying to write one set of information using two or more of the organizational patterns. For example, information about igloos can be written using description or as a comparison with Indian teepees.

Most of the research on students' ability to use the five organizational patterns has focused on upper grade and high school students. However, even primary grade students use the patterns in writing research reports. Excerpts from second graders' dinosaur reports that exemplify each of the five organizational patterns are presented in Figure 8–4. Teachers can help students organize their reports by first identifying key concepts, such as the two major types of dinosaurs—plant eaters and meat eaters—and possible reasons why the dinosaurs died. Then they draw a cluster with the concepts listed and ask students to develop the cluster as a prewriting activity. A cluster for dinosaurs with five rays focusing on the organizational patterns is presented in Figure 8–5.

Class Collaboration Reports

A crucial step in teaching students to write is the class collaboration in which students and the teacher write a composition together. Through this group writing activity, the students have an opportunity to practice the form of writing, and the

Step 1: Initiating

Introduce one of the organizational patterns using a chart that describes the pattern and lists a few cue words. Explain the pattern and cue words and then read a passage from a content area textbook or an informational tradebook that exemplifies the pattern. As additional cue words are found, add them to the list on the chart.

Step 2: Structuring

Share additional passages that exemplify the structure and have students identify cue words that signal the pattern and explain why the passage is an example of the particular pattern. Also, draw a graphic organizer or diagram with key words from the passage to illustrate the organization of the passage.

Step 3: Conceptualizing

Have students locate passages that exemplify the organizational pattern in content area textbooks or informational tradebooks. Have students share the passages they locate, identify cue words that signal the pattern, and draw a graphic organizer.

Step 4: Summarizing

Review the organizational pattern by rereading the chart presented in the first step and having students describe the pattern and list the cue words. Also, students can copy the chart in their writing journals and include a list of cue words that signal the pattern for readers.

Step 5: Generalizing

Have students locate additional passages that exemplify the organizational pattern in textbooks or tradebooks and share them with small groups of classmates.

Step 6: Applying

Have students write passages using the organizational pattern. Students should write about a topic they know well, such as a topic they are studying in social studies or science or about a hobby.

Figure 8–3   Instructional Strategy for Teaching Students
about Organizational Patterns

teacher can review the writing process and clarify any misconceptions about the writing activity. Writing research reports is no exception. Through a class collaboration research report, small groups of students work together to write parts of the report, which are then compiled to form the class research report.

The first step in writing class collaboration research reports is to choose a topic. Almost any social studies, science, or current events topic that can be subdivided into 4 to 10 parts works well for class collaboration reports. Possible topics in-

Description

How about Tyrannosaurus Rex? Tyrannosaurus Rex was 50 feet long and as tall as a telephone pole. This dinosaur had teeth 6 inches long and sharp claws on its feet. Its front legs were tiny, but its back legs were big and strong. All other dinosaurs were afraid of Tyrannosaurus Rex.

Danielle, age 8

Sequence

Before the dinosaurs there were fish and mollusks. There were insects. The land was bare. Plants started to grow but there were not very many. Not all the dinosaurs lived at once. There were three different periods: the Triassic Period, Jurassic Period, and Cretaceous Period. In the Triassic Period the dinosaurs were small and most of them walked on two legs. In the Jurassic Period the dinosaurs were real big. Allosaurus lived then. Birds appeared at this time also. In the next period, most of the dinosaurs were all different sizes. Tyrannosaurus Rex was the king. Eventually all of the dinosaurs died out. Then the first early humans appeared. I think this was probably the cave man. Today there are descendents of the dinosaurs. They are crocodiles, turtles, and cockroaches.

Amanda, age 8

Figure 8–4   Examples of Organizational Patterns from Second
Graders' Dinosaur Reports

clude dinosaurs, the solar system, the human body, life in the Middle Ages, and types of transportation. After identifying the main topic, students identify specific topics that small groups or pairs of students can research. They can brainstorm a list of specific topics such as parts of the body or develop a cluster of specific topics such as the cluster on dinosaurs presented in Figure 8–5. Next, students need to decide on key points to be covered in the report. In a report on the human body, for example, students studying each body part may decide to include the same key points, such as a description of the body part and its function in the body. In a report on dinosaurs, in contrast, a different set of key points may need to be developed for each specific topic. Then students divide into small groups or pairs and choose a specific topic.

Comparison

There are two kinds of dinosaurs. One of the kinds is the plant eaters. The other kind is the meat eaters. There are more plant eaters than meat eaters. Some of the names of the plant eaters are Trachodon, Brontosaurus, and Brachiosaurus. Some of the meat eaters' names are Tyrannosaurus Rex and a few others. Plant eaters have small heads and blunt teeth. Meat eaters are different. They have big heads and sharp teeth. Scientists say that when dinosaurs walk on two legs, it's usually a meat eater. When a dinosaur walks on four legs, it's usually a plant eater.

Stephanie, age 8

Cause and Effect

Some people think that the dinosaurs died because of Halley's Comet or a volcano erupted and ashes came and poisoned the plants. Then the plant eaters could have died. Then the meat eaters died because there was no food because the plant eaters had rotted. And some think that a great big asteroid came and blocked the light of the sun. It became cold and all the dinosaurs died. Or they think the sea monsters in the Bible were dinosaurs and then a great flood came and killed all the dinosaurs.

Caleb, age 8

Problem and Solution

Scientists know that dinosaurs lived because they found their fossils. You can see them at a museum. They are now skeletons.

Amanda, age 8

Figure 8–4 *Continued*

Before the students set to work researching and writing their parts of the report, the class works through the procedure using one of the specific topics the students did not choose. As a class, students gather information, organize it, and then write the section of the report using the drafting, revising, and editing stages of the writing process.

After this whole-class practice, students work in small groups or in pairs to research their self-selected specific topics. They gather information from a variety of reference materials, including both print and nonprint sources, and record important information they locate on notecards or data charts. (An example of a data chart was presented in the section on oral research reports in Chapter 4.) Students also compile a set of bibliography notecards, listing each reference source that

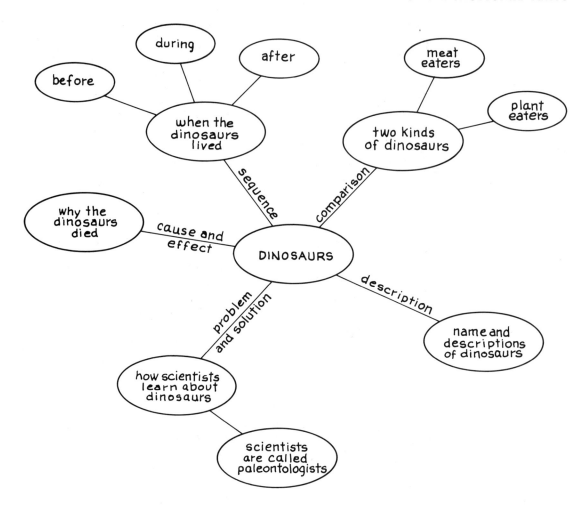

Figure 8–5   A Cluster on Dinosaurs with Rays Focusing on the Five
Organizational Patterns

they use. Collecting the bibliographic information as the materials are being used simplifies compiling the bibliography later.

After students collect the information they need for their section of the report, they organize it. It is often helpful for students to read over the information they have recorded on notecards or on a data chart and delete any unnecessary or redundant information. Then they consider how they will write the information and what organizational pattern or patterns they might use. As a last step in organizing information, students can number the pieces of information they have collected in the order they plan to use them in their composition.

With this preparation, students are ready to write their sections of the report using the process approach to writing. They write their first draft, skipping every other line to simplify revising and editing. Because students are working in pairs or small groups, one student can be designated as scribe to write the draft while the other students in the group dictate the sentences. Next, the students in the group revise the draft and then share it with students from other small groups. Students revise their compositions on the basis of feedback they have received. Then the same procedure is repeated for proofreading and correcting mechanical errors.

Students bring their completed sections for the research report and compile them. As a class, the students write the introduction, conclusion, and bibliography, and add them to the report. A list should also be added at the end of the report listing the authors of each section. After all the parts are compiled, it is a good idea to reread the entire report, looking for inconsistencies and redundant passages.

The last step in writing a class collaboration research report is to publish the report. A final copy with all of the parts of the report is made, and it can be typed or recopied by hand. Then copies are made for each student, and special bound copies can be constructed for the class or school library.

Students benefit from writing a large-group report before writing small-group or individual reports because they learn how to write a research report before they are asked to write individual reports. Also, by working in groups, the laborious work is shared. The steps in writing class collaboration reports are summarized in Figure 8–6.

Figure 8–7 presents the class collaboration human body report developed by a second-grade class. Together the class composed the introduction and the conclusion while students worked together in small groups to write the reports on the specific body parts.

Individual Reports

Students write individual reports following the same steps used in writing class collaboration reports. They choose their own topics related to their areas of interest. Toby Fulwiler (1985) explains that students should do "authentic" research in which they explore topics that interest them or hunt for answers to questions that puzzle them. The prewriting stage involves choosing a topic, gathering information and organizing it. Next, students draft their reports and revise and edit them. The audience is important in writing research reports just as it is in other types of writing. Often reports are published as informational books that are added to the class or school library.

Students can also organize their reports in a variety of formats—formats that they have seen used in informational books. One possibility is a question-answer format, and another possibility is an alphabet book. One group of upper grade students chose to organize their small-group report on the state of Vermont as an alphabet book, with one page for each letter of the alphabet. The *G* page is presented in Figure 8–8 (page 247).

Young Children's Reports

Even very young children can write reports which they dictate to their teacher who serves as scribe. After listening to a guest speaker, viewing films, or reading

1. *Choose a Topic*

   Brainstorm possible topics and choose an overall topic for the report.

   Use a cluster to identify specific topics.

   Divide students into small groups or pairs and have them choose specific topics.

   Decide on the key points to be covered in the report.

2. *Gather Information*

   Collect reference materials, including nonprint sources.

   Ask students to consult a variety of references in collecting information.

   Use notecards or a data chart (see Chapter 4) to record information.

   List all reference materials on bibliography notecards.

3. *Organize the Information*

   Read over the information on notecards or on a data chart.

   Delete unnecessary or redundant information.

   Identify possible patterns for organizing the report.

   Number the important information in sequence for the report.

4. *Write the Report*

   Write a draft, skipping every other line to simplify revising and editing.

   Share drafts in writing conferences.

   Ask students to first comment on the strengths of the report and then to ask clarifying questions and to make suggestions.

   Revise and edit the report based on the feedback received at the conference.

5. *Compile the Report*

   Write the introduction and conclusion together as a class.

   Sequence the small-group reports and compile them.

   List the names of students who wrote each section at the end of the report.

   Prepare the bibliography, listing all reference materials consulted.

6. *Publish the Report*

   Type or recopy the report.

   Make copies of the report for each student.

   Make bound copies for the class or school library.

Figure 8–6   Steps in Preparing Class Collaboration Research Reports

The Human Body

Your body keeps you alive. These are some of the things in your body. They are the bladder, blood, bones, brain, gall bladder, heart, intestines, kidneys, liver, lungs, muscles, pancreas, and stomach.

Bladder

The bladder is a storage tank for the urine. It is a stretchy bag. The waste comes from the blood. The blood goes to different parts of the body. Then it goes to the kidneys. The kidneys clean the blood. When the bladder is full, it sends a signal to the brain.

Blood

We have two kinds of blood cells. There are white blood cells and red blood cells. The white blood cells are shaped like a bean. The red blood cells are shaped like a circle. Red blood cells are smaller than white blood cells. Blood carries oxygen, food, and water.

Bones

Did you know there are 206 bones in your body? Your bones make you move. If you had no bones you would be flat and you could not walk. The bones are hard and smooth. All of the bones are called a skeleton.

Brain

The brain is located in your head. It is gray and wrinkly. The brain is soft. An average man's brain weighs three pounds. A woman's brain is smaller. Your brain tells you things. It helps you see. If we didn't have a brain, we couldn't think. It helps you move. Your brain is a very important part of your body.

Gall Bladder

The gall bladder is very little. It is a small bag that stores bile. The gall bladder is green. It's shaped like a pear. The gall bladder is by the pancreas and the left kidney.

Heart

Your heart is as big as your fist. It's also shaped like a pear. The heart is not like a valentine. There are door-like things in your heart. There are four of them. They are called valves. When the top ones close, the bottom ones open. When the bottom ones close, the top ones open. Your heart beats night and day. You can't live without your heart.

Intestines

We have two intestines. They are the large intestine and the small intestine. The small intestine empties into the large intestine. The large intestine is 5 feet long. The small intestine is 20 feet long. The intestines help digest food.

Kidneys

We have two kidneys. They are red and brown. The kidneys are 11 cm. long, 6 cm. wide and 35 cm. thick. They are bean shaped. The kidneys are near the lower part of the back. They weigh 400 grams. The kidneys get rid of 400 liters of liquid waste everyday.

(Figure continues on next page.)

Figure 8–7 *Continued*

Liver

The liver is the biggest organ in our body. It is brick red. It makes bile. It stores extra sugar. Some of the food that the body needs goes to the liver. It is stored there until the body needs it.

Lungs

The body has two lungs. The lungs are like balloons. They are also like two sponges. Your lungs weigh about one kilogram. Your lungs are pink. If you smoke, they'll turn black.

Muscles

Everyone has 600 muscles. Muscles are dark red. Each muscle is a different shape or size. Muscles work together in pairs. It takes muscle to move bones. Many of your muscles fasten to the bones of your skeleton. Some muscles are deep inside. One-fourth of the muscles are in the face and neck. You even use muscles when you read.

Pancreas

The pancreas is a small organ. It produces a digestive juice and the hormones insulin and glucagon. It is by the liver. The pancreas is light yellow. It looks like corn. If you lose your pancreas you will die.

Stomach

The stomach is located in the upper part of the abdomen under the heart. Your stomach is a bag with walls of muscles. It is shaped like a pear. The food goes through a tube called the esophagus. The stomach breaks up the food and mixes it. Without the stomach you cannot live. If the heart stops, the stomach will stop.

We studied about the most important body parts. We learned a lot of stuff about these organs. Now we're finished. It was fun!

The End

Bibliography

Baldwin, Dorothy and Claire Lister. *Your Body Fuel,* 1983.

Follett, Robert, Jr. *Your Wonderful Body,* 1961.

Gabb, Michael. *Secrets of the Human Body,* 1980.

LeMaster, Leslie. *Your Brain and Nervous System,* 1984.

Martin, Rhen. *Your Stomach and Digestive Tract, 1973.*

Ravielli, Anthony. *Wonders of the Human Body,* 1960.

Showers, Paul. *Hear Your Heart,* 1968.

Showers, Paul. *Use Your Brain,* 1971.

Showers, Paul. *You Can't Make a Move Without Your Muscles,* 1982.

Silverstein, Alvin. *The Digestive System,* 1970.

Zim, Herbert S. *Your Heart and How It Works,* 1959.

Zim, Herbert S. *Your Skin,* 1979.

Zim, Herbert S. *Your Stomach and Digestive Tract,* 1983.

Second graders

Figure 8–8 A Page from an ABC Book
about Vermont

Janet, Sarah, Sherrie, and Leslie, age 13

two or three books about a particular topic, kindergartners and first graders can dictate brief reports. A class of kindergartners compiled the book-length report on police officers presented in Figure 8–9. The teacher read two books aloud to the students and Officer Jerry, a police officer, visited the classroom and talked to the students about his job. Also, the students took a field trip to visit the police station. The teacher took photos of Officer Jerry, his police car, and the police station to illustrate the report. With this background, the students were well prepared to compose their report.

POINTS TO PONDER
How Can Newspapers Be Tied to Language Study?
How Can Elementary Students Write Class Newspapers?
What Kinds of Newspapers Can Students Write in Connection with Content Area Units?

Figure 8–9   Kindergartners' Dictated Report

Our Report about Police Officers

Page 1:   Police officers help people who are in trouble. They are nice to kids. They are only mean to robbers and bad people. Police officers make people obey the laws. They give tickets to people who drive cars too fast.

Page 2:   Men and women can be police officers. They wear blue uniforms like Officer Jerry's. But sometimes police officers wear regular clothes when they work undercover. They wear badges on their uniforms and on their hats. Officer Jerry's badge number is 3407. Police officers have guns, handcuffs, whistles, sticks, and two-way radios. They have to carry all these things.

Page 3:   Police officers drive police cars with flashing lights and loud sirens. The cars have radios so the officers can talk to other police officers at the police station. Sometimes they ride on police motorcycles or on police horses or in police helicopters or in police boats.

Page 4:   Police officers work at police stations. The jail for the bad people that they catch is right next door. One police officer sits at the radio to talk to the police officers who are driving their cars. The police chief works at the police station, too.

Page 5:   Police officers are your friends. They want to help you so you shouldn't be afraid of them. You can ask them if you need some help.

Page 6:   How We Learned About Police Officers for Our Report

    1. We read these books:
       Police by Ray Broekel
       What Do They Do? Policemen and Firemen by Carla Greene

    2. We interviewed Officer Jerry.

    3. We visited the police station.

Kindergarten class

NEWSPAPERS

Newspapers are one of the richest and least expensive sources of reading material and information about writing available today. Language is used for several different functions in newspapers, to inform and to persuade as well as to entertain. Reading newspapers can be tied to language study as well as to current events. Moreover, students learn to write different types of newspaper articles and to produce their own class newspapers.

Reading Newspapers

To appeal to all segments of their huge and diverse audiences, newspapers contain many different types of information. Sargent (1975) lists the following general categories of subject matter in newspapers:

general news or current events	opinions
sports news	business news
comics and cartoons	youth/teen features
women's news	society news
human relations/guidance articles	human interest features
arts features	leisure/recreation information
advertisements	real estate listings
weather information	legal notices

A student clips articles to use in examining the characteristics of newspaper articles.

Students discover these categories by reading and examining newspapers. Have students bring newspapers or order a class set of your local newspaper or *USA Today*. Working in pairs or small groups, students can investigate the parts of a newspaper. Students can list the categories that they discover on a chart and then cite examples of each category to add to the chart. For example, upper grade students might cite editorials, letters to the editor, syndicated columns, and editoral cartoons as examples of opinion articles.

Many different types of reading activities are possible using newspapers. These activities range from vocabulary study to considering the objectivity of news stories and interpreting cartoons, graphs, and maps. As they read news stories, students can check that all basic elements of a news story, the 5 *W*s plus one— *who, what, where, when, why* and *how*—are included. Newspapers can also be used for word study and other language activities. For example, students can hunt for different words used to describe movement (e.g., *tackle, run, leap*) in sports articles or search for adverbs or other parts of speech in news articles.

Organization of a Newspaper Article

Students can investigate the kinds of information included in each category of newspaper articles. For instance, a weather report includes different kinds of information and is written in a different way than a sports article or a news article. Most news articles are written to answer the 5 *W*s plus one questions. Ask students to read examples of a particular type of newspaper article, and then have them look to see how the article is structured. Next, list the characteristics on a chart. Repeat the procedure with other types of articles. Then students have the information they have learned available to use in writing their own newspaper articles for a class newspaper.

Writing Class Newspapers

After students have investigated newspapers and the types of information included in each category of newspaper articles, they apply what they have learned by writing their own class newspapers. Certain decisions must be made before starting to write the newspaper. For example, students will have to choose a name for the newspaper, decide what categories of articles to include in the newspaper, identify the audience for the newspaper, and develop a timeline for its production.

After these decisions have been made, students write articles for the various categories of articles that will be included in the newspaper. All students serve as reporters. Students can be assigned to write specific articles, but it is often more effective to have students sign up for the articles they wish to contribute. Students use the process approach to write their articles, and after completing their rough drafts, they meet in conference groups to revise and later to edit their articles. After the articles have been completed, they can be typed or recopied neatly by hand. Word processing programs such as *The newsroom* (1984) can be used to simplify formatting the newspaper.

Later, an editorial staff meets to make final decisions about which articles to include in this issue of the newspaper and what additional work needs to be done. After the articles are selected, they must be arranged on sheets of paper, either using traditional cut-and-paste layouts or using a word processing program to produce a very professional-looking publication. Then the newspaper is duplicated and distributed. Newspapers can be an on-going project throughout the year with issues being published periodically.

A class newspaper, *The Goggles Gazette,* produced by a class of third, fourth, and fifth graders is presented in Figure 8–10. Students wrote articles, revised and edited them, and then recopied them on paper cut into column-sized sheets. Then the teacher and student editorial staff reviewed the articles and selected the ones to put into the newspaper. They chose articles about news events as well as puzzles and riddles that would appeal to their audience. They also decided to include a letter the class had received from Patricia Lee Gauch, an author of children's books who had recently visited the class. Then the teacher and another group of students decided on the arrangement of articles and glued them on sheets of paper. Next, the teacher had the newspaper duplicated and the distribution staff collated and stapled the copies and then distributed them to each student in their class and to the other classes in the school. While it is nice to have the articles typed, it is not necessary as the newspaper in Figure 8–10 illustrates. Students can recopy their own articles neatly.

Kindergarten teachers often ask students to dictate accounts of the week's events to form a one-page class newspaper that students take home to inform their parents about what is going on in the classroom. Together the teacher and the children decide on several important events to write about, and the teacher records the children's dictation on the chalkboard. Next, the teacher reads the rough draft with the children and encourages them to suggest changes, additions, and deletions to improve the article. After children have made the changes and are satisfied with their articles, the teacher copies the articles on a sheet of paper and duplicates it for the children to take home. Not only is this an excellent way to keep parents informed about what is happening in the classroom, but it also introduces young children to another form and function of written language and helps them to learn to use the writing process to communicate effectively.

Simulated Newspapers

Students can also write simulated newspapers in connection with units in other content areas. In these newspapers, students can apply what they have learned about the historical events and characters as they write articles for the newspaper. In connection with a unit on the American Revolution, an upper grade class produced a simulated newspaper, *The Boston Patriot,* that might have been published in Boston on April 20, 1775, the day after the battles of Lexington and Concord. Simulated newspapers contain the same categories of articles as real newspapers—current events, weather, advertisements, editorials, and sports news.

Figure 8–10   A Middle Grade Class Newspaper

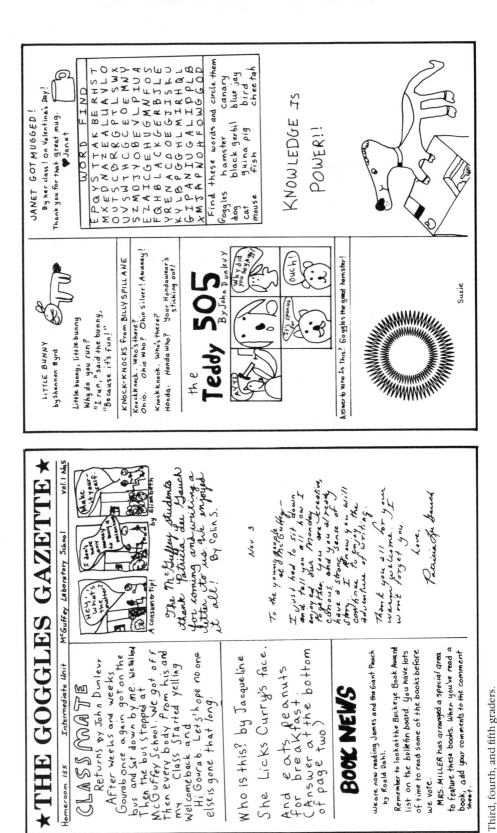

Third, fourth, and fifth graders.

POINTS TO PONDER
How Can Elementary Students Write About Themselves and Others?
How Can Students Collect Memories and Compile Autobiographies?
How Can Students Write About Community Members and Historical Figures
They Have Studied?
What Autobiographies and Biographies Can Elementary Students Read?

WRITING ABOUT SELF AND OTHERS

Students write about single events in their lives and in the lives of others through memory writing and memoirs, and they compile a series of events to form phase or entire-life autobiographies and biographies. By reading autobiographies and biographies written for young people, students examine the structure of life stories and use the books as models for the life stories they write.

In writing autobiographies and biographies, authors combine elements of transactional and poetic writing. They take factual information and present it in a story-like form, often in chronological sequence.

A student reads a biography to examine the structure of life stories and then uses the book as a model for the biography he will write.

Several different approaches are used in writing autobiographies and biographies (Fleming & McGinnis, 1985). The most commonly used approach is historical. In this approach, the author uses the sequence pattern and focuses on the dates and events of the person's life in a chronological order. Many autobiographies and biographies which span the person's entire life use this pattern.

A second approach is the sociological approach. Here the author describes what life was like during the historical period, providing information about family life, food, clothing, education, economics, transportation, and so on. For instance, in *Worlds apart: The autobiography of a dancer from Brooklyn* (1980), Robert Maiorano describes his childhood in an impoverished New York City neighborhood and how he escapes it through a career with the Metropolitan Opera Company.

A third approach is psychological, and the author focuses on the conflicts that the person faces. These conflicts may be with self, others, or society. This approach has many elements in common with stories, and it is most often used in event or phase autobiographies and biographies. One example is Jean Fritz's single event biography, *And then what happened, Paul Revere?* (1973), in which Paul Revere faces a conflict with the British army.

Memory Writing

In *memory writing,* students write about personally meaningful experiences (Moffett & Wagner, 1983). They recall these experiences from memory and write about them. The experiences should be mainly about the students themselves, but others may be involved to a limited degree. Students write these memories or memoirs from a first-person viewpoint. A fifth grader's memory writing about her grandfather is presented in Figure 8–11.

Memory writing can be about the milestones in students' lives such as the birth of a brother or sister, learning to swim, or a first camping trip. Students can write about humorous incidents in their lives, scary experiences, or events that seemed to them to be dangerous. Mark Hanson (1978) suggests a strategy that he calls "markings" to help students identify topics for memory writing. He gives students a broad and open-ended topic such as "things I've said good-bye to" and asks them to brainstorm a list of possible topics. Then students choose one entry from the list to write about. Consider all the things we say good-bye to: a favorite teddy bear that is outgrown, an older brother who goes away to college, a grandparent who dies, a best friend who moves away, a parent who moves out of the home in a divorce, or even baby teeth. Any one of the entries in this list could produce vivid memory writing. Other possible markings include things to keep secret, interesting people I've known, things I've begun but not finished, times I've cried (been mad, scared, etc.), things I've lost (or found), and games I've played (Hanson, 1978). Students can brainstorm other markings, too. Using markings is a valuable prewriting strategy that helps students inventory their past experiences and choose a topic for memory writing.

Figure 8–11   A Student's Memory Writing

Me and My Grandfather

My grandfather and I were best of all buddies until he died on February 16, 1981. We always played sports and games with each other. Every morning when I woke up, I would run into his room, wake him up, and then we'd stare out the window and tell each other jokes, happenings at school, and things we saw while we were looking around. Then, after breakfast, we'd play games, sports, take hikes, ride bikes or just sit around and talk. He was the nicest, kindest, happiest, and most loving person in the world.

Then my grandfather got sick and needed to have a lot of operations. He still played and did stuff with me like nothing had happened. Then one day he passed away while sleeping. It was the saddest and the worst day of my life. I cried for five straight days and then started to settle down. I still love him a whole lot today and I'll never forget him or his love as long as I live. He'll be in me wherever I go. And our memories will be with us as long as we live, just as well as our love.

Jennifer, age 11

Autobiography

An *autobiography* is the written story of a person's life narrated by that person. In writing an autobiography, students relate their life stories in chronological order. They describe the most important events in their life, the ones that are necessary to know and understand them, and they develop the important themes in their lives.

Autobiography can be introduced in kindergarten and first grade with students writing "All About Me" books. These first autobiographies usually contain information such as the child's name, age, birthdate, address, and telephone number as well as drawings and text about family members, pets, friends, and favorite activities. A page from a 6-year-old's "All About Me" book is reproduced in Figure 8–12.

Older students can tie the writing of an autobiography to journal writing and memory writing. When students have identified the milestones in their lives and have written a number of memories, they can connect the memories in a chronological order to compile an autobiography. It is also helpful to have students develop a lifeline or timeline of their lives to help them sequence these milestones and other memories. Students' memories can span their entire lives, or they can pick a phase

Figure 8–12   A Page from a 6-year-old's
"All About Me" Book

I am Kathy.
I am six years old.
I live in Noble, Oklahoma.
I am in kindergarten.

Kathy, age 6

of their lives to write about. Students may find that their memories relate more to one phase rather than to their entire lives. An example of a fourth grader's autobiography is presented in Figure 8–13.

Another strategy that students can use in preparing to write an autobiography is to collect three or four objects that symbolize their life and hang them on a lifeline clothesline or put them in a shoebox or "life box" (Fleming, 1985). Then students write briefly about each object, explaining what the object is and how it relates to their lives. Students can also decorate the box with words and pictures clipped from magazines to create an autobiographical collage.

Autobiographies written by other people can serve as models for the life stories that students write. Many life stories of scientists, entertainers, sports figures, and others are available for upper grade students, but only a few autobiographies have been written for younger children. A list of suggested autobiographies is pre-

Figure 8–13 A Fourth Grader's Autobiography

My Own Story

I was born in Greece on August 10, 1976 in a tent. When I was one I had an egg for the first time. When I turned dark blue my mom gave me Benadryl and took me to the hospital. If my mom didn't give me that Benadryl I would have died instantly. When we lived in Greece I knew a boy named Yorgo. He always flipped me and my brother over his back and he was three times as old as us!

Later on in my life I moved to Missouri. When I was 4 I met some kids named Russell and Stephen. We always had to walk to school. Russell beat me up but my brother beat him up so Russell never picked on me again.

When I was 6 we moved to Oklahoma and I met new friends and saw old friends. My friend Jeff was my best friend until he moved to Arkansas. I was very sad that he moved and I just had to accept the reason that he was gone.

A year later I moved to 813 Jay Drive in Noble. I met some friends. Their names were Bobby, Adam, Glenn, Justin, Cory, John, and Tim. Today I'm 9. I'm making good grades in school and have lots of new friends. I'm extremely smart and really improving my attitude.

Joke: Where do you go when you're 9 years old? Into your tenth year!

Aaron, age 9

A student adds a snapshot taken when he was one year old to a lifeline with classmates' personal items and photos strung across the classroom.

sented in Figure 8–14. These books provide examples of both entire-life and phase autobiography forms and their unique conventions. As students read autobiographies, they can note which events the narrator focuses on, how the narrator presents information and feelings, and what the narrator's viewpoint is.

Memoirs

Memoirs (Moffett & Wagner, 1983) are accounts of incidents which writers have observed as eyewitnesses but which have not happened to them personally. Al-

---

Ali, M. (with R. Durham). (1976). *The greatest: Muhammad Ali.* New York: Ballantine. (M–U)

Begley, K. A. (1977). *Deadline.* New York: Putnam, (U)

Chukosky, K. (1976). *The silver crest: My Russian boyhood* (B. Stillman, Trans.). New York: Holt. (U)

Collins, M. (1976). *Flying to the moon and other strange places.* New York: Farrar. (M–U)

Fisher, L. E. (1972). *The death of evening star: Diary of a young New England whaler.* New York: Doubleday. (U)

Fritz, J. (1982). *Homesick: My own story.* New York: Putnam. (M–U) P27 F919 Hₙ

Hamill, D. (with E. Clairmont). (1983). *Dorothy Hamill: On and off the ice.* New York: Knopf. (M)

James, N. (1979). *Alone around the world.* New York: Coward. (U)

Jenner, B. (with R. S. Kiliper). (1980). *The Olympics and me.* New York: Doubleday. (M)

Keller, H. (1980). *The story of my life.* New York: Watermill Press. (M–U)

Maiorano, R. (1980). *Worlds apart: The autobiography of a dancer from Brooklyn.* New York: Coward. (U)

Huynh. Q. N. (1982). *The land I lost: Adventures of a boy in Vietnam.* New York: Harper and Row. (M–U)

North, S. (1963). *Rascal.* New York: Dutton. (M–U)

O'Kelley, M. L. (1983). *From the hills of Georgia: An autobiography in paintings.* Boston: Little, Brown. (P–M–U)

Rudolph, W. (1977). *Wilma. The story of Wilma Rudolph.* New York: New American Library. (U)

Schulz, C. M. (with R. S. Kiliper). (1980). *Charlie Brown, Snoopy and me: And all the other Peanuts characters.* New York: Doubleday. (M–U)

Singer, I. B. (1969). *A day of pleasure: Stories of a boy growing up in Warsaw.* New York: Farrar. (U)

Sullivan, T., & Gill, D. (1975). *If you could see what I hear.* New York: Harper and Row. (U)

Figure 8–14 Autobiographies for Elementary Students

though the writer is not personally involved in the incident, a relative, friend, or acquaintance might have been. While these memoirs are often written in the first person, the writer's role is to narrate, describe, and inform the reader of the event from an objective point of view.

Students can begin writing memoirs by writing about incidents or events they have observed. Incidents that happen in the classroom or on the playground would be an immediate source. As students write memoirs, remind them that they are eyewitnesses and can record only what they see and hear. They can record the thinking and feelings of the participants only when they are told about them. Two memoirs are presented in Figure 8–15. In the first example, the student relates a

---

The Capture

The day is splendid. All is quiet. The sun's radiance shines in the few drops on the maple leaves. The cat pauses to swat at a butterfly. The air is clean and pure. The cat lies purring. She rises and spots a sparrow on a low perch.

She crouches, her eyes finding only the inert sparrow. She walks gracefully forward, her feet touching like feathers on the grass. She hesitates. On forward she goes. Again she pauses. She poses her feet beneath her, her poise so graceful.

She shrieks. Her back legs shoot like flaming rockets from beneath her. The startled bird flutters its wings, but it is too late. The cat lashes out her claws, ten shiny swords, at the bird.

Then it is over. The cat eats her prey and stalks off. All is quiet.

Laurie, age 11

My Brother Kyle

My brother Kyle is about three years old. He is three feet tall and weighs 27 pounds. Kyle goes by several names: Kermit, Willie, and Theodore. He got his first nickname, Kermit, while watching the Muppet movie on T.V. He loves to hop like a frog. Kyle goes by Kermit when he's in a cheery mood. His daddy made up his second name "Willie." Kyle is Willie when he is in a playful mood. Since Kyle is often playful, he is often Willie. My mom has a teddy bear which she named Theodore. Theodore gets up in the morning and climbs into bed with my parents, and he often pushes daddy out. This is how Kyle got his many names, but the only one he can spell is KYLE!

Steven, age 10

Figure 8–15   Students' Memoirs

dramatic account of an incident in which a cat stalks and captures a sparrow. Notice the short sentences that the 11-year-old writer uses to recount the action, and the vivid description she uses to set the mood and bring the account to life. In the second example, "My Brother Kyle," the student describes his 3-year-old brother and how he gained his three nicknames.

Biography

A *biography* is an account of a person's life. The account should be as accurate and authentic as possible. In constructing biographies, writers consult as many sources of information as possible. The best source of information is the person himself or herself. Other primary sources include diaries and letters written by the person, photographs, mementos, historical records, and recollections of people who knew that person. Secondary sources include newspaper articles and books written about the person.

While biographies are based on the facts known about a person's life, some parts are fictionalized out of necessity. In *The double life of Pocahontas* by Jean Fritz (1983), for instance, the author had to take what sketchy facts are known about Pocahontas and make some reasonable guesses to fill in the missing ones. To give one example, historians know that Pocahontas was a young woman when she died in 1617, but they are unsure how old she was when John Smith and the other English settlers arrived in Virginia in 1607. Fritz chose to make her 11-years-old when the settlers arrived. Moreover, dialogue and other details about daily life must often be invented after careful research of the period.

Students can write accounts of someone else's life after they have collected enough information. Students collect this necessary information in several different ways. First, they read books to learn about the person and the time period in which he or she lived. As they research, they may assume the role of that person and keep one or more simulated journals. Later, students may compile a list of the milestones in that person's life and write public memoirs focusing on several of these milestones. Then the memoirs can be used as the basis of the biographies they write.

Students can also interview family members and interesting people in the community and write biographical sketches of these people's lives. They can also borrow photographs, hobby collections, and other mementos from the person to use as a display to accompany the biography. A list of possible materials to collect is presented in Figure 8–16. This activity works well in conjunction with oral history and interview projects that were discussed in Chapter 4.

Reading and writing biographies can easily be coordinated with social studies, science, and other content areas. Biographies of well-known people such as explorers, kings and queens, scientists, sports figures, artists, and movie stars as well as "common" people who have endured hardship and shown exceptional courage are available for elementary students to read. Jean Fritz (1973, 1983) and the D'Aulaires (1936) have written excellent biographies for primary and middle grade students, and numerous authors have written biographies for older students. A list of recommended biographies is presented in Figure 8–17.

Figure 8–16   Materials to Collect for Biographical Displays

baby book	hobby collections
birth certificate	letters
citizenship papers	map with locations
death certificate	person has traveled or
diaries and journals	lived marked
drawings and other	marriage certificate
artwork	mementos
favorite books	newspaper clippings
favorite items of	photographs
clothing	report cards
favorite recipes	scrapbooks
favorite records	Social Security card
handmade crafts	stories and others
high school/college	writings
pennants and	stuffed animals/toys
yearbooks	trophies and awards

Adapted from Silverman, 1985, pp. 98–102.

Students in the primary grades can write brief biographies in which they research the answers to specific questions about a famous person and then compile
these answers to form a report. Students in a second-grade class became interested
in the presidents just before a presidential election and they each chose a United
States president to investigate. With their teacher, they brainstormed a list of questions about the presidents:

When and where was the president born?

When did he die?

What political party did he belong to?

How old was he when he was inaugurated?

How many terms did he serve?

What was his occupation before becoming president?

Who was his vice president?

What are two or three interesting facts about him?

These questions provided the structure for the students' research and writing. Students read articles and books about the presidents and listened to other information presented by the teacher. After they collected their information, they com-

Adoff, A. (1970). *Malcolm X.* New York: Crowell. (P–M)

Blassingame, W. (1979). *Thor Heyerdahl: Viking scientist.* New York: Elsevier/Nelson. (M–U)

Brandenberg, A. (1977). *The many lives of Benjamin Franklin.* Englewood Cliffs, NJ: Prentice-Hall. (P–M)

_____. (1965). *A weed is a flower: The life of George Washington Carver.* Englewood Cliffs, NJ: Prentice-Hall. (M)

Daugherty, J. (1939). *Daniel Boone.* New York: Viking. (U)

D'Aulaire, I. & D'Aulaire, E. P. (1936). *George Washington.* New York: Doubleday. (See other biographies by the same authors.) (P–M)

Dobrin, A. (1975). *I am a stranger on Earth: The story of Vincent Van Gogh.* New York: Warne. (M–U)

Felton, H. W. (1976). *Deborah Sampson: Soldier of the revolution.* New York: Dodd, Mead. (M)

Fritz, J. (1973). *And then what happened, Paul Revere?* New York: Coward. (See other biographies by the same author.) (P–M)

Greenfield, E. (1977). *Mary McLeod Bethune.* New York: Crowell. (P–M)

Hamilton, V. (1974). *Paul Robeson: The life and times of a free black man.* New York: Harper and Row. (U)

Latham, J. L. (1955). *Carry on, Mr. Bowditch.* Boston: Houghton Mifflin. (U)

Monjo, F. N. (1973). *Me and Willie and Pa: The story of Abraham Lincoln and his son Tad.* New York: Simon & Schuster. (M)

Provensen, A., & Provensen, M. (1984). *Leonardo da Vinci.* New York: Viking. (A moveable book) (M–U)

Quackenbush, R. (1981). *Ahoy! Ahoy! are you there? A story of Alexander Graham Bell.* Englewood Cliffs, NJ: Prentice-Hall. (See other biographies by the same author.) (P–M)

Wood, J. P. (1968). *Spunkwater, Spunkwater! A life of Mark Twain.* New York: Pantheon. (U)

Figure 8–17   Biographies Recommended for Elementary Students

Figure 8–18   A Second Grader's Biographical Report

John F. Kennedy
35th President (1961–1963)

John F. Kennedy was born May 29, 1917 in Brookline, Mass. He was a Democrat. His vice president was Lyndon B. Johnson. He was 43 years old and served part of 1 term. He became the fourth U.S. president to be assassinated. During World War II Kennedy commanded a navy P.T. boat in the Pacific. He became a hero to his crew by his courage in their rescue.

Dean, age 8

piled what they had learned in brief reports. One second grader's biography of John F. Kennedy is presented in Figure 8–18.

Older students can research the life of an historical character by reading textbooks and informational books and summarizing the key events and dates of the person's life in a lifeline. A lifeline for Paul Revere is presented in Figure 8–19. Then students choose several events from the lifeline, write about them, and compile them to make a biography. Three important events in Revere's life, for example, were his participation in the Boston Tea Party, his famous ride to warn the patriots that the British were coming, and his court martial trial.

Born January 1, 1735 in Boston, Massachusetts, the son of a silversmith ——————————————	1735
Attended grammar school in Boston —————————	
Learned the silversmith's trade ————————————	
Served in the French and Indian War ———————————	1756
Married his first wife, Sarah, and had eight children ————————	
Sarah died; married second wife Rachel several months later, and they had eight more children —————————————	1773
Took part in the Boston Tea Party —————————	
April 18–19, 1775, served as a messenger for the Boston patriots and rode to Lexington and Concord to warn about approaching British ————————————	1775
Commanded a garrison of troops in Boston —————————————	1776
Part of unsuccessful invasion of British-held lands in Maine ———————	1779
Court-martialed for cowardice and insubordination, but cleared of charges ——————————————	
Returned to silversmith trade in Boston with son after the war ————————	
Invented new way to cast bells using copper rolls —————————	
Died May 10, 1818 in Boston ———————	1818

Figure 8–19   Paul Revere's Lifeline

Summary

Transactional writing is the second of James Britton's three categories of writing. It is practical and formal and its purpose is to get things done. The boundaries between transactional writing and expressive and poetic writing are not clear, but transactional writing is described as more formal than expressive writing and more factual than poetic writing. Three types of transactional writing were discussed in this chapter: (a) research reports, (b) newspaper articles, and (c) autobiographies and biographies.

Transactional text is organized or structured in particular ways. Content area textbooks, informational tradebooks, and students' research reports use five basic organizational patterns called expository text structures. These five patterns are (a) description, (b) sequence, (c) comparison, (d) cause and effect, and (e) problem and solution. These patterns correspond with the traditional organization of main ideas and details within paragraphs. Students who are aware of these organizational patterns comprehend and remember what they have read better than students who are not aware of the patterns. Just as organizational patterns are important in reading, these patterns are valuable tools for writers. Students can use the five patterns in organizing the transactional texts that they write.

Research report writing is one of the most common types of school writing. The procedure used in teaching students to collect and organize information and write research reports is similar to the procedure presented in Chapter 4 for oral reports with the exception that students write the report instead of presenting it orally, and they use the stages of the writing process—prewriting, drafting, revising, editing, and publishing. One essential component of the procedure for writing research reports is writing class collaboration reports in which students divide into small groups or pairs and write parts that are then compiled for the research report. The value of class collaborations is that they provide teachers with the opportunity to model the writing process and to clarify students' misconceptions about the writing assignment.

Research reports can take many different forms. Students can write question-and-answer books as well as ABC books that include the information they have researched. Also, young chidren can compose and dictate research reports after listening to tradebooks read aloud, going on field trips, participating in interviews and other activities.

Newspapers are a rich and inexpensive source of reading material, and students can examine how newspaper articles are written and then write their own class newspapers. Classes can form their own newspaper, delegating students to serve as reporters, copy editors, and content editors. Through writing and publishing class newspapers, students experiment with another writing form and they also have a forum in which to inform their audience about events in their classroom and their opinions about current events and other topics of general interest. Students can also write simulated newspapers in connection with units in content areas such as social studies. Through writing simulated newspapers, students delve more deeply into the content being studied and they demonstrate their learning in valuable ways that tests often do not measure.

Students can also write about themselves and others through short memory writings and memoirs as well as longer autobiographies and biographies. These writings share many of the characteristics of both poetic and transactional writing because authors of autobiographies and biographies weave essential facts about a person's life into a story-like text. Mark Hanson's markings helps students focus on events in their lives which they can later compile to form an autobiography. Students can also collect three or four objects that symbolize their life and write about these objects. In writing about others, a lifeline often helps students focus on and tie together important events in the person's life. Reading autobiographies and biographies should be integrated with writing these forms because the tradebooks provide models students can use in writing their own compositions.

Extensions

1. Have middle and upper grade students locate examples of the five organizational patterns in their content area textbooks or in informational tradebooks. Ask students to identify cue words in the passages and to draw graphic organizers for the passages.

2. Write a class collaboration report on a social studies topic such as modes of transportation, types of houses, or the countries in Europe or on a science topic such as the solar system or the human body. Follow the guidelines presented in this chapter.

3. Write and publish a class newspaper according to the guidelines presented in this chapter or write and publish a simulated newspaper in conjunction with a social studies unit.

4. Ask a small group of students to brainstorm a list of things they have said good-bye to (or another of Mark Hanson's markings) and then choose one entry from the list to write about. Use the process approach and have students meet together to revise and edit their compositions.

5. Have students interview a community member and then write a biography about that person. If possible, have students borrow some of the materials listed in Figure 8–16 to use in preparing a display about the person to accompany the biography.

6. Have a small group of students develop a lifeline for an historical character or other well-known person, choose several events from the lifeline to write about, and compile the writings to form a biography.

References

Britton, J. (1970). *Language and learning*. New York: Penguin Books.

D'Aulaire, I., & D'Aulaire, E. P. (1936). *George Washington*. New York: Doubleday.

Fleming, M. (1985). Writing assignments focusing on autobiographical and biographical topics. In M. Fleming & J. McGinnis (Eds.), *Portraits: Biography and autobiography in the secondary school* (pp. 95–97). Urbana, IL: National Council of Teachers of English.

Fleming, M., & McGinnis, J. (Eds.). (1985). *Portraits: Biography and autobiography in the secondary school*. Urbana, IL: National Council of Teachers of English.

Flood, J., Lapp, D., & Farnan, N. (1986). A reading-writing procedure that teaches expository paragraph structure. *The Reading Teacher, 39,* 556–562.

Fritz, J. (1973). *And then what happened, Paul Revere?* New York: Coward.

———. (1983). *The double life of Pocahontas.* New York: Putnam.

Fulwiler, T. (1985). Research writing. In M. Schwartz (Ed.), *Writing for many roles* (pp. 207–230). Upper Montclair, New Jersey: Boynton/Cook.

Hanson, M. (1978). *Sources: Using personal journal entries to generate academic and creative writings.* Lakeside, CA: Interact.

Maiorano, R. (1980). *Worlds apart: The autobiography of a dancer from Brooklyn.* New York: Coward.

McGee, L. M., & Richgels, D. J. (1985). Teaching expository text structure to elementary students. *The Reading Teacher, 38,* 739–748.

Meyer, B. J., & Freedle, R. O. (1984). Effects of discourse type on recall. *American Educational Research Journal, 21,* 121–143.

Moffett, J., & Wagner, B. J. (1983). *Student-centered language arts and reading, K–13: A handbook for teachers* (3rd ed.). Boston: Houghton Mifflin.

The newsroom [Computer program]. (1984). New York: Scholastic.

Niles, O. S. (1974). Organization perceived. In H. L. Herber (Ed.), *Perspectives in reading: Developing study skills in secondary schools.* Newark, DE: International Reading Association.

Sargent, E. E. (1975). *The newspaper as a teaching tool.* South Norwalk, CT: Reading Laboratory.

Silverman, L. H. (1985). The biography kit. In M. Fleming & J. McGinnis, (Eds.), *Portraits: Biography and autobiography in the secondary school* (pp. 98–102). Urbana, IL: National Council of Teachers of English.

Taylor, B. M., & Samuels, S. J. (1983). Children's use of text structure in the recall of expository material. *American Educational Research Journal, 20,* 517–528.

IF YOU WANT TO LEARN MORE

Clem, C., & Feathers, K. M. (1986). I LIC SPIDRS: What one child teaches us about content learning. *Language Arts, 63,* 143–147.

DeMass, P., & Tway, E. (1984). Life sentences: Springboards to composition. *Middle School Journal, 15,* 7, 31.

Fleming, M., & McGinnis, J. (Eds.). (1985). *Portraits: Biography and autobiography in the secondary school.* Urbana, IL: National Council of Teachers of English.

Macrorie, K. (1985). *Telling writing* (4th ed.). Upper Montclair, New Jersey: Boynton/Cook.

McGee, L. M., & Richgels, D. J. (1985). Teaching expository text structure to elementary students. *The Reading Teacher, 38,* 739–748.

Moore, D. W., Moore, S. A., Cunningham, P. M., & Cunningham, J. W. (1986). *Developing readers and writers in the content areas.* New York: Longman.

Pehrsson, R. S., & Robinson, H. A. (1985). *The semantic organizer approach to writing and reading instruction.* Rockville, MD: Aspen.

Schwartz, M. (1985). *Writing for many roles.* Upper Montclair, NJ: Boynton/Cook.

Stotsky, S. (1984). Imagination, writing, and the integration of knowledge in the middle grades. *Journal of Teaching Writing, 3,* 157–190.

Tchudi, S. N., & Tchudi, S. J. (1983). *Teaching writing in the content areas: Elementary school.* Washington, DC: National Education Association.

Tchudi, S. N., & Huerto, M. C. (1983). *Teaching writing in the content areas: Middle school junior high.* Washington, DC: National Education Association.

CHAPTER NINE

Developing Students' Concept of Story

OVERVIEW. This chapter is the first of two chapters that focus on reading and writing stories. In this chapter, an approach which helps students learn about the structural elements of stories is presented. Literature is used as the source of information for examining seven basic elements of story structure: beginning-middle-end, motifs, plot, setting, story characters, theme, and point of view. An instructional strategy is discussed for teaching students to examine these elements in the stories they read and to incorporate them in the stories they write.

Why write stories? Story writing has become a popular writing form for children in the elementary grades, but how do students benefit from writing stories? Perhaps the most obvious reason for having students write stories is that through writing stories, they learn to read and to write. Children learn to write by writing, and story writing is a valuable means of providing opportunities for writing. Writing stories is also an effective way to help children learn to read because they read their own writing and that of their classmates. They also take a greater interest in reading stories to learn about the literary devices that authors use in their stories. Next, students write stories because they enjoy telling stories, and entertainment must be considered as a primary motive. Also, students explore some of the functions of written language through writing stories. Other reasons for writing stories include to foster artistic expression, to stimulate children's imaginations, and to learn to organize and clarify thinking (Tompkins, 1982).

Children, even preschoolers, have a rudimentary awareness of what makes a story, an understanding called *concept of story.* Their concept, or schema, includes information about the elements of story structure such as characters, plot, and setting as well as information about the conventions that authors use in stories. This knowledge is usually intuitive; that is, children are not conscious of what they know. Golden (1984) describes the concept of story as part of the cognitive structure: "a mental representation of story structure, essentially an outline of the basic story elements and their organization" (p. 578).

Researchers have documented that children's concept of story begins in the preschool years, and that children as young as 2½ years of age have a rudimentary sense of story (Applebee, 1978, 1980; Pitcher & Prelinger, 1963). Children acquire this concept of story gradually, through listening to stories read to them, later by reading stories themselves, and by telling and writing stories. Not surprisingly, older children have a better understanding of story structure and conventions than younger children do. Similarly, the stories that older children tell and write are increasingly more complex; the plot structures are more tightly organized, and the characters are more fully developed. Yet, Applebee (1980) states that "by the time they come to school, children ordinarily have a firmly developed set of expectations about what a story *is* — expectations that guide them both in their reactions to new stories and in their own storytelling activities" (p. 141). For example, he found that kindergartners could use three story markers: (a) the convention

Students read stories to learn about the elements of story structure that authors use in their stories.

"Once upon a time . . . " to begin a story, (b) the past tense consistently in telling a story, and (c) formal endings such as "The End" or "and they lived happily ever after."

Most of the research examining students' understanding of story structure and conventions has been applied to reading. Concept of story has been found to play an important role in students' ability to comprehend and recall information from the stories they read (Mandler & Johnson, 1977; Rumelhart, 1975; Stein & Glenn, 1979). However, children's concept of story is just as important in writing (Golden, 1984). Just as they draw on their concept of story in reading stories, students use this same knowledge in writing stories. Educators are now beginning to look for ways to help students expand and refine their concept of story. One strategy is to make story structure explicit, to talk with students about the elements of story structure, and to examine how authors use these elements in the stories they write (Stewig, 1980; Gordon & Braun, 1982).

When children learn to talk, they are immersed in a natural language environment, and they move from the general to the specific as they abstract certain aspects of the language they are learning and generalize rules of the grammar. This approach to reading and writing stories is similar, moving from general elements of story structure to more specific. The material is presented so that students first work with the general construct that stories have a beginning, a middle, and an end. Motifs, plot structure, setting, character development, theme, point of view, and stylistic devices are introduced as students learn to write stories and need a particular story structure. These elements are discussed in this chapter and Chapter 10.

POINTS TO PONDER

What Are the Seven Elements of Story Structure?

What Are the Characteristics of Each Element?

Which Books of Children's Literature Illustrate Each Element?

How Do Authors Use Each Element in the Stories They Create?

How Can Teachers Teach Students About These Elements?

ELEMENTS OF STORY STRUCTURE

One of the basic premises set forth in Chapter 6 was that students need to learn the structures of the different kinds of writing and that those structures can best be learned by using literature as a source of information. We approach story writing from the framework of using literature to illustrate how authors use various elements of story structure in their writing and to make explicit students' knowledge about these elements. Information gained from reading and interacting with stories is immediately put into practice by writing. The general procedure is that after teachers introduce an element, students read stories to see how the authors have used that structure, and then students write stories incorporating that element and the other elements they have learned.

Beginning-Middle-End

The most basic element of story structure is the arbitrary division of the main events of a story into three parts: (a) beginning, (b) middle, and (c) end. Middle grade students may substitute *introduction, development,* and *resolution* in place of beginning, middle, and end, and upper graders may use *exposition, complication,* and *denouement* instead. No matter what these three parts are called, their function remains the same. In *The tale of Peter Rabbit* (Potter, 1902), for instance, the three story parts can be picked out easily. The story begins as Mrs. Rabbit sends her children out to play after warning them not to go into Mr. McGregor's garden. In the middle, Peter goes to Mr. McGregor's garden and is almost caught. Then Peter finds his way out of the garden and gets home safely—the end of the story. Almost any story can be divided into these three parts; however, short stories are easier for students to manage. It is important to use short, familiar stories at first because these stories do not pose as many problems in recalling the story parts.

Throughout this chapter, we will provide lists of suggested stories for each element of story structure. A list of short stories to use in examining beginning-middle-end is presented in Figure 9–1. These lists are intended to be only suggestions; many other stories can be used, including stories in basal reader textbooks.

Authors have specific purposes in composing each of the three story parts. In the beginning, authors introduce and describe the story characters and the setting. Some central problem is introduced as the characters begin to interact and establish their relationships. The interrelationships that will exist among the characters, the locale, the societal concerns, and the events of the story are begun. These relationships will affect the actions that fill out the motif, establish the plot, and sustain the theme.

The major elements in the middle of a story keep the story moving along. Authors add to and combine the events established in the beginning and tie them to the climax and the end. Each event prepares readers for what comes later, and each detail is structured to show why the main event can happen. Conflict is introduced as the characters are faced with problems or are opposed by forces that keep them from reaching their goals. How the characters struggle against these forces or begin to find solutions to their problems adds the suspense that keeps readers interested.

Figure 9–1   Short Stories Illustrating Beginning-Middle-End

Andersen, H. C. (1979). *The ugly duckling.* New York: Harcourt Brace Jovanovich. (P–M)

Gag, W. (1956). *Millions of cats.* New York: Coward. (P)

Galdone, P. (1975). *The gingerbread boy.* New York: Seabury. (P)

Gallo, D. R. (Ed.). (1984). *Sixteen short stories by outstanding writers for young adults.* New York: Dell. (U)

Kellogg, S. (1973). *The island of the skog.* New York: Dial. (P)

London, J. (1960). To build a fire. *The call of the wild and other selected stories.* New York: Signet. (U)

Potter, B. (1902). *The tale of Peter Rabbit.* New York: Warne. (P)

Rogasky, B. (1982). *Rapunzel.* New York: Holiday House. (M–U)

Sendak, M. (1963). *Where the wild things are.* New York: Harper and Row. (P)

Van Allsburg, C. (1983). *The wreck of the Zephyr.* Boston: Houghton Mifflin. (M–U)

Zemach, H., & Zemach, M. (1973). *Duffy and the devil.* New York: Farrar. (P–M)

P = primary grades (K–2)
M = middle grades (3–5)
U = upper grades (6–8)

The major elements at the end of a story let readers know whether or not the central goals of the story will be achieved. The climax is the point in the story when readers know whether the characters' struggles against opposing forces will be successful. It is in the end of the story that authors must reconcile all that has gone on before. The outcome usually becomes clear at some point just following the climax. The complications of the plot are disentangled so that a clearer picture of all that has happened in the story is available. At this point in the story, readers

---

The Three Story Parts

What happened in the first part of the story?
What can we call this first part?
What happened in the second part of the story?
What can we call this second part?
What happened in the third part of the story?
What can we call this last part?

Beginnings of Stories

What kinds of information does an author put in the beginning of a
    story?
Which characters do you meet?
What do you learn about the setting or where the story takes place?
What happens in the first part of the story?
Is there a problem that will need to be solved?
Does the author give you any ideas about what will happen next?

Middles of Stories

What kinds of information does an author put in the middle of a story?
What happens to the characters?
Does the author add new characters?
What happens to the problem? Does it get worse? Is it solved?
What happens during the second part of the story?
How do you feel during this part of the story?

Ends of Stories

What kinds of information does an author put in the end of a story?
What happens to the characters?
What happens to the problem?
How do you feel during this part of the story?

Figure 9–2   General Questions About Beginning, Middle, and End
of Stories

should have an idea of what the story means to them. A list of general questions about the beginning, middle, and end of stories is presented in Figure 9–2.

Instructional Strategy.   The instructional strategy presented in the first chapter is used to teach the beginning-middle-end element of story structure as well as the other elements that will be presented in this chapter. Before introducing an element, teachers prepare by learning about the element, collecting stories that exemplify the element, and developing a set of instructional materials. Through this preparation, teachers gain valuable insights into how authors use beginning-middle-end and other elements of story structure in constructing their stories. Teachers are then ready to introduce their students to the element of story structure. The preparation activities and the instructional strategy for teaching elements of story structure are summarized in Figure 9–3.

The steps in the instructional strategy are easily adapted for teaching students about the beginning-middle-end element of story structure. To illustrate, the steps in the instructional strategy are outlined with specific adaptions for teaching this element.

Students retell the beginning, middle, and end of familiar stories using pictures on a flannel board.

Preparation

1. Review the information about the element of story structure presented in this chapter and in other reference books, including those listed in the "If You Want to Learn More" section at the end of this chapter.

2. Collect as many story examples of the element as possible. Folktales, other short stories, and longer stories can be used as examples. It is helpful to collect multiple copies of books that students will read independently. Stories can also be tape-recorded for students to listen to at a listening center. While some stories illustrate one or two elements of story structure more effectively than other elements, other stories exemplify all or almost all of the elements. Two "all-purpose" stories are Roald Dahl's short story *The enormous crocodile* (1978), and J. R. R. Tolkien's *The hobbit* (1966). Lists of stories that illustrate specific elements are presented with the information about that element in this chapter.

3. Read the stories to learn how authors have used the element in constructing their stories.

4. Write a set of specific questions from the general questions presented with the information about each element in this chapter. Adapt the general questions to reflect the specific stories that will be used in teaching the element. Be sure to identify specific characters and episodes in phrasing the questions.

5. Compile the information about the element and develop one or more charts to use in presenting the information to students. The charts should define the element and list characteristics of the element.

Instruction

Step 1: Initiating

Introduce the element of story structure and display the charts defining the element and/or listing characteristics of the element. Next, read several stories illustrating the element of story structure to students or have students read the stories themselves. After reading, discuss the story with students using the set of specific questions that was developed in advance.

Figure 9–3   Instructional Strategy for Teaching the Elements of Story Structure

The first component of the instructional strategy is preparation. The steps in preparing to teach students about the beginning-middle-end element include the following activities:

1. Review the information about the beginning-middle-end element.
2. Collect short stories with well-defined beginnings, middles, and ends that are appropriate for the students in your class. Stories may be chosen from the list in

Step 2: Structuring

Have students read one or more stories illustrating the element and explain how the author used the element in each story. Students should tie their explanations to the definition and characteristics of the element presented in the first step.

Step 3: Conceptualizing

Have students read additional stories illustrating the element, and then discuss the stories using the specific questions. Ask students to explain how the author used the element in constructing each story. Students can also participate in drama activities, storytelling, and other response activities to learn about the elements of story structure.

Step 4: Summarizing

Review the characteristics of the element being studied, using the charts introduced in the first step. Have students restate the characteristics in their own words and make their own charts, listing the important information about the element.

Step 5: Generalizing

Have students read additional stories and explain how the author used the element in each story. Also, ask students to restate the definition and characteristics of the element in their own words.

Step 6: Applying

Have students apply what they have learned about the element of story structure in a class collaboration story. Then have students write individual stories applying the element being studied and other elements of story structure that they have learned. Students should use the process approach to writing described in Chapter 6. The activities described in the first five steps of this model and class collaboration stories constitute the prewriting stage. In this step, students move through the drafting, revising, editing, and publishing stages of the writing process. They first write rough drafts of their stories and meet with classmates in writing conferences to share their writing. Next, students revise and edit their stories using the feedback they receive. In the final step, they make final copies of their stories and share them with an appropriate audience.

Figure 9–3 *Continued*

Figure 9–1, or stories included in basal reading textbooks may be used as long as they illustrate the beginning-middle-end element.

3. Read the stories to learn how authors have developed the three parts in each story and the types of information included in each part.

4. Write a set of specific questions based on the general questions about the beginning-middle-end element presented in Figure 9–2.

5. Develop a set of four charts to use in teaching students about the beginning-middle-end element. Make one chart that defines the element as shown in Figure 9–4 and three additional charts that list the characteristics of the three story parts. A sample chart listing the characteristics of story beginnings is presented in Figure 9–5. While teachers can list the characteristics of story beginnings on the chart in advance, it is preferable to simply write the title and laminate the chart. Then after reading several stories students can identify the characteristics and list them on the chart using a water-soluble marking pen. When the chart is no longer needed, it can be erased and used again with another group of students.

Figure 9–4   Chart for Beginning-Middle-End

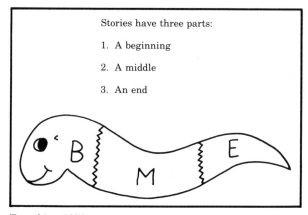

Stories have three parts:

1. A beginning

2. A middle

3. An end

Tompkins, 1979.

We found these things in the beginnings of stories:

1. You meet the main character and some of the other characters.

2. You find out where the story takes place.

3. You learn about a problem that the characters have to solve.

4. You get interested in the story and want to keep reading it.

Figure 9–5   Characteristics of Story Beginnings

The second component in the instructional strategy is the six-step instructional strategy. The six steps are listed with specific information about how to teach the beginning-middle-end element of story structure.

Step 1: Initiating. Read or tell a familiar story and ask, "What happened in the first part of the story?" "In the next part?" "In the last part?" Ask students to retell each part of the story. After the three parts of the story have been retold, introduce the terms *beginning, middle,* and *end,* or substitute other terms with older students. This discussion leads to the first generalization about stories, that they must have a beginning, a middle, and an end. Present the chart shown in Figure 9–4. Read another story and have students identify the beginning, middle, and end of that story.

Step 2: Structuring. Read the beginnings of several stories to students and discuss the common things found in these story beginnings using the specific questions about story beginnings that were developed in advance. From this discussion, have students compile a list of the characteristics of story beginnings and list these characteristics on a chart as shown in Figure 9–5. Read the beginnings of additional stories and ask students if they follow the characteristics of story beginnings they have developed. Add or delete characteristics from the chart as necessary. Then repeat this step for story middles and ends. Read and discuss the middles and ends of the same stories used for examining story beginnings.

Step 3: Conceptualizing. Read additional stories with well-defined beginnings, middles, and ends to students and discuss the stories using the set of specific questions. Ask students to explain how the author developed the three parts of each story.

Children practice retelling the beginning, middle, and end of familiar stories to learn about the element. Several approaches can be used to retell familiar stories. First, children can use flannelboard pieces to retell a familiar story. Divide the flannelboard into three sections and label the sections *beginning, middle,* and *end.* Children place the flannelboard pieces, which can be drawn or cut from inexpensive paperback versions of tradebooks and backed with flannel, in the beginning section as they retell the first part, and then put in the middle and end sections as they retell those parts. Many of the guidelines suggested in Chapter 5 about storytelling can be used in story retelling.

Next, primary grade students can draw pictures of the beginning, middle, and end and compile these pictures to make a story booklet (Buckley, 1968). Then students can use these three pictures as a prop to help them recall the story events as they retell the story. A 6-year-old's set of three drawings to retell *Where the wild things are* (Sendak, 1963) is presented in Figure 9–6.

Older students can draw story maps (Buckley & Boyle, 1983) to examine the beginning-middle-end structure. These story maps are a type of cluster diagrams. Students make the map by drawing rays from a central story hub and labeling the rays *introduction, development,* and *resolution* or whatever terms they are using for the three story parts. Then students list significant story events on each ray. Because the second part is the longest part of most stories, the development ray should include the most information. A story map for *The hare and the tortoise* (Galdone, 1962) is presented in Figure 9–7.

Step 4: Summarizing.   Review with students that stories have three parts—a beginning, a middle, and an end—using the chart shown in Figure 9–4. Ask students to name the three story parts. Then review the characteristics of each using the three charts that the students developed. Have students identify the characteristics and cite examples from the stories they have read. Have students make their own copies of the four charts about the beginning-middle-end element. Encourage them to restate the information in their own words and to draw pictures to illustrate them.

Step 5: Generalizing.   Read additional stories and have students retell the beginning, middle, and end of these stories. They may also draw pictures of the three story parts and draw story maps.

Step 6: Applying.   Before asking students to write individual stories, compose a class collaboration story. Through a class collaboration story, teachers can review the procedures, students have the opportunity to share ideas, and students' confusion about the assignment or misunderstanding about the element can be clarified.

Explain that as a class they will write a story with a beginning, middle, and end. Students start by discussing possible story ideas, and together decide on a topic. Often students will choose to model their story after one of the stories they have read recently. For example, *The three billy goats Gruff* can be rewritten as "The three red roosters." Divide the chalkboard into three sections and label them *beginning, middle,* and *end.* As a group, choose a topic for the story, identify the characters, and outline possible story events. With this preparation, students take turns dictating parts of the story as it is recorded on the chalkboard. Writing the first draft on the chalkboard is preferable to writing it on chart paper because it is easier to make additions, deletions, substitutions, and other changes on the chalkboard. After the first draft is completed, read it with the students and make whatever revisions and editorial changes they suggest. Also, add a title for the story. Later the story can be transcribed onto chart paper or typed so each student can have a copy.

After writing a class collaboration story, students are better prepared to write their own stories. It is often helpful for students to use several sheets of paper for their own stories, and label the first sheet as the *beginning,* one or more sheets as

Figure 9–6 Drawings of the Beginning, Middle, and End of Sendak's *Where the wild things are* (1963)

Anonymous

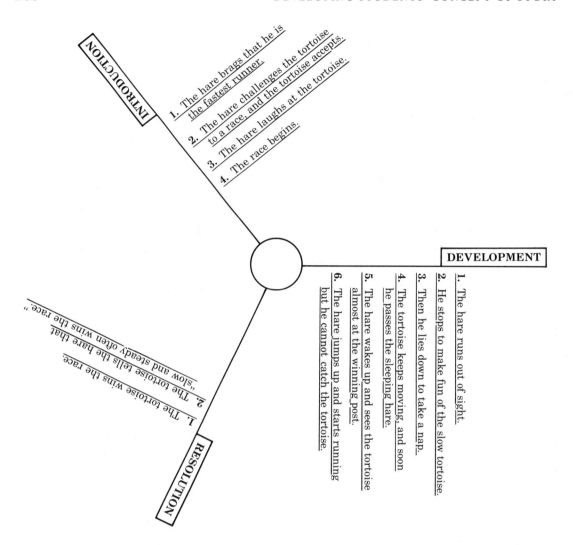

Figure 9–7   A Story Map for Galdone's *The hare and the tortoise* (1962)

the *middle,* and one sheet as the *end.* In this way, students are sure to include all three parts, including the often-neglected middle part, in their stories.

Students use the process approach in writing their stories. Learning about the beginning-middle-end structure and composing the class collaboration story is the prewriting stage. During drafting, students write and illustrate their stories. Next, they share their drafts in writing conferences and make revisions based on the feedback they received during the conference. After proofreading their stories and making editorial corrections, they publish and share them with an appropriate audience.

The instructional strategy is essentially the same for teaching motifs, plot, and the other elements of story structure we will discuss in this chapter, and it can easily be adapted to fit each element. There may, however, be a few differences in what is stressed depending on the element of story structure being presented and the grade level of the students. Teachers may need to simplify some of the terminology for young children, but many teachers find that students at all levels, even students in the primary grades, can examine these elements of story structure and write stories applying them.

Motifs

Folklorists have identified many different motifs, which they define as the smallest part of a tale that can exist independently. Their classification of motifs includes such things as a magic object (e.g., *Jack and the beanstalk*), a long sleep (e.g., *Rip Van Winkle*), and a spell (e.g., *Sleeping beauty*). However, in this chapter, we will consider a *motif* as the structural main idea from which the plot will be developed in a story. It is a general skeleton that must be fleshed out along with the theme. The devices used in the story generally depend on the motif or motifs to form the basic structure of the story.

The Four Motifs.   Four motifs found in folktales are easy for children to use in analyzing and writing their own stories. These four motifs were selected from *A curriculum for English* (1966):

1. *The journey motif* concerns a character's journey from home to isolation from home.
2. *The confrontation motif* concerns a character's journey from home to a confrontation with a monster.
3. *The rescue motif* concerns a character's rescue from a harsh home and the miraculous creation of a secure home.
4. *The trick motif* concerns a conflict between a wise character and a foolish character.

These motifs are not always found in their "pure form" in the stories students read, but the basic elements will be recognizable and can be pointed out to children. In the second motif, for example, a danger such as a forest fire may confront the characters instead of an actual monster. Examples of the motifs can be found in children's stories, and a list of stories illustrating each motif is presented in Figure 9–8.

Teaching Students About Motifs.   The instructional strategy presented in Figure 9–3 is adapted to teach students about motifs just as it was for the beginning-middle-end element. The same preparation and instruction steps are used. An example of a third grader's chart listing the four motifs with illustrations of stories representing each motif is presented in Figure 9–9.

It is important to note that in some stories more than one motif may have been used, or it may be difficult for students to decide which of several motifs was used. There may also be stories that have a main motif and other motifs that are

The Journey Motif

George, J. C. (1959). *My side of the mountain.* New York: Dutton. (U)

McCloskey, R. (1976). *Blueberries for Sal.* New York: Viking. (P)

Potter, B. (1902). *The tale of Peter Rabbit.* New York: Warne. (P)

Sendak, M. (1963). *Where the wild things are.* New York: Harper and Row. (P)

Taylor, T. (1969). *The cay.* New York: Doubleday. (U)

The Confrontation Motif

Galdone, P. (1974). *Little Red Riding Hood.* New York: McGraw Hill. (P)

LaFontaine, J. de. (1963). *The lion and the rat.* New York: Watts. (P–M)

L'Engle, M. (1962). *A wrinkle in time.* New York: Farrar. (U)

Lewis, C. S. (1981). *The lion, the witch and the wardrobe.* New York: Macmillan. (M–U)

Sperry, A. (1968). *Call it courage.* New York: Macmillan. (U)

The Rescue Motif

Brown, M. (1954). *Cinderella.* New York: Scribner. (P)

Gag, W. (1956). *Millions of cats.* New York: Coward-McCann. (P)

Galdone, P. (1984). *The elves and the shoemaker.* New York: Houghton Mifflin. (P–M)

Lawson, R. (1972). *Rabbit hill.* New York: Viking. (M)

Lionni, L. (1969). *Alexander and the wind-up mouse.* New York: Pantheon. (P)

The Trick Motif

Aesop. (1981). *Aesop's fables.* New York: Viking. (M–U)

Cooney, B. (1958). *Chanticleer and the fox.* New York: Crowell. (P–M)

de Paola, T. (1975). *Strega nona.* Englewood Cliffs, NJ: Prentice-Hall. (P)

Galdone, P. (1975). *The gingerbread boy.* New York: Seabury. (P)

Westcott, N. B. (1984). *The emperor's new clothes.* Boston: Little, Brown. (P–M)

Figure 9–8   Stories Illustrating the Four Motifs

subordinate to it. For instance, in Maurice Sendak's *Where the wild things are* (1963), students often claim that the story exemplifies all four motifs. Max does go on a *journey,* he does have a *confrontation* with a pack of monsters, the wild things do seem to *rescue* him from a harsh mother, and Max does use his *trick* of staring into the monsters' eyes to tame them. However, through discussion, students usually decide that the story is an example of either the journey motif or, perhaps, the confrontation motif. It is less important that students decide on a particular motif than it is that they analyze the underlying structure of the story and talk about how authors construct stories.

Figure 9–9   A Third Grader's Chart of the Four Motifs

Judy, age 9

Teachers may need to simplify the terminology used in motifs when working with young children; however, even kindergartners readily understand the four motifs and can tell stories representing each motif.

Plot

Plot is defined as the sequence of events involving characters in conflict situations (Lukens, 1986). It is based on the goals of one or more of the story characters and the processes involved in attaining these goals. Each character has some interest or some stake in achieving the main goal, which constitutes the reason for agreeing to help the other characters. Other characters are introduced to oppose or prevent the main characters and their supporters from achieving their goals. The story events, a series of cause and effect situations, are put in motion by characters as they encounter and resolve conflicts to reach their goals and solve their problems. The plot is built on the motif, which generally forms the basic structure of what will happen in the story.

The Four Conflict Situations.   *Conflict* is any tension or opposition between or among forces in the plot, and it is introduced to get the reader interested enough to read the story. The plot's conflict and suspense are instrumental in compelling the reader to read on. Conflict usually takes one of four forms:

1. conflict between a character and nature
2. conflict between a character and society
3. conflict between characters
4. conflict within a character (Lukens, 1986)

Examples of stories illustrating each of the four conflict situations are presented in Figure 9–10. In some short stories, such as Hans Christian Andersen's *The ugly duckling* (1979), there is one basic conflict situation, conflict between the cygnet and the ducks. Longer stories, however, consist of a series of conflict situations, and each conflict situation is a miniature story.

Plot Development.   The development of the plot involves four steps:

1. A problem is introduced.
2. Roadblocks (or complications) are placed in the path of the characters.
3. There is a high point (or climax) in the conflict situation.
4. The problem is resolved and the roadblocks are overcome.

A problem is introduced at the beginning of the story or story episode, and one or more characters are faced with trying to solve the problem. This problem determines the conflict situation. For example, in *The ugly duckling,* the problem is that the big, gray duckling does not fit in with the other ducklings, and conflict develops between the ugly duckling and other ducks. Once the problem has been introduced, the author must introduce conflict to throw a roadblock in the way of

Conflict Between a Character and Nature

Ardizzone, E. (1971). *Little Tim and the brave sea captain.* New York: Scholastic. (P)

George, J. C. (1972). *Julie of the wolves.* New York: Harper and Row. (M–U)

O'Dell, S. (1960). *Island of the blue dolphins.* Boston: Houghton Mifflin. (M–U)

Sperry, A. (1968). *Call it courage.* New York: Macmillan. (U)

Wilder, L. I. (1971). *The long winter.* New York: Harper and Row. (M)

Conflict Between a Character and Society

Hickman, J. (1978). *Zoar blue.* New York: Macmillan. (U)

Kellogg, S. (1973). *The island of skog.* New York: Dial. (P)

O'Brien, R. C. (1971). *Mrs. Frisby and the rats of NIMH.* New York: Atheneum. (M)

Speare, E. G. (1958). *The witch of Blackbird Pond.* Boston: Houghton Mifflin. (M–U)

White, E. B. (1952). *Charlotte's web.* New York: Harper and Row. (M)

Conflict Between Characters

Andersen, H. C. (1979). *The ugly duckling.* New York: Harcourt Brace Jovanovich. (P–M)

Blume, J. (1972). *Tales of a fourth grade nothing.* New York: Dutton. (M)

Hoban, R. (1970). *A bargain for Frances.* New York: Scholastic. (P)

Howe, D., & Howe, J. (1979). *Bunnicula.* New York: Atheneum. (M)

Raskin, E. (1978). *The westing game.* New York: Dutton. (U)

Conflict Within a Character

Byars, B. (1970). *Summer of the swans.* New York: Viking. (U)

Fritz, J. (1958). *The cabin faced west.* New York: Coward-McCann. (M)

Ness, E. (1966). *Sam, Bangs and Moonshine.* New York: Holt. (P)

Taylor, T. (1969). *The cay.* New York: Doubleday. (U)

Waber, P. (1972). *Ira sleeps over.* Boston: Houghton Mifflin. (P)

Figure 9–10   Stories Illustrating the Four Conflict Situations

an easy solution. As one roadblock is removed, another will be devised to thwart the characters as they strive to reach their main goal. *Conflict situations*, or roadblocks, are introduced to complicate the problem. As the problem is complicated or the goal made harder to achieve, additional conflict situations are introduced since the characters must find a way to overcome the roadblocks or to devise alternate solutions to the conflict situations. Complicating the solution to the main problem or achieving the main goal by introducing conflict is the core of plot structure.

The *climax* is the highest point of dramatic action where the story's main issue hangs in the balance. What happens determines the answer to the question

Students dictate and revise a class collaboration story after studying about plot development.

posed in the problem and whether the goal of the main characters will be achieved. The *resolution* is the deciding of the issue, how the problem is solved or how the goal is achieved. Students can use the list of general questions about plot in Figure 9–11 to examine plot in the stories they read.

The plot of a story can be diagrammed or charted. Figure 9–12 presents a basic diagram of plot development, and Figure 9–13 shows how the basic diagram can be applied to a specific story. Students can diagram the stories they read or are read to them to better understand how authors develop plot structure. They can also diagram the plot of the stories they write. These diagrams serve as useful checks on whether students have adequately developed the plot structure in their stories.

Setting

The *setting* is the environment or place in which the story occurs. It includes the natural environment as well as the communities, buildings, and objects created by the characters or the society in which they reside. Characters live and struggle in a world created by an author. This world must be believable and acceptable to readers. There must be dwellings with kitchens and other rooms, trees and flowers, roads and fences, day and night, good and bad weather, and rough and gentle terrain.

What is the character's main goal?

What problems do the characters face?

What conflict situations does the author use?

How does the author introduce the plot and get the story started?

What roadblocks (or complications) do the characters face in trying to reach the goal?

If one attempt is not successful, do the characters have the chance to try again to reach their goal?

Does the main character or one of the supporting characters resolve the conflict?

Do the characters gain in skill, strength, and wisdom as each roadblock is overcome? How?

Are the opposing characters endowed with powers that would make the outcome or resolution of the conflict doubtful? What kinds of powers?

Are the characters left to their own devices or does some outside force or character come to rescue or help them find new sources of strength within themselves?

How much complication does the author use before the high point (or climax) of the story?

Is there a shift from one form of conflict to another form?

Does the author use the device of foreshadowing? How?

Figure 9–11   General Questions About Plot

There are two types of settings according to Lukens (1986). The first type is the *backdrop setting,* which is barely sketched. The setting in many folktales, for example, is relatively unimportant and may simply use the convention, "Once upon a time . . . " to set the stage. The second type is the *integral setting,* which is greatly elaborated. How important the setting is to plot and character development determines how detailed and extensive the description must be. Some stories could take place anywhere and require little description; in others, however, the setting must be specific and much pain has to be taken to ensure the authenticity of the location and the description of the environment.

The Three Dimensions of Setting.   Location is a very important dimension of setting. The barn in *Charlotte's web* (White, 1952), the Alaskan North Slope in *Julie of the wolves* (George, 1972), and New York City's Metropolitan Museum of Art in *From the mixed-up files of Mrs. Basil E. Frankweiler* (Konigsburg, 1983) are in-

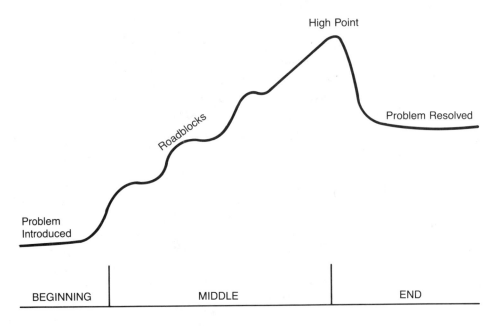

Figure 9–12 A Basic Diagram of Plot Development

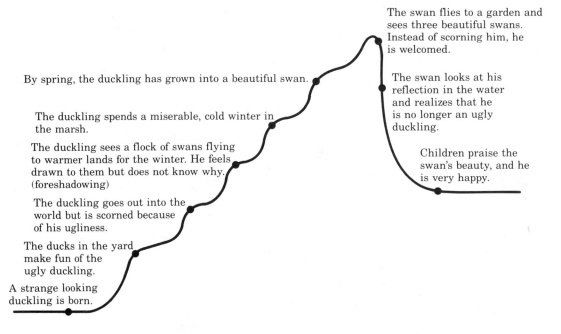

Figure 9–13 Plot Diagram for Andersen's *The ugly duckling* (1979)

tegral to these stories' effectiveness. However, location is only one dimension of setting; weather and time may also be important. For example, rainstorms are essential to the plot development in *Bridge to Terabithia* (Paterson, 1977) and *Sam, Bangs and Moonshine* (Ness, 1966) while frigid winter weather plays a crucial role in Laura Ingalls Wilder's *The long winter* (1971).

The time dimension includes both the passage of time and the historical era in which the story is set. Many short stories span a brief period of time, often less than a day, sometimes less than an hour. Consider how quickly the three billy goats Gruff crossed the bridge and disposed of the troll! Other stories, such as *The ugly duckling* and *Charlotte's web,* span more than a year during which the main characters grow to maturity. The historical period in which a story is set can also be necessary for the plot. If *The witch of Blackbird Pond* (Speare, 1958) and *The obstinate land* (Keith, 1977) were set in different eras, they would lose much of their impact. Today, few people would believe that Kit Tyler is a witch, and the settlement of Oklahoma would not be nearly so difficult with modern conveniences. A list of stories with integral settings is presented in Figure 9–14. These stories illustrate the three dimensions of setting—location, weather, and time.

How Authors Develop Setting.   Authors use a variety of devices to evoke a strong, integral setting in their stories. When the setting is integral to the story events, the author must describe it effectively and set the mood. Good description is important because it helps the readers visualize the location of the characters

---

Babbitt, N. (1975). *Tuck everlasting.* New York: Farrar. (M–U)

Frank, A. (1952). *Anne Frank: The diary of a young girl.* New York: Doubleday. (U)

George, J. C. (1972). *Julie of the wolves.* New York: Harper and Row. (M–U)

Grahame, K. (1961). *The wind in the willows.* New York: Scribner. (M)

Keith, H. (1977). *The obstinate land.* New York: Crowell. (U)

Konigsburg, E. L. (1983). *From the mixed-up files of Mrs. Basil E. Frankweiler.* New York: Atheneum. (M)

McCloskey, R. (1969). *Make way for ducklings.* New York: Viking. (P)

Ness, E. (1966). *Sam, Bangs and Moonshine.* New York: Holt. (P)

Norton, M. (1981). *The borrowers.* New York: Harcourt Brace Jovanovich. (M)

Paterson, K. (1977). *Bridge to Terabithia.* New York: Crowell. (M–U)

Speare, E. (1958). *The witch of Blackbird Pond.* Boston: Houghton Mifflin. (M–U)

Wilder, L. I. (1971). *The long winter.* New York: Harper and Row. (M)

Figure 9–14   Stories with Integral Settings

and what they are seeing, feeling, and hearing. Sensory description allows readers to draw mental pictures as they read. In *Charlotte's web* (1952), E. B. White describes the smells in Wilbur's barn so vividly that you feel as if you can smell them yourself:

> The barn was very large. It was very old. It smelled of hay and it smelled of manure. It smelled of the perspiration of tired horses and the wonderful sweet breath of patient cows. It often had a sort of peaceful smell—as though nothing bad could happen ever again in the world. It smelled of grain and harness dressing and of axle grease and of rubber boots and of new rope. And whenever the cat was given a fish-head to eat, the barn would smell of fish. But mostly it smelled of hay, for there was always hay in the great loft overhead. (p. 13)

Also, description can enhance suspense. In this excerpt from C. S. Lewis's *The lion, the witch and the wardrobe* (1950), Edmund has just entered the wicked White Witch's castle:

> He found himself in a long gloomy hall with many pillars, full, as the courtyard had been, of statues. The one nearest the door was a little Faun with a very sad expression on its face, and Edmund couldn't help wondering if this might be Lucy's friend. The only light came from a single lamp and close behind this sat the White Witch. (p. 93)

Too often students skip a description of the setting, and they lose an important element in making their stories interesting.

Writers often describe things in the setting to convey an emotion or to describe the feeling a certain setting creates. The author may choose a simple scene to establish this mood. The following paragraph from Tolkien's *The hobbit* (1966) illustrates the importance of using setting to create an impression on the reader, and letting the reader experience the emotion that the characters must be feeling. Bilbo and the dwarves are just entering the dreaded Mirkwood:

> They walked in a single file. The entrance to the path was like a sort of arch leading into a gloomy tunnel made by two great trees that leant together, too old and strangled with ivy and hung with lichen to bear more than a few blackened leaves. The path itself was narrow and wound in and out among the trunks. Soon the light at the gate was like a little bright hole far behind, and the quiet was so deep that their feet seemed to thump along while all the trees leaned over them and listened. (p. 140)

The setting in some stories may be almost as important as the plot structure and character development. In some stories the mood is established by the difficulties the characters have with the weather, the wildness, and the evilness of the country they must pass through. A set of general questions designed to draw students' attention to the setting in the stories they read is presented in Figure 9–15.

Characters

Characters are the people or personified animals who are involved in the story events. Often characters are considered the most important element in the story

Is the setting elaborated in great detail or barely sketched?

Is the setting of much importance to the story, or could the story take place anywhere?

Does the author take a great deal of effort to establish the authenticity and description of the environment?

Does weather or time play an important role in the story?

Is the scenic description interspersed with character description? How?

Is the mood engendered by the setting important to the story?

Would the story have as strong an effect if the setting were less involved?

Is the setting necessary for plot development?

Could the story characters be found in other kinds of settings?

Do the conflict situations depend as much on the setting as on the characters for the complications and resolutions of the problems?

Does the author use the setting to provide the kinds of complications that are believable?

Is the setting sometimes more important than the action or character description?

Figure 9–15   General Questions About Integral Settings

(Walker, 1981). Boynton and Mack (1985) explain the importance of characterization:

> Stories happen to people. If there is ever a story chiefly concerned with a tree, or a stone, or an ape, the story will exist only because these things will be treated as if they were human rather than as what we know they are in nature. (pp. 22–23)

The experience the author creates for readers is centered around a character or group of characters. Even though the experience is vicarious, readers must be able to identify with one of the characters. The writer must convince the readers that the characters experience the same feelings and emotions they feel.

Usually one fully rounded character and two or three supporting characters are introduced and developed in a story. Fully developed main characters have all the characteristics of real people: They have conflict and emotional ups and downs that surprise us from time to time; they are capable of ambiguous and contradictory behavior and thinking; and they are capable of doing almost anything or, perhaps, nothing at all. A list of fully developed main characters in children's stories is presented in Figure 9–16.

The supporting characters may be individualized, but they will be portrayed much less vividly than the main character. The extent to which the supporting characters are developed depends upon the needs of the story. They must help readers to experience the main character's emotion and conflict.

Character	Story
Catherine Hall	Blos, J. W. (1979). *A gathering of days: A New England girl's journal, 1830–1832*. New York: Scribner. (U)
Queenie	Burch, R. (1966). *Queenie Peavy.* New York: Viking. (U)
Harriet	Fitzhugh, L. (1964). *Harriet the spy.* New York: Harper and Row. (M)
Sam Gribley	George, J. C. (1959). *My side of the mountain.* New York: Dutton. (U)
Frances (the badger)	Hoban, R. (1976). *Best friends for Frances.* New York: Harper and Row. (P)
Anastasia	Lowry, L. (1979). *Anastasia Krupnik.* Boston: Houghton Mifflin. (M)
Arrietty	Norton, M. (1981). *The borrowers.* New York: Harcourt Brace Jovanovich. (M)
Karana	O'Dell, S. (1960). *Island of the blue dolphins.* Boston: Houghton Mifflin. (M–U)
Jess Aarons	Paterson, K. (1977). *Bridge to Terabithia.* New York: Crowell. (M–U)
Peter	Potter, B. (1902). *The tale of Peter Rabbit.* New York: Warne. (P)
Mafatu	Sperry, A. (1968). *Call it courage.* New York: Macmillan. (U)
Cassie	Taylor, M. (1976). *Roll of thunder, hear my cry.* New York: Dial. (U)
Laura	Wilder, L. I. (1959). *Little house in the big woods.* New York: Harper and Row. (M)
Chibi	Yashima, T. (1955). *Crow boy.* New York: Viking. (P)
Casey	Yep, L. (1977). *Child of the owl.* New York: Harper and Row. (M–U)

Figure 9–16   Fully Developed Characters in Children's Literature

How Authors Develop Characters. All writers of stories must determine how to develop and present characters to involve readers in the experiences they are writing about. To do this they use certain techniques that enable readers to understand and become involved in the conflict and emotions of the characters. Authors develop characters in three ways: (a) physical description, (b) dialogue, and (c) action.

Authors generally build the physical descriptions of characters as the story develops; however, they provide some physical description when characters are introduced. Readers come to know characters by the description of their facial features, body shapes, habits of dress, mannerisms, and gestures. Roald Dahl vividly describes James' two wicked aunts in *James and the giant peach* (1961):

> Aunt Sponge was enormously fat and very short. She had small piggy eyes, a sunken mouth, and one of those white flabby faces that looked exactly as though it had been boiled. She was like a great white soggy overboiled cabbage. Aunt Spiker, on the other hand, was lean and tall and bony, and she wore steel-rimmed spectacles that fixed onto the end of her nose with a clip. She had a screeching voice and long wet narrow lips, and whenever she got angry or excited, little flecks of spit would come shooting out of her mouth as she talked. (p. 7)

Their physical personalities are further developed or expressed in the actions the characters exhibit because of their physical makeup. The main problem for writers is how to use physical description to get readers to know their characters. Because not all physical characteristics are necessary for describing a character, writers need to know how to select appropriate details. Important details are those that mark characters as unique and that will play a role in the development of the story.

Dialogue and action are two better ways of describing characters than is physical description alone. To understand the motivation of characters, we must begin to know the feelings and sources of conflict that impel them to speak, think, and act the way they do. Plot and setting are tied to the development of the characters because the conditions in a story must be set up so that the motivation of the characters is believable.

When one character says something aloud to another character, that is *dialogue*. We learn about people by listening to what they say and how they say it. Dialogue is a reader's principal means of understanding story characters. Student authors must be careful to match the words and feelings expressed with the characters who are talking. Characters speak for specific reasons, and students need to know why their characters are speaking before they have them say anything. Dialogue clarifies situations, develops character, and moves the plot.

Characters are given separate paragraphs for what they say and for whatever qualifying statement or gesture an author includes as part of the situation. Students can introduce variety into their use of dialogue by placing some action or gesture within the dialogue. Facial expressions, actions, or pointed references to the locale are frequently used to interrupt the flow of dialogue. Consider this example from Armstrong's *Sounder* (1969):

"Where did you first get Sounder?" the boy asked.

"I never got him. He came to me along the road when he wasn't more'n a pup."

The father turned to the cabin door. It was ajar. Three small children, none as high as the level of the latch, were peering out into the dark.

"We just want to pet Sounder," the three all said at once.

"It's too cold. Shut the door." (p. 2)

The qualifying words used to introduce dialogue are very important. *Said* is most often used because it does not detract from the dialogue's effect. The situation or mood of the story may demand a different qualifying word, but these must be used carefully so the reader is not distracted from the mood being created. A variety of words may substitute for *said*. Some possible substitutions include *answered, asked, replied, whispered, shouted, screamed,* and *explained.* Qualifying words, however, are not necessary if the speaker's mood is already evident from the dialogue alone.

The best indicators of what people believe are their deeds. Likewise, what authors have their characters do gives readers the best insights into what type of individuals they are. What characters say and think are important; however, if there are inconsistencies among speech, thoughts, *and* actions, actions are the best means of knowing what the characters are really like. As readers, we are probably more impressed by what characters do than we are by what they say or think. Yet, we can fully understand characters only when we know the relationships among what they say, think, and do.

Our interest in the characters depends on their function in the story. To become interesting as individuals, characters must be portrayed in terms specific enough for us to understand them as people who live and think and act in certain ways that are credible and consistent with their roles in the story. The general questions about characters listed in Figure 9–17 can be used in discussing character development. The information you teach students will depend on the age of the students and how much they can understand and use in their stories. Children at any age, however, can understand what a character looks like, says, and does.

Theme

Theme is the psychological subject or meaning of a story. A *theme* embodies general truths about society, human nature, or the human condition and usually deals with the emotions and values of the story characters. The feelings that characters have toward each other amplify theme. If the theme is good versus evil, for instance, the feelings of love and hate should come through strongly. Other feelings and values that accompany love, such as being helpful, friendly, honest, trustworthy, and kind, will be evident in the characters who are on the side of good. Those characters on the side of evil will likely be mean, conniving, greedy, and so on. They put their own interests above all else and are not concerned about the welfare of anyone but themselves. By casting theme in the role of emotions and values, students will be able to understand it more easily.

Which character is developed the most?

Does the main character seem to be a real person?

How many supporting characters does the author include in the story?

Which characters support (or oppose) the main character?

How does each character get involved with the main character?

What does the character look like?

How do those physical characteristics affect the character's role in the story?

If the character had been bigger (smaller, older, stronger, etc.) would the character have behaved the same in the story?

Does the character use any specific mannerisms or gestures?

Is there a special relationship between how the character is described and how the character acts and talks?

Does the author use dialogue in the story? How?

Does the dialogue help you to predict what might happen because of what is said?

What do a character's actions tell us about that character?

Can we expect a character to behave in a certain way when we get to know that character?

Figure 9–17 General Questions About Characters

Contrasting themes and motifs can be helpful to students. While motifs are the structural main ideas, themes are the emotional forces that shape the goals that characters set out to achieve. The conflict situations that make up the plot result from the conflicting emotions and values of the story characters.

The Two Types of Themes.   There are two types of themes, explicit and implicit themes. *Explicit themes* are stated openly and clearly in the story. Lukens (1986) uses *Charlotte's web* to point out how friendship is expressed as an explicit theme:

> Charlotte has encouraged, protected, and mothered Wilbur, bargained and sacrificed for him, and Wilbur, the grateful receiver, realizes that "Friendship is one of the most satisfying things in the world." And Charlotte says later, "By helping you perhaps I was trying to lift up my life a little. Anyone's life can stand a little of that." Because these quoted sentences are exact statements from the text they are called explicit themes. (p. 102)

Implicit themes are implied in the story rather than explicitly stated in the text. Implicit themes are developed as the characters attempt to overcome the obstacles that would prevent them from reaching their goal. Plot and character development are interwoven with theme as the writer prepares the characters for the resolution of the complications introduced into their lives. Theme emerges through the thoughts, speech, and actions of the characters as they seek to resolve their conflicts. Lukens also uses *Charlotte's web* to illustrate implicit themes:

> Charlotte's selflessness—working late at night to finish a new word, expending her last energies for her friend—is evidence that friendship is giving oneself. Wilbur's protection of Charlotte's egg sac, his sacrifice of first turn at the slops, and his devotion to Charlotte's babies—giving without any need to stay even or to pay back—leads us to another theme: True friendship is naturally reciprocal. As the two become fond of each other, still another theme emerges: One's best friend can do no wrong. In fact, a best friend is sensational! Both Charlotte and Wilbur believe in these ideas; their experiences verify them. (p. 112)

A list of stories with explicit and implicit themes is presented in Figure 9–18 and a set of general questions about theme is presented in Figure 9–19.

Point of View

People see others and the world from different *points of view*, that is, they see things differently. Point of view is very important in writing because the focus of

---

de Paola, T. (1980). *The knight and the dragon*. New York: Putnam. (P)

Flack, M. (1931). *Angus and the cat*. New York: Doubleday. (P)

Freeman, D. (1964). *Dandelion*. New York: Viking. (P)

Lawson, R. (1972). *Rabbit hill*. New York: Viking. (M)

L'Engle, M. (1962). *A wrinkle in time*. New York: Farrar. (U)

Lewis, C. S. (1981). *The lion, the witch and the wardrobe*. New York: Macmillan. (M–U)

Merrill, J. (1964). *The pushcart war*. Reading, MA: Addison-Wesley. (M)

Miles, M. (1971). *Annie and the old one*. Boston: Little, Brown. (M–U)

Neville, E. (1963). *It's like this cat*. New York: Harper and Row. (U)

Piper, W. (1954). *The little engine that could*. New York: Platt and Munk. (P)

Wells, R. (1981). *Timothy goes to school*. New York: Dial. (P)

White, E. B. (1952). *Charlotte's web*. New York: Harper and Row. (M)

Yep, L. (1977). *Child of the owl*. New York: Harper and Row. (M–U)

Figure 9–18   Stories with Explicit and Implicit Themes

What does the story mean to you?

What is the most important idea the author tried to get across in the story?

Is this idea or theme explicitly stated or implied in the story?

Does the primary theme unfold primarily through the speech, thoughts, or actions of the characters?

Does the conflict the characters encountered help you to determine what the theme is? How?

Is the theme similar to the motif or rather different? How?

Are there other themes besides the primary one?

Are these other themes related to the primary theme or are they different? How?

Figure 9–19   General Questions for Theme

the narrator determines to a great extent readers' understanding of the story—the characters, events, and whether or not readers will believe what they are being told. Student authors must decide who will tell their stories and follow that viewpoint consistently in the stories they write.

Five points of view will be discussed: (a) the first-person narrator, (b) the objective third-person point of view, (c) the omniscient point of view, (d) the limited omniscient point of view, and (e) the character point of view. Examples of stories written from each viewpoint are presented in Figure 9–20.

The First-Person Narrator.   A story told in first person is easily accepted by readers because the narrator takes an active part in the story, speaking as an eyewitness and a participant in the events. As long as the narrator remains an eyewitness and limits the narration to only what he or she possibly can know, readers are very likely to accept what they are told.

There is one main limitation to the first-person point of view: the narrator cannot help readers fully understand the motives of the other characters unless they confess to the narrator. The first-person point of view is most effective when the narrator is the central character, because readers can enter the narrator's mind and discover what he or she thinks about the events and interrelationships among characters.

The Objective Third-Person Point of View.   Readers become an eyewitness and can only see, hear, and learn what is visible and audible and what others say about the characters and situations. The narrator and the readers are confined to the immediate scene and cannot enter the minds of the characters. Anything learned about the characters must be learned through what is said by the charac-

First Person Narrator

Danziger, P. (1978). *The pistachio prescription.* New York: Delacorte. (U)

Fritz, J. (1982). *Homesick: My own story.* New York: Putnam. (M–U)

Howe, D., & Howe, J. (1979). *Bunnicula.* New York: Atheneum. (M)

Viorst, J. (1977). *Alexander and the terrible, horrible, no good, very bad day.* New York: Atheneum. (P)

Objective Third-Person Point of View

Brown, M. (1954). *Cinderella.* New York: Scribner. (P)

Galdone, P. (1973). *The three billy goats Gruff.* Boston: Houghton Mifflin. (P)

Lobel, A. (1972). *Frog and toad together.* New York: Harper and Row. (P)

Wells, R. (1973). *Benjamin and Tulip.* New York: Dial. (P)

Omniscient Point of View

Babbitt, N. (1975). *Tuck everlasting.* New York: Farrar. (M–U)

Grahame, K. (1961). *The wind in the willows.* New York: Scribner. (M)

Lewis, C. S. (1981). *The lion, the witch and the wardrobe.* New York: Macmillan. (M–U)

Selden, G. (1960). *The cricket in Times Square.* New York: Dell. (M)

Limited Omniscient Point of View

Burch, R. (1966). *Queenie Peavy.* New York: Dell. (U)

Cleary, B. (1981). *Ramona Quimby, age 8.* New York: Random House. (M)

Lionni, L. (1969). *Alexander and the wind-up mouse.* New York: Pantheon. (P)

Lowry, L. (1979). *Anastasia Krupnik.* Boston: Houghton Mifflin. (M)

Character Point of View

George, J. C. (1972). *Julie of the wolves.* New York: Harper and Row. (M–U)

Norton, M. (1981). *The borrowers.* New York: Harcourt Brace Jovanovich. (M)

Figure 9–20   Stories Illustrating the Five Points of View

ters themselves or by what others say they have seen and heard. The limitation is that the author cannot probe very deeply into the characters.

The Omniscient Point of View.   Here the author sees all and knows all. The author tells the readers about the thought processes of each character without worrying about how the information is obtained. Readers may accept this convention but many will want to know by what authority the writer can tell us what goes on in the minds of different characters.

The Limited Omniscient Point of View.   This device is used when the author needs to overhear the thoughts of one of the characters but does not wish to be altogether all-knowing and all-seeing. The story is told in third person and the author generally concentrates on the thoughts, feelings, and significant past experiences of the main character. If needed, an author using this point of view might include the thoughts, feelings, and past experiences of one or two other characters and still be within this point of view.

The Character Point of View.   This device enables the writer to tell a story in third person but through the eyes of an important character. Once the character is selected and the point of view is established, that character tells the story. Readers will have accepted the point of view of the narrator, and a shift to another character would be hard for them to believe. The character point of view gives the writer the freedom to select the most perceptive character to tell the story. The limitation is that the character selected can only guess at the motives of the other characters. General questions about the five points of view are presented in Figure 9-21. These questions can be adapted to use in discussing stories illustrating each viewpoint.

Teaching Students About Point of View.   After students have been introduced to the five points of view, they need to experiment with them to understand how various viewpoints slant a story. To demonstrate to students how point of view changes according to the viewpoint of the person telling the story, read Judy Blume's *The pain and the great one* (1974) to students. In this book, the same brief story is told twice, first from the point of view of "The great one," an 8-year-old sister, and then from the point of view of "The pain," the 6-year-old brother. Even children in the primary grades are struck by how different the two versions of the same story are and how the narrator filters the information and presents it in a story.

Another way to demonstrate the power of different viewpoints is to have students retell or rewrite a familiar story such as *The three bears* (Galdone, 1972) from specific points of view—through the eyes of Mother Bear, Father Bear, Baby Bear, or Goldilocks. Mother Bear might be concerned about the messes Goldilocks has made in her home; Father Bear might be worrying about how he will catch the intruder; Baby Bear might be upset that it was his belongings that Goldilocks has damaged; and Goldilocks might be thinking about how to escape or how she will defend her actions. Then have students share the different versions and compare them.

As they shift the point of view, students learn that they can change some aspects of a story but not others. To help them appreciate how these changes affect a story, have them take a story such as C.S. Lewis' *The lion, the witch and the wardrobe* (1950), which is told from the omniscient point of view, and retell various episodes from the other four points of view. The omniscient point of view is a good one to start with because, in this viewpoint, the readers know all. As students shift to other points of view, they must decide what to leave out according to the

The First-Person Narrator

Who is telling the story?

Is the story told in first person?

Is the main character telling the story, or is another character telling it?

Is the narrator speaking as an eyewitness as well as a participant in the events?

Do we learn about the other characters only through what the narrator sees and what the other characters tell the narrator?

The Objective Third-Person Point of View

Who is telling the story?

Is what we learn about the story only by what we see and hear as eyewitnesses?

Are we restricted to only hearing dialogue and seeing actions and settings?

Can we listen in on a character's thoughts?

The Omniscient Point of View

Who is telling the story?

Do we know what the characters are thinking?

Does the narrator tell us how the characters feel?

Does the narrator tell what the character's ideas are before he or she tells anyone else?

Is the story told in third person?

The Limited Omniscient Point of View

Who is telling the story?

Are we limited to overhearing the thoughts of just one or two characters?

Does the narrator tell us how these characters feel?

Is the story told in third person?

Does the author stick to dialogue, action, and physical description when discussing the other characters in the story?

The Character Point of View

Who is telling the story?

Has the author selected one character through whose eyes the story will be told?

Is the story told in third person?

Does the author tell the entire story through the eyes of the same character?

Does the author tell us about the other characters only through their actions, dialogue, and physical descriptions?

Can we only overhear the thinking of the character through whom the story is being told?

Figure 9–21   General Questions on Point of View

new perspective. They must decide whether to tell the story in first or third person and what kinds of information about the characters they are permitted to share according to that viewpoint.

Summary

Information was presented in this chapter about seven elements of story structure: (a) beginning-middle-end, (b) motifs, (c) plot, (d) setting, (e) characters, (f) theme, and (g) point of view. These story structures are interrelated and build on one another. Beginning-middle-end is the most basic element. A motif is the structural main idea on which plot is developed. The plot consists of a series of events and conflict situations through which the characters strive to obtain their goals. Setting, with its three dimensions of location, weather, and time, is an important element that students often tend to glide over. We considered character development in terms of physical and psychological descriptions. Theme, or the meaning the author is trying to express, gives focus and direction to a story. Authors choose from a variety of viewpoints, and the point of view that an author adopts

has a significant effect on the way a story is told.

An instructional strategy based on the instructional model in Chapter 1 was presented to use in teaching students about the seven elements of story structure. In this approach, students learn to write stories by reading stories, by examining how authors use the structural elements, and by applying what they have learned through writing stories using the process approach.

Learning about the structure of stories not only influences students' abilities to comprehend and recall stories, but it also enhances their abilities to compose stories. By helping students to develop an explicit concept of story and by giving them time to write, they are far more capable of writing interesting and well-structured stories.

Extensions

1. Compile a list of books to use in teaching students to write stories at the grade level you teach or plan to teach. Write a brief summary for each book, commenting specifically on the elements of story structure that the book exemplifies.

2. Construct a set of charts to use in teaching the elements of story structure.

3. Interview several students about their concepts of stories and how they write stories. Ask questions such as:

   ■ Tell me about a story you have read that is really a good one.

   ■ What things do authors include in stories to make them good?

   ■ Do you like to write stories?

   ■ Tell me about some of the stories you have written.

   ■ Tell me some of the things you think about while you are writing a story.

   ■ What do you include in stories you write to make them good?

   ■ What have your teachers taught you about writing stories?

   ■ What would you like to learn about so you can be a better writer?

4. Teach one or more of the elements of story structure to a small group of students. Use the instructional strategy presented in Figure 9–3.

5. Collect samples of children's stories and examine them to see how students have used the elements of story structure presented in this chapter.

References

A curriculum for English. (1966). Lincoln, NE: University of Nebraska Press.

Applebee, A. N. (1978). *The child's concept of story: Ages two to seventeen.* Chicago: The University of Chicago Press.

———. (1980). Children's narratives: New directions. *The Reading Teacher, 34,* 137–142.

Andersen, H. C. (1979). *The ugly duckling.* New York: Harcourt Brace Jovanovich.

Armstrong, W. H. (1969). *Sounder.* New York: Harper and Row.

Blume, J. (1974). *The pain and the great one.* New York: Bradbury Press.

Boynton, R. W., & Mack, M. (1985). *Introduction to the short story.* New York: Hayden.

Buckley, M. H. (1968). A curriculum for the teaching of written expression in the elementary school. Unpublished Master's Thesis, University of California, Berkeley.

Buckley, M. H., & Boyle, O. (1983). Mapping and composing. In M. Myers & J. Gray (Eds.), *Theory and practice in the teaching of composition.* Urbana, IL: National Council of Teachers of English.

Dahl, R. (1978). *The enormous crocodile.* New York: Knopf.

———. (1961). *James and the giant peach.* New York: Knopf.

Galdone, P. (1962). *The hare and the tortoise.* New York: McGraw-Hill.

———. (1972). *The three bears.* New York: Houghton Mifflin.

George, J. C. (1972). *Julie of the wolves.* New York: Harper and Row.

Golden, J. M. (1984). Children's concept of story in reading and writing. *The Reading Teacher, 37,* 578–584.

Gordon, C. J., & Braun, C. (1982). Story schemata: Metatextual aid to reading and writing. In J. A. Niles & L. A. Harris (Eds.), *New inquiries in reading: Research and instruction.* Rochester, National Reading Conference.

Keith, H. (1977). *The obstinate land.* New York: Crowell.

Konigsburg, E. L. (1983). *From the mixed-up files of Mrs. Basil E. Frankweiler.* New York: Atheneum.

Lewis, C. S. (1950). *The lion, the witch and the wardrobe.* New York: Macmillan.

Lukens, R. J. (1986). *A critical handbook of children's literature* (3rd ed.). Glenview, IL: Scott, Foresman.

Mandler, J. M., & Johnson, N. S. (1977). Remembrance of things parsed: Story structure and recall. *Cognitive Psychology, 9,* 111–151.

Ness, E. (1966). *Sam, Bangs and Moonshine.* New York: Holt.

Paterson, K. (1977). *Bridge to Terabithia.* New York: Crowell.

Pitcher, E. G., & Prelinger, E. (1963). *Children tell stories: An analysis of fantasy.* New York: International Universities Press.

Potter, B. (1902). *The tale of Peter Rabbit.* New York: Warne.

Rumelhart, D. (1975). Notes on a schema for stories. In D. G. Bobrow (Ed.), *Representation and understanding: Studies in cognitive science.* New York: Academic Press.

Sendak, M. (1963). *Where the wild things are.* New York: Harper and Row.

Speare, E. (1958). *The witch of Blackbird Pond.* Boston: Houghton Mifflin.

Stein, N. L., & Glenn, C. G. (1979). An analysis of story comprehension in elementary school children. In R. O. Freedle (Ed.), *New Directions in Discourse Processing.* Norwood, NJ: Ablex.

Stewig, J. W. (1980). *Read to write: Using children's literature as a springboard for teaching writing* (2nd ed.). New York: Holt.

Tolkien, J. R. R. (1966). *The hobbit.* Boston: Houghton Mifflin.

Tompkins, G. E. (1979). *A kindergarten-first grade writing curriculum using literature as a model and based on cognitive developmental, psycholinguistic and metaphoric mode theoretical assumptions.* Unpublished doctoral dissertation, Virginia Polytechnic Institute and State University, Blacksburg, VA.

———. (1982). Seven reasons why children should write stories. *Language Arts, 59,* 718–721.

Walker, L. (1981). *Visions and revisions: A handbook for creative writing.* Palo Alto, CA: Peek.

White, E. B. (1952). *Charlotte's web.* New York: Harper and Row.

Wilder, L. I. (1971). *The long winter.* New York: Harper and Row.

IF YOU WANT TO LEARN MORE

Applebee, A. N. (1978). *The child's concept of story: Ages two to seventeen.* Chicago: The University of Chicago Press.

———. (1979). Children and stories: Learning the rules of the game. *Language Arts, 56,* 641–646.

Golden, J. M. (1984). Children's concept of story in reading and writing. *The Reading Teacher, 37,* 578–584.

Hoskisson, K. (1979). Writing is fundamental. *Language Arts, 56,* 892–896.

Lukens, R. J. (1982). *A critical handbook of children's literature* (2nd ed.). Glenview, IL: Scott, Foresman.

Moss. J. F. (1978). Literary awareness: A basis for composition. *Language Arts, 55,* 832–836.

Stewig, J. W. (1980). *Read to write: Using children's literature as a springboard for teaching writing* (2nd ed.). New York: Holt.

Stott, J. C. (1982). A structuralist approach to teaching novels in the elementary grades. *The Reading Teacher, 36,* 136–143.

Tompkins, G. E. (1982). Seven reasons why children should write stories. *Language Arts, 59,* 718–721.

CHAPTER TEN

Reading and Writing Stories: Exploring Stylistic Devices

OVERVIEW. In this chapter, we will explore additional elements of story structure, including the stylistic devices of repetition, imagery, personification, onomatopoeia, alliteration, and parody. These elements concern the way the story is written, that is, the author's style. Next, we will consider the words and phrases authors use to enhance the effectiveness of their writing. Helping students become aware of how they can create precise images with their words will make them better writers. In the third section of the chapter, we will examine specific genres or types of stories—folktales, fables, myths, epics and legends—that students read and can write using literature as a model.

Authors have different styles of writing because each writer is unique. Writers may use the same stylistic devices, but they will use them differently. How authors write depends on what they read, what they value, what relationships they have, and what they see in life. The same things hold true for students as they write.

The material presented in this chapter on story structure continues the general format we have been following of teaching the most general elements of story structure first and then teaching the more specific components. However, some stylistic devices can be introduced when the more general story structures are presented. For example, in conjunction with setting, teachers may want to introduce the stylistic device of imagery. The use of stylistic devices changes the focus of writing from the story line to the structure of paragraphs and sentences. When authors use stylistic devices, they are trying to obtain certain effects, and students recognize these effects as they read.

We will discuss style and stylistic devices because style is the essence or voice of a person's writing. Such devices help authors appeal to the reader's senses and to develop settings, moods, and characters. Students can begin to use stylistic devices in their stories as they attempt to use their own senses and words to translate into language what they see, hear, and feel.

The most specific elements of stories are the kinds of words and phrases that authors use. Words serve as labels for categories of experience, for feelings, and for plot. Words determine the effectiveness of an author's writing. As students become aware of how words and phrases can be used to obtain certain effects, they can begin to use their language deliberately, looking for words and phrases that will create the most precise images and communicate their ideas most effectively. When students realize that effective writing depends on the words and phrases used to relate a story, develop the plot and the setting, and create the story characters, they will be more interested in working on improving their writing. They will begin to develop their own style.

Students read a chart describing the characteristics of repetition, a commonly used stylistic device in folk tales such as The gingerbread boy.

POINTS TO PONDER
Why Do You Enjoy a Certain Author's Stories?
What Effects Can Authors Achieve by Using Stylistic Devices?

STYLISTIC DEVICES

Style is that quality which makes it possible to distinguish one writer from another. By a writer's style, "we mean the sound his words make on paper. Every writer, by the way he uses the language, reveals something of his spirit, his habits, his capacities, his bias" (Strunk & White, 1979, pp. 66–67). Style results from a combination of grammatical constraints and the stylistic devices a writer prefers, but "style takes its final shape more from attitudes of mind than from principles of composition . . . style *is* the writer, and therefore what a man is, rather than what he knows, will at last determine his style . . . . Full of his beliefs, sustained and elevated by the power of his purpose, armed with the rules of grammar, the writer is ready for exposure" (pp. 84–85).

With their style, writers bring readers closer to their personal visions. They engage readers in a sensory experience—to hear, to feel, and to see—by translating it into words, into an image. An *image* is an instantaneous picture that makes readers see, feel, and hear what is happening.

Eleven stylistic devices are presented in this section. Many have long and intimidating sounding names such as *onomatopoeia, consonance,* and *hyperbole.*

These names are just labels. Rather than having students memorize the labels and their definitions, teachers can help students in the elementary grades learn to use the terms by referring to specific structures in the stories they read, discuss, and write. What is important is that students explore how authors use these stylistic devices in their writing and that students experiment with them in the stories they write.

Repetition

Repetition is the easiest stylistic device for students to understand, and it is the starting point for introducing stylistic devices. Repetition provides younger students with a form or structure that enables them to produce more writing with fewer problems of invention. Moreover, the repetition of words, events, and feelings in stories has a strong appeal for children. The form itself affords the opportunity for endless variations. A variation that will probably be the easiest for kindergarten and primary grade students to begin with is to substitute new characters while repeating words and events. For instance, in Galdone's story *The gingerbread boy* (1975) the same words and the same events are repeated over and over again by adding a new character who has the same experiences with the gingerbread boy as the previous characters had. In one version of the story, the gingerbread boy runs away from a little old woman and a little old man, and then he continues running past one character after another. He shouts to each character:

> Run! Run! Run!
>
> Catch me if you can!
>
> You can't catch me!
>
> I'm the Gingerbread Boy,
>
> I am! I am! (unpaged)

He continues the refrain by listing all the characters he has run past. By the time he meets the fox at the end of the story, the gingerbread boy's list is quite long, and he boasts:

> I've run away from a little old woman,
>
> I've run away from a little old man,
>
> I've run away from a cow,
>
> I've run away from a horse,
>
> I've run away from a barn full of threshers,
>
> I've run away from a field full of mowers,
>
> And I can run away from you,
>
> I can! I can! (unpaged)

The repetition of words, events, and feelings in this story is what makes it fun for young children. Many folktales use repetition as a stylistic device. A list of folktales and other stories using repetition is presented in Figure 10–1.

Figure 10–1 Stories Using Repetition

Burningham, J. (1975). *Mr. Gumpy's outing*. New York: Holt. (P)

Ets, M. H. (1973). *Elephant in a well*. New York: Viking. (P)

Flack, M. (1958). *Ask Mr. Bear*. New York: Macmillan. (P)

Galdone, P. (1973). *The little red hen*. New York: Seabury. (P–M)

_____. (1973). *The three billy goats Gruff*. Boston: Houghton Mifflin. (P)

_____. (1975). *The gingerbread boy*. New York: Seabury. (P)

Haley, G. E. (1970). *A story a story*. New York: Atheneum. (P–M)

Kent, J. (1971). *The fat cat*. New York: Scholastic. (P)

McGovern, A. (1967). *Too much noise*. New York: Scholastic. (P)

Plume, I. (1980). *The Bremen town musicians*. New York: Doubleday. (P–M)

Tolstoy, A. (1969). *The great big enormous turnip*. Watts. (P–M)

Tresselt, A. (1964). *The mitten*. New York: Lothrop. (P)

Zemach, M. (1976). *It could always be worse*. New York: Farrar. (P–M)

P = primary grades (K–2)
M = middle grades (3–5)
U = upper grades (6–8)

The instructional strategy presented in Chapter 9 is also used in teaching repetition and the other elements of story structure and stylistic devices discussed in this chapter. A set of general questions is suggested for each stylistic device. These general questions can be used as a guide for writing specific questions. A set of general questions on repetition is presented in Figure 10–2.

After reading stories exemplifying the repetition structure and examining how authors use repetition to make their stories more interesting, students summarize what they have learned about repetition on a chart. A chart developed by a group of first graders is presented in Figure 10–3. These first graders focused on two types of repetition, repeating events and words, and they used *The gingerbread boy* as their model story. The teacher developed the chart and then the students added the illustrations and the gingerbread boy's refrain.

Students find the repetition device an easy one to understand and to incorporate in their own stories. This device provides the necessary structure, especially in the often underdeveloped middle part. A kindergartner dictated the repetition story presented in Figure 10–4 on pages 312–313. "The Runaway Crayon" is clearly based on *The gingerbread boy* and uses the repetition of events structure. The characters are the members of the student's family: her mother; Peter, her younger brother; and Sebastian, the family dog. In contrast to *The gingerbread boy*, Sarah creates a happy ending for her story. The purple crayon is caught and returned to the crayon box where it belongs.

Repetition of Words

Are some words repeated over and over in the story?
Which words or phrases are repeated?
Why are they repeated?

Repetition of an Event with Different Characters

Is an event repeated over and over with different characters?
What event is repeated?
Who are the different characters?
Why is the event repeated with different characters?
What effect does the repetition have on the story?

Repetition of an Event with Different Objects

Is an event repeated over and over with different objects?
What event is repeated?
What are the objects?
Why is the event repeated with different objects?
What effect does the repetition have on the story?

Repetition of a Feeling

Is a feeling repeated over and over as different characters strive to accomplish a task?
What feeling is repeated?
Why is the feeling repeated?
What effect does the repetition have on the story?

Figure 10–2   General Questions on Repetition

Imagery

Students use imagery daily as they see, smell, hear, and feel. The activities suggested in the section on Sensory Writing in Chapter 7 help students focus on the five senses. In the stories students read, they can discuss the vivid descriptions that appeal to the senses in more imaginative ways. The imagery in the stories children read must convince them they are smelling the same smells, hearing the same sounds, seeing the same things, and feeling the same emotions as the story characters. In *Rabbit hill* (1972), Lawson's descriptions of the house and property give us an image of the life on the Hill:

> As he picked his way through the long neglected garden the big brick house loomed up dark and lonely in the twilight. It looked very gloomy, no lights in the windows, no Folks about. The roof shingles were curled and rotting, blinds hung crookedly. In the walks and driveway tall, dried weeds rattled and

Repetition

There are two kinds of things that are repeated in stories.

1. Authors make events happen over and over in stories.

2. Authors have characters say the same things over and over.

Figure 10–3   A Chart on the Repetition Device

scraped whenever a breeze stirred. Now that all the earth was stirring with spring it seemed even more depressing. (pp. 13–14)

To stretch students' imaginations, point out how authors use imagery especially as they develop the setting. This device allows readers to see the world in new and interesting ways. Each experience with imagery must help them to see something new and indicate new possibilities for enjoying literature. General questions to use in discussing imagery with students are presented in Figure 10–5 on page 314.

Personification

Personification is the assignment of human traits, qualities, and powers to anything nonhuman. The author's task in using personification is to maintain the natural characteristics of whatever is being personified while creating distinct personalities. The personalities of other characters are less developed and remain within the bounds of their natural traits.

In *Bunnicula* (Howe & Howe, 1979), the two main characters, a dog named Harold and a cat named Chester, have been personified. Harold, the Monroe family dog, writes the story. He introduces himself, the Monroes, and Chester at the very beginning of the story:

Allow me to introduce myself. My name is Harold. I come to writing purely by chance. My full-time occupation is dog. I live with Mr. and Mrs. X (called here

Figure 10–4 A Kindergartner's Repetition Story Based on Galdone's *The gingerbread boy* (1975)

1. The RunaWay CraYon BY SARAh

2. Once there were 5 crayons in a box.

3. The purple crayon ran out of the box.

4. And the purple crayon got away.

7.

Then Peter tried to catch him and he did. And Peter put him back in the box.

5.

Then Sebastian tried to chase him but he couldn't catch him.

6.

Then Mommy tried to catch him. But she couldn't catch him.

Sarah, age 5

the "Monroes") and their two sons: Toby, aged eight, and Pete, aged ten. Also sharing our home is a cat named Chester, whom I am pleased to call my friend. (pp. xi–xii)

Harold's story is about what happened in the Monroe household after a rabbit named Bunnicula arrived. Chester, who is a well-read cat with a vivid imagination, concludes that Bunnicula is a vampire rabbit, and he tries without success to warn

---

Imagery

Can you imagine what the characters are seeing through the author's words?

Which words appeal to your sense of sight? Hearing? Smell?

How does the author make the setting seem real?

Does the author describe what the characters are hearing? How?

Does the author describe what the characters are feeling? How?

Can you imagine the same feelings the characters have? Why?

How does the author describe the action in the story?

Are all your senses engaged in the action?

Can you imagine the action because of the author's description?

Personification

Does the author give human characteristics to nonhuman beings and objects?

Are the main characters able to extend their natural traits to act in ways they would not normally act?

Do the supporting characters remain natural?

Is the personification believable?

Connotation

Does the author use words having meanings that call upon your own feelings for meaning?

What words have favorable connotations (i.e., feelings or images) associated with them?

What words have unfavorable connotations (i.e., feelings or images) associated with them?

Would it make a difference in the author's style if more connotative than denotative words were used?

Figure 10–5   General Questions on Imagery, Personification, and Connotation

Mr. and Mrs. Monroe about the rabbit. Harold tells us that he is not an ordinary dog and Chester is not an ordinary cat, but both characters still retain natural "pet" traits. One example is Harold's fondness for human food, especially for cream-filled chocolate cupcakes:

> It was Friday night, and on Friday nights, Toby gets to stay up and read as late as he wants to. So, of course, he needs lots of food to keep up his strength. Good food like cheese crackers, chocolate cupcakes (my very favorite, the kind with cream in the middle, mmmm!), pretzels and peanut butter sandwiches.... This particular evening, I stationed myself on Toby's stomach. Usually, I'm a little more subtle, but, having missed out on the bacon at breakfast, I was not about to take any chances on the chocolate cupcakes (with cream in the center). (pp. 37–38)

General questions about personification are included in Figure 10–5. These questions can be used in discussing *Bunnicula* and other stories with personified characters.

Connotation

The *connotation* of a word is what the word suggests. Connotation suggests emotional meaning or association with something a reader has in common with the writer but is not directly expressed. *Denotation,* on the other hand, is what a word specifically points to, its core of meaning. Denotative meanings of a word are found in the dictionary; connotative meanings are found in the word's suggestive power.

Words acquire their connotations from the experiences we have. The first time we hear a word we may not associate very much with it. However, the more times we hear a word the greater the number of connotations we will associate with the word. Our experiences and the subtle uses of words we hear add to the meanings we associate with words. Words heard in favorable situations often acquire pleasant connotations; words heard in unfavorable contexts often acquire unpleasant connotations.

In *Sounder* (1969), Armstrong used connotations very effectively in the scene in which the men who were coming to get the father pushed their way into the cabin: "The warm, but frozen circle of man, woman, and three small children around the stove jumped to their feet" (p. 21). The family is warm because of the stove's heat, but frozen because of the implications of the father's stealing the ham. Students can recognize words that are not used for their denotative meaning, but are used for their psychological implications. General questions on connotation are included in Figure 10–5.

Onomatopoeia

Onomatopoeia is a device in which authors use sound words to make their writing more vivid. These sound words (e.g., *crash, slurp, varoom, me-e-e-ow*) sound like their meanings. For instance, in *Blueberries for Sal* (1976), McCloskey used sound words in describing how Little Sal picked blueberries: "Little Sal picked three berries and dropped them in her little tin pail . . . kuplink, kuplank, kuplunk" (p. 8). General questions to use in discussing onomatopoeia are listed in Figure 10–6.

Students can compile a list of sound words found in the stories they read on a chart displayed in the classroom or in their writing journals, and they can refer to the list as they write their own stories. Peter Spier has compiled two books of sound words. *Gobble growl grunt* (1971) is about animal sounds, and *Crash! bang! boom!* (1972) is about the sounds people and machines make. These two books are excellent references for students to use in selecting sound words to use

---

Onomatopoeia

Does the author use any words that sound like their actions or meanings?

Do these words make the story more enjoyable?

Do the sound words give a clearer, more vivid image of the description?

Alliteration

Does the author use a sequence of words beginning with the same consonant sound in the story?

What effect does the alliteration have?

Consonance

Does the author use a close repetition of consonant sounds in any part of the story?

What effect does this repetition have?

Why do you think the author used this stylistic device?

Assonance

Does the author use a repetition of vowel sounds in any part of the story?

What effect does the repetition have?

Why do you think the author uses this stylistic device?

Hyperbole

Does the author use any deliberate exaggerations?

Do the characters exaggerate?

What kinds of exaggeration (e.g., comparisons, attributes, actions, feelings) does the author use?

Figure 10–6 General Questions on Onomatopoeia, Alliteration, Consonance, Assonance, and Hyperbole

in their writing. Students enjoy using sound words, and these words add interest and perhaps a touch of humor to their writing.

Alliteration

Alliteration is the repetition of the same initial consonant sound in consecutive words or in words very close to one another within a sentence. It is another device that emphasizes sound. Repeating sounds contributes to the enjoyment of reading a story; it can break the monotony of straight prose. In *Rabbit bill* (1972), Lawson has Tim McGarth say, "Grandpa always said, 'Readin' rots the mind . . . ' " (p. 71). Questions about alliteration are included in Figure 10–6.

Figure 10–7 presents an alliteration story written by a third grader. This humorous, tongue-twisting story demonstrates that students can have fun with language as they experiment with stylistic devices.

Consonance

The close repetition of consonant sounds in general is called *consonance*. Whereas alliteration depends on repetition of the same initial consonant sounds for its effect, consonance uses many consonant sounds closely packed together with few if any words beginning with vowel sounds. In Lawson's *Rabbit bill* (1972), Father's instruction, "Now recite your Dogs," is a parody on reciting the times tables or the alphabet as well as an excellent example of consonance:

> Little Georgie closed his eyes dutifully recited, 'Fat-Man-at-the-Crossroads: two Mongrels; Good Hill Road: Dalmatian; house on Long Hill: Collie, noisy, no wind; Norfield Church corner: Police Dog, stupid, no nose; On the High Ridge, red farmhouse: Bulldog and Setter, both fat, don't bother; farmhouse with the big barns: Old Hound, very dangerous.... (p. 37)

General questions about consonance are included in Figure 10–6.

Assonance

A stylistic device that adds interest to phrases and sentences by the repetition of similar vowels sounds without the repetition of consonant sounds is called *assonance*. It depends on a rhyming-like quality of one word with one or more other words by means of the correspondences of the vowels in the words. Meaning can be enhanced by the use of assonance. In *Rabbit bill* (1972), Porky's description of the dog that was trying to get him makes the incident more interesting: "And there he is, a-bellerin' and a-roarin' and a-rushin'..." (Lawson, p. 80). General questions about assonance are included in Figure 10–6.

Hyperbole

Hyperbole is a deliberate exaggeration which could not possibly be meant literally. Often a writer stretches a comparison for humor, for protest, or for another effect.

Figure 10–7 A Third Grader's Alliteration Story Using the Letter *S*

Señora Snowshoe Rabbit
Slid through the snow.
Señor Fox was right on her
Tail, smashing it to shreds.
Señora Snowshoe Rabbit slipped
And slid into a shed.
Señora Snowshoe Rabbit came
Out of the shed with her stom-
ach smeared with snow.

Señora Snowshoe Rabbit started
Hopping once again.
Señora Snowshoe Rabbit slipp-
ed and slid again.
This time into the sea.
And Señora Snowshoe Rabbit
Never saw Shore again.

Eddy, age 9

In *King of the wind* (1948), Henry uses hyperbole in the Sultan's description of the most perfect horses in the kingdom, which were to be chosen to send as a gift to the King of France: "If the distance of the fore part is greater than the hind part, the horse will travel like the wind, climb like the cat, and strike afar" (pp. 53–54). General questions about hyperbole are included in Figure 10–6.

Word Play

Students should become aware of the variety of ways authors play with words for their own amusement and to enhance the pleasure of reading their works. Sometimes, the structure of a familiar phrase is used to elicit description or narration that is fresh and interesting. In Lawson's *Rabbit hill* (1972), Father is talking about new Folks coming and concludes a comment to Porky with this question, "Is there any clear proof of this most desirable addition to our neighborhood, or is it mere hearsay?" (p. 16). Porky responds by prefacing six statements with, "I hearsay. . ." (pp. 16–17). the fun is in the repetition.

A second type of word play involves the use of puns, words with different meanings or homonyms. Peggy Parish's series of *Amelia Bedelia* stories (1963) contain many examples of word play. Amelia Bedelia is a housekeeper who follows directions too literally, producing hilarious results. When asked to draw the drapes, for instance, she draws a picture of them instead of closing them. Even young children can appreciate this kind of humor as the 6-year-old's retelling of *Amelia Bedelia* in Figure 10–8 illustrates.

Bunnicula (Howe & Howe, 1979) and its two sequels, *Howliday Inn* (1982) and *The celery stalks at midnight* (1983) contain other examples of puns that appeal to middle grade students. In *Bunnicula,* for example, Chester reads that to de-

Figure 10–8   A 6-Year-Old's Retelling of Parish's *Amelia Bedelia (1963)*

Page	*1:*	One day Amelia Bedelia had a list of things to do.
Page	*2:*	To sweep the floor.
Page	*3:*	To dust the counters.
Page	*4:*	To make the bed.
Page	*5:*	To ice the fish.
Page	*6:*	The people are coming. Amelia Bedelia, you are in a mess!
Page	*7:*	They tasted the fish. They didn't like the fish.
Page	*8:*	Everybody was mad at Amelia Bedelia.
Page	*9:*	And then everybody laughed. Ho! Ho! Ho!
Page	*10:*	The End

Jill, age 6

stroy a vampire's power, you must pound a sharp *stake* into the vampire's heart. So, he "borrows" the sirloin *steak* that is thawing on the kitchen counter for the Monroes' dinner, places it on top of the sleeping bunny, and pounds on it with his paws! A list of general questions to use in discussing word play in these and other stories is included in Figure 10–9.

Parody

Authors will sometimes vary or mimic the language and style of a well-known piece of writing or a way of talking for a humorous touch. If the reader is familiar with what is being parodied, knowing the old form gives a sense of satisfaction by seeing the contrast between the old form and the new and humorous meaning. An example of parody was cited earlier in the section on consonance, and a list of general questions on parody is included in Figure 10–9.

The stylistic devices writers employ become part of their style. The grammatical constructions they favor also determine style. Grammatical structures, similes, and metaphors will be discussed in the chapter on grammar.

Students will begin to see the differences in the style of authors and how the components of style are blended together when they discuss stories in great depth. Stories from children's literature and from basal reading textbooks can be used to discuss the structure of stories and to compare how various authors use these stylistic devices.

Word Play

How does the author use words in interesting and unusual ways?

Does the author use puns in the story?

Does the author invent new words in the story?

Does the author have any of the characters use logic in the story that adds humor?

Parody

Has the author used the form of another kind of story you know? What kind?

Has the author changed the wording of a saying that you recognize?

Has the author used a set of actions you might find in sports or some activity to describe some part of the story?

Figure 10–9   General Questions on Word Play and Parody

WORDS AND PHRASES

Choosing the right words to communicate the thought, impression, or description needed at any particular moment of writing is crucial. Meaning can be clarified by the right word or muddied by the not-quite-right-word. Writing can also be biased by including or leaving out words. Biased language is a deliberate attempt to prejudice a reader either positively or negatively. Students need to learn how to choose the right word for effect and communication as well as how to detect the wrong words and how to use and detect biased language. If writers want their readers to feel a certain way about a character, the language used to describe that character must influence readers' perceptions.

Words can be divided into various categories that draw attention to the special characteristics of their use. The following categories may prove helpful even though the boundaries between them are somewhat shadowy: (a) effective words, (b) exceptional words, (c) professional words, (d) effective phrases, (e) coined words and phrases, and (f) synonyms. Emphasis is always on the effectiveness of the words used to portray the image, emotion, and vision of the story or poem.

Effective Words

Students can identify *effective words,* words that create the most precise images and convey their ideas most effectively. It may be that a single word used appropriately will determine the effectiveness and essential meaning of an entire sentence or paragraph. Words that are nonspecific, broad, or general produce ideas and images that are nonspecific, broad, or general; they give information but have no color or precision. For example, compare the words written in italics in these two sentences:

He *held* the boy's shoulder with *strong fingers.*

"He *gripped* the boy's shoulder with *fingers as strong as the claws of an eagle."* (Henry, *King of the wind,* 1948, p. 24)

In the first sentence, the words written in italics are very general. In contrast, the italicized words in the second sentence are far more effective, producing precise images. Encourage students to work for more specificity in the nouns and verbs they use and more vividness and intensity in the adjectives and adverbs they choose.

Find sentences in children's literature in which precise, specific images and ideas are presented; take these and change the adjectives, nouns, verbs, and adverbs to more broad, nonspecific ideas or images. Mark the broad or general words in the sentences, and ask students to replace them with more specific words. Then have students compare their sentences with the author's original sentences. Ask questions similar to the following:

■ How did the words you substituted improve the sentences?

■ How did the words you used compare with those of the authors?

Examples of sentences to use are presented in Figure 10–10. Students should be able to see that when broad or general words are replaced with more limited and effective words, the ideas and images are more precise and the sentences are more emphatic.

Exceptional Words

An *exceptional word* is one that is rarely found or expected. It is used to express a thought in a manner that is clever, unusual, and effective. An exceptional word is

---

1. a. As the *boy* stood on watch, his mind was *at work*.

   b. "As *Agba* stood on watch, his mind was *a mill wheel, turning, turning, turning* (Henry, *King of the wind,* 1948, p. 28).

2. a. He waved toward the *weeds in the field* and the *bare places in the lawn.*

   b. "He waved disgustedly at the *weed-choked fields,* the *patchy lawn*" (Lawson, *Rabbit hill,* 1972, p. 16).

3. a. A fly that had been *walking* along Wilbur's trough had flown up and *gotten* into the lower part of Charlotte's web and was *stuck* in the sticky threads.

   b. "A fly that had been *crawling* along Wilbur's trough had flown up and *blundered* into the lower part of Charlotte's web and was *tangled* in the sticky threads" (White, *Charolotte's web,* 1952, p. 37).

4. a. Tucker *climbed* through the gate into the cage and *walked* all around inside it.

   b. "Tucker *scrambled* through the gate into the cage and *pranced* all around inside it" (Selden, *The cricket in Times Square,* 1960, p. 54).

5. a. Every moment more and more of the *snow melted off the trees.*

   b. "Every moment more and more of the *trees shook off their robes of snow*" (Lewis, *The lion, the witch and the wardrobe,* 1950, p. 116).

Figure 10–10 Sentences from Children's Literature with Effective Words

one that impresses you with its structure and the way the author has used it. Two examples are:

"Them last folks were *slops,* that's what they were, *slops."* (Lawson, *Rabbit hill,* 1972, p. 16)

"'Signor Achmet!' He *screaked.* 'I charge you, as head groom in the Service of the Sultan of Morocco, to select six of the most perfect steeds in the royal stables." (Henry, *King of the wind,* 1984, p. 50)

Find sentences in children's literature with exceptional words or sentences in which familiar words are used in exceptional ways, and replace the exceptional words with ordinary words. Give students copies of the sentences with ordinary words and ask them to replace the underlined ordinary words with exceptional words, words that they might not use normally in those places. Hand out copies of the original sentences and have students compare their exceptional words with the words used by the author. Examples of exceptional words from Norton's *The borrowers* (1981) are presented in Figure 10–11.

Figure 10–11   Examples of Exceptional Words from Norton's
The borrowers (1981)

---

1. a. She filed fish-bone needles to a *fine* sharpness.

   b. She filed fish-bone needles to a *bee-sting* sharpness . . ." (p. 55).

2. a. How strange her own voice sounded! *Very* thin and *quite* clear, it *sounded* on the air.

   b. "How strange her own voice sounded! *Crystal* thin and *harebell* clear, it *tinkled* on the air" (p. 72).

3. a. "Why?" she asked again, and the word *sounded*—icy cold it sounded this time, and *very* sharp.

   b. "'Why?' she asked again, and again the word *tinkled*—icy cold it sounded this time, and *needle* sharp" (p. 73).

4. a. They're drinking Fine Old Madeira, thought Arietty, and very carefully she set the stool upright and stood quietly beside it, looking up. She could see light through the crack, occasionally *darkened* with shadow as one person or another moved a hand or arm.

   b. "They're drinking Fine Old Madeira, thought Arietty, and very carefully she set the stool upright and stood quietly beside it, looking up. She could see light through the crack, occasionally *flicked* with shadow as one person or another moved a hand or arm" (pp. 103–104).

Norton, 1981.

Using the same examples from children's literature used in the previous exercise or by finding additional examples, have students discuss the use of the exceptional words or exceptional uses of ordinary words in the sentences. The emphasis of the discussion should focus on the effects of the words as used by the authors. Use questions similar to the following ones, which relate to the examples in Figure 10–11:

- How does the use of *flicked* sharpen the image of the shadows?
- How does the use of *tinkled* help you understand how Arriety's voice sounded on the air outside?

The questions should center on the senses. Use the words *how* and *what* to question what students feel, see, hear, and gain from the other sensory impressions they receive when reading.

Professional Words

When students use words that have a specific meaning in a professional field, they must be careful to use them correctly. Many words have special meaning in a particular field as well as a common meaning. Students should consult the dictionary to determine if they are using words with special meanings appropriately. This may not be an important use of words for younger students, but, on the other hand, noting specialized words may be a way of increasing their vocabularies.

To help students understand the use of professional terminology, find examples in children's literature and discuss the effect of the specialized words. There are two dimensions of specialized words. First, specialized words may be necessary to convey a concept that would take pages to explain. This is the case with the word *tesseract* in *A wrinkle in time* (L'Engle, 1962). After experiencing a tesseract, Calvin asks how they got to the planet they found themselves on. Mrs. Whatsit explains:

> "Oh, we don't travel at the speed of *anything* . . . . We *tesser.* Or you might say, we *wrinkle.*" (p. 61)

To help students understand what a *tesseract* is, the teacher may ask the students to read or reread pages 56–62 of *A wrinkle in time* and ask them what they know about a *tesseract.* This initial understanding is elaborated later in the story. The use of *wrinkle* as a synonym for *tesser* helps give a common word a specific meaning useful in explaining a specialized term. A second use of specialized words is to compare sentences in which loose, nonprecise words are used with sentences in which specialized words are used.

Effective Phrases

Sometimes authors write a phrase that evokes an interesting and sometimes complex thought. Such phrases are termed *effective phrases.* Watch for effective phrases in the material children read and make students aware of the impact of such phrases.

Students should also be on the lookout for effective phrases in stories, magazine articles, advertisements, and newspaper articles. As a writing exercise, teachers might ask students to express an idea in a few sentences and then try to collapse the sentences into a single phrase that has more force and is more interesting. The following are examples of effective phrases from children's literature that evoke interesting and complex thoughts:

> She had lost the protection of Calvin's hand. Charles was nowhere, either to save or to turn to. She was alone in a *fragment of nothingness.* No light, no sound, no feeling. (L'Engle, *A wrinkle in time,* 1962, p. 56)

> To Agaba, on that early morning of April, the road to Newmarket seemed never-ending. He was *in a fever of expectancy* . . . . He wanted to plunge ahead of Titus Twickerham on Galompus, the lead horse. But he must keep the pace set. (Henry, *King of the wind,* 1948, p. 158)

Coined Words and Phrases

Writers who seek to gain unusual effects in their writing sometimes deliberately vary from standard usage of a word or phrase and coin a new word or phrase or use words or phrases in ways that give poignant meaning to their words. Sometimes words used in new ways take on an almost metaphoric usage. A phrase from *King of the wind* that seems to be original, yet almost metaphoric, is "Yet *he closed the shutter on his dreams* and from force of habit rather than hope turned to look at the animal" (Henry, 1948, p. 85). Robert Lawson's use of the word *garbidge* for garbage by Phewie in *Rabbit hill* is an example of a spelling change to make ordinary garbage to be something else:

> Phewie slapped Father on the back gleefully. "Will there be *garbidge?* Will there? Oh my, oh my! I've never seen one that shape and size that didn't set out the elegantest *garbidge!* Lots of it too; chicken wings, duck's backs, hambones — and cooked to a turn!" (1972, p. 73)

Care should be taken in using familiar expressions that have lost their force. Cliches may be appropriate in conversation at times, but in writing they generally seem flat. They add little meaning and may make a bad impression. Encourage students to think of fresher, more concrete expressions to add clarity and precision to their writing. They can experiment with language and still be concerned with the effect and appropriateness of the results of their manipulations.

Lewis Carroll's poem "Jabberwocky" (Zalben, 1977) is probably the most famous example of coined words. Carroll termed his new words *portmanteau,* or suitcase, words because he created them by collapsing two words together in much the same way as one slams a suitcase shut. His best known portmanteau word is *chortle,* a blending of *snort* and *chuckle. Brunch, motel, smog* and *grumble* are other commonly used portmanteau words. Authors also invent new words simply by combining nonsense syllables such as *flummadiddle* in *Sam, Bangs and Moonshine* (Ness, 1966) and *bimulous* in *When the sky is like lace* (Horwitz, 1975).

Help students locate and discuss coined words and phrases. Advertisements are an immediate source. Children's literature should be the main source for students, however, so that they can discuss the structure of sentences and the effects of words and phrases in a literary context. Teachers who take a great deal of informal interest in all coined words that students find can stimulate their students to create original words or phrases to express a thought that just needs an original word or phrase.

Synonyms

Synonyms are words that have essentially the same meaning. When students begin to use synonyms in their writing, they must carefully choose substitute words since the sense of the sentence or paragraph may be altered slightly. One use of synonyms is to avoid the monotonous repetition of words. In the following excerpt from *King of the wind* (1948), Henry uses four synonyms for *smells: fragrance, perfume, aroma,* and *scent.*

> The world was full of wonders! If he stretched his nostrils to the wind, he could sift the most interesting smells — the delicious fragrance of clover, the biting smell of smoke from the burning stubble of cornfields, the perfume from orange and lime groves, the spicy aroma of pine woods beyond the city wall, the musky smell of the wild boar, the cool, moisture-laden scent of the clouds that blew over the snow-topped mountains. He could not label the smells as yet, but he was sorting them out in his mind. (p. 43)

A second use of synonyms is to increase the strength, clarity, and precision of writing. In the following sentence from *King of the wind,* Henry substitutes the word *larked* for *walked,* and the result is stronger, more vivid writing:

> He turned tail and *larked* across the paddock all by himself. (p. 42)

Students can select synonyms for common words and phrases. Read paragraphs to the class that have freshness and originality as a result of synonym selection. Replace the synonyms with more common words and reread the paragraphs. Discuss the differences in the effect of the words and paragraphs by asking questions similar to the following:

- How (or what) did the author's words make you feel, help you see, or help you hear?
- What effect did the use of the *synonym* have on the sense of the sentences or paragraph?
- Which sentences are stronger, clearer, and more precise?

A thesaurus may be a valuable aid to students. However, students must remember that there are subtle differences in the words listed as synonyms. The subtleties of word connotations and the sense of the sentence evoked by the right choice of synonyms must be guided carefully.

SPECIFIC STORY GENRE

In addition to the elements of story structure and the stylistic devices that authors use in writing stories, specific *genre,* or story types, such as fables and myths have their own unique characteristics. Just as students read and examine beginning-middle-end, plot, characters, and other structural elements of stories, they can read stories representing a particular genre to learn about that unique form of the stories. Then they apply what they have learned in writing that particular story genre. The instructional strategy that was presented in Chapter 9 is also used for reading and writing these stories. Students first read stories and examine them to develop a chart listing the unique characteristics, and then they write class collaboration and individual stories that follow the characteristics. One specific genre is mystery stories. The characteristics of mystery stories and an example of a class collaboration mystery story were presented in Chapter 2. In this section, we will discuss the unique characteristics of five story genre: (a) folktales, (b) fables, (c) myths, (d) epics, and (e) legends.

Folktales

Folktales including fairy tales are relatively short stories that originated as part of the oral tradition. Well-known folktales include "The Three Little Pigs," "Cinderella," and "Sleeping Beauty." These and other tales have a number of characteristics:

1. The story is often introduced with the words "Once upon a time."
2. The settings are not worked out in any detail; they are usually generalized and could be located anywhere.
3. The plot structure is simple and straightforward.
4. The problem usually revolves around a journey from home to perform some tasks, a journey that involves a confrontation with a monster, the miraculous change from a harsh home to a secure home, or a wise beast-foolish beast confrontation.
5. Characters are portrayed in one dimension: They are either good or bad, stupid or clever, industrious or lazy.
6. The ending is positive, and everyone "lives happily ever after."

A list of recommended folktales is presented in Figure 10–12, and the country of origin for each is listed. It is interesting to note that folktales have been collected from around the world.

Bruno Bettleheim (1976) argues that from the experience of literature, children gain access to "deeper meaning" in life and this meaning should be appropri-

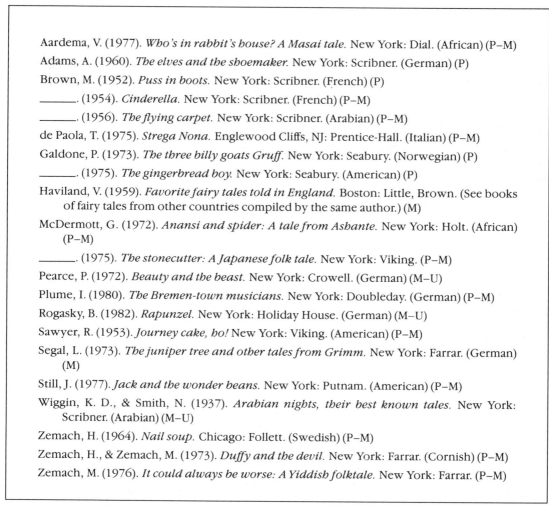

Aardema, V. (1977). *Who's in rabbit's house? A Masai tale.* New York: Dial. (African) (P–M)

Adams, A. (1960). *The elves and the shoemaker.* New York: Scribner. (German) (P)

Brown, M. (1952). *Puss in boots.* New York: Scribner. (French) (P)

———. (1954). *Cinderella.* New York: Scribner. (French) (P–M)

———. (1956). *The flying carpet.* New York: Scribner. (Arabian) (P–M)

de Paola, T. (1975). *Strega Nona.* Englewood Cliffs, NJ: Prentice-Hall. (Italian) (P–M)

Galdone, P. (1973). *The three billy goats Gruff.* New York: Seabury. (Norwegian) (P)

———. (1975). *The gingerbread boy.* New York: Seabury. (American) (P)

Haviland, V. (1959). *Favorite fairy tales told in England.* Boston: Little, Brown. (See books of fairy tales from other countries compiled by the same author.) (M)

McDermott, G. (1972). *Anansi and spider: A tale from Ashante.* New York: Holt. (African) (P–M)

———. (1975). *The stonecutter: A Japanese folk tale.* New York: Viking. (P–M)

Pearce, P. (1972). *Beauty and the beast.* New York: Crowell. (German) (M–U)

Plume, I. (1980). *The Bremen-town musicians.* New York: Doubleday. (German) (P–M)

Rogasky, B. (1982). *Rapunzel.* New York: Holiday House. (German) (M–U)

Sawyer, R. (1953). *Journey cake, ho!* New York: Viking. (American) (P–M)

Segal, L. (1973). *The juniper tree and other tales from Grimm.* New York: Farrar. (German) (M)

Still, J. (1977). *Jack and the wonder beans.* New York: Putnam. (American) (P–M)

Wiggin, K. D., & Smith, N. (1937). *Arabian nights, their best known tales.* New York: Scribner. (Arabian) (M–U)

Zemach, H. (1964). *Nail soup.* Chicago: Follett. (Swedish) (P–M)

Zemach, H., & Zemach, M. (1973). *Duffy and the devil.* New York: Farrar. (Cornish) (P–M)

Zemach, M. (1976). *It could always be worse: A Yiddish folktale.* New York: Farrar. (P–M)

Figure 10–12   Folktales for Elementary Students

ate for their stage of development. He believes that folktales can help children learn more about possible solutions to problems than they can learn from other types of stories. Folktales convey the advantages of moral behavior through characters and experiences that children relate to.

After reading folktales, children can compare versions of the same story. Look, for example, at the gingerbread stories, including Marcia Brown's Russian version, *The bun* (1972), Jacob's English version, *Johnny-cake* (n.d.), Asbjornsen and Moe's Norwegian version, *The runaway pancake* (1980), and Sawyer's American version, *Journey cake, ho!* (1953). Students can also "modernize" folktales such as "The Three Little Pigs." After students have read and examined a number of folktales, they are ready to apply what they have learned by writing their own.

Students listen as their teacher reads "The Hare and the Tortoise" in preparation for a discussion about the characteristics of fables.

Fables

Fables are brief narratives designed to teach a moral. They employ a story form to make the moral less abstract or to make the lesson easier to understand. The characters are usually animals who act wise or foolish, good or bad, or in a particular manner to illustrate the moral. The characters are not personalized with names or special characteristics and we do not become involved in their lives. The animals simply represent different characteristics of human nature. Our best known fables, including "The Hare and the Tortoise" and "The Ant and the Grasshopper," were written by a Greek slave, Aesop, in the sixth century B.C. Several collections of Aesop's fables are available for students: Eric Carle's *Twelve tales from Aesop* (1980); *Aesop's fables* selected by Michael Hague (1985); and Eve Rice's *Once upon a wood: Ten tales from Aesop* (1979). Other well-known fables include *Once a mouse,* an Indian fable retold by Marcia Brown (1961); Hans Christian Andersen's *The emperor's new clothes* (Westcott, 1984) and *The ugly duckling* (Cauley, 1979); and Chaucer's *Chanticleer and the fox* (Cooney, 1958). Also, Arnold Lobel (1980) has written a collection of 20 original fables. After students read fables, they choose a moral and then construct a brief story to illustrate it. An example of a sixth grader's fable using familiar animal characters but set in his language arts classroom is presented in Figure 10–13.

Figure 10–13   A Student's Modern Day Fable

The Peacock and the Mouse

The peacock was a very boastful bird who bragged and spread his feathers whenever he did something. He gave a report in front of our Language Arts class and bragged about it for three weeks.

The mouse

The mouse was very quiet and never bragged. She was just a quiet person who did her work.

Well it turned out at the end of the year the mouse's average was an "A" plus and the peacock's was a "D" minus.

Moral: Boastful People don't always come out on top.

Felton, age 12

Myths

People around the world have created *myths* to explain the origin of the world, how human beings were brought into existence, their relationship to gods; and how the sun and moon originated. Other myths were created to explain the seasons, the mountains and other physical features of the earth, the characteristics of various animals, and the constellations and other heavenly bodies. Myths of the past were used to explain many things that have more recently been explained by scientific theories and investigations. *Gods, stars, and computers: Fact and fancy in myth and science* (Weiss, 1980) provides an interesting comparison of ancient beliefs and scientific facts for middle and upper grade students. Myths about many different cultures have been compiled for children, and these myths provide a valuable way to tie literature to the study of history. The D'Aulaires have chronicled the Greek myths (1980) and the Norse myths (1967). Myths have also been compiled from Native American, Greek, Egyptian, Roman, African, and other cultures around the world. A list of myths recommended for elementary students is presented in Figure 10–14.

Myths that tell how something came to be are known as *pourquoi tales* (poor KWAH). The Greek myth about Persephone tells how spring originated (Hodges, 1973), and Rudyard Kipling's *Just so stories* (1972) tell about how the camel got his hump and how other animals acquired their unique characteristics. Native American pourquoi tales such as *The fire bringer* (Hodges, 1972) tell how natural phe-

---

Aardema, V. (1975). *Why mosquitoes buzz in people's ears: A west African folk tale.* New York: Dial. (Pourquoi Tale) (P)

Bernstein, M., & Kobrin, J. (1976). *The first morning: An African myth.* New York: Scribner. (P–M)

———. (1977). *The summer maker.* New York: Scribner. (American Indian) (P)

Colum, P. (1983). *The golden fleece and heroes who lived before Achilles.* New York: Macmillan. (Greek) (U)

———. (1984). *The children of Odin: The book of northern myths.* New York: Macmillan. (Norse) (M–U)

D'Aulaire, I., & D'Aulaire, E. P. (1967). *Norse gods and giants.* New York: Doubleday. (M–U)

———. (1980). D'Aulaires' book of Greek myths. New York: Doubleday. (M–U)

Dayrell, E. (1968). *Why the sun and the moon live in the sky: An African folktale.* Boston: Houghton Mifflin. (Pourquoi tale) (P)

de Paola, T. (1983). *The legend of the bluebonnet: An old tale of Texas.* New York: Putnam. (American Indian) (Pourquoi tale) (P)

Farmer, P. (1971). *Daedalus and Icarus.* New York: Harcourt Brace Jovanovich. (Greek) (M)

Hadithi, M. (1984). *Greedy zebra.* Boston: Little, Brown. (African) (Pourquoi tale) (P)

Hodges, M. (1973). *The other world: Myths of the Celts.* New York: Farrar. (M–U)

Maher, R. (1969). *The blind boy and the loon and other Eskimo myths.* New York: John Day. (M–U)

McDermott, G. (1977). *The voyage of Osiris: A myth of ancient Egypt.* New York: Dutton. (M–U)

Williams, J. (1979). *The surprising things Maui did.* New York: Four Winds Press. (Hawaiian) (Pourquoi tale) (P–M)

Figure 10–14   Myths for Elementary Students

nomena such as fire came to be. Children can read and compare pourquoi tales from various cultures. Later, students can write their own pourquoi tales. An 11-year-old's story of "How the Skunk Got Its Smell" is presented in Figure 10–15.

Greek and Roman myths have also contributed many words to our language—*atlas, echo, janitor, ocean,* and *volcano,* to name only a few. Names of gods and godesses such as Jupiter, Neptune, Mercury, Mars, and Venus were used to name the planets. Also, the names of some of the days of the week and some of the months of the year come from myths. Check Isaac Asimov's *Words from the myths* (1961) for more information.

Epics

Epics are long narratives or cycles of stories written about a hero such as Odysseus, Robin Hood, and King Arthur. Epics may be written in prose or poetry, and they deal with the heroic actions of this hero and those sharing the adventure or opposing the hero. Elements of the myth may be present in the epic, but the story is centered on a human hero rather than on the gods. The hero in the epic is strongly nationalistic, embodying the ideals of courage, sagacity, beauty, and other characteristics representing the code of chivalry.

Legends

Legends are stories coming down from the past that are thought to have some basis in history but are not verifiable. They may have elements of other literary forms such as myths and epics. The hero or main character (e.g., Johnny Appleseed and Davy Crockett) does something important enough to be remembered in story. The tall tales of Paul Bunyan, Mike Fink, John Henry, Casey Jones, and Pecos Bill are legends created as the American West was settled. A list of epics and legends appropriate for elementary students is presented in Figure 10–16. After students read these hero stories, they can create puppets of a favorite hero and tell their heroes' stories as well as writing their own legends.

Summary

Stylistic devices provide ways for students to add details, express emotions, create moods, and use description. They appeal to the senses. They are also used to structure stories in specific ways. Students can use each of these stylistic devices when writing stories and poems.

Stylistic devices are the specifics students will use to delineate the general elements of story structure they use in their writing. Repetition, for example, is used to structure the repeating of words and events in stories. Imagery, another specific structure, is used to describe settings, physical descriptions of characters, and the integration of action, setting, and characters. Effective writers often make subtle use of stylistic devices.

Words and phrases are the most specific of the structures students use in writing stories. The effective use of words is another manifestation of an author's style. Students need to be conscious of how authors use words ef-

Figure 10–15 A Student's Pourquoi Tale

How the Skunk Got Its Smell

Long ago, when the Lord of the Animal Kingdom was still creating animals, a problem was discovered. "All of my animals have a means of defense except you," said the Lord to the skunk. "My tiger has its sharp teeth and claws, my birds have their great wings, my cheetah has its fast speed, and my porcupine has its prickly quills. But you, my skunk, are defenseless."

The poor skunk felt terrible. He was so depressed that he decided to run away. He ran across the fields and through the forest. Soon he came to a tiny village. By now the skunk was starved. Behind the village was a bunch of rotten vegetables that smelled horrible. The skunk began to dig in and eat them. When he was done he smelled awful.

Now the skunk began walking through the village. The Indians of the village had never seen a skunk before. They started walking toward him but when they got too close to him and smelled the awful odor, they ran in the opposite direction, yelling, "Phew! Phew!"

Now the skunk was crushed! He began to realize how wrong he was to run away. He decided to go back home.

Every time he met an animal on the journey back it would run away, yelling, "Phew! The new animal called Skunk smells! Phew!"

The skunk was afraid to go near the Lord for fear that he would run away too, but he decided to give it a try.

The Lord was very wise and kind. He sat patiently (bearing the smell) while the skunk told his sad story. When the skunk got to the part about the animals running away when they smelled him, the Lord started yelling, "That's it! That's it!"

"What's the matter?" the skunk asked.

"Nothing. The smell will be your means of defense!" exclaimed the Lord.

"Yes, but I don't want to smell bad all the time," said the skunk.

"I will invent a way that you can spray your smell whenever you need to," said the Lord.

The Lord worked frantically for almost a week. Finally he had invented a potion for the skunk. After the skunk had drunk it, he was able to spray the smell anytime he wanted to.

And to this day, the skunk still uses the smell as a means of defense.

Scott, age 11

Colum, P. (1962). *The children's Homer: The adventures of Odysseus and the tales of Troy.* New York: Macmillan. (U)

de Paola, T. (1981). *Fin M'Coul: The giant of Knockmany Hill.* New York: Holiday House. (P)

Felton, H. W. (1968). *True tall tales of Stormalong: Sailor of the seven seas.* Englewood Cliffs, NJ: Prentice-Hall. (See other tall tales written by the same author.) (M)

Hastings, S. (1981). *Sir Gawain and the green knight.* New York: Lothrop. (M–U)

Haviland, V. (Ed.). (1979). *North American legends.* New York: Collins. (U)

Highwater, J. (1977). *Anpao: An American Indian odyssey.* Philadelphia: Lippincott. (U)

Hodges, M. (1984). *Saint George and the Dragon.* Boston: Little, Brown. (P–M)

Houston, J. (1973). *Kiviok's magic journey: An Eskimo legend.* New York: Atheneum. (M)

Keats, E. J. (1965). *John Henry: An American legend.* New York: Pantheon. (P–M)

Malcolmson, A. (1941). *Yankee Doodle's cousins.* Boston: Houghton Mifflin. (M–U)

Nye, R. (1982). *Beowulf.* New York: Dell. (M–U)

Picard, B. L. (1963). *Hero-tales from the British Isles.* New York: Criterion Books. (U)

Pyle, H. (1952). *The merry adventures of Robin Hood.* New York: Grosset & Dunlap. (M–U)

———. (1984). *The story of King Arthur and his knights.* New York: Scribner. (U)

Robbins, R. (1970). *Taliesin and King Arthur.* Boston: Houghton Mifflin. (M)

Rounds, G. (1976). *Ol'Paul, the mighty logger.* New York: Holiday House. (M)

Seredy, K. (1965). *The white stag.* New York: Viking. (Hungarian) (U)

Shephard, E. (1941). *Paul Bunyan.* New York: Harcourt Brace Jovanovich. (M–U)

Stoutenburg, A. (1966). *American tall tales.* New York: Viking. (M)

Sutcliff, R. (1977). *The chronicles of Robin Hood.* New York: Oxford University Press. (M)

———. (1981). *The sword and the circle: King Arthur and the knights of the round table.* New York: Dutton. (U)

Synge, U. (1978). *Land of heroes: A retelling of the Kalevala.* New York: Atheneum. (Finnish) (U)

Figure 10–16   Epics and Legends for Elementary Students

fectively. Teachers can begin with primary grade students to comment informally on good word usage in the stories they read and write. Both teachers and students can locate examples of effective words in the stories students are reading and discuss how these words and phrases are effective. Teachers can also design specific lessons similar to those discussed in this chapter when they are needed and would be appropriate for students.

Students can also examine the characteristics of specific story genre including folktales, fables, myths, epics, and legends. They read stories and examine the unique characteristics of these stories and then write stories using the instructional strategy presented in Chapter 9.

Extensions

1. Search for examples of the 11 stylistic devices in books of children's literature and develop a file of examples to use in teaching students about stories. Choose tradebooks that are appropriate for the level of students you teach or plan to teach.

2. Plan and teach a lesson on repetition to a group of primary grade students. Following the instructional strategy presented in Chapter 9, have students read stories exemplifying repetition, develop a chart about repetition, write a collaborative repetition story, and then write or dictate individual stories.

3. Read aloud a tradebook, such as *Charlotte's web* (White, 1952) or *Sounder* (Armstrong, 1969), that is rich with stylistic devices and words used in clever, unusual, and exceptional ways to a group of middle or upper grade students. As you read, point out examples of stylistic devices and effective words that the author has used. Then ask students to listen for other examples and to list the examples on a chart to be displayed in the classroom or noted in their writing journals.

4. Choose a specific genre and teach a lesson to middle to upper grade students using the instructional strategy presented in Chapter 9.

References

Armstrong, W.H. (1969). *Sounder.* New York: Harper and Row.

Asbjornsen, P., & Moe, J. (1980). *The runaway pancake.* New York: Larousse.

Asimov, I. (1961). *Words from the myths.* Boston: Houghton Mifflin.

Bettleheim, B. (1976). *The uses of enchantment: The meaning and importance of fairy tales.* New York: Random House.

Brown, M. (1961). *Once a mouse.* New York: Scribner.

_____. (1972). *The bun: A tale from Russia.* New York: Harcourt Brace Jovanovich.

Carle, E. (1980). *Twelve tales from Aesop.* New York: Philomel Books.

Cauley, L.B. (1979). *The ugly duckling.* New York: Harcourt Brace Jovanovich.

Cooney, B. (1958). *Chanticleer and the fox.* New York: Crowell.

D'Aulaire, I., & Parin, E. (1967). *Norse gods and giants.* New York: Doubleday.

_____. (1980). *D'Aulaires' book of Greek myths.* New York: Doubleday.

Galdone, P. (1975). *The gingerbread boy.* New York: Seabury.

Hague, M. (1985). *Aesop's fables.* New York: Holt.

Henry, M. (1948). *King of the wind.* Chicago: Rand McNally.

Hodges, M. (1972). *The fire bringer: A Paiute Indian legend.* Boston: Little, Brown.

_____. (1973). *Persephone and the springtime.* Boston: Little, Brown.

Horwitz, E.L. (1975). *When the sky is like lace.* Philadelphia: Lippincott.

Howe, D., & Howe, J. (1979). *Bunnicula.* New York: Atheneum.

Howe, J. (1982). *Howliday Inn.* New York: Atheneum.

_____. (1983). *The celery stalks at midnight.* New York: Atheneum.

Jacob, J. (n.d.). *Johnny-cake.* New York: Putnam.

Kipling, R. (1972). *Just so stories.* New York: Doubleday.

Lawson, R. (1972). *Rabbit hill.* New York: Viking.

L'Engle, M. (1962). *A wrinkle in time.* New York: Farrar.

Lobel, A. (1980). *Fables.* New York: Harper and Row.

Luckens, R.J. (1982). *A critical handbook of children's literature* (2nd ed.). Glenview, IL: Scott, Foresman.

McCloskey, R. (1976). *Blueberries for Sal.* New York: Viking.

Ness, E. (1966). *Sam, Bangs and Moonshine.* New York: Holt.

Norton, M. (1981). *The borrowers.* New York: Harcourt Brace Jovanovich.

Parish, P. (1963). *Amelia Bedelia.* New York: Harper and Row.

Rice, E. (1979). *Once upon a wood: Ten tales from Aesop.* New York: Greenwillow.

Sawyer, R. (1953). *Journey cake, ho!* New York: Viking.

Spier, P. (1971). *Gobble growl grunt.* New York: Doubleday.

———. (1972). *Crash! bang! boom!* New York: Doubleday.

Strunk, W., Jr., & White, E.B. (1979). *The elements of style* (3rd ed.). New York: Macmillan.

Weiss, M.E. (1980). *Gods, stars and computers: Fact and fancy in myth and science.* New York: Doubleday.

Westcott, N.B. (1984). *The emperor's new clothes.* Boston: Little, Brown.

White, E.B. (1952). *Charlotte's web.* New York: Harper and Row.

Zalben, J.B. (1977). *Lewis Carroll's jabberwocky.* New York: Warne.

IF YOU WANT TO LEARN MORE

Beaver, J.M. (1982). Say it! Over and over. *Language Arts, 59,* 143–148.

Bradley, B. (1976). *Growing from word play into poetry.* Palo Alto, CA: Learning.

Frank, M. (1979). *If you're trying to teach kids how to write, you've gotta have this book!* Nashville: Incentive Publications.

Geller, L.G. (1985). *Wordplay and language learning for children.* Urbana, IL: National Council of Teachers of English.

Jett-Simpson, M. (1981). Writing stories using model structures: The circle story. *Language Arts, 58,* 293–300.

Stacy, C.S. (1974). *Write: Finding things to say and saying them.* Glenview, IL: Scott, Foresman.

Tompkins, G.E. (1981). Gingerbread boys, johnny-cakes, and buns: More than just good things to eat. In L. L. Lamme (Ed.), *Learning to love literature: Preschool through grade 3* (pp. 55–58). Urbana, IL: National Council of Teachers of English.

CHAPTER ELEVEN

Reading and Writing Poetry

O*VERVIEW.   In this chapter, we will consider ways to involve students with poetry. First, research concerning the types of poetry that children prefer will be presented, and then guidelines for sharing poetry with elementary students will be discussed. In the second part of the chapter, a strategy for teaching students to write poetry as well as information on a variety of poetic forms will be presented.*

This is a golden era of poetry for children. Today more poets are writing for children, and, since 1970, more books of poetry for children have been published than ever before. Yet, despite its current popularity, poetry—both reading it and writing it—is often neglected in the language arts classroom, and the term *poetry* is often misunderstood. In this chapter, we hope to demystify poetry. Poetry is something everyone can understand and enjoy. No longer is poetry confined to rhyming verse about daffodils, clouds, and love.

Children, too, are writing poetry as never before. The current attention on writing and publishing students' writing makes poetry a natural choice. Poems are usually short and can easily be revised and edited. They lend themselves to anthologies more readily than stories and other longer forms of writing. In addition, many of the authors who visit classrooms are poets, and students are encouraged to write poems. Too often children's poetry writing activities are limited to haiku and other syllable-counting formulas. Instead, through a variety of poetry writing activities, students can paint word pictures, make comparisons, and express themselves in imaginative and poignant ways. The poems in Figure 11–1 illustrate the power of children's poetry when it is not constrained by rhyme or syllable counts. In the poem, "Unwanted," for example, a sixth grader expresses her feelings as a new student at a middle school. The student explains, "I write poems when I get inspirations. I wrote this when I was a newcomer at Irving. I guess you can see how I felt. Most of my poems don't rhyme. I have a hard time making the poem sound good."

POINTS TO PONDER

What Kinds of Poetry Do Children Like?

Which Contemporary Poets Write for Children?

Which Poems Written for Adults Can Elementary Students Appreciate?

POETRY AND CHILDREN

Children grow rather naturally into poetry. The Opies (1959) have verified what we know from observing children: that children have a natural affinity to verse, songs, riddles, jokes, chants, and puns. Babies and preschoolers are introduced to poetry when their parents repeat Mother Goose rhymes, read A. A. Milne's *The house at Pooh Corner* (1956) and the Dr. Seuss stories, and sing little songs to

Unwanted

I am like a clam—all shut up inside myself
    Letting nothing in except for particles
Of dust. No one here to be called mine. Why
    Couldn't they let me stay back where we
Used to live: I am scared. Who is the first
    Person that will pry off this shell of
Loneliness and make the darkness light
    Again? Who will be the first to smile,
Bringing warmth back into my confinement?
    Like a clam I am. No one yet wants to
Claim me as theirs. I am lonely and afraid.
    I am in a world of my own. Something that
Is mine—and I am happy! In my very own world.

Malia, age 12

A Man

I am a little man standing all alone
In the deep, dark wood.
I am standing on one foot
In the deep, dark wood.
Tell me quickly, if you can,
What to call this little man
Standing all alone
In the deep, dark wood.

Who am I?

(Answer: a mushroom)

Bonnie, age 10

**Thoughts after a
Forty-Mile Bike Ride**

    My feet
    And seat
    Are beat.

Roy, age 11

Figure 11–1 Poems Written by Elementary Students

them. During the elementary grades, youngsters often create jump-rope rhymes and other ditties on the playground. Yet children often seem to lose interest in poetry during the elementary grades. Poetry books sit unopened on library shelves and poetry is often a forgotten part of the language arts curriculum.

Types of Poetry

Poetry assumes many different forms. The most common type of poetry is rhymed verse, such as Robert Louis Stevenson's "Where Go the Boats?", Vachel

Lindsay's "The Little Turtle," and "Mummy Slept Late and Daddy Fixed Breakfast" by John Ciardi. Poems that tell a story are called *narrative poems.* Examples of narrative poems include Clement Moore's "The Night Before Christmas," "The Pied Piper of Hamelin" by Robert Browning, and Henry Wadsworth Longfellow's "The Song of Hiawatha." A Japanese form, haiku, is popular in anthologies of poetry for children. *Haiku* is a 3-line poem containing just 17 syllables. Because of its brevity it has been considered an appropriate form of poetry for children to read and write. *Free verse,* a relatively new form of poetry, has lines that do not rhyme, and rhythm is less important than in other types of poetry. Images take on a greater importance in free form verse. Langston Hughes' "Subway Rush Hour" and "This Is Just to Say" by William Carlos Williams are two examples of free verse. Other forms of poetry include *limericks,* a short five-line rhymed verse form popularized by Edward Lear, and *concrete poems,* or poems with words arranged on the page to create a picture or image. A list of books of poetry appropriate for elementary students is presented in Figure 11–2.

In addition to the well-known children's poets from the last century, such as Robert Louis Stevenson, Lewis Carroll, A. A. Milne, and Vachel Lindsay, many poets are writing for children today. They include Arnold Adoff, Byrd Baylor, Gwendolyn Brooks, John Ciardi, Aileen Fisher, Karla Kuskin, Myra Cohn Livingston, David McCord, Eve Merriam, Lilian Moore, Mary O'Neill, Jack Prelutsky, and Shel Silverstein. Thumbnail sketches of six of these contemporary children's poets are presented in Figure 11–3. Children are just as interested in learning about favorite poets as they are in learning about authors whose stories they read. When children view poets and other writers as real people, people they can relate to and who enjoy the same things as they do, they begin to see themselves as poets, a necessary criterion for successful writing. Information about poets is available from many of the sources about authors listed in Chapter 6. Inviting poets to visit the classroom to share their own poetry is one of the most valuable poetry experiences for children. For example, Chapman (1985) shares what happened when poet Arnold Adoff visited her classroom, and Parker (1981) relates a visit by Karla Kuskin.

Poems for Adults that Children Can Appreciate.   In addition to the poetry written specifically for children, some poetry written for adults can be used effectively with elementary students, especially at upper grade levels. Apseloff (1979) explains that poetry originally written for adults uses more sophisticated language and imagery and provides children with an early introduction to poems and poets they will undoubtedly study later. For instance, elementary students will enjoy Shakespeare's "The Witches' Song" from *Macbeth,* Carl Sandburg's "Fog," and William Blake's "The Piper" and "The Tyger." A list of poems written for adults that may be appropriate to use with elementary students is presented in Figure 11–4 on page 344.

Which Poems Do Children Like Best?

Children have preferences about which poems they like best just as adults do. Fisher and Natarella (1982) surveyed the poetry preferences of first, second, and

Adoff, A. (Ed.). (1974). *My black me: A beginning book on black poetry.* New York: Dutton.

Atwood, A. (1971). *Haiku: The mood of earth.* New York: Scribner.

Dunning, S., Lueders, E., & Smith, H. (Eds.). (1966). *Reflections on a gift of watermelon pickle . . . and other modern verse.* Glenview, IL: Scott, Foresman.

Froman, R. (1974). *Seeing things: A book of poems.* New York: Crowell.

Hopkins, L. B. (Ed.). (1976). *Good morning to you, valentine.* New York: Harcourt Brace Jovanovich. (See books for other holidays compiled by the same editor.)

Jones, H. (Ed.). (1971). *The trees stand shining: Poetry of the North American Indians.* New York: Dial.

Kennedy, X. J., & Kennedy, D. M. (Eds.). (1982). *Knock at a star: A children's introduction to poetry.* Boston: Little, Brown.

Kuskin, K. (1980). *Dogs and dragons, trees and dreams.* New York: Harper and Row.

Larrick, N. (Ed.). (1968). *Piping down the valleys wild.* New York: Dell.

Livingston, M. C. (1976). *4-way stop and other poems.* New York: Atheneum.

_____. (1982). *A circle of seasons.* New York: Holiday House.

McCord, D. (1974). *One at a time.* Boston: Little, Brown.

O'Neill, M. (1966). *Words, words, words.* Garden City, NY: Doubleday.

Prelutsky, J. (1983). *The Random House book of poetry for children.* New York: Random House.

_____. (1984). *The new kid on the block.* New York: Greenwillow.

Rothenberg, J. (1972). *Shaking the pumpkin: Traditional poetry of the Indian North Americans.* Garden City, NY: Doubleday.

Silverstein, S. (1974). *Where the sidewalk ends: The poems and drawings of Shel Silverstein.* New York: Harper and Row.

Viorst, J. (1981). *If I were in charge of the world and other worries.* New York: Atheneum.

Figure 11–2   Books of Poetry Appropriate for Elementary Students

third graders, Terry (1974) investigated fourth, fifth, and sixth graders' preferences, and Kutiper (1985) researched seventh, eighth, and ninth graders' preferences. The results of these three studies are important for teachers to consider as they select poems to read to their students. The most popular forms of poetry were limericks and narrative poems, and the most disliked forms were haiku and free verse. In addition, children preferred funny poems, poems about animals, and poems about familiar experiences. The most important elements were rhyme, rhythm, and sound. While primary grade students preferred traditional poetry (e.g., Vachel Lindsay's "The Little Turtle"), middle graders preferred modern poetry (e.g., a modern version of "Little Miss Muffet" by Paul Dehn), and upper grade students preferred rhyming verse. The 10 best liked poems for each of the three grade groups are presented in Figure 11–5 on page 345. The researchers found

Arnold Adoff

I am the darker brother (1968)
Black out loud (1970)
Ma nDa la (1971)
Black is brown is tan (1973)
Make a circle keep us in: Poems for a good day (1975)

Arnold Adoff grew up in New York City, and he taught at a public school in Harlem for 12 years. During his teaching, Adoff was frustrated by the lack of materials about black culture and he began to collect the work of black writers to use with his students. His writing focuses on black life; however, Adoff says that he sees himself as a student rather than an expert on black culture. Several of his books of poetry and a biography, *Malcolm X* (1970), have been chosen as American Library Association Notable Books. He is married to award-winning children's author Virginia Hamilton, and they live in Yellow Springs, Ohio.

Karla Kuskin

Roar and more (1956)
Any me I want to be (1972)
Near the window tree (1975)
Dogs and dragons, trees and dreams (1980)

Karla Kuskin is a native New Yorker who wrote and published her first book, *Roar and more,* as a class assignment while a student at Yale University. Kuskin writes both humorous picture books for preschoolers and books of poetry for older children. Her poems are often short, written with a gentle rhythm and whimsical tone. "Knitted Things" is a good example. She says that she writes from her memories of childhood, and she is especially successful in capturing the essence of childhood experiences in poems such as "I Woke Up This Morning." Kuskin discusses how she writes poetry on "Poetry Explained by Karla Kuskin," a sound filmstrip available from Weston Woods.

Myra Cohn Livingston

Whispers and other poems (1958)
Wide awake and other poems (1959)
What a wonderful bird the frog are (1973)
A circle of seasons (1982)

Myra Cohn Livingston was born in Omaha, Nebraska and began writing poems and stories as soon as she could read. She had a special interest in both writing and music. As a teenager, she played the French horn in the California Junior Symphony and wrote for her high school newspaper. Livingston wrote her first book of poems, *Whispers and other poems,* while she was in college, but it was not published until 12 years later. Since then, she has written nearly 30 books of poetry. Today Livingston lives in Beverly Hills, California. She teaches creative writing at the University of California, and she has written a book on teaching children to write poetry, *When you are alone/It keeps you capone* (1974), which is based on her work with teachers.

Figure 11–3 Thumbnail Sketches of Six Contemporary Poets Who Write for Children

David McCord

Far and few (1952)
Take sky (1962)
All day long (1966)
Everytime I climb a tree (1967)
Once at a time: Collected poems for the young (1977)

David McCord was born in New York City and raised there and in Oregon. After completing undergraduate studies in physics and graduate studies in English at Harvard University, McCord became a professional fund raiser for the Harvard Fund Council. He began writing poetry when he was 15, and as an adult he turned his attention to writing poetry for children. During his long career, he has composed more than 400 poems for children. McCord is called "an acrobat with language" and he uses surprising rhythm, sound effects, and word play in the poetry he writes. In 1977, David McCord was the first recipient of the National Council of Teachers of English Award for Excellence in Poetry for Children.

Jack Prelutsky

Circus (1974)
Nightmares: Poems to trouble your sleep (1976)
It's Halloween (1977)
The snopp on the sidewalk and other poems (1977)
The Random House book of poetry for children (1983)

Jack Prelutsky was born in New York City, and his career has included singing and acting jobs as well as writing poetry. He has sung with opera companies in Boston and Seattle. Prelutsky has written more than 30 books of poetry. His poetry is delightful nonsense in rhymed, rhythmic verse, and his poems are often about imaginary animals such as "The Snopp on the Sidewalk." His nonsense verse has definite child-appeal. Jack Prelutsky now makes his home in Albuquerque, New Mexico, and he frequently travels around the country to visit libraries and schools and share his poems with children.

Shel Silverstein

The giving tree (1964)
Where the sidewalk ends (1974)
The missing piece (1976)
The light in the attic (1981)

Shel Silverstein was born in Chicago, but he now divides his time among homes in Greenwich Village, Key West, and a houseboat in Sausalito, California. Silverstein began to write and draw when he was a teenager, and when he served in the US armed forces in the 1950s he was a cartoonist for the military newspaper, *Stars and Stripes.* Silverstein never planned to write or draw for children, but friends convinced him that his work had appeal for children as well as adults. He says that he hopes readers will experience "a personal sense of discovery" as they read his poems. Silverstein has other interests in addition to writing poetry; he is a folksinger, lyricist, and playwright.

Figure 11–3 *Continued*

Poet	Poems and/or Books of Poetry
William Blake	"The Lamb," "The Tyger," "The Piper," and other selections from *Songs of experience* and *Songs of innocence*. Compare with Nancy Willard's *A visit to William Blake's inn: Poems for innocent and experienced travelers* (Harcourt Brace Jovanovich, 1981).
Emily Dickinson	"I'm nobody! Who are you?," "There is no frigate like a book," and other favorite poems from *I'm nobody! Who are you? Poems of Emily Dickinson for children* (Stemmer House, 1978).
T. S. Eliot	Poems about cats from *Old possum's book of practical cats* (Harcourt Brace Jovanovich, 1967).
Robert Frost	"The Pasture," "Birches," "Fire and Ice," "Stopping by Woods on a Snowy Evening," and other favorites are included in *The poetry of Robert Frost,* edited by E. C. Latham (Holt, 1969). Also check the picture book version of *Stopping by woods on snowy evening,* illustrated by Susan Jeffers (Dutton, 1978).
Langston Hughes	"Dreams," "City," "April Rain Song," and other selections are included in *The dream keeper and other poems* (Knopf, 1960). Also, Lee Bennett Hopkins has compiled a collection of Hughes' poetry for young people: *Don't you turn back: Poems by Langston Hughes* (Knopf, 1969).
D. H. Lawrence	William Cole has prepared a selection of Lawrence's poetry suitable for upper grade students: *D. H. Lawrence: Poems selected for young people* (Knopf, 1967). Also, Alice and Martin Provensen have illustrated a collection of D. H. Lawrence's poems for students, *Birds, beasts and the third thing: Poems by D. H. Lawrence* (Viking, 1982).
Carl Sandburg	"Fog," "Daybreak," "Buffalo Dusk," and other poems for elementary students are included in *Wind song* (Harcourt Brace Jovanovich, 1960), *Chicago poems* (Harcourt Brace Jovanovich, 1944) and other books of Sandburg's poetry. Also, see Lee Bennett Hopkins' collection of Sandburg's poems: *Rainbows are made: Poems by Carl Sandburg* (Harcourt Brace Jovanovich, 1982).
Walt Whitman	Elementary students will enjoy "I Hear America Singing," "I Believe in a Leaf of Grass," and other selections from *Leaves of grass* (Doubleday, 1926).

Figure 11–4   Adult Poems Appropriate for Elementary Students

First, Second, and Third Graders' Favorite Poems

Rank	Title	Author
1	"The Young Lady of Lynn"	Unknown
2	"The Little Turtle"	Vachel Lindsay
3	"Bad Boy"	Lois Lenski
4	"Little Miss Muffet"	Paul Dehn
5	"Cat"	Eleanor Farjeon
6	"Adventures of Isabel"	Ogden Nash
7	"Mummy Slept Late and Daddy Fixed Breakfast"	John Ciardi
8	"The Lurpp is on the Loose"	Jack Prelutsky
9	"A Bookworm of Curious Breed"	Ann Hoberman
10	"The Owl and the Pussy-cat"	Edward Lear

Fisher & Natarella, 1982, p. 344.

Fourth, Fifth, and Sixth Graders' Favorite Poems

Rank	Title	Author
1	"Mummy Slept Late and Daddy Fixed Breakfast"	John Ciardi
2	"Fire! Fire!"	Unknown
3	"There was an old man of Blackheath"	Unknown
4	"Little Miss Muffet"	Paul Dehn
5	"There once was an old kangaroo"	Edward S. Mullins
6	"There was a young lady of Niger"	Unknown
7	"Hughbert and the Glue"	Karla Kuskin
8	"Betty Barter"	Unknown
9	"Lone Dog"	Irene Rutherford McLeod
10	"Eletelephony"	Laura E. Richards

Terry, 1974, p. 15.

Seventh, Eighth, and Ninth Graders' Favorite Poems

Rank	Title	Author
1	"Sick"	Shel Silverstein
2	"Oh, Teddy Bear"	Jack Prelutsky
3	"Mother Doesn't Want a Dog"	Judith Viorst
4	"Mummy Slept Late and Daddy Fixed Breakfast"	John Ciardi
5	"The Unicorn"	Shel Silverstein
6	"Why Nobody Pets the Lion at the Zoo"	John Ciardi
7	"Homework"	Jane Yolen
8	"Dreams"	Langston Hughes
9	"Questions"	Marci Ridlon
10	"Willie Ate a Worm Today"	Jack Prelutsky

Kutiper, 1985, p. 51.

Figure 11–5 Children's Poetry Preferences

Students enjoy sharing favorite poems with classmates.

that children in all three studies liked poetry, enjoyed listening to poetry read aloud, and could give reasons why they liked or disliked particular poems.

POINTS TO PONDER

How Can Teachers Share Poetry with Their Students?

Should Students Memorize Poetry?

What Is Choral Reading?

SHARING POETRY WITH CHILDREN

Perhaps one of the main reasons poetry is neglected in elementary classrooms is because teachers are not sure what to do with it. The answer is simple: Teachers should choose a poem they like and then share it with students. It is an easy task to browse through an anthology of poems, find a favorite poem, read it silently several times, and then share it with students. In her poem "How to Eat a Poem" (1966), poet Eve Merriam provides some useful advice. She compares reading a poem to eating a piece of fruit and advises to bite right in, letting the juice run down your chin.

Poetry sharing time does not need to be scheduled for a particular time of day. Poems can be shared anytime. First thing in the morning or right after lunch are good times, but because poems can be shared quickly, they can be tied in with almost any activity. Often poems are coordinated with a holiday, a social studies unit, a story being read to the class, or even with homonyms and other language skills being taught.

Guidelines for Sharing Poetry

The following nine guidelines provide suggestions about how to share poetry with children in the elementary grades.

1. Read or recite only poems that are personal favorites. Students can tell when a teacher does not particularly care for a poem.

2. Rehearse the poem several times to get the feel of the words and the rhythm. Decide where to pause and which words or phrases to accent.

3. Start a collection of favorite poems. Jot them down on notecards and have a poem ready to share during any free moment during the day.

4. Keep a collection of poetry books handy in the classroom for children to browse through. Students may want to use bookmarks to mark favorite poems to share or add to their copybooks. (See Chapter 14 for more information on copybooks.)

5. Set up a listening center with records or audiocassettes of poems. Also, students may want to record their favorite poems for the listening center.

6. Poetry is meant to be shared orally, not silently. Do not ask students to read poems silently.

7. Have children become the primary readers and sharers of poetry as quickly as possible. Try group poetry reading or reciting and choral reading activities.

8. Do not assign children to memorize a particular poem, but allow children to volunteer to learn favorite poems to recite to the class.

9. Do not ask students to analyze the meaning of the poem or its rhyme scheme. Many students tell us that they stopped enjoying poetry when teachers required them to analyze poems.

Response Activities

There are many ways to share poetry with children and to involve them in sharing poetry with their classmates. Choral reading and a variety of other ideas are presented in the following paragraphs.

Choral Reading.   When children take turns reading a poem together, they are participating in *choral reading*. (This activity is called *choral speaking* when children recite rather than read the poem.) Through active participation with poetry, students learn to appreciate poetry, its sounds, its feelings, and its magic. Moreover, Donald Graves (1983) explains that through reading and reciting poems, children internalize language, and later this language becomes a part of their writing.

There are a number of things to consider when selecting and preparing a selection for presentation. First, how will four of the basic elements of oral language enhance the interpretation? These elements are *tempo* (how fast or slow to read the lines), *rhythm* (which words to stress or say the loudest), *pitch* (when to raise or lower the voice), and *juncture* (when to pause and how long to pause) (Stewig, 1981). As students select a poem and prepare it for presentation, they will need to consider these four elements and experiment with each element to create the desired interpretation. Encourage students to ask themselves the 5 Ws plus one as they experiment with each element. For example:

- What should the tempo be?
- Why do we want to have a pause here?
- Where should we raise or lower our voices?
- Which words should we pronounce the loudest?

By questioning themselves as they decide how to present the poem, students will learn how to experiment with oral language and to take responsibility for their own learning. Copy the poem on a large chart or on a transparency so that students can underline particular words and use arrows or other marks to indicate the tempo, rhythm, pitch, and juncture they have decided on for their choral reading. This procedure is similar to the one used by composers to mark tempo and other considerations on their musical scores.

The second consideration concerns how to arrange the poem for choral reading. Students may read the poem together in unison, in small groups, or individual students can read particular lines or stanzas. There are four possible arrangements:

1. *Echoic.*   The leader reads each line and the group repeats it.
2. *Refrain.*   The leader reads the main part of the poem and the group reads the refrain or chorus in unison.
3. *Antiphonal.*   Divide the class into two or more groups and each group reads one part of the poem.
4. *Cumulative.*   A cumulative effect is created by adding voices as the poem is read. Start with one student or one group reading the first line or stanza, and add another student or group as each line or stanza is read (Stewig, 1981).

The arrangement can easily be marked on the copy of the poem together with the information about tempo, rhythm, pitch, and juncture.

Almost any poem can be used in a choral reading activity. For example, try Shel Silverstein's "Boa Constrictor," "Full of the Moon" by Karla Kuskin, Laura E. Richards' "Eletelephony," and "Catch a Little Rhyme" by Eve Merriam. Many of the poems contained in the books of poetry listed in Figure 11–2 can also be used in choral reading interpretations.

Compiling Collections of Poems.   Some students enjoy compiling anthologies of their favorite poems. The activity often begins quite naturally as students read poems. They copy favorite poems to keep, and soon they are stapling their collections together to make books. Copying poems can also be a worthwhile handwriting activity because students are copying something meaningful to them, not just words or sentences from a workbook. Poet and anthologist Lee Bennett Hopkins (1972) suggests setting up a dead tree or an artificial Christmas tree in the classroom as a "poetree" for students to hang copies of their favorite poems on for their classmates to read and enjoy.

Other Activities.   Informal drama, art, and music activities can be used to accompany favorite poems. For instance, students can role-play Karla Kuskin's "I Woke Up This Morning" or construct monster puppets for the Lurpp creature in Jack Prelutsky's "The Lurpp is on the Loose." Students may also compile picture book versions of narrative poems such as "Mummy Slept Late and Daddy Cooked Breakfast" by John Ciardi, or they may make their own filmstrip versions of a poem using a filmstrip kit. Several frames from a filmstrip illustrating "Mummy Slept Late . . ." are presented in Figure 11–6.

Children may also compile a book of poems and illustrate them with photographs. In *A song in stone: City poems* (1983), Lee Bennett Hopkins compiled a collection of city poems and Anna Held Audette selected black and white photographs to illustrate each poem. Children can create a similar type of book, and photocopies of the book can be made so each child will have a personal copy.

POINTS TO PONDER
Why Have Students Write Poetry?
How Do You Teach Students to Write Poetry?
What Poetic Forms Can Elementary Students Use?

WRITING POETRY WITH CHILDREN

Writing poetry helps students explore ideas and feelings. Children bring to the writing of poetry their feelings, imagination, and funny and touching experiences. The atmosphere of writing and sharing should be one of openness and acceptance. The things children discover and the feelings they explore by freely associating one thing with another can be of great pleasure to them.

The same basic ingredients needed to write stories are needed to write poetry. Students need time, exposure to the structure of poetry by reading poems, and an audience that appreciates their efforts and gives them encouraging feedback. Students are endowed with the power to see the world in strong, fresh, and beautiful ways. The desire to express that vision is a strong creative force.

Instructional Strategy

The strategy for teaching children to write poetry is similar to the one used for writing stories, and it is based on the instructional strategy developed in Chap-

Text
Daddy fixed the breakfast.
He made us each a waffle.
It looked like gravel pudding.
It tasted something awful.

"Ha, ha," he said, "I'll try again.
This time I'll get it right."

But what *I* got was in between
Bituminous and anthracite.

"A little too well done? Oh well,
I'll have to start all over."
***That* time what landed on my plate**
Looked like a manhole cover.

I tried to cut it with a fork:
The fork gave off a spark.

I tried a knife and twisted it

Into a question mark.

I tried it with a hack-saw.

I tried it with a torch.

It didn't even make a dent.
It didn't even scorch.

The next time Dad gets breakfast
When Mummy's sleeping late,
I think I'll skip the waffles.
I'd sooner eat the plate!

Figure 11–6   Excerpt from a Filmstrip Illustrating John Ciardi's "Mummy Slept
Late and Daddy Fixed Breakfast" (1962)

ter 1. The strategy involves two components, preparation and instruction. To prepare to teach a particular poetic form, teachers need to learn as much as possible
about the form, gather examples of the form, and prepare a chart to explain the
form. Next, the instruction component involves six steps.

Step 1: Initiating.   Display a chart describing the poetic form and its formula,
and explain it to your students. Figure 11–7 displays a chart with the formula for
one poetic form, wish poems.

Step 2: Structuring.   Read examples of the poetic form and point out how each
poem adheres to the formula. Share poems written by other students as examples
whenever possible. Samples of students' work are provided for most of the poetic
forms discussed in this chapter. Also, poems written by students can be located in
student anthologies and magazines that publish student writing. Student examples

```
                              Wish Poems
   Formula:                                          Student Samples:

   Begin each line with the words I WISH.            [                    ]

                                                     [                    ]

   Examples:                                         [                    ]

   I wish I were a movie star and I would be Dolly Parton.   [            ]

   I wish I were the President and lived in the White House. [            ]

                                                     [                    ]
```

Figure 11–7   A Chart Describing the "I Wish" Poems Formula

are preferable to poems written by adults in many cases because they show the students that they, too, can write poems.

Step 3: Conceptualizing.   Read several more poems, and have students explain how each poem adheres to the formula.

Step 4: Summarizing.   Review the formula, and have students restate the formula in their own words or make individual copies of the chart.

Step 5: Generalizing.   Compose class or small-group collaboration poems in which students write a poem together. As in writing stories, writing collaboration poems is an essential step in the writing process. Through this group experience, students have many of their misunderstandings clarified, and they are able to practice writing a poem using a particular formula with the support of their classmates. Because of this step, students are far more confident and successful when they write individual poems.

Step 6: Applying.   Have students write individual poems following the formula. Use the process approach to writing described in Chapter 6. The first five steps in this strategy constitute the prewriting stage, and in this step, students move through the remainder of the writing process stages by writing rough drafts, and then revising, editing, and sharing their poems.

Types of Poetry

Elementary students can easily have successful experiences writing poetry using the poetic formulas presented in this section. They can write short, two-word hink-pinks or formula poems that begin each line with particular words such as "I wish . . .", count syllables for haiku, or even design concrete poems in which the

Students write and illustrate poems using formulas such as "I wish. . . ."

words are arranged to create a picture. Because poetry writing is short and guidelines are provided, children can use the writing process to revise, edit, and share their writing without a time-consuming process of making changes, correcting errors, and recopying. Poetry also allows students more freedom in how they use the mechanics of writing—punctuation, capitalization, and page arrangement.

Many of the types of poetry that children write do not use rhyme. Rhyme is the sticking-point for many would-be poets. In searching for a rhyming word, children often create inane verse such as this example from *Anastasia Krupnik* (Lowry, 1979):

> I have a dog whose name is Spot.
> He likes to eat and drink a lot.
> When I put water in his dish,
> He laps it up just like a fish (p.10).

Ten-year-old Anastasia, the main character of the story, is unimpressed with this poem written by a classmate. Among other things, she knows that the child who wrote the poem has a dog and the dog's name is *Sputnik,* not *Spot*! In the story, Anastasia also wrote a poem and her poem was very different. She wrote about the little creatures who swim around in tidespools:

        hush   hush   the sea-soft night is aswim
            with wrinklesquirm creatures
                                                        listen(!)
      to them   move   smooth   in the moistly dark
            here in the   whisperwarm wet (pp. 11–12)

What a contrast between the two poems! Anastasia paints a word picture and uses several invented words. Unlike the earlier "I have a dog . . ." poem, Anastasia's poem touches us. Too often children sacrifice their ideas when they are pressured to string together rhyming words. This is not to suggest that children should not be allowed to write rhyming poetry, but rhyme should not be imposed as a criterion for acceptable poetry. Children should feel free to use rhyme when it fits naturally into their writing. As children write poetry during the elementary grades, they are searching for their own voices, and they need freedom to do that. Freed from the pressure to create rhyming poetry or other constraints, children often create sensitive word pictures, vivid images, and unique comparisons in the poems they compose, as the students' poems presented throughout this chapter illustrate.

Formula Poems

Just as structure is important in writing stories, it is also useful in helping students to write poetry. Poet Kenneth Koch (1970) has worked with students in the elementary grades and has developed some simple structures that make it easy for nearly every child to become a successful poet. At first some of these forms may seem more like sentences than poems, but the dividing line between poetry and prose is very fine, and these poetry writing exercises help direct children toward poetic expression. Koch suggests a structure for student poems in which children begin every line the same way or insert a particular kind of word in every line. This structure involves the use of repetition, a stylistic device that is much more effective for young poets than rhyme.

    These poetic forms provide a structure that is easy for students to follow and fun to do. Many teachers are at first somewhat skeptical about the effectiveness of formula poems. However, after they introduce their students to formula poems, they often report that these poetry writing activities are among the most successful writing experiences their students have ever participated in. The formulas for five types of poems are described below and student examples are presented with each formula.

I Wish Poems.   Children begin each line of their poems with the words "I wish" and then complete the line with a wish (Koch, 1970). Children's first poems are lists of wishes. Later they can take one of their wishes and expand on the idea in several more lines. Figure 11–8 presents examples of children's wish poems.

Color Poems.   Students begin each line of their poems with a color. The same color may be repeated in each line, or a different color may be used (Koch, 1970).

Class Collaboration Wish Poem

I wish I had all the Cabbage Patch dolls in the world.
I wish my great-great grandmother didn't die.
I wish I had a new bicycle.
I wish there were no hungry children in Africa.
I wish I could live on the moon for two hours.
I wish a unicorn would come to my house.
I wish I could burp at the table.
I wish Care Bears were real.
I wish my daddy would come home.
I wish everyone would be quiet.
I wish I could fly.

Five- and six-year-olds

I Wish

I wish I could be an All American in sports,
Especially in football.
Because it's rough, tough, lean and mean
Because I wanna be Mean Joe Green.

Johnny, age 10

"I Wish" Poems Written in Music Class

I wish I was a harp
And for someone to pluck my strings.

I wish I was a tuba
Made of brass and two big rings.

Christy, age 9

I wish I was a trumpet
and played some mellow notes.

I wish I was a snare drum
and played a rat-a-tat-tat beat.

Mark, age 9

Figure 11–8 Students' "I Wish" Poems

Examples of elementary students' color poems are presented in Figure 11–9. Mary O'Neill's book of color poems, *Hailstones and halibut bones: Adventures in color* (1961) may also be shared with students; however, O'Neill's poems all use rhyme as an important poetic device, and it is important to stipulate that students' poems need not rhyme.

Writing color poems can be coordinated with teaching young children to read and write the color words. Instead of having kindergartners and first graders read the color words on worksheets and color pictures the designated colors, give

Color Poems

Red Seasons

Red is a bright umbrella
Red is a yummy strawberry
Red is a bright, new wagon

Red is a hot, new car
Red is a painful sunburn
Red is an opening flower

Red is oozing blood
Red is the cold night sky
Red is a dead leaf in autumn

Red is hot chili
Red is a fire in the fireplace
Red is giftwrapping
Red is a running fox in the snow

Thomas, age 12

What is White?

White is an invisible door
        that I open and close
    to go in and out.

White is light
        like a leaf
    and the softness of a cloud.

White is very proud.

Anonymous, age 10

"If I Were" Poems

If I were a Tyrannosaurus Rex
I would terrorize other dinosaurs
And eat them up for supper.

Robbie, age 7

If I were a clown
I'd hang by a wire
And do tricks
And go pow on the trampoline.

Heather, age 6

Figure 11–9   Students' Color Poems and "If I Were" Poems

students booklets of paper stapled together and have them create color poems. They write one line of the poem on each page and draw a picture to illustrate each line.

"If I Were" Poems.   Children write about how they would feel and what they would do if they were something else—a dragon, a chair, or the wind, for instance (Koch, 1970). They begin each poem with "If I were" and tell what it would be like to be that thing. Students use the stylistic device of personification in composing "If I were" poems. They explore ideas and feelings and consider how the world looks from a different vantage point. Poet Karla Kuskin has also written several "If I were" poems (1980) that can be used as models for students. Examples of students' "If I were" poems are also included in Figure 11–9.

"I Used to/But Now" Poems.   Students begin the first line (and every odd numbered line) with "I used to" and the second line (and every even numbered line) with "But now" (Koch, 1970). One sixth-grade teacher adapted this formula for her social studies class, and these students wrote "I used to think/But now I know" poems using the information they were learning during a unit on the American Revolution. Their class collaboration poem and other "I used to/But now" poems are shown in Figure 11–10.

Noise Poems.   Children include a noise or sound word (e.g., *bow-wow, z-z-z, splash*) in each line of their poems (Koch, 1970). Before writing their poems, it may be helpful to have children collect sound words they find in the stories they

---

I used to be a kernel
but now I am a crunchy,
tasty, buttery cloud
popped by Orville Redenbacher.

Tony and Christina, age 9

I used to be a pile of junk
but now I'm a mechanical machine
I went from a brainless nothing
to a fast computerized motor-mouth.

Jeanie and Kristie, age 11

Class Collaboration "I used to think/But now I know" Poem on the American Revolution

I USED TO THINK	that Florida was one of the thirteen colonies,
BUT NOW I KNOW	it belonged to Spain.
I USED TO THINK	the War for Independence was one big battle,
BUT NOW I KNOW	it was made up of many battles.
I USED TO THINK	that Americans and the British fought the same way,
BUT NOW I KNOW	they had different military styles.
I USED TO THINK	when the War for Independence ended, our troubles were over,
BUT NOW I KNOW	we still had trouble with Britain.
I USED TO THINK	that the Constitution was our first set of rules,
BUT NOW I KNOW	that the Articles of Confederation was.
I USED TO THINK	that the United States was founded all at once,
BUT NOW I KNOW	it grew little by little.
I USED TO THINK	that war was exciting and glamorous,
BUT NOW I KNOW	that it was not that way at all.

Fifth graders

Figure 11–10   "I used to/But now" Poems

Poetry, whether written for children or by children, should be shared orally.

are reading or in cartoons and comics. For other resources on sound words, check the section on onomatopoeia in Chapter 10. A class collaboration noise poem and two other poems that each use a single noise word for emphasis are presented in Figure 11–11.

Other Unrhymed Formulas

While most students rank haiku and other unrhymed formula poems low on their lists of favorite poems to read and share, many students like to write these formula poems. The formula provides a structure, which helps students succeed in their writing; however, the need to adhere to a syllable count in these poems restricts students' freedom of expression. In other words, the structure of these poems may both help and hinder students. The exact syllable counts force students to search for just the right words to express their ideas and feelings and provide a valuable opportunity for students to use thesauruses and dictionaries. The formulas for four of these poetic forms are presented next.

An Excerpt from a Class Collaboration Noise Poem

Bees go buzz.
The phone is ringing R-R-R-ING-G-G.
The snow is cold, burr-rrr.
When I see a mouse, I say EEEEEK.
I threw a pie and it went splat.
The ghost goes BOOOOOOOOOOOOOOOOOOOOOOOOOOOOOOOOOOOO!
My dog B-A-R-R-R-KS.
SPLAT! Oops, I stepped in a mud puddle!!!

Second graders

Loneliness

Loneliness is
    a deep gnawing pain in your empty stomach.
It starts with a soft growl
But it builds up to a deep agonizing rumble.
           GRRR
           GRRR
It is not satisfied until you
    feed it friendship.

Maureen, age 14

Elephant Noses

Elephant noses
Elephant noses
Elephants have big noses
Big noses
Big noses
Elephants have big noses
through which they drink
SCHLURRP

Christopher, age 5

Figure 11–11   Students' Noise Poems

Haiku.   *Haiku* (high KOO) is a Japanese poetic form that consists of 17 syllables arranged in 3 lines, 5-7-5. Haiku poems deal with nature or seasons and present a single clear image. They are written in a concise form, much like a telegram. Books of haiku poems to share with students include *My own rhythm: An approch to haiku* (Atwood, 1973), *Haiku: The mood of the earth* (Atwood, 1971), *In a spring garden* (Lewis, 1965), *Cricket songs* (Behn, 1964), and *More cricket songs* (Behn, 1971). Also, Richard Lewis (1968, 1970) has written about the lives of two of the greatest Japanese haiku poets, Issa and Basho. In these books, Lewis provides biographical information as well as a collection of poems. Figure 11–12 presents examples of haiku poems written by elementary students.

Tanka.   *Tanka* (TANK ah) is a Japanese verse form containing 31 syllables arranged in 5 lines, 5-7-5-7-7. The form is very similar to haiku except that two additional lines of seven syllables each are added to the haiku form. One book of tanka poetry that elementary students will enjoy is Baron's *The seasons of time: Tanka poetry of ancient Japan* (1968). Students' tanka poems are presented in Figure 11–13.

The mud feels slimy
As it splashes through my toes
Making them vanish.

Shawn, age 10

Trees almost naked
Leaves sit quietly waiting,
Then drift with the wind.

Shannon, age 11

The music to me,
Is the rushing of the stream,
On a cool, spring morn.

Such a dreary day,
With air so dark and heavy,
And a dark, dark sky.

Let the sun shine in!
For today I saw snowdrops,
The first ones to see!

The morning is lost,
But today is well begun,
Evening yet to come.

A chill in the air,
A cool, crisp breeze at my back,
The sun fading low.

On a lovely day,
The sun shining through the trees,
The twittering birds.

Wandering around,
With nothing at all to do.
Just writing haiku.

Larissa, age 13

Figure 11–12 Students' Haiku Poems

Cinquain. A *cinquain* (SIN cane) is a 5-line poem containing 22 syllables in a 2-4-6-8-2 syllable pattern. Cinquain poems usually describe something but they may also tell a story. Encourage students to search for words and phrases that are precise, vivid, and sensual. Have students ask themselves what their subject looks like, smells like, feels like, sounds like, and tastes like. The formula is

Line 1: a one word subject with two syllables

Line 2: four syllables describing the subject

Line 3: six syllables showing action

Line 4: eight syllables expressing a feeling or observation about the subject

Line 5: two syllables describing or renaming the subject

The summer dancers
Dancing in the midnight sky,
Waltzing and dreaming.
Stars glistening in the night sky.
Wish upon a shooting star.

Amy, age 14

The bass breaks the water,
beautiful and powerful,
climbing higher and higher
to catch its prey
and re-enter the water without a ripple.

Randal, age 14

Trees are budding out;
Grass is sprouting everywhere.
Birds chirping again,
They are signs of happiness
Spring is coming once again.

Quenton, age 14

Figure 11–13   Students' Tanka Poems

An alternate cinquain form contains five lines but does not follow the syllable count. Instead, each line uses the specified number of words rather than syllables. Thus, the first line contains a one-word title, the second line has two words that describe the title, the third line has three words that express action, the fourth line has eight words that express feelings, and the fifth line contains a two-word synonym for the title. Examples of students' cinquain poems are presented in Figure 11–14.

Diamante.   Iris Tiedt (1970) invented the diamante (dee ah MAHN tay) to provide another poetry writing form for elementary students. *Diamante* is a seven-line contrast poem written in the shape of a diamond. In this poetic form, students apply their knowledge of opposites and parts of speech. The formula is

Line 1:   one noun as the subject

Line 2:   two adjectives describing the subject

Line 3:   three participles (words ending in *-ing*) telling about the subject

Line 4:   four nouns (the first two related to the subject and the second two related to the opposite)

Snake   Spider
Scary, slimy   Creepy, black
Slides, eats, sleeps   Spins, crawls, eats
He will bite me   Scared, nervous, surprised
Rattlesnake   Tarantula

Lisa, age 7   Alison, age 7

Rainbow
Colorful, bright
Glowing, shimmering, shining
An arch of colors
Enchanting

Stephanie, age 12

Figure 11–14   Students' Cinquain Poems

Line 5:   three participles telling about the opposite

Line 6:   two adjectives describing the opposite

Line 7:   one noun that is the opposite of the subject

When the poem is written, it is arranged in a diamond shape:

noun

adjective   adjective

participle   participle   participle

noun   noun   noun   noun

participle   participle   participle

adjective   adjective

noun

The poem creates a contrast between the subject represented by the noun in the first line and the opposite noun in the last line. Creating the contrast gives students the opportunity to play with words and extend their understanding of opposites and words used to describe opposites. The fourth line begins the transition from the subject to its opposite. A class collaboration diamante poem and other diamante poems are presented in Figure 11–15.

Rhymed Verse Forms

Several rhymed verse forms such as hink-pinks, clerihews, and limericks can be used effectively with middle and upper grade students. In using these forms, it is

BABY
wrinkled tiny
crying wetting sleeping
rattles diapers money house
caring working loving
smart helpful
ADULT

Third graders

WINTER
cold, bare
sledding, slipping, skating
snow, ice, sunshine, breeze
swimming, fishing, boating
hot, dry
SUMMER

Scott, age 11

CALIFORNIA
hot, sunny
surfing, swimming, running
beaches, sunsets, gangsters, crowds
patrolling, fighting, running
violent, tough
NEW YORK

Chad, age 11

Figure 11–15   Students' Diamante Poems

important that teachers try to prevent these forms and rhyme schemes from restricting students' creative and imaginative expression.

Hink-Pinks.   *Hink-pinks* (also called *terse verse*) are short, two-word poems that either take the form of an answer to a riddle or describe something. Longer versions of the poetic form have also been developed. Hink-pinks are composed with two one-syllable words, hinky-pinkies with two two-syllable words, and hinkity-pinkities with two three-syllable words (Geller, 1981). Figure 11–16 presents examples of students' hink-pinks. A group of eighth graders composed riddle hink-pinks and then turned their hink-pinks into games. They wrote the riddle question on a manila envelope and the hink-pink answer on a sheet of posterboard which they then cut into jigsaw puzzles. The puzzle which answers the question, "What do you call a finicky chicken?" is presented in Figure 11–17.

Limericks.   The *limerick* is a form of light verse that uses both rhyme and rhythm. The poem consists of five lines, and the first, second, and fifth lines rhyme while the third and fourth lines rhyme with each other and are shorter than the other three lines. The rhyme scheme is a-a-b-b-a. Often the last line contains a funny or surprise ending. The poem is arranged this way:

Ghost	**Garfield**	**Astronaut**
White	Fat	Sky
Fright	Cat	Guy
Marshall, age 12	Mark, age 14	Tara, age 12

What do you call a *weird stinker*?

PUNK SKUNK

Burgundy, age 14

Figure 11–16   Students' Hink-Pink Poems

Figure 11–17   An Eighth Grader's Hinky-pinky Poem

What do you call a finicky chicken?

Robin, age 13

Line		Rhyme
1	_____	a
2	_____	a
3	_____	b
4	_____	b
5	_____	a

Limericks are believed to have originated in the city of Limerick, Ireland, and they were first popularized over a century ago by Edward Lear (1812–1888). Poet X. J. Kennedy (1982) reports that limericks are the most popular type of poem in the English language today. Introduce your students to limericks by reading aloud some of Lear's verses so that your students can appreciate the rhythm (stressed and unstressed syllables) of the verse. One fine edition of Lear's limericks is *How pleasant to know Mr. Lear!* (Livingston, 1982). Another book of limericks that students will enjoy is *They've discovered a head in the box of bread and other laughable limericks* (Brewton & Blackburn, 1978). Arnold Lobel has also written a book of unique pig limericks, *Pigericks* (1983). After sharing Lobel's pigericks, students will want to write "dogericks," "catericks," or maybe "fishericks." Examples of students' limericks are presented in Figure 11–18.

Clerihews. *Clerihews* (KLER i hyoo) are four-line rhymed verse that describe a person. The poetic form is named for Edmund Clerihew Bentley (1875–1956), a British detective writer who invented the form. The formula is:

Limericks

There was an old lady named Betty
Who feasted on only spaghetti.
When to her surprise
She met her demise
By eating instead some confetti.

Kim, age 11

There lives an old man in my boot.
He's purple and covered with soot.
I told him one day,
"You have to pay."
And he said, "Sorry, but I have not loot."

Joe, age 12

Clerihews

John Wayne
Is in the Cowboy Hall of Fame
In movies he shot his gun the best,
And that's how he won the West.

Johnny, age 14

Albert Einstein
His genius did shine
Of relativity and energy did he dream,
And scientists of today hold him in high esteem.

Heather, age 12

Figure 11–18   Students' Limericks and Clerihews

Line 1:   the person's name

Line 2:   the last word rhymes with the last word in line 1

Lines 3 and 4:   the last word in these lines rhymes with each other

Clerihews can be written about anyone: historical figures, characters in stories, athletes, and even the students themselves. Figure 11–18 also includes two clerihews written by upper grade students.

Model Poems

Students can also write poems that are modeled on poems composed by adult poets. Kenneth Koch suggests this approach in his book, *Rose, where did you get that red?* (1973). According to this approach, children read a poem and then write their own poems following the same main ideas and feelings expressed in the model poem. Presented below are two of Koch's writing activities and another writing activity based on poems written by adults, which can serve as models for students' poems.

Apologies.   Using William Carlos Williams' poem, "This Is Just to Say," as the model poem, children write a poem in which they apologize for something they are secretly glad they did (Koch, 1973). Middle and upper grade students are very familiar with offering apologies and they enjoy writing humorous apologies. Examples of students' apology poems are presented in Figure 11–19.

Invitations.   Students write poems in which they invite people to a magical, beautiful place full of sounds and colors and where all kinds of marvelous things happen. The model poem is William Shakespeare's poem, "Come Unto These Yellow Sands" (Koch, 1973).

Prayers for the Ark.   Students write a poem or prayer from the viewpoint of an animal following the model poems in Carmen Bernos de Gasztold's *Prayers from the ark* (1965). Examples of students' poems are included in Figure 11–19.

Concrete Poems

Students can also make word pictures by arranging words on a page and by combining art and writing. Perhaps the easiest type of concrete poems are those in which a single word is written in a special way as the illustrations in Figure 11–20 show. Invite students to experiment with writing these words concretely:

box	broken	cracked	cross
disappear	divide	down	elephant
explode	football	heart	invisible
long	merry-go-round	narrow	nervous
point	rough	squash	television

Apology Poems

This is just to say
I have mowed
Over the rosebush
You were growing
For the rosebush contest;
I know you wanted me
To mow your lawn,
Not your bush;
Forgive me,
I couldn't help it;
I mowed over it
Because it was in my way
And the steering wheel
Wouldn't turn.

Nicole, age 12

This is just to say
I wore
Your white socks
That were in
The top drawer
So I washed them
Just for you;
Forgive me,
But I didn't have any;
Your white socks are now pink.

Jennifer, age 12

Prayers from the Ark Poems

Monkey's Prayer

Dear Lord,

I forgive you for making my face so ugly.
I thank you for giving me hands.
Thank you for placing the trees so
     high away
from my enemies.
I almost forgot,
Bless you for last month's big crop
     of bananas.

                    Amen.

David, age 12

Elephant's Prayer

Dear God,

I am the elephant.
Why did you make me so fat?
The ground moans when I walk.
Yet I thank you for keeping the grass
sweet and green so I can be strong.
Thank you for keeping the mud puddles soft.
I ask you one favor.
Could you keep me with this fine herd
for as long as I live.

                    Amen.

Mattson, age 12

Figure 11–19   Students' Model Poems

Also, words, phrases, and sentences can be written in the shape of an object. In the "Ants" poem in Figure 11–20, you can easily imagine the setting: a picnic. Several books of concrete poems that will give students ideas for their poems include Barbara Pilon's *Concrete is not always hard* (1972), Robert Froman's *Seeing things* (1974), and *Walking talking words* by Ivan Sherman (1980).

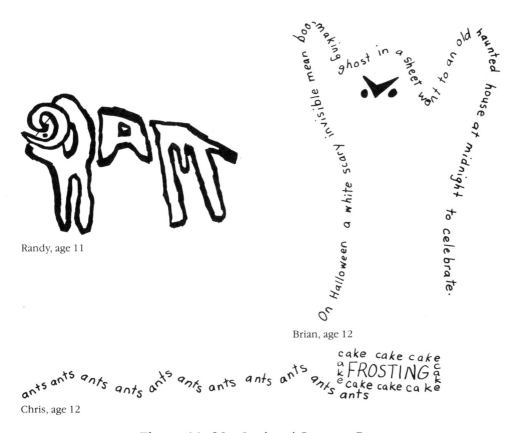

Randy, age 11

On Halloween a white scary invisible mean boo making ghost in a sheet went to an old haunted house at midnight to celebrate.

Brian, age 12

ants ants ants ants ants ants ants ants ants ants
cake cake cake
cake FROSTING cake
cake cake cake
ants

Chris, age 12

Figure 11–20 Students' Concrete Poems

What children learn about playing with words when they write concrete poems often influences their story writing as well. Children experiment with words, move them around on a page, and change the size of print for emphasis. In her very realistic poem, "I Woke Up This Morning" (1980), Kuskin writes each line in a progressively larger type to show her frustration and determination that tomorrow morning she is staying in bed! Similarly, in *The three billy goats Gruff,* the words "trip-trap," which mark the movement of each goat across the bridge, are often written in progressively larger type. Children quickly begin to use the same techniques in their own story and poetry writing.

Evaluating Students' Experiences with Poetry

Teachers share poetry with students in the elementary grades to provide them with a variety of experiences with poetry—to listen to poems read aloud, to read poems themselves, to share poems through choral reading, and to respond to poems through art, drama, and other modes. It is difficult to evaluate students' experiences with poetry because of the nature of the experiences. Observing students while they participate in poetry experiences and talking to them about poetry may be the most useful approaches. These questions can serve as an observation or discussion guide:

- Does the student read poems?
- Does the student share favorite poems with classmates?
- Does the student copy favorite poems to keep?
- Does the student respond to favorite poems through some of the response activities (e.g., informal drama, art) suggested in the chapter?
- Does the student have a favorite poet?
- Can the student tell about that poet and the poems the poet has written?

At the same time students are reading and responding to poems written by others, they are writing their own poems. Students use the process approach in writing poems, and the process evaluation checklist presented in Chapter 6 is one possible evaluation tool. In this chapter, we have presented a variety of poetry formulas. These formulas provide options for students as they experiment with ways to express their thoughts. Although students should experiment with a variety of forms during the elementary grades, they should not be tested on their knowledge of particular forms. Instead, the forms should be posted in the classroom for students to refer to as they write.

Evaluating the quality of students' poems is just as difficult as evaluating the quality of their stories. We recommend that instead of trying to give a grade for quality, students be evaluated on two other criteria: (a) whether or not they have written poems using the process approach and (b) whether or not they have experimented with the formulas presented in class. Teachers might also ask students to evaluate their own progress in writing poems. Students should keep copies of the poems they write in their writing folders so they can also review and assess their own work. Also, if a grade for quality is absolutely necessary, students should be permitted to choose several of the poems in their writing folders to be evaluated.

Summary

Too often poetry is neglected in the elementary language arts curriculum. Sometimes students seem resistant to poetry, and sometimes teachers feel unprepared to share poetry with students or to help them write poetry. The information presented in this chapter suggested ways to involve children with poetry.

Guidelines were presented for sharing poetry with students. The teacher begins by reading or reciting poetry, and soon children are encouraged to share poetry with their classmates. Educators suggest that children should not be required to memorize particular poems, but rather they should be asked to "learn" a poem they especially enjoy to share with their classmates. In addition, educators caution that children quickly lose interest in poetry when they are forced to analyze poems and discuss their meanings. Enjoyment and word play are the primary reasons for sharing poetry in the elementary grades. Several strategies for sharing poetry were presented. Choral reading was described as a good way to actively engage students in sharing poetry.

Children learn to write poetry easily using formulas. The formulas provide the structure that allows students to be successful in their writing. Many of these poetic forms do not rhyme, allowing students to share intense feelings and create vivid descriptions in their poems instead of searching for pairs of rhyming words. Several poetic forms were described in the chapter, including formula poems such as "I wish" poems, color poems, and "If I were" poems and other unrhymed forms such as haiku, cinquain, and diamante. Rhymed verse forms—hink-pinks, limericks, and clerihews—were presented, as were model poems and concrete poems.

Extensions

1. Invite a small group of students to study a favorite poet. Students can read poems written by the poet and learn about the poet's life. They may also want to arrange to place a conference telephone call or write letters to the poet. (Note: You can arrange for a conference call by contacting the poet's publisher and renting a special telephone from the telephone company.)

2. Share poetry with a group of students and allow students to participate in one or more of the response activities, such as participating in choral reading, dramatizing a poem, compiling a picture book version of a poem, or creating a filmstrip of a poem.

3. Copy favorite poems on index cards and compile a collection of poems appropri-

ate for the grade level you teach or plan to teach.

4. Make a set of charts listing the formulas for the various types of poems presented in the second half of the chapter to use in teaching elementary students to write poetry.

5. Teach a small group of students to write several types of poems (e.g., formula poems, rhymed verse poems, model poems, concrete poems) presented in the second half of the chapter. Use the instructional strategy and student examples presented in the chapter. Then have students compile the poems they write in hardbound books. (The procedure for making these books was presented in Chapter 6.)

References

Apseloff, M. (1979). Old wine in new bottles: Adult poetry for children. *Children's* Literature in Education, *10,* 194–202.

Atwood, A. (1971). *Haiku: The mood of the earth.* New York: Scribner.

_____. (1973). *My own rhythm: An approach to haiku.* New York: Scribner.

Baron, V. C. (Ed.). (1968). *The seasons of time: Tanka poetry of ancient Japan.* New York: Dial.

Behn, H. (1964). (Trans.). *Cricket songs.* New York: Harcourt Brace and World.

_____. (1971). *More cricket songs.* New York: Harcourt Brace Jovanovich.

Brewton, J. E., & Blackburn, L. A. (1978). *They've discovered a head in the box of bread and other laughable limericks.* New York: Crowell.

Chapman, D. L. (1985). Poet to poet: An author responds to child writers. *Language Arts, 62,* 235–242.

Ciardi, J. (1962). *You read to me, I'll read to you.* New York: Harper and Row.

de Gasztold, C. B. (1965). *Prayers from the ark.* New York: Penguin Books.

Fisher, C. J., & Natarella, M. A. (1982). Young children's preferences in poetry: A national survey of first, second and third graders. *Research in the Teaching of English, 16,* 339–354.

Froman, R. (1974). *Seeing things: A book of poems.* New York: Crowell.

Geller, L. G. (1981). Riddling: A playful way to explore language. *Language Arts, 58,* 669–674.

Graves, D. H. (1983). *Writing: Teachers and children at work.* Exeter, NH: Heinemann.

Hopkins, L. B. (1972). *Pass the poetry, please! Using poetry in pre-kindergarten–six classrooms.* New York: Citation Press.

———. (1983). *A song in stone: City poems.* New York: Crowell.

Kennedy, X. J., & Kennedy, D. M. (1982). *Knock at a star: A child's introduction to poetry.* Boston: Little, Brown.

Koch, K. (1970). *Wishes, lies, and dreams: Teaching children to write poetry.* New York: Random House.

———. (1973). *Rose, where did you get that red? Teaching great poetry to children.* New York: Random House.

Kuskin, K. (1980). *Dogs and dragons, trees and dreams.* New York: Harper and Row.

Kutiper, K. (1985). *A survey of the poetry preferences of seventh, eighth, and ninth graders.* Unpublished doctoral dissertation, Universtiy of Houston.

Lewis, R. (Ed.). (1965). *In a spring garden.* New York: Dial.

———. (1968). *Of this world: A poet's life in poetry.* New York: Dial.

———. (1970). *The way of silence: The prose and poetry of Basho.* New York: Dial.

Livingston, M. C. (Ed.). (1982). *How pleasant to know Mr. Lear!* New York: Holiday House.

Lobel, A. (1983). *Pigericks: A book of pig limericks.* New York: Harper and Row.

Lowry, L. (1979). *Anastasia Krupnik.* Boston: Houghton Mifflin.

Merriam, E. (1966). *It doesn't always have to rhyme.* New York: Atheneum.

Milne, A. A. (1956). *The house at Pooh corner.* New York: Dutton.

O'Neill, M. (1961). *Hailstones and halibut bones: Adventures in color.* Garden City, NJ: Doubleday.

Opie, I., & Opie, P. (1959). *The lore and language of schoolchildren.* Oxford, England: Oxford University Press.

Parker, M. K. (1981). A visit from a poet. *Language Arts, 58,* 448–451.

Pilon, A. B. (1972). *Concrete is not always hard.* Middletown, CT: Xerox Education Publications.

Prelutsky, J. (1977). *The snoop on the sidewalk and other poems.* New York: Greenwillow.

———. (1982). *The baby uggs are hatching.* New York: Greenwillow.

Sherman, I. (1980). *Walking talking words.* New York: Harcourt Brace Jovanovich.

Stewig, J. W. (1981). Choral speaking: Who has the time? Why take the time? *Childhood Education, 57,* 25–29.

Terry, A. (1974). *Children's poetry preferences: A national survey of upper elementary grades* (NCTE Research Report No. 16). Urbana, IL: National Council of Teachers of English.

Tiedt, I. (1970). Exploring poetry patterns. *Elementary English, 45,* 1082–1084.

IF YOU WANT TO LEARN MORE

Esbensen, B. J. (1975). *A celebration of bees: Helping children write poetry.* Minneapolis: Winston Press.

Freeman, R. H. (1983). Poetry writing in the upper elementary grades. *The Reading Teacher, 37,* 238–242.

Hopkins, L. B. (1972). *Pass the poetry, please! Using poetry in pre-kindergarten–six classrooms.* New York: Citation Press.

Koch, K. (1970). *Wishes, lies, and dreams: Teaching children to write poetry.* New York: Random House.

———. (1973). *Rose, where did you get that red? Teaching Great Poetry to Children.* New York: Random House.

Larrick, N. (Ed.). (1971). *Somebody turned on a tap in these kids: Poetry and young people today.* New York: Delacorte.

Lipson, G. B., & Romatowski, J. A. (1981). *Calliope: A handbook of 47 poetic forms and parts of speech.* Glenview, IL: Good Apple.

Livingston, M. C. (1973). *When you are alone/it keeps you capone: An approach to creative writing with children.* New York: Atheneum.

Markham, L. R. (1983). Writing cinquains: Start with a word or two. *Language Arts, 60,* 350–354.

Rogacki, J. M. (1984). Poetry in motion. *Language Arts, 61,* 261–264.

Whitin, D. J. (1983). Making poetry come alive. *Language Arts, 60,* 456–458.

Winkeljohann, R., Sr.(1981). How can I help children to enjoy poetry? *Language Arts, 58,* 353–355.

CHAPTER TWELVE

Writers' Tools: Grammar

*O*VERVIEW. *In this chapter we focus on the sentence as the grammatical unit of language. Students examine sentences from children's literature and from their own writing and consider the use of modification added to nouns and verbs to make sentences clearer and more interesting. The nature of descriptive modification is discussed in terms of qualities and attributes, details, and comparisons. Sentence building activities in which students add modification to sentences are also discussed.*

Grammar is the description of the structure of a language. It involves principles of word and sentence formation. In contrast, *usage* is "correctness" or the appropriate word in a sentence. It is the socially preferred way of using language within a dialect. Fraser and Hodson (1978) explain the distinction between grammar and usage this way: "Grammar is the rationale of a language; usage is its etiquette (p. 52)."

While there is much controversy about teaching grammar and its value for elementary students, grammar is a part of the elementary language arts curriculum and will undoubtedly remain so for some time to come. Given this fact, it is only reasonable to suggest that grammar should be taught in the most beneficial manner possible. Researchers suggest that integrating grammar study with reading and

Grammar deals with the structure of a language and involves principles of word and sentence formation.

writing produce the best results (Noyce & Christie, 1983). Also, Peter Elbow (1973) and Shirley Haley-James (1981) view grammar as a tool for writers and recommend integrating grammar instruction with the revising and editing stages of the writing process.

The approach to teaching grammar described in this chapter integrates reading and writing. Students examine the structure of sentences and types of modification. Then they investigate how authors of children's books use these structures and experiment with the grammatical structures in their own compositions. This approach is based on three premises:

1. Students learn to use grammatical structures in their writing by experimenting with alternative structures and the effects they achieve.

2. Students learn to use grammatical structures by studying how authors use these structures and the effects they achieve.

3. Students learn to use grammatical structures by substituting different but appropriate grammatical structures in the sentences that authors have written as well as in the sentences they themselves have written.

An explicit knowledge of grammatical structures and how to use them enables students to write more effectively. Understanding grammatical structures and modification techniques gives students the same options that adult writers have. As they write, authors must decide whether or not to use words, phrases, clauses, or complete sentences to express their ideas most effectively. In *Charlotte's web* (1952), for instance, author E. B. White had to decide whether to use phrases or sentences in the following excerpt:

> " 'Run!' commanded Mrs. Arable, taking the pig from Fern and slipping
> a doughnut into her hand." (p.7)

White chose to use two participial phrases rather than two additional sentences. Instead, he could have written:

> "Run!" commanded Mrs. Arable. Mrs. Arable took the pig from Fern.
> Mrs. Arable slipped a doughnut into Fern's hand.

Breaking these actions apart into three sentences slows down the action. In White's version, however, the two participial phrases help speed up the action. Fern is in a hurry, and Mrs. Arable is spurring her on to catch the school bus.

POINTS TO PONDER
What Are the Two Basic Parts of a Sentence?
What Types of Words Are Used to Modify Nouns and Verbs?
What Are the Three Types of Phrases and How Are They Used in Sentences?
What Is the Instructional Strategy for Teaching Students about Parts of Sentences?

PARTS OF SENTENCES

Nouns and verbs are the basic building blocks of sentences. Writers add adjectives, adverbs, and phrases to build upon the nouns and verbs. These modifiers add qualities and attributes, details, and comparisons to sentences. John Erskine explains:

> When you write, you make a point, not by subtracting as though you sharpened a pencil, but by adding . . . The noun, the verb, and the main clause serve merely as a base on which the meaning will rise. The modifier is the essential part of any sentence. (quoted in Christensen & Christensen, 1978, pp. 46–47)

The instructional strategy for teaching students about nouns, verbs, and other parts of sentences is based on the instructional model presented in Chapter 1. In the strategy students examine sample sentences from children's literature and from their own writing. The steps in the strategy are presented in Figure 12–1.

Nouns and Verbs

To introduce students to the function of nouns and verbs in sentences, scramble the words in several sentences or in a paragraph and prepare a chart or transparency with these word strings. The sentences from the first paragraph of William Armstrong's award-winning book *Sounder* (1969) are presented in scrambled order:

> Of the porch the stood at the man tall edge. Sagged from head roof posts two the the rough held which it, closing the almost between gap his and rafters the. Dim the cabin from light cast window equal from posts shadows long and man. Nearby stood shivering cold a in October boy wind the. Over the broad Sounder fingers a head and back of he crown forth dog ran the coon of named his.

Ask students to rearrange the words to construct the sentences in English word order. Compare their sentences with the original:

> The tall man stood at the edge of the porch. The roof sagged from the two rough posts which held it, almost closing the gap between his head and the rafters. The dim light from the cabin window cast long equal shadows from man and posts. A boy stood nearby shivering in the cold October wind. He ran his fingers back and forth over the broad crown of the head of a coon dog named Sounder. (p. 1)

After the strings of words have been rearranged into sentences and compared with the original, ask questions in order to separate, identify, and classify the nouns and verbs of each sentence. Use questions similar to the following:

- In the first sentence, which two words carry the general meaning of the sentence? (man stood)
- Where did you put them?
- When you rearranged the words, how did you know where to put them in the sentence?

Preparation

Locate sample sentences in children's literature or in basal reader stories that use the grammatical structure or concept being taught.

Define and list characteristics of the structure on a chart.

Instruction

Step 1: Initiating

Introduce the grammatical structure (e.g., adjectives, prepositional phrases) using a chart defining and listing characteristics of the structure and explain its function in a sentence. Then present sentences using the structure and explain the structure's function in each sentence. Discuss the structure's effect in the sentences. Use the questions listed in this chapter to probe students' thinking about the grammatical structure.

Step 2: Structuring

Manipulate the sentences by removing the structure from a sentence or by substituting another structure. Read the changed sentences and discuss the effect that removing or replacing the structure has on the meaning of the sentence.

Step 3: Conceptualizing

Have students locate examples of the grammatical structure in their own writing. Ask them to explain why they used the particular structure. Discuss its use and effect in each sentence read.

Step 4: Summarizing

Review the grammatical structure and its function using the chart presented in the first step. Share another set of sentences taken from children's literature or students' own writing and have students identify the grammatical structure and explain its function in each sentence.

Step 5: Generalizing

Have students locate sentences in their compositions where the addition of the structure being studied would improve the meaning. Ask students to read those sentences and suggest how they would revise the sentences.

Step 6: Applying

Encourage students to use the grammatical structure being studied in their writing. Also, during revising conferences, ask students to point out opportunities where writers might revise their compositions and incorporate the structure to improve the meaning.

Figure 12-1   An Instructional Strategy for Teaching Grammatical Structures

Repeat the questions for each of the rearranged sentences. Ask students to study the words carefully and to divide and classify them into two groups. Ask questions similar to the following:

- What words seem to have something in common?
- Why should we put *man* and *roof* in the same group?
- Why should we put *stood* and *sagged* in the same group?
- Why can't we put *man, roof,* and *sagged* in the same group?

Continue with the same line of questioning until all the words have been put into one group or the other. Then explain that the group or category with the words *man, roof, light,* and *boy* are called nouns; and the group of words *stood, sagged, cast,* and *stood* are called verbs.

Ask the following questions to begin to define nouns and verbs:

- Why did we classify the words *man, roof, light* and *boy* as nouns?
- Why did we classify the words *stood, sagged, cast,* and *stood* as verbs?

After students respond, explain that nouns are labels of things (e.g., *roof* and *light*) and of persons (e.g., *man* and *boy*), and verbs are labels of actions (e.g., *stood, sagged,* and *cast*). Verbs also say something about the nouns, for example, *man stood, roof sagged, light cast shadows,* and *boy stood.* We can get a picture in our

After examining the nouns in an excerpt from a favorite tradebook, a student develops a functional definition of the label "noun."

minds of *a man standing, a roof sagging, light being cast by a lamp,* and *a boy standing.*

Word Order.   There is also another relationship between the main noun and verb in each of these sentences. The main noun precedes the verb in each sentence. The usual word order in English sentences (other than questions) is *noun-verb.* Children learn the word order of English when they learned how to talk as young children. Now they use this knowledge of word order in rearranging the sentences in the paragraph from *Sounder.* This activity is useful in pointing out to students that they already have some knowledge of grammar, the rules of the language.

Noun Determiners.   Nouns can also be identified by the determiners that precede them. The nouns in the paragraph from *Sounder* are marked as follows:

Determiner Marking the Noun	*Noun*
the	man
the	edge
the	porch
the	roof
the	posts
the	gap
his	head
the	rafters
the	light
the	window
a	boy
the	wind

Nouns will usually be preceded by determiners; some sentences require them or they sound awkward. Determiners can be listed and pointed out to students. Locating the noun determiners is an easy way for students to identify nouns, the headwords to which they will add modifiers.

Modifiers

Students will quickly see the need for modification if all the modifiers are omitted from a paragraph. For example, the paragraph from *Sounder* (1969) rewritten in skeletal form, using only nouns, verbs, and the necessary determiners, follows:

> The man stood. The roof sagged. The light cast shadows. A boy stood. He ran fingers.

This skeleton paragraph carries the general idea or narrative, but the interesting information, the modification the writer adds to these nouns and verbs, is missing.

Using either this paragraph from *Sounder* or another paragraph, students can determine what modification has been added to the nouns and verbs to give them the impressions the author intends to convey. The following questions direct students' attention to the role of modification:

- What does the author want you to know about the man?

- Where was he standing?

- How does this information help you to know more about the man and the story?

- What does the author want you to know about the porch?

- Why does he want you to know about the porch?

- What do you know about the family from the words the author added to the nouns and verbs, the modification?

Adjectives.   After the need for modification has been established, students can identify adjectives and discuss their function. *Adjectives* are words that modify nouns by indicating a quality or attribute and in some cases a detail. Adjectives change the words they modify in special ways. The noun *light,* for example, can be dim only when the modifier *dim* has been added to it. Adjectives answer the question, *what kind.* The first paragraph from *Sounder* can again be used to dem-

---

Adjectives

Locate a noun.
Which word modifies that noun?
Do any other words modify it?
Where is the adjective located in the sentence?
Does the adjective answer the question, what kind?
What effect does the adjective have on the meaning of the sentence?
Could a different word be substituted for the adjective without changing the meaning?

Adverbs

Locate an adverb.
What word does it modify?
Does the adverb modify a verb, an adjective, or another adverb?
Where is the adverb located in the sentence?
Does the adverb come before or after the word it modifies?
What effect does the adverb have on the word it modifies?
Delete the adverb and read the sentence. What effect does this change have on the meaning of the sentence?

Figure 12–2   General Questions About Modifiers

onstrate how authors use adjectives to modify nouns. Ask students to read the paragraph and underline each noun in the paragraph:

> The tall <u>man</u> stood at the <u>edge</u> of the <u>porch</u>. The <u>roof</u> sagged from the two rough <u>posts</u> which held it, almost closing the <u>gap</u> between his <u>head</u> and the <u>rafters.</u> The dim <u>light</u> from the cabin <u>window</u> cast long equal <u>shadows</u> from <u>man</u> and <u>posts</u>. A <u>boy</u> stood nearby shivering the cold October <u>wind</u>. He ran his <u>fingers</u> back and forth over the broad <u>crown</u> of the <u>head</u> of a coon <u>dog</u> named <u>Sounder.</u>

Then they can locate the modifiers in front of many of the underlined nouns. Ask questions similar to the following to focus students' attention on the modifying words:

- What word is in front of *man?*

- Does the word *tall* change your idea of *man* in any way?

- If the word *tall* wasn't in front of the word *man,* what would you see?

- What does the word *tall* do?

Follow the same procedure with the other underlined words.

Students can classify the words used as modifiers and nouns as this chart illustrates:

Modifier	*Noun*
tall	man
rough	posts
dim	light
cabin	window
long, equal	shadows
cold, October	wind
broad	crown
coon	dog

The list of general questions about adjectives presented in Figure 12–2 can be used to help students classify nouns and modifiers.

After introducing students to adjectives, students can reread compositions they have written and underline the adjectives and the nouns they modify in brief excerpts. Ask students to discuss their selection of adjectives and the effect those modifiers created in their compositions. Students can rewrite parts of their compositions, leaving out all the adjectives to understand the function of adjectives more clearly. They might also want to revise their compositions by adding adjectives to modify nouns.

Adverbs. *Adverbs* are modifiers that change or add meaning to verbs, adjectives, and other adverbs in special ways. These modifiers answer the questions suggested by the words *how, where, when, how much,* and *how many.* Present sentences from a story and discuss the function of the adverbs in the sentences by asking questions similar to those following each quoted sentence below from *Charlotte's web* (White, 1952):

> "When he had finished the last drop, he grunted and walked *sleepily* into the box." (p. 9)
>
> What word tells how Wilbur walked?
>
> Do you know more about how Wilbur felt after eating because the author added *sleepily* to the verb *walked?*
>
> "Wilbur amused himself in the mud along the edge of the brook, where it was warm and moist and *delightfully* sticky and oozy." (pp. 10–11)
>
> What adjectives does *delightfully* modify?
>
> How does Wilbur feel about amusing himself in the sticky and oozy mud?

After introducing adverbs, students can examine the compositions they have written and locate the adverbs they have used in their writing. They can also revise particular sentences in their compositions by adding adverbs.

Students can examine how authors use adverbs to modify verbs, adjectives, and other adverbs. Select one or two paragraphs rich with adverbs from a story such as Robert Lawson's *Rabbit hill* (1972) and write the excerpt on a transparency. Display the transparency on an overhead projector, and ask students to read the paragraphs and to mark the adverbs. The following paragraph from *Rabbit hill* is used as an example:

> Haste and excitement made Willie <u>inexcusably</u> careless. He should have remembered that the lid of the <u>rainwater barrel</u> was old and rotted, that there were several dangerous holes in it. He did <u>not</u>, and his leap from the window sill landed him <u>squarely</u> in one of the holes. He grabbed <u>frantically</u> as he went <u>through</u>, but the rotten wood crumbled under his claws and with a sickening shock he plunged into the icy water. (p. 88)

Questions can be used to probe students' understanding of the function of adverbs in the paragraph and the effect adverbs have on the words they modify. For instance, ask students to read the third sentence in the excerpt from *Rabbit hill*, omitting the adverb *not*. How is the meaning of that sentence and the sentence before it affected by this three-letter word? A list of general questions to use in discussing the function of adverbs is included in Figure 12–2.

Phrases

We will discuss three types of phrases and their functions in sentences. These three types are (a) prepositional phrases, (b) participial phrases, and (c) absolute phrases. Examples of all three types of phrases are easily located in children's literature.

Prepositions and Prepositional Phrases. *Prepositions* are words that take nouns as objects, relate those objects to other words in the sentence, and modify those words or structures. The *prepositional phrase* is a phrase formed by the preposition and its object. It is important for students to understand the structure of prepositional phrases so that they can construct them to function as adjectival or adverbial modifiers when simple adjectives or adverbs would not serve their purposes.

Prepositions belong to the closed class of words; that is, new prepositions are not being added to English regularly as nouns and other open class words are. Because prepositions are a closed class, it is simpler to list the most frequently used prepositions on a chart, identify them in sentences, and discuss their functions. This discussion should help students more easily recognize prepositional phrases and their adjectival and adverbial functions. Questions to use in examining prepositions and prepositional phrases are presented in Figure 12–3.

Students can make a list of prepositions on a chart and use it as a reference throughout the year. There are three general classes of prepositions: (a) simple prepositions, (b) compound prepositions, and (c) phrasal prepositions. *Simple*

Prepositional Phrases

Locate a prepositional phrase.
What is the preposition?
What is the prepositional phrase?
What is the structure of the prepositional phrase?
How does the prepositional phrase function in the sentence?
Does it function as an adverb?
What effect does the prepositional phrase have on the meaning of the sentence?

Participial Phrases

Locate a participial phrase.
What participle is used in the participial phrase?
Is the participial phrase used as an adjective or as an adverb?
What effect does the participial phrase have on the meaning of the sentence?
Drop the participial phrase from the sentence. What effect does it have on the sentence?
Substitute a different structure for the participial phrase.
What effect does it have on the sentence?
Why did the author use the participial phrase?

Absolute Phrases

Locate an absolute phrase.
What is the structure of the absolute phrase?
What is the effect of the descriptive detail added by the absolute phrase?
Substitute a different structure for the absolute phrase. What effect does it have on the sentence?
Why did the author use the absolute phrase?

Figure 12–3 General Questions About Phrases

prepositions (e.g., *in, to*) contain one word. *Compound prepositions* (e.g., *according to*) are made up of two prepositions that function as one. *Phrasal prepositions* (e.g., *in spite of*) are phrases used as prepositions and may include compound prepositions. A list of prepositions representing the three classes is presented in Figure 12–4. Students should be encouraged to add other prepositions to the chart as they discover them in their writing and reading. The dictionary is an important tool for verifying the structure and function of prepositions.

Participles and Participial Phrases.   Present participles and past participles are two of the four principal parts of verbs. The present participle is formed by adding *-ing* to the verb, and the past participle of regular verbs is formed by adding *-ed* to the verb. The past participle forms of irregular verbs include *frozen, thought,* and *written.* Participles by themselves usually function as adjectives. When they are combined with auxiliary verbs, they function as parts of verb phrases. When they are used to form the head words in participial phrases, these phrases usually function as adjectives or adverbs.

Students should examine participial phrases for their structure and function. A participial phrase has a participle at its head and takes the same complements as a corresponding finite verb to form its phrase. Depending on its function, it may also take modifiers. A participial phrase may function as a bound or as a free modifier (Christensen & Christensen, 1978). Generally, a *bound modifier* contains in-

---

Simple Prepositions

abroad	about	above	across	after
against	along	amid	among	around
at	before	behind	below	beneath
beside	between	beyond	by	down
during	except	for	in	into
of	off	on	outside	over
round	since	through	throughout	to
with	within	without		

Compound Prepositions

according to	from among	from between
from under	over against	out of
round about		

Phrasal Prepositions

by the side of	in spite of
in accordance with	with regard to

Figure 12–4   Three Types of Prepositions

formation needed to identify the structure it modifies; it is not set off with commas. A *free modifier* adds descriptive detail about whatever structure is being modified but it is not necessary to identify it; it is set off with commas. Dropping a bound modifier will generally change the meaning of whatever is being modified; dropping a free modifier will not. The following examples from *Charlotte's web* (White, 1952) should help to clarify this distinction:

> *Bound Modifiers*
> "Wilbur stood in the sun *feeling lonely and bored.*" (p. 16)
>
> *Free Modifiers*
> "'Certainly not,' he said, *looking down at his daughter with love.*" (p.3)
>
> "'I see no difference,' replied Fern, still *hanging on to the ax.*" (p.3)

In the first sentence, if the phrase "feeling lonely and bored" is dropped, the meaning of the sentence is changed. However, in the second sentence, if the phrases "looking down at his daughter with love" and "hanging on to the ax" are dropped, descriptive detail is lost, but the meaning of the sentence is not changed. Questions about participial phrases are included in Figure 12–3.

Absolute Phrases.   The *absolute phrase* is a free modifier since, by definition, its subject does not have any grammatical function in the sentence in which it occurs. It adds information about the situation, the subjects, or the action in the sentence in which it occurs. An absolute phrase has a subject and a predicate. The predicate, however, lacks a complete verb. The absolute phrase has a substantive for its subject, and, most often, a participial phrase for its predicate. The following examples of absolute phrases are taken from *The king of the wind* (Henry, 1948):

> "Swiftly and silently the Signor turned upon his heel, *his white mantle fluttering behind him like moth wings.*" (p.27)
>
> "She was standing patiently in a corner of her stall, *her head lowered, her tail tucked in.*" (p.27)

Questions to use in discussing absolute phrases are included in Figure 12–3.

Absolute phrases is a difficult grammatical concept for elementary students, but some upper grade students will be using them in their writing and will be familiar with them from their reading. It is appropriate to introduce absolute phrases to those students who are already experimenting with them in their writing.

POINTS TO PONDER

What Are the Three Types of Descriptive Modifiers that Can Be Added to Nouns and Verbs?

What Is the Function of Descriptive Modifiers?

What Are Similes and Metaphors?

DESCRIPTIVE MODIFICATION

Elementary students can use three techniques for adding descriptive modification to nouns, verbs, and main clauses. These three techniques are (a) qualities and attributes, (b) details, and (c) comparisons (Christensen & Christensen, 1978). The words that modification is added to are called *headwords.* Nouns and verbs are the headwords used with descriptive modifiers.

Qualities and Attributes

Descriptive modifiers may point to a quality or attribute and produce in the reader's mind an overall modification of whatever is being labeled by the headword. Adjectives and adverbs are the descriptive modifiers that are normally used to designate qualities or attributes. Adjectives modify the nouns and adverbs modify the verbs. Sometimes authors use adjectives and adverbs following verbs of action to make sentences more interesting. For example:

Adjective: The *round* door closed quietly.

Adverb: He ate *slowly.*

Adjective: John stood, *heavy* and *rigid,* his face flushed with anger.

In these examples, *round* is a characteristic of some doors in general. It is an overall modification of a door. *Slowly* is an overall modification of the act of eating. *Heavy* and *rigid* are adjectives that modify the overall action expressed by the verb *stood.*

Introduce descriptive modifiers by discussing how they modify the headword. Students can look for examples of modifiers in basal reader stories and in children's literature. Examples of qualities and attributes from children's literature are presented below:

"It had a perfectly *round* door . . . ." (*The hobbit,* Tolkien, 1966, p.15).

"In the walks and driveway *tall, dried* weeds rattled and scraped whenever a breeze stirred." (*Rabbit hill,* Lawson, 1972, p.13)

"Mrs. Arable shifted *uneasily* in her chair." (*Charlotte's web,* White, 1952, p. 109)

"Wilbur ate his breakfast *slowly."* (*Charlotte's web,* White, 1952, p. 120)

General questions about qualities and attributes are presented in Figure 12–5. These questions can be used in discussing how the modifiers function in these and other sentences.

Students can characterize qualities and attributes of objects, people, and actions using pictures cut from magazines. Have students cut from magazines an interesting picture with an object, person or action that they will describe. Students brainstorm a list of adjectives to describe the object or person or adverbs to describe the action. Then they write a sentence or two using the words they have

---

Qualities and Attributes

How does the modifier change the overall impression of the head-
    word?
What quality or attribute is being suggested for the headword?
What is the function of the modifier in this sentence?
Would the headword have the same meaning without the modifier?
Does the modifier make the headword clearer and more precise?

Details

Which words add detail?
What headword does the detail modify?
Is the detail added before or after the headword?
What happens to the effect if the detail words are moved around in the
    sentence?

Comparisons

Locate a comparison in a sentence.
Is the comparison a simile or a metaphor?
Is the comparison in simple form or is it expanded?
What headword does the comparison modify?
What is the function of the comparison in the sentence?
How does the comparison sharpen the image of the headword?

Figure 12–5   General Questions About Descriptive Modification

listed to describe the qualities or attributes of that object, person, or action. Students next meet in small group conferences to share their pictures, list the descriptive words they brainstormed, and read the sentences they composed using the
descriptive words.

Excerpts from children's literature can also be used for a practice activity.
Working in small groups, students locate paragraph-long excerpts from stories
they are reading that use descriptive modifiers and copy the excerpts, omitting all
modifiers. Then groups exchange excerpts and add modifiers to the nouns and
verbs that will describe their qualities and attributes. Students share their revisions
and discuss their use of modifiers using the questions on qualities and attributes included in Figure 12–5.

Students can reread the stories and other compositions they have written and
identify the adjectives and adverbs that modify the headwords. Urge students not
to use abstract adjectives, such as *beautiful* or *nice,* to point to a quality or attribute because these adjectives summarize; at best they modify in a very general and
nonspecific way.

Details

Descriptive modifiers used as details specify parts of a whole. While a quality or attribute provides an overall modification of the image suggested by the headword, a detail suggests that some part of the image needs to be highlighted.

Details are indicated by (a) prepositional phrases, (b) participial phrases, and (c) absolute phrases. Prepositional phrases beginning with *in, with,* and *without* are used most often for adding details. Participial phrases are used more often to add descriptive details to verbs than to nouns because they use a form of a verb in their structure. Absolute phrases are excellent vehicles for adding descriptive details to verbs because they contain both a subject and predicate. The following are examples of descriptive details added to nouns:

> "It had a perfectly round door like a porthole, *painted green, with a shiny yellow brass knob* in the exact middle." (*The hobbit,* Tolkien, 1966, p.15)

> "The cook could not see the face of the man, but he noticed the brutish size of him—*hands big and broad, legs shaped like water casks.*" (*King of the wind,* Henry, 1948, p.81)

"With a shiny yellow brass knob" is a prepositional phrase, "painted green" is a participial phrase, and "hands big and broad" and "legs shaped like water casks" are absolute phrases. The following are examples of descriptive details added to verbs:

> "Like a barn swallow in flight Sham wheeled, and *with a beautiful soaring motion* he flew to the safety of his stall." (*King of the wind,* Henry, 1948, p.101)

> "Sham was sucking for breath, *his nostrils going in and out, showing the red lining. . . .* The onlookers were pulling with him, *breathing heavily, tensing their muscles as one man, straining, straining to help.*" (*King of the wind,* Henry, 1948, p.92)

"With a beautiful soaring motion" is a prepositional phrase, "breathing heavily" and "tensing their muscles as one" are participial phrases, and "his nostrils going in and out" is an absolute phrase.

The strategy and activities for teaching qualities and attributes can be used to help students learn to recognize descriptive details and use them in their writing. Locate examples of descriptive details in books of children's literature and in basal reader stories. Questions to use in examining details are included in Figure 12–5. The picture activity used in the previous section can also be used to practice brainstorming details and writing sentences with details. As a final step, have students read compositions they have written and locate details they have added to headwords. Also, encourage students to use descriptive details in their writing.

Comparisons

Descriptive modifiers may also be used to compare the image or action denoted by the headword to something else. Descriptive comparisons go beyond the object, person, or action being compared and suggest a likeness to something else. Similes and metaphors are used for descriptive comparisons. They can be used in simple form or be expanded by the addition of an adjective, prepositional phrase, or a participial phrase.

A *simile* is an explicit comparison of one thing to another by stating that one object is *like* another object. A *metaphor* compares two things by implying that one *is* something else. Two forms of a simile are (a) a *like* phrase that consists of the preposition *like* and a noun, such as "like a moonbeam," and (b) an *as . . . as* phrase that consists of *as* followed by an adjective and then *as* followed by a noun, for example, "as cold as silence." The following examples of similes and metaphors are categorized according to form:

Similes: Like Comparisons

Simple form: "like a *shout*" (*Wind in the willows,* Grahame, 1961, p.2)

Expanded by an adjective: "like a *tiny star*" (*Wind in the willows,* Grahame, 1961, p. 5)

Expanded by a prepositional phrase: "like the drone *of a distant bee*" (*Wind in the willows,* Grahame, 1961, p. 36)

Expanded by a participial phrase: "like someone *walking in carpet slippers that were too big for him*" (*Wind in the willows,* Grahame, 1961, p. 62)

Similes: As . . . as Comparisons

Simple form: "as thin as a *pencil*" (*Fantastic Mr. Fox,* Dahl, 1970, p. 2).

Expanded by an adjective: "as clean as a *newly polished spoon*" (*The sign of the beaver,* Speare, 1983, p. 5)

Expanded by a prepositional phrase: "as high as the level *of the latch*" (*Sounder,* Armstrong, 1969, p. 2)

Expanded by a participial phrase: as helpless as a man *shackled in irons.*

Metaphors

Simple form: "when he flees under the sun he is the wind" (*King of the wind,* Henry, 1948, p. 53)

Expanded by an adjective; "His legs were *steel* rods" (*King of the wind,* Henry, 1948, p. 139)

Expanded by a prepositional phrase: "He was a machine *with pistons for legs,* pistons that struck out in perfect rhythm." (*King of the wind,* Henry, 1948, p. 13)

Expanded by a participial phrase: "It [the mineret] was a sharp needle *pricking the blood-red reflection of the sun.*" (*King of the wind,* Henry, 1948, p. 22)

The instructional strategy for teaching descriptive comparisons is the same whether the comparisons are used to describe nouns or verbs. Read some comparisons to students using the *like* form, show them some pictures of objects or the objects themselves, and ask them to compare the objects to something else. Write their comparisons on the chalkboard. Explain the structure of a simple *like* comparison. Have students write comparisons using *like.* Compile them and read them as a class collaboration poem. Repeat for the other forms of *like* comparisons.

Next, have students look for *like* comparisons in stories or poems they have read. As they find them, list them on the chalkboard with separate columns for the categories: simple, expanded by an adjective, expanded by a prepositional phrase, and expanded by a participial phrase. Then discuss the structure and function of each form. The list of questions about comparisons included in Figure 12–5 can be used to probe students' thinking.

Students can review the compositions they have written to see if they have used any *like* comparisons. Let them read the sentences or paragraphs in which the comparisons occur to the class. Have them select sentences from their compositions that could be improved by using a *like* comparison. Ask them to concentrate on sharpening the image of a character, a mood, a setting, or an object by adding a *like* comparison.

Follow the same type of activities as those listed above for *like* comparisons for comparisons using *as . . . as similes and metaphors.*

POINTS TO PONDER

What Is Sentence Slotting?

What Are the Seven Basic Sentence Patterns?

What Is Sentence Expansion?

What Is Sentence Combining?

How Do Sentence Building Activities Help Students Communicate More Effectively?

SENTENCE BUILDING

Students can experiment with the grammatical structures they have learned through a variety of sentence building activities. In this section, we will discuss four sentence building activities: (a) sentence slotting, (b) sentence patterns, (c) sentence expansion, and (d) sentence combining. Through sentence slotting activities, students experiment with the functions of words and phrases in a sentence, and in sentence patterns, they construct sentences following each sentence pattern. Students learn about the effects of adding modifiers through sentence expansion activities; in sentence combining, they combine short, choppy sentences to build more complex sentences. Through these activities, students experiment with techniques for adding modification to sentences, manipulate sentences, and experiment with different sentence patterns to communicate more effectively through writing.

Sentence Slotting

Students can experiment with words and phrases to see how they function in sentences by filling in sentences that have *slots,* or blanks. Sentence slotting can be used to teach students about several different grammatical concepts. First, students can experiment with parts of speech using a sentence like this:

> The snake slithered _____ the rock.
>
> over
>
> around
>
> under
>
> to

Students can brainstorm a number of words to fill in the slot, all of which will be prepositions. Adjectives, nouns, verbs, and adverbs do not make sense when they are used to fill in the slot. This activity can be repeated to introduce or review any part of speech.

Sentence slotting can also be used to demonstrate to students that parts of speech can substitute for each other. In the following sentence, common and proper nouns as well as pronouns can be used in the slot:

> _____ asked his secretary to get him a cup of coffee.
>
> The man
>
> Mr. Jones
>
> He

A similar sentence slotting example can be used to demonstrate how phrases can function as an adverb:

> The dog growled _____.
>
> ferociously
>
> with his teeth bared
>
> daring us to reach for his bone

In this example, the adverb *ferociously* can be used in the slot as well as prepositional and participial phrases. Sentences with an adjective slot can be used to demonstrate that phrases function as adjectives.

Teachers can create sentences for sentence slotting activities or may take them from children's literature. The goal of these activities is to demonstrate the function of words in sentences. Many of the sentence slotting activities, such as the last sample, also illustrate that sentences become more specific with the addition of a word or phrase. Through these activities, students experiment with the grammatical options they have been learning.

Sentence Patterns

The seven basic sentence patterns provided in structural grammar can help students learn the structure and function of sentence elements. The basic sentence parts consist of nouns, verbs, and complements. The noun by itself serves as the subject of the sentence; the verb by itself or with complements serves as the predicate of the sentence. Modifiers are added to the nouns, verbs, and complements. Connectives are used to join words, phrases, and clauses. Students can build sentences by adding modifiers to the basic patterns.

N-V.   The first pattern, N-V, consists of a subject and predicate with no complements. The verb is an intransitive verb, so it does not take any complements. Both the noun and the verb may take modifiers that will expand the possible sentences and make them more interesting. In this N-V sentence pattern and in all the succeeding sentence patterns, each pattern, may be expanded by adding adjectives, adverbs, prepositional phrases, participial phrases, and absolute phrases. The basic sentence will be given and then, to save space, only one expanded sentence is included.

Lions roared.

Hungry *lions,* searching for food, their mouths open wide, *roared* angrily in frustration.

N-V-N.   The second pattern, N-V-N, consists of a subject, a transitive verb, and a direct object complement. The direct object receives the action initiated by the subject and specified by the verb. The verb carries the action from the subject to the object, as the following sentences illustrate:

The lion stalked the jungle.

The hungry *lion,* swaying from side to side, his skin stretched taut, *stalked the jungle* menacingly.

N-LV-N.   The third pattern, N-LV-N, consists of a subject, a linking verb, and a complement. In this pattern the complement is a subjective complement because it completes the meaning of the subject. The linking verb links a description of the subject to the subject. The subjective complement further identifies the subject:

Lions are animals.

Lions, penned in cages, their freedom taken from them, *are* very unhappy *animals.*

N-LV-Adj.   The fourth pattern, N-LV-Adj, consists of a subject, a linking verb, and a predicate adjective. The predicate adjective is a subjective complement that points out a quality of the subject. The linking verb links the description of the adjective to the subject:

Lions are cautious.

The young *lions,* stalking their prey in the African grasslands, their tails twitching nervously, *are* extremely *cautious.*

N-V-N-N. The fifth pattern, N-V-N-N, consists of a subject; a transitive verb; and two complements, an indirect object and a direct object. The verb specifies an action that is passed from the subject to the object, but another person or thing is also involved in the action. The subject passes the object on to someone or something else, the indirect object:

> Lions give cubs meat.
>
> Moving away from the kill, the *lions,* their paws red with blood, *give* their hungry *cubs meat.*

N-V-N-N. The sixth pattern, N-V-N-N, consists of a subject; a transitive verb; and two complements, a direct object and an objective complement. The objective complement completes the meaning of the object by identifying what the verb is passed on to the object and completed by the objective complement. The objective complement refers to the same person or thing as the object:

> Lions make cubs hunters.
>
> *Lions,* living at the edge of the jungle, painstakingly *make* their young *cubs hunters* of small game.

N-V-N-Adj. The seventh pattern, N-V-N-Adj, consists of a subject; a transitive verb; and two complements, a direct object and an objective complement. The objective complement in this pattern is an adjective; it, however, still completes the meaning of the action passed on from the subject to the object. The adjective points out a quality of the object. If the objective complement is a noun, as in pattern six, it renames the object rather than pointing out a quality of the object:

> Lions make cubs happy.
>
> The old *lions,* pacing back and forth, their heads swinging from side to side, *make* the *cubs* very *happy.*

These seven basic sentence patterns are summarized in Figure 12–6.

The sentence patterns can be expanded even further by using phrases and clauses as the subjects of the sentences. The sentences can also be joined by coordinating and subordinating conjunctions. One of the potential problems with an approach based on building sentences from basic patterns is that such sentences are often stilted. The sample sentences about lions constructed from the basic patterns are in some respects awkward. The value of the exercises, however, lies in the practice they give students in manipulating language structures for different effects.

As each basic sentence pattern is introduced, have students locate examples of the patterns in stories they are reading as well as in their own writing. Practice in sentence building can be integrated with writing stories and other compositions. Examples of expanded sentences are easily found in children's literature:

> He made his prayers (N-V-N) in Sham's stall (prepositional phrase), carefully (adverb) spreading his mantle to kneel on (participial phrase), and facing the eastern sky (participial phrase) that showed itself through the round window at the back of the stall (clause). (*King of the wind,* Henry, 1948, p. 42)

Pattern	Description	Sample Sentence
1. N-V	Subject and intransitive verb with no complements	Lions roared.
2. N-V-N	Subject, transitive verb, and direct object	The lion stalked the jungle.
3. N-LV-N	Subject, linking verb, and complement	Lions are animals.
4. N-LV-Adj	Subject, linking verb, and predicate adjective	Lions are cautious.
5. N-V-N-N	Subject, transitive verb, indirect object, and direct object	Lions give cubs meat.
6. N-V-N-N	Subject, transitive verb, direct object, and objective complement	Lions make cubs hunters.
7. N-V-N-Adj	Subject, transitive verb, direct object, and objective complement	Lions make cubs happy.

Figure 12–6   Seven Basic Sentence Patterns

Variations and combinations of these seven basic sentence patterns are used to produce almost all sentences that we speak and write. For example, sentences can be changed from positive to negative by adding a form of *not* and an auxiliary verb, and questions are formed by transposing the subject and an auxiliary verb or by adding *who, what,* or other *wh-* words. Sentences are made more complex by joining two sentences or embedding one sentence within another. Linguists have identified a number of transformations that change sentences from one form to another. A list of the most common transformations is presented in Figure 12–7. While these transformations are presented separately, several transformations can be applied to the same sentence simultaneously. Elementary students already know and use most of the simple transformations, but the more complex joining and embedding transformations are often taught through sentence combining activities.

Sentence Expansion

Students can take basic or kernel sentences, such as *A frog leaps* or *The car raced,* and expand them by adding descriptive modifiers. The words and phrases used to expand the basic sentence can add qualities and attributes, details, and compari-

Figure 12-7 Transformations of Sentence Patterns

Transformation	Description	Sample Sentence
Simple Transformations		
1. Negative	*Not* or *n't* and auxiliary verb inserted	Lions roar. Lions don't roar.
2. Yes-No Question	Subject and auxiliary verb switched	The lion stalked the jungle. Did the lion stalk the jungle?
3. *Wh-* Question	*Wh-* word (*who, what, which, when, where, why*) or *how,* and auxiliary verb inserted	Lions roar. Why do lions roar?
4. Imperative	*You* becomes the subject	Lions give cubs meat. Give cubs meat.
5. There	*There* and auxiliary verb inserted	Lions are cautious. There are cautious lions.
6. Passive	Subject and direct object switched and the main verb changed to past participle form	Lions make cubs hunters. Cubs are made hunters by lions.
Complex Transformations		
1. Joining	Two sentences joined using conjunctions such as *and, but, or*	Lions roar. Tigers roar. Lions and tigers roar.
2. Embedding	Two (or more) sentences combined by embedding one into the other	Lions are animals. Lions are cautious. Lions are cautious animals.

Malmstrom, 1977

sons. The "5 Ws plus one" help students focus on expanding particular aspects of the sentence. For example:

Basic sentence:	A frog leaps.
What kind?	green, speckled
How?	high into the air
Where?	from a half-submerged log and lands in the water with a splash
Why?	to avoid the noisy boys playing nearby
Expanded sentence:	To avoid the noisy boys playing nearby, *a* green, speckled *frog leaps* high into the air from a half-submerged log and lands in the water with a splash.

Depending on the questions asked and the answers given, many other expanded sentences are possible from the same basic sentence. Students enjoy working in small groups to expand a basic sentence so that they can compare the expanded versions each group produces. Instead of using the "5 Ws plus one" to expand sentences, older students can be asked to supply a specific part of speech or modifier at each step of expansion.

Basic sentences for sentence expansion activities can be created by students or the teacher, or they can come from children's literature. Very few basic sentences are found in stories, but the basic sentence within an expanded sentence can be identified and used. Students enjoy comparing their expanded versions of the basic sentence with the author's. When students are familiar with the story the sentence was taken from, they can try to approximate the meaning of the author's sentence. Even so, it is likely that they will go in a variety of directions as they expand the basic sentence. Because students' expanded sentences may vary greatly from the author's, they realize the power of modifiers to transform a sentence.

Sentence Combining

The rise of transformational grammar has led many educators to seek ways of operationalizing it for classroom use. The method that seems most promising is sentence combining. Sentence combining was the focus of a study by Mellon (1969). His work suggested that sentence combining activities might be a profitable way to increase the rate of students' syntactic development. Work by Hunt and O'Donnell (1970) and by O'Hare (1973) showed that students could improve their writing when sentence combining exercises were taught. Since their efforts, many teachers have introduced sentence combining activities to their students.

Students use complex transformations in sentence combining activities. Sentences can be joined or embedded in a variety of ways. Two sentences (S) are transformed to create a matrix (or combined) sentence (M) in these examples:

(S)	Tom found a wallet.
(S)	The wallet was brown.

> (M1)   Tom found a wallet which was brown.
>
> (M2)   Tom found a brown wallet.

Two possible matrix sentences (M1 and M2) were presented in which the adjective *brown* was embedded. In matrix sentence M1, a relative clause transformation was used, and an adjective transformation was used in matrix sentence M2. Neither matrix sentence is right or wrong. Rather, they provide two options. The goal of sentence combining is for students to experiment with different combinations. Examples of other sentence combining exercises are presented in Figure 12–8.

    Teachers can incorporate sentence combining activities with the study of the syntactic patterns used by authors. Analyze the authors' sentences and paragraphs

Figure 12–8   Sentence Combining Exercises

Examples of Sentence Joining

1. (S)*   Joe is tall.
   (S)   Bill is tall.

   (M)**   Joe and Bill are tall.

2. (S)   John fell off his bike.
   (S)   Mary screamed.

   (M)   When John fell off his bike, Mary screamed.

3. (S)   Tom hit the ball over the wall.
   (S)   Tom ran around the bases.

   (M)   Tom hit the ball over the wall and ran around the bases.

Examples of Sentence Embedding

1. (S)   The boy is fat.
   (S)   The boy is eating cake.

   (M)   The boy who is eating cake is fat.
   (M)   The fat boy is eating cake.

2. (S)   John fights fires.
   (S)   John is a fireman.

   (M)   John who is a fireman fights fires.
   (M)   John, a fireman, fights fires.

3. (S)   The bird is beautiful.
   (S)   The bird is flying over the tree.

   (M)   The bird which is flying over the tree is beautiful.
   (M)   The bird flying over the tree is beautiful.

*S = sentence to be combined
**M = matrix or combined sentence

for sentences that can easily be used to demonstrate sentence combining. For example, this sentence about Wilbur from *Charlotte's web* (White, 1952) can be broken down into three short sentences:

"He crawled into the tunnel and disappeared from sight, completely covered with straw." (p. 9)

1. He crawled into the tunnel.
2. He disappeared from sight.
3. He was completely covered with straw.

When sentences from children's literature are used for analysis, always stress the effect the author was trying to have on the reader. Sentence combining activities become "busy work" if the effect on potential readers is not stressed. Students can ask themselves these questions:

■ Would the effect be different if I combined these sentences?

■ Which way of combining these sentences would be most effective?

Sentence combining activities give students opportunities to manipulate sentence structures; however, they are rather artificial. They are most effective when combined with other writing assignments. Weaver (1979) cautions that "sentence combining activities are only an adjunct to the writing program and the writing process and should never be used as substitutes for actual writing" (pp. 83–84).

Summary

This chapter focused on helping students understand how the modification of nouns, verbs, and clauses is used for more precise descriptions. When students understand how authors use descriptive modifiers for certain effects on their readers, they can begin to experiment with the grammatical structures that are used as modifiers. They can test these structures in the sentences they have written for the effects they have on their readers. They can decide whether an adjective, a prepositional phrase, a participial phrase, or an absolute would be the best structure to use as a modifier.

Sentence slotting and sentence patterns were presented to help students experiment with the modifiers they can add to the nouns,

verbs, and complements that make up the basic sentence patterns. As students experiment with these activities, they should not just load the patterns. It is important that students use these patterns to obtain the effects they want by having classmates react to their sentences.

Sentence expansion and sentence combining activities can be used with students who tend to use short, choppy sentences when they write. When they understand the possibilities for manipulating grammatical structures, students can experiment with the structures in their writing. They can integrate their practice with sentence combining, sentence expanding, and modification in their writing.

Extensions

1. Examine your own feelings about whether grammar should be taught in elementary schools. If you decide it should be, how should it be taught? Compare your opinions with the arguments for and against teaching grammar presented in Frederica Davis' "In defense of grammar" (1984) and Robert Small's "Why I'll never teach grammar again" (1985) or "Grammar should be taught and learned in our schools," by Ronald I. Goba and Polly Ann Brown (1982).

2. Examine language arts textbooks to see how grammar is presented in them. What percentage of the textbook pages is devoted to grammar instruction? What types of activities are included? Is grammar instruction tied to literature and writing activities?

3. Interview students about their knowledge of grammar and how they apply it in their writing. Questions such as these may be used:

   ■ Do you study grammar in school?

   ■ What kinds of grammar activities does your teacher assign?

   ■ What have you learned about grammar?

   ■ Do you think it's important to learn about grammar? Why or why not?

   ■ Do authors need to know about grammar? Why or why not?

   ■ Do you use what you know about grammar when you write? Why or why not?

4. Collect sample sentences and paragraphs to use in teaching grammar from books of children's literature that are appropriate for students at the level you teach or expect to teach.

5. Plan and teach a lesson on nouns, verbs, or modifiers using the instructional strategy presented in Figure 12-1.

6. Plan and teach a lesson on sentence building using one of the four types of activities presented in the chapter.

References

Armstrong, W. H. (1969). *Sounder.* New York: Harper and Row.

Christensen, F., & Christensen, B. (1978). *Notes toward a new rhetoric: Nine essays for teachers* (2nd ed.). New York: Harper and Row.

Dahl, R. (1970). *Fantastic Mr. Fox.* New York: Knopf.

Davis, F. (1984). In defense of grammar. *English Education, 16,* 151–164.

Elbow, P. (1973). *Writing without teachers.* New York: Oxford University Press.

Fraser, I. S., & Hodson, L.M. (1978). Twenty-one kicks at the grammar horse. *English Journal, 67,* 49–53.

Goba, I., & Brown, P. A. (1982). Grammar should be taught and learned in our schools, *English Journal, 73,* 20–23.

Grahame, K. (1961). *The wind in the willows.* New York: Scribner.

Haley-James, S. (Ed.). (1981). *Perspectives on writing in grades 1–8.* Urbana, IL: National Council of Teachers of English.

Henry, M. (1948). *King of the wind*. Chicago: Rand McNally.

Hunt, K. W., & O'Donnell, R.C. (1970). *An elementary school curriculum to develop better writing skills*. Washington, DC: US Government Printing Office.

Lawson, R. (1972). *Rabbit hill*. New York:Viking.

Malmstrom, J. (1977). *Understanding language: A primer for the language arts teacher*. New York: St. Martin's Press.

Mellon, J. C. (1969). *Transformational sentence combining: A method for enhancing the development of syntactic fluency in English composition* (NCTE Research Report No. 10). Urbana, IL: National Council of Teachers of English.

Noyce, R. M., & Christie, J. F. (1983). Effects of an integrated approach to grammar instruction on third graders' reading and writing. *Elementary School Journal, 84*, 63-69.

O'Hare, F. (1973). *Sentence combining: Improving student writing without formal grammar instruction* (NCTE Research Report No. 15). Urbana, IL: National Council of Teachers of English.

Small, R. (1985). Why I'll never teach grammar again. *English Education, 17*, 174-178.

Speare, E. G. (1983). *The sign of the beaver*. New York: Dell.

Tolkien, J. R. R. (1966). *The hobbit*. Boston: Houghton Mifflin.

Weaver, C. (1979). *Grammar for teachers: Perspectives and definitions*. Urbana, IL: National Council of Teachers of English.

White, E. B. (1952). *Charlotte's web*. New York: Harper and Row.

IF YOU WANT TO LEARN MORE

Holbrook, H.T. (1983). Whither (wither) grammar? *Language Arts, 60*, 259–263.

Hutson, B.A. (1980). Moving language around: Helping students become aware of language structure. *Language Arts, 57*, 614–620.

Lamb, P. (1977). *Linguistics in proper perspective* (2nd ed.). Columbus,OH: Merrill.

Noyce, R.M. & Christie, J.F. (1981). Using literature to develop children's grasp of syntax. *The Reading Teacher, 35*, 298–304.

Perron, J. (1976). Beginning writing: It's all in the mind. *Language Arts, 53*, 652–657.

Schiff, P.M. (1980). But they make me use that grammar text! *English Journal, 69*, 23–25.

Van Hook, B. (1979). Grammatic surgery. *Teacher, 96*, 78–80.

Weaver, C. (1979). *Grammar for teachers: Perspectives and definitions*. Urbana, IL: National Council of Teachers of English.

Willis, S. (1977). Some ideas for teaching grammar. In B. Zavatsky & R. Padgett (Eds.), *The Whole Word Catalogue 2*. New York: McGraw-Hill.

CHAPTER THIRTEEN

Writers' Tools: Spelling

OVERVIEW. Because spelling practices are undergoing change as a result of new information about the English orthographic system and how children learn to spell, this chapter has been divided into two main sections: current practices and emerging practices. We will consider current practices first to give you some information about teaching spelling using a textbook approach. In the second section, we will examine what linguists have discovered about lexical spelling and young children's stages of invented spelling as well as the implications of this research for spelling instruction.

Learning to spell involves learning the *orthographic,* or spelling, system of English, which specifies the standard way words should be spelled. The orthographic system and the grammar work together to determine how words are spelled and used correctly in writing. The phonological, syntactic, and semantic systems determine how words will be spelled according to how they are to be used in sentences, and the orthographic system determines what letters are used in the spelling. For example, a word used as an adjective in one part of a sentence may be spelled differently when it is used as a noun in another part of the sentence. Consider the following sentence: The man was *sane,* but his *sanity* was being questioned by the courts. The noun *sanity* is derived from the adjective *sane* by the addition of the noun suffix *-ity.* The spelling of *sane* is altered by dropping the *e* before the suffix *-ity* is added. In the orthographic system of English, a rule specifies that when a suffix beginning with a vowel is added to a word that ends in "silent" *e,* the *e* is dropped before the suffix is added. There are, however, exceptions to the general rules of English orthography and to other more specific rules that govern a very small set of words. Because English has borrowed so many words from other languages, it is impossible to establish spelling rules that are invariant across all words in the English language.

At least two approaches to instruction in spelling exist in schools today: current practices and emerging practices. Current practices involve the use of some type of spelling textbook and daily periods of work on a list of spelling words and on related activities. In contrast, emerging practices are integrated with writing and involve students in spelling situations in a more natural way. Students do not memorize words to pass a weekly spelling test; rather, they gradually develop an understanding of the orthographic system in much the same manner as they developed their knowledge of the oral language system.

POINTS TO PONDER

What Is the Textbook Approach to Spelling Instruction?

What Phonological and Morphological Information Do Students Need to Know to Be Good Spellers?

Which Spelling Rules Should Students Learn?

*Spelling is a tool for writers, and it is learned most
efficiently by writing every day.*

CURRENT PRACTICES

Current practices in spelling tend to be based on spelling textbooks and the methods of teaching tend to stress the spelling of words in relation to phoneme-
grapheme (sound-symbol) correspondences. Emphasis is placed on listening for
the sounds students hear in words and then matching those sounds to corresponding letters. The other emphasis is on morphology, studying words in terms of root
words, prefixes, and suffixes.

The Spelling Textbook Approach

The spelling textbook approach is the most commonly used means to help students learn to spell. While some variation exists in the content of the textbooks
and in the methods suggested for teaching the spelling words, five common characteristics can be noted: (a) study and testing procedures, (b) unit arrangements,
(c) spelling words, (d) instructional strategy, and (e) time.

Study and Testing Procedures.   Most spelling textbooks use a variation of the *test-study-test* plan in which students are given a pretest on Monday, encouraged to study the words they missed on the pretest during the week, and are retested on Friday. Some teachers omit the pretest and use a *study-test* plan in which students study all words, even those they already know, and other teachers add a midweek trial test (*test-study-test-study-test* plan). Researchers have found that the pretest is a critical component in the study procedures. The pretest helps to identify those spelling words that students already know how to spell. By eliminating the words they can already spell, students can direct their study toward the words that are difficult for them. Students need immediate feedback about their efforts to learn to spell. According to Thomas Horn (1947), the best way to improve students' spelling is to have them correct their own pretests and trial tests to receive immediate feedback.

Unit Arrangement.   Spelling textbooks use a weekly plan in which lessons are included for each of the five days. On Monday, the words in the new unit are intro-

A student corrects his own pretest to identify the words he already knows how to spell and the words he needs to study.

duced, and students typically copy the word list and sometimes use the words to write sentences or to fill-in-the-blanks to complete a paragraph. On Tuesday, spellers usually have a set of exercises that provide practice for an aspect of word structure such as phoneme-grapheme correspondences, spelling patterns, or root words and affixes. In many programs, Wednesday is used for the trial test, and some programs also include additional word study activities on Wednesday. On Thursday, spelling textbooks provide a variety of activities, ranging from grammar, dictionary, and handwriting activities to enrichment word activities. Friday is reserved for the final spelling test. A sample textbook unit is presented in Figure 13–1.

Spelling Words. Lists of spelling words usually include the most frequently used spelling words. During the elementary grades, spelling textbooks present at least 3,000 words, and researchers have found that these 3,000 most frequently used words account for more than 97% of all the words children and adults use in writing. Even more interesting, the three most frequently used words—*I, and, the*—account for 10% of all words written, and the 100 most frequently used words represent more than 50% of all the words written (E. Horn, 1926). Thus, a relatively small number of words account for an amazingly large percentage of words students use in their writing. A list of the 100 most frequently used words is presented in Figure 13–2 on page 408.

The words in each unit are often grouped according to spelling patterns or phonetic generalizations; that is, all the words in one spelling list may follow a vowel rule (e.g., *i-e*) or a spelling pattern (e.g., *-igh*). Researchers have questioned this approach. Johnson, Langford, and Quorn (1981) found that "the effectiveness of teaching spelling via phonic generalizations is highly questionable" (p. 586). Too often students memorize the rule or spelling pattern and score 100% on the spelling test, but later they are unable to choose among spelling options in their writing. For example, after learning the *i-e* vowel rule and the *-igh* spelling pattern in isolation, students are often stumped about how to spell a word such as *light*. They have learned two spelling options for /ay/, *i-e* and *-igh,* and *lite* is an option, one they often see in their environment. Instead of organizing words according to phonetic generalizations and spelling rules, many educators recommend that teachers simply point out these rules whenever they occur rather than teaching according to them.

Instructional Strategy. Students need to learn a systematic and efficient strategy for learning to spell words. The strategy should focus on the whole word rather than breaking it apart into sounds or syllables, and it should include visual, auditory, and kinestethic components. An eight-step strategy that meets these two criteria is presented in Figure 13–3 on page 408. Strategies similar to this one are presented in most spelling textbooks. Research indicates that a whole-word approach to spelling instruction is more successful than phonetic or syllable approaches (T. Horn, 1969).

Figure 13–1 Sample Unit from a Third-Grade Spelling Textbook

23 /ôr/

OUR WORDS

sport pour score
order or poor
storm corner sore
forget snore course
horn fort fourth

_____
_____
_____
_____

PATTERN POWER

Say each spelling word.

1. Write the three spelling words in which /ôr/ as in **born** is spelled **ore.**
_____
_____
_____

2. Write the eight spelling words in which /ôr/ is spelled **or.**
_____
_____
_____
_____

3. Write the three spelling words in which /ôr/ is spelled **our.**
_____
_____
_____

4. Write the spelling word in which /ôr/ is spelled **oor.**
_____

In most words, /ôr/ as in born is spelled or, ore, or our.

90

MEANING MASTERY

Mr. Gibben has a very unusual store.
Use the spelling words below to complete
this paragraph about his strange shop.

sore   order   sport   corner   storm   horn

Mr. Gibben owns an odd store just around the (1) _____. He has
everything you can think of. If you like to play music, you can buy a
_____. If your back is (3) _____, you can buy
(2) _____ something to make it feel better. You can buy equipment for any kind of
_____ you want to play. You can even buy a coat to keep you
(4) _____. If you want something he does not
warm in a snow (5) _____.
have, Mr. Gibben will (6) _____ it for you.

DICTIONARY SKILLS

Pretend *forget* and *snore* are guide words on a dictionary page. Write in
alphabetical order the ten spelling words that would appear on this page.
Be sure to include the guide words. The first one is done for you.

1. *forget*
2. _____
3. _____
4. _____
5. _____
6. _____
7. _____
8. _____
9. _____
10. _____

WORD BUILDING

You can make new words by adding **-ly** at the end of some base words. Add the suffix **-ly** to each base word below. Write the new words. The first one is done for you.

1. loud   *loudly*
2. poor
3. proud
4. order
5. high
6. deep
7. even
8. certain

sport
order
storm
forget
horn
pour
or
corner
snore
fort
score
poor
sore
course
fourth

WRITING ACTIVITIES

Write two sentences using spelling words to describe what is happening in the picture to the right.

HANDWRITING PRACTICE

A. Practice writing **our** and **ore**. Be sure the **o** is closed at the top. Be sure the **u** is pointed at the top, so it does not look like an **n**.

our   *ore*

B. Now practice writing these sentences.

1. *The fourth score is yours.*

2. *Of course I snore.*

CHALLENGE WORDS

Use the challenge words to complete each sentence below.

fifty   **forty**   **age**   **thirty**   **twenty**

1. If you want to know a person's _____, ask, "How old are you?"

2. There are _____ states in the United States.

3. Two times ten is _____.

4. April and June each has _____ days.

5. Halfway between thirty and fifty is _____.

Cook, Esposito, Gabrielson, & Turner, 1984, pp. 90–93.

Figure 13–2 The 100 Most Frequently Used Words

I	there	to	around
and	with	do	see
the	one	about	think
a	be	some	down
to	so	her	over
was	all	him	by
in	said	could	did
it	were	as	mother
of	then	get	our
my	like	got	don't
he	went	came	school
is	them	time	little
you	she	back	into
that	out	will	who
we	at	can	after
when	are	people	no
they	just	from	am
on	because	saw	well
would	what	now	two
me	if	or	put
for	day	know	man
but	his	your	didn't
have	this	home	us
up	not	house	things
had	very	an	too

Hillerich, 1978, p. xiii.

Figure 13–3 Steps in the Instructional Strategy

1. LOOK at the word and say it.
2. READ each letter in the word.
3. CLOSE your eyes and spell the word to yourself.
4. LOOK at the word. Did you spell it correctly?
5. COPY the word from your list.
6. COVER the word and write it again.
7. LOOK at the word. Did you write it correctly?
8. If you made any mistakes, repeat the steps.

Cook, et al., 1984, p. 1.

Time. Assignments in spelling textbooks often require at least 30 minutes per day to complete, totaling 2½ hours per week devoted to spelling instruction. However, research indicates that only 60 to 75 minutes per week should be spent on spelling instruction, and greater periods of time do not result in increased spelling ability (Johnson et al., 1981). Many of the activities included in spelling textbooks involve language arts skills that are not directly related to learning to spell (Graves, 1977). If these activities, which often duplicate other language arts activities, were eliminated and students were to focus for 15 minutes each day on practicing their spelling words using the instructional strategy, then students could learn to spell more quickly and more easily.

A checklist for evaluating spelling textbooks according to these five criteria and recommendations made by researchers in the area of spelling is presented in Figure 13–4.

Study and Testing Procedures

Does the textbook use a test-study-test plan (or a variation of that plan)?
Do students take a pretest before studying the list of spelling words?
Do students correct their own pretests and trial tests?
Do students study all words in the list or only those that they do not know how to spell?

Unit Arrangement

Does the textbook use a five-day approach?
Do the activities focus on learning to spell the words or on related activities such as grammar, dictionary skills, or handwriting?

Spelling Words

How are the spelling words selected?
Are the spelling words grouped according to spelling patterns or phonetic generalizations?

Instructional Strategy

Does the textbook present a systematic and efficient strategy for learning to spell words?
Does the strategy focus on whole words rather than breaking words apart into sounds or syllables?
Does the strategy include visual, auditory, and kinesthetic components?

Time

How much time is required for students to complete the assignments in the textbook?

Figure 13–4   A Checklist for Evaluating Spelling Textbooks

Phonological Representation in Spelling

Phonemes are the smallest units of sound in a language that make a difference in meaning. For example, in the words *pit* and *bit,* both words have the same phonemes except for the initial sounds, /p/ and /b/.

Students can be made aware of consistent phoneme-grapheme correspondences in words by recognizing the consonants that almost always have a one-to-one phoneme-grapheme correspondence. The phoneme /b/ and the grapheme *b* can be used to demonstrate this. The grapheme *b* almost always represents /b/ as in *baby;* although in a few words such as *lamb* and *doubt* it is not pronounced. Other consonants and vowels can be discussed as students begin to observe both regularity and irregularity in the spelling system.

The alphabetic principle suggests that there should be a one-to-one correspondence between graphemes and phonemes so that each letter represents one sound consistently. English, however, does not have this correspondence. The 26 letters are used to represent 40 to 50 phonemes. Moreover, three letters — *c, q,* and *x* — are superfluous as they do not represent unique phonemes. Letter *c,* for instance, is used either to represent /k/ as in *cat* or /s/ as in *decide.* It can also be joined with *b* to represent the digraph /ch/. To further complicate the problem, there are more than 500 spellings to present these 40 to 50 phonemes. Long *e,* according to E. Horn (1957), is spelled 14 different ways in common words! This situation is known as a *lack of fit.*

The reasons for this lack of fit can be found by examining events in the history of the English language. Approximately 75% of our words have been borrowed from languages around the world, and many of these words have retained their native spellings. The spellings of other words have been tinkered with by linguists. More than four hundred years ago, for instance, in an effort to relate the word *island* to its supposed French or Latin origin, the unnecessary and unpronounced *s* was added. However, *island* (spelled *ilond* in the Middle Ages) is a native English word, and the spelling change sends a false message about the word's etymology.

The controversy about whether English spelling is regular or irregular has been waged for years. Recently, linguists have begun to examine the deeper, underlying structure of language, and they have been able to account for many of the seeming irregularities in English. They suggest that English spelling is indeed regular, not at the phoneme-grapheme level, but at a deeper, more abstract level.

Because of the number of spelling options available for many phonemes, it is helpful to develop a set of spelling option charts to display in the classroom. Write a phoneme (e.g., long *e*) at the top of a chart and then ask students to list possible spelling options for the phoneme (e.g., *e* as in *be, ee* as in *tree, ea* as in *sea, ie* as in *chief,* and *eo* as in *people*). Compiling the list of spelling options and sample words can continue as a year-long activity. As students locate words in their reading and writing activities, they can add them to the charts.

English is an affixing language. New words are constantly being formed by adding prefixes and suffixes to words or to borrowed root forms. *A root word* is often defined as the basic part of a word to which prefixes and suffixes are added to derive new words but it is essentially a free morpheme. English borrows many root words from other languages. Some are whole words and others are parts of words. Some root words have become free morphemes and can be used as separate words while others cannot. For example, the word *act* comes from the Latin words *actus,* meaning *doing.* English uses part of the Latin word *actus* and treats it as a root word that can be used independently, or in combination with affixes as in *actor, activate, react,* and *enact.* In the words *alias, alien, unalienable,* and *alienate* the root word *ali* comes from the Latin *alius* meaning other; it is not used as an independent root word in English. A list of root words is presented in Figure 13–5.

Students can compile lists of words developed from root words presented in Figure 13–5, and they can draw root word clusters to illustrate the relationship of the root word to the words developed from it. A root word cluster for the Greek root *graph,* meaning to write, is presented in Figure 13–6. Recognizing basic elements from word to word helps students cut down on the amount of memorizing necessary in learning to spell. Knowing word roots also increases students' vocabularies and gives them clues to word meanings based on morphological considerations (Dale & O'Rourke, 1971).

Prefixes. A *prefix* is essentially a bound morpheme added to the beginning of a root word. A *bound morpheme* is the smallest unit of meaning that cannot be used separately (e.g., *in-, pre-, sub-*). Prefixes change the meaning of derived words, and they may also change the part of speech. Some prefixes have more than one form of the same morpheme. For example, the prefixes *il-, im-,* and *ir-* are forms of the prefix *in-* with the meanings of *in, into,* and *on* and are used with verbs and nouns. The prefixes *il-, im-, ir-,* and *ig-* are also forms of another prefix *in-* with the meaning *not* and are used with adjectives. Both the *in-* prefixes are borrowed from Latin. The prefix *a-* and its alternate form *an-* are borrowed from Greek and also mean *not.*

Suffixes. A *suffix* is essentially a bound morpheme added to the end of a root word or derived word. A suffix generally changes the part of speech of the derived word as well as its meaning. Some suffixes are alternate forms of the same morpheme. For example, the suffix *-ible* is an alternate form of the suffix *-able.*

Students can experiment with adding prefixes and suffixes to the root words presented in Figure 13–5 to create both real and invented words. A list of affixes is presented in Figure 13–7 on page 414. Examples of invented words that students have created include

- phonomatic (makes sounds by itself)
- monoscript (written once)
- jector (hurler)
- astrometer (measures stars)
- solarscope (sunviewer) (Dale & O'Rourke, 1971, p. 12)

An understanding of morphology can be a big help to students. Knowing that there is some system to the way words are spelled and how to change a word from

ann/enn (year): anniversary, annual, biennial, centennial, perennial

ast (star): aster, asterisk, astrology, astronaut, astronomy

auto (self): autobiography, automatic, automobile

bio (life): biography, biology, autobiography, biodegradable

cent (hundred): cent, centennial, centigrade, centipede, century

circ (around): circle, circular, circus, circumspect

corp (body): corporal, corporation, corps

cycl (wheel): bicycle, cycle, cyclist, cyclone, tricycle

dict (speak): contradict, dictate, dictator, predict, verdict

geo (earth): geography, geology, geometry

graph (write): biography, graphic, paragraph, phonograph, stenographer

gram (letter): diagram, grammar, monogram, telegram

grat (pleasing, thankful): congratulate, grateful, gratitude

jus/jud/jur (law, right): injury, judge, justice

man (hand): manacle, manual, manufacture, manuscript

mand (order): command, demand, mandate, remand

mar (sea): aquamarine, marine, maritime, submarine

meter (measure): barometer, centimeter, diameter, speedometer, thermometer

min (small): miniature, minimize, minor, minute

mort (death): immortal, mortal, mortality, mortician, post-mortem

ped/pod (foot): pedal, pedestrian, podiatry, tripod

phon (sound): earphone, microphone, phonics, phonograph, saxophone, symphony

photo (light): photograph, photographer, photosensitive, photosynthesis

quer/ques/quis (seek): query, question, inquisitive

rupt (break): abrupt, bankrupt, interrupt, rupture

scope (see): horoscope, kaleidoscope, microscope, periscope, telescope

struct (build): construction, indestructible, instruct

tele (far): telecast, telegram, telegraph, telephone, telescope, telethon, television

terr (land): terrace, terrain, terrarium, territory

tract (pull, drag): attraction, subtract, tractor

vict/vinc (conquer): convince, convict, evict, victor, victory

vis (see): television, visa, vision, visual

viv/vit (live): survive vitamin, vivid

volv (roll): involve, revolutionary, revolver

Figure 13–5   Root Words

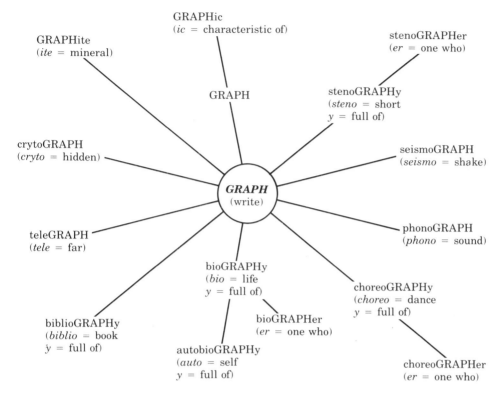

Figure 13–6 A Cluster for the Root Word *Graph*

one part of speech to another will help them express themselves in writing. The reason we learn to spell words, after all, is to express ourselves and to communicate with others through writing.

Spelling Rules

Because so many words have been borrowed from other languages, most spelling rules have exceptions. The classic long vowel rule, "when two vowels go walking, the first one does the talking," has been found to be regular only 14% of the time (Grief, 1981). Some of the commonly used exceptions are *said, air,* and *head*. However, some rules are regular, and only those rules that apply to a majority of words and have few exceptions should be taught to students. Ernest Horn (1960) lists six types of rules that are regular enough to be of use to students: (a) rules for adding suffixes, (b) that letter *q* is followed by *u,* (c) that words do not end in *v,* (d) that proper nouns and most adjectives formed from them begin with a capital letter, (e) rules for using periods in abbreviations, (f) rules for using an apostrophe in possessives and in contractions. As students become aware of the regularities that exist in our spelling system, they can learn these rules and apply them in their

Prefixes

a/an- (not): atheist, anaerobic
amphi- (both): amphibian
anti- (against): antiseptic
bi- (two, twice): bifocal, biannual
contra- (against): contradict
de- (away): detract
di- (two): dioxide
ex- (out): export
hemi (half): hemisphere
il-/im-/in-/ir- (not): illegible, impolite, inexpensive, irrational
in- (in, into): include
inter- (between): intermission
kilo-/milli- (one thousand): kilometer, milligram
micro- (small): microfilm
mis- (wrong): mistake
mono- (one): monarch
multi- (many): multimillionaire
omni- (all): omnivorous
poly- (many): polygon
post- (after): postwar
pre-/pro- (before): precede, prologue
quad-/quart- (four): quadruple, quarter
re- (again): repay
retro- (back): retroactive
sol- (alone): solitary
sub- (under): submarine
super- (above): supermarket
trans- (across): transport
tri- (three): triangle
un- (not): unhappy

Suffixes

-able/-ible (worthy of, can be): lovable, audible
-ance/-ence (state or quality): annoyance, absence
-ant (one who): servant
-ard (one who is): coward
-ary/-ory (person, place): secretary, laboratory
-dom (state or quality): freedom
-ee (one who is): trustee
-er/-or/-ar (one who): teacher, actor, liar
-er/-or (action): robber
-ern (direction): northern
-et/-ette (small): booklet, dinette
-ful (full of): hopeful
-hood (state or quality): childhood
-ic (characterized by): angelic
-icle/-ucle (small): particle, molecule
-ify (to make): simplify
-ish (like): reddish
-ism (doctrine of): communism
-less (without): hopeless
-ling (young): duckling
-logy (the study of): zoology
-ly (in the manner of): slowly
-ment (state or quality): enjoyment
-ness (state or quality): kindness
-ship (state or, art or skill): friendship, seamanship
-sion/-tion (state or quality): tension, attraction
-ster (one who): gangster
-ure (state or quality): failure
-ward (direction): homeward
-y (full of): sleepy

Figure 13–7 A List of Affixes

spelling. A list of spelling rules with few exceptions is presented in Figure 13–8. Have students verify the usefulness of each rule by making a list of words from their reading and writing that follows the rule as well as any exceptions they find.

POINTS TO PONDER

Why Is English Spelling More Consistent than Phoneme-Grapheme Correspondences Indicate? ·

What Are the Stages of Invented Spelling that Children Move Through as They Learn to Spell?

Why Is Spelling a Tool for Writers?

What Is Contract Spelling?

How Do Students Develop a Spelling Conscience?

EMERGING PRACTICES

Transformational linguists (e.g., Noam Chomsky, 1965; Chomsky & Halle, 1968) began several decades ago to take a more careful look at the role phonology plays in the orthographic system. They found that morphological aspects of English orthography indicate a greater regularity in the spelling system than might otherwise be expected if the phoneme-grapheme correspondences were considered alone. Certain nonphonetic aspects in the orthographic system pertain to a deeper level of representation that considers the lexical (morpheme or word) nature of the orthography. The lexical relations are those that would be identified if you were attempting to write a dictionary that represented all the grammatical information about each word or lexical item (e.g., *major-majority*). One of the problems you would face would be to determine the spelling of the entry word and its phonological, syntactic, and semantic relationships to the grammar and orthography.

The emerging practices in spelling are based on a combination of the research on the lexical nature of the orthography, on the invented spellings children create, and on the manner in which children proceed developmentally from invented spellings to correct spellings.

Lexical Spelling

English spelling is often considered to be irregular, if not chaotic, when considered on the basis of phoneme-grapheme correspondences alone. Transformational linguists have found that English orthography's regularity is not at the phonological level, but at a deeper, lexical base level. Tying the spelling system too closely to the pronunciation of English words raises some problems because pronunciation shifts occur in English words when suffixes are added to them (C. Chomsky, 1970). For each suffix added and for each pronunciation shift that occurs, a new word is created and a new spelling of the derived word would be necessary if spellings

Figure 13–8   Spelling Rules with Few Exceptions

1. Some rules governing the addition of suffixes and inflected endings include the following:

   a. Words ending in silent *e* drop the *e* when adding a suffix or ending beginning with a vowel and keep the *e* when adding a suffix or ending beginning with a consonant.

bake	manage
baking	managing
baker	management

   b. When a root word ends in *y* preceded by a consonant, the *y* is changed to *i* in adding suffixes and endings unless the ending or suffix begins with *i*.

fly	study
flies	studying
flying	studious
	studies

   c. When a root word ends in *y* preceded by a vowel, the root word is not changed when adding suffixes or endings.

play	monkey
playful	monkeys

   d. When a one-syllable word ends in a consonant with one vowel before it, the consonant is doubled before adding a suffix or ending beginning with a vowel.

run	ship
running	shipping
	shipment

   e. In words of more than one syllable, the final consonant is doubled before adding a suffix or ending if (a) the last syllable is accented, (b) the last syllable ends in a consonant with one vowel before it, and (c) the suffix or ending begins with a vowel.

begin	admit
beginning	admittance

were created solely on the basis of the phoneme-grapheme correspondences. For example, the word pairs *nation-national* and *sane-sanity* illustrate the shift from the long vowel sound /ey/ to /ae/. If you were to spell by pronunciation, the shift in the vowel sound would signal a change in spelling. Thus, one lexical entry or spelling would be created for *nation* and another lexical spelling for *national.* Shifts in

Figure 13–8 *Continued*

2. The letter *q* is always followed by *u* in common English words.

   queen quequiet

3. No English words end in *v*.

   love glove

4. Proper nouns and most adjectives formed from proper nouns should begin with capital letters.

   America American

5. Most abbreviations end with a period.

   etc. Nov.

6. The apostrophe is used to show the omission of letters in contractions.

   don't haven't

7. The apostrophe is used to indicate the possessive form of nouns but not pronouns.

   boy's its
   dog's theirs

8. When adding *s* to words to form plurals or to change the tense of verbs, *es* must be added to words ending with the hissing sounds (*x, s, sh, ch*).

   glass watch
   glasses watches

9. When *s* is added to words ending in a single *f,* the *f* is changed to *v* and *es* is added.

   half shelf
   halves shelves

10. When *ei* or *ie* are to be used, *i* usually comes before *e* except after *c* or when sounded like *a*. (Note these exceptions: leisure, neither, seize, and weird.)

    believe neighbor
    relieve weigh

Allred, 1977, pp. 27–28.

vowel sounds would result in many new entry words and would mask the underlying lexical relationships that exist between the word pairs.

Vowel alternations are common in English. The same principles that govern the /ey/ to /ae/ alternation also govern other vowel alternations such as the /iy/ to /e/ shift in *extreme-extremity* and the /ay/ to /i/ alternation in *wide-width*. These and other examples of vowel alternations are listed in Figure 13–9. We recognize that these pairs, though phonemically different, are variant forms of the same word. If the dictionary had just one spelling, a lexical spelling, the vowel and pronunciation shifts would be the result of rules of pronunciation. The lexical spelling, therefore, operates at a deeper level than the surface level phoneme-grapheme correspondences.

Other surface phonemic variations are better represented by phonological rules. These rules operate on lexical spellings. The lexical spelling is able to present an underlying relationship in words that a phonemic representation would fail to capture. English has a number of consonant alternations, such as the /k/ to /s/ shift in *medicate-medicine,* which are not expressed in the lexical spelling. A list of consonant alternations is presented in Figure 13–10. As you examine this list, note the influence of the vowels in the affixes on the consonants nearest to them. For example, in the *medicate-medicine* example, the shift from *a* to *i* in the suffixes, results in the /k/ to /s/ consonant alternation.

Carol Chomsky (1970) makes the point "that the orthography bears an *indirect* rather than a direct relation to pronunciation. The direct correlation is to lexical spelling, a level of linguistic processing that is beneath the surface, related to

Figure 13–9   Vowel Alternations

Alternations	*Sample Word Pairs*
/ey/→/ae/	courageous-courage
	explain-explanation
	major-majority
	nation-national
	nature-natural
	sane-sanity
/iy/→/e/	convene-convention
	extreme-extremity
	precede-precedent
/ay/→/i/	expedite-expeditious
	preside-president
	revise-revision
	sign-signature
	wide-width
/ow/→/a/	compose-composition
	democratic-democracy
	phone-phonic
	photograph-photography

C. Chomsky, 1970.

Figure 13–10 Consonant Alternations

Alternations	Sample Word Pairs
/k/→/s/	medicate-medicine
	critical-criticize
	romantic-romanticize
v	
/g/→/j/	sagacity-sage
	prodigal-prodigious
v	
/d/→/j/	grade-gradual
	mode-modular
v	
/t/→/s/	resident-residential
	expedite-expeditious
v	
/t/→/ts/	fact-factual
	quest-question
	right-righteous
v	
/z/→/z/	revise-revision
/s/→/z/	sign-resign
	gymnastics-gymnasium

C. Chomsky, 1970.

pronunciation by regular phonological rules that are part of the child's normal linguistic equipment" (p. 298). An example of this dependence can be observed in the addition of suffixes to root words. The root *cour-* needs to have a suffix such as *-age* or *-ageous* added before the pronunciation can be determined.

Students need to be aware of the spelling of words with close phoneme-grapheme correspondences and those that are systematic in terms of lexical spellings with vowel and consonant alternations. As students examine the relations that exist among words according to their lexical spellings, they are adding cognitive categories and discovering new relationships among these categories. Teachers can help students realize that spelling is systematic and that many spelling errors can be avoided if they will look for relationships that exist among words.

The suggestion by linguists that the orthography has a lexical base and is more regular than was supposed has helped spelling researchers move beyond the notion that phoneme-grapheme correspondences were the basic unit of study in spelling. The view that words, not phoneme-grapheme correspondences, are the appropriate unit of analysis for studying the orthography helped them to realize that "*both* phonological and morphological relationships play fundamental roles in establishing the spelling patterns within words" (Hodges, 1982, p. 286).

Invented Spelling

Charles Read (1971, 1975) studied preschoolers' efforts to spell words and found that they used their knowledge of phonology to invent spellings for words. These children used letter names to spell words such as U (*you*), ME (*me*), and R (*are*), and they used consonant sounds rather consistently: GRL, (*girl*), TIGR (*tiger*), and NIT (*night*). The preschoolers used several unusual but phonetically based spelling patterns to represent affricates. They spelled *tr* with *chr* (e.g., CHRIBLES for *troubles*), spelled *dr* with *jr* (e.g., JRAGIN for *dragon*), and substituted *d* for *t* (e.g., PREDE for *pretty*). Words with long vowels were spelled using letter names: MI (*my*), LADE (*lady*), and FEL (*feel*). The children used several ingenious strategies to spell words with short vowels. These 3-, 4-, and 5-year-olds rather consistently selected letters to represent short vowels on the basis of place of articulation in the mouth. Short *i* was represented with *e* as in FES (*fish*), short *e* with *a* as in LAFFT (*left*), and short *o* with *i* as in CLIK (*clock*). While these spellings may seem odd to adults, they are based on phonetic relationships. The children often omitted nasals within words (e.g., ED for *end*) and substituted *-eg* or *-ig* for *-ing* (e.g., CUMIG for *coming* and GOWEG for *going*). Also, they often ignored the vowel in unaccented syllables as illustrated in AFTR (*after*) and MUTHR (*mother*).

These children had clearly developed some strategies for their spellings based on their knowledge of the phonological system, their knowledge of letter names, their judgments of phonetic similarities and differences, and their ability to abstract phonetic information from letter names. Read suggested that from among the many phonetic properties in the phonological system, children abstract away certain phonetic details and preserve other phonetic details in their invented spellings.

Based on Charles Read's seminal work, other researchers began to systematically study the development of children's spelling abilities. Henderson and his colleagues (Beers & Henderson, 1977; Gentry, 1978, 1981; Templeton, 1979; Zutell, 1979) have studied the manner in which children proceed developmentally from invented spelling to correct spelling. The chart in Figure 13–11 on pages 422–423 illustrates the developmental patterns of first through fourth graders' spelling of short vowels, long vowels, past tense markers, consonant doubling, and vowel alternations. This research puts spelling into a developmental framework that is more closely akin to the pyscholinguistic view of language learning, which stresses that students construct their own knowledge of language systems, including the orthographic system.

Stages of Invented Spelling

Researchers have found that while all children do not invent spellings in exactly the same way, or at the same speed, they do develop spelling strategies in roughly the same sequence (Henderson, 1980a). The five stages that children move through on their way to becoming conventional spellers are (a) precommunicative spelling, (b) semiphonetic spelling, (c) phonetic spelling, (d) transitional spelling, and (e) correct spelling (Gentry, 1978, 1981, 1982a, 1982b). Each of the five stages will be discussed in the following paragraphs, and examples of three words spelled at each of the stages of invented spelling are presented in Figure 13–12 on page 424.

Stage 1: Precommunicative Spelling. In this stage, children string scribbles, letters, and letter-like forms together but they do not associate the marks they make with any specific phonemes. Precommunicative spelling represents children's natural, early expression of the alphabet and other concepts about writing. They may write from left-to-right, right-to-left, top-to-bottom, or randomly across the page. Some precommunicative spellers have a large repertoire of letter forms to use in writing while others repeat a small number of letters over and over. Children may use both upper and lower case letters, but they show a distinct preference for upper case letters. At this stage, children have not discovered how spelling works or the alphabetic principle that letters represent sounds in words. This stage is typical of preschoolers, ages 3–5.

Stage 2: Semiphonetic Spelling. At this stage, children begin to represent phonemes in words with letters, indicating that they have a rudimentary understanding of the alphabetic principle, that a link exists between letters and sounds. The spellings are very abbreviated, and children use only one, two, or three letters to represent an entire word. Examples of stage two spelling include: DA (*day*), KLZ (*closed*), and SM (*swimming*). As these examples illustrate, semiphonetic spellers use a letter-name strategy to determine which letters to use in spelling a word, and their spellings represent some sound features of words while ignoring other equally important features. Semiphonetic spellers include 5- and 6-year-old children.

Stage 3: Phonetic Spelling. In this third stage, children's understanding of the alphabetic principle is further refined. They continue to use letter names to represent sounds but they also use consonant and vowels sounds at this stage. Examples of stage three spelling include: LIV (*live*), DRAS (*dress*), and PEKT (*peeked*). As these examples show, children choose letters on the basis of sound alone without considering acceptable English letter sequences (e.g., using -*t* rather than -*ed* as a past tense marker in *peeked*) or other spelling conventions. These spellings do not resemble English words, and although spelling does not look like adult spelling, it can be deciphered. The major achievement of this stage is that for the first time children represent *all* essential sound features in the words being spelled. Henderson (1980b) explains that words are "bewilderingly homographic" at this stage because children spell on the basis of sound alone. For example, *bat, bet,* and *bait* might all be spelled BAT at this stage (Read, 1971). Phonetic spellers are typically 6-year-old children.

Stage 4: Transitional Spelling. Transitional spellers come close to the correct spellings of English words. They spell many words correctly, but words with irreg-

Figure 13–11   Developmental Patterns for Five Categories of
Spelling Knowledge

Category	Strategy	Score	Examples of Children's Spellings
Short Vowel	unclassifiable	0	krof (craft), scod (skid)
	vowel omitted	1	krft, scd
	closest tense vowel	2	crift, sced
	transitional	3	creft, scad
	vowel correct, incorrect form	4	kraf, scid
	correct form	5	craft, skid
Long Vowel	unclassifiable	0	crop (creep), slom (slime)
	letter-name	1	crep, slim
	transitional	2	crip, slam
	vowel correct, marking incorrect	3	creyp, sliym
	vowel correctly marked, incorrect form	4	creap, sime
	correct form	5	creep, slime
Past Tense	unclassifiable	0	rake (raked), cet (cheated)
	letter-name	1	rakt, chetd
	d-marker	2	rakd, cheatd
	vowel (not e, not o) + d	3	racid, cheatud

ular spellings continue to be misspelled. Examples of stage four spelling include
HUOSE (*house*), TRUBAL (*trouble*), EAGUL (*eagle*), and AFTERNEWN (*afternoon*).
This stage is characterized by children's increased ability to represent the features
of English orthography. First, they include a vowel in every syllable as the *trouble*
and *eagle* spellings show. Next, they demonstrate knowledge of vowel patterns
even though they might make a faulty decision about which marker to use. For example, *toad* is often spelled TODE when children choose the wrong vowel marker
or TAOD when the two vowels are reversed. Also, transitional spellers use com-

Figure 13–11 *Continued*

Category	Strategy	Score	Examples of Children's Spellings
	marker correct, incorrect form	4	raced, cheeted
	correct form	5	raked, cheated
Consonant Doubling	unclassifiable	0	flop (flopped), wad (wading)
	letter-name	1	flpt, wadn
	lax, undoubled	2	floped
	tense, doubled	3	wadding
	doubling correct, incorrect form	4	floppid, weding
	correct form	5	flopped, wading
Derivational Pairs	unclassifiable	0	xpln-xplntn (explain-explanation)
	letter-name	1	xplan-xplnashon
	vowel present, unextended	2	explain-explinashon
	vowel incorrectly extended	3	explain-explaination
	vowel correctly extended, incorrect form	4	explain-xplanashon
	correct form	5	explain-explanation

Zutell, 1979, p. 72.

mon letter patterns in their spelling such as YOUNIGHTED for *united* and HIGHCKED for *hiked*. In this stage, children use conventional alternatives for representing sounds, and although they continue to misspell words according to adult standards, transitional spelling resembles English orthography and can easily be read. As examples presented above show, children stop relying entirely on phonological information and begin to use visual clues and morphological information as well. Transitional spellers generally include 7- and 8-year-old children.

Figure 13–12   Examples of Invented Words
at Each Stage of Invented Spelling

Precommunicative Stage	btBpa	iBALI	LYilAWO	IDMitL
Semiphonetic Stage	MTR	BTM	BD	U
Phonetic Stage	MOSTR	BOTM	BRD	UNITID
Transitional Stage	MONSTUR	BODUM	BRID	YOUNIGHTED
Correct	MONSTER	BOTTOM	BIRD	UNITED

Gentry, 1982b.

Stage 5: Correct Spelling.   As the name implies, children spell many, many words correctly at this stage. However, this is not to suggest that they spell all words correctly. Children have mastered the basic principles of English orthography, and this achievement indicates that children are ready for formal spelling instruction (Gentry, 1981; 1982a). Children typically reach stage 5 and are ready for formal spelling instruction by age 8 or 9. During the next four or five years, children learn to control homonyms (e.g., *road-rode*), contractions, consonant doubling and adding affixes (e.g., *runing/running*), and vowel and consonant alternations. And, they learn to spell most common irregularly spelled words. Spellers also learn about spelling alternatives—different ways to spell the same sound.

Researchers have not yet thoroughly studied children's spelling development beyond age 8. With additional research, it seems reasonable that several additional stages will be added after this stage to more accurately describe children's spelling development through eighth grade. The characteristics of each of the five stages of invented spelling are summarized in Figure 13–13.

In a short period of three or four years, young children move from precommunicative spelling to correct spelling, and this learning happens informally rather than through direct instruction. When formal spelling instruction begins before children have reached the fifth stage, their natural development is interrupted. Typically, children are advised to sound-out words or to memorize the spelling of words during spelling instruction. Sounding-out is a stage children naturally progress through in the developmental sequence. If instruction interrupts their progress at that point, they are less likely to generalize the morphemic component of spelling. Similarly, the fourth and fifth stages are cut short when children memorize words.

Figure 13–13   Characteristics of the Invented Spelling Stages

Stage 1: Precommunicative Spelling

Child uses scribbles, letter-like forms, letters, and sometimes numbers to represent a message.

Child may write from left-to-right, right-to-left, top-to-bottom, or randomly on the page.

Child shows no understanding of phoneme-grapheme correspondences.

Child may repeat a few letters again and again or use most of the letters of the alphabet.

Child frequently mixes upper and lower case letters but shows a preference for upper case letters.

Stage 2: Semiphonetic Spelling

Child becomes aware of the alphabetic principle, that letters are used to represent sounds.

Child uses abbreviated one, two, or three letter spelling to represent an entire word.

Child uses letter-name strategy to spell words.

Stage 3: Phonetic Spelling

Child represents all essential sound features of a word in spelling.

Child develops particular spellings for long and short vowels, plural and past tense markers, and other aspects of spelling.

Child chooses letters on the basis of sound without regard for English letter sequences or other conventions.

Stage 4: Transitional Spelling

Child adheres to basic conventions of English orthography.

Child begins to use morphological and visual information in addition to phonetic information.

Child may include all appropriate letters in a word but reverse some of them.

Child uses alternate spellings for the same sound in different words, but only partially understands the conditions governing their use.

Child uses a high percentage of correctly spelled words.

Stage 5: Correct Spelling

Child applies the basic rules of the English orthographic system.

Child extends knowledge of word structure including the spelling of affixes, contractions, compound words, and homonyms.

Child demonstrates growing accuracy in using silent consonants and doubling consonants before adding suffixes.

Child recognizes when a word doesn't "look right" and can consider alternate spellings for the same sound.

Child learns irregular spelling patterns.

Child learns consonant and vowel alternations and other morphological structures.

Child knows how to spell a large number of words.

Adapted from Gentry, 1982, pp. 192–200.

Moving through these stages is dependent on immersion in a written language environment with daily opportunities to read and write. Also, teachers should de-emphasize standard spelling during this period and be tolerant of children's invented spelling, even celebrating students' nonstandard spellings. Teachers can use these "mistakes" to identify the stage of invented spelling the child is in and to determine when the child has reached stage 5 and is ready for formal spelling instruction.

Word Sorting.   A useful technique for examining students' developing awareness of spelling is *word sorting* (Gillet & Kita, 1980). In this technique, students sort or categorize a set of word cards using their knowledge of phoneme-grapheme correspondences, spelling patterns, root words and affixes, consonant and vowel alternations, and so on. Depending on their stage of development, students will focus on different features as they categorize the word cards. Some students, for example, might focus on beginning letters of words or vowel patterns while other students might use suffixes or consonant or vowel alternations in categorizing the word cards. This technique not only expands students' understanding of spelling, but it is a valuable diagnostic tool. By observing students as they sort the cards, teachers can note the types of categories students use and the features they consider most important in grouping words together. Through this exercise, teachers can collect important information about students' knowledge of spelling and their stage of spelling development.

Spelling Instruction

These emerging practices suggest that spelling is best learned through writing and that students' spelling programs should be individualized so that they can learn to spell the words they need for their writing. Spelling is viewed as a tool for writers and as a part of the editing stage of the writing process. Words that students study should come from their writing, and an individualized approach known as contract spelling can be used for spelling instruction. Also, the research on lexical spelling and children's invented spelling suggests two additional components of a spelling program: (a) developing a spelling conscience and (b) learning to use a dictionary to locate unknown words.

Learning to Spell by Writing

Spelling is a writer's tool, and it is best learned through writing. Students who write daily and are encouraged in kindergarten and first grade to use invented spellings will move naturally toward correct spelling. As they begin to write, young children guess at how words are spelled using their knowledge of letter names and sounds. Through reading and writing, they gradually recognize that the words they are reading and writing are spelled the same way each time. When students recognize that words have consistent spellings, they are ready to be helped in a direct way. Teachers can then begin to point out the conventions of the spelling system.

As they write, primary grade students write commonly used words over and over, providing the necessary practice to master these words. They also invent spellings for unknown words, and through this cognitive, problem-solving process, students advance through the stages of invented spelling.

Emphasis on correct spelling, like handwriting and other mechanics, belongs in the editing stage of the writing process. As children write and revise their rough drafts, they should be encouraged at all grade levels to not worry about correct spelling and to use invented spelling as needed. Stopping to ask a classmate or the teacher how to spell a word or going to check the correct spelling of a word in a dictionary while pouring out ideas in a rough draft interrupts the writer's train of thought. Through the process approach, children recognize spelling for what it is—a courtesy to the reader. As they write, revise, edit, and share their writing with genuine audiences, students will begin to learn that they need to spell correctly so that their audience will be able to read their compositions.

It is important to underscore that students' invented spellings are not errors. Rather, they represent developmental trends in students' knowledge about English orthography. Treating invented spellings as errors sends a false message to students about the importance of mechanics in writing and discourages them from attempting to develop reasonable spelling options. Often students become very dependent on the teacher or on classmates to spell words for them when they feel that correctness in spelling is of primary importance. Students will quit taking risks if their efforts are treated as being wrong. Rather, they should be encouraged to invent spellings as necessary during the drafting and revising stages and then move toward correct spelling as they edit and prepare to publish their writing.

Moving to a writing base for spelling means that you will give up the spelling period and textbook. Predetermined lists of words will be eliminated. Spelling will be taught as part of the ongoing process of learning to write. Spelling will be included as one of the mechanics of writing and will be taught individually as part of the editing stage of the writing process. All students will not be working on the same words at the same time; instead they will be working on the words they are using in their writing but at the moment cannot spell.

Teachers need to learn about the phonology and morphology of English so that they can help students understand how words are structured. Students need help to recognize that when they write and pronounce words, they pay more attention to some letters than to others. They need to recognize and listen for the letters they are ignoring in the words they are writing. Students will need to know how derivational affixes (e.g., *re-, -ly*) and inflectional endings (e.g., *-s, -ed*) affect words and the way the words are spelled. It will also be helpful for them to understand how vowel and consonant alternation affect the pronunciation and spelling of words. They should also begin to understand that our spelling system is essentially based on word meanings rather than on phoneme-grapheme correspondences.

Students may have trouble with words having the schwa sound /ə/ (such as *circus, gallop,* and *pollen*). It occurs in unaccented syllables and is represented by all vowels. Have students pay special attention to the letters used to represent the schwa sound in words they continue to misspell.

Faulty pronunciation and poor handwriting are two other causes of spelling problems. Ask students to pronounce words they habitually misspell to see if pronunciation or dialect differences may be contributing to spelling problems. Students need to recognize when pronunciation does not always predict spelling. Students in some parts of the United States pronounce the words *pin* and *pen* as though they were spelled with the same vowel. Also, we pronounce *better* as though it were spelled *bedder* and *going* as though it were spelled *goin'*. Ask students to spell words orally that they spell incorrectly in their writing to see whether or not handwriting difficulties are contributing to spelling problems. Sometimes a handwriting lesson on how to connect two cursive letters (e.g., *br*) or a reminder about the importance of legible handwriting will solve the problem.

The Role of Reading

Reading plays an enormous role in the progress students make in passing through the developmental stages of spelling. As students learn to read, they store the words that they can recall on sight. This ability to recall how words look aids students in deciding when a spelling is or is not correct. If a word does not look right, they must check the spelling. Students have two choices when they decide that a word does not look right: They can rewrite the word in several different ways until it does look right, or they can ask the teacher or a classmate who knows the spelling.

Spelling ability seems to develop in much the same manner that oral language develops. Much of what is learned is learned incidentally, in the context of doing something. It is becoming apparent that many, if not most of the words students will learn to spell are learned incidentally through reading and writing. Learning to read establishes a memory bank of how words look; writing establishes a memory bank of how words are spelled. The brain ensures that every time we see a word when reading or writing, we do not have to figure it out again. Teachers capitalize on incidental spelling learning by providing daily opportunities for both reading and writing.

Contract Spelling

Contract spelling offers an alternative to the textbook approach. In contrast to spelling book programs, contract spelling is tied to students' writing and their spelling needs. Teachers often complain that their students cannot spell the words they need when writing stories, reports, letters, and other compositions. Even the students who spell all or nearly all the words correctly on weekly spelling tests often do not transfer this learning to other spelling situations. Through contract spelling, students learn to spell the words they use in their writing, and because they are using these words in their writing, they remember how to spell them more easily.

In contract spelling, students develop a contract with the teacher to learn specific words during the week. Having a voice in determining the words they will study is more motivating for students because they can see the relevance of what

*Reading plays an enormous role in the progress
students make in learning to spell.*

they are asked to learn. Contract spelling places more responsibility on students for their own learning, and when students have responsibility, they tend to perform better.

Developing the Word List.   Contract spelling begins with the development of a weekly word list from which teachers and their students select the words to be learned. The words for this master list are drawn from all the words needed by students in their writing activities during the previous week. One way to accumulate words for the word list is for students to keep a slip of paper taped on their desks, and for teachers to record the words students need help with on the slips of paper. Or, teachers can write the needed words on slips of paper, which students return to a box on the teacher's desk after they are used. If a spelling textbook is used, the week's word list can also be added to this master word list. This list may include 30, 40, or even 50 words for middle and upper grade students.

The master word list can also provide an opportunity to point out aspects of the orthography. Students can look for phoneme-grapheme correspondences and develop lists of words to discover which letters are used most frequently to represent each phoneme and whether the letters are in initial, medial, or final position in the words. Students can also examine inflectional endings and the rules that operate on them as these words occur in the sentences students read and write. In addition, students can check for applications of the spelling rules with few exceptions in these words.

Pretest.   The master list of words is used as the pretest. This test is administered at the beginning of the week, and the results of the pretest will be used in developing each student's spelling contract for the week. After students have corrected their own pretests, distribute the "Spelling Contract and Word List" form that is shown in Figure 13–14. This form contains the master list of words and is used for the individual contracts teachers and students will develop. Students circle the words they spelled correctly on the pretest and transfer this information to the word list by circling the number of each word they spelled correctly. Then they draw a box around the number of each word they plan to learn that week. By including the word list and spelling contract on the same form, students have less trouble keeping track of their work.

The master word list used for the pretest will include words at several levels of difficulty because of the differing spelling needs of the students. Because of the range of words included on the master word list, students will be able to select words at their own level for their spelling contracts. They will need to experiment to determine the appropriate difficulty level for them and the number of words they can learn each week. Good spellers will be able to learn both more difficult words and a greater number of words each week than poor spellers will. For some students, learning 5 words each week will be an achievement while other students may be able to learn 10, 20, or more words.

Developing the Spelling Contract.   Students negotiate with the teacher for the number of words they believe they can learn in one week. This number includes the words they spelled correctly plus an additional number of words they misspelled on the pretest that they think they can learn. Through these negotiations, students learn to be realistic about their spelling ability.

Word Study.   Students select the methods they will use to study their spelling words during the contract negotiations. Students should try auditory, visual, kinesthetic, and integrated strategies to learn which method works best for them. Prepare a chart describing the steps in each of the word study procedures students may use. An example of an integrated approach was presented in Figure 13–1. On the back of the "Spelling Contract and Word List" form, students can record the study methods agreed upon for that week. After the final test on Friday, they can judge how well the method worked for them and make a note on the back of the form. After several weeks, students should try to decide which method is most effective for them.

Weekly Final Test.   A final test is administered at the end of the week on the words that the students have contracted to learn. The teacher reads the master list

Figure 13–14   Spelling Contract and Word List

Name: _____

Week: _____

SPELLING CONTRACT

Number of words spelled correctly on the pretest: _____

Number of words to be learned: _____

Total number of words contracted: _____

1.* _____		16. _____
2. _____		17. _____
3. _____		18. _____
4. _____		19. _____
5. _____		20. _____
6. _____		21. _____
... _____		... _____
15. _____		30. _____

Instructions

1. Circle the number of each word you spelled correctly on the pretest.
2. Draw a box around the number of each word you plan to learn. Use a pencil so that you can make changes if necessary.

*The teacher writes the master list on these lines before the form is duplicated.

of words, and students write only those words they have contracted to learn. To make it easier to administer the test, have students list the numbers of the words they have contracted to spell on their spelling test papers in advance of the test. They can locate the numbers of their contracted spelling words on their "Spelling Contract and Word List" forms. In this way, students are reminded which words they have contracted to learn.

The final test scores can be recorded on "Spelling Contract Record" forms to determine whether students have met their contracts. This information is used to negotiate the new contract for the following week. On the next contract, students may change the number of words or their study methods. A sample of the "Spelling Contract Record" is presented in Figure 13–15.

Name: _____

SPELLING CONTRACT RECORD

Week	Words Correct on Pretest	Words to Learn	Words Contracted	Study Methods			Final Test Score
				T	W	TH	
Oct. 14	5	5	10	A	C	A	9
Oct. 21	6	4	10	A	B	C	10

Figure 13–15   Spelling Contract Record

Developing a Spelling Conscience

Spelling involves more than just learning to spell specific words, whether they are drawn from children's writing or from words listed in spelling textbooks. Robert Hillerich (1977) believes that students need to develop a *spelling conscience,* or a positive attitude toward spelling and a concern for using standard spelling. He lists two dimensions of a spelling conscience: (a) understanding that standard spelling is a courtesy to readers, and (b) developing the ability to proofread to spot and correct misspellings.

Using standard spelling is a courtesy to readers. Students in the middle and upper grades need to learn that it is unrealistic to expect readers to try to decipher numerous misspelled words as they read a piece of writing. This first dimension develops as students write frequently and for varied audiences. By writing for a variety of audiences, students acquire a concept of audience and realize that there are readers who will read their writing. As students move from writing for self to writing that communicates, they internalize this concept. Teachers help students to recognize the purpose of standard spelling by providing meaningful writing activities directed to a variety of genuine audiences.

The second dimension, proofreading for spelling errors, is an essential part of the writing process. As discussed in Chapter 6, proofreading is part of the editing stage, and it should be introduced in kindergarten and first grade rather than post-poning it until the middle grades. Young children and their teachers can proofread class collaboration and dictated stories together, and students can be encouraged to read over their own compositions and make necessary corrections as soon as they begin writing. With this beginning, students will accept proofreading as a nat-ural part of both spelling and writing, and together with their growing awareness of audience, students will appreciate the importance of proofreading to correct misspellings and other mechanical errors.

Learning to Use a Dictionary

Students need to learn to locate the spellings for unknown words in the dictionary. Approximately 450,000 entry words are included in unabridged dictionaries, and students typically learn to spell about 3,000 of these words by the end of eighth grade. Subtracting 3,000 from 450,000 leaves 447,000 words unaccounted for! Obviously, students will need to learn how to locate the spellings for many of these additional words. While it is relatively easy to find a "known" word in the dictionary, it is much harder to locate an unfamiliar word, and students need to learn what to do when they do not know how to spell a word. They can consider spelling options and predict possible spellings for the unknown words and then check their predicted spellings by consulting a dictionary. This strategy involves six steps:

1. Identify root words and affixes.
2. Consider related words (e.g., medicine-medical).
3. Determine the sounds in the word.
4. Generate a list of spelling options.
5. Select the most likely alternatives.
6. Consult a dictionary to check the correct spelling.

The fourth step is undoubtedly the most difficult one in the strategy. Using both knowledge of phonology and morphology, students develop a list of possible spellings. For some words, phoneme-grapheme relationships may rate primary consideration in generating spelling options, while for other words root words and affixes or related words may be more important in determining how the word is spelled.

Evaluating Students' Progress in Spelling

Grades on weekly spelling tests are the traditional measure of students' progress in spelling. Both the textbook spelling and contract spelling approaches provide teachers with a convenient way to evaluate students, based on the number of words spelled correctly on weekly tests. However, this method of evaluating stu-dent progress is somewhat deceptive because the goal of spelling instruction is not simply to spell words correctly on weekly tests but for students to use the words they have spelled correctly on the weekly spelling tests in their writing. Grades on weekly spelling tests are meaningless unless students can use the words in their writing.

Samples of student writing should be collected periodically to determine whether or not the words that students have spelled correctly on weekly spelling tests are being spelled correctly in writing assignments. If students are not applying what they have learned through the weekly spelling instruction in their writing, they may not have learned to spell the words after all. Oftentimes students memorize the words or the spelling pattern for the spelling test but do not really learn to spell the words.

In addition to the grades reflecting students' performance on weekly spelling tests, it is essential that teachers keep anecdotal information and samples of children's writing to monitor their overall progress in learning to spell. Teachers need to examine students' patterns of error and their use of spelling strategies in these samples. Checking to see if students have spelled their spelling words correctly in writing samples provides one type of information while examining students' writing samples for patterns of error and spelling strategies provides an additional type of information. It is important to note that misspelling fewer words does not necessarily indicate progress. To learn to spell, students must experiment with the spellings of unfamiliar words, which will result in spelling errors from time to time. Many times students will misspell a word by misapplying a newly learned spelling pattern. The word *extension* is a good example. Upper grade students begin by spelling the word *extenshun* and then change their spelling to *extention* after they learn the suffix *-tion*. While they are still misspelling the word, students have moved from using sound-symbol correspondences to spell the word to using a spelling pattern. Even though the word is misspelled according to adult standards, students have moved from using a less sophisticated spelling strategy to a more sophisticated one.

Students' behavior as they proofread and edit their compositions also provides evidence of their progress in spelling. They should become increasingly able to spot misspelled words in their compositions and to locate the spelling of unknown words in a dictionary. It is easy for teachers to calculate the number of spelling errors students have identified as they proofread their compositions and to chart students' progress in learning to spot errors. Locating errors is the first step in proofreading and correcting the errors is the second step. It is fairly easy for students to correct the spelling of known words, but for students to correct the spelling errors of unknown words, they must consider spelling options and predict possible spellings before they can locate the words in a dictionary. Teachers can also document students' growth in locating unfamiliar words in a dictionary by observing their behavior as they edit their compositions.

For primary grade students, teachers should collect writing samples to document children's progression through the stages of invented spelling. While young children's invented spelling usually spans two or more stages, it is possible to analyze their writing samples and determine a general stage of development.

Summary

We have discussed some of the current practices in spelling. Most schools use the spelling textbook approach to organize the content and sequence the words to be learned. Characteristics of the textbook approach include study and testing procedures, weekly unit arrangement with daily lessons, lists of spelling words, and an instructional strategy. Exercises dealing with phoneme-grapheme correspondences, morphological considerations, spelling patterns, and dictionary use generally make up the content of the spellers.

We continued with some information on the development of spelling ability. The assumptions that children pass through stages of development are based on the view that the orthography has a lexical base and that invented spellings show that children use phonetic information in spelling before they become adept at conventional spellings. Incidental learning through reading and writing are valuable means of learning the correct spelling of words, and contract spelling is an individualized approach to spelling instruction that allows students to study words that they need to learn for their writing. In addition, students need to develop a spelling conscience and learn to locate unknown words in a dictionary.

Extensions

1. Examine several spelling textbooks at the grade level you teach or expect to teach and evaluate them using the checklist presented in Figure 13–4. How well do the textbooks adhere to the research findings about how spelling should be taught?

2. Observe how spelling is taught in a classroom in which the textbook approach is used and in another class in which contract spelling or another writing-based spelling approach is used. Compare the two approaches. If possible, assist in teaching a lesson in each classroom.

3. Collect samples of young children's writing and analyze their invented spellings. While children's invented spellings often span two or more stages, at what stage of development does each child appear to be? Also, check upper grade students' writing for examples of invented spellings.

4. Interview a middle or upper grade student about spelling. Ask questions such as:

- Who do you know who is a good speller? Why is he/she a good speller?

- Are you a good speller? Why? Why not?

- What do you do when you do not know how to spell a word? What else do you do?

- How would you help a classmate who did not know how to spell a word?

- Are some words harder for you to spell than other words? Which words?

- What rules about how to spell words have you learned?

- Do you think that "sound it out" is a good way to try to figure out the spelling of a word you do not know? Why or why not?

- Do you use a dictionary to look up the spelling of words you do not know how to spell?

- ■ Do you have a list of words to learn to spell each week?

- ■ How do you study these words?

5. Help students proofread their writing and identify possible misspelled words. Watch the strategies that students use to identify and correct misspelled words.

6. Students ask many questions about the seeming inconsistencies of English words and their spellings. For example, primary grade students often ask why there are silent *e*'s. Consult *Answering students' questions about words* by Gail E. Tompkins and David B. Yaden (1986) to find answers to students' questions. Use the answers and activities suggested in the book to prepare and teach a spelling lesson to a small group of students.

References

Allred, R. A. (1977). *Spelling: An application of research findings.* Washington, DC: National Education Association.

Beers, J. W., & Henderson, E. H. (1977). A study of developing orthographic concepts among first graders. *Research in the Teaching of English, 11,* 133–148.

Chomsky, C. (1970). Reading, writing, and phonology. *Harvard Educational Review, 40,* 287–309.

Chomsky, N. (1965). *Aspects of the theory of syntax.* Cambridge, MA: M.I.T. Press.

Chomsky, N., & Halle, M. (1968). *The sound pattern of English.* New York: Harper and Row.

Cook, G. E., Esposito, M., Gabrielson, T., & Turner, G. (1984). *Spelling for word mastery.* Columbus, OH: Merrill.

Dale, E., & O'Rourke, J. (1971). *Techniques of teaching vocabulary.* Palo Alto, CA: Field Educational Publications.

Gentry, J. R. (1978). Early spelling strategies. *Elementary School Journal, 79,* 88–92.

———. (1981). Learning to spell developmentally. *The Reading Teacher, 34,* 378–381.

———. (1982a). An analysis of developmental spellings in *Gnys at wrk. The Reading Teacher, 36,* 192–200.

———. (1982b). Developmental spelling: Assessment. *Diagnostique, 8,* 52–61.

Gentry, J. R., & Henderson, E. H. (1980). Three steps to teaching beginning readers to spell. In E. H. Henderson & J. W. Beers (Eds.), *Developmental and cognitive aspects of learning to spell: A reflection of word knowledge.* Newark, DE: International Reading Association.

Gillet, J. W., & Kita, J. (1980). Words, kids, and categories. In E. H. Henderson & J. W. Beers (Eds.), *Developmental and cognitive aspects of learning to spell: A reflection of word knowledge.* Newark, DE: International Reading Association.

Graves, D. H. (1977). Research update: Spelling texts and structural analysis methods. *Language Arts, 54,* 86–90.

Grief, I. P. (1981). 'When two vowels go walking,' They should get lost. *The Reading Teacher, 34,* 460–461.

Henderson, E. H. (1980a). Developmental concepts of word. In E. H. Henderson & J. W. Beers (Eds.), *Developmental and cognitive aspects of learning to spell: A reflection of word knowledge* (pp. 1–14). Newark, DE: International Reading Association.

———. (1980b). Word knowledge and reading disability. In E. H. Henderson & J. W. Beers (Eds.), *Developmental and cognitive aspects of learning to spell: A reflection of word knowledge* (pp. 138–148). Newark, DE: International Reading Association.

Hillerich, R. L. (1977). Let's teach spelling—Not phonetic misspelling. *Language Arts, 54,* 301–307.

———. (1978). *A writing vocabulary for elementary children.* Springfield, IL: Thomas.

Hodges, R. E. (1982). Research update: On the development of spelling ability. *Language Arts, 59,* 284–290.

Horn, E. (1926). *A basic writing vocabulary.* Iowa City: University of Iowa Press.

————. (1957). Phonetics and spelling. *Elementary School Journal, 57,* 233–235, 246.

————. (1960). Spelling. In C. W. Harris (Ed.), *Encyclopedia of educational research* (3rd ed.) (pp. 1337–1354). New York: Macmillan.

Horn, T. D. (1947). The effect of the corrected test on learning to spell. *Elementary School Journal, 47,* 277–285.

————. (1969). Spelling. In R. L. Ebel (Ed.), *Encyclopedia of educational research* (4th ed.) (pp. 1282–1299). New York: Macmillan.

Johnson, T. D., Langford, K. G., & Quorn, K. C. (1981). Characteristics of an effective spelling program. *Language Arts, 58,* 581–588.

Read, C. (1971). Pre-school children's knowledge of English phonology. *Harvard Educational Review, 41,* 1–34.

————. (1975). *Children's categorization of speech sounds in English* (NCTE Research Report No. 17). Urbana, IL: National Council of Teachers of English.

Templeton, S. (1979). Spelling first, sound later: The relationship between orthography and higher order phonological knowledge in older students. *Research in the Teaching of English, 13,* 255–265.

Tompkins, G. E., & Yaden, D. B. (1986). *Answering students' questions about words.* Urbana, IL: ERIC Clearinghouse on Reading and Communication Skills and National Council of Teachers of English.

Zutell, J. (1979). Spelling strategies of primary school children and their relationship to Pia-get's concept of decentration. *Research in the Teaching of English, 13,* 69–79.

IF YOU WANT TO LEARN MORE

Beers, C. S., & Beers, J. W. (1981). Three Assumptions about learning to spell. *Language Arts, 58,* 573–580.

Bissex, G. L. (1980). *Gnys at wrk: A child learns to read and write.* Cambridge, MA: Harvard University Press.

DiStefano, P. P., & Hagerty, P. J. (1985). Teaching spelling at the elementary level: A realistic perspective. *The Reading Teacher, 38,* 373–377.

Hanna, P. R., Hodges, R. E., & Hanna, J. (1971). *Spelling: Structure and strategies.* Boston: Houghton Mifflin.

Henderson, E. H. (1981). *Learning to read and spell: The child's knowledge of words.* DeKalb, IL: Northern Illinois University Press.

————. (1985). *Teaching spelling.* Boston: Houghton Mifflin.

Henderson, E. H. and J. W. Beers (Eds.). (1980). *Developmental and cognitive aspects of learning to spell: A reflection of word knowledge.* Newark, DE: International Reading Association.

Hillerich, R. L. (1977). Let's teach spelling—Not phonetic misspelling. *Language Arts, 54,* 301–307.

Hodges, R. E. (1981). *Learning to spell* (TRIP Booklet). Urbana, IL: ERIC Clearinghouse on Reading and Communication Skills and the National Council of Teachers of English.

Marino, J. L. (1980). What makes a good speller? *Language Arts, 57,* 173–177.

Temple, C. A., Nathan, R. G., & Burris, N. A. (1982). *The beginnings of writing.* Boston: Allyn and Bacon.

CHAPTER FOURTEEN

Writers' Tools: Handwriting

OVERVIEW.   *In this chapter, we will describe handwriting as a functional, support skill for writing. We will present two traditional forms of handwriting, manuscript and cursive, as well as the innovative D'Nealian handwriting forms. An instructional strategy for teaching handwriting will be presented and the sequence of children's handwriting development is outlined. Lastly, we will identify the special adaptions for teaching left-handed writers.*

Like spelling, handwriting is a functional, support skill for writing. Donald Graves (1983) explains further:

> Children win prizes for fine script, parents and teachers nod approval for a crisp, well-crafted page, a good impression is made on a job application blank . . . all important elements, but they pale next to the *substance* they carry. (p. 171)

It is important to distinguish between *writing* and *handwriting.* Writing is the substance of a composition, while handwriting is the formation of alphabetic symbols on paper. Students need to develop a legible and fluent style of handwriting so that they will be able to fully participate in all written language activities.

Most teachers spend a great deal of time insisting that their students perfect their handwriting until it closely approximates the samples in handwriting textbooks. However, the goal in handwriting instruction is to help students develop legible forms to communicate effectively through writing. The two most important criteria in determining the quality in handwriting are (a) *legibility,* that the writing can be easily and quickly read, and (b) *fluency,* that the writing can be easily and quickly written.

Handwriting is a motor skill, not an art form! It is not particularly important that the letters be artistically formed. Even though a few students take great pleasure in developing flawless handwriting skills, most students feel that handwriting instruction is boring and unnecessary. It is imperative, therefore, to recognize the functional purpose of handwriting and convey the importance of developing legible handwriting to your students. And, writing for genuine audiences is the best way to convey the importance of legibility. A letter sent to a favorite author that is returned by the post office because the address on the envelope is not decipherable, or a child's published, hardcover book that sits unread on the library shelf because the handwriting is illegible makes clear the importance of legibility. Illegible writing means a failure to communicate, a harsh lesson for a writer!

POINTS TO PONDER

What Are the Two Traditional Handwriting Forms That Elementary Students Learn to Use?

How Do the D'Nealian Handwriting Forms Differ from the Traditional Forms?

HANDWRITING FORMS

Two forms of handwriting are currently used in elementary schools, the *manuscript,* or printing, form and the *cursive,* or connected-writing, form. These two forms are illustrated in Figure 14–1. Typically, students in the primary grades learn and use the manuscript form, and students switch to cursive handwriting in the middle grades. The transition to the cursive form usually occurs in second or third grade.

Manuscript Handwriting

Until the 1920s, students learned only cursive handwriting. Marjorie Wise is credited with introducing the manuscript form for primary grade students in 1921 (Hildreth, 1960). Manuscript handwriting is considered to be superior to the cursive form for young children because they seem to lack the fine motor control and eye-hand coordination needed for cursive handwriting. In addition, manuscript handwriting is very similar to the style of type used in primary level reading textbooks. Only two lower case letters, *a* and *g* are different in typed and handwritten forms. The similarity is assumed to facilitate young children's introduction to reading and writing.

Barbe and Milone (1980) suggest several additional reasons why students in the primary grades should learn the manuscript form before the cursive form. First, manuscript handwriting is easier to learn. Studies have shown that young children can copy letters and words written in the manuscript form more easily than when they are written in the cursive form. Also, young children can form the vertical and horizontal lines and circles used in manuscript handwriting more easily than the cursive strokes. Next, they remind us that manuscript handwriting is more legible than cursive handwriting. Because it is more easily read, signs and advertisements are printed in letter-forms closely approximating manuscript handwriting. Lastly, people are often requested to print when completing applications and other forms. For these reasons, manuscript handwriting has become the preferred handwriting form for young children as well as a necessary handwriting skill for older children and adults.

Too often children's use of the manuscript form disappears in the middle grades after they have learned cursive handwriting. It is essential that middle and upper grade teachers learn and use the manuscript form with their students. Manuscript handwriting should remain an option for older students. Second and third graders are learning cursive handwriting, a new handwriting form, just when they are becoming proficient in the manuscript form. It is not surprising, then, that some students want to switch back and forth between the two forms. Frequently the need to develop greater writing speed is given as the reason for the quick transfer to cursive handwriting. However, research has shown that students can write as quickly in manuscript as in the cursive form (Hildreth, 1960).

Criticisms.   There have also been criticisms of the manuscript form. A major complaint is the reversal problem caused by some very similar lower case letters. The letters *b* and *d* are particularly confusing for young children. Other detractors

Figure 14–1 Manuscript and Cursive Handwriting Forms

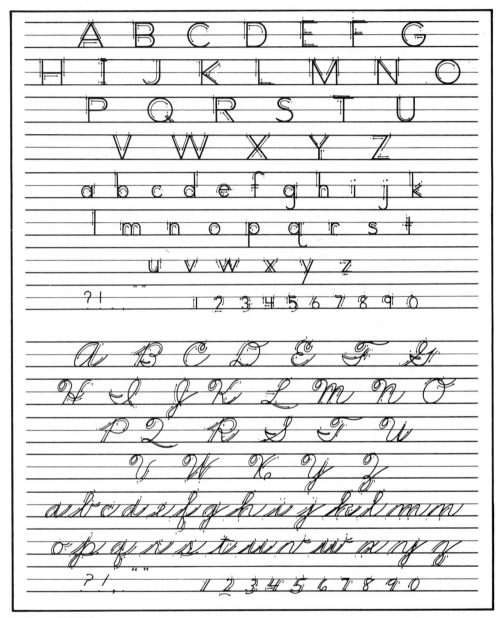

Barbe, et al., 1984.

have argued that using both the manuscript and cursive forms in the elementary grades requires teaching students two totally different handwriting forms within the span of several years. Also, they complain that the "circle and sticks" style of manuscript handwriting requires frequent stops and starts, inhibiting a smooth and rhythmic flow of writing.

D'Nealian Handwriting

A new manuscript and cursive handwriting style, D'Nealian, was developed in 1968 by Donald Neal Thurber, a teacher in Michigan. The D'Nealian handwriting forms are presented in Figure 14–2. In the D'Nealian manuscript form, the letters are slanted and formed with a continuous stroke, and in the D'Nealian cursive form, the letters are simplified, lacking the flourishes of the traditional cursive form. Both forms were designed to increase legibility and fluency and to ease the transition from manuscript to cursive handwriting.

Figure 14–2 D'Nealian Manuscript and Cursive Handwriting Forms

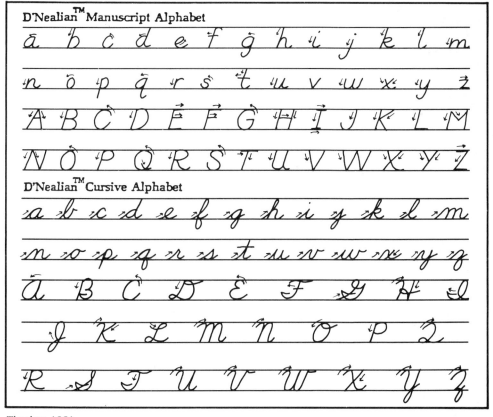

Thurber, 1981.

Thurber's purpose in developing the D'Nealian style was to ameliorate some of the problems associated with the traditional manuscript form (Thurber, 1981). The D'Nealian manuscript form uses the same basic letter forms that students will need for cursive handwriting as well as the slant and rhythm required for the cursive form. Another advantage of the D'Nealian style is that the transition from manuscript to cursive involves adding only connective strokes to most manuscript letters. Only five letters—*f, r, s, v,* and *z*—have a different shape in the cursive form. Figure 14–3 shows the transition from D'Nealian manuscript to cursive handwriting. Research is currently underway to compare the effectiveness of the D'Nealian style with the traditional handwriting forms.

POINTS TO PONDER

What Are the Steps in Teaching Handwriting?

What Types of Authentic Writing Activities Can Be Used to Apply Newly Learned Handwriting Skills?

What Are the Elements of Legibility?

How Do Elementary Students Learn to Diagnose and Correct Their Handwriting Problems?

INSTRUCTIONAL STRATEGY

Handwriting is best taught in separate periods of direct instruction and teacher supervised practice. As soon as skills are taught, they are applied in real-life writing activities. Too often students are required to copy lists of words and sentences from the chalkboard under the guise of handwriting instruction. Such assignments are "busy work" and lack educational significance. Moreover, students may develop poor handwriting habits or learn to form letters incorrectly when they practice without direct supervision. It is much more difficult to correct bad habits and errors in letter formation than to teach handwriting correctly in the first place!

Figure 14–3   Transition to the Cursive Form Using the D'Nealian Style

Thurber, 1981.

The periods of handwriting instruction and practice should be brief. Short 15 to 20 minute periods of instruction several times a week are more effective than a single lengthy period weekly or monthly. Regular periods of handwriting instruction are necessary when first teaching the manuscript form in kindergarten and first grade and the cursive form in second and third grade. In the middle and upper grades, instruction depends on specific handwriting problems that students demonstrate and periodic reviews of both handwriting forms.

The instructional strategy can be used to teach both manuscript and cursive handwriting forms. It is based on the research in the field of handwriting (Askov & Greff, 1975; Furner, 1969; Hirsch & Niedermeyer, 1973). This approach is multisensory, involving visual, auditory, and kinesthetic components and is based on the instructional model presented in Chapter 1. The five steps of the strategy are:

1. *Initiating.* The teacher demonstrates the specific handwriting skill as students observe. As the skill is demonstrated, the teacher describes the steps involved in executing it.

2. *Structuring and Conceptualizing.* Students describe the skill and the steps involved in executing it as the teacher or a classmate demonstrates the skill again.

3. *Summarizing.* The teacher reviews the specific handwriting skill, summarizing the steps involved in executing the skill.

4. *Generalizing.* Students practice the skill using pencils, pens, or other writing instruments. As they practice the skill, students softly repeat the steps involved in executing it that they learned in steps 1 and 2. The teacher circulates, providing assistance as needed.

5. *Applying.* Students apply the skill they have learned in their writing. To check that they have learned the specific skill, students can review their writing over a period of several days and mark examples of the skill used correctly.

An example of how to apply this strategy in teaching manuscript letter formation is presented in Figure 14–4.

As in most language arts activities, the teacher plays a crucial role in handwriting instruction. The teacher *teaches* the handwriting skill and then *supervises* the students as they practice it. Research has shown the importance of the teachers' active involvement in handwriting instruction and practice.

One aspect of the teacher's role is particularly interesting. To save time, teachers often print or write handwriting samples in advance on practice sheets. Then they distribute the sheets and ask students to practice a handwriting skill by copying the model they have written. However, researchers have found that moving models, that is, observing the teacher write the handwriting sample, is of far greater value than copying models that have already been written on the paper (Wright & Wright, 1980). When the teacher circulates around the classroom, stopping to demonstrate a skill for one student and moving to assist another student, moving models are possible. Circling incorrectly formed letters and marking other errors with a red pen on completed handwriting sheets is of little value. As in the writing process, the teacher's assistance is far more worthwhile while the student is producing handwriting, not after the handwriting has been completed.

1. *Initiating*

   Demonstrate the formation of a single letter or family of letters (e.g., the manuscript circle letters—*O, o, C, c, a, e, Q*) on the chalkboard while explaining how the letter is formed.

2. *Structuring and Conceptualizing*

   Have students describe how the letter is formed while you or a student forms the letter on the chalkboard. At first you may need to ask questions to direct students' descriptions. Possible questions include:

   > How many strokes are used in making the letter?
   > Which stroke comes first?
   > Where do you begin the stroke?
   > In which direction do you go?
   > What size will the letter be?
   > Where does the stroke stop?
   > Which stroke comes next?

   Students will quickly learn the appropriate terminology such as *baseline, left-right, slant line, counterclockwise,* and so on to describe how the letters are formed.

3. *Summarizing*

   Review the formation of the letter or letter family with students while demonstrating how to form the letter on the chalkboard.

4. *Generalizing*

   Have the students print the letter at the chalkboard, in sand, and with a variety of other materials such as clay, shaving cream, fingerpaint, pudding, and pipecleaners. As students form the letter, they should softly describe the formation process to themselves.

   Have students practice writing the letter on paper with the accompanying verbal descriptions.

   Circulate among students providing assistance and encouragement. Demonstrate and describe the correct formation of the letter as the students observe.

5. *Applying*

   After practicing the letter or family of letters, have students apply what they have learned in authentic writing activities. This is the crucial step!

Figure 14–4   Using the Instructional Strategy to Teach Letter Formation

Practice Activities

As Donald Graves (1983) reminds us, "handwriting is for writing" (p. 171), and for the most meaningful transfer of skills, students should be involved in writing for varied purposes and for genuine audiences. Students apply their handwriting skills whenever they write. In addition to the writing activities discussed in previous chapters, two additional writing activities are presented in this section. The first,

"Let's go on a Bear Hunt" (Tompkins, 1980) adapts the familiar language game to practice basic manuscript letter strokes. Children can use the strokes to create re-bus stories, too. Students at all grade levels can use second activity, copy books, to compile a collection of favorite poems, quotes, and excerpts from stories.

Activity 1: "Let's Go on a Bear Hunt."   "Let's Go on a Bear Hunt" is a favorite language game of young children, and it can also be adapted for a handwriting activity. The teacher takes the children on a bear hunt using the basic handwriting strokes to represent the actions of the hunt. Straight sticks become grass and forests to hike through, slanted sticks become hills and mountains to conquer, and circles become bears' paw-prints to track. As the teacher tells the story and demonstrates the handwriting strokes on the chalkboard, the children practice making the strokes on their papers.

The steps in this approach are

1. Provide the students with lined or blank paper and crayons or pencils.
2. Explain that you are going to tell the students a story, and they will draw lines and pictures for the story.
3. Tell the first section of the story and demonstrate the first handwriting stroke on the chalkboard.
4. Have the children copy the stroke on their papers and practice making the stroke several times.
5. Circulate to check that the children are making the stroke correctly.
6. Repeats steps 3, 4, and 5 with each section of the story.
7. At the end of the story have the children draw a picture about the story. Also, record children's dictation about their pictures or have the children write a sentence about the story on their papers.

Let's Go on a Bear Hunt

The teacher says:

1. Let's go on a bear hunt! Here we are hiking through the grass looking for a bear. Let's make a row of grass on our papers.
2. Shh! Do you hear anything? No? Let's keep hunting. Now we're walking through a forest. The forest is filled with many trees.
3. Do you see any bears? No? Let's keep walking. Oh, the walking is getting harder and harder. We're climbing over hills and mountains. Let's make some hills and mountains.

The teacher demonstrates, and the children copy on their papers:

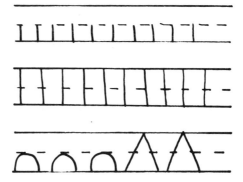

4. Watch out for bears! These mountain trails are so curvey and dangerous. Be careful! Stay on the trail!

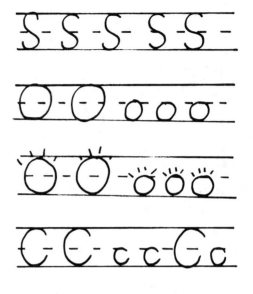

5. Look! I see some marks that look
like circles on the ground. Let's
make big and little circles.

6. These circles look like paw-prints
to me. Could they be bear paw-
prints? Make circles into paw-
prints by adding little claw marks.

7. These paw-prints lead up to a cave.
Do bears live in caves? Let's make
some big and little caves.

8. Listen! Do you hear a bear? Do you
see a bear? Draw a picture of what
you think the bear might look like.

A 5-year-old's bear hunt is shown in Figure 14–5. As a variation, have the children finish the story themselves. Let them decide what was in the cave. Six- and 7-
year-olds wrote these endings:

"The cave wus empey."
"It's a Easter bunny."
"Woodstock was in the cave."
"a gerbil was in the cave."
"I was ni th cav."

The bear hunt activity can be adapted to other topics; children can hunt for
dinosaurs, Santa Claus, ghosts, the Easter Bunny, other animals, or even Big Foot.
Figure 14–6 shows a 5-year-old's hunt for Big Foot.

Figure 14–5 A 5-Year-Old's
Bear Hunt

Figure 14–6 A 5-Year-Old's Hunt
for Big Foot

Adaptations of Circle and Stick Stories.   Teachers can make up new and different stories by adapting the basic circle and stick stories to represent other pictures. Here is a Halloween story:

Jack-o-Lanterns

The teacher says:

1. Let's make a jack-o-lantern. We need a nice round pumpkin. Let's make a pumpkin patch full of big and little pumpkins.
2. When we turn a pumpkin into a jack-o-lantern, we give it a face. Let's make triangle eyes and noses. This way.
3. And this way.

4. Let's add happy and sad mouths.

5. And lots of teeth to fill the mouths.

6. Now draw a picture to show how the jack-o-lantern might look.

The teacher demonstrates:

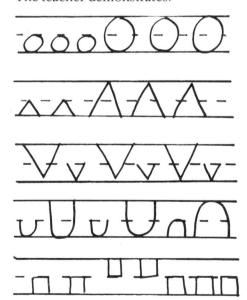

A Snowy Day

The teacher says: The teacher demonstrates:

1. One day it began to snow. At first it
   was just a snow flurry. Then it began to snow very hard. (Remind
   children to have the snowflakes
   come from the sky down to the
   ground.)

2. At first the snow wasn't very deep.
   Then, as it snowed harder and
   harder, the snow got deeper and
   deeper.

3. Then we decided to go outside and
   make a snowman. We started roll-
   ing snowballs. At first the snowballs were very small. Then they
   got larger and larger.

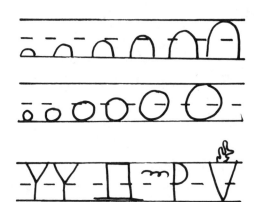

4. After we made the snowballs, we
   needed some things to make our
   snowballs become a snowman.
   Can you guess what we needed?
   We needed sticks for arms, a hat, a
   pipe, and a carrot.

5. Now draw a picture to show how
   you think our snowman looked
   when he was all put together.

A 5-year-old's version of the snow story is shown in Figure 14–7. Children can compose their own handwriting stories using the basic strokes. Figure 14–8 shows

Figure 14–7 A 5-Year-Old's   **Figure 14–8** A 7-Year-Old's
Snow Story   Fossil Hunt

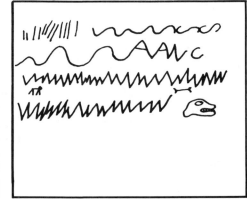

*A student practices handwriting skills by copying poems, riddles, and quotes
in his copy book.*

a fossil hunt written by Robbie, a 7-year-old who cleverly manages to involve dinosaurs in almost every activity. Robbie describes his fossil hunt this way:

> A paleontologist was going on a fossil hunt. He went over short grass and long
> grass and over little hills. (See, I made the hills with a sideway S's.) Then he
> came to mountains and high mountains and high mountains with snow on
> them. Then he went in a cave. It had lots of icicles. He crawled down low. He
> crawled some more. Then he found it — a Tyrannosaurus skull.

The teacher's excitement makes these stories believable. By setting the mood
and responding to the children's comments, the teacher stimulates children's interest in the handwriting activity. The rapid tempo of the activity allows for intensive drill without losing the children's interest. As the children practice each letter
form, the teacher can instruct individual children about proper letter formation
and spacing between letters.

Activity 2: Copy books. *   Students in the middle and upper grades need many
opportunities to practice manuscript and cursive handwriting forms through
meaningful activities. One way to provide this practice is through the use of copy

---

*The authors are grateful to Janet Kretchmer, principal and teacher at the McGuffey Foundation
School, Oxford, Ohio, for this activity idea.

books. For this activity, students need spiral-bound notebooks or the blank boundbooks available at bookstores. Students choose poems, quotes, paragraphs from stories they are reading, riddles, or other short pieces of writing that they would like to write and save in their copy books. Usually students make one or two entries in their copy books each week, and they may choose to write in either manuscript or cursive handwriting. Students can concentrate on their handwriting as they make entries in these books because they do not have to worry about creating the content at the same time. Examples of students' copy book entries are presented in Figure 14–9.

Copy books are especially beneficial because they provide a meaningful context for handwriting practice. Instead of requiring students to write rows of letters and isolated words, students are immersed in language and literature. For many students, copy books become valued, personal anthologies of favorite literary selections.

Figure 14–9 Entries from Students' Copy Books
for Galdone's *The three bears* (1972) and
Sterne's *Tyrannosaurus wrecks:*
A book of dinosaur riddles (1979)

"Someone has been sleeping in my bed,"

said Baby Bear,

in his biggest teeny-tiny voice,

"and she is still there!"

Jennifer, age 6

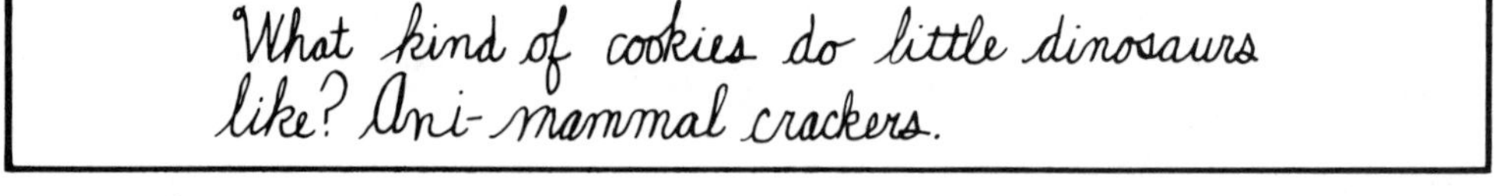

What kind of cookies do little dinosaurs like? Ani-mammal crackers.

Aaron, age 9

Elements of Legibility

The goal of handwriting instruction is for students to develop legible handwriting. For students to reach this goal, they must first understand what qualities or elements determine legibility and then analyze their own handwriting according to these elements. The six elements of legible handwriting according to the Zaner-Bloser handwriting program (Barbe, Lucas, Wasylyk, Hackney, & Braun, 1984) are (a) letter formation, (b) size and proportion, (c) spacing, (d) slant, (e) alignment, and (f) line quality. Each of these elements is described in the following paragraphs.

Letter Formation.   The letters are formed with specific strokes. In manuscript handwriting, letters are composed of vertical, horizontal, and slanted lines plus circles or parts of circles. For example, the letter *b* is composed of a vertical line and a circle, and *M* is composed of vertical and slanted lines. The cursive letter forms are composed of slanted lines, loops, and curved lines. The lower case cursive letters *e* and *l*, for instance, are composed of a slant stroke, a loop, and an undercurve stroke. In cursive handwriting, an additional component is the connecting strokes used to join letters.

Size and Proportion.   Through the elementary grades, the size of students' handwriting decreases, and the proportional size of upper to lower case letters increases. For manuscript letters, upper case letters are twice the size of lower case letters. When second and third grade students are first introduced to cursive handwriting, the proportional size of letters remains 2:1. Later, the proportion of upper case to lower case cursive letters increases to 3:1 for middle and upper grade students. These three sizes are illustrated in Figure 14–10.

Spacing.   Students must leave adequate space between letters in words and between words and sentences if their handwriting is to be read easily. For manuscript handwriting, spacing between words, according to Zaner-Bloser, should equal one lower case letter *o*. Spacing between sentences should equal two lower case letter *o*'s. For cursive handwriting, the most important aspect of spacing within words is consistency. For correct spacing between words, the beginning stroke of the new word should begin directly below the end stroke of the preceding word.

Figure 14–10   Size and Proportion of Elementary Students' Handwriting

Manuscript Handwriting	Transition to Cursive	Cursive Handwriting
(proportion 2:1)	(proportion 2:1)	(proportion 3:1)

Spacing between sentences should equal one upper case letter *O,* and spacing between paragraphs should equal two upper case letter *O*'s.

Slant.   Letters should be consistently parallel. In manuscript handwriting, the letters are vertical. In the cursive form, letters slant slightly to the right for both right-handed and left-handed students. To ensure the correct slant, right-handed students tilt their papers to the left and left-handed students tilt their papers to the right.

Alignment.   For proper alignment in both manuscript and cursive handwriting, all letters are uniform in size and consistently touch the baseline.

Line Quality.   Students should write at a consistent speed and hold their writing instruments correctly and in a relaxed manner in order to make steady, unwavering lines of even thickness.

Correct letter formation and spacing receive the major focus in handwriting instruction during the elementary grades. While the other four elements usually receive less attention, they, too, are important in developing legible and fluent handwriting. The characteristics of these six elements of legibility are summarized in Figure 14–11.

Diagnosing and Correcting Handwriting Problems

Students can use the characteristics of the six elements of legibility in diagnosing their handwriting problems. Primary grade students, for example, can check to see if they formed a particular letter correctly, if the round parts of letters are joined neatly, or if slanted letters are joined in sharp points. Older students can examine a piece of handwriting and check to see if their letters were consistently parallel or if the letters touched the baseline consistently.

Checklists for students to use in evaluating their own handwriting can be developed from the characteristics of the six elements of legibility. A sample checklist for evaluating manuscript handwriting is presented in Figure 14–12. Checklists can also be developed for cursive handwriting. It is important to involve students in developing the checklists so that they can appreciate the need to make their handwriting more legible.

Another reason students need to diagnose and correct their handwriting problems is because handwriting quality influences teacher evaluation and grading. Markham (1976) found that both elementary student teachers and experienced classroom teachers consistently graded papers with better handwriting higher than papers with poor handwriting regardless of the quality of the content. Students in the elementary grades are not too young to learn that poor quality or illegible handwriting may lead to lower grades.

POINTS TO PONDER

How Does Handwriting Develop During the Elementary Grades?

What Types of Writing Paper and Writing Instruments Are Most Appropriate for Elementary Students?

Letter Formation

Letters are formed with specific strokes.
Cursive letters are joined carefully.

Size and Proportion

Letter size decreases for middle and upper grade students.
Proportion of upper to lower case manuscript letters is 2:1.
Proportion of upper to lower case cursive letters increases from 2:1 to 3:1.

Spacing

Adequate space is left between letters.
Adequate space is left between words and sentences.
Spacing is consistent.

Slant

Letters are consistently parallel.
Manuscript letters are vertical.
Cursive letters are slanted slightly to the right.

Alignment

Letters are uniform in size.
Letters consistently touch the baseline.

Line Quality

Lines are steady and unwavering.
Lines are of consistent thickness.

Figure 14–11   Characteristics of the Six Elements of Legibility

1. Did I form my letters correctly?

   Did I start my line letters at the top?
   Did I start my circle letters at 1:00?
   Did I join the round parts of the letters neatly?
   Did I join the slanted strokes in sharp points?

2. Did my lines touch the midline or top line neatly?

3. Did I space evenly between letters?

4. Did I leave enough space between words?

5. Did I make my letters straight up and down?

6. Did I make all my letters sit on the baseline?

Figure 14–12   A Checklist for Diagnosing Manuscript Handwriting

What Factors Should Be Considered in Deciding When to Introduce Students to Cursive Handwriting?

What Is the Difference between Public and Private Handwriting?

CHILDREN'S HANDWRITING DEVELOPMENT

During the elementary grades, children grow from using scribbles and letter-like forms in kindergarten to learning the manuscript handwriting form in the primary grades and the cursive form beginning in the middle grades. Students in the middle and upper grades use both forms interchangeably for a variety of handwriting tasks.

Handwriting Before First Grade

Children's handwriting grows out of their drawing activities. Young children observe words all around them in their environment: *McDonald's, Coke, STOP.* They also observe parents and teachers writing messages. From this early interest in written words and communicating through writing, 3-, 4-, and 5-year-olds begin to write letter-like forms and scribbles. In kindergarten, children observe as the teacher transcribes experience stories, and they begin to copy their name and familiar words. Once they are familiar with most of the letters, they use invented spelling to express themselves in writing. Through this drawing-reading-writing-handwriting connection, youngsters discover that they can experiment with letters and words and communicate through written language. And, handwriting becomes the functional tool for this written communication.

A New Zealand educator, Marie Clay (1975), has identified five principles that document the development of children's early writing/handwriting skills: (a) recurring principle, (b) directional principle, (c) generating principle, (d) inventory principle, and (e) contrastive principle.

Recurring Principle.   Children repeat patterns of designs, letters, and words over and over. In writing, children often repeat a single word or phrase again. Clay suggests this phenomenon may be due to a child's feeling of accomplishment in knowing how to write the word or phrase.

Directional Principle.   At first, children place their written marks randomly on a paper. Through experience with writing, children learn to follow our conventional pattern, moving from left to right and sweeping to the left side of the next line to continue writing.

Generating Principle.   Children extend their writing options when they realize that letter elements can recur in variable patterns. They can string together letters to create word-like arrangements of letters.

Inventory Principle. Children "take inventory" or list all the letters or words in their writing repertoire. Sometimes they limit their lists to names of family members or words beginning with a particular letter.

Contrastive Principle. Children perceive likenesses and differences among letters and words that they write. They compare reversed letters such as *b* and *d,* words spelled in upper and lower case letters (e.g., *THE, the*), and antonyms such as *boy* and *girl.*

These principles develop through drawing as well as through real-life writing activities. Teachers can observe children as they draw and write, noting children's use of these principles as they manipulate letters and letter-like forms and play with words. These principles need not be taught because children will exhibit them spontaneously as they draw and write.

Young children enter kindergarten with differing backgrounds of handwriting experience. Some 5-year-olds have never held a pencil before although many others have written cursive-like scribbles or manuscript letter-like forms. Some preschoolers have learned how to print their names and some letters with importance for them.

Handwriting in kindergarten typically includes three types of activities: (a) stimulating children's interest in writing, (b) developing their ability to hold writing instruments, and (c) refining their fine motor control.

Stimulating Interest in Writing. Adults can be very influential as role models in stimulating children's interest in writing. Parents can encourage children's interest at home through their own writing activities, such as writing letters, telephone messages, and grocery lists. Also, parents can provide children with a supply of paper, pencils, and pens so that they can imitate their parents' writing. At school, picture journals and experience stories stimulate children's interest in writing.

Developing the Ability to Hold Writing Instruments. Students develop the ability to hold a pencil or other writing instrument through modeling their parents and teachers and through numerous opportunities to experiment with pencils, pens, paint brushes, crayons, and other writing instruments.

Refining Motor Skills. Young children develop and refine their fine motor skills through a variety of motor activities and experiences with manipulative materials. Possible activities include building with blocks, stringing beads, completing parquetry designs and puzzles, drawing, cutting, pasting, and other art activities.

Handwriting instruction in kindergarten typically focuses on teaching children to form the upper and lower case letters and to print their names. Many kindergarten teachers use a multisensory approach for learning letter forms. Students trace letters in shaving cream, sand, and fingerpaint; they glue popcorn in the shape of letters; and they arrange blocks or pipecleaners to form letters. Children learn to print their names through similar multisensory activities and through daily practice writing their names on attendance sheets, their experience stories, their paintings, and other papers.

*Forming letters in shaving cream is a good way for young children to practice
fine motor skills.*

Handwriting must be linked with writing at all grade levels, beginning in kindergarten or even earlier. Young children write labels, draw and write stories, keep
journals, and write other messages (Klein & Schickedanz, 1980). The more they
write, the greater their need becomes for instruction in handwriting. Writers need
to know how to grip a pencil, how to form letters, and how to space between letters and words. Instruction is necessary so that students will not learn bad habits
that later must be broken. Too often students look at a letter and devise their own,
rather bizarre way to form that letter. As students write more, these bad habits will
cause problems as they need to develop greater writing speed.

Handwriting in the Primary Grades

Formal handwriting instruction begins in first grade. The instructional strategy
presented earlier is used to teach manuscript handwriting. Students learn how to
form the manuscript letters, how to space between them, and to develop skills related to the six elements of legibility. Researchers have found that primary grade
students have more difficulty forming the lower case letters than the upper case
letters, and by third grade, some students still have difficulty forming *r, u, h,* and *t*
(Stennett, Smithe, & Hardy, 1972).

A commonly used handwriting activity requires students to copy short writing samples from the chalkboard. This type of handwriting activity is not recommended for several reasons. First, young children have great difficulty with far-to-near copying (Lamme, 1979). When copying a piece of writing, it should be placed close to the child. Children recopy their own compositions to publish them, copy their language experience stories, and copy self-selected writing samples in their copy books. Other types of copying should be avoided. It is far better for children to create their own writing than to copy words and sentences that they may not even be able to read!

Writing Instruments and Paper. Special pencils and handwriting paper are often provided for handwriting instruction. Kindergartners and first graders commonly use "fat" beginner pencils, 13/32 inch in diameter, because it has been assumed that these pencils are easier for young children to hold. However, most children prefer to use regular size, 10/32 inch, pencils that older students and adults use. Moreover, regular pencils have erasers! Research now indicates that beginner pencils are not better than regular-sized pencils for young children (Lamme & Ayris, 1983). Likewise, there is no evidence that specially shaped pencils and little writing aids that slip onto pencils to improve children's grip are effective.

Many types of paper, both lined and unlined, are used in elementary classrooms. Paper companies manufacture paper lined in a range of sizes. Typically, paper is lined at two inch intervals for kindergartners, 7/8 inch intervals for first graders, 3/4 inch intervals for second graders, 1/2 inch intervals for third graders, and 3/8 inch intervals for older students. Lined paper for first and second graders has an added midline which is often dotted to guide students in forming the lower case letters. Also, a line is sometimes added below the baseline to guide the placement of letters such as lower case *g, p, q,* and *y* that have "tails" that drop below the baseline.

The few research studies that have examined the value of lined paper in general and paper lined at these specific intervals offer conflicting results. One recent study suggests that younger children's handwriting is more legible using unlined paper while older children's handwriting is better using lined paper (Lindsay & McLennan, 1983). Most teachers seem to prefer that students use lined paper for most handwriting activities, but students easily adjust to whichever type of writing paper is available. Children often use rulers to line their paper when they are given unlined paper, and, likewise, they ignore the lines on lined paper when they interfere with their drawing or writing.

Transition to Cursive Handwriting

Students' introduction to cursive handwriting typically occurs in the second semester of second grade or in the first semester of third grade. Too often parents and students attach great importance to this transition from manuscript to cursive form, thus adding unnecessary pressure for the students. The time of transition is usually dictated by tradition rather than by sound educational theory. Usually all students in the school or school district are introduced to cursive handwriting at the same time regardless of their readiness to make the change.

Some of your students may indicate an early interest in cursive handwriting by trying to connect manuscript letters to create cursive letters or by having their parents demonstrate how to write their names in the cursive form. Because of individual differences in motor skills and levels of interest in cursive writing, it is better to introduce some students to cursive handwriting in first or second grade and to provide other students with additional opportunities to refine their manuscript skills. These students can then learn cursive handwriting in third or fourth grade.

The transition to cursive handwriting requires a full semester of instruction. Before students learn to form the cursive letters, they must learn to identify them. First, students learn to recognize the upper and lower case cursive letters. Flash cards and bingo and lotto games are useful in teaching cursive letter recognition. Next, students learn to read words and sentences written in the cursive form.

Invariably, the first thing that students will want to write in cursive handwriting is their own names. With individual and small group instruction, your students can quickly learn to write their names and then progress to learning the basic strokes used in forming the cursive letters.

The practice of changing children from manuscript to cursive handwriting only a year or two after learning the manuscript form is receiving increasing criticism. The argument has been that students need to learn cursive handwriting as early as possible because of their increasing need for handwriting speed. It has been assumed that because of its continuous flow, cursive handwriting is faster to write than manuscript. However, research suggests that manuscript handwriting can be written as quickly as cursive handwriting (Jackson, 1971). The controversy over the benefits of the two forms and the best time to introduce cursive handwriting is likely to continue for some time.

Handwriting in the Middle and Upper Grades

In second and third grades, students are introduced to the cursive handwriting form. The instructional strategy presented earlier is used in teaching cursive as well as manuscript handwriting. Typically, the basic strokes that make up the letters (e.g., slant stroke, undercurve, downcurve) are taught first. Next, the lower case letters are taught in isolation and then the connecting strokes are introduced. Upper case letters are taught later because they are used far less often and are more difficult to form.

Which cursive letters are most difficult for students to form? According to the results of a study that examined sixth graders' handwriting, the lower case letter *r* is the most troublesome letter. The other lower case letters that students frequently form incorrectly are *h, i, k. p,* and *z.* The lower case letters found to be least difficult for students are *a, b, c, i, l, m, n, u, v,* and *x* (Horton, 1970).

Once students have learned both manuscript and cursive handwriting, they need to review both forms periodically. By this time, too, they have firmly established handwriting habits, both good and bad habits. At the middle and upper grade levels, the emphasis is on helping students diagnose and correct their handwriting trouble-spots in order to develop a legible and fluent handwriting style. Older students both simplify their letter forms as well as add unique flourishes to their handwriting to develop their own "trademark" styles.

Private and Public Handwriting.   Too often teachers insist that students demonstrate their best handwriting every time they pick up a pencil or a pen. This requirement is very unrealistic; certainly there are times when handwriting is important, but at other times speed or other considerations outweigh neatness. Children need to learn to recognize two basic types of writing occasions, *private* writing and *public* writing. Legibility counts in public writing, but when students make notes for themselves or write a rough draft of a composition, they are doing private writing, and students should decide for themselves whether neatness is important.

POINTS TO PONDER
What Is "Handedness"?
What Special Adaptations Are Necessary for Left-Handed Writers?

LEFT-HANDED WRITERS

Approximately 10% of the American population is left-handed, and two or three left-handed students may be found in most classrooms. Until recently, teachers have insisted that left-handed students change over and use their right hands for handwriting because left-handed writers were thought to have inferior handwriting skills. Parents and teachers are more realistic now and accept children's natural tendencies for left or right handedness. In fact, research has shown that there is no significant difference in the quality or speed of left- or right-handed students' writing (Groff, 1963).

Handedness

Most young children develop *handedness* or the preference for using either the right or left hand for fine motor activities before entering kindergarten or first grade. However, kindergarten and first grade teachers must help those few students who have not already developed handedness to choose and consistently use one hand for handwriting and other fine motor activities. Your role consists of observing the student's behavior and hand preference in play, art, writing, and playground activities. Over a period of days or weeks, observe and note the hand the child uses in these types of activities:

■ building with blocks

■ catching balls

■ cutting with scissors

- holding a paintbrush
- holding a pencil or crayon
- manipulating clay
- manipulating puzzle pieces
- pasting
- pouring water or sand
- stringing beads
- throwing balls

During the observation period, teachers may find that a young child who has not established hand preference uses both hands interchangeably. For example, a child may first reach for several blocks with one hand and then reach for the next block with the alternate hand. During drawing activities, the child will sometimes switch hands every few minutes. Also consult the child's parents and ask them to assist in observing and monitoring the child's behavior at home, noting hand preferences when eating, brushing teeth, turning on the television, opening doors, and so on. The teacher, the child, and the child's parents should then confer, and based on the results of joint observations, the handedness of family members, and the child's wishes, a tentative decision about a hand preference can be made. At school the teacher and the child will work closely together so that the child will only use the chosen hand. As long as the child continues to use both hands interchangeably, neither hand will develop the prerequisite fine motor control for handwriting. Therefore, teachers should postpone handwriting instruction until the child has developed a dominant hand.

Teaching Left-handed Students

Teaching handwriting to left-handed students is not simply the reverse of teaching handwriting to right-handed students (Howell, 1978). Left-handed students have unique handwriting problems, and special adaptations of procedures used for teaching right-handed students are necessary. In fact, many of the problems that left-handed students have can be made worse by using the procedures designed for right-handed writers (Harrison, 1981). These special adjustments are necessary to allow left-handed students to write legibly, fluently, and with less fatigue.

The basic difference between right- and left-handed writers is physical orientation. Right-handed students pull their hands and arms toward their bodies as they write while left-handed writers must push away. As left-handed students write, they move their left hands across what has just been written, often covering it. Many children adopt a "hook" position to avoid covering and smudging what they have just written.

Because of their different physical orientation, left-handed writers need to make three major types of adjustments: (a) how they grip their pens or pencils, (b) how they position the writing paper on their desks, and (c) how they slant their writing (Howell, 1978).

First, left-handed writers should hold pencils or pens an inch or more farther back from the tip than right-handed writers do. This change will help them to see what they have just written and to avoid smearing their writing. Left-handed writers need to work to avoid "hooking" their wrists. Have them keep their wrists straight and elbows close to their bodies to avoid the awkward hooked position. Practicing their handwriting on the chalkboard is one way to help students develop a more natural handwriting style.

Second, left-handed students should tilt their writing papers slightly to the right, in contrast to right-handed students who tilt their papers to the left. Sometimes it is helpful to place a piece of masking tape on the student's desk to indicate the proper amount of tilt.

Third, while right-handed students are encouraged to slant their cursive letters to the right, left-handed writers often write vertically or even slant their letters slightly backward. The Zaner-Bloser handwriting program (1984) recommends that left-handed writers slant their cursive letters slightly to the right as right-handed students do, but other educators, such as Harrison (1981), advise teachers to permit any slant between vertical and 45 degrees to the left of the vertical. These and other special adaptations are summarized in Figure 14–13.

Left-handed writers need special support, and one way to provide this support is by grouping left-handed students together for handwriting instruction. Right-handed teachers should consider asking a left-handed teacher, parent, or an older student to come into the classroom to work with left-handed writers. Lastly, it is important to carefully monitor left-handed students as they are forming handwriting skills because bad habits such as "hooking" are very difficult to break.

---

1. Group left-handed students together for handwriting instruction.
2. Provide a left-handed person to serve as the model if you are not left-handed. Perhaps another teacher, parent, or an older student could come to the classroom to assist left-handed students.
3. Direct students to hold their pencils farther back from the point than right-handed students do.
4. Encourage students to practice handwriting skills at the chalkboard.
5. Have students tilt their papers to the right rather than to the left as right-handed students do.
6. Encourage students to slant their cursive letters slightly to the right, but allow them to form them vertically or even with a slight backhand slant.
7. Encourage students to eliminate excessive loops and flourishes from their writing to increase handwriting speed.

Figure 14–13 Special Adaptations for Left-Handed Writers

Summary

Handwriting is a functional, support skill for writing, not an art form! The teacher's goal in handwriting instruction is to help students develop legible and fluent handwriting skills and to understand the functional nature of handwriting.

Two forms of handwriting are taught in the elementary school. Manuscript handwriting is the print form, and cursive handwriting is a connected, flowing writing form. A new handwriting style, D'Nealian, has been developed to ameliorate some of the problems associated with manuscript handwriting and the transition to cursive handwriting.

A five-step instructional strategy based on the instructional model introduced in Chapter 1 was presented to use in teaching manuscript and cursive handwriting. The most crucial step is the last step, in which students apply the skills they have practiced in real-life writing activities.

Six elements of legible handwriting have been identified. These elements are (a) letter formation, (b) size and proportion, (c) spacing, (d) slant, (e) alignment, and (f) line quality. Students can learn to evaluate their own handwriting using these six elements. One strategy for helping students identify their handwriting problems is using checklists based on the elements of legibility.

Children's handwriting development was outlined. Young children's handwriting grows out of their drawing, and some preschoolers learn to print their names before they enter kindergarten. Primary grade students are taught manuscript handwriting; in second or third grade, students are introduced to cursive handwriting. Critics have complained that it is unrealistic to expect students to master two completely different handwriting forms in such a short time span.

Teachers can expect to have two or three left-handed students in their class, and these left-handed writers have special needs. We presented a list of seven ways to adapt your handwriting program to meet these students' special needs.

Extensions

1. Practice forming the manuscript and cursive letters presented in Figure 14–1 until your handwriting approximates the models. Practicing these two handwriting forms will prepare you for working with elementary students. However, be sure to take note of the manuscript and/or cursive handwriting forms displayed in the students' classroom before beginning to work with students because there are several different handwriting programs used in schools. The programs are very similar, but some students, especially younger children, are quick to point out when you are not forming a letter correctly!

2. Observe in a primary grade classroom where the D'Nealian handwriting program is used. Talk with teachers and students about this innovative form. How do the students like it? Do the teachers believe that it ameliorates some of the problems with manuscript handwriting and the transition to cursive as Thurber claims?

3. Practice manuscript handwriting skills with a small group of kindergartners or first graders using the "Let's Go on a Bear Hunt" activity.

4. Practice manuscript and cursive handwriting skills with a small group of middle or upper grade students using copy books. Supply students with small notebooks and have them copy favorite poems, quotes, excerpts from stories they are reading, and other short pieces of writing in the books. Meet with students weekly for several weeks as they work in their copy books.

5. Work with a small group of students to develop a checklist similar to the one presented in Figure 14–8 to evaluate their handwriting. After developing the checklist, have students evaluate their handwriting and set goals for improving both the legibility and fluency.

6. Observe a left-handed writer and compare this student to right-handed writers in the same classroom. How does the left-handed student's handwriting differ from right-handed students'? What types of special adaptions has the teacher made for teaching the left-handed student?

References

Askov, E., & Greff, K. N. (1975). Handwriting: Copying versus tracing as the most effective type of practice. *Journal of Educational Research, 69,* 96–98.

Barbe, W. B., & Milone, M. N. Jr. (1980). *Why manuscript writing should come before cursive writing* (Zaner-Bloser Professional Pamphlet No. 11). Columbus, OH: Zaner-Bloser.

Barbe, W. B., Wasylyk, T. M., Hackney, C. S., & Braun, L. A. (1984). *Zaner-Bloser creative growth in handwriting* (Grades K–8). Columbus, OH: Zaner-Bloser.

Clay, M. (1975). *What did I write?* Auckland, NZ: Heinemann.

Furner, B. A. (1969). Recommended instructional procedures in a method emphasizing the perceptual-motor nature of learning in handwriting. *Elementay English, 46,* 1021–1030.

Galdone, P. (1972). *The three bears.* New York: Houghton Mifflin.

Graves, D. H. (1983). *Writing: Teachers and children at work.* Exeter, NH: Heinemann.

Groff, P. J. (1963). Who writes faster? *Education, 83,* 367–369.

Harrison, S. (1981). Open letter from a left-handed teacher: Some sinistral ideas on the teaching of handwriting. *Teaching Exceptional Children, 13,* 116–120.

Hildreth, G. (1960). Manuscript writing after sixty years. *Elementary English, 37,* 3–13.

Hirsch, E., & Niedermeyer, F. C. (1973). The effects of tracing prompts and discrimination training on kindergarten handwriting performance. *Journal of Educational Research, 67,* 81–83.

Horton, L. W. (1970). Illegibilities in the cursive handwriting of sixth graders. *Elementary School Journal, 70,* 446–450.

Howell, H. (1978). Write on, you sinistrals! *Language Arts, 55,* 852–856.

Jackson, A. D. (1971). A comparison of speed of legibility of manuscript and cursive handwriting of intermediate grade pupils. Unpublished doctoral dissertation, University of Arizona. *Dissertation Abstracts, 31,* (1971), pp. 4384A.

Klein, A., & Schickedanz, J. (1980). Preschoolers write messages and receive their favorite books. *Language Arts, 57,* 742–749.

Lamme, L. L. (1979). Handwriting in an early childhood curriculum. *Young Children, 35,* 20–27.

Lamme, L. L., & Ayris, B. M. (1983). Is the handwriting of beginning writers influenced by writing tools? *Journal of Research and Development in Education, 17,* 32–38.

Lindsay, G. A., & McLennan, D. (1983). Lined paper: Its effects on the legibility and creativity of young children's writing. *British Journal of Educational Psychology, 53,* 364–368.

Markham, L. R. (1976). Influences of handwriting quality on teacher evaluation of written work. *American Educational Research Journal, 13,* 277–283.

Stennett, R. G., Smithe, P. C., & Hardy, M. (1972). Developmental trends in letter-printing skill. *Perceptual and Motor Skills, 34,* 183–186.

Sterne, N. (1979). *Tyrannosaurus wrecks: A book of dinosaur riddles.* New York: Crowell.

Thurber, D. N. (1981). *D'Nealian handwriting* (Grades K–8). Glenview, IL: Scott, Foresman.

Tompkins, G. E. (1980). Let's go on a bear hunt! A fresh approach to penmanship drill. *Language Arts, 57,* 782–786.

Wright, C. D., & Wright, J. P. (1980). Handwriting: The effectiveness of copying from moving versus still models. *Journal of Educational Research, 74,* 95–98.

IF YOU WANT TO LEARN MORE

Barbe, W. B., Lucas, V. H., & Wasylyk, T. M. (Eds.). (1984). *Handwriting: Basic skills for effective communication.* Columbus, OH: Zaner-Bloser.

Clay, M. M. (1975). *What did I write?* Auckland, NZ: Heinemann.

D'Angelo, K. (1982). Developing legibility and uniqueness in handwriting with calligraphy. *Language Arts, 59,* 23–27.

Graves, D. H. (1978). Research update: Handwriting is for writing. *Language Arts, 55,* 393–399.

Howell, H. (1978). Write on, you sinistrals! *Language Arts, 55,* 852–856.

Lamme, L. L. (1979). Handwriting in an early childhood curriculum. *Young Children, 35,* 20–27.

_____. (1984). *Growing up writing.* Washington, DC: Acropolis.

Strickland, R. W. (1983). Thoughts from a concerned parent: Reading, writing and D'Nealian? *Childhood Education, 60,* 28–30.

CHAPTER FIFTEEN

Teaching Language Arts to Students with Special Needs

OVERVIEW.   In Chapter 15 we will examine the learning characteristics of exceptional students who are mainstreamed in regular classrooms and suggest ways to modify the language arts program to meet the needs of these students. Three categories of exceptionality will be considered: mildly handicapped students, language different students, and gifted students.

In 1975 Congress passed the Education for All Handicapped Children Act (PL 94–142). This act requires the handicapped children "to the maximum extent appropriate" be educated "with children who are not handicapped" and that "removal of handicapped children from the regular educational environment occurs only when the nature or severity of the handicap is such that education in regular classes with the use of supplementary aids and services cannot be achieved satisfactorily" (*Federal Register,* August 23, 1977, p. 821). This legislation does not stipulate that every exceptional child will be placed in regular classrooms. It does mean, however, that mildly handicapped children who can benefit from being in regular classrooms will spend part or all of each school day in the mainstream of education, in regular classroom.

Mainstreaming is the placement of handicapped students in the least restrictive environment. For many mildly handicapped students, such as learning disabled and emotionally disturbed students, the least restrictive environment may be the regular classroom with or without supplemental "pull-out" programs. This placement involves more than just the physical integration of handicapped students into a regular classroom. Exceptional students have educational and social needs that must also be met. Classroom teachers can modify their language arts programs to meet these students' individual needs and to integrate them socially into the classroom by allowing them to participate fully in classroom activities.

In this chapter we will consider the learning characteristics and instructional needs of the exceptional students who are most likely to be placed in regular classrooms. Because it is not possible to examine all categories of exceptional learners, we will focus only on three categories of students with special learning needs: (a) mildly handicapped students, (b) language different students, and (c) gifted students. While school districts may use slightly different labels for these learners, we will use the terms specified in federal guidelines. For exceptionalities not defined by federal legislation, we will use the currently accepted terminology. Also, it should be noted that students do not always fit neatly in the categories identified above. For example, some students may be both bilingual and gifted while others may have multiple handicapping conditions such as cerebral palsy.

Our position is that students with special needs benefit from the same language arts content and teaching strategies that other students do. Instructional strategies that allow students to use their natural language ability and concrete, real-life activities facilitate *all* students' oral and written language development. The material presented in this book capitalizes on the natural ways children learn, and it can be used effectively with exceptional students. Glass, Christiansen, and

*Classroom teachers can modify their language arts
programs and provide special assistance to meet
exceptional students' educational needs.*

Christiansen (1982) point out that "beyond some global considerations, there is no one way to teach mentally retarded students that is distinctly different from how we might teach learning disabled, emotionally disturbed, physically handicapped, or normal students" p. 43.

POINTS TO PONDER
What Types of Mildly Handicapped Students Might Be Mainstreamed in Regular Classrooms?
What Are the Characteristics of These Special Learners?
What Instructional Strategies and Activities Can Be Used with These Special Learners?

MILDLY HANDICAPPED STUDENTS

Mildly handicapped students are those who are identified as being learning disabled, mentally retarded, and emotionally disturbed. PL 94–142, which deals with the education of these handicapped students, mandates that these youngsters be mainstreamed as much as possible in regular classrooms. Thus, it is likely that teachers will have one or more of these students in their classrooms. In this section, we will examine characteristics of these mildly handicapped students and suggest instructional strategies and activities to meet their educational needs.

Learning Disabled Students

Learning disabled students (LD) are children who exhibit severe and specific learning difficulties in areas related to language or mathematics. Learning disabilities is defined as:

> a disorder in one or more of the basic psychological processes involved in understanding or in using language, spoken or written, which may manifest itself in an imperfect ability to listen, think, speak, read, write, spell, or to do mathematical calculations. The term includes such conditions as perceptual handicaps, brain injury, minimal brain disfunction, dyslexia, and developmental aphasia. The term does not include children who have learning problems which are primarily the result of visual, hearing, or motor handicaps, of mental retardation, of emotional disturbance, or of environmental, cultural, or economic disadvantage. (*Federal Register,* August 23, 1977, p. 786)

Learner characteristics of LD students that affect instruction are listed in Figure 15–1. These characteristics suggest an academic handicap, and language arts disabilities, particularly in reading, are common academic problems. In addition, these students frequently exhibit socially inappropriate behaviors and may have difficulty relating to their classmates. Certainly not all learning disabled students exhibit all the characteristics presented in Figure 15–1, and some of the characteristics are also associated with other learning problems and handicapping conditions.

Many different diagnostic labels have been applied to LD students, and the term *learning disabilities* is relatively new. It was coined by a special educator, Samuel Kirk, in 1963 (Lerner, 1985). Depending on the labels and criteria used, the prevalence of learning disabilities has been estimated to range from 3% to 5% of the school-aged population.

Instructional Implications.   Learning disabled students are typically mainstreamed in regular classrooms for much of the schoolday and pulled out to a resource room for special instruction. Perhaps the most important consideration in planning instruction for learning disabled students is that the instructional approach be structured. The approach to instruction suggested in Chapter 1 is a structured approach, and strategies based on this approach have been identified for teaching many oral and written language skills. The strategies for teaching listening skills and elements of story structure are two strategies that are especially beneficial for LD students.

Figure 15–1 Behavior and Learning Characteristics of
Learning Disabled Students

Behavior

moves constantly
has difficulty beginning or completing tasks
is generally quiet or withdrawn
has difficulty with peer relationships
is disorganized
is easily distracted
displays inconsistencies in behavior
seems to misunderstand oral directions

Oral Language

hesitates often when speaking
has poor verbal expression for age

Reading

looses place, repeats words
does not read fluently
confuses similar words and letters
uses fingers to follow along
does not read willingly

Spelling

uses incorrect order of letters in words
has difficulty associating correct sound with appropriate letter
reverses letters and words

Handwriting

cannot stay on line
has difficulty copying from board or other source
uses cursive and manuscript handwriting in same assignment
is slow in completing written work

Writing

uses poor written expression for age

Summers, 1977, p. 42.

A second important consideration is that learning disabled children must be allowed to experience success, even in nontraditional ways. For example, students can compose stories orally using a tape recorder or prepare oral reports rather than written reports. It is essential that teachers develop innovative strategies to work around LD students' handicapping conditions.

Other strategies and activities presented in this book that are appropriate for LD students include:

1. Try predictable books with LD students because the repetitive patterns allow students to feel immediate success as well as learning prediction strategies (McClure, 1985). (Check the list of predictable books presented in Figure 1–11.) Vocabulary study as well as writing activities can grow out of the reading experiences.

2. Allow LD students with severe handwriting problems to use a typewriter or a microcomputer with word processing software for writing all types of compositions as well as for practicing spelling words. Poor handwriting skills contribute to many children's spelling errors.

3. Use journal writing to help LD students learn to express their feelings and develop writing fluency. Because the teacher does not correct spelling and other mechanical errors on journal assignments, this activity is less threatening to LD students than other more formal writing activities.

4. Wordless picture books are an especially valuable instructional material for LD students. (A list of wordless picture books was presented in Figure 4–4.) Students can tell stories based on the pictures, learn vocabulary words related to the stories, and dictate or write their own stories based on the books (D'Angelo, 1980; McGee & Tompkins, 1983).

5. Provide extensive prewriting activities (e.g., brainstorming, clustering, markings) to give LD students the necessary warm-up before writing (Tompkins & Friend, 1986). Even though the prewriting stage of the writing process is valuable for all students, learning disabled students especially benefit from prewriting activities in which they generate ideas and organize these ideas for writing. A third grader's cluster and autobiographical writing are presented in Figure 15–2. Notice how the student gathered and organized ideas in the cluster and expanded the ideas in the autobiography.

Mentally Retarded Students

Because the media has enhanced the public's knowledge of mentally retarded children and adults through their coverage of the Special Olympics, mentally retarded students are probably the most familiar of all types of exceptional students. *Mental retardation* is defined as "significantly subaverage general intellectual functioning existing concurrently with deficits in adaptive behavior, and manifested during the developmental period [ages 0–18], which adversely affects a child's educational performance" (*Federal Register,* August 23, 1977, p. 785). This definition involves two dimensions: To be considered mentally retarded, a student's general intellectual functioning must be significantly below average, and the student must also have deficits in adaptive behavior. *Adaptive behavior* refers to students' ability to meet standards of personal independence, self-care, and social responsibility expected of their age and cultural group. *Subaverage intellectual functioning* is usually indicated by an intelligence quotient score (IQ) of 70 or less (approximately

Figure 15–2 A Student's Cluster and Autobiography

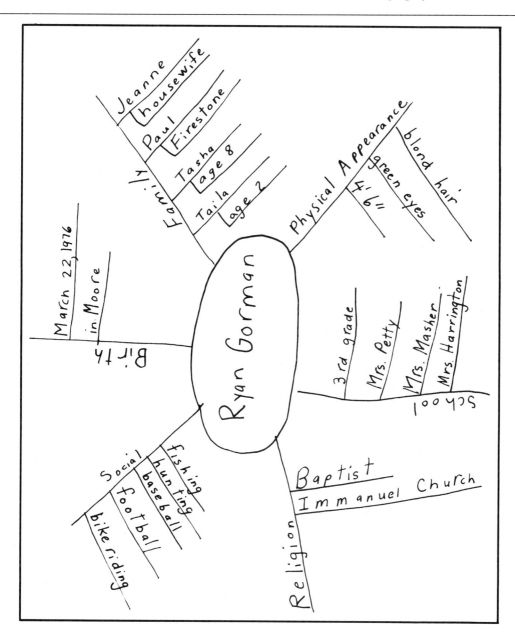

My name is Ryan Gorman. I was born March 22, 1976. I was born in Moore, Oklahoma. I have blond hair. My eyes are green. I am 4′6″.

My favorite sports are football and baseball. I like bike riding. I like fishing. I like hunting.

My mom's name is Jeanne. She is a housewife. My dad's name is Paul. He works at Firestone. I have two sisters. One's name is Tasha. She is 8. My other sister's name is Talia. She is 2.

I am Baptist. I go to Immanuel Church.

The school I go to is Southgate. I am in third grade. My homeroom teacher is Mrs. Petty. My lab teacher is Mrs. Harrington. I have a science teacher. Her name is Mrs. Masher. My favorite subject is math. My worst subject is reading.

two standard deviations below the mean *IQ* score, 100) on a standardized intelligence test. Mentally retarded students are classified into three or more levels according to severity. Psychologists use the terms *mild, moderate, severe,* and *profound* as labels for the categories, but educators typically use terms with educational implications, *educable mentally retarded* (EMR) (55–70 IQ range), *trainable mentally retarded* (TMR) (40–55 IQ range), and *severe/profound mentally retarded* (less than 40 IQ). School districts, however, may use different IQ scores to define the categories of mental retardation and to identify the students they will serve in each program.

Instructional Implications. Programs for the mentally retarded focus on helping students develop functional skills considered essential to living independently. The more severely retarded students are typically not mainstreamed into elementary classrooms. Educable mentally retarded students, in contrast to the more severely retarded students, are often placed in a regular class for most of the school day, leaving to go to a resource room for special instruction.

Educable mentally retarded students can be included in many regular instructional activities with slight modifications. The most valuable activities for EMR students, as well as for other students, are those that are concrete, meaningful, and based on personal experience. When the pace of classroom activities is too fast, individualized instruction with peer-tutors can be provided. This individualized instruction should involve more repetition and practice than is necessary for other students. EMR students need to "overlearn" a concept or skill by continuing practice even after they have demonstrated proficiency.

The most valuable language arts activities for EMR students are functional and involve skills that the students really need to know. These students are capable of learning to communicate through oral and written language, and they need to learn many of the same basic skills that other students learn in the elementary grades. Activities that are appropriate for educable mentally retarded students include the following:

1. Have peer-tutors read with EMR students using the assisted reading strategy that was presented in Chapter 1. The assisted reading strategy allows students to move naturally into reading and provides the repetition and practice these students need.

2. Have EMR students tell and dictate stories using wordless picture books. (Wordless picture books from the list in Figure 4–4 may be used.) These books without words are useful for introducing book handling skills and the concept of "story." An example of a story from a wordless picture book that was dictated by a mentally retarded student is presented in Figure 15–3.

3. Focus on functional learning through reading, spelling, and writing activities. For example, take a walking field trip through the community, taking pictures of functional words (e.g., *STOP, exit, women*) that students spot. Paste the photos in a booklet for students to read. Add students' dictated sentences below the pictures to show the word used in context. A list of essential survival words and phrases is presented in Figure 15–4. Also share concept books, such as

Figure 15–3 A Mildly Handicapped Student's Retelling of Alexander's
Out! Out! Out! (1968)

Out! Out! Out!

The little boy is pulling the train. The mother is feeding porridge to the baby while the baby feeds the porridge to a bird. The mother screams and the bird flies into the cabinet. The bird is getting into everything. A man is bringing groceries to mom. The bird flies out of the bag. The trashman shoos the bird out with a broom. The bird is trying to run away from the men. The little boy is spilling food. The bird is eating the food the little boy spilled. The little boy puts food on the window and the bird follows it. The mother is happy because the bird went away. The mother hugs the little boy.

Lisa, age 14

Figure 15–4 A List of Survival Words and Phrases

---

50 Most Essential Survival Words

1. Poison	26. Ambulance
2. Danger	27. Girls
3. Police	28. Open
4. Emergency	29. Out
5. Stop	30. Combustible
6. Hot	31. Closed
7. Walk	32. Condemned
8. Caution	33. Up
9. Exit	34. Blasting
10. Men	35. Gentlemen
11. Women	36. Pull
12. Warning	37. Down
13. Entrance	38. Detour
14. Help	39. Gasoline
15. Off	40. Inflammable
16. On	41. In
17. Explosives	42. Push
18. Flammable	43. Nurse
19. Doctor	44. Information
20. Go	45. Lifeguard
21. Telephone	46. Listen
22. Boys	47. Private
23. Contaminated	48. Quiet
24. Ladies	49. Look
25. Dynamite	50. Wanted

50 Most Essential Survival Phrases

1. Don't walk	26. Wrong way
2. Fire escape	27. No fires
3. Fire extinguisher	28. No swimming
4. Do not enter	29. Watch your step
5. First aid	30. Watch for children
6. Deep water	31. No diving
7. External use only	32. Stop for pedestrians
8. High voltage	33. Post office
9. No trespassing	34. Slippery when wet
10. Railroad crossing	35. Help wanted
11. Rest rooms	36. Slow down
12. Do not touch	37. Smoking prohibited
13. Do not use near open flame	38. No admittance
14. Do not inhale fumes	39. Proceed at your own risk
15. One way	40. Step down
16. Do not cross	41. No parking
17. Do not use near heat	42. Keep closed
18. Keep out	43. No turns
19. Keep off	44. Beware of dog
20. Exit only	45. School zone
21. No right turn	46. Dangerous curve
22. Keep away	47. Hospital zone
23. Thin ice	48. Out of order
24. Bus stop	49. No smoking
25. No passing	50. Go slow

Polloway & Polloway, 1981, pp. 446–447.

Signs (Goor & Goor, 1983), which include photos of signs with these essential survival words and phrases.

4. Use pattern books to teach oral language patterns such as *wh-* questions and past tense markers. In addition, students can dictate or write their own books following the patterns. Pattern books are a special kind of predictable book in which a phrase or sentence is repeated again and again. A list of predictable books that may be helpful was presented in Figure 1–11.

5. Try writing without a pencil (Tompkins, 1981). EMR students can practice handwriting skills using clay, fingerpaint, sand, shaving cream, and shaping their bodies like letters. They can also practice spelling words using these techniques and using magnetic letters, foam letters, letter stamps, and letter pillows.

6. Invite EMR students to write "I wish" poems, color poems, If I were . . . poems and other formula poems presented in Chapter 11. While EMR students may not be successful with haiku, limericks, and other more difficult syllable-counting and rhyming poetic formulas, they can write poems with repetitive patterns.

Emotionally Disturbed Students

Emotionally disturbed students (ED) are children with behavior disorders that interfere with learning. Typically, they are either aggressive with acting-out behaviors or withdrawn with nonresponsive behaviors. The term *emotionally disturbed* is defined as "a condition exhibiting one or more of the following characteristics over a long period of time and to a marked degree, which adversely affects educational performance:

1. an inability to learn which cannot be explained by intellectual, sensory, or health factors;

2. an inability to build or maintain satisfactory interpersonal relationships with peers and teachers;

3. inappropriate types of behavior or feelings under normal circumstances;

4. a general pervasive mood of unhappiness or depression; or

5. a tendency to develop physical symptoms or fears associated with personal or school problems. (*Federal Register,* August 23, 1977, pp. 785–786)

While any student can exhibit one of these behavior patterns for a brief period, children who are identified as emotionally disturbed exhibit one or more of these age or context inappropriate patterns to a marked degree or consistently over time.

Approximately 2% of students have an emotional handicap, but only the most severely maladjusted students are typically identified and served. Emotionally disturbed students are frequently underachievers because their emotional problems interfere with learning.

Instructional Implications. Scant attention has been given to developing instructional strategies and instructional materials to meet the special needs of ED students. However, the behavior of these exceptional learners suggest that they need a structured and positive school environment. Instruction in oral language skills may help ED students to express their emotions more appropriately. Teachers must closely monitor ED students' frustration levels and help students find ways to communicate their frustration. Behavior modification is an effective technique for helping students learn to control their disruptive and socially inappropriate behavior. Also, teachers must consider the ED students' social and emotional needs as well as their academic needs.

Many of the oral and written language strategies and activities discussed in this book can be used effectively with ED students. The following are some recommended activities:

1. To develop ED students' oral language and socialization skills, involve them in a variety of functional oral language activities. Younger children can participate in dramatic play and children at all ages can engage in informal conversations with classmates and with the teacher.

2. Emotionally disturbed students can express themselves with less anxiety using puppets. Encourage these students to use puppets in developing oral reports and retelling stories.

3. Have students write in journals and record their feelings or behaviors. This activity provides ED students with a pressure-release valve as well as necessary writing practice.

Drawing is an especially valuable prewriting activity for students with special learning needs.

4. Use drawing and other art activities as a prewriting strategy for ED students. For children who have trouble expressing themselves, art is an alternative form of communication. Students might also try creating their own wordless picture books.

5. Some ED students benefit from reading books with characters who exhibit behavior and learning problems similar to their own. In this way, students recognize that other children cope with similar problems. A list of books with characters who exhibit aggressive or withdrawn behavior is presented in Figure 15–5. Also, these books, rather than those suggested in Chapter 9, might be more appropriate for ED students to use in examining elements of story structure.

6. Special care is necessary in introducing ED students to the revising and editing stages of the writing process. Some ED students will have difficulty allowing their classmates to critique their writing. Teachers must nurture the writing process and demonstrate the importance of revising and editing to improve writing quality. Begin with one-on-one revising and editing, and then move slowly into group work.

POINTS TO PONDER
What Types of Language Different Students Might Be Placed in Your Classroom?
What Are the Characteristics of These Special Learners?
What Instructional Strategies Can Be Used with These Students?

LANGUAGE DIFFERENT STUDENTS

Language different students are children who cannot communicate effectively in standard English for other than physical or emotional reasons. They may be delayed in developing language, live in non-English speaking communities and have limited proficiency in English, have recently arrived in the United States and not speak English, or speak a nonstandard English dialect. In this section, we will consider the learning characteristics of these students and discuss strategies for teaching them language arts.

Language-delayed Students

Students are classified as *language-delayed* when their language development is significantly slower than the rate for other children. Despite a chronological delay, these students' language development usually follows the same stages as other children's development, but at a slower rate. Scofield (1978, p. 720) lists these characteristics of language-delayed students: They may (a) speak in markedly childlike phrases, (b) lack the sentence-producing ability of their classmates, (c) lack the ability to use language purposefully, (d) talk very little in school situations, and (e) lack many concepts that are part of day-to-day living. Many of these same

Figure 15–5   Stories with Characters Who Exhibit Aggressive or Withdrawn Behaviors

Brooks, B. (1984). *The moves make the man.* New York: Harper and Row. (U)

Bulla, C. R. (1975). *The shoeshine girl.* New York: Crowell. (M)

Byars, B. (1977). *The pinballs.* New York: Harper and Row. (U)

Cormier, R. (1977). *I am the cheese.* New York: Pantheon. (U)

Cunningham, J. (1977). *Come to the edge.* New York: Pantheon. (U)

Dana, F. (1978). *Crazy eights.* New York: Harper and Row. (U)

Fassler, J. (1971). *The boy with a problem.* New York: Behavioral Publications. (P)

Greenberg, J. (1979). *A season in-between.* New York: Farrar. (U)

Greene, C. C. (1979). *Getting nowhere.* New York: Viking. (M–U)

Heide, F. P. (1976). *Growing anyway up.* Philadelphia: Lippincott. (U)

Hunt, I. (1976). *The lottery rose.* New York: Scribner. (M–U)

Konigsburg, E. L. (1970). *George.* New York: Atheneum. (M)

Kroll, S. (1976). *That makes me mad!* New York: Pantheon. (P)

Ness, E. (1966). *Sam, Bangs and Moonshine.* New York: Holt. (P)

Platt, K. (1979). *The ape inside me.* Philadelphia: Lippincott. (U)

Preston, E. M. (1976). *The temper tantrum book.* New York: Viking. (P)

Sachs, M. (1971). *Bear's house.* New York: Doubleday. (M)

Slote, A. (1974). *Tony and me.* New York: Harper and Row. (M–U)

Stolz, M. (1963). *The bully of Barkham Street.* New York: Harper and Row. (M)

Udry, J. (1961). *Let's be enemies.* New York: Harper and Row. (P)

Viorst, J. (1972). *Alexander and the terrible, horrible, no good, very bad day.* New York: Atheneum. (P–M)

Yashima, T. (1955). *Crow boy.* New York: Viking. (P)

Zolotow, C. (1969). *The hating book.* New York: Harper and Row. (P)

P = primary grades (K–2)
M = middle grades (3–5)
U = upper grades (6–8)

language problems are also exhibited by learning disabled, mentally retarded, and emotionally disturbed learners.

Instructional Implications.   Language-delayed students need intensive experience with language, and many meaningful opportunities for learning language, both directly and indirectly, can be provided for them in the regular classroom. Scofield (1978) suggests three strategies for working with these special students.

Language-delayed children need (a) systematic instruction, (b) experience with a range of language functions, and (c) opportunities for spontaneous speech in the context of genuine interpersonal relationships.

Many of the activities suggested in Chapters 4 and 5 on talk and drama can be used effectively with language-delayed students. A list of 10 language functions was presented in Chapter 2, and this list can be used in planning language experiences for these special learners. The following is a list of activities recommended for language-delayed students:

1. Encourage language-delayed students to participate in conversations and small group interactions. Also, primary grade students can use spontaneous speech as they participate in dramatic play.

2. Use predictable books to provide structured practice of targeted language patterns. (A list of predictable books was provided in Chapter 1.) Also, Bromley and Jalongo (1984) recommend using song picture books with particular language patterns. Ezra Jack Keats' *Over in the meadow* (1971), for instance, can be used to practice person-number agreements. Other song picture books include: *Six little ducks* (Conover, 1976), *Roll over! A counting song* (Peek, 1981), and *She'll be comin' round the mountain* (Quackenbush, 1973).

3. Involve language-delayed students in informal drama activities such as role-playing and puppetry. Retelling familiar stories using the puppets is one possible activity. Movement activities can also be used to teach language concepts such as opposites, prepositions, and directional terms.

4. Teach language and content-area concepts by applying Piaget's theory of cognitive development. Introduce concepts to language-delayed students, provide concrete experiences, and help students identify both the features of the concept and the relationships between the concept and the child's other experiences. Drawing cluster diagrams may also be helpful.

5. Have language-delayed students write caption books in which they draw pictures or cut pictures from magazines and add word or phrase captions. Students can read the captions in the books and also talk about the pictures or use the captions in complete sentences. In this way, students learn concepts about written language while preparing materials for oral language practice.

6. Involve language-delayed children with books. Read and reread books to them and use the assisted reading strategy. Through experiences with books, these students will hear and perhaps repeat a rich variety of words and language patterns as well as learn to enjoy books. For a very moving account of the crucial role books played in the early development of a severely handicapped and nonverbal child, read Dorothy Butler's *Cushla and her books* (1979).

Bilingual and Non-English Speaking Students

Because many children living in the United States come from Hispanic, French, Asian, and Native American backgrounds, they acquire a native language at home which is different than the language used by their teachers at school. These children are called *bilingual speakers* because they speak one language in the home and English in the outside world. Bilingual students speak some English but often mix it with their native language, shifting back and forth between their native language and English, even within sentences. This phenomenon is called *code-switching,* and it is often misunderstood. Rather than a confusion between the two languages or a corruption of the native language, code-switching is a special linguistic and social skill (Troika, 1981).

One conflict for bilingual students is that learning and speaking standard English is often perceived by family and community members as a rejection of family and culture. Cultural pluralism has been gradually replacing the "melting pot" point of view. People in minority ethnic groups are now not as willing to give up their primary culture and language to join the mainstream Anglo culture. They want to live and function in both cultures, having free access to their cultural patterns, switching from one culture to the other as the situation demands.

Also, millions of immigrants enter the United States each year speaking Spanish, Farsi, Vietnamese, and other languages from around the world. These immigrant children who do not speak English are called *non-English speakers.* They are immersed in an English language environment as soon as they enter this country and learn to speak English with varying degrees of success depending on a variety of factors.

Research suggests that second-language acquisition is similar to first-language acquisition. Carole Urzua (1980) lists three principles culled from the research:

1. When people learn languages, they use many similar acquisition strategies; this is true whether they are small children learning their first (or native) language or older children or adults learning a second language.

2. Second-language learners go through several stages as they acquire their new language.

3. First- or second-language learning can only take place when and if the learner is placed in a situation that has meaning for that individual. (p. 33)

These stages of second-language acquisition are listed in Figure 15–6. At the same time students are acquiring the syntactic structures listed in Figure 15–6, they are also progressively using longer and more complex sentences. You will note many similarities to the stages of first-language acquisition discussed in Chapter 1.

Instructional Implications. Educational programs for bilingual and non-English speaking students usually take one of two forms: (a) transitional programs in which instruction in students' native language is used as a bridge to learning English and the native language is phased out as students' English proficiency increases and (b) maintenance programs in which instruction in both English and students' native language continues through school with the goal of bilingualism and the maintenance of the native language and culture. No single approach has been found to be most successful for all students; however, Troika (1981) urges that instruction in the students' native language continue until they are 10 or 11 years old. By that age, students have consolidated their linguistic skill development.

Figure 15–6 Stages of Second-Language Acquisition

Stage 1

    Yes/no answers
    Positive statements
    Subject pronouns (e.g., *he, she*)
    Present tense/present habitual verb tense
    Possessive pronouns (e.g., *my, your*)

Stage 2

    Simple plurals of nouns
    Affirmative sentences
    Subject and object pronouns (all)
    Possessive (*'s*)
    Negation
    Possessive pronouns (e.g., *mine*)

Stage 3

    Present progressive tense (-*ing*)
    Conjunctions (e.g., *and, but, or, because, so, as*)

Stage 4

    Questions (*who? what? which? where?*)
    Irregular plurals of nouns
    Simple future tense (*going to*)
    Prepositions

Stage 5

    Future tense (*will*)
    Questions (*when? how?*)
    Conjunctions (e.g,. *either, nor, neither, that, since*)

Stage 6

    Regular past tense verbs
    Question (*why?*)
    Contractions (e.g., *isn't*)
    Modal verbs (e.g., *can, must, do*)

Stage 7

    Irregular past tense verbs
    Past tense questions
    Auxilliary verbs (*has, is*)
    Passive voice

Stage 8

    Conditional verbs
    Imperfect verb tense
    Conjunctions (e.g., *though, if, therefore*)
    Subjunctive verb mood

Gonzales, 1981a, pp. 156–157.

To help bilingual and non-English speaking students learn English as a second language, teachers need to develop an understanding and appreciation of the culture and language their students bring with them. Teachers' attitudes toward their students' language and culture will be the key to success or failure in teaching these language different students.

The first priority in instructing a non-English speaking student is to teach survival vocabulary and to orient the child to the school and classroom environment. English speaking students can serve as peer-tutors and "buddies" for the new students. Wagner (1982) reports that her students took turns teaching the non-English speaking students in her class. After a semester the program was terminated because the non-English speaking students had learned to speak English! Suggestions for orienting non-English speaking students into an English speaking class appear in Figure 15–7.

In the regular classroom, bilingual and non-English speaking students at second-grade level or above should be immersed in both oral and written language, but bilingual educators suggest that younger students concentrate on oral

Figure 15–7 Suggestions for Orienting Non-English Speaking Students into an English Speaking Classroom

1. Teach the non-English speaking student survival vocabulary including courtesy words and phrases such as "hello," "thank you," "my name is _____," and "I need to go to the bathroom."
2. Try to locate an adult or older student who speaks both the child's native language and English to teach English speaking students a few survival words and phrases in the child's native language and to serve as a volunteer aide to ease the non-English speaker's transition to the classroom.
3. Orient the non-English speaking student to the school setting and the classroom. Take the child on a "survival tour" of the school, pointing out the cafeteria, library, bathroom, principal's office, and other essential locations. Continue with a classroom "survival tour," and add labels for classroom objects. If possible, write names of objects in both the child's native language and English on the labels. Also, draw maps of the classroom and school with the student.
4. Ask students to volunteer to serve as peer-tutors for the non-English speaking student. These peer-tutors serve as "buddies" and involve the non-English speaking student in hands-on and natural language activities such as playing basketball, erasing the chalkboard, delivering messages to other classrooms, or working on a jigsaw puzzle.

Gonzales, 1981b.

language first (Rodrigues & White, 1981). Language different students can be immersed in oral language by means of conversations, discussions, and other activities suggested in Chapter 4. Students also can participate in the informal drama, role-playing, and puppetry activities suggested in Chapter 5. Students can be immersed in written languages by reading to them and by using assisted reading. Other strategies for immersing these language different students in oral and written language include the following:

1. Have students write in journals. Journal writing is an effective way to help students develop writing fluency (Rodrigues & White, 1981). Shea and Fitzgerald (1981) report that non-English speaking kindergartners can draw pictures in their journals and gradually grow into dictating and later writing labels and captions to accompany their drawings.

2. Teach the survival words and phrases presented in Figure 15–4. Non-English speaking students and those with limited English proficiency will need to learn these words and phrases quickly to function successfully in the mainstream culture.

3. Use concept books such as Gail Gibbons' *Trucks* (1981) and Tana Hoban's *A, B, see* (1982) to teach basic vocabulary words. A list of concept books appropriate for elementary students is presented in Figure 15–8. In addition, students can draw pictures or cut pictures from magazines and add labels to create their own concept books.

4. Show filmstrip versions of stories to limited English speaking students before asking them to read the story. (Filmstrip versions of many stories are available from Weston Woods, Weston, CT 06880). Also, have students pantomime stories or retell them using puppets. Another possibility is to tape-record reading materials or have limited English speaking students read with a peer-tutor who can answer questions as they arise.

5. Involve students in the sentence pattern and sentence-combining activities presented in Chapter 12 to refine students' oral language skills after they have developed some fluency in English.

6. Non-English speaking and bilingual students often have difficulty understanding our idioms (e.g., "rocks in his head," "out in left field"). Use pantomime to act out literal and figurative meanings. Later, have children develop a class collaboration book in which they draw pictures and write sentences using both meanings. Books, such as *Put your foot in your mouth and other silly sayings* (Cox, 1980), *In a pickle and other funny idioms* (Terban, 1983), *Easy as pie: A guessing game of sayings* (Folsom & Folsom, 1985), can be used as examples. A student's drawing of the literal meaning of "butterflies in my stomach" is presented in Figure 15–9.

Nonstandard English Speaking Students

A single "pure" form of English does not exist, and all English speakers speak one dialect or another. These dialects vary across geographic regions, ethnic back-

Anno, M. (1975). *Anno's counting book.* New York: Crowell.

Banchek, L. (1978). *Snake in, snake out.* New York: Crowell.

Beller, J. (1984). *A-B-C-ing: An action alphabet.* New York: Crown.

Burningham, J. (1969). *Seasons.* Indianapolis: Bobbs-Merrill. (See also *Sniff shout* and other books about sounds by the same author.)

Carle, E. (1974). *My very first book of colors.* New York: Crowell. (See other concept books by the same author.)

Crews, D. (1982). *Harbor.* New York: Greenwillow. (See other beautifully illustrated concept books by the same author.)

Gibbons, G. (1981). *Trucks.* New York: Crowell. (See other concept books including *The boat book, Fire! Fire!* and *New road* by the same author.)

Goor, R., & Goor, N. (1983). *Signs.* New York: Crowell.

Hoban, T. (1982). *A, B, see.* New York: Greenwillow. (See *More than one, Over, under & through (and other spatial concepts), Push-pull, empty-full: A book of opposites,* and other concept books by the same author.)

Maestro, G. (1974). *One more and one less.* New York: Crown.

Oxenbury, H. (1981). *Dressing.* New York: Simon & Schuster. (See other basic concept books by the same author.)

Robbins, K. (1981). *Trucks of every sort.* New York: Crown.

Rockwell, A. (1984). *Trucks.* New York: Dutton. (See *Cars* and other concept books by the same author.)

Rockwell, A., & Rockwell, H. (1972). *Machines.* New York: Macmillan. (See other concept books by these authors.)

Rockwell, H. (1975). *My dentist.* New York: Greenwillow. (See *My doctor* and other concept books by the same author.)

Supraner, R. (1978). *Giggly-wiggly, snickety-snick.* New York: Parents.

Wildsmith, B. (1962). *Brian Wildsmith's ABC.* New York: Watts. (See *Brian Wildsmith's circus* and other concept books by the same author.)

Figure 15–8 Concept Books to Use with Non-English Speaking Students

grounds, and socioeconomic levels. Speakers of particular dialects are distinguished by their pronunciations, particular word choices, and grammatical forms. Consider the different pronunciations of Bostonians, New Yorkers, and Texans; the different words—*pop, soda, soft drink, soda pop,* and *tonic*—used to describe the same carbonated beverage; and the double negatives used by speakers of some dialects. This diversity reflects the cultural pluralism of our society. Some dialects, however, command more respect than others. The dialect used by television reporters and commentators, by authors of books and newspaper and magazine articles, and in school is known as *standard English* (SE). The other dialects

Figure 15–9   A Student's Literal Drawing of an Idiom

Robert, age 10

are collectively termed *nonstandard English* (NSE). Students who use nonstandard speech patterns in 20% to 30% of their conversation are generally referred to as nonstandard English speakers.

In the past, Black students, Appalachian students, and others who spoke a dialect different from standard English were considered to have little language ability. Myths about Black English and other nonstandard dialects that were perpetuated for generations have been disproved. Nonstandard English dialects are not inferior language systems; rather they are different, rule-governed systems which have patterns of their own (Labov, 1969). The children and adults who speak these dialects are neither cognitively or linguistically deficient.

Children who speak NSE dialects develop language competency in the same way and at a rate that parallels standard English development. Distinctive phonological and syntactic features of Black English and other nonstandard dialects are listed in Figure 15–10. Researchers have found that NSE speakers gradually incorporate some features of standard English into their speech and writing during the elementary grades. The increasing use of SE features may be due to peer interaction, exposure to standard English on television, or instruction in standard English at school.

Instructional Implications.   William Labov (1966) has identified eight areas of language arts instruction necessary for NSE students. These areas are listed in or-

Contrast	Standard English	Nonstandard English
Phonological Contrasts		
1. *r*-lessness	guard, fort	god, fought
2. *l*-lessness	help, you'll	hep, you
3. Final consonant cluster simplified	past, desk, meant	pass, des, men
4. Substitutions for /th/	then, mouth	den, mouf
5. Substitution of /n/ for /ing/	coming	comin'
Syntactic Contrasts		
1. Plural marker	two girls	two girl
2. Possessive marker	a dog's bone	a dog bone
3. Double negatives	don't have any	don't got none
	doesn't have	ain't got no
4. Preposition	at his friend's house	to his friend's house
	lives on 3rd Street	live 3rd Street
5. Indefinite article	an apple	a apple
6. Pronoun form	we have	us got
	his ball	he ball
7. Double subjects	John runs	John he run
8. Person-number agreement	she walks	she walk
	Bill has	Bill have
9. Present participle	he is coming	he comin'
10. Past marker	Mother asked	Mother ask
11. Verb form	I said	I say
12. Verb "to be" (present tense)	she is busy	she busy
		she be busy
13. Verb "to be" (past tense)	we were happy	we was happy
14. Future form	I will go	I'ma go, I gonna go
15. "If" construction	I asked if	I ask did

Figure 15–10   Contrasts Between Standard and Nonstandard English

der of priority: (a) understanding spoken SE, (b) reading books written in SE, (c) communicating effectively through talk, (d) communicating effectively through writing, (e) using SE forms in writing, (f) spelling words correctly, (g) using SE forms in talk, and (h) using SE pronunciation. Notice that the sequence moves from competency in basic oral and written to communication to the acquisition of standard English syntactic and phonological features. Using standard English in writing precedes oral language proficiency.

The teacher's role is three-fold: (a) to become sensitive to the needs of NSE speakers; (b) to learn about the distinctive features of NSE in order to understand the difficulties and frustrations that NSE students face in learning to read, write, and spell in standard English; and (c) to accept and show respect for students' language. Rejection of students' nonstandard dialects as well as teachers' confusion about nonstandard English interferes with students' learning (Goodman & Buck, 1973). Teachers should establish a climate in their classrooms where students will feel that their language is accepted. Students' language reflects their culture, and it is essential to respect them. Teachers should also demonstrate that they truly believe that their students are capable of handling two or more dialects. Teachers usually assume that non-English speakers who have recently arrived in the United States will learn to speak standard English, but this same confidence is rarely shown to NSE speakers.

Students naturally use their NSE dialect in reading aloud. Even though students comprehend the standard English they are reading, they often "translate" the language of the textbook into their dialect. This phenomenon can be explained using transformational grammar terminology: While the surface structure of NSE and SE are different, the deep, meaning level is the same, and these dialectal errors do not interfere with meaning (Goodman & Buck, 1973).

Accepting students' linguistic differences, however, is not synonymous with not teaching standard English. Students who speak a NSE dialect need to participate in oral language activities in order to use the forms of standard English. Many of the activities provided in Chapter 4 on oral language can be used with these students to help them expand their use of sentence patterns and grammatical structures. It is important to note, however, that interrupting students while they are speaking or reading aloud to correct their NSE "errors" is not an effective practice. In fact, students may choose not to talk or read aloud if they do not feel their language will be accepted. Activities to teach standard English are suggested in the following paragraphs:

1. Use children's literature that involves SE patterns in teaching standard English. Programs using chidren's literature as a model (Strickland, 1973; Cullinan, Jaggar & Strickland, 1974) have been found to be successful in expanding students' language repertoire. A three-step approach has been developed to introduce NSE speakers to SE syntactic patterns (Tompkins & McGee, 1983). The three steps are: (a) introduce an SE pattern by reading a predictable book that repeats the syntactic pattern; (b) provide extensive practice with the pattern through reading, role-playing, puppetry, and dictating or writing the story; and (c) have students manipulate the pattern by inventing new content for the pattern they are practicing. Emphasis in this approach is placed on imitating and repeating the pattern. At first students will use their own dialect in repeating the pattern, but as they feel comfortable with the pattern, students should be encouraged to substitute the SE form. Emphasize the specific contrast between the dialect and the standard form. The list of predictable books with patterns and sample activities to teach some NSE/SE contrasts is presented in Figure 15–11. Teachers can locate additional predictable books to use in introducing other

NSE/SE syntactic and phonological contrasts. (A list of predictable books from Chapter 1, Figure 1–11, may be useful.)

2. Teachers can use stories and short pieces of writing that children write or dictate in teaching standard English (Gillet & Gentry, 1983). The four steps of this approach are: (a) compose a story with a child, (b) present a SE version of the story, (c) revise the original story using SE forms, and (d) expand selected sentences from the story using a transformation strategy. The teacher begins by writing a story with a child or selecting a story the child has already written. Next, a SE version of the story is developed in which the teacher replaces the NSE sentence patterns and grammatical structures with standard English ones but retains as many of the child's words as possible. This version is introduced as "another story" and the child reads it aloud. This second story is compared with the original story. Then the student revises the original story by expanding the sentences. Even in the revisions, several nonstandard elements are likely to remain. In the final step, sentences selected from the revised story are used to generate new sentences by substituting words and phrases:

Original sentence:	It sits on a log.
Transformation:	*A rabbit* sits on a log.
Transformation:	A rabbit *with long ears* sits on a log.
Transformation:	A rabbit with long ears *hops* on the log.

These sentence transformations allow students to expand their vocabularies and invent new, more elaborate sentences while modeling SE sentence patterns and grammatical structures.

3. Use the editing stage of the writing process to correct NSE "errors" in students' writing and to teach selected NSE/SE contrasts. Emphasize that the purpose of these changes is to communicate more effectively, not to criticize the student's language. It may be helpful for students to keep a checklist of NSE/SE contrasts they have learned to aid in locating their own errors. Sometimes students will write dialogue in a nonstandard dialect to more fully develop the characters and setting of a story. Many adult authors use this strategy to depict characters and settings more authentically, and teachers should be supportive of this writing strategy.

4. While NSE students' writing is less influenced by their dialects than their oral language is, dialect does have an impact on students' writing. Research indicates that the two NSE features that have the greatest influence on spelling errors are verb marker omissions and consonant omissions (Cronnell, 1984). One strategy for helping NSE speakers keep track of their standard English errors involves the use of spelling and grammar logs (VanDeWeghe, 1982). Students divide pages in their learning logs (a section in their journals or a special notebook) into columns as shown in Figure 15–12 on page 492, and record spelling errors in one section and grammar errors in the second section. In their learning logs, students record their errors and corrections and then analyze possible reasons for their errors. This is a strategy that many students use intuitively, but

Figure 15–11 A List of Pattern Books and Sample Activities to Teach some NSE/SE Contrasts

SE/NSE Contrast	Sample Book	Book's Pattern	Steps 2 and 3 Sample Activities	Other Books
Plural	*The very hungry caterpillar*	The very hungry caterpillar eats through: 1 apple 2 pears 3 plums, etc.	Have children draw pictures of more foods for the caterpillar to eat. Use a hole punch to make holes in the foods. Record children's dictation to accompany the pictures.	*Goodnight Moon, Millions of cats*
Possessive	*Ask Mr. Bear*	Danny asks Mr. Bear and other animals, "Can you give me something for my mother's birthday?"	Have children make labels using possessives for their desks, pencils, and other belongings. Then have them read the labels aloud.	*Whose nose is this?*
Person-Number Agreement	*The judge*	Each prisoner describes the horrible thing in more detail: It growls, it groans It chews up stones It spreads its wings And does bad things	Have children use collage materials to construct their own horrible things. Then record children's descriptions of their horrible things.	*Over in the meadow The green grass grows all around, Seven little monsters The maestro plays When it rains . . it rains*
Past Tense	*I know an old lady who swallowed a fly*	This is a cumulative tale about an old lady who swallows a fly and a series of other animals to catch the fly.	Have the children make a set of finger puppets to use in retelling the story.	*Elephant in a well Too much noise Goodnight, owl Where the wild things are The haunted house Roll over! The enormous turnip*

Present Participle	Chicken Licken	Chicken Licken warns everyone that "The sky is falling!"	Have the children act out the story.	Someone is eating the sun The chick and the duckling Crocodile and ben Henny penny The fat cat Brown bear, Brown bear, What do you see?
Negative	A flower pot is not a bat	This pattern is repeated on each page: A ___ is not a ___.	Have children compose new sentences and record them on a chart or in individual booklets. Have children draw pictures to illustrate the sentences.	It looked like spilt milk Never bit a porcupine Have you seen my cat? One Monday morning The grouchy ladybug Crocodile and ben
Verb "to be" (Present tense)	Where in the world is Henry?	Two children use questions and answers to look for Henry: Where is the bed? The bed is in the bedroom.	Have children compose new questions and answers following the same pattern. Record them on sentence strips for children to match.	A ghost story King of the mountain The judge The house that Jack built
Verb "to be" (Past tense)	10 bears in my bed	A little boy tries to get 10 bears out of his bed. Each page begins: There were (number) in his bed and the little one said, "Roll over!"	Tape-record the story leaving space on the tape for children to repeat the sentence pattern.	There was an old woman The very hungry caterpillar What good luck! What bad luck!

Tompkins & McGee, 1983, pp. 466–467.

Figure 15–12   Sample Spelling and Grammar Logs

Spelling Log Entry

Correct Spelling	My Misspelling	Why the Word Confuses Me	Helps for Remembering the Correct Spelling
meant	ment	I spell it like I think it sounds.	It's the past of *mean*.
demonstrate	demenstrate	I use *e* instead of *o*.	A dem*o* is used to demonstrate.
coarse	course	I get it mixed up with *course* as a class.	a = co*a*rse is h*a*rd.

Grammar Log Entry

Personal Grammar	Written Grammar	Reasons for Differences
my brothers house	my brother's house	I need to put in an apostrophe (') to show ownership.
We took the following items, a camera, a backpack, and a canteen.	We took the following items: a camera, a backpack, and a canteen.	I should use a colon (:) when I introduce a series of things.

Van DeWeghe, 1982, pp. 102–103.

by formalizing the strategy in their learning logs, NSE students are more likely to learn SE patterns.

5. Because of pronunciation differences between dialects, students may have difficulty with pairs of words that are not homonyms in standard English but are homonyms in their dialects. For example, these pairs of words are homonyms for some students: *poke/pork, told/toll, pin/pen, all/oil* (Barnitz, 1980). Teachers who are sensitive to their students' spelling and word choice errors can catch these homonym confusions and develop activities to help students distinguish between the pairs. One possible activity is the class collaboration homonym book discussed in Chapter 1.

6. Introduce students to the variety of dialects spoken in the United States. Records such as "Our Changing Language" (Burack & McDavid, 1965) can be shared so that students can hear the phonological, syntactic, and semantic differences among dialects. (For a list of language recordings, check *The sound of*

English: A bibliography of language recordings compiled by Linn and Zuber, [1984]). Books of children's literature with dialogue written in different dialects can also be used. Through these experiences, students can learn about the richness and variety of language as well as the prestige associated with some dialects. Research suggests that before adolescence children are not even aware that standard English is the prestige dialect (Labov, 1970).

POINTS TO PONDER
What Are the Learning Characteristics of Gifted Students?
What Instructional Strategies Can Be Used with These Students?

GIFTED STUDENTS

In contrast to mildly handicapped students who have intellectual or emotional problems that interfere with their learning and language different students who have language barriers, *gifted students* are academically advanced students. Because they learn quickly and have advanced language skills, these students also require special programs to meet their needs.

National interest in gifted students was sparked in 1957 with Russia's launch of the Sputnik satellite, and federal programs were soon developed to encourage students to excel academically. Gifted children usually score two standard deviations or higher (approximately 130+) above the mean IQ score of 100 on intelligence tests, and their level of academic functioning is often two or more grade levels above that of their classmates. It must be noted, however, that many school districts set their own guidelines for identifying students who will be included in gifted programs.

Educators acknowledge that giftedness is more than an IQ score, and they are working to broaden the concept and definition of giftedness by including other dimensions of intelligence. Certainly, intelligence is far more than a single ability. Guilford (1967) identified 120 specific abilities related to intelligence! Characteristics of gifted students are included in Figure 15–13. While a gifted child may exhibit many of these characteristics, no one child exhibits them all.

In addition, not all gifted students are high achievers. Some are underachievers who do not work up to their potential because of lack of motivation, peer pressure, or fear of success. Too often teachers identify students who are well behaved or complete their assignments accurately and punctually as possibly gifted students. In contrast, other students who appear to be bored or show a lack of interest in class activities may also be gifted but have not demonstrated their potential.

Instructional Implications.   Gifted students have special needs just as other exceptional learners do, and the greater the student's ability, the more that student needs an individually tailored program. Four options are available to meet the needs of gifted students: (a) segregating gifted students in a special "gifted class" or

Figure 15–13 Characteristics of Gifted Students

The gifted child tends to

1. have a unique learning style
2. learn faster than most children do
3. develop earlier (e.g., walking, talking, reading)
4. ask complex questions and display a high degree of curiosity
5. give complicated, detailed explanations
6. grasp relationships quickly
7. organize information in new ways
8. see many solutions to a problem
9. have an unusually good memory
10. use abstract thought processes
11. see ambiguity in factual materials (e.g., true-false questions)
12. have a large vocabulary
13. express self well
14. have varied interests
15. delight in discovery and problem solving
16. enjoy working independently
17. have a longer attention span than peers
18. persevere in areas of interest
19. have a highly developed sense of humor (e.g., punning)
20. be perfectionistic
21. be highly energetic
22. prefer the company of older children and adults
23. exhibit strong personal values
24. be highly sensitive about self and others
25. show a high level of self-awareness

Silverman, 1982, p. 494.

in magnet schools, (b) accelerating gifted students by "telescoping" or "skipping" them to a higher grade, (c) mainstreaming gifted students in regular classrooms, (d) enriching mainstreamed gifted students through special pull-out programs (Schwartz, 1984).

Independent study assignments are recommended as the best way for classroom teachers to work with mainstreamed gifted students (Silverman, 1982). Before assigning independent study activities, though, teachers should be certain that students know how to study independently. Students need to learn how to collect resources, use study skills, manage time, and complete products. Teachers should teach or review these skills before allowing students to work individually. Also gifted students, like other students, need teacher supervision as they work, and they need to know their teacher is interested in their work and available for guidance as needed.

In designing these independent study activities, the following variables should be considered:

1. *Pacing.* Instruction for gifted students should be rapidly paced to suit their learning style.

2. *Level of Abstraction.* Gifted students can engage in hypothetical reasoning, discuss complex issues, make higher order inferences, and utilize systematic procedures in their quest for knowledge.

3. *Type of Subject Matter.* Interdisciplinary units are well suited to the complex minds and synthesizing abilities of the gifted.

4. *Depth of Study.* For gifted students, depth is preferable to breadth.

5. *Range of Resources.* Gifted students can be given access to a greater variety and more advanced level of resources than the norm . . . Human resources should also be used to a greater extent.

6. *Dissemination.* High quality student products should be shared with the community in some way—through science fairs, editorials, speeches to parents, learning centers for other classes, submitting work for publication, and so on (Silverman, 1982, pp. 505–506).

One approach to self-directed, independent study is Joseph Renzulli's enrichment triad (1977). This approach involves three steps to lead gifted students through a series of experiences that culminate in products that have value for society. Through the enrichment triad, prospective scientists, artists, or young historians, writers, or computer programmers can have an impact on the adult world.

Step 1. The first step consists of exploratory activities in which students investigate one or more avenues of interest and then decide on a topic or problem they would like to study further. Through an interview, the teacher and the gifted student discuss a topic to be studied further and together develop a written plan of study listing the activities the student will engage in, the types of resources to be consulted, and a timeline for completing the activities.

Step 2. Experiences in Step 2 provide students with the technical skills and tools they will need to complete the scientific investigations and other products they develop in the third step. The technical skills that each student learns will depend on the topic or problem identified earlier. After completing these training activities, students brainstorm products which they complete in the third step.

Step 3. In the third step, students investigate real-life problems working individually or in small groups. Using appropriate methods of inquiry, they develop a product that is meaningful to them and to society. These products may include reports of scientific investigations that are submitted for publication, computer programs, artistic creations and productions, or students serving as docents at a local museum.

Throughout this book, we have encouraged the notion of independent study assignments without calling them by name. We have discussed oral history projects, research reports, class newspapers, writing biographies, composing and performing scripts, and speechmasters clubs. All of these activities are appropriate for gifted students. Other activities include the following:

1. Invite community persons with particular areas of expertise to serve as mentors for gifted students (Boston, 1976; Jackson, 1981). Mentors offer students enthusiasm as well as expertise, and they can guide and counsel students as they work on independent study assignments. Mentors can provide assistance in almost any area in which students indicate interest—from aerospace engineering to computer programming to writing for publication.

2. Encourage students to publish their writing in a variety of ways. They can compile class anthologies, publish class newspapers, and produce plays or puppet shows from scripts they have written. They can create books with pop-ups or movables on each page (Abrahamson & Stewart, 1982) and share these or other stories they have written with younger children.

3. Gifted students can write and produce story and informational films (Cox, 1983). In this strategy, students begin by brainstorming a film and developing it into a cohesive composition. Next, students write the script using a story board. Finally the film properties (e.g., illustrations, title card, credits list, and other props) are collected or created, and the film is shot using either a movie camera or a video camera. (See Chapter 5 for more information on scripts, films, and video productions.)

4. In addition to using microcomputers for writing, gifted students can learn computer languages such as BASIC and PASCAL and create computer programs.

Gifted students can create learning centers and other curricular materials for their classmates to use.

Gifted students are often encouraged to study a foreign language, an alternative form of communication. Similarly, computer languages are alternative forms of communication, and learning to program computers provides students with an additional communication mode.

5. Encourage gifted students to use higher-level thinking skills. Bloom's *Taxonomy of educational objectives* (1956) identifies six levels of thinking skills ranging from knowledge to evaluation. Too often instruction focuses on the lower-level thinking skills, knowledge and comprehension, but especially for gifted students, the emphasis should be on the higher levels—analysis, synthesis, and evaluation. In planning independent study assignments, teachers should design activities involving these higher-level thinking skills. An example of an interdisciplinary unit on ancient Egypt with activities planned at each of the six levels according to Bloom's taxonomy is presented in Figure 15–14. Another

Figure 15–14   Activities from an Interdisciplinary Unit on Ancient Egypt at the Six Levels of Bloom's *Taxonomy* (1956)

Level 1: Knowledge

Make a flow chart showing the power structure of government during the New Kingdom.

Learn about at least five Egyptian gods. Write a paragraph on each.

Level 2: Comprehension

Write biographical sketches of five famous Egyptians.

Draw a crosscut diagram of a pyramid.

Level 3: Application

Make a scrapbook of gods and godesses.

Make an annotated bibliography of 10 sources about ancient Egypt.

Level 4: Analysis

Write a poem that describes the ancient Egyptian army.

Make a chart of sacred animals showing their purposes.

Level 5: Synthesis

Write a fairy tale about the flooding of the Nile River.

Create your own writing system using hieroglyphics.

Level 6: Evaluation

Solve the problem of how to play "senet." Write your own rules and teach others to play.

Write a report about the motifs of ancient Egyptian art.

Mrs. Diane Lewis, Irving Middle School, Norman, OK.

way to encourage higher-level thinking is the reflective discussions described in Chapter 3.

6. Provide opportunities for gifted students to create curricular materials for classroom use. Developing these materials provides students with the opportunity to apply their knowledge in particular content areas and to create a product with a functional use. For instance, two upper grade gifted students developed a unit on survival. They began by collecting survival stories (e.g., Defoe's *Robinson Crusoe,* 1966, and Taylor's *The cay,* 1969), autobiographies/biographies (e.g., Read's *Alive,* 1984), and informational tradebooks such as *Outdoor survival skills* (Olsen, 1973). Next, the students developed the unit and organized it according to six hazardous geographic environments: (a) arctic, (b) sea, (c) swamp, (d) forest, (e) tropical forest, and (f) desert. They developed activities for each environment based on Bloom's taxonomy and produced the unit as a center with survival books and related activity cards. A list of the activities on tropical forest survival that the students developed for the unit is presented in Figure 15–15. After the unit was constructed, it was set out in the classroom for other students to use.

Figure 15–15   Tropical Forest Survival Activities from a Unit Developed by Gifted Students

Knowledge:	Make a list of all the materials you would need to construct a shelter in a tropical forest. Explain why the materials are needed.
Comprehension:	Explain why you need more preparation concerning first aid and insects in a tropical forest than in a regular forest.
Application:	Draw a picture to illustrate at least 10 dangers of a tropical forest and tell how you can avoid them.
Analysis:	Survey 10 adults and ask them what they think are the 10 most essential items for survival in a tropical forest.
Synthesis:	Collect facts and make a scrapbook on surviving in a jungle and other tropical rain forests.
Evaluation:	Compare the necessities for surviving in a forest to the necessities for surviving in a tropical forest.

Brian and Brady, age 14

Summary

In this chapter we considered three categories of students with special learning needs: (a) mildly handicapped students, (b) language different students, and (c) gifted students. For each category, learning characteristics were discussed and instructional implications were suggested. The approach presented in this chapter was that the content and strategies in this book are appropriate with some modifications for all students who are mainstreamed or placed in regular classes.

Mildly handicapped students, including learning disabled, mentally retarded, and emotionally disturbed students, are high-incidence handicapped students who are frequently mainstreamed in regular classrooms. All three types of mildly handicapped students benefit from structured environments in which they can learn more easily and feel successful. Suggested strategies included assisted reading, journal writing, and using peer-tutors.

Three types of language different students were considered: (a) students who are language-delayed; (b) students who come to school not speaking English or who have limited English proficiency because they speak another language at home; (c) and nonstandard English speaking students. These students need to be involved in extensive language activities that expand their use of language patterns and develop their knowledge of the world in general. It is also important to note that teachers must accept these students' language differences and respect their cultures.

The third category of students with special needs were gifted students. In contrast to other groups of exceptional students, gifted students have advanced language development and accelerated academic achievement. In the regular classroom, these students benefit from independent study assignments. Renzulli's enrichment triad and interdisciplinary units with activities requiring higher-level thinking skills were suggested as two enrichment techniques.

Extensions

1. Observe mildly handicapped students, language different students, or gifted students working in regular classrooms as well as in supplemental "pull-out" programs. Which of the activities recommended in this chapter are teachers using with these special students?

2. Develop and teach a lesson to one or more mildly handicapped students. Choose one of the activities listed in this chapter for learning disabled, educable mentally retarded, or emotionally disturbed students. Keep a log describing the students you are working with and how you adapt the activity to meet the students' needs. After teaching, evaluate the lesson and describe how students benefited from it in your log.

3. Repeat extension 2 with language different students and with gifted students.

References

Abrahamson, R. F., & Stewart, R. (1982). Movable books—A new golden age. *Language Arts, 59,* 342–347.

Alexander, M. (1968). *Out! out! out!* New York: Dial.

Barnitz, J. G. (1980). Black English and other dialects: Sociolinguistic implications for reading instruction. *The Reading Teacher, 33,* 779–786.

Bloom, B. S. (1956). *Taxonomy of educational objectives, handbook I: Cognitive domain.* New York: McKay.

Boston, B. O. (1976). *The sorcerer's apprentice: A case study in the role of the mentor.* Reston, VA: The Council for Exceptional Children and the ERIC Clearinghouse on Handicapped and Gifted Children.

Bromley, K. D., & Jalongo, M. R. (1984). Song picture books and the language disabled child. *Teaching Exceptional Children, 16,* 114–119.

Burack, E. G., & McDavid, R. I., Jr. (1965). Our changing language (record). Urbana, IL: National Council of Teachers of English.

Butler, D. (1979). *Cushla and her books.* Boston: Horn Book.

Conover, C. (1976) *Six little ducks.* New York: Crowell.

Cox, C. (1983). Young filmmakers speak the language of film. *Language Arts, 60,* 296–304, 372.

Cox, J. A. (1980). *Put your foot in your mouth and other silly sayings.* New York: Random House.

Cronnell, B. (1984). Black-English influences in the writing of third- and sixth-grade black students. *Journal of Educational Research, 77,* 223–236.

Cullinan, B. E., Jaggar, A. M., & Strickland, D. (1974). Language expansion for black children in the primary grades: A research report. *Young Children, 39,* 98–112.

D'Angelo, K. (1980). Wordless picture books and the learning disabled. In G. Stafford (Ed.), *Dealing with differences: Classroom practices in teaching English 1980–1981* (pp. 46–49). Urbana, IL: National Council of Teachers of English.

Defoe, D. (1966). *Robinson Crusoe.* New York: Penguin.

Federal Register (vol. 42). (1977, August 23). Washington, DC: Department of Health, Education, and Welfare.

Folsom, M., & Folsom, M. (1985). *Easy as pie: A guessing game of sayings.* Boston: Houghton Mifflin.

Gibbons, G. (1981). *Trucks.* New York: Crowell.

Gillet, J. W., & Gentry, J. R. (1983). Bridges between nonstandard and standard English with extensions of dictated stories. *The Reading Teacher, 36,* 360–364.

Glass, R. M., Christiansen, J., & Christiansen, J. L. (1982). *Teaching exceptional students in the regular classroom.* Boston: Little, Brown.

Gonzales, P. C. (1981a). Beginning English reading for ESL students. *The Reading Teacher, 35,* 154–162.

———. (1981b). How to begin language instruction for non-English speaking students. *Language Arts, 58,* 175–180.

Goodman, K. S., & Buck, C. (1983). Dialect barriers to reading comprehension revisited. *The Reading Teacher, 27,* 6–12.

Goor, R., & Goor, N. (1983). *Signs.* New York: Crowell.

Guilford, J. P. (1967). *The nature of human intelligence.* New York: McGraw Hill.

Hoban, T. (1982). *A, B, see.* New York: Greenwillow.

Jackson, L. A. (1981). Enrich your writing program with mentors. *Language Arts, 58,* 837–839.

Keats, E. J. (1971). *Over in the meadow.* New York: Scholastic.

Labov, W. (1966). *The social stratification of English in New York City.* Washington, DC: Center for Applied Linguistics.

_____. (1969). The logic of non-standard English. *The Florida FL Reporter, 7,* 60–74.

_____. (1970). *The study of nonstandard English.* Urbana, IL: National Council of Teachers of English.

Lerner, J. (1985). Learning disabilities: Theories, diagnosis, and teaching strategies (4th ed.). Boston: Houghton Mifflin.

Linn, M. D., & Zuber, M. (1984). *The sound of English: A bibliography of language recordings.* Urbana, IL: National Council of Teachers of English.

McClure, A. A. (1985). Predictable books: Another way to teach reading to learning disabled children. *Teaching Exceptional Children, 17,* 267–273.

McGee, L. M., & Tompkins, G. E. (1983). Wordless picture books are for older readers, too. *Journal of Reading, 27,* 120–123.

Olsen, L. D. (1973). *Outdoor survival skills.* New York: Pocket Books.

Peek, M. (1981). *Roll over! A counting song.* Boston: Houghton Mifflin.

Polloway, C. H., & Polloway, E. A. (1981). Survival words for disabled readers. *Academic Therapy, 16,* 443–448.

Quackenbush, R. (1973). *She'll be comin' round the mountain.* Philadelphia: Lippincott.

Read, P. P. (1984). *Alive: The story of the Andes survivors.* New York: Harper and Row.

Renzulli, J. S. (1977). *The enrichment triad model: A guide for developing defensible programs for the gifted and talented.* Mansfield Center, CT: Creative Learning Press.

Rodrigues, R. J., & White, R. H. (1981). *Mainstreaming the non-English speaking student* (TRIP Booklet). Urbana, IL: ERIC Clearinghouse on Reading and Communication Skills and the National Council of Teachers of English.

Schwartz, L. L. (1984). *Exceptional students in the mainstream.* Belmont, CA: Wadsworth.

Scofield, S. J. (1978). The language-delayed child in the mainstreamed primary classroom. *Language Arts, 55,* 719–723, 732.

Shea, P., & Fitzgerald, S. (1981). Raddara's beautiful book. *Language Arts, 58,* 156–161.

Silverman, L. (1982). Giftedness. In E. L. Meyen (Ed.), *Exceptional children in today's schools: An alternative resource book* (pp. 485–528). Denver: Love.

Strickland, D. S. (1973). A program for linguistically different, black children. *Research in the Teaching of English, 7,* 79–86.

Summers, M. (1977). Learning disabilities . . . A puzzlement. *Today's Education, 66,* 40–42.

Taylor, T. (1969). *The cay.* New York: Doubleday.

Terban, M. (1983). *In a pickle and other funny idioms.* Boston: Houghton Mifflin.

Tompkins, G. E. (1981). Writing without a pencil. *Language Arts, 58,* 823–833.

Tompkins, G. E., & Friend, M. (1986). On your mark, get set, write! *Teaching Exceptional Children, 18,* 82–89.

Tompkins, G. E., & McGee, L. M. (1983). Launching nonstandard speakers into standard English. *Language Arts, 60,* 463–469.

Troika, R. C. (1981). Synthesis of research on bilingual education. *Educational Leadership, 38,* 498–504.

Urzua, C. (1980). Doing what comes naturally: Recent research in second language acquisition. In G. S. Pinnell (Ed.), *Discovering language with children* (pp. 33–38). Urbana, IL: National Council of Teachers of English.

VanDeWeghe, R. (1982). Spelling and grammar logs. In C. Carter (Ed.), *Non-native and nonstandard dialect students: Classroom practices in teaching English, 1982–1983* (pp. 101–105). Urbana, IL: National Council of Teachers of English.

Wagner, H. S. (1982). Kids can be ESL teachers. In C. Carter (Ed.), *Non-native and nonstandard dialect students: Classroom practices in teaching English, 1982–1983* (pp. 62–65). Urbana, IL: National Council of Teachers of English.

IF YOU WANT TO LEARN MORE

Ashton-Warner, S. (1971). *Teacher.* New York: Bantam Books.

Brooks, C. K. (Ed.). (1985). *Tapping potential: English and language arts for the black learner.* Urbana, IL: National Council of Teachers of English.

Butler, D. (1979). *Cushia and her books.* Boston: Horn Book.

Carter, C. (Ed.). (1982). *Non-native and nonstandard dialect students: Classroom practices in teaching English, 1982–1983.* Urbana, IL: National Council of Teachers of English.

Hammill, D. D., & Bartel, N. (1978). *Teaching children with learning and behavior problems* (2nd ed.). Boston: Allyn and Bacon.

Pinnell, G. S. (Ed.). (1980). *Discovering language with children.* Urbana, IL: National Council of Teachers of English.

Polloway, E. A., & Smith, J. E., Jr. (1982). *Teaching language skills to exceptional learners.* Denver: Love.

Pooley, R. C. (1974). *The teaching of English usage.* Urbana, IL: National Council of Teachers of English.

Rodrigues, R. J., & White, R. H. (1981). *Mainstreaming the non-English speaking student* (TRIP Booklet). Urbana, IL: ERIC Clearinghouse on Reading and Communication Skills and the National Council of Teachers of English.

Shafer, S. (1976). Messin' wif language. *Elementary School Journal, 76,* 500–506.

Stafford, G. (Ed.). (1980). *Dealing with differences: Classroom practices in teaching English, 1980–1981.* Urbana, IL: National Council of Teachers of English.

Subject Index

Author and Title Index

Dr. Kenneth Hoskisson teaches courses in reading and language arts at Virginia Tech in Blacksburg, Virginia. He has published in the *Elementary School Journal, Language Arts,* and *The Reading Teacher.* Dr. Hoskisson is well known for his conceptualization and development of assisted reading. He earned a Ph.D. in curriculum and instruction with emphasis in reading and language arts at the University of California, Berkeley. His major interests are writing and helping teachers examine the relationships between theory and practice. Dr. Hoskisson was both a teacher and an administrator with the Department of Defense schools in Europe for 10 years.

Gail E. Tompkins is an Associate Professor of Language Arts Education at the University of Oklahoma in Norman. She teaches language arts courses for preservice and inservice teachers as well as graduate courses in writing and language development. In 1986, Dr. Tompkins received the University of Oklahoma's prestigious Regents' Award for Superior Teaching. She is also Director of the Oklahoma Writing Project, one of more than 150 affiliates of the National Writing Project. Through this project, Dr. Tompkins works with teachers, kindergarten through college level, introducing them to new strategies for teaching composition. Dr. Tompkins is co-author of a recently published book about the history of the English language, *Answering Students' Questions About Words,* published by the ERIC Clearinghouse on Reading and Communication Skills and the National Council of Teachers of English, and has written more than 20 articles on topics related to language arts that have been published in *Language Arts, The Reading Teacher,* and other professional journals.